It's an eye-opening book "not about finding a job, but about creating a life" that all high school and college kids should read to help them think outside the last-century box in this new millennium... That's one recurring theme in *Shake the World*, a hot new book about a growing number of young, socially conscious entrepreneurs who, in an age of avarice, measure their own success by how much they give back.

—*New York Daily News*

What Reilly discovered in these in-depth interviews were career paths that defy prediction. The thoughtful strategizing beloved by old-school career counselors does aspiring entrepreneurs little good, Reilly found. Instead, they need to learn to dabble, experiment, and most of all redefine their understanding of risk.

—*Inc.* magazine

It's a grim time out there, with millions of unemployed or underemployed out of work for months if not years, whether newly minted college graduates or corporate veterans. Having interviewed a good handful of entrepreneurs (as well as drawing on his own youthful success), Reilly is ready to share his take on what makes career changers succeed. His enthusiasm and spirit are contagious and might just provide a good boost to the weary job seeker.

—*Booklist*

A powerful blend of inspiration and action, *Shake the World* offers a life-and-career plan handcrafted for the new millennium. Read this book, then head out to set the world on fire.

—Jonathan Fields, author of *Uncertainty*

At Zappos, one of our core values is to "Embrace and Drive Change." This book is for anyone interested in inspiring their own life to change for the better, both personally and professionally!

—Tony Hsieh, *New York Times* bestselling author
of *Delivering Happiness*

A new generation wants work to be about far more than making money—they want their jobs to make a positive difference to the world. James Marshall Reilly has written a compelling and optimistic firsthand account of what it means to put this excellent goal into practice.

—Matthew Bishop, New York Bureau Chief of *The Economist*
and coauthor of *Philanthrocapitalism*

Reilly is part of a cohort of young entrepreneurial leaders who will change this country over the next few years. Their fascinating stories and his insights will inspire and guide you as you invent your career and life while making a *big* difference.

—Peter Sims, author of *Little Bets* and founder
and CEO of BLK SHP, Inc.

"Charity: Water" was founded out of a desire to inspire a new generation of givers to solve the water crisis. In this book, Reilly introduces you to many of our friends who had the fearlessness to break the mold and think incredibly big. Prepare to be inspired, and then to act!

—Scott Harrison, founder and CEO of Charity: Water

In this ever complex, dynamic, and demanding world, everyone needs to design their lives, and James Marshall Reilly shows how. If you want a principled, consequential, and successful life, read this book.

—Don Tapscott, author of *MacroWikinomics*

This book shifts the mindset for anyone who reads it. Define your own success and then do what the best have already done to achieve it. Reilly has uncovered the secrets of the most hypersuccessful people of this generation. If you internalize their lessons, you will accelerate the rate at which you achieve the success goals you have for yourself.

—Cameron Herold, author of *Double Double*
and former COO of 1-800-GOT-JUNK?

Forget triple-bottom-line companies, James Marshall Reilly documents triple-bottom-line individuals—a cadre of brilliant business adventurers devoted to building a better world and, just as importantly, finding a better way to live in that world. With great storytelling and penetrating insight, *Shake the World* adds an entrepreneurial twist to the quest for the meaning of life.

—Steven Kotler, author of *Abundance*,
A Small Furry Prayer, and *West of Jesus*

One Great Speech

One Great Speech

Speech

SECRETS, STORIES, AND PERKS OF THE PAID SPEAKING INDUSTRY

(AND HOW YOU CAN BREAK IN)

JAMES MARSHALL REILLY

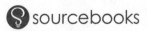

Published by Sourcebooks
P.O. Box 4410, Naperville, Illinois 60567-4410
(630) 961-3900
sourcebooks.com

Library of Congress Cataloging-in-Publication Data

Names: Reilly, James Marshall, author.
Title: One great speech : secrets, stories, and perks of the paid speaking
    industry (and how you can break in) / James Marshall Reilly.
Description: Naperville, IL : Sourcebooks, [2020] | Includes
    bibliographical references and index.
Identifiers: LCCN 2019053663 (hardcover)
Subjects: LCSH: Public speaking--Vocational guidance.
Classification: LCC PN4098 .R45 2020 | DDC 808.5/1023--dc23
LC record available at https://lccn.loc.gov/2019053663

Printed and bound in the Unites States of America.
SB 10 9 8 7 6 5 4 3 2 1

For Elizabeth and River

Table of Contents

Introduction

What would you say if I told you that you could make an additional $5,000 per year by only putting in a few hours of work?

How about $10,000?

What would you say if I told you that you could make an additional $100,000 per year with no special skills or additional education and no up-front investment other than a few hours of your own time?

And what would you say if I told you that you could quit your current job—if you wanted to—and make more money by simply *sharing your own story*?

I must be crazy. Right?

I assure you, I'm not.

Welcome to the largely misunderstood, highly secretive, enormously lucrative paid speaking industry.

A $100 million industry with little transparency and few barriers to entry. And yet very few people understand how it works, or how to tap into it. Or, if they think they know, the information they have is often incorrect because it wasn't explained to them by someone on the inside.

On top of that, there are very few outside resources that make this information available. While there are a ton of books on speech prep, speech delivery, and how to speak for free, there aren't any books that explain how to actually get *paid* to speak.

Yet there are thousands—if not tens of thousands—of organizations in America that pay for speeches each year. Global opportunities make this market even larger. *As a speaking agent, over the course of just a few years, I generated in excess of $25 million in offers for my clients.*

And that $25 million is only a fraction of the money out there. As an agent, I've had more money *turned down* by speakers than booked. In fact, as an agency owner, my agents and I once had a cumulative sum of $1 million *turned down in a matter of hours.* And of course, as an individual agent—and even as an agency owner—I represented only a tiny segment of the total market.

Plus, it's likely that you've never even heard of most of the people I booked. They weren't famous politicians. They weren't celebrities. For the most part, they weren't household names. *They were ordinary people.* Schoolteachers. College professors. Small business owners. Nonprofit founders. Health experts. Cancer survivors. Because speaking builds profiles and visibility fast, you may be familiar with some of these speakers now—but the point is that anyone can participate in the highly lucrative paid speaking business—*that is, if they know how.*

"But," you say, "we've heard grandiose claims like this before."

In 2009, Tim Ferriss and *The 4-Hour Workweek* made an equally extraordinary promise: *Escape 9–5, live anywhere, and join the new rich.*

By working only four hours a week. *Half a day.*

The brilliance of this promise is obvious; it's so big and so compelling that everyone wants to sign on. In fact, there have been a ton of other life-hack books that offer ways to get rich quick and free up time.

But what I'm outlining in *One Great Speech* will be, for most people, a far more accessible and actionable version of this same promise: *work less and earn more.* For some, what I'm offering in this book might manifest as a four-hour workweek. And, for a handful of people, it might even manifest as a four-hour work *month.* A week or a month in which you fly, all expenses paid—often first class—to a speaking engagement. A single speaking engagement for which you'll be paid four, five, or potentially even six figures.

How many offers you accept, and how much you earn, is largely controlled by you. And you don't need to own a company or to have done something extraordinary to join the party. *You just need a story. A story you already have.*

In my experience, *everyone* wants to be a speaker. TED made speaking sexy. And TEDx made speaking accessible to the masses. But the thing is, TED and TEDx don't pay speakers. And getting paid to speak is much better than speaking for free—even at TED. *Paid speakers are the new rock stars.* And the money can be *huge.*

In this book I am going to explain every detail and inside secret of the paid speaking industry so that anyone—and everyone—can monetize it. I am going to invite "regular people" to participate in what is one of the most misunderstood and surprisingly accessible markets available for personal wealth-building in the world today. I will also expose the inner workings of this elusive and lucrative industry and the people who inhabit it.

If you think that the kind of democratization and market

creation I'm talking about isn't possible or hasn't been done before—that inviting "normal" people into what has traditionally been a closed marketplace can't be done—you're wrong. Consider Uber and Airbnb.

In 2011, Uber launched to the masses with a unique value proposition: *You own a car, so let us help you monetize it.* What made Uber so successful was that it repositioned the concept of owning a car by presenting it in a different light—your car is a distressed asset, and one you can put into service. Uber invited people to be taxi drivers who would have otherwise never considered driving taxis. They invited new people—new drivers— into a market in which very few car owners had previously participated. Actors, students, retirees, the unemployed, and others suddenly had the means—and better yet, the opportunity and mindset—to generate additional income by putting their car to work for them.

A few years earlier, in 2008, Airbnb launched to the masses with an equally compelling promise: *We can help you cover your mortgage or your rent, or simply add to your bottom line, by providing a bridge to positive revenue based on leveraging something you already have—your home.* Just like Uber, Airbnb invited people into an income-generating market in which most had not previously participated.

Despite the mass appeal of these two companies and the billions of dollars they generate for everyday people, both have a costly barrier to entry. *You can only drive for Uber if you own or lease a new model car. And you can only earn money through Airbnb if you are willing to let someone else move into the home you rent or own for a while.*

According to Uber, "the median wage for an UberX driver working at least forty hours a week in New York City is $90,766 a year."* According to the *Washington Post*, this isn't realistic, and, in most markets, drivers make closer to minimum wage. When *Money* analyzed the income generated in the "sharing economy," it was estimated that the average Uber driver's income was $364 a month—$4,368 per year—and that the average Airbnb earnings were $924 a month—$11,088 a year.

Regardless of which numbers you believe, as a paid speaker, sharing your story, *a fully utilized YOU* can make far more money than the average Uber or Airbnb participant makes in a year—*in an hour.* And without the up-front investment. *There is a zero-dollar entry fee to the speaking market, and enormous potential for earnings.*

I am essentially going to show you *how to rent yourself*—and your life experience—instead of your car or your house. *And for a lot more money.*

. . . .

Here are examples of just ten of the individuals I've represented as a speaking agent, followed by the cumulative dollar value of what they were offered† for speaking engagements in a single year. Keep in mind, *each individual offer was for what would have amounted to a few hours of work*:

---

* Matt McFarland, "Uber's Remarkable Growth Could End the Era of Poorly Paid Cab Drivers," *Washington Post*, May 27, 2014, https://www.washingtonpost.com/news /innovations/wp/2014/05/27/ubers-remarkable-growth-could-end-the-era-of-poorly -paid-cab-drivers/.

† For clarity, not all speakers accept all offers. In this book I will discuss both *offers* (a firm and binding contract for a speaker to give a talk for a specific fee on a specific date) and *bookings* (an offer accepted by a speaker).

Social Entrepreneur: $2,500,000

Diversity Expert: $96,000

T-shirt Entrepreneur: $600,000

Nonprofit Founder: $780,000

Science Writer: $650,000

Schoolteacher: $212,000

College Professor No. 1: $400,000

College Professor No. 2: $325,000

Food Expert: $550,000

Happiness Expert: $200,000

In this book, I'm going to teach you how you can become a paid speaker and generate income to cover your annual grocery bill or pay your monthly mortgage—and entertain you with fun, insider stories. I'm going to show you how you can generate a new revenue stream to help pay for your vacations and cover your kid's college expenses. I'm going to teach you how to potentially fund your retirement, buy a sports car—or anything else you want—by being paid to simply *talk*.

But wait, you don't mean me. *I can't be a paid speaker, can I?*

Yes, you can.

Some of the speaking requests I've received over the years that weren't for a specific speaker were based on topics that weren't suitable for any of the speaking clients I exclusively represented. This means that I booked quite a few of the incoming inquiries based on one of two things: Either *spin*, which is exactly what it sounds like—I would take my biographical knowledge of my exclusive speakers and spin their stories to meet the needs of the enquiring parties. Or *cold-calling*—I would locate someone who had never given a speech and convince that person to do so. Which means that I had to track down and call an unrepresented "expert" and say, "Hi, I read your story about guerrilla marketing online. I know you've probably never given a paid speech before, but I work with a Fortune 500 company that is looking for someone to talk about guerrilla marketing on March 15. I have a signed, firm-and-binding offer to pay you $10,000 plus first-class travel and expenses to give a forty-five-minute speech. Are you interested and available?"

How would you like to get that call out of the blue?

As a speaking agent, one of my biggest challenges was locating and identifying unrepresented "experts" in various fields based on the incoming requests of buyers and event sponsors.* Experts, who—in the speaking world—are unknown and therefore "not on the menu." People just like you who are not being pitched for paid speaking engagements because they aren't represented by an agent.

And don't be confused.

When NASA wants to pay for a speaker, they're not looking for an astronaut.

When Bank of America wants to pay for a speaker, they're not looking for a banker or a financial services expert.

And the State Department isn't looking for a diplomat.

These organizations have plenty of their own in-house.

Instead, these organizations are looking for someone who has founded a small business, is an exercise guru, runs a women's group, or sailed a boat through a storm. They are looking for someone with a unique perspective, a new idea—someone who

---

* Technically, "buyers" and "event sponsors" are the organizations, committees, or governing bodies that are holding an event and footing the bill for the speakers. For simplicity, in this book, when I refer to buyers and event sponsors I am often referencing the individual who is the point of contact for the overall event and who executes bookings.

has information to share. And passion; they are looking for someone with *a story that resonates.*

For example, I once booked Sarah Jones, a Tony Award–winning playwright, actress, and poet, to give a forty-five-minute presentation at one of the largest aerospace companies in the world. For this speech she was paid $45,000 plus first-class travel and expenses. And she knew nothing about aeronautics.

Hold on, you're thinking. *I'm not a Tony Award–winning playwright, actress, and poet. So, you don't really mean me, right?*

Wrong! I do mean you, and this book will explain why.

OK, but don't I need a published book in order to get paid to speak?

Nope.

▸ If you already wrote and published a book—great. It will help you to secure representation at a speaking agency.

▸ If you don't have a book, I'll explain why you don't need one to become a successful paid speaker. And then I'll explain that you may be able to leverage your speaking career to secure a book deal, if you want one.

Because paid speaking engagements can *get you a book deal.* I'll explain how I was able to negotiate five- and six-figure book deals with some of the biggest publishers in the world simply based on the platforms I built for my speaking clients and the demand for their future speeches.

Who is this book for?

▸ This book is for *people who never thought that they could give a paid speech—and who still think that.* And it will show them how they can make additional, reliable income every year by doing so.

▶ This book is for *people who already want to be paid speakers and would like to have a speaking agency represent them.* And it will show them how to get one.

▶ This book is for *people who already have speaking agency representation.* And it will show them how to better monetize their relationships: How to get their agents to work harder, smarter, and more efficiently—to the tune of higher-profile, higher-paying gigs. And how to leave agents, event sponsors, and audiences pleased.

▶ This book is also for *people who may not want to speak themselves, but who are interested in learning about the behind-the-scenes workings of an industry that few people know anything about.*

What this book will teach you:

▶ How to identify, hone, and frame your personal story in such a way that other people will be willing to pay you a ton of money to tell it.

▶ How to rethink your personal brand—and if you think that you don't have a personal brand, I'll convince you that you do.

▶ How to craft the best materials, and the type of agencies to approach, to ensure representation.

▸ How to position your topics, bio, and collateral marketing materials in such a way that you are best positioned to be signed to a speaking agency.

▸ How to differentiate between the "levels" of speaking agencies. For example, why you likely shouldn't be targeting household-name speakers bureaus unless you're extremely well known or retired from the Senate yesterday; the difference between agencies that simply field incoming calls versus those that actively sell; and, if you have a book, why the in-house speakers bureau at your publishing company might not be all it's cracked up to be.

▸ How to secure an exclusive speaking agent or agency, and what to do when you are offered representation.

▸ What your speaking agent is thinking but isn't telling you, and how to get ahead of prospective challenges simply by being prepared.

▸ Why signing with a speaking agency is only 50 percent of the battle.

▸ How to get your agents to pitch you and book you, and how to empower those agents to make you the most money possible.

▸ How to set a speaking fee that best positions you for success based on the dynamics of the market.

▸ How to increase your speaking fees over time.

▶ How to further monetize your speeches without being pushy or coming off like you're selling something.

▶ Best practices when it comes to data capture, list-building, and interacting with audiences after the speech.

▶ How to use the paid speaking industry to attract customers, build your profile, and generate revenue if you run a business or nonprofit.

▶ When and where and why—and if—you should speak for free.

▶ Why everything you know, or think you know, about sales and marketing is likely irrelevant in the paid speaking space.

▶ And, most importantly, *One Great Speech* will teach you the language and inner workings of the paid speaking industry so you are better positioned to monetize it.

What this book isn't:

▶ This is not a book about *how* to give a speech.

▶ I will never tell you where to stand on stage.

▶ I will never tell you to envision the audience naked.

▶ I will never tell you to conform to cookie-cutter standards.

▶ I will never tell you how to write your speech. In fact, I might tell you *not* to write a speech at all.

▶ I will never tell you how to build a killer PowerPoint presentation—although I will explain why you might not need one.

▶ I will never tell you how to dress. Though I will tell you that a few of my most successful speakers go on stage barefoot, or may not have showered in the previous three days, and I'll tell you why this doesn't necessarily matter.

▶ I will never tell you not to say "um" or "like." Though I will advise you that being yourself—regardless of flawed grammar, how you look, or if you stumble—is the most endearing thing that you and your agents are selling.

So Who Am I, and Why Should You Listen to Me?

I've been working in the speaking industry for over a decade. In 2011, I founded a speaking agency based in midtown Manhattan. At the time, I represented no one—not a single client.

I didn't have a list of buyers or event sponsors, either. I had Google, a basic website, an email address, and a few years of experience working as an agent at an international speaking agency.

When I started my company, I was still in my twenties. Five years later, I represented over one hundred speakers exclusively and began generating between $6 million and $10 million a year in offers for them.

I represented a few big names. But more importantly, I represented a lot of "nobodies." Regular, hardworking people just like you and me. I've also worked with just about every speakers bureau in the world. Not just major speakers bureaus, but the small ones too. In fact, some of my biggest customers were other speaking agencies, and I'll explain later in the book why that matters and what it means.

I've worked with companies that are household names—Bank of America, Facebook, Disney, Coca-Cola, Chick-fil-A, FedEx, Viacom, and Gatorade, among others. I've worked with hundreds of high-profile nonprofit and government organizations—including NASA, the U.S. Department of State, Phi Beta Kappa, Children's Miracle Network, Doctors Without Borders, Girl Scouts of the USA, and the United Nations. I've worked with hundreds of colleges and universities—Harvard, Yale, UCLA, Notre Dame, USC, University of Chicago, Wharton School of Business, and University of North Carolina, to name a few. I've also arranged speeches in countries all over the world, including England, Peru, Australia, Belgium, France, South Africa, Taiwan, and Colombia.

One insider secret of the speaking industry? *Most of the money for paid speeches lies not with big, recognizable names, but with speakers and organizations you've never heard of.*

As a speaking agent, I got *hundreds* of emails each week from organizations looking to pay for a speaker. But most of these organizations had less than $5,000 to spend. This means that, in a traditional speaking agency mindset, these inquiries were unserviceable because the dollars weren't large enough to bother with. So, in addition to teaching you how to get an agent to go after the bigger dollars, this book will also teach you how to motivate your agent to convert these "unserviceable" and "small" dollars for your benefit.

Like most marketplaces, the speaking industry has a high end and a low end. Both are lucrative. And there's mobility between the two extremes—I've taken speakers no one has ever heard of from getting $500 a night to $60,000 a night. And I'll demonstrate how.

Because I've been in this industry for so long, I also have a lot of stories.

Funny stories. Hard-to-believe stories. Insider stories about a world very few people know anything about. Stories about famous people—Academy Award winners, celebrities, bestselling authors, powerful businesspeople, high-profile entrepreneurs, influential nonprofit leaders, former heads of state, Nobel and Pulitzer Prize nominees—and about regular people like you and me.[*]

I've had speaking clients who didn't want event sponsors, or the public, to know that they were flying in on private jets to give their speeches. (Depending on your branding, it's not necessarily good optics—or good PR—to take a flight that costs tens of thousands of dollars.) I've had speaking clients who have led event sponsors to believe that their five- and six- figure speaking fees were going to charity when, in fact, the fees were going into their own bank accounts. But I've also had clients who have donated their speaking fees back to the universities where they spoke; who used their speaking platform to build nonprofits and better the world; who worked to improve awareness of global social issues; and who improved the lives of tens of thousands of people around of the globe because they got massive exposure as paid speakers.

In this book I am going to teach you how I helped a specific group of people make tens of millions of dollars by *simply talking*—and I am going to teach you how you can get a piece of

---

[*]   Every story in this book is true. However, in many cases the names and details have been altered slightly in order to protect the privacy of the individuals and institutions discussed. In each case, I preserved enough of the details to make sure the core value of each story remained intact.

that market too. On the pages that follow I will share the closely guarded knowledge and insider secrets of the paid speaking industry so that they can be monetized by you.

1.

Show Me the Money

HOW IT ALL WORKS

Here are the short answers to three of the most common questions every aspiring speaker asks:

1. *How much money can I get paid to give a speech?*
   How much speakers make can vary from a few thousand dollars to hundreds of thousands of dollars for a single speech. More specifically, unless you're a celebrity, you can expect to make somewhere between $5,000 and $30,000 for a single booking.

2. *How often can I get booked?*
   Anywhere from never to constantly. Vague, I know, but it's the truth. I've represented speakers who have never been booked. I've represented speakers who set limits, saying, "I only want to speak four times a year." I've also represented speakers who get so many offers that they could never

possibly accept them all. Perhaps most importantly, I've represented speakers who start out small and unknown who go on to build highly lucrative careers by following the rules set forth in this book. On the flip side, I've also represented speakers who get booked once and never again—and later on I'll explain why that happens and how to prevent it.

3. *How does my agent get paid?*
    Just like literary agents and real estate agents, speaking agents work on commission.* The best part of that is *there's no up-front cost to you.* But while a real estate agency might get 5–6 percent and a literary agency gets 15 percent, a speaking agency will generally commission 20–25 percent of what you get paid for a speech. That means that if you get booked four or five times, your agency will make as much as you do for giving a single speech—and I'll explain why your agent is worth every penny of that money.

This said, here are two critical questions speakers never ask, but should:

1. *Who controls the dollars?*

2. *And how can knowing this enable a speaker to make more money?*

---

*   Some speaking agencies pay a flat salary to agents. Many pay a draw against commission. Generally what this means is that the more an agent books, the more money he or she makes. With few exceptions—and even if you are on a flat salary—if you don't get enough bookings to cover what you are being paid, you won't last at your job.

Sometimes, after a speech is booked, on the days leading up to the event I worry that something will happen and that the speaker won't show up for one reason or another. It's important to note that, as an agent, I only get paid if the event actually *occurs*. And I work on a draw against commissions, so a no-show can have a disastrous impact on both my current income and my relationship with an event sponsor—which can hugely impact my future income. Now, a no-show can happen due to bad weather, flight delays, and unexpected work conflicts—among other things. I once had a speaker who had a heart attack right before a speech. I even had a speaker who "forgot" that she had a speech in Switzerland and didn't show up for her flight from Los Angeles. And I once had a speaker—a Pulitzer Prize–winning author—who passed away seventy-two hours before his scheduled speech.

Mind you, things like this rarely happen. But as an agent, the possibility of a speech—which is on a fixed date typically booked many months in advance—being canceled or forfeited by the speaker and therefore not paying out is top of mind, particularly on big-dollar bookings. And while we, as agents, put measures in place to prevent cancellations from happening—such as not letting a speaker fly in on the day of a speech or on the last flight out the evening prior—I've still sweated it out over more events than I can count.

Consider these four actual examples:

1. *I had a CEO flying in on a private jet with a full security detail— armed to the teeth—on a flight to Bogota, Colombia, to give a forty-minute speech to a group of South American businesspeople. The speaker would be in and out in a matter of hours*

and was being paid $250,000. I was having a panic attack the entire time because there were so many things that could go wrong—including that the speaker could be kidnapped.

2. *I had filmmaker Spike Lee booked on a private jet for a Black History Month speech at a private school.* The fee was $25,000 (net to him) and there was a snowstorm on the morning of the event that jeopardized his flight. To add to the pressure, the event couldn't be rescheduled because Spike was slated to begin filming a new movie the following week.

3. *I booked Supreme Court Justice Sandra Day O'Connor to speak for one of my favorite event sponsors at a college in Tennessee for $10,000.* As we got closer to the event date, I worried that the relatively low fee* might be easy for someone of her stature to walk away from, especially at the last minute. Plus, when I initially cold-called her to see if she was interested and available, her assistant said she had never given a paid speech and insisted that she wouldn't be interested. So I was worried that she might not be highly incentivized to show up, that her team wouldn't know the protocol, and that she might back out on the day of the event—especially if something more important popped up.

4. *I booked MSNBC's Rachel Maddow for what I was told was her first-ever paid speech at an event where I already had Dr. Sanjay Gupta booked for high five figures.* The invitation was for Rachel to give a twenty-five-minute keynote presentation to

---

*   She should have asked me for more money—a lot more—but didn't know to. I'll talk more about pricing in chapter 12.

a group of Phi Beta Kappa members within the community college system for $65,000. The invitation included a private jet and—to sweeten the pot—a prearranged fishing trip for Rachel and her partner with bestselling author and Pulitzer Prize nominee (and well-known golf and fishing enthusiast) Carl Hiaasen.

Four events, five speakers, $450,000 gross. The net agency commission? Twenty-five percent—$112,500.

The reason these particular events caused me so much angst wasn't because the speakers were a famous CEO, or well-known members of the media, or a Supreme Court justice, or celebrities. It wasn't because I was trying to please the speakers. And it wasn't only—as most people might assume—because the six-figure commission due to my agency might be at risk. It also wasn't because I was particularly worried about protecting my relationship with the speakers themselves. In fact, at no time during any of these bookings, or on the days of those speeches, was I particularly worried about the speaker having an enjoyable experience.

At no point was I worried about the speaker's time.

The speaker didn't matter all that much.

The speaker was replaceable.

If that CEO, or Spike Lee, or Sandra Day O'Connor, or Rachel Maddow, or Sanjay Gupta had *the worst experience of their lives* at any of these paid speaking events, it would have bothered me, but it wouldn't have been the end of the world. After all, they were making a significant amount of money. And there's a reason the speaker's experience at a given event wasn't all that important to me—just as it's not that important to any other speaking agent. The reason is this: *In the paid speaking industry, the event sponsors are the most important players, and these are the most important relationships an agent has to protect. The speakers might be that agent's clients, but the buyers are that agent's largest source of income.* Which means that my anxiety and concern about those speakers not showing up was rooted in dollar preservation much larger than the commission on these four individual events.

Typically, and with few exceptions, a speaker will be booked for a paid speech by a given event sponsor only *one time* in his or her entire career. It doesn't make sense for a buyer to pay five figures for a speaker in 2022 if they already paid five figures for that speaker in 2019—few speakers are that relevant.

We have a term for this: *One and done.*

However, that event sponsor—if pleased with the speaker and the content that speaker delivered—will continue to book speakers from that agent or agency (me) a couple of times a year for the foreseeable future. Event sponsors often control large budgets for yearly conferences and events, and they need fresh faces and innovative talks on an ongoing basis.

If we break down the numbers, the agency is getting 25 percent of the gross spend of any given buyer in perpetuity—as long as the agent doesn't lose the buyer—whereas any given speaker is getting 75 percent of the gross spend *once*. This means that if that private school books Spike Lee for $32,500 and he receives a $25,000 net fee after my commission,* the maximum value of that relationship for Spike is $25,000. That private school will likely never book him again even if he gave the greatest speech in the history of the world.

Assuming that buyer books two events with me each year, however, the maximum value of the relationship for me, the

---

* I am using round numbers here to keep things simple.

agent, is $7,500 per speech twice a year over, potentially, ten years—$150,000. That means that my potential earn-out from this one particular relationship with this one particular buyer is six times Spike's upside. Which means that I had six times more to lose than Spike Lee did if he didn't show up. And if he had angered or upset the buyer by complaining about something, or was in a bad mood, or didn't participate in an extra classroom visit, or didn't give a great presentation, he still would have been paid and I would have gotten my commission—but I'd be at risk of losing my buyer forever. Even though any poor performance by a speaker has nothing to do with me.[†]

In the speaking industry, the speaker is making the most absolute dollars from *each individual event*, but the agent has a potential upside that could play out over the next several years that will far outearn the commission from each individual event. So, *the person making the most money from any individual event sponsor is the agent, but that means that the agent also shoulders the outcome regardless of who controls the variables that contributed to that outcome.*

The next time I call Spike with $25,000 for a speech, he will either accept the offer or he won't. But if the *buyer* from his previous event is unhappy, I might lose her business forever. And buyers are one thousand times harder to find than speakers.

So every time I have an event booked, I have a delicate, highly monetizable, sometimes decade-long, critical financial relationship that I am worried about maintaining. And those relationships are with people you've never heard of.

---

† Luckily, all of these speakers showed up and had great events—and Spike killed it. He risked his life getting on a small private plane in a snowstorm, stayed late, visited an extra class, and, according to the buyer, was the best speaker they ever had.

The event sponsors who booked those events with me.

Not the speakers.

And every speaker needs to know that.

Why?

Because understanding this will change your behavior and greatly improve your outcomes. Leveraging this information will give you power. It will help you get an agent. It will affect your relationship with your agency once you sign with one. It will also affect your relationship with the buyers and the audiences where you speak. And that will impact how often you are booked, as well as how much money you can make.

So why am I admitting to you—a potential speaker—that I, your potential agent, think you matter less to me than my buyers?

Because it's the truth and it's to your advantage to know that.

What most paid speakers don't realize is that any good speaking agency could replace most of their speakers—with few exceptions—with new speakers and still generate the same annual revenue.* The truth is that there are very few people in the world who would say no to the kind of money paid to speakers for a few hours of work—which means that speakers, generally, are not hard to sign.

So not only were the speakers' experiences not my first priority on the days of the aforementioned events, but also if that CEO, Spike Lee, Sandra Day O'Connor, Rachel Maddow, or Sanjay Gupta had turned those bookings down, there's an excellent chance that I would have simply replaced them with

---

*   Marquee speakers that generate mid to high six-figure fees are obviously hard to replace. But good, solid speakers, say a CEO who speaks about leadership or a wellness guru or a robotics expert, can be subbed out for another highly qualified speaker with an equally compelling résumé and speaking topics pretty easily.

different speakers—*just like that*. Why? Because each of those events *required a speaker,* regardless of who it was.

Of course, there are times when a buyer calls with a specific offer for a specific speaker and is inflexible as to who they host— it's "the speaker we're calling about, or bust." But more often than not, the agent is the critical gatekeeper and is a suggestive resource because that buyer *has to book a speaker* for their event. An agent can easily say, "I know you called looking to book Speaker A, but she isn't available. Have you heard about Speaker B?"

As a speaker you need to understand that not only do you not matter to your agent nearly as much as the buyers do, but also that your agent has almost immeasurable power to choose which speakers to pitch to buyers. Better yet, your agent has the power to change the buyer's mind when he or she calls in with an offer for one particular speaker simply by strategically subbing in someone else. *As a speaker, you always need to remember that you were booked because an agent sold you. And—as great as you are—that agent who sold you could have easily sold someone else.*

If you're smart, knowing this arms you with information that you can use to change outcomes and get more gigs. So, the question a speaker should be asking himself or herself is, *If my agent will be protecting his or her relationship with the buyer, not with me, and that agent has a lot of discretionary power and leeway as to whom to "sell," what are the best strategies for leveraging this information to my advantage?*

Case Study: The Stale Bagel

In 2009, I heard a particular comment from a buyer about a stale bagel that cost a whole lot of people a whole lot of money. This particular speaker—let's call her Speaker A—made a snide and nasty comment to the buyer about the quality of the bagels served at the breakfast event where she was booked. And it bothered the event sponsor so much that he called and told me about it. Keep in mind that the speaker was being paid $15,000 for the event, and a bagel costs in the vicinity of a dollar.

So now let's say I get a phone call from a different trusted buyer who regularly books two events a year with me. He informs me that he has narrowed his list of potential speakers down to two people: Speaker A (who complained about the stale bagel) and Speaker B. Speaker A has a $15,000 fee, Speaker B has a $10,000 fee, and the buyer is willing to host either speaker at their full-fee asking price depending on who's available. I'm being trusted to call this buyer back with a confirmed acceptance from either Speaker A or Speaker B. And as an agent, I have a lot of power to swing this one way or the other.

Here are my most recent pieces of feedback about Speaker A and Speaker B, which I received the previous week from two separate buyers:

▸ Speaker A spoke at an entrepreneurship conference and didn't seem excited to be there. She was five minutes late to the community breakfast she was contracted to attend and complained that her bagel was stale. Her speech was also exactly the same as the TEDx talk she gave eighteen months ago—and was therefore too short. My buyer thought the event was "pretty good," but wouldn't rush to recommend this speaker to other organizations—the buyer was expecting content that wasn't already available for free online (the TEDx presentation), and the bagel comment was off-putting, and quite frankly, the tipping point.

I did my job as an agent. The buyer did his job. But the speaker didn't do hers.

The speaker made the buyer look bad at his job by delivering unoriginal, recycled material and by not being "nice." And the speaker made me look bad to my buyer.

▶ Speaker B spoke at a community college and was absolutely amazing—a delight to work with. She visited two extra student groups on campus, despite the visits not being mandated in her contract, and had dinner with the dean. The dean was thrilled, as was everyone on the board of directors.

I did my job as an agent. The buyer did his job. And the speaker did her job too—she made this buyer look good at his job. And she made me look good at mine.

As an agent, what would you do? I now have an offer that I can bring to either of these speakers. The difference is that if I bring the offer to Speaker B, there is a good chance that the buyer will have a good experience and continue to book from me twice a year at $10,000 to $15,000 a pop. Whereas if I bring the offer to Speaker A, there's a good chance that this is the last deal, and the last commission, I will ever receive from this particular buyer—and I've already lost another buyer largely due to this speaker's behavior.

As you can see, the decision is incredibly easy. In fact, it's a foregone conclusion. Speaker B is booked for the event. In fact, *Speaker A never knew that the offer existed.* And the thing is, I will happily forgo the commission on the extra $5,000—the difference in price between Speaker A and Speaker B—to preserve the long-term relationship with that buyer. Plus, remember, *I am serving the buyer by doing this* as I'm increasing the chance that the buyer will have a positive experience.

Speakers need to know that speaking agencies play favorites. More specifically, agents within speaking agencies play favorites. And they do it in a very calculated, justifiable manner—with the sole focus on self-preservation. I have my go-to speakers, and the agent sitting next to me has her go-to speakers. And agents talk—we know who is reliable, who killed it yesterday, and which speakers are hard to deal with. We also know who has a misplaced ego—who complains about bagels—and how badly that can play out. Having just one agent who has your back, let alone several agents within a single agency who have your back, can be the difference between making hundreds of thousands of dollars a year or making a fraction of that—or nothing at all.

And the thing is, the difference between one speaker making hundreds of thousands of dollars and another speaker making absolutely nothing *looks exactly the same* on paper and *feels exactly the same* to those speakers over the course of the year—at least on the surface. Speaker A and Speaker B both had new books out. They both had a new TEDx video being circulated by their speaking agency. They both had companies or organizations that had been in the press. In other words, things were happening for both of them. With the one giant exception being that Speaker B's phone rang ten times a year for paid speeches, while Speaker A's phone only rang once. And Speaker A had no idea that *every* agent at her agency knew about the stale bagel and was therefore pitching her ten times less than before—if at all.

If a speaker isn't on the menu, the buyer can't book him or her. And if a speaker *is* on the menu, an agent can take that speaker off the menu very quickly, very easily, and without a disparaging word simply by saying Speaker B is a better fit for the buyer. And Speaker A will never even know this is happening.

What Speaker A should have said was *that was the best bagel she'd ever eaten.* Or better yet, not commented at all because saying the bagel was stale cost her a fortune in lost bookings. After all, we're here for five-figure fees, not bagels.

A *great* speaker can easily make a solid mid-five figures per year if she knows what she's doing. And yet a *good* speaker, who may not have as compelling a topic or the same pedigree, who is easy to work with, empowers his or her agency, and shows up on time can make six figures per year if she understands who matters and how to play the game. In other words, a big part of success in this industry is understanding how it works and using that information to your advantage. That's just the truth.

TAKEAWAYS

Paid speaking can be very lucrative

Frequency of booking varies

Agents generally work on commission, but either way—salary or commission—there is no cost to entry for speakers

Buyers matter more than speakers—use that knowledge to your advantage

Treat agents, buyers, and audiences with the highest respect—it's the difference between success and failure

It's important to have an agent who is motivated to work hard to sell you

2.

Come Join the Paid Speaking Party

WHY NOT YOU?

How Paid Speaking Inverts the Traditional Pay-to-Play Advertising Model

Companies and brands pay to advertise their products and services—often spending millions of dollars each year to build brand awareness, brand loyalty, and brand identity. And, of course, to increase sales. Similarly, nonprofits pay to advertise to build their brand identity, raise capital, generate donations, and promote their messages. If these businesses and organizations are really lucky, they might, on occasion, get some free advertising. But the norm is that in order to grow a brand, you have to spend money to advertise.

Now imagine a world where that equation is inverted and brands not only get free advertising, but also they actually *get paid to advertise their products and services*. Then imagine a world where *you are a brand*. A brand that needs awareness, loyalty, and identity, because—just like a company selling consumer packaged goods or a nonprofit organization promoting social change—you are selling something too. That thing that you are selling might be tied to a product or a service related to a business or nonprofit you run, or it may simply be a message that you gleaned from a life experience that you'd like to share.

The paid speaking industry creates a platform to do just that. It inverts the traditional advertising model by paying individuals to advertise whatever it is that they are selling. It functions as a marketplace for individuals to become branded "products." The paid speaking industry provides one of the best high-paying, low-risk advertising forums in the world. And this means that whoever you are—if you have a business, run an organization, or are an author, a scientist, a hobbyist, or simply an average person with a message you want to communicate—you can be a paid speaker. And smart speakers can leverage paid speaking engagements as an extremely lucrative platform to generate profit and proliferate ideas.

Take this example from an actual client I worked with:

Joan is the author of a business book. To generate book sales, Joan can opt to pay a publicist an up-front fee—out of pocket—to *try* to secure media placements and reviews. She's quoted a fee of $50,000 a month from a top literary PR firm to promote her book—with no guarantee that they will generate a single placement or sell a single copy of the book.

The other option is that Joan can skip the PR firm and, with little or no out-of-pocket cost to her, she can focus her energies toward trying to get signed to a speaking agency. That agency will pitch her for paid speaking engagements where she will talk about a message tied to her book, or perhaps about the writing process, or something else she happens to be passionate about.

Joan decides to go with the second option and signs with a speakers bureau.

During her first month at the speaking agency, she accepts an offer to give a keynote address at a university for which she'll be provided first-class travel and be paid a net fee of $20,000. On top of that, in the deal negotiated by her speaking agent, the university has agreed to purchase two thousand copies of her book—which, based on her agreement with her publisher and the standard royalty rate, adds an additional dollar value of roughly $6,000 to Joan.

The swing between these two options is enormous.

In the pay-to-play PR example, Joan is in the red for $50,000. She would have to have a bestselling book to even *begin* to recoup that amount of money. In fact, doing some loose math, if she netted three dollars a copy on her hardcover sales after her publisher and literary agent took their cut, Joan would have to sell roughly seventeen thousand copies of her book that month *just to cover the first month's PR bill.*

And what does Joan do on day thirty when the month is up? If she's sold seventeen thousand copies of her book, she has now paid all of her profit to the publicist and she's at breakeven for the month. If she's had few or no media placements and there's no visible uptick in book sales, she is now faced with a dilemma. Does she sign up with the PR firm for month two at an additional $50,000? After all, the PR agency claims they are just getting their feet wet and expect things to start rolling soon. Joan is not only out the $50,000, but she's facing something called *sunk cost fallacy*—she feels that she can't quit now because she is already in the hole for $50K. So she reluctantly signs up for month two with the PR firm.

Joan now has $100,000 invested for just sixty days of book promotion—book promotion that quite possibly generated little or no media placements and no book sales.

In the second option—signing with a speaking agency—Joan pays nothing up front, she has agents pitching her and getting the word out about her book, and she gives a forty-five-minute keynote speech at the university followed by fifteen minutes of Q&A and a brief meet-and-greet with the students and faculty. In this scenario, Joan is *guaranteed* $26,000 in profit for her efforts—the $20,000 speaking fee and $6,000 in book royalties.

On top of that, she is *guaranteed* that she will get to promote her book and message to her target audience. She also will likely get booked for future paid events with similar payouts to this one. And to boot, Joan's publisher is happy because they just moved two thousand copies of her book and received their portion of the profit on those sales. But here's the kicker: Joan may also have earned media* coverage for her keynote address—media coverage the PR firm couldn't get for her. Of course, there was no guarantee from the speaking agency either, but at least Joan didn't go out of pocket.

Now consider a different example—also from a real client I represented. Instead of paying to advertise his venture or speaking for free at high schools, Bob, a nonprofit founder who was raising money to provide school supplies to students in impoverished regions of the world, signs with a speaking agency. That agency gets Bob a gig to give a keynote speech about his experience building a nonprofit from the ground up before an audience of three thousand people. For this speech Bob will be paid a $65,000 net fee, which goes directly into his pocket—not into the coffers of the nonprofit. Bob's message to that targeted audience is so powerful that the audience is motivated to act. During his

---

*   Earned media is free publicity attained via promotional efforts. For example, the university likely secured some media coverage for the event.

talk, many of the three thousand attendees reach out to their contacts and collectively raise $50,000 for Bob's nonprofit. Bob benefits personally to the tune of $65,000 and on top of that, raises $50,000 for his nonprofit.

Read that again: Bob cleared $65,000. *For less than a day's work.* And he was a kid in his twenties. His nonprofit raised substantial capital—$50,000—and built awareness. And there was no expenditure to do so or any financial risk whatsoever on Bob's end.

Both of these stories are real-life examples of win-win inversions of the standard advertising model. And they required no out-of-pocket cost, required little work, and offered both financial and nonfinancial gains for both Joan and Bob.

But what if I don't have a book and I don't run a nonprofit?

A common concern that many potential speakers have is that they haven't been published and they haven't founded a company and therefore aren't qualified to speak. This couldn't be more wrong. In fact, sometimes a small speaking career can lead to a book deal—or even a new business venture—down the line. The reality is that having a book or a company is great—the bigger your platform, the better—but there are very few speaking programs that *require* the speaker to have written a book or founded a company. With the exception of "common reads" on college campuses and at corporations that mandate authors, most event sponsors simply want to feel comfortable that the speaker is qualified and be confident that the speaker is delivering accurate information and an impassioned, compelling message to their audience.

Case Study: The Speaker Who Got a Book Deal

In 2011, I represented the founder of a line of natural beauty products. The speaker got a few gigs here and there, in the vicinity of $10,000 apiece. He was, however, speaking to fairly large audiences, which enabled him to promote his business and core message. But we decided that a book about the growth of his company would be an additional brand-building tool. So we leveraged his growing speaking platform—publishers love it when authors have an existing speaking career—and worked with him to get a book deal, securing a $50,000 publishing advance from Amazon.

The lesson here is that the book deal likely never would have happened without his speaking platform—and if he *had* gotten a book deal without a speaking background and the promise of future engagements, it would have been for a lower advance. At the same time, having a book in the works—and then later, a recently released book—increased his marketability for speaking events. We began to receive additional speaking invitations, some of which we designed as exclusive book buys with no honorarium.* This made the publisher extremely happy—and those good sales numbers set the speaker up for a second book down the line. In other cases, he received invitations that included both an honorarium and a book buy—the best combination a speaker can hope for. And of course we still got speaking invitations that were strictly that—speaking invitations with no book sales involved. And these invitations were for larger fees. *Paid speaking is the gift that keeps on giving.*

Realistically, who can get paid to give a speech?

This is one of the most misunderstood aspects of the paid

---

*   Throughout the book I use the terms *honorarium* and *speaking fee* interchangeably to refer to the amount paid to a speaker for an event.

speaking industry. Absolutely anyone who is an expert in a given field—and I am using the term *expert* loosely here—can get paid to speak. This includes anyone who is running a for-profit or a nonprofit business, anyone who is employed at a company, anyone who is unemployed, abled or disabled, a veteran, hobbyist, parent, or educator—anyone who has a message or a story to tell. That message or story can range from your experience rescuing cats, being a Girl Scout leader, operating a small business, being an entrepreneur, an immigrant, a teacher, a survivor, and so on. In fact, the only people who *cannot* give a paid speech are people who have nothing to say—or who never try.

Over the course of the past decade I've worked with people as diverse as a toy designer, an architect, a "happiness expert," a female pilot, a schoolteacher, a barista, and a female hockey player. And these are just a few examples of "small," seemingly unbookable individuals who were able to generate income by giving speeches.

Why It's Often Easier to Book an Unknown Speaker than a Celebrity

When I first started out in the speaking industry, I assumed that big-name speakers—the intellectual or entertainment celebrities of the world—would yield the most bookings and the highest dollars. As it turned out, I was completely wrong. And there are several reasons for this, the largest being that celebrities are expensive to book but, more importantly, celebrities and successful businesspeople are often only available to speak for a limited number of days each year. How this translates is that high-profile celebrities who are household names might get lots of *offers*, but they get few actual *bookings*. The odds of one of these speakers being available on the date of a given event are slim. In other words, they get lots of offers but they don't accept them.

I've represented a number of very high-profile speakers who regularly received over one hundred speaking inquiries a year, but only accepted a few of the offers they received due to the obligations of their day jobs and, frankly, a lack of interest in the money. This leaves a wide-open marketplace for an agent to move an event sponsor's interest from their "dream speaker"—who isn't available and is often priced out of their budget anyway—to a more practical, more affordable speaker who *is* available.

Case Study: How I Made a Social Entrepreneur a Million Dollars

When I signed the founder of TOMS, Blake Mycoskie, as a speaker, his hope was to get paid $10,000 per speech. TOMS was a relatively unknown brand at the time, so introducing prospective event bookers to Blake's message was a challenge. In fact, it was a challenge to convince the other agents in my office to get behind Blake's value as a speaker. I'll never forget receiving an email from a senior agent with two decades of experience in the speaking market asking me, "How are we ever going to book a guy who is talking about giving away shoes?"

The TOMS model is simple; for every pair of shoes that they sell, they give a pair to a child in need. Blake introduced something that, while commonplace now, was new at the time—buy one, give one. Buy an item for yourself and, in turn, yield a positive benefit for someone in need. So, rather than speaking about "giving away shoes" as that agent had incorrectly assumed, Blake was going to be talking to businesspeople about how companies can incorporate philanthropy into their for-profit business models in a new and very specific way, and to college students about how young people can make purposeful and powerful decisions about where and how they spend their money. He was also going to be speaking to college students about his life experience and how he built his company.

The shoes were secondary to the larger message.

And that's a key point—not just about Blake's story but also about yours. Blake wasn't *really* going to be talking about giving away shoes, and there's a good chance that by the time you get to the end of this book you're not going to be speaking about what you think you will be speaking about either.

The first event that I booked for Blake was at the University of North Carolina for $7,500. A little less than what he had been hoping to receive. But a number of years later, I was regularly receiving six-figure offers—that often included a private jet—for Blake to give speeches. Over the course of the few years that I booked and represented him, he earned over a million dollars in speaking fees. And what about that agent who said he couldn't be booked? He was referring to it as the "speaker signing of the decade" just a few weeks after we signed him.

But aren't most paid speakers motivational?

Absolutely not. Over the course of my career, I've booked a grand total of one motivational speaker.* This said, *all great speakers motivate.*

If inspiration can be gleaned from a presentation, the topic doesn't matter nearly as much as that inspired message. Is a

---

* A motivational speaker's main purpose is to inspire transformation in audience members. This transformation is intended to be applied to a personal goal of each audience member, rather than be directed toward a specific cause or message the speaker offers.

twenty-year-old who helped build hundreds of schools in the developing world a motivational speaker? No. But does she *motivate* audiences because her message about hard work, giving back, and nontraditional fund-raising techniques speak to a larger, aspirational message? Most definitely, *yes*.

If it's so easy, why isn't everyone doing it?

For a variety of reasons. First, public speaking is the biggest fear of all Americans—even outranking *death*. So, there's a segment of the population that is simply afraid to speak in front of audiences. That said, the biggest reason that more people aren't pursuing paid speaking is because the general public has no idea that this industry is available to them. And the segment of the population that *is* aware of the paid speaking industry often doesn't think they are qualified to participate. After all, when we think about speaking agencies and getting paid to speak, we think of big household names. Celebrities and politicians and billionaires—not nurses and teachers and everyday people. We don't think it includes us. But it does—or at least it can.

What does success look like in the speaking industry?

Invitations and bookings!

That being said, there are many different reasons that people decide to become speakers, and many aren't motivated by money alone. Now, while I've observed that money motivates most speakers, perhaps you are hoping to give back by sharing your story. Perhaps you are a research scientist who wants to invite more girls into the science field. Perhaps you are the founder of a growing company and you want to share the lessons you learned building that company from the ground up, your experience hiring millennials, overcoming challenges, or failing and starting over.

Paid speaking is a great way to accomplish all of these goals.

Now, no agency is going to want to sign a client who doesn't want to be compensated for speeches, because the agency won't make any money. That said, I've worked with many speakers who donate all of their speaking fees to charitable causes. I've also worked with speakers who allow their agency to charge a small fee to the event sponsor for arranging a no-fee event.

So to answer the question of what success looks like to a paid speaker, it simply depends on you and your goals. If you are the research scientist mentioned above, success likely looks like speaking engagements at conferences and universities that are interested in your experience and ideas. If you are the founder of a small but growing company, success might look like a small speaking fee of $5,000–$10,000 along with the opportunity to talk to targeted audiences of potential customers or investors. But real success comes when a speaker—and I've represented many— has the tools to work with his agency to build his personal brand and hone his message to become someone who has a story that resonates. He goes from generating small fees and a few bookings to generating large fees and a lot of bookings—what he does with the money is up to him.

But how do I know if I have what it takes?

You'll never know if you don't try, but the simple act of picking up this book probably signifies that you do indeed have what it takes. Giving a keynote speech is no different than talking in front of students if you are a teacher or giving a presentation at work if you have a corporate job—except that you will be far better compensated.

I always recommend that people start out by giving a few free speeches, ideally before even contacting an agency. Free presentation opportunities aren't that hard to find. Your local library, an Elks Club meeting, or talking to the parents of the soccer team you coach are all good examples. And your practice speech doesn't need to relate to the content you plan on presenting at paid events. This is simply an exercise to get you comfortable with talking to groups, particularly if that's not something you're used to doing.

What Does a Successful Potential Speaker Look Like?

When seeking agency representation, this speaker understands that she is a brand and that paid speaking is a lucrative option available to her. She has a clear idea as to what she is qualified to speak about, has a curated message, and knows what she wants to get out of speaking—which may or may not be strictly financial. It may be proliferation of message, generating donations, moving product, up-selling, or building brand awareness. She has an agent, is at the right agency for her, and is being marketed to the right event sponsors and under the right umbrella. Understanding her purpose—her reasons for giving speeches—is the key. It will affect everything from her speech topics to the speaking agency she chooses, to which offers she accepts and which offers she politely turns down. And all of this will have a big impact and affect how successful she is and how much she is paid.

TAKEAWAYS
Paid speaking inverts the pay-to-play advertising model

There is little or no up-front cost and no risk

You don't need to be an author or run a company to be a paid speaker

And you don't have to be a celebrity or a high-powered professional either

Most paid speakers aren't motivational, but they do motivate

Don't fall into the trap of thinking that if it's so easy, everyone
would be doing it

Invitations and bookings are the definition of success in the paid
speaking industry

3.

But What If I'm a Poet or a Beekeeper?

CREATE YOUR OWN LANE

Early in my career, the majority of the speakers I was assigned to book fell into the $5,000–$20,000 range. And at first, bookings were hard to come by. This was for a variety of reasons, but for starters, selling a speaker has a lot to do with having relationships of trust with event sponsors. Because I was new to the industry, I didn't have those relationships. As much as I knew that this would resolve itself with time, there was one thing I noticed that I *could* fix immediately.

As I spoke with potential event sponsors on the phone, I realized that they were all looking for something fairly specific—but on occasion, I didn't represent speakers who were a perfect match for their programs. In those cases, I was faced with either trying to force-fit one of the speakers I did represent or taking the time to try to *find someone* who was a better fit. Typically that meant finding a person who wasn't represented by a speaking agency and probably had never even considered the possibility of being a speaker.

I was once contacted by an event sponsor from a private girls school in Tennessee who wanted someone young to give a talk about community-building. I must have pitched every speaker on my roster three times—the Pulitzer Prize–nominated author who worked in dog rescue, the founder of an education nonprofit, and a woman who ran a wellness initiative, to name a few. These were all high-profile individuals who had paid speaking experience and *could* have talked about community-building. But none of them got the event sponsor excited. I knew this buyer was probably speaking with other agencies and I didn't want to lose the chance to deliver for a buyer who I was hoping would become a long-term client. Nor did I want to let the commission slip through my fingers. So, I did what most people do when they don't have the answer to something—I hopped on Google.

An hour or so into reading random articles about community-building, I stumbled upon a fascinating piece written by a young beekeeper. The article touched on the way that bees form communities and how they are members of hives with intricate power structures and methods of communication with one dominant female force—the queen—at the helm. The author, Jill, appeared to be perfect for my buyer. She was in her twenties, seemed passionate, and even if she didn't know it—her article was specific to bees—she had a unique angle on community-building.

On the downside, from what I could glean online, Jill had no prior public speaking experience—save her classroom presentations in college. Her article, as good as it was, wasn't published by a well-known media outlet—and worse than that, I had no idea if I could even reach her. This was a time-sensitive booking and all I had to contact her was the email address listed on her website. I had no way to know how long it might take to get a response, I had no idea if she'd be interested and available, and I also had no idea if the event sponsor would be as excited about her as I was.

I knew that the best approach would be to first see if the event sponsor would be interested in Jill. But this approach had inherent risk. Jill was not my client. In fact, she had never heard of me or spoken to me before. I had no idea if she would have interest in giving a lecture, let alone a lecture in Tennessee on a specific date. And if I were to sell her to my buyer and then couldn't deliver because Jill declined, I'd be nowhere.

I took the gamble anyway and pitched Jill for the event. The event sponsor was excited after reading the article and wrote an offer for $15,000—plus travel expenses—for Jill to come to campus, give a keynote speech, and visit a few classes. While this was great, Jill had no clue that I had just sold her to a client and spun her article into a speech topic about community-building.

I wrote Jill a short but to-the-point message and sent it to the email address on her website. It went something like this:

> I read your most recent article, and I represent speakers for paid speaking opportunities around the world. I was inspired by your story, and shared your work with one of my clients. They would like to invite you to give a presentation on their campus. They can offer you a speaking fee of $15,000. Please call me at the number below if you are interested.

Jill called my office twenty minutes later a little shell-shocked and guarded—but excited. She accepted the engagement and two months later visited the school in Tennessee. She talked about the importance of bees and their communities—relating it to forming communities based around everything from friendship to shared beliefs, from neighborhoods to schools. *But she primarily talked about bees.*

It was a fresh angle on community-building. One she was well-versed in and passionate about. She had a great time, the audience was engaged, and the sponsor was thrilled with her visit. It's important to note that Jill only had to add a little bit of non-bee-related information to her speech to make her forty-five-minute keynote address relevant to the needs of this particular event sponsor. The girls in the audience learned primarily about bees but left with a strong message about community.

I learned two important lessons here pertaining to me as an agent:

▸ I would have better luck finding the perfect fit than trying to force a square peg into a round hole.

▸ There are many experts out there who aren't even aware that they have a message they can get paid to share.

Going forward, I made it my mission to find the perfect speakers for event sponsors even if that meant reaching beyond the clients who were signed exclusively to my agency. But there are also a couple of lessons here that pertain to you as a potential paid speaker:

▸ No matter how unlikely you might think it is that someone will pay you to speak, don't be afraid to put your hat in the ring. The most essential key to success in the paid speaking industry is simply "showing up." In other words, the one way to ensure that you never make money as a paid speaker is by never putting yourself out there. The simple act of putting yourself on the menu is the single biggest step you can take toward finding success as a paid speaker and changing your life—both professionally and financially.

▶ Story trumps everything. And finding your lane—what I think about as *personal brand development*—is another key to success in the paid speaking industry. If Jill wanted to earn money as a paid speaker, she had to stop narrowly defining herself as a beekeeper and instead brand herself as an expert with a fascinating and unique spin on community-building.

Why Story Trumps Everything

I once signed an Iraqi poet named Nadia. Nadia was of interest to me—and my event sponsors—for a few reasons: A) Iraq was all over the news following 9/11, B) women were—and still are—oppressed in Iraq, so the very nature of her content was stimulating and different, and C) she is a poet. Female Iraqi poets are not something you find every day. This was highly relevant because most event sponsors had never even *met* someone from Iraq, let alone heard an Iraqi speaker and poet give a speech.

In the speaking world, poets are a bit of a novelty and often difficult to book. But after meeting Nadia, I determined that her speeches—which focused on her poetry about the empowerment of women—would appeal to three different sets of event sponsors: A) English programs at colleges and universities (the poetry aspect), B) international studies programs at institutes of higher education (the Iraqi aspect), and C) corporations and nonprofits that wanted to learn about "life on the ground" in war-torn Iraq (the politics/humanitarian aspect).

I subsequently took these three categories and began

developing a marketing plan. And since Nadia wasn't looking for a large payday—anywhere between $2,500 and $10,000 a speech—she was an easy booking. What we were selling here was the power of story. And this translates across the board. Her *story* is what sold her—not her speaking ability or her stage presence.

Nadia's story was widely framed, uniquely positioned, and in a lane with no competition. If an event sponsor was looking for a management speech, or a speech about leadership, Nadia would have been competing against hundreds of other speakers. But by defining her uniqueness, she was able to carve out a nice little niche for herself that added tens of thousands of dollars to her annual income for very little work. The fact that she was a paid speaker helped her gain status as a university professor and also increased her book advances* from her publisher. Although my agency wasn't getting paid directly for her book sales, the books helped scale her speaking fee. In the speaking world, this is often called a *virtuous circle*. Give a speech, publish a book—in her case a book of poetry—and then go speak more, and for higher fees.

How to Find Your Lane and Think about Yourself as a Brand

The issue that I often run into—as was the case with Nadia—is that she didn't think of herself as a brand. Rather, she viewed herself as a college professor who specialized in poetry—just as Jill viewed herself as a beekeeper. On top of the fact that they both defined themselves too narrowly, neither of these women saw their value as paid speakers.

---

*   A book advance is the money paid to an author prior to publication and is an advance against future royalties.

Jill had never even considered giving a paid speech or "putting herself on the menu," and Nadia didn't think of herself as worthy of the speaking fees being offered—to the degree that she would often call me apologizing, asking if we should reduce her rate—likely because one speech earned her more money than she was making in a month as a professor. I also had to convince Nadia that marketing herself solely as a poet was narrow and shortsighted. To me, and to my event sponsors, Nadia offered a perspective otherwise unseen in the speaking world. In other words, *she owned her own niche.* As an Iraqi woman with credentials, she had a wide variety of interested clients ranging from college English programs who were seeking a poet, nonprofits who were working with women from war-torn countries, and corporations that were seeking an inspiring message for their employees. Where Nadia saw herself as a poet, I was able to brand her as a triple threat.

Case Study: Creating Your Own Lane

The Public School Teacher Who Was Passionate about Gardening

In 2012, I signed a school teacher named Steve who taught in New York City. His passions revolved around healthy eating and gardening. And he went so far as to start growing vegetables at his school to empower students to eat healthfully. Now, to be honest, I originally thought that Steve was going to be a very difficult booking. After all, what were we going to do, sell him to elementary schools? Generally, elementary schools don't have budgets for speakers, and the only high schools that have speaking budgets—for the most part—are private high schools, and those opportunities are few and far between.

To solve that problem, we had to take Steve's narrow

interest—gardening and nutrition for kids—and find its broad appeal. By framing his lectures around innovation in the classroom—he was using hydroponic technology to grow fruits and vegetables in the inner city and showing his students an alternative to traditional school lunch and junk food—we were able to move him into the speaking categories of leadership and innovation.

The first place we booked Steve was at a leadership conference for CEOs of mid-level companies. And they loved him. Remember, Steve wasn't a CEO and he wasn't a high-level businessperson—he was talking about growing vegetables on rooftops with school kids in the city. But the audience responded to him because they identified with the challenge he was facing in trying to solve a significant problem—an epidemic of obesity and poor nutrition in the inner city. That is, after all, what companies, leaders, and innovators do—they solve problems.

Now, the organizations that booked Steve could have easily brought in innovation experts, authors, or journalists who'd written about innovation for C-level executives for years—established experts who speak to this topic. But Steve was competing for these gigs in a lane all by himself.

He was as unique as a beekeeper or an Iraqi poet.

Event sponsors were either going to book one of the other guys, most of whom looked the same on paper, or Steve, the one outlier who offered a message that no one could ever have predicted. And that was Steve's primary selling point. When you have your own lane—an approach that is slightly different than all of the other speakers being pitched—the competition tends to be canceled out quite quickly.

What are the first few steps you can take to expand your view of yourself, find your lane, and monetize your story?

▶ Begin to think of yourself as a brand.

▶ Consider both your broad appeal—for example, community-building (Jill), the empowerment of women (Nadia), or innovation (Steve)—and own your narrow, unique angle—beekeeping, the empowerment of women, or school gardening.

▶ Think about the three different audiences and what you would share with them. These audiences should be university, corporate,* and nonprofit. While you may not be able to develop suitable topics for each, this is a good exercise.

▶ Write down the message for each audience—bullet points for what you want to convey—knowing that the message may be exactly the same for all three audiences or it may be different. Then write down the stories you have that demonstrate that message in a unique manner.

And don't be afraid to think outside the box, not just in terms your lane, but in terms of the speaking venue marketplace as well.

Case Study: Chuck Klosterman and the Hard Rock Cafe

From 2007 thru 2009 I was lucky to be one of the agents who represented pop culture critic Chuck Klosterman. At the time, Chuck regularly received speaking invitations in the $5,000–$7,500 range, mainly from colleges and universities.

On a rainy Monday afternoon, I called Chuck with an

---

*   For purposes of simplicity, I'm including conferences, consortiums, and similar events
under the corporate umbrella.

interesting offer—speaking at a music venue in New York City. But here was the catch. Instead of a guaranteed offer to cover his fee, we would be selling tickets. This is very uncommon because universities and companies generally have fixed budgets that guarantee payment to a speaker. It was also uncommon because speakers don't typically speak at music venues. A speaking fee based on ticket sales alone is a fairly aggressive—and risky—play. When I called Chuck with the offer, he told me that he "couldn't imagine people paying twenty dollars a ticket to see a living author." Quickly, and perhaps somewhat glibly, I told Chuck that no one would pay twenty dollars to see a dead author either, so maybe we should give it a try.

He agreed and we did our first event in New York City. It sold out quickly, and he killed it. On top of that, I convinced NPR's Ira Glass to appear as a surprise guest. The audience went nuts when Ira unexpectedly took the stage. And they went equally wild for Chuck, who was previewing a chapter from his yet-to-be-released first book of fiction. As agents, when we try something new—a new speaker, a different speech topic, a new type of venue, a slightly different audience—we're always looking for proof of concept, and this sold-out event was exactly that.

Subsequently we booked an event for him at the Hard Rock Cafe in Boston. And this event generated earned media that college and university events couldn't. For example, we booked Chuck on the largest morning drive radio show in Boston—with hundreds of thousands of listeners—on the day of the Hard Rock Cafe event.

Now, I know you're probably thinking: *Chuck Klosterman is a top-selling author and acclaimed journalist and I'm not.* But here's the thing—that's not what mattered. What mattered is that we were putting something different on the menu. The Hard Rock

Cafe didn't book speakers, nor did the venue he was booked at in New York City. What we did, essentially, was carve out a new market for Chuck that didn't previously exist. And that's what we did for Jill, Nadia, and Steve. So think about this as you consider carving out a career as a paid speaker. Put yourself on the menu, and find your unique angle.

TAKEAWAYS

Don't be afraid to throw your hat in the ring

Story trumps everything

Think about yourself as a brand and find your lane

Consider how to marry your narrow uniqueness with broad appeal

Own your niche

4.

How to Avoid the Most Common Mistakes

NEVER MISTAKE MOTION FOR ACTION

The biggest, most common problems potential speakers face are having improperly formatted materials and the wrong content.

To be considered for representation by an agency, an aspiring speaker has to submit a few sample speaking topics and descriptions, a bio, a list of his or her accomplishments along with endorsements (blurbs or praise), and a photo. Basically, whatever materials you have to explain who you are, what you want to speak about, and why you're qualified to do so. If all goes well, you'll receive offers of representation and sign an exclusive contract with an agency.

The most common mistake I've seen is that the materials being presented by aspiring speakers—their topics, bio, and praise—aren't written in the language of the speaking world. Your bio may be perfect for a job interview or your LinkedIn profile, and your speaking topics might sound interesting to *you*, but they're not right for the speaking market. Generally, agencies have limited time to work on this material with you—and agents don't help to develop speaking topics with new speakers to the degree that most aspiring speakers require. Because *agents have to sell to survive,* any time they spend not on the phone selling means that they're not making money. So as much as in a perfect world this wouldn't be the case, more often than not *the agents put in some work but essentially use the materials they are given.*

As such, the most important thing you can do is create killer, industry-specific marketing materials *preemptively.* If you show up with well-crafted and perfectly formatted speaking topics (chapter 5), an industry specific bio (chapter 6), professionally presented marketing collateral (chapter 7), and create a killer one sheet* (chapter 8), it will not only increase your chances of getting signed for representation, but also once you are signed it will empower the agents at your agency to get you more bookings, higher-profile bookings, and more money.

And there's something else you have to do. *You also have to make sure you sign with the right agency.*

Case Study: The Speaker Who Made No Money at a Major Hollywood Agency
Bad Speaker or Wrong Agency?

I once represented a speaker who left a major, household-name Hollywood talent agency to sign with my relatively unknown agency. He was a fantastic speaker with an incredibly inspiring story about his work building schools around the world.

The problem was that the major Hollywood agency didn't

---

*   A one sheet is a single page document—typically in PDF form—that reflects the speaker's profile page on an agency's website.

secure any bookings for him. Part of this had to do with the fact that his requested fee was too low for him to be top of mind at such a top-tier agency that represented celebrities—movie stars, television hosts, and Olympic athletes. After all, if you're an agent working on commission, would you focus your efforts on booking a $5,000 speaker or the $50,000 speakers your agency also represents for film deals? The latter comes with ten times the commission.

This particular speaker had great, timely topics. His bio was perfect. He just needed someone motivated to push him from a marketing standpoint—to be top of mind with his agents. When I signed him, the first booking we got was for $500 at MasterCard. But within eighteen months, he was regularly receiving $20,000 per speech, and he occasionally received offers in the $40,000–$60,000 range. He found huge success by going with a less prestigious agency that was a better fit for him.

So if you're "repped" by an agency and you're not getting booked but your materials are top-notch, you have to ask yourself, *Am I not a qualified speaker, or is the agency I'm with simply not a good fit?* In my experience, it's likely the latter. And if you are just starting out, I'm going to help you make sure you get signed to the right agency for *you* (chapter 9).

You also need to temper expectations.

Why Some Speakers Find Instant Success While Others Build over Time

Instant success is rare in the speaking industry. Looking at the hundreds of speaking clients I've worked with over the course of my career, only a handful met with instant success. I always like to tell new speakers that it's going to be at least a year before we see any tangible results; part of this is managing expectations, but mostly it's simply the truth. Even if you're an established speaker, it's important to allow some "runway" when working with a new agency. Agents have to learn your story inside and out, become comfortable pitching you, and work you into their event sponsors' list of potential speakers.

I've also found that speakers who meet with instant success often can't sustain it. Sometimes this is due to their early success being tied to a specific timely event—a particular topic becomes hot, or a speaker releases a new book—maybe even hitting a best-seller list. Other times it's because a few agents are particularly motivated to book a speaker because he or she is new. It can also be that an agent simply gets lucky—and then interest wanes.

Early in my career I came close to booking a brand-new speaker to the agency for a $40,000 keynote at a university, and it came down to a choice between that speaker and one other. They had radically different backgrounds and were both being pitched for a program on creativity. Not only did my speaker lose that gig by a hair—a toss of the coin, the event sponsor told me—but we never booked that speaker for anything else. Flukes happen, and even the best agents have clients they can't book. But given the choice between flash-in-the-pan instant success and a slow, organic build, most speakers and agents would—and should—choose the latter.

Agents know full well that a speaker can't be forced on an event sponsor. That the decision to hire one speaker over another is typically made by a panel or committee—not by one person. You could be the second choice speaker in every committee vote, and you'll never see a dollar. You also may never know that you were the second choice. But if you have a good agent, she will know how close you are getting—tell you so—and keep pitching you for appropriate programs. And this takes time. The most important thing you can do is have something specific to say and make sure you present it with sizzle and spin.

Case Study: Don't Rely on a Job Title or an Award Alone
The Former Head of State from a Middle Eastern Country

I once worked at an agency that signed the former president of a well-known country that was always in the news. Upon signing him, all of the agents were super excited to have a former head of state on the roster. We figured we could book him frequently for six figures plus a private jet.

Boy, were we wrong. We couldn't book him at all. Everyone at the agency pitched him like crazy—with very poor results. But as I tried to figure out why, I analyzed his material and learned a very important lesson—*titles alone mean very little in the speaking world.*

And that's basically all he had given us. There was nothing fresh or exciting about his material. He was being pitched as the ex-president of a Middle Eastern country—he had a prestigious title, but no distinct message for American paid speaking audiences. And we could read about the Middle East every day in the newspapers. Also, remember that speakers compete for these coveted engagements with an odd mix of bedfellows. The ex-president of a country might be competing with the founder of PostSecret and the founders of Ben & Jerry's, who are very popular speakers.

I believe that the conclusion arrived at by most event sponsors— all of whom were based in the college market since the ex-president had little value to provide to corporations—was that he was a political figure and nothing more. And this was not because of who he was, but because of how he was framed in his speaking materials— and that's something that speakers can change.

It's helpful to reframe prior rejections and failures and repurpose them for future success. I've represented many speakers who have failed their way to success. What I mean by this is that they were willing to take the feedback from speeches that weren't well-received and from the pitches that didn't result in bookings and modify their content.

This may sound basic, but most speakers I've worked with are married to their topics and their message and resist change. The ex-president could have reframed his marketing materials to address their flaws. He didn't. At least not when I worked with him.

Now, this isn't to say you shouldn't stick to your guns if you have a message you believe in. But if you aren't getting booked and you are market-savvy and market-sensitive, you can often work with a good agent to subtly change your content—and the way in which it's presented can make all the difference.

You have to be willing to make changes if you are failing either at the pitch level or at the event level. It's great to hear the feedback from event sponsors who said no when you were being pitched. Is it your topics? Your bio? Why, specifically, are you being turned down? But also consider the feedback you receive after your speeches—if you're giving them. Is there anything you can do to improve future events? Figuring this out is something your agent can and should help you with.

Consider if there are any "magic bullets" that you haven't thought to tell your agents but should. You might not be getting booked because there is something you didn't tell them. While speaking agents don't want to waste time listening to your entire life story, they are looking for "magic bullets." They are looking for something that separates you from the pack—including the other speakers represented by their agency. If everyone looks the same, sounds the same, and is espousing the same message—or close to the same message—all the agency is doing is building a basket of speakers who will be competing against each other. And agencies don't like to have competition in-house for obvious reasons. If an agency has two speakers who talk about robotics and they are in the same price range, they will both get fewer bookings because they're competing with each other for the same events.

When looking for your magic bullets, it's important to consider that there are likely pieces of information that you aren't sharing with your agency and should be. It could be that you served in the military in Afghanistan prior to becoming a yoga instructor. It could be that prior to becoming a biologist you were a touring musician; an Eagle Scout; a self-published mystery writer; the first in your family to go to college; a marathon runner. Or it could be an interesting anecdote from your childhood. And here's the thing—it's not that you're going to lecture about these topics, it's just that they help to define you in a unique way, make you relatable, and can help establish a platform that separates you from the other speakers being pitched.

And finally, treat your agents and agency well—failure often occurs because speakers don't interact with the agency correctly. Earlier, I gave the example of the stale bagel. That speaker didn't show the respect that an event sponsor writing a large check expects and deserves to receive. Bringing a highly compensated speaker to an event is a *big deal* to the sponsor—as it should be. The organization he or she works for is spending a lot of money for an important event. Often times the fee the sponsor is paying a speaker is more money than the sponsor makes in several months—or even a year—at his or her job.

But before a potential speaker even gets to interact with an event sponsor or an audience, they interact with the agents at their speaking agency. And there are ways of doing this correctly and ways of doing this incorrectly. How you work with your agency will have a great impact on whether you get booked, where you get booked, how often you get booked, and how much money you get.

Case Study: Speaker A or Speaker B

Speaker A signed with a speaking agency two years ago. She's only been booked a couple of times but speaks with her agent every two weeks, staying on the phone for a long time despite the agent's attempts to end the call. She also sends frequent emails asking how bookings are going, who she's being pitched to, and what sort of feedback she's receiving from prospective event sponsors. She scoffs at and dismisses any market feedback she's offered, balks at any suggestions to update her lecture topics in a market-sensitive way, and comes to the conclusion that her agents simply aren't pitching her correctly—or enough. Then she starts calling to check in even more frequently, and these calls are to offer new strategies that she thinks the agents should be using to book her.

Speaker B also signed with the same speaking agency two years ago. He too has only been booked a couple of times, but he speaks with the agents at his agency once every six months or so, only touching base more frequently if he has significant news or important updates. Just like Speaker A, he too asks what type of feedback he's getting—and over the course of the last two years he's modified his speaking topics based on the feedback from his agent—so much so that his speaking topics now look nothing like the topics he presented when he initially signed with the agency.

Speaker A is demonstrating a series of problematic behaviors. For one, she's contacting her agency too often, which means she's likely being pitched less because agents hate being bothered about booking results they cannot control. Further, she's making no attempt to advance her career by taking the constructive feedback from the event sponsors she *is* being pitched to and incorporating it into new—or modified—topics.

On the flip side, Speaker B is demonstrating a series of forward-thinking, agency-friendly, agency-respectful behaviors. He's contacting his agency at appropriate times with appropriate updates. He's also taking constructive criticism from the market into account and modifying his topics to fit what event sponsors seem to be looking for. He's making every effort to benefit not only himself, but also the agents responsible for booking him. As a result, these agents are likely pitching him more frequently than they are pitching Speaker A. Armed with refined market information and happier agents, he's more likely to get booked.

TAKEAWAYS

Make sure you have the best speech topics, bio, and marketing materials possible

Many speakers struggle with their *first* agency, but that can be prevented by signing with *the right* agency (for you)

Temper expectations—building a speaking career takes time

Have something specific to say, and make sure you present it with sizzle and spin—don't rely on a title (job or otherwise) alone

Reframe prior speaking failures and use them as fuel for future paid speaking success

Identify any magic bullets that you didn't think to tell your agent about, but should

Failed speaking careers often occur because the speaker doesn't interact with their agency correctly: *Make sure to give your agent and agency what they need so they can get you what you want*

5.

How to Create Your Speaking Topics

CHANGE THE FRAME, CHANGE THE GAME

Now that we've taken a broad, 35,000-foot view of the paid speaking industry, let's explore how best to determine your potential speaking topics, how to title them, and how to write compelling, descriptive copy.

Selecting your speech topics is arguably the most important first step in getting a speaking agent for this reason: it's the first step in *defining yourself as a brand*. And defining yourself as a brand will not only frame and direct the other component pieces of your speaking materials—your bio and collateral marketing— but it will also dictate where (which markets) and to whom (which event sponsors) you can potentially be "sold." In other words, your speech topics will define what shelf you should sit on—or as I think of it, which speaking bucket you fall into—and how marketable you are.

Now, technically you don't need to have your speech topics prepared before you approach speaking agencies for representation. But if you do, you'll have a much better chance of a successful outcome—especially if you're new to the paid speaking industry and aren't someone who is already a household name and has a large platform.

The best way to explain this is to remind you that in order to become a paid speaker, you'll need to be sold to event sponsors. And before that can happen, you have to first sell yourself to a speaking agency. The better and more professional your introduction is to those speaking agencies, the better your chances are of getting offers for representation. Arriving in speaking agents' inboxes with defined speaking topics, intriguing titles, and great descriptive copy will give agents a good idea of your viability and potential value in the paid speaking market. It also shows a level of professionalism and presents you as a candidate who may be easy and fast to get to market—and that gives you a significant leg up.

I can't tell you how many times extremely credentialed people who could have had great paid speaking careers contacted me with poorly thought-out speaking topics—speaking topics that obviously sounded good to them but that wouldn't fly in the paid speaking market. I have also been inundated with queries from potential speakers that contained no speaking topics at all.

In fact, the most common introduction I've gotten over the years is, "I'm contacting you because everyone says I should be a speaker." This is a statement that is often delivered with little else. I might get a CV, résumé, or bio suited for other outlets— not the paid speaking industry—forwarded by an individual with little or no knowledge of what sells or how the industry works.

When this happens, it means that I—and all of the other agents who receive that query—have to do the work of figuring out what this particular speaker's message is, or should be.

We then have to determine why he or she may or may not be uniquely qualified to deliver that message, and which market segment that message may or may not be marketable to. In other words, the agents have to figure out exactly what the speaker wants to speak about, if he or she is really qualified to do so, and where he or she can be sold. And that's a lot of work—work agents are eager to do to sign particularly appealing new speakers, but more work than most agents are willing or able to do for the majority of the potential speakers who contact them. So that means that many highly qualified want-to-be-paid speakers looking to be represented heard a *no* from me (and likely from other agents too) that could have been a *yes* if only they had been better prepared. I would also argue that, in most cases, you are the person who is best suited to figure out what you should speak about and what your message should be—assuming of course that you understand how the industry works.

To put it in simple terms, approaching an agency with professionally presented speech topics makes the agents' jobs easier and gives you the strongest chance of getting signed to an exclusive agency contract. That gives you the best shot at a great career as a paid speaker. And doing the heavy lifting up front also puts you in the driver's seat; it allows you to forge and define your own brand.

Where to Start? First Find Your "Bucket"

I like to think about the speaking industry's needs as falling into eighteen general buckets.

- ▶ Distinguished/Celebrity
- ▶ Authors

▶ Leadership/Management   ▶ Health/Wellness

▶ Innovation   ▶ Politics/Economy

▶ Diversity/Race   ▶ Entrepreneurship

▶ Women/Gender/Sexuality ▶ Social Entrepreneurship

▶ Science   ▶ Business

▶ Arts   ▶ Technology

▶ Education   ▶ Spirituality

▶ Inspiration   ▶ Big Think/Futurism

Of course, there are other categories and subcategories within these buckets, as well as speakers and speeches, that don't fit neatly into any of the above categories. Sports, for example, is a category. But generally the only people being booked to talk about sports are household-name athletes and coaches—all of whom are typically retired and who also fall into the distinguished/celebrity bucket. The key is to start thinking about where your topic(s) will fit, while understanding that there will likely be overlap. For example, you might be pitched as an author who speaks about health and wellness with a spiritual spin.

Once You've Found Your Bucket or Buckets, You Have to Zero In on Specific Topics

I once got an email from an aspiring speaker who included a bullet point list of ten topics she could speak to without a single description of any of the topics. First of all, no one can speak to ten different topics no matter how smart they might be, and rattling off a list of topics is a red flag to any agent because it shows a lack of understanding as to how the speaking industry works.

When I replied to the aspiring speaker—let's call her Mary—I asked her to write up a few topic descriptions using five or six sentences. But when Mary responded back to me, she couldn't provide more than one or two sentences for any of the topics she submitted. This is an important lesson because it's one thing to say that you can speak to multiple topics, but when it comes down to providing a description—let alone a forty-five-minute lecture—it's a lot more difficult than it might seem. So ask yourself this: How many topics can you talk about—uninterrupted—for forty-five minutes straight? Typically the answer is two or three. And this is the goal. Speak to what you know, stay in your lane, and focus on quality over quantity. As you'll see later on in this book, one well-positioned topic—your *one great speech*—can be sold over and over again. Potentially for years. So it's worth taking the time now to cull through the list of potential topics you think you might be able to speak about with authority and conviction to find a few topics that might end up being your one great speech.

What Is the True Value Measure of an Authentic Voice?

The most important aspect of public speaking, especially paid speaking, as I'll keep pounding home, is *authenticity*. This may sound obvious, but I can't count how many times I've seen speakers focus too much on what they think agents and event sponsors want, abandon their own voice, and in turn lose the importance of their expertise and message along the way. Agents want to

understand who you are, what about your background is potentially valuable to event sponsors, and what you'll talk about specifically. Your topics should reflect this. When applying to an
agency for representation, don't try to be more than you are, and
don't try to speak to topics you can't address at an expert level.
This said, it's wise to try to connect your expertise and topic(s) to
larger ideas in order to be appealing to an agency, to event sponsors, and prospective audiences.

Why the Topics You Think You Should Be Speaking About Are Likely the Exact Things You Shouldn't Be Speaking About

As mentioned earlier, I recommend that anyone hoping to get
paid to speak begin to think about themselves as a brand—
because that is exactly what paid speakers become. *Neatly packaged intellectual products that are being sold in incremental time
segments to event sponsors.*

In order to begin the process of branding and marketing
yourself as if you were a consumer packaged good, you have to
determine what the great advertising luminary Rosser Reeves of
Ted Bates & Company called back in the 1940s your *Unique Selling
Proposition (USP)*. And your USP is the single sales point that
differentiates you from the pack. This works brilliantly for both
branding products and for branding people, and it will become
the defining element of your personal brand identity and the cor-
nerstone of your speaking platform.

According to Reeves, a USP for a brand can't simply be generic
"fluff" or empty words that sound good. Instead, to be successful,
a USP for a consumer packaged good must do three things:

1. It must say, "Buy this product, for *this specific benefit.*"

2. It must be unique—offer an appealing attribute or claim that your competition can't make.

3. And it must be compelling enough to "move the masses."

On the consumer product level, think of the slogan for M&M's: *melts in your mouth, not in your hand.*

1. The specific benefit to the consumer is clear:

    ► *The outer coating on the candy prevents messy fingers.*

2. It is a unique claim:

    ► *At the time, no other chocolate candy offered this particular attribute.*

3. And based on sales, it was a need that resonated with many chocolate eaters:

    ► *It appealed to the masses.*

Now consider that the concept of a Unique Selling Proposition is an effective conceptual template to use as you begin to think about yourself as a brand. And also consider that it's an effective filter through which you should run any ideas you have for potential speaking topics.

To be successful, a USP for a speaking topic must do the same three things it does for a consumer packaged good:

1. Your speech topic must identify a specific benefit to the

audience—a specific message that people will be able to take away from your talk.

2. It must be a topic that you are uniquely qualified to speak about—you must establish that while plenty of other people might be able to deliver a similar message, very few—if any—people could give this speech the way you can. (Think the beekeeper speaking about community-building. While community-building itself is not that unique of a speech topic, when it's told through the lens of a beekeeper it is singularly unique.)

3. Your content and takeaways must contain a message that moves the masses—one that appeals to a lot of people.
   As close to perfect as Reeve's USP rubric is, when applying it as a template for selecting speaking topics, I'd add a fourth parameter:

4. The speech topics you choose should be wrapped around a compelling, engaging, and authentic story.

So how does this work exactly?

Now, let's say you've found your bucket. You're a scientist—a physicist with a PhD—who's conducting cutting-edge research in nanotechnology and you want to get paid to speak. You have a huge reputation in the academic world, but most people outside of your field have never heard of you—including the speaking agents you'll be contacting in the hope of getting signed. If you contact an agency introducing yourself as a physicist from MIT doing cutting-edge research on nanotechnology and say that you'd like to be a paid speaker, the agent is likely to feel intrigued but a bit overwhelmed, perhaps thinking, *She sounds impressive and brilliant, and nanotechnology is interesting, but what exactly would she speak about and to whom? What's her message?*

But let's say our physicist goes a step further and introduces herself to the speaking agent by saying, *I would like to speak about recent technical developments I've made in nanotechnology.* The problem with this is that there's not much of a market for people to be paid to speak about something this specific and this technical beyond academic conferences, unless the agent can convince our physicist to frame her fascinating research in nanotechnology to underpin a *larger, more universal message.* In other words, technical developments in nanotechnology probably don't fulfill item three of the USP directive—*appealing to the masses.*

Now, the physicist will likely be able to speak to audiences comprised of other scientists at academic conferences on nanotechnology—and has probably been doing that—but those conferences often don't have big budgets for speakers and aren't where agents at most speaking agencies normally book clients.* *We book speakers to give talks to "regular" people at colleges and corporations and nonprofit organizations.* And that's where the big dollars are and the big exposure lies in the paid speaking market—not scientists speaking to other scientists at academic conferences. So that means that our physicist will have to define her brand *on a consumer-friendly level,* understanding that the audiences she'll be speaking before aren't made up of other PhDs with interest in highly technical developments. *She will have to find her Unique Selling Proposition.*

---

* There are some very high-end conferences that pay significant fees for highly specialized speakers and a few agencies who will represent these speakers.

1. She will have to clearly define the message the audience will walk away with.

2. She will have to differentiate herself from all the other scientists who are available to speak, and explain how she is uniquely qualified to deliver that message.

3. She will have to establish that her speech topic has appeal to a wide audience.

4. And she will have to wrap it in an engaging, enlightening story.

If she crafts potential speech topic descriptions that do this, she'll likely generate agency interest. And don't think for a second this requires that our physicist dumb herself down or that she shouldn't speak about nanotechnology. It simply requires that she make her message *more universal and more relevant to an audience comprising non-scientists.* When she does that, it will be game changing for her as it expands her brand beyond her previously narrow academic niche, makes her far more commercially viable as a paid speaker and, as I've seen numerous times, allows her to start thinking about herself in an entirely new way.

So, how does our physicist actually do this?

By simply asking herself a few questions about her interests. For example, I would suggest that to begin the process of speech topic selection, she first ask herself this:

Thinking in the broadest sense, what's the most compelling message I want to convey to a general audience? What's the biggest, most significant takeaway that ties my experience in nanotechnology to the rest of humanity?

Remembering of course that her topic must offer a significant takeaway like *melts in your mouth, not in your hands*, that it should be something that she is uniquely qualified to deliver, and is something that will appeal to a wide audience and can be delivered in an engaging manner.

But first she has to consider the audience and take into account the three specific speaking markets: college, corporate, and nonprofit. And how and where her topics fit in.

Of course, there are always exceptions, and some speakers can be booked successfully in all three categories—but most speakers will find that their message and experience make them most appropriate for just one of the three markets. The speakers who have experiences that are highly relevant to all three segments of the paid speaking market will find that in some cases they can simply adjust the language, tone, and content of a speech for it to work well for all three audiences, while others will find that they have to write completely different speeches for each audience.

Obviously, a speech topic written for college students will have different *content* as well as a different *tone* and *message*—and significantly different *language*—than one written to be delivered to a group of C-level executives in corporate banking. But stepping back from that extreme, there can be a lot of overlap— particularly between speeches written for employees of for-profit corporations and nonprofits. For example, if your speech is about productivity or customer acquisition, that message can be relevant to people working in both the for-profit and the nonprofit business sectors with very little adjustment to the content, tone, or takeaways.

There's also significant overlap between the college and nonprofit speaking markets. For example, a young founder of a nonprofit can speak to an audience of employees of other nonprofits about public service or career paths, then speak about the same topic at a college or university. But he will have to write a completely different speech for the corporate market—perhaps focusing on customer acquisition or scaling an organization.

It's important to keep these three markets in mind when thinking about your speaking topics, and then write your speech titles and descriptive copy with that (or those) specific target market(s) in mind. Bearing in mind that—depending on who you are and what market you think your message is more relevant to—your three speech topics may all be geared toward one of these markets. Or you may, for example, write one topic appropriate for a corporate speech and two oriented for the college market.

So how does this work?

Now let's apply our eighteen buckets and three markets back to our physicist. She might start off by saying there are a lot of possibilities to bridge her (narrow) experience doing research in nanotechnology to a broader category of interest. She could talk about the roadblocks to getting girls more interested in science, because she faced them herself in this male-dominated field. This speech topic would hold interest at colleges where there are female students trying to break through these barriers and professors teaching them who are interested in how to facilitate change. It might also be a speech topic that is marketable to the corporate and nonprofit speaking markets, where there are companies and organizations trying to invite more gender-diverse talent to the marketplace and that have programs and interests in promoting gender equality in the job market.

But she might also gravitate toward something completely different. Once she's thinking big and broad, she might decide that she wants to talk about the future and the role nanotechnology will play in it. Or she might decide that she really wants to speak about the importance of creativity in science—perhaps her greatest inspirations and technical breakthroughs have come to her while she was painting, and for her this was life-changing.

But that might not be it either. She might want to speak about how she relied on faith—not science—when she faced a life crisis and how that surprised her.

Regardless of what particular topic or topics that she selects, she has to bridge her highly technical knowledge and her highly personal experience with the commercial mass market—and you can see how that opens her up to being salable in the different industry buckets.

This illustration underscores just how important it is for a potential speaker to think through his or her own personal branding options and determine his or her USP and potential speech topics before approaching a speaking agency seeking representation. It would be almost impossible and incredibly time-consuming for an agent who doesn't know you to learn enough about you to come up with speech topics as personally relevant as the ideas above.

Case Study: The Female European Olympic Hockey Player

I once worked with a female European hockey player who competed in the Olympics. She wasn't well known enough to fall into the distinguished/celebrity bucket, but she had recently beaten cancer and she wanted to speak about an in-depth analysis of her disease and how she fought it. Not being a scientist, she didn't fall into the science bucket, which landed her cancer talk in the health and wellness and/or inspiration categories. The problem was that she made it clear that she really wanted to focus very narrowly on *her* cancer experience and *her* treatment.

I suggested that if she broadened her message, she might receive more offers than she was getting. I felt that if she could speak about perseverance, overcoming adversity, and what really matters in life (the inspiration bucket) or had a broader health message (the health and wellness bucket) it would open her up to wider audiences. I stressed that she could still focus her talk on her battle with cancer, but she needed to highlight her experience as an Olympian. After all, that's what made her unique. Unfortunately, she balked at the idea and stuck to her guns, wanting to discuss the specifics of her recovery, which was a topic I couldn't book.

Her speech content, while engaging, didn't fulfill any of the original three USP mandates:

1. She couldn't explain what the audience would take away from her speech.

2. Her story wasn't unique. After all, there are many people who have survived cancer. So, unless she tied her recovery back to being an Olympic athlete, she wasn't making a point her competition couldn't make just as well.

3. And, as the market proved when we couldn't book her, her personal recovery story didn't have particular mass appeal either.

When I called her with an offer and explained that if she accepted she couldn't just talk about her specific experience with cancer, but had to relate that experience to a larger construct, she reluctantly agreed and got a great response from the audience and event sponsor. And in the months that followed we saw her bookings triple with her fee increasing significantly. Will this happen for everyone? No. But it's important to remember not to confine your message too narrowly, and that sometimes there are small shifts you can make that change everything.

Here's why. The content of her successful speech didn't need to be presented all that differently than the cancer speech she wanted to give. Speaking is about *the power of story* and the ability of the speaker to *touch home plate** a few times during the speech. She just had to reframe her story a bit and add a few references related to the larger takeaway and she now had a powerful and potentially lucrative offering.

How many speaking topics do I need?

I've always advised my speakers to have *three sample speaking topics,* complete with a title and a five-to-six-sentence description for each. This is what most speaking agencies look for and need in order to sell you. The ability to speak about three topics makes you pitchable to a larger pool of event buyers. You can look at this as one topic for each market—college, corporate, and nonprofit—which is appropriate for some speakers, but it's more likely that it will be three topics within just one or two of these sectors.

Why three?

While there are speakers who consistently get booked for the same speech over and over again—their *one great speech*—they likely didn't find that speech on their first try. Remember that you are competing for the attention of an agent as well as the attention of prospective event sponsors. Three well-written sample topics, with compelling titles, will increase your chances

---

* This is a phrase I use to reference the importance of always bringing your speech back to its core message.

of signing with an agency and getting booked, as your agent will be able to pitch you for a wider range of events.

What are the key elements of a successful speaking topic description?

Here are the critical elements of any five-to-six-sentence topic description:

▶ A compelling title

▶ Posing a question with hook and intrigue

▶ Statement of supporting fact(s)

▶ What the audience will learn

▶ A piece of biographical context

▶ Supporting credentials

Limit the topic descriptions to five or six sentences each, and make it clear as to what the audience will learn. This can be difficult to be sure. We often begin with drafts of topic descriptions that are fifteen sentences, and the challenge is to whittle that down to five or six powerful, punchy, and clear sentences with no wasted words. When approaching an agency with your topics, your mastery of this approach will be very apparent and will increase your chances of getting an exclusive contract.

The most obvious topics aren't necessarily the best topics. This isn't in any way suggesting that you should speak to a topic you don't know. Rather, it's a question of how we, the agents, think about you and more importantly how—and how often—we will be able to present you to prospective event sponsors. The number of calls that come in for speeches about beekeeping are zero. The topic of community-building—with a unique spin—casts a much wider net.

How to Effectively Position Your Topics without Overcommitting

When writing your topic descriptions, try to think like your (prospective) agent. Agents need to be able to spin your topics to event sponsors who have different needs and who likely work in radically different industries, so always consider how specific you want to be when you write your topic blurbs. If you're a teacher or college professor, it's likely that your target market is going to be universities and the occasional high school—but if you construct your topics correctly, it could be nonprofits and corporations too. If this is the case, you might write one topic where you reference what students will take away from your speech. By mentioning students specifically, you are better positioning yourself than if you simply mention "the audience." This makes it easier for your agent to submit you to schools and colleges— event sponsors want to feel like they are special, and that your message is geared toward their needs.

Similarly, if you are a hedge fund manager or an entrepreneur, your target audience will likely be corporations and nonprofit organizations. If this is the case, make sure to include a reference to working professionals or employees in your description. While this may sound obvious, you'd be surprised as to how many aspiring speakers write topics without a specification as to the audience.

For a great number of speakers, the backstory and spin can

basically be the same, but the speech will need to be altered and tweaked to meet the needs of each different audience. For example, if you are a successful entrepreneur, your message to students might be about overcoming the fear of failure, how passion can drive success, or how to get your idea off the ground with little funding. Whereas your message to an audience at a corporate conference might need to be different—say, about how to effectively build teams, increase brand exposure, or diversify your offerings.

The wider your appeal, the greater your chances of getting booked. So, if you can, draft a speech topic for the college market, the nonprofit sector, and the corporate sector. And if you are not well-suited for all three markets, decide where you best fit and draft three topics for the one or two markets that are applicable to you.

What does a bad speaking topic description look like?

A bad speaking topic focuses too much on the biographical information of the speaker. It doesn't indicate or even hint at what the audience will learn. It is too long—more than six sentences. And, most important, the topic fails to convey to the prospective agency—and later prospective event sponsors—*what* it is exactly that they are signing or paying for.

Case Study: How the Founder of a Nonprofit Organization Made over a Million Dollars Giving Speeches

Charles is the cofounder of an education nonprofit based in Tulsa, Oklahoma. When he first contacted my agency, I was uncertain as to whether or not we could book him. He had no speech topics worked out, let alone titled and presented with descriptive copy. But my agency was new at the time and we were willing to work harder with new clients, so we signed him and got to work.

At first, it seemed to me that the logical target audiences were either college students or other nonprofits, and we constructed his speech topics using the USP rubric—making sure that each topic had a significant audience takeaway that Charles was uniquely qualified to deliver, that they appealed to a wide audience, and were wrapped up in a compelling story.

We then discovered that Charles might also be great for corporate audiences based on his understanding of business and money management, so we decided to create a single speech topic that would work—with minor adjustments—in each category. We began to see that with only a few changes this was a speech that he could give anywhere simply by adjusting some of the dynamics to suit each audience.

We then set an affordable price—$7,500—and began to pitch him. By creating a wide net, with an appeal to all three of the major audience types—university, corporate, and nonprofit—we were well positioned to maximize his bookings. And we were able to secure bookings quickly across sectors—he saw immediate results. Because of his speaking platform, other nonprofits began partnering with him after hearing him speak. His donations were up. College students who couldn't make large donations were starting campus clubs to raise awareness after he spoke at their schools. For-profit businesses began raising money after hearing his keynotes. In other words, Charles was *building his brand.*

Charles also did a lot to help himself. He was constantly updating his speeches based on the needs of a given audience, which sponsors—and audiences—loved. And before too long, we were receiving $20,000 offers for him. A lot of them.

Then one day a major article about Charles ran in the *Los Angeles Times.* The article referenced his speaking as many times as it mentioned his nonprofit—talk about a speaking agent's dream. Suddenly our phones began to explode—including one phone call from an event sponsor in South America who had a $150,000 budget for a speaker. At this point Charles was receiving, on average, $30,000 for a speech, and he had generated about $350,000 over the course of two years.

Because such a massive fee increase felt unethical, we explained to the event sponsor in South America that their budget was too large, and that they should make an offer more in tune with his standard fee—something we rarely do— suggesting perhaps a slight fee increase due to the international travel required. Unbelievably, the event sponsor said, "We've followed his nonprofit and watched some of his speeches. We want our money to go to good use, and we know that Charles will do exactly that."

So we brought the offer for $150,000 to Charles for one speech. Then things really started to get interesting.

I began to share with other speaking agencies that Charles had received a six-figure offer, which put him on their radar. So, as agencies do, they began pitching Charles to their event sponsors in hopes of co-brokering him with my agency.* Charles earned an additional $400,000 the following year at an average fee of $50,000. And remember, we started him off at $7,500 just a couple of years prior. Within the next few months, we passed

---

* A co-broker deal is when an agency other than the exclusive agency secures an offer for a speaker and splits the commission—assuming the offer is accepted—with the exclusive agency. This benefits both sides: the exclusive agency gets a booking, and half of the commission, without having to do much work in addition to potentially gaining a new event sponsor they can call in the future. The co-brokering agency gets a commission from a speaker they do not represent, which benefits them—they keep a sponsor happy by getting them who they want and profit from another agency's exclusive roster at the same time.

the $1 million mark for a speaker who ran a small education non-profit in the Oklahoma. And what did Charles do? Being the man that he is, he gave every penny to his organization and continued to pay himself a small salary.

Now, there are certain elements of this story that involve luck. Charles found an agency hungry for new clients that was willing to work with him on topic development. And there is no question that he also got lucky with the phone call from the South American sponsor.

But there is a larger message here.

Charles had the trifecta—he had a message that was applicable to all three speaking markets with very little adaption. He had speech topics that used the original USP template—significant audience takeaways delivered by someone uniquely qualified and with mass appeal.

But he also perfectly executed the fourth mandate; he was able to emotionally connect with the audiences through story.

He found his *one great speech*. Granted, it had to be adapted slightly for each audience, but he was able to use it over and again. And he found his *one great speech* by uncovering the right emotional hook. He told real stories about real kids, and he did it with passion and commitment. Remember that the power is always in real stories, authenticity of voice, and relatability—and of course heart.

Case Study: Winning and Losing Topics

Annie is in the process of writing speaking topics to submit to agencies—hoping she'll be offered representation by at least one of them. Over the course of the past ten years, Annie has been an independent sales consultant for a variety of companies in the

South. At her core, Annie is a people person, and that's how she's found success. She works from home, doesn't have a support staff, and manages to care for her two children while making six figures a year.

When thinking about how to position her first speaking topic, Annie thinks back to the days when she was starting out and realizes that things haven't changed all that much—she's still a one-person shop with no investors, and still has to make cold calls to generate new business. She also realizes that her biggest asset is her people skills—and that's what has enabled her to succeed in client acquisition. As she begins to sketch out her first topic blurb, she decides to write a speech topic that will focus on *new client acquisition without spending a lot of money:*

> What would you do if you had no clients, no funding, and no employees—and your next paycheck was contingent on winning an account by delivering a ten-thousand-word financial analysis to a midsize bank in two days? With more than a decade in sales and customer acquisition, Annie outlines the methods she's used to build a cutting-edge consulting business and recruit new clients from various industries that include manufacturing, banking, and B2B sales companies. In this compelling presentation, Annie explains not only how she found success—beating out larger firms for business from the comfort of her own home—but how you can find it too, whether working for a company or as a solo practitioner.

Annie decides to title this topic "The Art of Lean Customer Acquisition."

What Annie has done here is ask a question, establish her

credibility, and outline what the audience will learn from her speech. *She's also done it in three sentences.* In asking a question, she hooks the reader—in this case any agents reviewing it—and drives the reader to continue reading. She's also created a compelling title using industry buzzwords. Corporations and nonprofits are used to working in lean environments and circumstances, and the title tells the reader exactly what the takeaway will be—in this case customer acquisition strategies that she's used to find success.

Bryce works as a part-time ghostwriter and he's writing his own book about how he discovered a seven-carat diamond in a national park. During his time as a ghostwriter—writing nonfiction books for other businesspeople—he's become familiar with the speaking circuit and decides that his story about finding the diamond might be interesting enough to generate additional income.

When thinking about how to position his first speaking topic to submit to agencies to be considered for representation, he thinks about the day that he discovered the diamond. He was digging for gemstones, using specialized equipment, and knew the moment he saw it that he had discovered something huge. After thinking about it for a while, Bryce decides to sketch out a topic blurb around the value of chasing your dreams.

Bryce is twenty-nine years old and lives in Wyoming. In 2015, he discovered a seven-carat diamond while digging for gemstones in a national park. While his career is focused on writing, he always dreamed of becoming a geologist. Bryce tells audiences the incredible story of how he discovered the diamond, what equipment he used to find it, and how it changed his life. Most importantly,

Bryce explains how the power of chasing your dreams
can help you to find what you are meant to do and who
you are meant to be.

Bryce decides to title this topic "Dream Chasing."

What Bryce has failed to do here is establish an area of expertise, ask a question, and deliver a topic that is bookable by an
agency. Generally, speeches about pursuing one's dreams are difficult to book, and the ones that are successful come from people
who have had massive success in their respective industries. He
also includes too much biographical information. His age and
where he lives are absolutely meaningless and shouldn't appear
in a topic description. Nothing about this description hooks the
reader and the intended audience is unclear. Is he targeting college students? Is this a talk for corporations? Further, his topic
title is weak and vague.

Annie had something specific, tangible, and broadly applicable to offer—instructional tips on client acquisition—something
every business has to deal with. This message wouldn't work
for the college market, but all corporations and nonprofits—
regardless of the field they are in—have to acquire customers.

Bryce, theoretically, to a novice, might appear to have the
bigger story. He found a seven-carat diamond in a national park.
But he failed to relate it to anything beyond that. If he had redirected his topic back to his expertise—after all, as a ghostwriter
he had to find the diamonds in the rough as he culled through
which material to include in a nonfiction book—and perhaps
titled his speech topic "Diamond in the Rough: What I Learned
as a Ghostwriter for Some of the World's Brightest Minds," he
might have had something. This topic has relevance in the corporate, nonprofit, and college markets—many businesspeople want

books and want to learn how to write them, and many colleges have writing programs.

But the end result is that Annie secured speaking representation and Bryce didn't—not because Bryce didn't have a message deserving of representation, but because he didn't identify it.

When writing your topic descriptions, always use the USP rubric, ask a question that you will answer in your speech, remember to establish facts, and make reference to your qualifications. These steps will get you halfway through the door when it comes to landing an agent.

Case Study: The Authenticity Equation

Speaker A or Speaker B?

Speaker A worked in the finance industry, but his company recently went out of business. While looking for a new job, he decides to try to get represented by a speaking agency to generate income. Although Speaker A was a mid-level manager, he tries to sound as impressive as possible. After all, he does have a lot of knowledge about the finance industry—information that could be important for C-level executives to hear.

Speaker B runs a nonprofit that helps oppressed young women in the developing world. She's given a couple of speeches that she wrangled herself and is now looking for agency representation. Speaker B works in the field—she rarely has access to running water, her clothes are worn through, and she doesn't deliver perfectly scripted speeches. After two years, she decides to return to the United States to write a book and, hopefully, get picked up by an agency.

Speaker A puts together his topics and uses a lot of sales copy—he sounds like a prepackaged speaker. There isn't anything particularly special about his "Financial Management in Hard Times" topic, and there are a hundred other speakers who are more qualified to be delivering a speech like this. He has no individual hook or personal story to wrap his message around. In fact, there is nothing unique about his offering. It says "ordinary, boring, and so what?"

Speaker B puts together a from-the-heart topic description about the oppression of girls and women in the developing world, titling it "What I Learned about Gender Pay Equity in America from Living in the Developing World."

Right off the bat, this is a special topic. Further, it's clear simply from the title that Speaker B is the only person qualified to give this exact speech. It is *What I learned*. And it is *What I learned* about a current, hot topic. And it is *What I learned in a unique way*—in the fields of developing nations. It screams *No one else can tell this story the way I can.* And because she was addressing a current topic of interest—one not going anywhere for a long time—she made her unique perspective relevant to large audiences while promising that they would learn something too.

Sure, there are lots of speakers who also have speeches addressing the gender pay gap, but her experience is completely unique to her, and therefore her viewpoint will be unique to audiences. Look at what we can learn simply from a topic title and nothing else. We don't even need to read the descriptions to know which talk will resonate as authentic. Speaker A is going to give a canned talk that practically anyone in his industry could deliver, while Speaker B is going to speak from her unique experience. She is authentic, and we know it right away.

Now, this isn't to say that Speaker A couldn't have a wildly successful speaking career—but his topic lacked authenticity. In the speaking world, authenticity is king, and if your authenticity can be seen on the page, then it will most certainly be seen on the stage.

So now let's flip them. Speaker A, instead of approaching agencies with the boring topic, recasts it and comes up with a speaking topic that he titles: *What Losing My Job in Finance Can Teach You about Change in Difficult Times.*

Let's say Speaker B, the woman who worked in the fields in the developing world, had a generic speech topic titled *The Plight of Women in the Developing World,* the tables would then turn and Speaker A would be more bookable and Speaker B would be less bookable. A big part of the reason why is that we can tell from Speaker A's topic title that there are going to be takeaways from his speech. Speaker B sounds like she is going to get on stage and tell a story—it might be a great story but that's not enough. Story is essential, but it has to underpin a message—especially when trying to grab the attention of agents and event sponsors.

TAKEAWAYS

To be booked for paid speaking you'll need a speaking agency to represent you

You'll increase your chances of getting signed by a speaking agency if you approach agencies with professional, market-ready speaking topics

Speech topics can be difficult to pin down, so take your time and get it right—*one great speech* can last a lifetime

The most obvious topics aren't necessarily the best topics—think *What is my unique spin and how does it have broad appeal?* (e.g., the physicist who speaks about faith or creativity and how that relates back to science)

To find your topics, start thinking about yourself as a brand and identify your *Unique Selling Proposition*—a message that you are singularly qualified to deliver, sets you apart from the competition, and has broad market appeal—and wrap that in story

Consider which of the eighteen broad speaking industry buckets—e.g., innovation, diversity, management, health and wellness—your topics fit into

It's best to have three speech topics—it widens your net, allows you to test the market, and shows a little diversity. Then hone these three topics for three different markets if you can: college, corporate, and nonprofit

Develop your speaking topics with each audience in mind

Each topic needs an intriguing title and hook and will be defined by your USP

Write compelling topic blurbs that are only five to six sentences each

Position your topics effectively without overcommitting—adapt with market feedback and to each audience

An authentic voice with a message delivered with heart is more valuable than anything else

6.

The Art of the Speaker Bio

THERE ARE A MILLION WAYS TO TELL THE SAME STORY

Even if that story is about you.

To be a successful paid speaker, agents will be pitching *a very specifically branded version of you*. This means that you're going to need a specific speaking-industry-friendly bio that likely looks nothing like the other bios that you might already have on your LinkedIn profile or work website.

The previous chapter explained that the first step in building your brand as a paid speaker is to figure out what you want—and are qualified—to speak about. It then guided you in selecting three speech topics, explained the importance of giving each of those topics an intriguing title, and writing catchy, descriptive copy for them.

The next step in your personal branding as a paid speaker is to prove the second component of your Unique Selling Proposition—namely, that you are singularly qualified to give the three speeches that your agent will be pitching you for.

And your speaking bio is the sales copy that does that.

The good news is that when you go back and reread your speech topic descriptions, if they're written well, one of the key things that should jump out at you is how clearly they'll dictate the content and structure of your bio. Not only pointing to *what you should say in your bio*, but also *how you should say it*. And, *in what order*. In other words, once you know exactly which bucket(s) your speaking topics land in—diversity, innovation, spirituality, technology, and so on—what broad message you are driving toward (the takeaways), and the specific spin you'll use to illustrate those points, the key elements you should emphasize in your bio will quickly become apparent.

The first step in preparing your speaking bio is to make a list of any specific elements of your biographical information that directly support you as an expert in the area(s) your speech topic(s) reference.

If we look back at the beekeeper, it's easy to see that once we'd determined that she'd be framing her experience with bees to speak about community-building, we would instantly know that we should build her bio around those two factors—not her four years working as a CPA, or her training as a classical pianist, or the fact that she grew up on Staten Island. Instead, the smart thing to do would be to open her bio with a bold statement about her lifelong fascination with the complex social structure of honeybee colonies.

Similarly, if we use the physicist from the previous chapter as an example, we can easily see how her biographical content should flow directly from the speech topics she eventually decides upon. We can also see how greatly her bio would differ if she decided to write her speech topics about the importance of creativity in science rather than about how, as a scientist, she relied on faith when she faced a harrowing life crisis. Her life events and qualifications would be the same of course, but the speech topic(s) she selects would dictate which biographical elements to highlight, how to present them, and in what sequence. *Poorly positioned biographies are probably the biggest preemptive barrier to both landing an agent and securing paid speaking gigs.*

The challenge in creating a great speaker bio is finding the right content—content that sets up and reinforces your authority to speak about your proposed topics—then putting it in the correct order and illustrating it with compelling language that will intrigue both prospective agents and prospective event sponsors.

If you're thinking, *My bio can't be that important,* consider that when you approach potential agents you'll only have their attention for a few minutes, and you don't want to lose their attention with a bio that's completely unrelated to your potential speaking topics—or worse yet, one full of mundane, unrelated copy. With a clear, concise, and interesting story of who you are—which is what agents are selling and what event sponsors are buying—you are more likely to get the response you want. And if you walk through the door with a bio that is close to a finished product, agents can begin pitching you almost immediately.

You also don't want to get signed to a speaking agency with a weak bio only to have your agent pitching event sponsors with material that isn't selling you as strongly as it could be. Just as when you approach potential speaking agents with your bio and topics, when agents approach event sponsors they only have their attention for a few minutes during the pitch phase. Because of that, the speaker bio becomes one of our *most valuable tools.* For this reason: *It's often the first thing an event sponsor looks at.* And yes, both agencies and event sponsors will quit reading after the first paragraph if they aren't engaged.

Lead with Sizzle

Since prospective agents and event sponsors generally read your bio first—*before they read your speaking topics or collateral marketing material*—we have to get them *past your bio* before they'll even consider your speaking topics. It also means that if you're bio *is* interesting, and you are positioned correctly in it, it will be obvious that you are uniquely qualified to deliver the speeches your agent is pitching you for.

Once you understand that your bio is key sales copy, it will make sense that every line of it should be architected as a pitch— and you'll want to start with a first line that has a strong hook and leaves the reader wanting to find out more. For example, let's say that a bio from a prospective speaker looking for me to represent her lands in my inbox and it begins with this:

"Gina Jones is a professor of art history who's lectured at dozens of universities about fifteenth-century Italian painting."

OK. But could it be stronger? Remember, she's got my attention for a minute or two—is this the best thing Gina can lead with?

Probably not.

What if Gina's bio began with something different, perhaps a provocative statement? Something like: "Throughout history, art has rarely been appreciated in its own time. Gina Jones has..."

Or, "In 1497, something happened in Florence, Italy, that completely changed human development. Gina Jones has..."

The second and third statements have me itching to read the next sentence, while the first example offers little to hold my interest. In fact, *the first statement reads like a generic line from a résumé.* It offers no *opinion* or *position,* and it could be a line from the bio of just about any art history professor—including all the art history professors working at the colleges where Gina is hoping to be booked as a speaker. Also remember that, as Gina's potential agent or event sponsor, *I don't know Gina or her accomplishments, and the amount of time I'll spend trying to get to know her is limited.* Potential agents and potential event sponsors are hers to lose.

I'm not saying that the second two statements are the only—or even the right—options for Gina. They're just better options than the first one. For these reasons:

The second and third options separate Gina from the pack. They also are—or will be—statements that are directly tied to her speaking topics. This is extremely significant. It means that it will be highly unlikely that anyone I currently represent—and anyone else a search committee is looking at for a particular event—will be making the same statement or proposing a speech about the same topic(s) as Gina. And if her bio is done correctly, it will support this fact. If Gina listens to the advice in this book, she'll very purposefully craft unique speaking topics and gear her speaking bio to support them. Gina will be branded with a powerful USP. One that no other speaker has.

Now, if Gina happens to have a significant, show-stopping credential—say she just won a coveted art history award—she might also decide to lead with that. Why? Even though it's a *credential* rather than an intriguing statement with a hook, it's still unique because very few people can make that particular claim. To put it another way, there are some biographical details and awards that can separate you from the pack in a distinguishing way.

But you might be thinking, *What about that ex-president who you couldn't book?* His bio led with a powerful, singular credential—ex-president of a country; *that has to be better than winning some art prize—and you couldn't book him?*

Here's why that scenario was different:

He was relying *solely* on his credentials and title of

ex-president to get bookings. When you do that, you fail. A title or award alone isn't enough. His mistake was that his speech topics were generic and his bio was generic—all he offered was the implied stature of his previous position.

Now, I'll never know *for sure* why we couldn't book that ex-president. Some would argue that it was because he was expensive—but I've booked a lot of six-figure speakers. So I'll say this: We could book a beekeeper, a poet, a schoolteacher, and hundreds of other people who were—at least in theory—far less impressive than the ex-president, and yet we couldn't book him. And I can't tell you how many times I have seen this happen— highly credentialed people with *generic topics and generic bios* are impressive on the surface but don't spark interest.

And with good reason: They don't offer agents, event sponsors, or audiences a Unique Selling Proposition. They don't say *"Buy this product (me and my speech) for this specific benefit."*

They don't scream *unique*. They don't offer an appealing attribute or claim that the competition can't make. And they're simply not compelling enough to *move the masses*. So don't ever underestimate the value of good sales copy and the importance of *specificity* and *individual branding* when it comes to your bio and speaking topics.

Other Examples of When to Lead with Titles and Awards

I once worked with an entrepreneur named Klaus who ran a football (soccer) nonprofit. The role of the nonprofit was different depending on the country in which they were working, but the causes they helped ranged from HIV/AIDS awareness and testing for inner-city youth who couldn't afford it, to bringing members of gangs in Peru together to play football against each other—with a clear focus on nonviolence, friendly collaboration, and learning to work together. We booked Klaus regularly to give speeches around the world. He had been awarded a $1 million grant and was named European Social Entrepreneur of the Year by a very well-known international bank. So, in his case, we led his bio with the European Social Entrepreneur of the Year award rather than a statement about his football nonprofit or a provocative statement. In his case, we led with a credential.

Why? Because even though it was biographical, it was *unique* and *compelling*. It had a hook, and when tied to his speech topics, it wasn't a stand-alone. Instead it had an intriguing "WOW" factor and validated him as the most significant person to give the talk(s) we were pitching him for.

I once had a *New York Times* bestselling author sheepishly ask me if adding that he was nominated for a Pulitzer Prize to his bio might help his booking prospects. Since I had no idea that he had been nominated—he hadn't told me and it never occurred to me to ask—I couldn't believe what a great piece of sales information we had left out of his bio. I also couldn't believe that he didn't tell me sooner. Using this piece of information, by placing it at the very top of his bio, his bookings—and his fees—increased dramatically. The key in this example is the same as it was with Klaus; we didn't rely on that credential as a stand-alone claim. We wouldn't have been able to book the bestselling author simply because he was a Pulitzer Prize nominee. He also had interesting speaking topics—supported by his bio—and a unique offering that validated his credentials. He wasn't relying solely on the status of a title to drive bookings.

So how do I determine the best first sentence for my bio?

I recommend making a list of possible options. Make sure they all have a compelling hook and are strong lead-ins to your speaking topics. Then cull through them and go with the strongest one.

Here's a tip: I've noticed that most people start their bios with broad generic statements and put the good details at the bottom—remember, we want to invert that here and *start with the sizzle*. The hook generally won't be your job title, and it will almost never be a piece of biographical information like where you were born or went to school. What we want to do with the first sentence of your bio is grab the reader with something striking and compelling. So, in the case of Gina, our art history professor, we'll leave the fact that she's lectured at dozens of universities for the end of her bio.

Why is this tip so important?

The most important aspect of any speaker bio is to engage the reader—and quickly. Remember that you are potentially competing with a hundred other speakers for representation at the same agency, and having a great bio will increase your chances of getting an agency to sign you.

Much like with your speech topic descriptions, when it comes to your bio we want to capture prospective agencies' attention and demonstrate that you understand how the industry works. If you can do that, you're far more likely to receive a callback from the various agencies to which you've applied. By arriving armed and ready with a solid bio, even if it needs to be adjusted a bit by your agent—which it undoubtedly will be—you are taking work off your potential agent's desk. This will make agencies more inclined to sign you because you've demonstrated that you understand not only the *how*, but the *why*, when it comes to your speaker bio.

Once you have an agent, you are also competing for each booking with other speakers. And what we want to do is hook the prospective event sponsor from sentence one. It's also important to remember that most people making the decisions as to which speakers will be booked for an event do this in addition to their day jobs; a university English professor gets assigned the task of booking this year's speakers, or the senior vice president of sales at an insurance company is charged with organizing the speakers for their annual corporate retreat. Most event planners have limited time to review potential speakers, and if your bio doesn't spark interest from the first sentence, you're likely going to be knocked out of contention at the very beginning of the pitch process.

The pitching and booking process often takes months. And agents need to keep the attention of the event organizer every time there's an interaction. As agents, we call this *time-engaged*, and it's exactly what it sounds like. The longer your agent can keep the event sponsor interested in booking you, the more likely the odds of you being booked. It's also extremely rare for the event sponsor to be the only person involved in the selection process. There will be many sets of eyes on your materials and we want to make sure that every piece of that material is as strong as it can be.

So, how does an agent create ongoing engagement? At first, it's the agent's pitch on the phone. Then we direct the buyer to your material on our website and forward your one sheet via email. Following this, there might be a request for additional information. For example, the event sponsor may say, *I love the speaker's bio and speech topics. Can you tell me more about him?* This process can be long and drawn out—three months may pass before you get an offer. Sometimes longer. During this time, your bio is likely being shared with other members of the event sponsor's committee and every line has to be strong, relevant sales copy. I may speak with an event sponsor about you on the phone for an hour, but when she takes your bio to the committee members, they only see what they have in front of them on paper and only hear what the event sponsor recalls from our conversations. Therefore, it's important to make sure your strongest selling points are in writing.

When writing your bio, think about how journalists write articles. Start with a compelling headline, followed by the hook of your story, followed by the meat of your experience. Then put your most significant speech-topic-related qualifications in the next two paragraphs, followed by any ancillary information at the end (generally where you work, awards you've won, other places you've spoken, and so on). If you think about this in terms of a short-form five-paragraph essay contained to three-quarters of a page, you'll be in good shape.

Speaking bios are all about how to position yourself with a strategic, thoughtful, less-is-more approach that sets up your speaking topics where every line is a powerful statement of fact about why you are qualified to speak about whatever it is you hope to speak about. When writing your speaking bio, a good approach is to think about things in reverse. We're not writing your life story here. "Wendy Jones was born on December 12, 1976, and was raised in Northern Arizona until the age of twelve when she moved with her family to New Hampshire," isn't what we want to see. In fact, we don't want to see this information anywhere in a speaker bio unless it's relevant to your speaking topics. We want your biggest accomplishments to be highlighted in the first paragraph. We lead with sizzle, follow with support and proof, and exclude the irrelevant.

But what if I don't have enough biographical material to fill up five paragraphs?

Not to worry, it's simply time to get creative. A bio can just as easily explain *why* and *what* and highlight your personality to help fill up that extra space. What I mean here is that your bio can be used artfully and strategically to precede and set up your topics. It can be just as impressive for an event sponsor to hear about your work with children or dogs, or your summer building boats, as it is to hear about your Nobel Prize nomination—as long as it offers them a significant takeaway and it relates to your topics.

Case Study: What Can Happen if I Don't Take This Advice?

I once represented the founder of a very large international nonprofit focused on men's health and promoting awareness, particularly around colon and testicular cancer. He was smart, good-looking, could speak articulately, and had a huge media presence—social and otherwise. I thought his bio needed to be rewritten, but he was well known enough that I figured we could sign him and adjust his bio to be more booking-friendly afterward. The thing is, after I signed him, I found out that he didn't want to change his bio. And we couldn't book him. At least, not as often as he could have been booked.

I spent months ripping my hair out, trying to convince the speaker to change his bio—which was the same bio he used on his nonprofit's website—to be more speaker industry–friendly. Again and again he refused, citing the fact that he wanted his branding to be the same across all platforms, insisting that his LinkedIn bio read the same as the bio on his nonprofit's website as well as the bio included with his speaking materials.

So, I took matters into my own hands. Rather than linking event sponsors to the bio on our agency website, I cut and pasted a new bio I had crafted into email pitches for event sponsors.

Guess what happened? As soon as I did that, we generated three five-figure bookings for the speaker in one week—and he finally agreed to the change.

Don't assume everyone knows who you are—even if you're "someone." I once pitched Salman Rushdie to the head of a college English department over the phone—without sending a bio—and she replied by saying that they only booked "known authors." Rushdie is arguably one of the most important writers of the past fifty years, was the recipient of the Booker Prize, and was knighted by Queen Elizabeth—a fact that I had to delicately point out to her. The lesson here is that, even if you are at the top of your field—even a lauded celebrity—it's essential to get your bio right because chances are not everyone knows who you are.

Case Study: The Celebrity Author and the Journalist You've Never Heard Of

Who Gets More Offers?

When I was first starting out as an agent, I felt lucky to have the opportunity to work with a number of very famous bestselling authors. One of them in particular I imagined would be an oft-requested speaker. After all, at that time, he had sold roughly one hundred million books worldwide and his books were being made into Hollywood blockbusters. This said, I was receiving more requests for the relatively unknown journalists and authors we also represented than I was getting for him. And it certainly wasn't because he wasn't well known or was a poor speaker.

As I tried to figure out *why*, I considered all the options.

Could it have been his high fee?

Maybe, I thought, but I'd booked plenty of speakers for six figures and a jet.

Then, as I reviewed his speech topics and bio, what I noticed was that we were selling him on his celebrity alone—*nothing more.*

The other "smaller" journalists and authors on our roster were being pitched not based on their celebrity (they didn't have it), but on intriguing educational angles with bios that related to topics and takeaways that were tied to larger issues. The other lesser-known authors and journalists were positing a different value proposition to event sponsors and audiences both in their speech topics and their bios. *They had branded themselves in a manner that led to more interest.*

The celebrity author presented himself *as him* and his bio referenced his books and film adaptations, while many of the other authors and journalists we represented offered the audience more. Their bios emphasized their specific writing techniques, or their expertise and qualifications to present big-think ideas around topics that ranged from race to psychology. I realized that they were fulfilling the first mandate of Rosser Reeves's Unique Selling Proposition—they were offering audiences a very specific product benefit.

Just like with the beekeeper, the poet, and the schoolteacher from the previous chapters, there was a greater value proposition for the audience in those less well-known writers' speaking materials than there was in the celebrity author's. And that was exactly the same problem we had faced when trying to book the ex-president of the Middle Eastern country.

What I took away from my experiences with these individuals and so many others over the years, from speakers we were *sure we could book,* but couldn't, and speakers I was *sure we couldn't book but had great success doing so,* is that except for a small handful of celebrities, speaking is almost never about *who you are.* Rather, it's almost always about *actually having something to say.* And the fact that you actually have something to say is what you want to make sure you communicate not only in your speech topics, but in your bio. Without question, success and failure in the paid speaking market is all about how well you are branded.

TAKEAWAYS

You need a specific speaking industry bio. Don't copy and paste from an existing bio—write a new one

Don't forget that you are building a brand, and every piece of information about you as a speaker—including your bio—should support your brand identity

Your bio is where you prove item two in the USP—that you are uniquely qualified to give the particular speeches we are pitching you for—so make sure the content of your bio supports that

Don't forget that every line of your bio should read like sales copy, not a résumé

Always lead with sizzle, and support that with relevant and intriguing facts

Less is more. Keep your speaking bio to a three-quarters of a page, single-spaced

7.

Collateral Advantage

WRAP YOURSELF IN QUALITY

Once you have your speaking topics and bio nailed down, the next thing to tackle is your marketing collateral. I've found that too often—probably because the speech topic(s) and bio feel so defining—this is something that speakers don't pay enough attention to. And yet, your marketing collateral is a critical component of your personal branding, one I liken to the packaging and ad copy for a consumer product. If we think about the product we're selling as *you and what you have to say* (your topics and bio), and your marketing collateral as *what we wrap you up in,* you can begin to see how the content and quality of your marketing collateral can have a huge impact on your overall branding and salability. It can make a big difference in whether or not you attract a speaking agent and, assuming you do, your marketing collateral can also be the difference between an enormously successful paid speaking career and no career at all.

To understand what your marketing collateral actually comprises, ask yourself these three general questions:

▸ Beyond what I've already included in my bio, what else do I have to support the fact that I have the authority to speak about my particular topic(s) in the venues where I'd like to speak?

▸ What pertinent, defining, additional information can I offer about myself and my topic(s) that is most likely to attract an agent?

▸ What are the key points that agent can use—or better yet, *leverage*—to sell me to event sponsors once I'm signed to an agency?

Then consider these more specific questions:

▸ What specific materials are worthy of inclusion? How much do I have, and what's the most valuable?

▸ What photo will I use? What should I be wearing in it? Should it be a headshot? Do I need a professional photographer?

▸ Do I have prior speaking engagements to reference? Do I currently have any endorsements—validating quotes or "blurbs?" If not, can I get some? If so, who will they be from? Do I know whose personal endorsements matter the most? Do my blurbs need to be about speaking? What if I don't have any at all?

▸ Should I include book praise and book reviews, if I have any?

▶ What about degrees, awards, or related industry recognition?

▶ Should I hyperlink videos? What if I have a TEDx video? Can
   I use video footage from a lecture I've given at a work event
   or conference? What if I don't have any video footage at all?

▶ What about other relevant web links—to a blog, articles, or
   my business site? What about web links to articles about my
   topic(s) that I *haven't* authored—could they be relevant?

▶ Should I direct people to my personal website if I have one?
   And if I don't have a personal website, do I need to build one?
   If so, how much should I spend doing so?

▶ What about my internet presence? What comes up if someone Googles me? How about social media accounts? Am I
   on social media now? How am I branded? Which platforms?
   How am I controlling for uniform branding across platforms?
   What about handles? Content? Followers? Should I provide
   this information on my one sheet?

▶ If I have a lot of possible marketing collateral, how do I pri-
   oritize? What order should I put it in? How much room is
   there on my one sheet? What takes precedence? And if I
   have nothing—what do I do then?

As you can see, when it comes to marketing collateral, there's a
lot to consider—and you need to think about all of it. And not as
ancillary, unimportant filler to rush through and "get done," but
as critical sales copy to promote your brand.

To jump-start the process, I recommend using the questions

above as a rough guide. Then simply jot down everything you can think of that you *currently have or that you may be able to easily obtain*. And then decide—based on the advice that follows— which of these potential pieces of marketing collateral have the most value to your brand.

Obviously, if you already have a lot of the above available to you—say you've done a few speaking events, have blurbs, have written a book, and have published articles to reference and perhaps even have some video footage from an event you've done— you'll be culling through all of it to determine the most significant pieces to use and what to cut, for this important reason: *while we absolutely need some form of external endorsements and validation, we have limited space on your one sheet.* And it's worth noting that even if we didn't have limited space, it's never a good marketing strategy to include *everything* that you have. As you think about your marketing collateral, it's helpful to think about the value of *clean package design*—one that has just enough of the right ad copy to *sell*, but not so much that it makes your presentation look noisy and cluttered.

For potential speakers who are just starting out and who don't have a lot, or any, of this material available to use—if you haven't written a book, don't have any articles, have no speaking experience or blurbs, and very little in terms of external validation— this process can feel daunting. But here's the good news: We can create some of these components pretty easily—or work around their absence—and still make you look market-ready and salable by simply getting creative. And we can do it without spending a whole lot of time or money. Further, if you don't have much in terms of marketing collateral *now*, we're going to do the best we can with what we have to launch you as a speaker, and then sub out that weaker material with any stronger material that becomes available as your speaking career and personal brand advances.

You're going to need a photo.

It's almost always best to use a head shot taken from the shoulders up, and make sure to use a clean backdrop. Smile—or don't. But be yourself. It can be in black and white or in color. Make these decisions based on your branding. If you have a picture of yourself standing behind a lectern, or can get one, that's even better. Now you *look like a speaker*. A good way to help frame how you think about selecting a photo is to remember that as event sponsors are reviewing your bio and topics, the photo helps them visualize you speaking at their event. That means you want a photo that gives them a good idea as to who you are, and what you'll look like standing on their stage—and that means you want a photo that depicts you—who you are as a *brand*, not necessarily who you are as an individual.

In other words, when it comes to your photo, consider the message you're sending.

Ask yourself, *Are my speech topics serious or humorous? How do I present myself in my bio? As an intellectual or as a "regular" person? What should an expert giving the speech I plan to give look like?*

I once represented a scientist who wanted to speak about serious, highbrow material and in the photo he sent to me he was at the beach wearing board shorts. I had to explain that while I understood his desire to communicate his personality, the photo wasn't in line with the rest of his material (it wasn't on brand) and, as a result, the event sponsors at the types of organizations we'd be pitching him to for keynotes might not take him seriously.

So always aim for brand consistency. At the end of the day, if that scientist had insisted on going with the board shorts photo, I would have let him. And your agent will likely permit you to make branding mistakes if you push for them as well. As an agent, my job is to advise clients the best that I can adhering to my experience and knowledge of what will "float" and what won't, but also keep in mind that I have a limited amount of time to work with them and that I'll rarely override a client if that client feels passionate about something. But also bear in mind that if you do override your agent on a branding decision and insist on a choice that is, in the eyes of that agent at least, clearly wrong, you might be undermining the confidence that agent has in pitching you—which may mean that he or she pitches you less often. A lot less often.

Before you select a photo, consider not only your branding, but also your audience. If you're targeting the corporate market only, it might make sense to wear business clothes in your photo. If you're only going to be pitched to the college market, you can consider using a less formal and more relaxed photo. It you expect to target both the college and corporate sectors, perhaps land somewhere in between. The key is to give even these seemingly small decisions careful thought.

If you don't have a professional photo, don't stress about it. In fact, I recommend *not* hiring a professional photographer. I've had countless speakers drop hundreds of dollars on professional headshots, and we've gotten better quality pictures using a smartphone. This is about *smart* branding, not *expensive* branding.

What about praise and blurbs?

We are going to need to include some validation of your expertise. And the best validation is *praise for speaking from prior event sponsors.* So, if you've already given some speeches, you'll want to provide blurbs—a few sentences of praise about your performance—from prior event sponsors. Complimentary praise about your speaking performances proves that you are capable of delivering on the stage. A happy event sponsor in your past lets potential future event sponsors know that someone else "bought" you before and that you delivered. And that's important—it means that you're more likely to make them look great.

Your marketing collateral should include any speaking praise you have, even if the places you've spoken aren't all that impressive. The event sponsors you'll be pitched to in the future are generally less concerned about *where the praise is coming from* and more concerned with *the content of the praise itself.* So even if you've only given free speeches, a few sentences of praise from the sponsors of those events can be very beneficial— especially considering that future event sponsors most likely won't have any idea whether you were compensated to speak at those events.

If you've given any speeches in the past, but never got testimonials from the event sponsors, don't hesitate to reach out to request a few sentences of written feedback now. In my experience, event sponsors are more than happy to accommodate requests like this. And certainly include links to video if you have any, so long as it's high quality footage.* If you've given a TEDx talk—or a speech at any other event that provides video—include a link to the video as part of your marketing collateral. One of the great offerings TEDx provides, typically, is high quality video. This can be a tremendous asset and the link to your talk should most certainly be included on your one sheet.

If you haven't given any speeches yet, consider widening

---

* I can't tell you how many speaker bookings I've lost over poor quality video despite the speeches being great.

your concept of *where you've spoken*. Maybe you haven't been paid to speak or even spoken for free, but perhaps you lecture as a professor at a university and the department chair can provide a blurb about your riveting lectures. Or maybe you've spoken at a work conference or an organization where you volunteer. Consider approaching colleagues or people you've done business with in the past to request praise about your engaging presence or compelling content.

If you have no speaking praise at all, we next look to praise for any writing you may have done as validation of your expertise. If you have a book out, consider using reviews and blurbs that praise your book. Or you can include links to articles or blog posts you've written. Keep in mind that we want the strongest statements of praise from external validating sources as we can get.

If I've never given a speech and haven't written a book, how do I include praise?

If you don't have any praise for speaking or writing, consider if you can get quotes of praise about your performance, rather than from content that you've created. We can use a statement of validation of your status as an expert in a particular field or even simply affirmation of your personal integrity as sales copy. If you're hoping to speak about leadership—where have you led? And who has the credentials to comment on your ability to do so? For example, you might be able to get a quote from a manager where you work. *Bill Murphy has led teams of divers in deep sea rescues for more than a decade. He is highly skilled and has an admirable ability to command small groups under high-stress situations where lives are at stake.* Or perhaps get a quote from the principal of your local high school: *In addition to being an award-winning guidance counselor, Ben Hamilton has been a soccer coach working with at-risk teens for the past eight years and has led three unlikely teams to league championships.* The key here is to consider the source. That praise has to come from a respected individual with some level of authority in your field. What event sponsors are looking for is something that completes the package and will justify their interest in booking you.

But what if I'm just starting out and have absolutely nothing in terms of praise?

This is a fairly common challenge for new speakers. With a lack of speaking experience and no blurbs, no publishing history, and very little in terms of external validation, how does one get around the problem?

The first thing you should do is step back and assess if you are in fact an "expert" on your selected topic(s) and, assuming that you are, revisit whether there is someone who can validate that on some level. But if there still is nothing available to you in terms of external validation and you still believe that you have something important to say that offers a tangible takeaway for audiences, the solution is to fill the extra space on your one sheet with substitute material until you do get some praise. In some cases, this filler can be something as simple as adding a fourth speaking topic. In other cases, you might provide links to articles or blog posts *you didn't write,* but that reinforce the relevance—or wide appeal—of your particular speech topic(s).

And if you've never written an article or blog post, consider starting now. Try to see if you can write an article or opinion piece for your local newspaper or a blog you follow about the topic(s) you're hoping to speak about. And don't be shy. Bloggers love guest posts—they have to deliver fresh content to readers on a regular basis. So reach out to a few bloggers in your field of interest and suggest a few article topics you could write, or offer to be interviewed, which usually involves nothing more than typing answers to a few questions they submit to you.

Case Study: How Changing Two Blurbs Created an Additional $100K in Speaking Fees

I once worked with a speaker named Sarah who had authored a small book about the job market. We'd been able to book her five times the first year she was signed with us for $7,500 per event. We were targeting colleges and universities, as corporations don't bring in speakers to talk about the job market because they generally don't want their employees thinking about quitting their jobs to look for new ones. We had two reviews on her one sheet, both from community college sponsors who praised Sarah's speaking abilities and presentations.

Then one day I received a call from an event sponsor who was running a conference about the job market and who expressed interest in Sarah as a potential speaker. This was a great opportunity for Sarah because it offered her a chance to speak before a different target audience and opened a new market for her. We were able to book Sarah for the conference, she got rave reviews, and we got really lucky—there was another event sponsor in the audience who loved her speech. That sponsor approached Sarah during the meet-and-greet after her keynote and expressed his interest in booking her for his upcoming conference. Sarah gave him her agency contact info, and we booked Sarah for that event a few months later.

Following each of these two conference speeches, I connected with the event sponsors and asked them to write blurbs about Sarah's performance—*Since you had such a great event with Sarah we'd love to put a blurb from you on our website.* We then subbed in these higher-profile blurbs on her one sheet and removed the community college praise. The reason being that the conferences were more prestigious than the community colleges, and also because it differentiated Sarah from other job-related speakers since these were noncollege events.

Based on the success of these events and the great feedback she'd received, we also decided to increase Sarah's fee to $10,000. Although she was still an unlikely speaking candidate at corporate events, there are a lot of conferences that have corporate sponsors where she could speak about the job market in a manner that didn't directly threaten specific employers. This opened up opportunities for her because it put her on a stage in front of audiences of corporate employees instead of only college students.

When we did our next marketing blast—a monthly agency email that speaking agencies often send to event sponsors—we featured Sarah alongside her new blurbs and referenced her conference speeches. We subsequently booked her five times in ten days. Our agents were also able to share the feedback from these events during their phone calls, exciting event sponsors in the college market in a way that they hadn't been able to before. Over the course of the next six months, we booked Sarah an additional ten times, making her annual gross $137,500. *That was $100,000 more than she earned the previous year.*

The prestige of where the two blurbs had come from opened Sarah up to a new market and made a huge difference not only in the number of bookings she received, but also in her audience reach and speaking fee. Were it not for these blurbs, Sarah likely would have remained a $7,500 speaker who continued to get booked only a few times a year at colleges. The blurbs gave Sarah a *higher level of market validation* than she'd previously had, which made other event sponsors feel more comfortable booking her for their events and for higher fees. It's amazing how a simple change—in this case higher-profile reviews from a new market—can make a huge difference in how the broader market perceives, and more importantly reacts to, your message *even when that message is essentially the same*. In Sarah's case, her content stayed the same except for a few tweaks and adjustments to accommodate a slightly different audience, but her collateral marketing was adjusted, and that changed everything.

What Additional Material beyond a Photo, Blurbs, and Media Links Are Worthy of Inclusion on Your One Sheet and Why?

Think about anything else you might fight to mention in a job interview or put on your résumé, and consider including that here—as long as it directly relates to your branding. Have you won a relevant industry award or been nominated? This is a great place to highlight those successes. Think of your marketing collateral as an opportunity to brag—as a slot for all the "extras" that didn't fit in your bio. Remember, we are *selling you*—so include anything that positions you as a validated expert qualified to speak about your chosen topic(s).

Do I need to build a personal website?

Most of the successful speakers I've worked with don't have personal websites and don't need them. But there are a couple of exceptions to this. Speakers who already have a business branded around themselves—say they are a consultant or personal trainer or a blogger—likely have websites for that business. Most authors have websites too—in fact, it's often a mandate from their publisher that they have one.

If you do have a website because of your personally branded

business, or because you're an author, add a speaking tab to your contact info and link it directly to your agency's site. List your speaking topics and update the site anytime you give a speech—and include any praise. If you have any video links, you can embed them or provide a link to YouTube or Vimeo, or wherever else your videos are hosted. There are many speakers with enough traffic on their own websites to drive speaking inquiries to their agencies—and that has tremendous value.

Beyond these two exceptions, most speakers shouldn't build a website solely for speaking for this reason: *it will likely be redundant, and we want traffic to flow to your speaking agency's website, not your own.* In other words, if your website is basically a clone of your agency's speaker profile, there isn't much of a point to having it and it can create market confusion.

If you do decide to build a website—perhaps you are launching a larger business around your speaking brand or are writing a book—keep it clean and simple. And consider building it yourself. There are a number of great options for building a free website where you only have to pay for hosting, which is relatively inexpensive. Remember, our goal is for you to spend as little money up front as we launch your speaking career. A simple homepage with your bio and topics, and a secondary page that includes the contact information for your agency is all you need.

How to Handle Social Media

Since you're building a brand, it's smart to use all the media available to you as a tool. But recognize that there's a huge difference between *personal* social media accounts and *branded* social media accounts. Do your Facebook page and Instagram account have pictures of your family and friends and include comments about your cousin's birthday party? Or are those accounts very purposefully branded to support and promote you as an expert who is passionate about your topics? For example, our beekeeper might—and probably should—have a branded Instagram account with images of people building communities and bees in hives alongside interesting information about both community-building and the behavior of bees. Or if our physicist chooses to speak about girls in science she might—and probably should—build her social media presence around that topic. She'd be smart to post links to articles about woman and girls in science, links to her own research or writing, pictures of girls at science fairs, and so on. And all of her branding—including her handles—should be consistent across platforms.

It's essential to understand that separating your personal life from your brand is critical. You don't want to include personal information—say about your last vacation—on social media any more than founders of major consumer packaged-good brands would on their company accounts. There are all sorts of problems with the optics of this—with an exception, of course, being made for people who are actually making their personal life part of their brand. Everyone needs to look professional, serious, and worth the dollars we will be asking for. If a potential event sponsor finds you on social media standing in the parking lot of a cheap motel wearing a T-shirt of your favorite indie band, and you're listed as a $20,000 speaker who gives talks about neuroscience on your agency's website, that can backfire. It can look equally bad if they see you standing next to your expensive sports car, where the takeaway message for event sponsors can be "I'm using our foundation's money to help pay for that." So, if you have a personal presence on social media, you need to clean it up—or make it private—and then rebrand yourself with "work" accounts before you launch yourself as a paid speaker because we are always aiming for a high level of professionalism and brand consistency.

One of the biggest questions that potential speakers who are just starting out ask is, *If I'm not currently on social media as a brand, am I better off staying off social media and being completely invisible, or starting out now knowing I'll only have a few followers?* In other words, is it better to be a ghost, or is it better to start building an internet presence now knowing that for a while you might not have many followers? The best-case scenario is to get ahead of this problem and build something quickly, even if it's not that substantial. Before contacting speaking agencies, as you're working on your topics and bio and perhaps trying to give a few speeches locally—generally taking any steps you can to brand yourself around your topic(s)—also attempt to build your internet presence on whichever platforms you feel are best for you. But even if you don't have the runway to get in front of it, the answer for most is to make the leap—it's better to start building your digital brand now and own it across platforms.

Why?

Because everything will change once you start speaking.

You'll be speaking at an event, and a few hundred people might start following you—if you're not on social media they can't do that. It's not uncommon for audience members to livetweet during speeches, and without a Twitter handle there is no one for them to tweet at or reference. In other words, there's the important element of *accessibility*. People want to feel that they are connected to the speakers they see and hear. And building your presence on social media is also a pivotal way for you to reach your growing audience with outbound marketing. You can send out messages about upcoming speaking events or factoids or comments about related topics that will increase your followers. You can use your social media presence to grow your brand and build a following that will impress event sponsors who are considering booking you in the future.

What about my broad internet presence beyond social media?

As an agent, when I received submissions from an aspiring speakers, the first thing I did was Google them. If those Google searches revealed a substantial number of matches—let's say a few thousand—and their social media presence was decent, they were far more likely to get a call from me or one of my agents. Remember that much of the speaking industry is based on optics, so not only is it important to produce content that is in line with the way you are presenting yourself to your agency and event sponsors, but also to make sure that this information is easily accessible.

If you have enough content available on the web, it can be wise to set up a Wikipedia page. This is easier than it sounds and you can get a professional who knows the rules and standards for Wikipedia to set up a page for you for less than $100. Websites like UpWork and Mechanical Turk usually have professionals who can perform these tasks quickly and efficiently. When searching for your name online, Wikipedia typically comes up first. This can be a powerful selling tool because Wikipedia profiles carry weight and help legitimize and validate your qualifications to event sponsors.

Case Study: When It Comes to Your Marketing Collateral, Less Is Always More—Except When It's Not

Speaker A or Speaker B?

Speaker A is a popular speaker who covers the economy for many well-known publications, including the *Wall Street Journal*. He has been on the speaking circuit for a few years, is represented by a midsize agency, and generally gets booked for about one gig a month. Over the years, he's collected dozens of blurbs related to his speaking. But his one sheet contains just three of them—and he's worked with his agent to identify the best blurbs based on the types of speaking engagements he is trying to secure.

Speaker B is also a popular speaker who covers the economy and is represented by the same agency. In fact, on paper, he's even higher profile than Speaker A, as he runs one of the most prestigious economic publications in the world. Speaker B doesn't have many speaking blurbs—his agents haven't been diligent about requesting them from event sponsors or updating his one sheet, and he doesn't speak as often as Speaker A. However, he does have a lot of reviews for his books and from industry colleagues.

An agent who represents Speaker A begins to review his marketing collateral and realizes that the speaking blurbs that aren't included on his one sheet are just as impressive as the ones that are—which gets the agent thinking. He also notices that Speaker A's blurbs are almost listed at random and decides to call Speaker A to get his opinion about reworking his one sheet, and talk about what to do with all the impressive extra praise he has for the speeches he's given. After discussing it for a while, they realize that there is enough high-quality content to turn Speaker A's one sheet into a two sheet—filling the entire second page with the praise he'd received giving speeches at high-profile events.

An agent at the same agency who represents Speaker B begins to review his marketing collateral, calls him, and they come to the same conclusion as Speaker A and his agent—they decide to create a two sheet. In Speaker B's case, since they didn't collect feedback about the speeches he'd given, they fill the entire second page with book reviews and personal endorsements from colleagues—even though most of them aren't well known outside of academic circles.

Armed with his revamped two sheet, Speaker A begins to see an increase in the number and quality of his bookings. He receives more offers from prestigious venues and for higher fees. Speaker B, who's also been relaunched with expanded marketing collateral, doesn't see any uptick in offers. In fact, the following year, the quantity and quality of the offers that come in for him actually *decrease*.

There are a number of possible explanations for this. Was it random luck? Did the marketplace change? Was Speaker A speaking about topics that were more in demand? Did the agents push him harder and pitch him more frequently than Speaker B?

The conclusion the agents came to was *no*.

Both of these speakers were speaking about the economy, and they had similar topics and backgrounds. Remember, Speaker B, whose bookings *went down*, was, objectively speaking, even more impressive than Speaker A. They were both at the same agency and were both being pitched with equal zeal for the same events. The only factor that had changed was the transition both speakers made from a one sheet to a two sheet.

Here's what they concluded: The difference in bookings was due to *the significant difference in the quality and relevance of the blurbs themselves*. Speaker A had blurbs that spoke directly to his speaking ability and referenced the corporate events where he'd given keynotes. Speaker B's additional praise related to *him as a person or to his writing.*

But we then have to ask, *Why did Speaker B's additional blurbs actually appear to hurt him?*

The conclusion the agents came to is that in all likelihood those additional blurbs overwhelmed the buyers; they were what Rosser Reeves would have called unrelated "fluff." For Speaker B, because the blurbs were unrelated to speeches, we'd moved too far away from our core sell message—breaking the cardinal rule of the USP mandate.

In Speaker A's case, since the extra content was specifically related to speaking, the blurbs helped him get more gigs and increase his fee. In Speaker B's case, since the extra content was specifically related to either his writing or to him as a person, the blurbs hurt him because they just created *noise and clutter.* The key piece of the equation is to understand when less is more.

TAKEAWAYS

Your marketing collateral is a key *additional* component of a strong one sheet—think of it as the product packaging and copy

Your photo should look professional, but not necessarily be *done professionally.* The most important thing is that your picture reflects your brand and personality

Get the best outside validation you can for your speaking ability and your status as an authority on your topics. Approach prior event sponsors, colleagues, and professionals in the same field to request blurbs

If you don't have speaking blurbs, use praise for your writing. If you don't have that, work around this problem by being creative. Fill

in the empty space with alternative sales material such as links
to articles that support your topic/position

Having a personal website is right for some, but isn't right for everyone who wants to be a paid speaker

Remember that being on social media makes you accessible—
people can reach out to you with queries about speaking that
you can forward to your agency and with offers for you to do
blog posts and interviews. As you give speeches, you'll also gain
followers and build your brand

Go for *professionalism, brand consistency,* and *focused messaging* across all social media platforms

Be cognizant of your internet presence—and do what you can to
build it strategically

When it comes to all of your marketing collateral, go for *quality*
and *focused message* over quantity, with an aim to inform with
precision but not to overwhelm potential event sponsors

Make sure to update all collateral marketing as your profile im-
proves

8.

All Together Now

HOW TO MAKE 1+1=3

Now that you've created well-crafted and well-branded content, it's time to put your speech topics, bio, and marketing collateral together on a one sheet—the comprehensive marketing document where all of these smaller components are assembled. The one sheet is what you will submit to agencies, and eventually the document that sales agents will use to pitch you to prospective event sponsors. Our goal is to make sure that the one sheet is professional and concise, with clean design. And, as with everything else you've done, you need to make sure that it's put together with your branding top of mind.

As you begin to think about layout and graphic design, pay attention to everything from placement, to font and font size, to use of color. Keeping in mind of course that there are no universal, correct choices. For example, I might suggest a different overall look for a one sheet for the beekeeper speaking about community-building than I would for the businesswoman speaking about client acquisition. In making that decision I am thinking about their different branding and different audiences as well. For the beekeeper, who's young and hoping to speak to students, I might suggest capturing some youthful exuberance—using some extra color and aiming for a bit of a fun vibe. Whereas I might recommend a more serious tone for the established businesswoman who speaks about client acquisition—perhaps suggesting that she lean toward an understated, business formal one sheet. In both cases, whatever we finally decide, we want conscious decisions, brand consistency, a clean uncluttered look, and professionalism.

One page or two?

As demonstrated in the previous chapter, unless they have a tremendous amount of speaking praise, most speakers should stick to a single page—and certainly should to start. As you assemble your one sheet and try to fit everything onto a single page, you'll see how important it is to keep everything short and concise. Even if you abided by the sizing parameters for your speech topic descriptions, bio, and marketing collateral—you may find that you have to trim further to get everything to fit onto one page without looking overly cluttered and busy.

Where does everything go?

In terms of layout, in my experience, the best one sheets look something like this:

▸ A small headshot of the speaker in the upper left corner.

▸ Contact information—start with your contact info, then change it to your agency's after you get one—on the upper right, opposite the picture.

▶ Your name under the picture.

▶ Your job title beneath your name.

▶ Your bio beneath name and title.

▶ Praise/accolades/links to media in the left margin.

▶ Speaking topics with descriptions at the bottom of the page.

Now that you've got a rough draft, fiddle with the placement. Adjust content and header sizes until you have a great looking page with appropriate margins.

Case Study: What Does a Successful Speaker One Sheet Look like, and What Happens if I Get It Wrong

Speaker A or Speaker B?

Speaker A approaches agencies with the hope of getting signed to an exclusive contract. When she puts together her material, she doesn't create a one sheet. Rather, she simply attaches a picture and her work bio to her introductory email, which includes a couple of generic speaking topic titles but no descriptive copy. She's really hoping to generate income speaking but hasn't given any speeches yet—not even any free ones—so she doesn't have any quotes or blurbs either. She has, however, written blog posts for a few online media outlets and she pastes links to the articles beneath her bio. Speaker A doesn't know enough to understand that her topics aren't fleshed out enough for an agent to make much of them, and they don't present her as a unique and interesting speaker. Rather, she appears to be just another person in a pool of thousands of people who have interesting jobs. She, of course, doesn't see it this way. She's hoping to snag an agent who will help her figure all the other stuff out—after all, she thinks, *That's what speaking agents do, isn't it?*

Speaker B also approaches agencies with the hope of getting signed. He knows enough to put together a one sheet and includes three sample speech topics—even though he isn't sure about two of them—a bio he branded carefully to reflect his speech topics, and links to a few articles he's written. He also includes a quote praising his recent TEDx talk written by one of the TEDx organizers, along with a link to his TEDx speech, which is posted on YouTube.

Both speakers send emails with their attachments and they land in the inbox of the same agent. Speaker A's clearly needs a lot of work. The agent reads what she sent, thinking that he'll have to figure out what she'll speak about and that he will possibly have to help her write her speech topics. Without the content of the speech topics already specified, this agent knows that her bio will also likely need tweaking after the topics are fleshed out. She seems interesting, and he has a few ideas about holes in the market she *might* be able to fill, but he can't tell from the info she's provided if she's actually a good fit or where her interests lie.

Speaker B basically got it right—with the exception of the missing picture, which is an easy fix—he's put the agent in a good position to ascertain his market value. Even though Speaker B is uncertain about two of his proposed speaking topics, the agent decides that's something he can work around because Speaker B's sample topics are specific and interesting enough to give him some idea as to what he actually wants to speak about. So, the agent decides to reach out to Speaker B and talk further, knowing that if the call goes well these speech topics can always be modified during the signing process.

Beyond being closer to market-ready than Speaker A, because his three speech topics gave the agent a really good idea as to his key areas of expertise, the agent can determine Speaker B's overall marketability. And the agent starts to think about a price point for him while he also starts to think about a few upcoming events for which he can pitch Speaker B. As he's typing an email to him requesting that they get on the phone, the agent has a good idea if Speaker B will be in demand, and—this is important—because Speaker B carved out a unique lane for himself by taking his area of broad expertise and giving it a unique spin in his topics, the agent knows that Speaker B won't be in direct competition with other exclusive speakers at the agency. Speaker B talks with the agent, and even though his one sheet wasn't perfect and the agent will have to make a few adjustments to it, he gets signed by the agency.

Speaker A doesn't get signed. In fact, she never hears back from the agent. The agent decides that Speaker A is just too much work, largely because he can't determine her marketability from the little that she sent. She didn't define herself well enough for the agent to decide to take her on—or even call her back—especially considering all of the other clients he has.

But something else very important happened here. Speaker A, by not being prepared, has likely lost her chance to pitch this agency—and all of the other agencies she approached with her weak material—at some point in the future. It's pretty hard to show up in an agent's inbox a second time after you've been rejected already.

So, Speaker B gets signed and has a solid speaking career.

But here's something that I know because I'm very familiar

with both Speaker A and Speaker B. *Speaker A would have been the better choice for the agency to take on than Speaker B—it's just that the agent had no way of knowing this, because Speaker A didn't present herself with well-branded content.*

If Speaker A had presented better—if she had fleshed out her topic descriptions and found her lane and branded herself with a USP that clearly demarked what audiences would get from her presentations—she would have made a fortune speaking.

How do I know this? Because I was the agent who signed Speaker B and rejected Speaker A. Then, Speaker A got really, really lucky. I took Speaker A on several years *after* she'd been rejected by me and all the other speaking agencies she'd contacted.

Through a series of coincidences and mutual acquaintances, I was reintroduced to Speaker A. And because I took the time to get to know her, I was able to see her value and work with her to develop her content. I was starting a new agency at the time and therefore had the motivation to do so. She now makes more money speaking than Speaker B does.

But that's not going to happen for too many others. So, get it right the first time. Make sure you get your one sheet as close to perfect as you can *before* you go out with it to speaking agencies because, unlike Speaker A, you probably aren't going to get a second chance.

Case Study: The Rudder Effect
The CEO Who Got It Wrong, Then Got It Right

Stephan is the founder and CEO of a relatively young consumer packaged-goods company. His company's products can be found in various national chain stores ranging from CVS and Duane Reade to Target and Walmart. He has a growing brand and he's a funny character—oozing personality and a great storyteller with a salable, relevant message. Exactly the type of person an agency would love to represent for speaking engagements.

When we first began working with Stephan, he had three corporate topics that we felt were strong. One talk focused on building a positive corporate culture for employees. Another focused on how to win new customers with a unique spin on acquisition and retention. His third topic was about work-life balance for both entrepreneurs and their employees, explaining how to succeed at work while maintaining a healthy lifestyle and work-life-family balance. These are all powerful, in-demand corporate topics. Stephan also had a strongly branded bio and great references from industry leaders. Even though he hadn't given any speeches yet, he had a very solid one sheet and we received interest in him from event sponsors almost immediately.

The first speech we booked for Stephan was at a technology start-up in Silicon Valley. The company hiring him had done about $40 million in revenue the prior year and had close to one hundred employees. The event sponsor explained to me that they were looking for a speaker who could address corporate culture, employee engagement, and how to provide moments of fun and levity in an otherwise stressful work environment. This was a perfect fit for Stephan's talk about building a positive culture in the workplace, and after the event sponsor saw his one sheet, she agreed.

When Stephan arrived on the day of the event, the sponsor met him and loved his energy and enthusiasm. Stephan then delivered a keynote address to a small group of executives, and the speech fell flat. Stephan spent most of the speech referencing his own company. Sure, it was within the context of developing positive culture, but it was too focused on his specific company and needs—not theirs. So, the message didn't coincide with what he presented on his one sheet, and as such, his speech came up short.

After the event, the sponsor reported back to me that she didn't think Stephan's bio captured his outsized personality but, more importantly, she felt that his speech would have been better if the references to his company were less of a focus and more attention had been paid to building corporate culture in a relatable, actionable way. What she essentially told me was that Stephan hadn't delivered the first promise of the USP—he hadn't given the audience a specific takeaway, a clear benefit they were able to extract from his talk.

This was great feedback for me to have, particularly because this was constructive criticism that I could share with Stephan to make his speech topic description on his one sheet—and his speech—better. When I called Stephan to share this information with him, he understood immediately. "I knew something was off," he told me, "but I couldn't put my finger on what it was." I told him that the event sponsor's feedback was that not everyone in the room was familiar with his brand and he strayed too far from the topic on his one sheet, so while the company culture pieces were well received, the audience members were a little bit lost when he talked about his company in so much detail. I explained that it felt like he was promoting something, not teaching or offering the audience something. After all, the speech we sold them was about what they could learn from his experience about creating a healthy workplace environment at their company, and Stephan hadn't related it to them enough— his takeaways seemed to fit his own particular company's needs, but not necessarily theirs.

I advised Stephan to think about his speech like it was a boat that had simply gone a little off course, and that all we needed to do was adjust the rudder slightly in order to land where we wanted to land. Rather than throwing the entire talk out or dropping his topic concept around company culture—we were, after all, getting a great response to this topic—we simply needed to make a few small adjustments to the actual speech topic description and he had to alter the speech he delivered so it was closer to what we promised on his one sheet.

In Stephan's case, it meant acknowledging his giant personality in his bio, adjusting his speech topic description to include more tangible takeaways, and eliminating many of the references to his company in the actual speech. Instead, he needed to focus more on the specific, extractable methods that he used when employee morale was suffering, and explain how other businesses could improve their company culture doing so as well. We also talked about the importance of establishing authority when speaking to audiences who aren't necessarily familiar with a given industry or brand—he could certainly begin his speech with a quick overview of what his company does for contextual reasons, and tell colorful relatable industry-specific stories, but after that he had to focus on culture-building examples without reference to his company by name or by industry.

The great thing is that Stephan took the constructive criticism, and while he kept the same speech topic title about company culture, he reworked his topic description and speech content, along with his bio. About two months later Stephan was booked to give a keynote presentation at a conference in Phoenix, Arizona, based on company culture, but with new and improved speech content. Stephan was confident that his revised speech was now closely aligned with the topic description on his one sheet and would be far more relatable to his audience.

When he arrived at the event there were over 1,500 people

from different industries in attendance—some of whom were familiar with his brand but, just like with the previous group, most of whom weren't. During the first three minutes of his speech, Stephan established his credentials and what he was going to be talking about. And this got the audience's attention. But then he spent the next forty-two minutes focused specifically on relatable takeaways about developing company culture—all gleaned from his experience at his company—without actually mentioning his company by name. And this made all the difference in the world. He got a standing ovation.

If you have a great speech topic on your one sheet, make sure the actual speech is closely aligned with it. Think about this as delivering the product attributes that were promised in the ad copy. And if a speech still doesn't land as well as you'd hoped, it doesn't necessarily mean you should throw the baby out with the bathwater. Small changes to content—or delivery—can make a tremendous difference.

It would have been a mistake for Stephan—or me as Stephan's agent—to assume that he was a bad speaker, or to draw the conclusion that his one sheet was weak, or that his topic didn't work based on the feedback from his first event. In reality, all it took was listening to a little bit of constructive criticism to get things on track. And the best news? This ended up being Stephan's *one great speech*. He was booked more than fifty times over the course of two years to discuss company culture, much to his delight and much to the delight of audiences both in the United States and Europe. His gross revenue from these speeches was roughly $600,000, despite his original speech falling flat.

The specifics you provide on your one sheet—who you are, what you do, what your company does, your blurbs, and what you speak about—validate you as someone who is worth listening to. But you have to make sure that the speech you give actually delivers the promise offered on your one sheet, and if it doesn't, you have to go back and make the necessary adjustments.

TAKEAWAYS

You will have to assemble your component pieces—sample topics, bio, and marketing collateral—into a cohesive industry-specific document called a *one sheet*

Don't underestimate the value of thoughtful graphic design and keep brand consistency in mind as you consider layout, font, color, and overall tone

Double-check that, in total, your one sheet really reflects who you are and what you have to say

Do the work and get it right with an eye on branding—it's hard to get a second chance

Never forget that what is in the sales copy has to be delivered by the product or you won't get a good response—or future bookings

Your speech must deliver what is promised on your one sheet—but if it doesn't, don't assume that it can't be fixed; perhaps it needs just a few subtle tweaks

9.

How to Get a Speaking Agent

FINDING THE PERFECT FIT

Now that you are armed with a strong, well-branded one sheet, it's time to explore how to secure speaking agency representation. What follows is a best-practices guide for what to do—and what not to do—once you're ready to begin shopping for an agency.

In order to make sure that you target the best agencies for *you*, the first step is to consider the different types of speakers agencies, who they represent, and the differing ways agents at those agencies are motivated when booking speakers—and how that differing motivation impacts the strategies they employ to get bookings. I'll explain the types of agencies to approach, and how to approach them—including *what* and *how much* additional information, beyond what's already on your one sheet, to put in your introductory email. Then I'll explain how to follow up if you hear back from a number of agencies, one agency, or no agencies at all. I'll cover how to talk to—and interview—potential speaking agents (and agencies) based on the responses you receive to your submissions. I'll also explain the ins and outs of commission rates, the value of exclusivity, and how—and what—to negotiate with an agency when it comes time to sign a contract. And finally, I'll also touch on what to do if you are a speaker—or become a speaker—with agency representation who has reached a certain level of success and are thinking it might be time to switch to a larger agency.

There are basically five broad types of speaking agencies:

▸   Massive, brand-name, 360-degree Hollywood-level talent agencies that, in addition to repping clients for music, film, television, literary—and possibly sports—also have speaking divisions that, for the most part, represent highly successful, high-profile individuals in the entertainment industry. Think celebrity-level musicians, actors, comedians, authors, and athletes who are also available for paid speaking.

▸   Large, prestigious "speaking only" agencies that are primarily populated with big-name clients and that sometimes specialize in a particular arena—for example, politics, the economy, or business.

▸   Midsize boutique, workhorse agencies that tend to have a broad range of exclusive, mid-level speakers in the $5,000–$50,000 range, a few high-fee, marquee names, and a tier of newer, inexperienced speakers who are hoping to establish themselves and climb the ranks. (This category encompasses the majority of the speakers agencies in America.)

▸   Mom-and-pop agencies that generally don't represent any big names at all, often have few—or no—exclusive speakers, and that generally exist by either booking low-fee events, or pitching and trying to co-broker speakers signed to other agencies.

▶ In-house speakers bureaus at large publishing houses that only represent the authors they publish and primarily handle incoming speaking inquiries for them.*

Of course, there are some subcategories within each of these, but, as you can see, the above categories encompass differences in size, reach, and prestige—and best serve different types of speaking clients. And, as you're about to see, the agents who work within each of these types of agencies often operate under a different set of motivating factors and, as a result, use different selling strategies—which means that they are not all right for every speaker.

But if I can get one of the giant agencies to sign me, why not? Even though I'm just starting out, I'm thinking I should start at the top, right?

If by "the top" you're thinking big, Hollywood-type agency, then *no*—unless you're a celebrity.

I'm asked this question all the time and there are a couple of reasons why starting at the top might not be the right thing for your career. I've had both inexperienced speakers and very experienced speakers who, in order to justify the fact that they think that they should be repped by a large well-known "Hollywood"

---

* If you are a published author who is represented by your publisher's speaking agency, I highly advise also working with another agency that does more outbound marketing, has access to event sponsors beyond the scope of most publishing houses, and has interest in your brand beyond just your book. Also note, some corporations have industry-specific in-house speaking divisions meant to serve their employees only.

agency say *But everyone I know—or every event sponsor who's hosted me—says I'm the best speaker they've ever heard!*

That statement from your friends and family—and even when it's from event sponsors—is meaningless. And it can even be misleading and counterproductive too. News flash: your friends and family are probably just being nice. As for those event sponsors? Even if you *are* the best speaker a particular event sponsor has ever had—and you probably aren't—it still doesn't mean that it's in your best interest to be represented by one of the big dogs. Or that you should want to be, either.

Large, prestigious, speaking-only agencies tend to sign celebrities, politicians, well-known public intellectuals, and people who already have well-established speaking careers and high fees to match. They largely represent people who receive honoraria[*] that are in the mid-five-figure range and higher and who—and this is important—get incoming speaking inquiries. *Lots of them.* So even if you are an established speaker, this may not be competition that you want or a sales situation that will work to your advantage.

And yet, I've seen a number of new, first-time speakers who had something impressive enough going on—or a connection— that enabled them to get offers of representation from large, prestigious agencies. When this happens, they tend to feel empowered by the implied status of the brand-name representation—who wouldn't?—only to get frustrated when they get little attention from the agency and few—or no—bookings.

This speaks to issues of *fit*. And more importantly, *differences in agent motivation and sales practices at the different size*

---

[*]   *Honoraria*, or *honorarium*, is another term for the fee paid to the speaker.

agencies. So, anyone looking for speaking agency representation should consider that, rather than a flashy name, you're looking for a good fit. In fact, looking for a speaking agency is a lot like shopping for a pair of shoes—if you get a pair that looks great but don't fit well, they won't take you very far.

Earlier in the book we looked at the story of the new speaker who was a little fish in the big pond of a huge Hollywood agency and didn't get booked. He left that agency to sign with my boutique agency and got lots of bookings.

Why were we so successful booking that new speaker when the big agency wasn't?

Because we were the right fit for him. We worked with the right types of event sponsors. And we were properly motivated. We were motivated to build his career because he was a big fish in our relatively small pond. And we paid attention to him. *A lot of attention.* Attention to the tune of well over half a million dollars in speaking fees for him. And we did it by employing a different selling strategy than that huge agency—by making *outbound marketing calls.* In other words, he wasn't well known enough to be getting incoming speaking requests either at the large agency or at my boutique agency. The difference is we *aggressively pitched him* to event sponsors who didn't know who he was. We were *selling him* while the large agency was *waiting for the phone to ring with inquiries*—because that's what their other speaking clients get.

When you're an agent with a roster full of high-fee clients who generate large volumes of incoming inquiries, which is typical at the brand-name agencies, the agents do far less outbound marketing in general. Let alone *aggressive outbound marketing.* Instead, agents with rosters full of household-name speakers spend a lot of time answering the phones to field these incoming inquiries. Which means that if you don't think people will be calling your agency to invite you to speak—chances are one of the giant talent agencies isn't the right choice for you.

And yet, I've found a lot of speakers—both new to the industry and established ones—get blinded by the bright light of a brand-name agency when what they should want is to sign with—or stick with—an agency that's a better fit for them. What celebrities need is someone to handle incoming requests. What every other speaker needs is an agency with agents eager to sign them. Agents who are chomping at the bit to build speakers' careers and push them to event sponsors via outbound marketing. They need agents who make time for them and who have the right contacts to generate offers and get them bookings. So, unless you have a celebrity-level household name (or are not intending to actually speak, but want to be listed on a big-name agency's website for optics) most new to mid-level speakers are better off being signed to a midsize agency with a lot of reach— one that can generate bookings—rather than to a larger prestige agency that may hardly pitch them at all.

So, if you're a celebrity and want paid speaking gigs, those brand-name Hollywood agencies with speaking divisions are great places for you—in fact, they already rep you. If you're a former politician or an industry titan, there are speaking agencies that handle similarly pedigreed speakers that will also be an equally good shop for you. But for everyone else who is not on that level, these large conglomerate talent agencies and the pedigreed specialty agencies are often the wrong choice. If you need further convincing consider this—many of these massive agencies have a category for the new, inexperienced speakers they sign. It's listed right alongside the other categories—*authors, scientists,* and *CEOs*—and it's called "Under $5,000."

For a smaller speaker repped by a big-name agency, landing in the under $5,000 category is a lot like being thrown into the bargain bin at a high-end retail store. And if you're in the under $5,000 bin at a big prestigious agency, there's a reason the agents are rarely doing any outbound selling for you: *There are only so many hours in a day.*

An agent who has a long list of high-profile, six-figure, exclusive speakers on her roster who spends her days fielding incoming inquiries for them is not going to spend the time necessary to pitch a $5,000 speaker who is just starting out unless they're really in a bind—trying to accommodate an event sponsor who calls in looking for an expensive speaker but only has a small budget. Why? *The math simply doesn't work.*

If you look at the numbers, that agent would have to book that $5,000 speaker ten times to make the same commission he or she would make on one booking for one of her $50,000 speakers. That means a lot of outbound calls and selling. And that agent's phone is ringing with incoming inquiries and offers. So, instead of taking those incoming calls and bringing the offers to their high-profile clients, that agent would have to make outgoing marketing calls to try to sell you. And that not only means making all the calls to actually generate ten separate sales, but also it means ten sets of contracts, ten different sets of travel arrangements, ten chances for problems of a no-show, and ten follow-ups—all for the same commission on that single $50,000 booking that involved little more than answering the phone. This is work that no agent wants to do unless they have to.

And all of those logistics and additional work—sales, contracts, travel, follow-up—take time and cut into profit on other events that agent now can't book because he or she is spending time handling the logistics of those ten smaller deals. And the work of a single $5,000 deal is basically the same as it is for a single $50,000 deal—in fact, a $5,000 event often requires more attention and requires just as much paperwork as a high-fee event.

But the fact that no one is doing much outbound marketing and actually selling you and you are getting no bookings isn't even the biggest problem with landing in the under $5,000 category— even at a big, prestigious agency. The biggest problem is that it defies everything we know about branding. All that work we did to position you as an expert with a strong Unique Selling Proposition fades fast when someone dumps you in the bargain bin and stamps "Under $5,000" across the front of your profile.

Assuming the big dogs aren't right for me, which type of agencies might be a good fit?

It's important to remember that there are dozens upon dozens of speaking agencies in the United States that fall into the two middle categories—mid-level boutique agencies and mom-and-pop agencies—and an agency that's perfect for one person might be completely ineffective for another. Assess where you are and look at your one sheet. Then look for an agency that represents people of similar stature and experience. This isn't to say that you should seek out an agency that represents people who speak about the same topics as you, but rather that you should search for an agency that represents similar "size" speakers.

The bottom line? The best speaking agencies for most small to midsize speakers are midsize boutiques that represent their speakers exclusively. They are often great places for speakers who are starting out and want to grow their careers and increase their fees. You'll get attention, be actively pitched, and the agents will be eager for your career to grow so they can earn more money. And these midsize boutique agencies have a lot more pull and prestige in the industry than the mom-and-pop agencies do. That means higher-profile bookings, for higher fees, and a better chance for growth. And that isn't to say that a mom-and-pop agency can't be effective, but if you can get signed by a midsize boutique agency, in my experience they are a great fit for most and you should go for it.

So how do I find them?

Simply Google *speaking agencies* or *speakers bureaus* and read a little bit about each agency that pops up, because there are big differences between the agencies within each of these broad categories when it comes to performance, personnel, and personality. Look at the speaking categories on each agency's website, read a few speaker bios and topics, and start thinking about which agencies feel like they might be the right choice for you—not only in a broad sense, but also in terms of personality and vibe. Also keep an eye out for *themes* when applying to agencies for representation. If you are an author, try to target agencies that represent a number of other authors. Then check out where they've given speeches; that way you'll see if they're getting booked. If you are a social entrepreneur, do likewise. This is easy to determine by simply poking around websites. The same rules apply to scientists, diversity speakers, and so on. While few agencies specialize in one particular area and most represent a variety of speakers across a variety of categories, you might find an agency that only represents one category—say, women—and that might be spot on for you and your branding. I find these smaller details relating to fit are important to consider when applying for agency representation as you want to be represented by the best agency for *you*.

Once I have some agencies in mind, how do I approach them, and with what material?

Much like submitting to a literary agent or applying for a job, you want to put your best foot forward with clear, concise materials. Agencies generally have an email address or a submission form—use that. Don't call. Use email. In fact, if you want to ensure that you *won't* get signed, call a speakers bureau—or show up at their door—and ask if they want to sign you.* In the email, be polite, brief, and professional. Introduce yourself and indicate that you are familiar with the agency—*I am contacting you because I'm interested in being represented for paid speaking and I see that you represent a number of speakers similar to me. I saw so-and-so speak at the such-and such-conference and...* Or, *After looking at your website, I feel I would be a great fit for you because you don't seem to have many speakers in the category of...* Give your key sales points, including your speaking topic titles, key audience takeaways, and proof of your expertise. Hit them hard with sell lines and professionalism in your email. End with your contact info and attach your one sheet, knowing that a lot of your competition won't be sending a one sheet. Instead, they'll be sending an email that simply says something vague and unprofessional like, "I'm a great speaker and I talk about animal rescue (or the environment or marketing) and I'd like to get on the phone and talk to you about representing me." This is *not* the way to go about this. Not because of the specific topics mentioned, but because of how unprofessional it is. It screams, *I have no idea how the industry works, I've made no effort to brand*

---

*   Of course, there are exceptions to this rule. *NYT* bestselling author of *On the Edge*, Alison Levine, tells a funny story about standing outside on the street in front of a speaking agency every day and finally getting an agent to talk to her. She then got a phone call from that agent when he was in a jam and had a speaker cancel an event, asking Alison if she could be in Las Vegas for a speech the following day. And that jump-started her speaking career.

or position myself, and I might not even be qualified to speak about these topics in the first place.

As a speaking agent, I received about fifty emails each week just like this and few, if any, of the applicants got called back, let alone got signed. However, the speakers who sent a professional email and a well-put-together, well-branded one sheet almost always got a return call. And I ended up signing many of them in the process. That's because those aspiring speakers demonstrated that they knew how the speaking industry functions, they'd already done a lot of the heavy lifting for us and provided us with the information we needed to make an informed decision—and make it quickly.

If I don't hear back from an agency, how soon should I follow up?

Tread lightly. Agencies are busier than you can imagine, so wait six to eight weeks and if you haven't heard back by then, you can follow up—also via email.

Do *not* call an agency to follow up unless you are asked to.

No one will be available to take your call, and it will actually work against you. Speaking agents know what they are looking for and who they can sell. And most importantly, they know what they're *not looking for.*

You should follow up via email sooner than six to eight weeks only if you have a significant update:

▶ A development that might enhance or improve your speaking profile and/or potential speaking fee—a significant career update, a book deal, an upcoming media event, or a paid speaking offer.

▶ If you receive an offer for representation from a competing agency.

Emailing with a significant update is a way to reach out a second time and might prompt a response, especially if that update is a speaking offer. You've now demonstrated that you're a viable paid speaker. And with an offer in hand, a polite update will nudge agencies to take a second—or a closer—look at your materials.

And, of course, you're always more desirable looking to an agency if they know that the competition is interested. If the perception is that you are in hot demand, it might be possible to leverage an offer for exclusive representation from one agency to get the attention of another agency you feel is a better fit.

What should I do if I get a response?

You can hear back from an agency either by phone or email. Either way, give yourself a pat on the back—getting interest from a speaking agency is difficult to do and you are competing against tons of prospective speakers. This said, the next step is to send an email to alert any other agencies you have interest in but haven't heard back from in order to nudge them to respond. Then you should arrange a call (if you were contacted by email)—or perhaps even an in-person meeting if you're in the same city—with the agency that contacted you to see if there is synergy.[*]

When you do get on the phone (or meet) with the agent(s) who contacted you, they will talk about you and how you present on your one sheet—discussing your speech topics, bio, and collateral marketing. They will likely ask you questions about your goals, the fee you are hoping to receive per event, and discuss commission percentages with you. They will also provide guidance and have opinions as to your target market, how much they can sell you for, and tell you their thoughts as to your overall fit in the

---

[*]   If you're not in the same city do *not* spend money to fly out to visit the agency—it's not necessary because everything can be done on the phone.

paid speaking marketplace and at their particular agency. Listen to them. Since agents live and breathe speakers every day—and more importantly, since they interact for hours every day with event sponsors—they know the market better than anyone. But also, present yourself in the best possible light—they're interviewing you for *speaking*. Think about your voice, personality, presence, and appearance, and demonstrate how well you think on your feet.

And don't be afraid to ask questions.

How many speeches do they think they can book in year one and year two? Is there anyone on their roster who might be in direct competition with you? How do they see you fitting in? What are your strong points? Are there any visible weaknesses to work around? If so, how will they do this? (For example, if you have no speaking experience, what is their strategy for getting you a first gig?) *How's your bio? What about your speech topics? Do your topics need work or repositioning? Which of your three topics do they see as most salable? What do they think of your one sheet overall? How's the layout? Does it fit within the format they use? Are there any points you're missing? Will they work with you to refine it, or go with it as is? Is there anything hot in the speaking market right now that pertains to you that you should know about or reference? What price point do they envision for you to start? Will they post your fee online? Why or why not? Is there a target number of events they have in mind for you? How do they commission? How long is the term of the contract you would be signing? Have they ever worked with someone like you before? If so, what were the results? How many agents work at their company? How many will be pitching you and in what markets? How soon? Will you have a single contact at the agency? Who will it be? If you have a question or update, do they prefer that you call or email? How often will you get updates from them?*

It's also important to establish *why* you want to speak—this will help the agency understand your motivation. So always talk about brand-building and what your short- and long-term goals are. It may sound surprising, but not all speakers are motivated by money. It's possible that you are looking to speak in order to secure a book deal. Or perhaps it's more important to you to have the chance to spread a message that you are passionate about. Or you see speaking as an avenue to generate brand awareness for your company or to open strategic alliances and network. This information helps an agency help you. Knowing that you might be open to working for a lower fee can open up opportunities for bookings that they wouldn't have otherwise pitched you for. Whatever the case, it's important that the agency knows *why* you want to speak as it will affect the way in which—and how often—they pitch you. And to whom. If all goes well—and if you don't hear back from any other agencies you nudged—your goal should be to sign an exclusive contract.

Hold on, what's this about exclusivity?

Most agencies will shy away from working with you unless you sign an exclusive contract. The reason for this should be relatively obvious—if the only place you can purchase a particular product is at one store, that store can control both the *messaging* and the *pricing*. Agents want this power while negotiating to get you gigs. Therefore, nonexclusivity is a disadvantage to both the speaker and the agency. Further, if a number of agencies are pitching you to event sponsors on a nonexclusive basis, no single agency is going to pitch you as often as they should be pitching you. Which means you get fewer offers. And the offers you do get will likely be of lesser dollar value that the offers you *should* get. In other words, if more than one agency is working with you, the problem isn't only that you're less likely to be actively pitched—when you are pitched, you may end up getting less money than you deserve.

Here's an example:

In scenario one, Josephine gets interest from three agencies and signs an exclusive contract with one of them, and the agency sets a price of $7,500 for speaking events.* This agency knows that there are no other agencies pitching her and therefore no agency that can interfere with their efforts by stealing a booking while driving her price down.

In scenario two, Josephine has interest from three agencies and, thinking she's being smart, decides to work on a nonexclusive basis with all of them. The agent at Agency A works hard and pitches Josephine for $7,500 to an event sponsor. Then, since the event sponsor knows that the speaker is nonexclusive (Josephine is on the website of two other agencies), the event sponsor who got the quote of $7,500 from Agency A calls Agency B and tells Agency B that they were quoted $7,500 by Agency A. Agency B immediately tells the event sponsor that they can do the deal for $6,500. The sponsor is thrilled, and then calls Agency C where Josephine is also on the website and—after sharing the prior quotes of $7,500 and $6,500 respectively—receives a price quote of $5,000. The sponsor logically decides to go with Agency C, who provided the lowest price and sends Agency C an offer for $5,000. Agency C calls Josephine, who has no idea what just transpired, and she decides to accept the gig for $5,000 even though it's below her asking price. In fact, Josephine's thrilled and thinks that Agency C did a really good job for her.

They didn't.

---

* This does not imply that they publish that rate on their website (some agencies do, some don't). In this example it's just the price the agents use internally.

In fact, they took $2,500 out of her pocket and they're getting the credit as the good guys. Here's what really happened. Agency A was actively pitching Josephine—in fact they had pitched her for ten or fifteen events before getting the interest from the event sponsor who then decided to price shop. Think about that. *The event sponsor was going to hire Josephine and pay her $7,500.* Had Josephine been exclusive with Agency A, that's what would have happened. But now when Agency A does the follow-up call with the event sponsor and finds out what happened, the event sponsor glibly tells him, *Oh, I didn't get back to you because we got Josephine for $5,000 from another agency.*

Josephine just inadvertently angered the agent at Agency A, who had been working hard to pitch her and get that gig. They now decide not to bother to actively pitch her anymore. So, she still sits on the three agencies websites—but no one is pitching her. All Agencies B and C did was answer incoming calls and undercut the price—they had never pitched Josephine to anyone. Had Josephine signed exclusively with Agency A, she would have gotten the gig for $7,500 and would still be being pitched. This kind of thing happens all the time.

Nonexclusive speakers are difficult to get behind, difficult to handle, and pose a risk because there's uncertainty in nonexclusive relationships. If I represent someone exclusively, I fight tooth and nail to get them as many offers as possible—and I feel safe doing so. If I am working with someone on a nonexclusive basis, I'll likely pitch them 95 percent less frequently because my commission isn't guaranteed and I risk being undercut by another agency.

I learned this lesson on my first day as a speakers agent. I connected with an event sponsor who wanted a celebrity type to speak at an annual conference. Based on the description of the type of speaker they were looking for, I suggested the actress Alyssa Milano—who wasn't exclusive with my agency but who I thought would be perfect—at a fee that I knew the sponsor could afford. A week later, when I followed up with the sponsor, I found out that they had booked Alyssa Milano through another agency and—as it turns out—for a significantly lower fee than I had quoted. And this didn't happen because I quoted too high a fee—I quoted her exact price. But the other agency was willing to take the risk of saying they could secure her for less. And they did. I was naive and it was my first day, and I lost about $10,000 in agency commission—which would have meant $2,500 to me. And the worst part? I was the agent who had given the event sponsor the idea to book Alyssa in the first place. I did 95 percent of the work and lost out on the booking—and the commission—to an agency that did only 5 percent of the work.

The lesson is that agents will hesitate to pitch you as often and as passionately if you aren't exclusive and, as we just saw, that can lead to price erosion. "If we sign you exclusively, we're all committed" is what I often say to speakers—the speaker can rest assured that she has a team of dedicated agents pitching her, and the agency can rest assured that the speaker isn't listed with competing agencies.

But isn't it worth it to have more agents pitching you even if they're pitching you less and it sometimes works against you?

Nope. And here's why.

Almost every exclusive agency is willing to co-broker their speakers. Meaning that if an event sponsor wants you and is working with a different agency than the one that represents you, that agency can call your agency and present an offer without diluting the value of that offer. So, for example, if another agency gets an offer for $10,000 for you to give a speech, they can simply call your exclusive agency to get the deal done. The agencies split the commission and you still net the same amount of money for your speech—so exclusivity is a win-win for all involved. Exclusive speakers are the speakers who are pushed hard, pushed often, and pushed with passion. And passion is one of the key elements agents rely on when pitching and booking speakers. If I'm excited about a speaker, I'll pitch her to almost anyone who is willing to listen. I'll even push her to my family over Thanksgiving dinner just to create interesting conversation.

And exclusivity does more than allow your agency to control your speaking fee and increase the chances that you are being pitched often and pitched hard. Having an exclusive agent means you have a partner in your branding and control over the language used when pitching you. Nonexclusive speakers don't get this treatment. Exclusivity also creates great optics, which can be leveraged both with event sponsors and beyond. To give you an example, I've also functioned as a literary agent for some of my exclusive speakers and generated five- and six-figure book advances for them.* The reason I was able to accomplish this was largely because the publishers knew that my agency booked a lot of speakers, and that in signing a publishing deal with one of my speakers the book would receive exposure and generate sales—specifically bulk book buys—at the events at which they were speaking. Being signed as a speaker made my clients better prospects for publishing houses. It also increased the advances they got for their books. Why? Because I was able to talk about branding and marketing, and promised to bake book promotion into their speaking platforms in a manner that was to everyone's financial benefit.

---

* Please note that it is very uncommon for a speaking agent to also act as a literary agent.

Exclusive representation facilitates greater interest on the agents' part in working on long-term strategies even beyond a book deal when it comes to building your speaking career. These agents are invested in your success and want you to grow—which is exactly why I worked with clients to get them book deals—and are working hard to make sure that you have a presence in the market for years to come. Without exclusivity, you aren't going to get very much help in terms of planning and scaling for the long term.

Since agencies work on commission, what percentage should I agree to pay?

The average commission is generally between 20 and 25 percent. Occasionally, you'll run into an agency that asks for 30 percent—in those situations, it's usually because the agency doesn't think they can book you all that often, and not at a particularly high fee. So, 30 percent makes the work worth their while. And there is nothing wrong with agreeing to a 30 percent commission if you are just starting out or have a relatively low fee—$5,000 or less—because you can always revisit it later when you are more established.

Paying a speaking agency the standard 20 to 25 percent is worth every penny. Remember, for you, this is "found money," and your agency is working on spec—if you don't make money, they don't make money. And agents love to—and need to—make money. So, what you want to do is strategically assess your value to them and their value to you. If you are an established speaker who gets lots of incoming requests—lots of event sponsors calling the agency with high-fee offers—you have great value to the agency. But if you need a lot of brand-building and outbound marketing because you're not known and in demand, you can see how the motivations of your agent can be swayed by a lot of factors—including the commission rate. When an event sponsor calls and says, *I need to book a speaker for our upcoming conference on diversity*, that agent has a lot of options as to who to suggest and who to push. And a lot of variables come into play in that decision—from the obvious, like how applicable each speaker is, to the less obvious, like how easy they are to work with, how likely they are to accept an offer, and what commission they are contracted for. For example (assuming all the other variables are the same), if an agent has two $50,000 speakers and one is at 20 percent commission rate and another is at 25 percent, guess who gets pushed harder?

Case Study: Speaker A or Speaker B?

Speaker A sends out his one sheet and marketing materials to five agencies that range in size and presence. He's hopeful that he might receive interest from at least two of the agencies so he can negotiate the commission rate down. Speaker A has spoken at a few conferences for free, and his marketing materials are strong—he even includes links to two different videos of his speeches on his one sheet.

Speaker B also sends out her one sheet and marketing materials—which are equally as strong as Speaker A's—to five agencies that range in size and presence. She's hopeful to get interest from a few of them so she has some options. Speaker B has a few friends and colleagues who are already represented by agencies, and she's aware of and accepts the fact that the going commission rate for noncelebrities is 25 percent.

Speaker A receives interest from three of the five agencies he contacted and is thrilled. After speaking on the phone with agents from all three agencies—all of whom explain that they get a 25 percent commission rate—he lets the owner of each agency know that he has interest from two other agencies and that he is asking which of them will negotiate a reduced commission of 20 percent. The owner of the first agency, the largest of the three, says there is absolutely no way they'll take Speaker A at 20 percent, and gives him a day to consider their offer of representation at a 25 percent commission. An agent at the second agency informs Speaker A that they regularly receive a 30 percent commission for new speakers like himself, so Speaker A is already getting a deal at 25 percent. The owner of the third agency is annoyed by the request and simply tells Speaker A that he is no longer interested.

Speaker B also receives interest from three agencies. After speaking with agents from each, she narrows her decision down to two—eliminating the largest agency from the running because she feels she won't be top of mind with the agents. Her friends who have speaking representation have advised her that it's best to be at an agency where she is sure she'll get the attention of the agents, be pitched frequently, and fits within the budgets of the event sponsors those agencies serve—and Speaker B judges that the biggest agency is simply too big for her. Commission percentage hasn't even come up on the phone calls—Speaker B is more interested in asking questions about how these agents envision her, what they think her potential is in the marketplace, and where they would set her speaking fees.

Speaker A now has two agencies interested but takes a week to think about who to sign with and ignores the owner of the first agency who gave him a day to make a decision. In the end, Speaker A calls the second agency and tells the owner that he is going with the first agency. He then calls the first agency, leaves a message, and doesn't hear back. He calls five more times over the course of a month and still doesn't hear back. Finally, one day he receives a phone call from an assistant at the first agency who is passing along a message that they aren't going to be pursuing a relationship as the agency is currently too busy. Speaker A had three interested parties and managed to lose all three because of misplaced greed. To put this in perspective, the 5 percentage point difference in commission Speaker A was trying to negotiate down—20 percent instead of 25 percent—on a $10,000 speaking gig is $500.

Speaker B speaks with the second agency on her list and tells the agents that she would like to proceed. Still, no commission percentage has been discussed. When the contract arrives in her inbox, she sees the expected 25 percent commission, signs the contract, is up on the company website forty-eight hours later, and is being pitched by agents to event sponsors almost immediately. She also has the foresight and wherewithal to call the third agency to thank them, very nicely explaining that she was very impressed with them and torn, but ultimately decided to go with a different agency. The agent she speaks with thanks her for the opportunity and tells Speaker B to be in touch if anything ever changes with the agency she selected.

Speaker B went on to have a great relationship with her agency and she made $400,000 speaking—before commissions— during her first three years as a speaker. She also got her message, brand, and face out before large audiences, got a book deal, and leveraged the fact that she was speaking to expand her personal network. Speaker B was smart enough to figure out that 80 percent of nothing is nothing. And that 75 percent of the $400,000 she made speaking takes a nice chunk out of the cost of even the most expensive private colleges for her two kids. Speaker A, as far as I know, never signed with an agency and never spoke at a paid event. On the other hand, at least he didn't have to pay an agency that extra 5 percentage points he was so worried about.

When I sign a contract for representation, how long should it be for?

Generally, speakers bureaus sign speakers for exclusive representation for a term of two or three years. I've encountered many speakers who want to sign a one-year contract in order to see how the agency does. This is a complicated two-way street—with pros and cons for everyone on both sides. But a one-year contract is almost universally a bad idea unless you're an extremely established speaker who's already receiving significant offers on your own and will drive business to an agency. Why? Because of buying cycles.

Buying cycles have to do with how far ahead sponsors plan and book events, and that time frame impacts your agency's willingness to pitch you. If you sign a one-year contract, the agents at your agency know that they only have you for one year and that it's likely going to be anywhere from three to nine months before they book you—because event sponsors typically plan this far out. The problem is that you're possibly leaving the agency not long after signing. As such, your agents have less incentive to pitch you—or to work hard to get you plum bookings or drive up your price— since you have one foot (potentially) out the door. This means that they may be competing against you next year—pitching their long-term exclusive speakers to the same event sponsors that your new agent will be pitching you to. If you do leave, the new agency reaps the rewards of all the hard work done by your old agency.*

---

*   Agency agreements have clauses that try to protect the agency against this type of loss, but they are very limited, hard to enforce, and are rarely collected on. For example, if I introduce a speaker to an event sponsor by pitching him or her for an event they don't get booked for and nine months later that sponsor decides to book that speaker through the speaker's new agency, I don't collect a commission even though I made the introduction.

Now, the counterargument to this is that you'll sign a one-year contract but stay at the agency if they do a good job during your first year. But this is a flawed proposition and agents know this. The agency won't perform at full potential or full capacity if you aren't willing to show a commitment to them—that means they'll be pushing their clients signed to longer contracts harder. Signing with an agency should be the "We're all committed" sentiment I mentioned earlier by all parties involved, and that includes the speaker. The agency should feel safe working with you, and you should feel safe knowing that your agency is going to work hard for you.

What do I do if multiple agencies want to sign me?

First, pat yourself on the back—again. This means you and your materials are well branded enough to garner wide interest. Next, schedule a call with each agency, and view each and every one of these calls as opportunities to present yourself as professional, engaging, and just as interesting as you branded yourself on your one sheet.

Also, view these calls as an opportunity to assess the professionalism and ethos of the agent(s) and agency. Are these people you can get excited about working with? Do they sound enthusiastic about working with you? Are they smart and articulate? (After all, they may be representing—and presenting—you to event sponsors.) Make sure to review the agency's website before the call so you can ask informed questions: *I see you represent (insert name) and since he also speaks about (insert topic), I was wondering what you think about...*

If it isn't evident on their websites, ask your agency contact if they are more focused on one specific market—if so, is it college, corporate, or nonprofit? How does that work for your brand? Note if the call is with the agency owner or one of the agents. If it's an agent, ask which division that agent works in: college, corporate, or nonprofit. Listen to what they have to say and ask the same list of questions to each agency you speak with.

As you digest all of the answers, remember that the best fit isn't necessarily the agency that is offering you the lowest commission rate or the shortest-term contract. And you shouldn't automatically go with the biggest agency. Listen to what they all have to say. Judge fit and personality—and strive for comfort. Consider the agency's branding and USP, just like you do your own.

Help! I feel overwhelmed. They all seem great!

I've found that, at least when starting out, it's better to have a more hands-on agency where you are a top priority. If I was offered representation by two different agencies tomorrow, and at the first agency I'd be in their top 20 percent of speakers, but at the second, I'd be in their bottom 20 percent, I'd choose the first agency every time. You want agents who keep you top of mind and who are actively pushing for engagements on a daily basis. You don't want to be an afterthought or perceived as not a valuable asset for the agency to have on their roster, or just be filler for their website. But you also don't want to be in the top ranks of an agency without reach. So, look at—or ask—where each agency books the majority of their speakers and how much of their time is dedicated to their exclusive speakers. And if you are in the position that you have a number of agencies interested in signing you, and at all of them you'll be at the top of the heap, go with the agency that seems to have the strongest market pull. Obviously, if you have the option, you don't want to be the top speaker at a mom-and-pop agency that primarily books other agencies' speakers and only books their exclusive speakers at low-end venues— and is hoping to sign you to generate incoming inquiries.

What if I've already been at an agency for a year or more and I'm thinking about switching?

First, ask yourself why you want to leave. And be honest. Are you legitimately being underserved by the agency where you're now signed? Or are you doing extremely well? Maybe you're getting a lot of bookings, your fee has moved up, and you're speaking at much better venues than when you started—but now you simply feel that a bigger agency will be able to do more for you.

In other words, is the potential move because you are dead in the water and stagnating? Or because you are now a superstar looking for an agency with more prestige?

Let's say you're dead in the water and stagnating. You're sitting on your agency's website and haven't gotten many—or any—offers, and your gut tells you the problem's not *you*, it's *them*. You've tried talking to your contact at the agency about it and got nowhere, and now your contract is up for renewal and you're thinking that maybe it's time to move on and look for an agency that's a better fit. And you might be right.

If you reach out to other agencies and they express interest, ask them why they think you aren't being booked—or booked enough—by your current agency and see what they say. Do they think it's your speech topics? Your bio? Your lack of speaking experience? The current marketplace? The agency? Then ask yourself if what the agent(s) at the new agency are telling you resonates. *How does it fit in with what my current agency has been telling me about why I haven't been booked?* Then ask the agent(s) at this new agency what they'll change when they pitch you, and who they'll be pitching you to—and why. In fact, ask them all the same questions you asked agencies when you first signed. If, after all of that, you still feel that you haven't been properly served by your current agency, and you have another—hopefully better—offer of representation, then a move might be in order. But be warned. Agencies are going to tell you what you want to hear—especially if you've been generating income for your other agency. For example, if a speaker calls and tells a new agency that they were "only" booked ten times for $10,000 a gig the prior year and they aren't happy, that new agency is going to think that they will be able to make at least $25,000 in commission on you next year simply based on incoming inquiries. They are going to want sign you. And they might overpromise.

But what about the tougher call? The superstar looking for a more prestigious agency?

This happens all the time. A speaker signs to an agency. They have a great compelling message, but little or no speaking experience. The agents go all out to get the speaker a first event for a few thousand dollars. The speaker gets rave reviews, and the agency gets the speaker another event for a higher fee, and then another and another. They've held the speaker's hand through the process, taught her the ropes, and worked with her to build her platform, hone her marketing materials, and give her advice. Both the agency and the speaker are killing it. Event sponsors love them. The agents are thrilled, the speaker is thrilled, and her brand grows. She starts pulling in the big bucks. She's able to leverage her speaking gigs to not only earn money, but also in a whole slew of other ways—maybe that manifests as a better job, more donations to her nonprofit, increased sponsorships for her brand, a book deal, or more growth opportunities all around.

And then the speaker gets greedy. Her ego gets big. She doesn't ever forget how far she's come, but she forgets *how she got there.* She forgets that the agents at the agency where her speaking career started—and exploded—took risks, worked for free, and pushed her when they weren't sure that she could deliver and when they could have pushed someone else, someone who was already proven and a safer bet. Those agents did that expecting loyalty—they pushed that new speaker and took on risk because they wanted to profit from their hard work too.

For speakers who start at the bottom with an agency that helps build them to have not only a great speaking career, but also all the ancillary benefits that come along with that, it's best to be careful that you aren't leaving a great agency that was right by your side growing your career to where it is now. That current agency built your career on spec—spent months or even years selling you and building your brand, struggled to get you your initial booking, got your fee up, and is now still getting you great gigs. That's a lot of sweat equity they deserve to profit from now that your bookings are finally at a higher fee and a bit easier to get.

I believe in loyalty when loyalty is due, and my advice is that you should probably stick with them.

With two caveats.

One—you may want to negotiate a lower commission. If you are bringing a lot of new event sponsors their way and you are turning the offers down because you have so many high-fee offers that you can't—or don't—take them all, and the agency can flip those inquiries that came in for you to their other speakers, you can consider asking for a lower commission rate on the gigs you do accept.

Two—there's one very specific, legitimate reason for an established speaker to leave a great agency that has served them well. And it's this: Since you aren't likely to be booked at the same events where you've already spoken, if you feel that the agency that did such a good job growing your brand has exhausted their reach and your bookings are dwindling, you might want to talk to them about the current fit.

In other words, if your sense is that you've already spoken at all of the events they book for the sponsors they work with, and the agency's ability to book you is diminishing, it might be time to move on because you've outgrown them and they're no longer a good fit for you. If you fear that this is the case, discuss this with your agency and see if they have a solution—or if they can explain that your fear is misplaced. Ask them why your growth was spectacular and then stagnated. Where are they pitching you now? What response are they getting? What new conferences, businesses, and college programs do they have targeted for you over the next twelve months?

If you don't get an answer you like, consider moving on to a different, similarly sized, or bigger agency.

Why?

A new agency likely has a completely different set of event sponsors they work with and can now sell you to.

Just think long and hard about a move like this. If your current agency took you from nowhere to somewhere, from small brand to big brand, consider how much of that growth was because of your speaking agency's efforts. And then consider how hard they worked to get you where you are now and whether they deserve to participate in those higher profits now that—with their expert hand-holding—you've "made it."

TAKEAWAYS

When making a decision on who to approach for representation, consider the different types of speakers agencies—they vary in terms of size, clientele, agent motivation, sales practices, market presence, and personality

After you realistically assess your relative position in the paid

speaking marketplace, approach a smattering of agencies that
you think are a good fit for you

After your initial query, if you don't hear back from prospective
agencies right away, wait six to eight weeks before following up
unless you have a significant update

When offered representation, interview the agency as much as
they are interviewing you. Ask a lot of questions, and make informed decisions—find that perfect fit

Understand that it's to your advantage to pay the standard 20 to
25 percent commission rate, and don't attempt to negotiate it
down unless you are already a successful speaker with a track
record and are capable of generating incoming offers

Agency contracts are typically exclusive—and that benefits you
enormously as you build your brand. In fact, *exclusivity is king.*
It's good for you as a speaker, and it is good for your agency too

Expect your speaking agency contract to have a term of two to
three years—mutual commitment, just like exclusivity, is good.
It gives the agency a comfort level to keep selling you for events
in the future without fear that you will soon leave for another
agency—and it gives you enough time to prove yourself to them

Be loyal—leave your agency only if they truly aren't delivering or
because you've legitimately outgrown them. Don't leave out of
greed, misplaced loyalty, or an inflated ego

10.

What Your Agent Actually Does

...AND HOW KNOWING THAT WILL HELP YOU

Now that we've covered *how to get a speaking agency*, this chapter will discuss exactly what to do with—and expect from—that agency now that you have one. I'll explain what speaking agencies—and more importantly the agents at them—actually do. I'll cover the detailed nuances of what goes on behind the scenes day in and day out, from relationship-building and relationship management (agent–speaker and agent–event sponsor) to the art of the pitch, deal closing, contract negotiation, and post-event follow-up, so that you fully understand what is being—or at least, should be—done on your behalf.

The reason that it's so vital for you to understand what your agent's* job entails is so you'll be able to *adjust your behavior* in

---

* Generally, a speaker will have one agent who is a point of contact at their agency, but other agents at the agency will also be pitching him or her. I am, at times, using the term *agent* to encompass all of the agents at your agency.

a manner that will both facilitate and enable them. Supportive behavior on the part of speakers leads to better outcomes. It frames you as both professional and easy to work with, and that inspires agents to be even more excited about representing you and your growing brand. That means that they're more likely to pitch you, which translates to more offers and greater opportunities.

So, what exactly do speaking agencies, and speaking agents, do?

Once you're signed by an agency, your profile and speech topics will be posted on their website and you—or more specifically, your ideas and a few hours of your time—will be listed for sale. So, your speaking agency is essentially an online store that is your portal to event sponsors. And the agents are the sales force and lifeblood of that "store." They have contacts and relationships of trust with event sponsors. Agents have an in-depth knowledge of the speaking market—what's selling, who's buying, how to negotiate, where to set fees—and, for the most part, agents spend their days pitching speakers to event sponsors on the phone. Granted, agents do spend some time on things like contracts, travel arrangements, working to modify and update one sheets and web profiles, speaking with other agents in-house to discuss new signings and speaker developments, and updating their current speakers as needed. Agents also bring speakers offers, go over contract points, follow up on recently completed events, and discuss significant new developments—but the vast majority of a speaking agent's time is dedicated to making outbound sales calls.

Speaking agents essentially smile and dial.

They sell.

All day. Every day.

Generally, a speaking agent is expected to make a *minimum* of thirty-five outbound calls each day, pitching event sponsors to generate speaker bookings. That's four to five calls an hour. These calls include pitching speakers to event sponsors for upcoming events, updating them on speaker news, following up on any events that just occurred, and inquiring about any events the sponsors might have in the pipeline. The rest of these phone calls involve cold-calling event sponsors who the agent doesn't currently have a relationship with in order to introduce themselves to try to establish one. All of this is a means to extract dollar value from their current relationships and increase their database of potential buyers.

Now, if the agency has notable clients who are capable of generating incoming inquiries—warm leads—the job is decidedly easier. Picking up the phone and fielding a call from an event sponsor who says something like *I see that you represent Bill. We were hoping he might be interested in speaking at our conference on May 10. We have a budget of $50,000* makes it a lot easier to get an actual booking than cold-calling event sponsors to find—or drum up—that interest. But either way—outgoing or incoming, long shots or shoo-ins—speaking agents spend their days on the phone. And if you dissect the calls a typical speaking agent makes on any given day, you'll see that they all revolve around the two, very intertwined, components of the job—relationship management and selling.

Building those relationships isn't easy. The first thing a new speaking agent has to do is establish relationships with event sponsors at organizations that book speakers—corporations, nonprofits, and colleges and universities.* A new agent who joins

---

* Some speaking agencies have agents in separate divisions—so one agent may only book at colleges and another at corporations and nonprofits, but other agencies have the same agents work all three markets. And some agencies don't service all three markets and may focus solely, for example, on corporate.

an agency will likely be given a database of event sponsors to call in order to establish those relationships, and once they're established, the goal is to have a comfortable back-and-forth where the agent can reach out to those event sponsors saying something like *I'm checking in to see where you are with the speaker booking for your April conference on thought leadership. I sent over one sheets for Laura and Mary last Wednesday, both of whom I think would be great for your event, and I was wondering if you had any questions.* If that agent is lucky, he'll hear that the event sponsor presented both of his speakers' one sheets to their committee and they'll be voting next week. And if he's really lucky, that agent will also hear that the sponsor has two new events scheduled in the fall that they're starting to think about speakers for.

Once a speaking agent and an event sponsor have done a deal together, after the event takes place, the agent will also call for a postmortem, saying something like *Just checking in to hear how the event went last night.* And, of course, he's hoping to hear that the event they'd hosted the previous night with his speaker was fantastic and the speaker got a standing ovation—which is exactly what the speaker reported. At this point in the relationship, hopefully, the sponsor will also be calling that agent with leads like *We have an event coming up for Women's History Month and we've set a budget of $30,000. I was wondering who you might think would be great for the keynote.*

For new agents who are trying to establish contacts and build relationships, or for the agent who is carving out new territory, he or she might cold-call an event sponsor and say, *I book speakers at corporate events and I wanted to introduce myself to see if you have any upcoming events for which you need speakers. We just began working with someone I'm very excited to share with you who talks about leadership and women in technology.* In this case, event sponsor responses can range from an out-and-out *I'm-so-not-interested-where-did-you-get-my-number* hang-ups, to wary or even warm welcomes. Whatever the response, building these agent-event sponsor relationships is a slow and often discouraging process. But, at the end of the day, what gets you through the event sponsors' doors as a speaking agent is the same thing that works for all salespeople regardless of what they are selling:

▸ You need a great product.

▸ You need (ideally) to be the only one selling it.

▸ The buyer has to trust you.

In other words, there has to be demand for what you are selling. You have to control the supply. And you have to own the seller-buyer relationship.

In my first job as a speaking agent, I was assigned to the college booking division of the boutique agency that had hired me and, on day one, I was given a database of names and phone numbers left behind by an agent no longer with the company. It was a list of college event planners at schools that, for the most part, I'd never heard of. These were the schools that none of the other agents had time to deal with, and I was tasked with seeing how much money I could generate from the list. When I first saw the names, I was disappointed. I assumed that bigger, well-known schools were where the money was, but in the end, that part turned out OK. I came to learn that it's often schools that you've never heard of that have the biggest speaking budgets. To give you an idea, as an agent I'd often book speakers at tiny colleges and state universities that have funded programs with massive budgets. And then I'd get calls from event sponsors at Ivy League schools who were looking to book speakers but who claimed to have little or no money. In lieu of a five-figure honoraria, these lofty institutions often offered, as agents like to joke, "a cheeseburger and a Coke," as if the prestige of speaking at their institution was enough compensation.

In any event, although I was eventually able to build relationships with event sponsors and generate a few million dollars in bookings from that list of neglected schools, my first few calls landed extremely badly. When I called and asked to speak with the first event sponsor on my list, I was told by the person who answered the phone that he'd passed away—which made for a difficult comeback for someone like me who was brand-new and looking to sell something.

But as I stumbled through that first day of painfully awkward phone calls peppered with responses of "he no longer works here" and more than a few hang-ups, I learned the value of both *a great database* and *the importance of relationships in sales.*

It became exceedingly clear to me that no one—at least no one at a corporation or institution of higher learning—is going to trust a stranger on a phone who is trying to sell them *anything*, let alone a high-priced intangible like a speaker. Especially a speaker they may have never heard of before, and especially a speaker who only works for a few hours and comes with a price tag of $10,000 or $20,000 or $30,000 or more—that is, unless the buyer has a strong relationship of trust with the person doing the selling.

That trust takes time to build. And so do sales. In my experience, even with established relationships the average time it takes for an agent to close a deal is between two and three months. During that time the agent is pitching speakers to an event sponsor who is usually talking with other speaking agencies and considering their suggestions for speakers as well. In the case of a keynote, the event sponsor might need to narrow down their list of possible speakers from perhaps the fifty or so they start with to the one speaker who is eventually hired. And, of course, that agent isn't only handling one pitch—he or she is juggling many speakers and many pitches and deals simultaneously.

In fact, agents typically need to make ten sales per month if they want to keep their jobs. To wrap this in dollars and put all of this in perspective, a speaking agent who works on a draw against a 25 percent commission who wants to make $100,000 for the year (generally) has to book $400,000 in agency commissions, which is (generally) $1.6 million in speaking revenue for speakers—that's a lot of bookings and a lot of phone time.

OK, I get it. It's a tough job. But as a speaker, how do I leverage the fact that I know this?

Understanding that your agents are trying very hard to make each and every sale and—this is essential—that your agents *have to get bookings to keep their jobs* is valuable insight. It's also important to understand that agents generate an agency commission *no matter who they sell,* meaning that your agent—any agent—isn't committed to pitching and booking you alone. An average agent probably makes anywhere from three to ten speaker pitches per event—perhaps more—which, mathematically speaking, means that the odds of getting hired for any particular event are *always* against you. While your agents can't control the outcome, the agents do decide *whom to pitch, how hard to pitch them,* and *whom not to pitch at all.* This is important to remember because the reality is an agent will pitch whomever they need to pitch to secure a booking and maintain a good relationship with the event sponsor so the event sponsor will book with that agent again and again.

Knowing this should make light bulbs turn on in your head—
*agents' time is valuable, so don't waste it. Agents have a lot of options
over whom they pitch, so make sure that it's you. And agents have
to protect the buyer relationship more than the speaker relationship.*
Hopefully, understanding all of this will help shape your behavior
as you build your relationship with your agent(s) and agency—
and when you speak. Here's why: There are things that you can
do to improve your chances of being pitched and booked, and to
increase your odds of being pitched and booked *a lot.*

Understand How Your Agents Actually Make Money, and How Not to Interfere with That

I explained that in a common pay model an agent on a $100,000
draw has to generate $400,000 in agency commissions, which
is roughly $1.6 million in speaker bookings. The operative word
here is *bookings.* An offer that is not accepted doesn't count as a
booking—obviously because *it wasn't booked* and the agency and
speaker made no money. Leaving money on the table in the form
of an unaccepted offer is really painful for agents. In most cases,
they worked for months to get that offer and if the speaker turns
it down—which can be for a legitimate reason like a work conflict, but it can also be because the speaker feels that the offer
isn't high enough or he doesn't want to, say, fly to Philly—it can
be disheartening. So, it is really important to be respectful of how
hard those offers are to generate, and to inform your agents if
you won't be accepting offers during certain times—or if there
are any other automatic no's for you. Try to remember how
easily inquiries and pitches can be redirected away from you and
toward other speakers if you prove to be difficult to work with.

Since the sales process is so drawn out and challenging,

getting full-fee offers for someone who only accepts 20 percent of the invitations sent their way is frustrating to say the least. And if that happens, it likely means that the agents will pitch that speaker less frequently and try to steer event sponsors in the direction of other speakers in order to generate offers that the agents are confident will be accepted.

I've run into this challenge many times over the course of my career, and it can become complicated. What I typically try to accomplish when an event sponsor is fixated on booking a particular speaker I have concerns about, is to generate a backup offer at the same time. For example, if I get an offer for Speaker A and I'm relatively certain he won't accept it, I'll ask the event planner to write me a separate offer on contingency for another speaker—Speaker B—who I know is more likely to accept it. I'll bring the offer to Speaker A first, knowing that I've got an offer in my back pocket for Speaker B should Speaker A turn it down.

But while this is a challenge for me, for you as a speaker, there are very easy ways to avoid these problems and to keep your agent happy. If you aren't going to accept many of the invitations you receive, for whatever reason—let's say you are a professor and have classroom obligations—have your agency either increase your speaking fee to a number that justifies taking a day off of work to fly across the country to give a speech, or make it clear to your agency which days you are available. Another way to accomplish this is to cap the number of speaking engagements that you are willing to accept each year and inform the agents well in advance of any blackout dates. This will help the agents who are working on your behalf to present offers that fit your criteria and your needs without eroding your relationship by rejecting offers they worked hard to generate.

The best way to empower your agent is to:

1. Sign an exclusive contract.

2. Sign a full-fee commission deal.

3. Make it clear to the agent that you want to work as much as possible—unless you don't—and then accept all reasonable offers.

4. Treat everyone at the agency with respect.

5. Do a great job when you speak.

Case Study: As an Agent, Who Am I Pushing and Why?
Speaker A or Speaker B?

I once represented a speaker—Speaker A—who only accepted offers at universities because she was uncomfortable with corporate audiences. Unfortunately, it took me about a year and six rejected corporate offers to figure this out. This means that I lost six bookings and, as an agent, believe me, it was frustrating. If she had explained this to me up front, I wouldn't have pushed her for corporate gigs at all and likely would have been able to push event sponsors in a more viable direction by securing those offers for a different speaker—say Speaker B—on my roster.

I represented a lot of Speaker Bs who had no problem speaking to corporate audiences, and I could have pushed any one of them for the corporate talks and focused on pitching Speaker A exclusively for university presentations. This is why clear communication with your agent is important. Not only does it maximize results for you and your agency, but it helps to avoid a situation of hard work and high expectations that results in disappointment and no pay. Remember, the agents at your agency should be well informed. You can be honest with them about your concerns, your goals, and ultimately where you want to land as a speaker. From there, the job of your agents is to deliver for you. But they only know what you tell them. If you, the speaker, can give them clear guidelines and clear goals, they'll not only work more efficiently for you, but also more effectively.

Just as you shouldn't call when looking for representation, make sure that you email your agent—don't call—when you have questions or updates. In general, email is a great way to keep your agent engaged and keep your name top of mind without being too intrusive or cutting into the agent's phone time. Do some quick math. If fifty speakers call into an agency each week to ask if they've been booked, or to report that they posted a new blog piece, and those calls each takes five minutes, that's 250 minutes—or over four hours—of phone time. If the average length of the phone calls were sixty minutes, this would mean that your agent is spending fifty hours a week on the phone with speakers—meaning your agent isn't making *any* outbound sales calls. This is not a good thing—for anyone. Especially you, the speaker. And yet agents can read an email while they're on the phone pitching.

And if the update in your email is substantial, your agent will likely call you on the phone pretty quickly anyway.

Unobtrusive communication not only updates your agent appropriately, but it also keeps you top of mind with the agent and indicates to that agent that you've got them top of mind. A short, professional email that has a useful update—a timely sales point—and requires no response is a reminder that you're vested in your speaking career and that you understand the agents are important and are worthy of updates. And because you have news, it's also a reminder that you are relevant in the marketplace.

Empower Your Agent(s)

It's important to remember that your agency likely represents anywhere from ten to a hundred speakers, and as great as it is to get signed to an agency, you are still competing for your agents' time and attention. The goal is to provide your agents with the necessary tools to book you, while simultaneously being mindful of your agents' time.

Empowering your agents is simple. Provide them only with information relevant to bookings. If you constantly have updates, decide which pieces of information can be shared over email and which updates actually require a phone call. Your agents love speaking with you, no doubt, but the best thing you can do to empower your agents is respect their time and get out of your own way—you want your contact at your agency to have a clear understanding as to who you are as both a speaker and as a person.

One of my favorite go-to pitches when talking with event bookers is to share that I've recently been in contact with my speakers and received an update. If I can say *Michelle, I've been thinking about your fall semester speaker and I just got an email with some really interesting updates from Speaker A. Would it be OK to send over some of their content?* Not only does this demonstrate mastery by the agent, but also it demonstrates to the event sponsor that your agent isn't just blindly suggesting speakers— hoping for a sale at any cost. The agent is reaching out with fresh information and is entirely focused on finding the right speaker at the right price for the event.

On the flip side, too much information can be overwhelming for both the agent and the event sponsor. Be wise when it comes to your agent's time and consider that when events are booked, you end up on the phone with your agent anyway—which is also a great time to share updates. There is nothing an agent loves more than being able to call a speaker with a great offer. And there is no better call to receive than one from an agent sharing that they have an offer for you. I've been on both sides of this coin, both as an agent and a speaker, and the excitement is both contagious and scalable. By scalable, I mean that as momentum builds, your agent can fall into a rhythm because she is more and more inclined to pitch you due to prior success. The more often I pitch Susan for a speaking engagement, and the more often I book her, the easier it becomes. As an agent I can replicate my pitch that worked, I become more and more comfortable telling Susan's story, and if Susan is being booked based on that pitch, I'm going to pitch her more often.

Be Judicious: Why Constant Content Updates—Even by Email—Can Work against You

When building your speaking brand, it can be tempting to not only bring general news to your agent, but to also update your speech topics, bio, and marketing materials. And in some cases, these updates are warranted. However, constant content updates can work against you—think about how constant product updates to a consumer good would be confusing to both the sales team and to buyers. It means your brand is continually changing, which means we don't know who you are or what we are buying. Or as agents, what we are selling. You don't want your agent to pitch you and refer an event sponsor to your online speaker profile and one sheet, then hear the following week that you want to make significant changes. This can get confusing for event sponsors and can chase them away. Your agent needs something consistent to work with, which means that your branding has to be consistent over time. When developing your speaking brand, make sure that changes to your topics, bio, and marketing collateral are done at the right time and for the right reasons.

So how much contact is too much? The "don't take up my time" rule.

This is fairly straightforward—call if there is huge news. Otherwise, send an email once a month or so with a list of relevant updates and the respective links. If you have a new topic you'd like your agent to pitch, email him with a sample description *first*. Making an unexpected phone call to your agent during prime selling time is about the worst thing you can do because it interrupts your agent's flow. And no matter what, don't call your agent to ask how bookings are going. It's not like you're going to get a response like *Oh, we forgot to tell you! We have three offers sitting here that we didn't get around to calling you about.*

When agents get offers, they will immediately call or email you because they are excited to have an offer for your services and they don't want to lose their commission by finding out that you have a conflict on the day of the event. As an agent, when I got an offer, I was dialing the speaker's phone number practically before I got off the phone with the event sponsor. Getting an offer is exciting, and it's time-sensitive. The event sponsor wants to hear back as quickly as possible and your agent wants to ensure the gig will work for you.

Work with your agent without getting in the way.

Incoming phone calls from speakers can derail the outbound sales process and ultimately hurt not only you, but also everyone else represented at your agency. So, why should you care about the other speakers represented by your agency? Because when they get booked for an event, it *increases* the chance that you will be booked for the next one also—whether the following month or the following year. The success of an individual speaker directly affects the success of the group. If there are five speakers on an event sponsor's short list to potentially book this year, and they are all represented by your agency—and one of the other speakers gets selected—your odds of being booked by that same organization next year, assuming your agent is still working with that event sponsor and the list didn't change, just went up. It's important to note that many event sponsors only work with one agency, so the mentality should be that the success of one can lead to the success of many.

A Couple of Exceptions to the "Don't Take Up My Time" Rule

Offering to meet with your agent face to face—assuming you are in the same city—can be a great way to get several agents at your agency on board with your message. It enables the agents to put a real face with the name, and it places you top of mind. As an agency owner, I often met with new speakers before I signed them, and we sometimes had speakers come into the office to meet the whole sales team. While this does take up time, it offers a good opportunity to get to know a speaker in depth, and that can be valuable when we pitch to sponsors. We've seen you in person and can assess your personality and presence, and we can then communicate that familiarity and firsthand interaction to event sponsors.

Another option, which only happens on occasion and under unusual circumstances, is that you may have a chance to invite your agent to a speech you are giving nearby. Do it. Of course, the stars have to align in this situation—the odds of a speaking event being held in a public venue in the same city as your agency aren't great—but seeing a compelling speaker who you represent in action can be the best form of motivation for agents.

It's important to note that both the agency meet and greet and attending a talk given by a speaking client are both *planned activities*. They are not unexpected disruptions during the day. And there is another key difference here. Unlike a short phone interruption, *the meet-and-greet and speech attendance are both constructive*. Meeting you for a sit-down in the office or sitting in the audience for a speech gives your agents valuable selling information they can use going forward. Conversely, when a speaker calls to ask if they have been booked or to ask the agent why they haven't been booked, the agent is not getting anything useful at all. The only thing happening in that phone call is the sales clock is ticking down on the workday with no offers, and the agent is getting annoyed.

What new developments does my agent need to know about?

This is relatively simple and straightforward, and depending on how often you are getting booked—and how big a speaker you are—it will affect how often you should update your agent. I've found that the speakers who get booked the most spend the least amount of time on the phone with their agents, whereas the speakers who don't get booked that often—or at all—spend the most time on the phone with their agents. A speaking agent's time, like most economic factors, operates under the 80/20 rule—or the Pareto Principle. It translates to this: 80 percent of agent's time is taken up by the least productive 20 percent of their speakers, leaving us to spend the most time in an unproductive manner dealing with the *Trivial Many* instead of the *Vital*

Few—a concept attributed to Italian economist Vilfredo Pareto around the turn of the twentieth century.

Simply understanding this will encourage you to streamline your communication.

In terms of what your agent needs to know, it's good to think about how impactful your update is. If you are a successful author and are about to receive a book review in the *New York Times*, this is something we would want to know about as soon as possible. If the same author receives a review on a relatively small blog, the agent doesn't need an update—perhaps an email at best. Conversely, if you are a first-time author and don't have many reviews, that small blog might be the best thing you could possibly share with your agent. The goal is to empower your agent—to give him the tools to book you without getting in his way. Again, every minute you spend on the phone with your agent is a minute that he isn't on the phone with event sponsors pitching you.

Remember That Your Agent Is Working on Spec

The most irritating thing for any agent is getting an angry phone call from a speaker who is miffed that he or she isn't being booked—or booked enough. These speakers fail to take a lot into consideration. Understand that while we have a lot of sway, we can't actually control who books you—or how many times you are booked. All we can do is provide our best possible pitch to as many event planners as possible and, believe me, we *want* to succeed and make every speaker happy—but there's a lot of competition out there.

With that said, I've received phone calls from speakers screaming at me that they aren't getting bookings. I've also received rude responses from speakers who simply don't understand how things work. For example, I call with a $40,000 offer for a well-known scientist, he yells at me that his fee is $45,000. Guess what? The client's budget was $40,000, and I can't control that. I'm not suggesting that there aren't times when speakers should stick to their guns when it comes to honoraria and compensation, but if speakers understood how difficult it is to generate offers, they would definitely treat the agents at their agencies differently.

On the flip side, I've called speakers with offers that are *higher* than their asking price. This is an incredible feeling both for the agent and the speaker. Remember that our goal as agents is to generate as much money as possible for our speaking clients, so if we see an opportunity to book you for more money, we'll act on it. This isn't to say that we're ruthlessly price gouging or aren't protecting the interests of our loyal event sponsors, but rather it demonstrates that, when appropriate, we're willing to let the market set the price.

If I'm working with a corporation that has a $10,000 budget and they are interested in a speaker who asks for $7,500, believe me, I'm going to shoot for the full $10,000. Speaker pricing is arbitrary to a large degree—we make up a number that we think is palatable the day we sign you. After you're signed, if you're generally being booked for $7,500 and are getting good reviews and offers, there's no reason to maintain the fee at that price point if there's an opportunity to increase it. And this can have a domino effect. Once I've booked the $7,500 speaker for $10,000—pending a good review from the sponsor—I can start pitching that speaker at the higher fee knowing that the speaker will still accept less. It also gives me the opportunity to pitch event sponsors based on the idea that the speaker is growing in popularity and therefore might not be available within their budget in a year's time. This is a way to increase the value of your brand and increase your speaking fees and bookings across the board.

I once represented a former VP of a major airline who was being booked based on her writing as opposed to her professional experience as an executive at a major airline. Despite offering topics from both her book and her professional experience, all of her bookings fell into the author category and she generally received about $5,000 for her talks. One day, I was speaking with an event sponsor at a major food company who needed a speaker to address market disruption and innovation. I immediately suggested the airline executive and shared her corporate topic blurb, explaining that her corporate fee was different from her book talks because she had to customize the content in order to fit the sponsor's needs. Forty-eight hours later, I had an offer in my inbox for $35,000—seven times her standard rate. After emailing the offer to the speaker, she wrote back to me a few minutes later saying, "I just fell out of my chair—is this real?" And here's the thing—to the event sponsor at the food company, she was worth every penny. Value, especially when it comes to speakers, is in the eye of the beholder. The sponsor was thrilled with the presentation and told me afterward that they couldn't have imagined receiving such great content.

How far below fee should I accept?

If your speaking fee is $10,000, there's nothing wrong with accepting one invitation at $5,000 and another at $15,000. The money will average out. Plus, you have the advantage that you just gave two speeches instead of one. And the benefit of giving two speeches is a plus because speeches often have value to the speaker beyond the honorarium. It may turn out that the $5,000 speech yielded $30,000 in donations toward your cause or led to an interesting connection, while the $15,000 speech yielded no additional benefits other than the flat speaking fee. Further, accepting these two events will likely increase your mailing list, increase your reach, and generally give you access to more people. The additional below-fee speech might be before a critical audience, or on a panel with significant colleagues or great contacts and may, potentially, provide more blurbs for your one sheet. Plus, since the amount paid to a speaker usually isn't published, very few people will ever know how much you were paid. This is why I like to look at speeches from an average per-night perspective. If it all comes out in the wash, why would you *not* accept a speaking invitation at a reduced rate? The exposure can be invaluable.

In accepting a lower fee offer, you are keeping your agent happy too. It gets them a booking and commission. This is important. If your agent knows that you are flexible with your pricing, not only are you more inclined to get offers, but you're also more likely to be pitched since your agent knows that you're willing to accept most reasonable offers. Now some people do have restrictions—say they are a teacher and can only miss twelve days a year—but for many other speakers who do not have those restrictions I often say, *What else are you doing that day? I know your fee is $10,000, but $8,000 is nothing to sneeze at.*

Which begs the question, How do you set your speaking fee in the first place?

Listen to your agent. Unless you have specific knowledge of your value or a proven history of paid speaking at a particular rate, and as long as your agent isn't posting your fee on their website—something I advise against—go with what they recommend and discuss with them the process of increasing that fee as you get more experience and great feedback under your belt.

A good agent knows event sponsors' budgets, and understands your motivation and what you need for your career to advance. Some speakers just need experience, and what they get paid for those first few gigs is irrelevant. Other speakers have so much value at their day job that anything below a certain fee isn't worth it to them. You can see how all the motivational components—why you are speaking in the first place and what your goals are—contribute to setting your rate.

Contract Negotiation and Deal Closing

Once a speaker is selected, the way an actual deal is executed generally works like this: The event sponsor makes a firm and binding offer for the speaker to his or her agent—usually in writing. This is after fee and travel arrangements, and anything like book buys or classroom visits, have already been negotiated. The agent then calls the speaker to present the offer. Assuming the speaker accepts, the agency then signs a contract with the event sponsor, and the speaker signs a deal memo with the agency. That deal memo and contract both cover the specifics—date and speech length, location where it will be delivered, and technical details. It lists any other deliverables—perhaps a dinner with the board, a fifteen-minute Q&A, a classroom visit, or book buys—anything that was agreed on during the negotiation. The contract will cover the specifics of travel, who's paying, whether it's a flat rate buyout and, if not, who will make the arrangements. It will also cover things like event insurance, liability, and have force majeure and mutual hold harmless clauses. There might also be a rider with specifics. Perhaps the sponsor will provide a smart podium and wireless mic, a pitcher of water and a glass, a deli platter or an organic salad; and a small fee is generally added for incidentals—$100 or $200 for taxis to and from the airport. The deal is technically firm and binding at the offer stage, but the deal isn't really complete until the speech is actually given. Hopefully, this denotes the serious nature of a speaker booking, and the sum total of what your agency is doing to earn that 25 percent commission.

Understand the Difference between a Good Agent and a Great Agent

A good agent pitches you when appropriate. A *great* agent pitches you (practically) all of the time. "While John—the speaker you called about—is fantastic, have you ever heard of Fred?" This isn't to suggest that agents bait and switch—or are trying to undercut or sabotage John—it's just that agents know things. Perhaps John rarely takes offers that are so far out of town, or he's difficult to work with, has gotten a few lukewarm reviews, is hesitant to craft his speech to be more relevant to a specific audience, is on a book deadline, or has a much higher fee than this sponsor's budget will accommodate. There's also this: Great agents build the careers of upcoming speakers assuming they will be grateful and stick with the agency. In other words, if John is already established and getting warm leads—he's getting a certain fee and is really easy to book for the number of incoming requests he gets—if an agent pushes Fred and increases his fee the agent now effectively has two Johns. Further, a great agent will find a way to spin you into various pitches regardless of what the event sponsor is looking for, assuming you are easy to work with— accommodating, respectful of the agent, sponsor, and audience, and get great reviews. The thing to remember is that your agent is focused on getting bookings and making money; your job is to make sure the agent sees you as a streamlined way to do that. Why? Because the difficult-to-work-with speaker, the one who complains, turns down offers, grumbles about travel, fees, event sponsors—and stale bagels—will get bypassed whenever possible, for a speaker an agent perceives as a better sell.

Things You Should Never Do When Dealing with Your Agent

One of the most frustrating things an agent can hear is complaints about a commission when they are calling you with a booking. You signed a contract. You set a fee. You're getting paid. Don't begrudge your agency getting its share.

Another no-no is complaining about the event sponsor, either before or after the event. For example, if your agent calls you with a full-fee offer from a community college, don't complain that you are better than that. And don't call your agent complaining after an event either. You should certainly share negative aspects of the event for future reference—for example, if the sponsor didn't have the right equipment for your PowerPoint presentation despite it being stipulated in your contract, your agent needs to know that. This can be helpful to the agent when booking future events with this sponsor for other speakers, but you can't hold it against your agent. It's important to remember that your agent is hundreds—if not thousands—of miles away from the event and has no control over day-of missteps.

Another common complaint speakers will call agents about is about the size of the audience. I've booked a number of speakers with substantial fees to speak in two-thousand-person theaters, only to find that a few hundred people turned out for the speech. Getting a call from a speaker complaining about the size of the audience for a speech booked many months in advance is one of the most annoying things an agent can experience, particularly because we have no control over attendance. I once had a speaker booked in a theater at a university in Ohio where his book was a common read—meaning that a large portion of the freshman class was required to read it. We were expecting a packed house. But the school made attending the speaking engagement optional. And unfortunately for the speaker, there was a football pep rally the night of his speech. This meant that only a few hundred students attended the event despite the fact that thousands of students had read the book and had been expected to turn out.

The speaker was furious. He felt misled, and when he called me, he said he wanted an explanation. I calmly explained to him that I have no control over turnout and that he should consider the upside—he sold several thousand books and got paid a five-figure speaking fee regardless of the attendance. In fact, his fee and his book sales were guaranteed even if the room was empty.

And that's the point. If you're being paid your speaking fee, objectively it shouldn't matter to you—that much—if there are six people in the audience or six thousand. Obviously, everyone would prefer a packed house, and the more faces you get in front of the better. But your fee is guaranteed regardless of turnout and you're making the same amount of money, full house or empty.

There are a lot of factors that can affect turnout for an event that don't reflect on the speaker and shouldn't bruise his or her ego. I once booked a gig at Rutgers University in New Jersey for four speakers to take part in a panel discussion—and I was one of the four speakers. On the night of the event, it snowed heavily and only about twenty students turned out. Four speakers, a cumulative fee of five figures, and a disappointed sponsor. But, for our part, we made the best of it. Rather than a panel discussion we split the audience up into groups of five and each of us did small, personal sessions with the attending students. The sponsor was suddenly thrilled to have smaller, dedicated group sessions—as were the students—and as speakers, we had a great time despite the low turnout.

Don't Neglect to Handle the Post-Event Follow Up like a Pro

When working with speakers, post-event feedback from event sponsors is often a difficult course to navigate. Great feedback, of course, is what we're all hoping to receive. That said, when an agent gets great feedback and passes it along to you, the speaker, don't let it inflate your ego. If the event sponsor loved you, that's great—everyone is thrilled—but it's also expected. Anyone getting paid five or six figures for an hour or two of work is *expected* to kill it. That's why the fees are so high.

Obviously, the larger problem is when event sponsors aren't happy. Nobody wants to hear disappointing news. But speakers need to be able to take any criticism and determine if it is actually something they could have controlled. If a Pulitzer Prize–winning author is booked to give a talk at a college and no one shows up, believe me the event sponsor and the board will be embarrassed and upset, but that's not something the speaker can control and might actually be a failure of the sponsor. For example, to ensure that an event is well attended, some schools make attendance mandatory or encourage it by inviting students to bring stamped event tickets to class for extra credit. But if the criticism offered by the event sponsor is something the speaker could have controlled, he or she better listen—because your agent is listening. If you can work to improve something, make changes accordingly, because the speakers who do that—those who take ownership of the problem and fix it—are ultimately the speakers who achieve the most success. With regard to post-event feedback, my advice to speakers is:

▶ It's expected to be glowing, so set your standards high and perform as expected or better.

▶ Not all problems are the fault of the speaker. So, own what's yours, and dismiss the rest.

▶ When an event doesn't go well, listen to any criticism and, moving forward, try to fix what didn't work.

▶ And as Quincy Jones told the group of world-class musicians when they arrived to record "We Are the World": "Leave your egos at the door."

And, finally, be patient.

Case Study: Best of the Best. Worst of the Worst.

One Speaker Who "Got It Right" with Their Agency and One Speaker Who "Got It Wrong."

In 2015, I signed a new speaker—Speaker A—who was a certified yoga instructor hoping to speak to corporate audiences about health and wellness. She hadn't done any paid speaking, but she had a successful book and had appeared on a few television shows both promoting—and validating—her expertise and brand. We worked with her on a one sheet, put her up on our website, and pitched her internally to our agents—making sure we were well-versed in her expertise and interests and understood how to present her to sponsors. Then we got to work presenting her to event sponsors any time it seemed appropriate—*Here's an interesting new speaker whose book got rave reviews. She speaks about work-life balance and health*—and we were encouraged, because dozens of corporate event sponsors had expressed interest in her.

The same week that I signed Speaker A, I also signed another speaker to the agency—Speaker B. He spoke about learning disabilities—specifically about attention deficit hyperactivity disorder (ADHD)—to audiences interested in education. Speaker B was already a successful paid speaker when we signed him and, unlike Speaker A, arrived at our door fully branded and neatly packaged with a one sheet that had intriguing speech topics, a spot-on bio, and compelling marketing collateral—including rave reviews from his previous event sponsors. Speaker B also had his own website, had written several books, and had even appeared on *The Oprah Winfrey Show* a few years back.

Speaker B's assistant was our main point of contact, and she was incredible to work with—any time a potential event sponsor needed additional information about one of his books or his presentation, she got back to us immediately with the material and information we had requested.

In addition to his assistant, Speaker B was also great. He was willing to get on the phone with event sponsors even *before* being offered an event. This is unusual, as most agencies won't allow their speakers to have a conference call with an event sponsor until the event is booked and the contract signed and, frankly, most speakers don't want to do this because they view it as a waste of time. But in Speaker B's case, he saw these conference calls as a way to further impress event sponsors, make them feel confident and seal deals, and he had no problem taking fifteen to twenty minutes out of his schedule to speak with them.

We loved it because he was terrific on the phone and said just enough, and just the right things, to close each deal. This proved to be a tremendous asset—both for our agency and for Speaker B. By participating in these calls, he showed the event sponsors his interest and enthusiasm for their particular event, and also showed respect for the magnitude of their decisions—no one wants to be responsible for the decision to bring a $10,000, or $20,000, or $30,000 speaker to an event and have it be bad. And it also showed valuable authenticity and transparency on the part of the speaker. That made the event sponsors appreciate his professionalism, allowed them to get a feel for what he would sound like, and gave them the confidence to pull the trigger on offers. Of equal importance, Speaker B knew enough to not step on our toes—during those calls he didn't ask the buyer about compensation or logistics, nor did he attempt to hard sell or push for the booking as he understood that this was the job of his agent.

Because he was so well known, we started booking Speaker B almost immediately, but despite our efforts, a few months in, Speaker A—the new health and wellness speaker—hadn't gotten any gigs. For me, this was par for the course, and I was optimistic, but three months after we signed her, Speaker A called me yelling and screaming because she hadn't been booked yet. She ranted on and on about how she had signed with the wrong agency and that we weren't meeting her expectations. I calmly told her to think back to our first meeting when I'd told her that it might take up to twelve months just to secure her first booking—that we'd hoped that wouldn't be the case, but it could be. I reminded her that I'd explained that the speaking industry moves slowly, results aren't guaranteed, and emphasized that we were getting interest from event sponsors when we pitched her, and that while nothing had stuck yet, we were only three months in and

I thought we were getting close. I then nicely reminded her that the entire agency had been—and still was—working hard on her behalf, explaining that we were all regularly pitching her to event sponsors on the phone, and that when we pitched *her*, we weren't pitching any one of a number of other speakers who were more proven commodities. Then I reminded Speaker A that we were doing all of this on spec—that it had cost her nothing to sign with us, but I was paying the agents who were pitching her, and that although we were going cash out of pocket, we hadn't yelled at her—or recouped a dime for those efforts either.

As fate would have it, while I was still on the phone with Speaker A as she threatened to fire me, an email appeared in my inbox with an offer of $12,500 for her to give a keynote and run a yoga session with the employees at a Fortune 500 company. It was an incredible opportunity, above her fee, and at an impressive venue.

Talk about fortuitous—and ironic—timing.

While she continued to go on about how we had underserved her, I was reading the email and interrupted her to say, "You're not going to believe this, but I just got an offer for you in my inbox."

It was an uncomfortable moment for her, peppered, I suspect, with a dose of excitement and awkward embarrassment. It was a mixed moment for me also. As much as I had been fighting for her up until this phone call, now I felt disenfranchised.

Speaker A, of course, accepted the offer, but she burned a bridge with me because agents want—and deserve—to be appreciated. Speakers need to understand that their agents are working hard and working on spec. They need to understand that a *good* agent won't overpromise or underrepresent a new speaker—but instead will explain the lumbering, uncertain, nothing-is-guaranteed-but-we'll-try-our-best-at-no-cost-to-you process to them.

In this case, Speaker A got it wrong. And Speaker B got it right. Even though Speaker A was less qualified than Speaker B, she felt entitled. Speaker B felt gratitude. Speaker A said, *You're not doing enough.* Speaker B said, *How can I help?* Speaker B understood that participating in the process without getting in our way was a valuable tool to help advance his speaking career, while Speaker A effectively landed on a sword wielded by her own hand.

As much as we all want instant results, it's imperative to think about any type of brand-building as a marathon, not a sprint. And the booking process for a paid speaker is more like an ultramarathon. The important thing is to do a frank and honest assessment of your value in the marketplace, know how that can change—in either direction—depending on what you do and don't do, and understand that as long as you're confident that your agency is working hard for you, you can step back and let them do their job.

TAKEAWAYS

Learn how to work with your agent without getting in their way

Never forget that your agent is working on spec—or that speaking is big business

Understand that your agent wants to book you and *is* pitching you—don't become 80 percent of the work but only 20 percent of the profit

Know that your agents are trying *very hard* to make a sale and that they get a booking and earn a commission *no matter who they sell.* Which means your agents aren't committed to pitching

and booking you alone. And that means you have to behave in a
manner that defines you as easy to work with

Respect the fact that your agent rarely wants to speak with you
on the phone because he or she needs that time for sales calls

Don't constantly update your agent on news or new topics or marketing materials. Instead, empower your agent with significant,
relevant updates—only do it judiciously, by email, and with respect for their time

Most of all, accept all reasonable offers

When giving a speech, set your standards high and perform as
expected—or better

Post-event, listen to any criticism, but be objective. Dismiss any
issues that are not "on you" and learn from and own the rest.
Moving forward, strive to fix what didn't work. In other words,
now that you've defined and packaged your brand, make sure
that you as a product perform well in the marketplace

11.

Find Your Audience

WHAT SHELF DO YOU SIT ON?

After you sign with an agency, you should work with your agents to identify the ideal target audience(s) for your paid speeches because your agents can't, shouldn't—and won't—pitch you to everyone, or for everything. Of course, your agents will have strong ideas about what types of organizations and programs they think are best to target based on their existing relationships with buyers and how they match up with your background, topics, and, most importantly, your overall branding. If they didn't, they probably wouldn't have signed you in the first place. In fact, during the signing process, the agents likely had very specific places, events, and sponsors already in mind for you. But this doesn't mean you should assume that your agents will do all of the heavy lifting. The more informed you are, the more you'll be able to contribute in a constructive manner to the decisions regarding where you should be pitched, and why.

To start, the three most important things to understand are these:

▶ The types of organizations your agents will target—corporations, nonprofits, or colleges—will largely be determined by your speech topics and how they are framed.

▶ There are a wide range of specific programs and events within each of these three markets that may—or may not—be well suited for you and your topics.

▶ To whom you are pitched, and what you are pitched for, will not necessarily be the groups or places you might initially think.

As a newly signed speaker, identifying your key target audience(s) is one of the most important decisions that will be made. If we relate it back to the analogy of you as a consumer packaged good, deciding where and to whom you should be pitched is akin to choosing the type of stores you should be sold in and on which shelf you should sit. And here's why this matters so much: Proper product placement is a key component of successful branding and has a big impact on sales.

To secure the best possible outcome, it's vital to consider:

▶ How you can utilize your agents' unique knowledge of what dozens of organizations are paying for in any given buying cycle to find your best target audiences.

▶ How, once you've been pitched or have given a few speeches, you and your agents can use the reactions of event sponsors to those pitches and/or audience responses to your early speeches to confirm—or refine—the validity of the audience(s) you've targeted, as well as help to identify additional viable groups to pitch.

▸ In case you're not getting booked at all—or enough—consider what strategies you can use to completely rethink who to target and why.

How to Define Your Best Audience, and Why the Most Obvious Audience Is Not Always Going to Be Your Bread and Butter

If you're an academic, you might think that your primary targets are universities. If your experience is on the corporate side, you might similarly assume that your target audiences—in general— will be found at events and conferences held by other corporations. And speakers who hail from the world of nonprofits might logically conclude that their speaking agencies will be targeting other nonprofits. For many speakers this will be the case. I once represented a speaker named Alan, a corporate HR specialist who spoke about employee morale to other corporations over and over again, and he made a great income doing so. He never spoke anywhere other than corporations. But for many speakers it's also important to consider the opportunities to *stand out* and *diminish and skirt the competition* by crossing over.

I've booked nonprofit founders to speak at Fortune 100 corporations, and I've booked corporate leaders at colleges, universities, and high schools. I've booked a food expert and authors at tech companies; actors at nonprofits; recent college grads at Fortune 500 companies; and—as previously referenced—a school teacher turned gardener at corporations and business conferences; a beekeeper at a girls school; an Oscar-winning filmmaker at a private high school; and a poet at an aerospace company— just to give a few examples.

What I generally find—with some exceptions—is that when

it comes to audience, both speakers and agencies have a propensity to think *narrowly* when it's best to think in the broadest sense possible. For example, if you are speaking about business management strategies and you want as many gigs as possible, since your lecture topics are geared toward people who want to learn how to manage, your first step might be to target those groups at corporations with events focused on management. Just don't stop there. *That's only one store and one shelf.* Remember that those companies have a lot of management experts on staff already, and you may have better success trying to be sold to MBA and business programs at universities and to nonprofits that are interested in resource management.

Why?

For one, this strategy puts you on a shelf with *less competition*. That means you'll stand out as more unique. Think back to the school teacher who gardened—when his one sheet landed on each event sponsor's desk, it stood out in a pile of similar looking one sheets from highly qualified people who all sounded the same and basically talked about the same thing. Further, a corporation full of managers may very well be more interested in booking that inner-city schoolteacher turned gardener to speak about the power of the individual to enact change, or a wellness coach who speaks about stress management, or a spelunker who speaks about what caving taught her about the decision-making process than another corporate manager who sounds just like everyone already on their payroll.

If you think you can be pitched to more than one of the speaking categories—*college, corporate, and nonprofit*—it's important that you suggest that to your agency. And hopefully that's something you were thinking about as you framed and wrote your speech topics.

Case Study: Your Message and Your Best Audience Can Often Feel like a Counterintuitive Fit—until They Don't

I once represented a speaker named Jack who was the founder of a nonprofit that advised college students about how to incorporate smart financial planning into their lives at a young age. Although Jack wanted to speak to the college market, we found that we were getting more responses from corporations and nonprofit organizations than we were from universities. It turned out that most colleges didn't see him as a fit, since they were focused on more academic and celebrity-type speakers in order to generate large crowds, and a speech about smart financial planning didn't fit those needs. The general feedback we were getting from event sponsors was that students wouldn't turn out for a financial planning talk.

The corporations and nonprofits we pitched Jack to saw the value in his presentation for a variety of reasons. Nonprofit audiences wanted to learn how to better financially plan, and also liked the fact that they shared something in common—Jack had founded a nonprofit. Corporations wanted to book Jack because they viewed a financial planning talk as a value add for their employees—how to incorporate fiscal responsibility into their daily lives as well as the lives of their college-age children. But there was something else. Since corporate audiences can make presentations mandatory, Jack was guaranteed to have the sizable crowds that the universities couldn't offer. And corporations were better for generating donations and sponsorships for Jack's nonprofit than the college market was anyway. As a result, Jack tweaked his topics a bit with the help of our agents and started getting booked about fifteen times per year at nonprofits and corporations. He found his *one great speech* by understanding that his audience was different than what he—and his agency—initially

imagined. And this was true even though he had a product specifically aimed at college students.

It isn't only standing out and reducing the competition—or
good fit—that can drive successful shelf placement for speakers.
It can also be personal. I once had the CEO of a major corporation speak at private high schools about the power of giving.
This particular CEO could have spoken to other CEOs about
team-building and leadership, but he *wanted* to be booked at high
schools. He had an affinity for talking with students since he
founded his first company—a cookie delivery service—when he
was still in high school, and he felt a strong obligation to share
his story and give back to teens. Now, a corporate CEO giving
a speech at a high school doesn't sound like a good fit unless
the story, message, and delivery were designed for a young
audience—and in this case we made sure that they were. But here
is where this story gains traction. Obviously, a high school has a
lot of speaker options that likely sound a whole lot more interesting to students than a corporate CEO. And while we understand
why the CEO wanted to speak to high schoolers, why were these
private high schools eager to have a leader of a Fortune 500 company speak to their students? The answer to this raises a critical
set of questions:

▶   Why are event sponsors hiring speakers in the first place?

▶   Why are they paying so much?

▶   And how does understanding this help you choose your best
    target audiences?

We know that the speaker is using the event to build his or

her brand with the purpose of driving toward an end goal—generating income, spreading a message, increasing donations to a nonprofit or a cause, selling books, and so on. But it's important to remember that event sponsors are building their brands too.

And hiring a speaker is often a PR move. It's advertising and promotion.

In the case of the CEO, the private high schools wanted to build their image and drive alumni donations—and the CEO of a major corporation did that better than, say, a pop star or a mixed martial arts celebrity.

So, hiring you to speak is an *investment*. No different than running a TV commercial or taking out an ad in a magazine. And it's a PR move that sponsors will promote and advertise in order to spread their brand message, improve value for their consumers, and potentially generate more revenue.

If your alumni or children's school magazine arrives in the mail and an impressive speaker—say a corporate CEO—is on the cover standing at a podium, and there's an article inside about how this person spoke at a school event and a large number of people turned out, it advertises a very specific value proposition—*look what we're offering students!* And that does two things. *It builds the school's brand image in a very specific direction and it often drives alumni giving.* So, if a university spends $35,000 on a speaker and sees a significant increase in alumni donations well above that, it means that they are seeing a valuable return on investment. Clearly, in most cases, the exact dollar correlation may not be directly measurable—after all, a school does a number of PR initiatives and there are numerous outlying factors that drive donations. But there is a very significant mathematical truth here: when an event sponsor hires a speaker, they aren't *spending money*, they are *investing money*.

That investment may manifest as a value add-on for students or employees who attend a stress management lecture at lunch and leave feeling empowered. Or it may be a value add-on for students who get to hear a famous author speak. Those speaking dollars may be an investment to drive donations through alumni giving. They may be a revenue generator through ticket sales. Or it may simply be a means to communicate something about an institution—*we are diverse, or liberal, or conservative, interested in the environment, forward thinking, care about our employees/students,* and so on. But in all cases, speaking events are PR opportunities related to brand-building in one way or another, and this is true for both the organization that hosts these events as well as for the speakers who are hired. So, while speaking events may *seem* expensive or frivolous, they are, in fact, not expensive at all. In fact, speaking engagements are often very cost-effective ways for event sponsors to improve image, drive donations, and attract or retain students and employees.

This is true for schools, corporations, and nonprofits. They all use speakers not only to espouse messages but also as branding collateral. If someone is interviewing for a job at a company and learns that twice a year the company hosts events with big-name speakers, suddenly that company may seem more appealing to work for than one that doesn't have a robust speaker program. Schools, nonprofits, and corporations showcase their speakers in annual reports and press releases and on their websites. Savvy sponsors are well aware of the power of speakers as brand-builders, and speaker bookings are often a significant part of a larger branding strategy and not just a frivolous expense. Which helps to *clarify your value as a speaker* and what *drives the dollars* spent on these programs.

A demonstrative example of this is the branding mistake

made by The State University of New Jersey (Rutgers) when they booked a speaker for an event. Rutgers went off brand—at least according to the press, public opinion, and the state of New Jersey—when in 2011 they hired Nicole Polizzi, a.k.a. Snooki of MTV reality show *The Jersey Shore* fame, for $32,000 to deliver her "study hard but party harder" message to one thousand students on campus, and it backfired badly. The students may have loved it, but the taxpayers, politicians, and parents—not so much. There was quite an uproar in the press and layers of complications. For example, some parents and alumni didn't like what it said about the school. It also miffed some people that Toni Morrison, the Nobel laureate, was paid $30,000–$2,000 less than Snooki to speak at commencement that same year held at Rutger's 52,000-seat football stadium. Others objected because they thought tax dollars were used to pay Snooki. The outcry was so great that the state of New Jersey passed and signed a bill into law that prevented state funds from being used to pay speakers. This was mostly a symbolic move because no state funds were actually used to cover Snooki's speaking fee. (Instead, she was paid out of student fees collected alongside tuition.)

Now, Snooki was typically booked to make appearances at bars and clubs—not to give speeches at colleges. But no matter who a speaker is or where a speaker is booked, there are always powerful issues of brand image and brand-building—or erosion—as well as significant underlying economics at play.

Catherine Rampell's April 8, 2011, article in the *New York Times* called "Snookinomics: Profits From a Tan" outlines some rough math for a Snooki club event demonstrating just how mind-boggling the profits for sponsors can be. Rampell estimates that Snooki's $25,000 appearance fee for a single club event generated an additional $259,406 in revenue for the club. The same economic premise holds for corporations and nonprofits and colleges—*paid speakers are investments, not expenses.*

How can a speaker leverage this information to find the best audience(s) possible? And how can speakers (subtly) reposition themselves to appeal to different audiences?

Whether speaker or sponsor, the "Snookinomics" of the Rutgers story exemplifies the fact that a brand should never stray too far from its core message. This is true for sponsors like Rutgers, and it's true for speakers hoping to be sold to different target markets. Having said this, there's a subtle art to widening your brand appeal by slightly altering the description of your speaking topics and tweaking your bio in a manner that addresses more directly the needs of specific markets you are hoping to be pitched to while still staying on brand. But once you set yourself up with the right topics and take a broad, open-minded approach to whom you should be pitched, you can change your booking potential and economic prospects.

Case Study: How One Speaker Successfully Put Himself on a New Shelf

I once worked with a speaker who wrote a bestselling book about the environment, and the book was a popular common read at a number of universities and high schools. On paper, there was no specific corporate message to glean from the book. We spent a few years booking him at educational institutions knowing that his message about the environment appealed to college students and he was affordable in that market—we pitched and sold him in the $10,000 range. But after a couple of years, he wanted to increase his speaking fees. I explained to him that an increased fee for universities would likely work against him as it would make him less affordable and less likely to get as many gigs. But I also advised him that if we could find a corporate angle for his speeches based on his book, we could open him up to the corporate market where his fees could increase.

So, we sat down and started hammering out ideas. And where we landed was with a topic about corporate social responsibility as it relates to environmental issues—which was a perfect reframing of his book and its message. We only changed about a dozen words in his topic description, eliminated references to common reads and students, put it up on our website, and added it to his one sheet as a corporate topic. We then got to work pitching him to business entities on the corporate social responsibility topic, setting his fee at $20,000, which was a comfortable price point for the types of companies we were working with. The end result was that he was booked frequently. He still spoke at universities for $10,000, but the corporate fee not only doubled his rate, it also doubled his chances of getting booked since we were now pitching him to two markets instead of one.

It's better to be sold in a wider range of outlets if possible. So take a second look at your topics, and ask yourself, *Are there any missed opportunities?* Because if you can increase your reach, it will almost always generate more bookings and possibly increase your fees without creating very much additional work.

Why You Should Think of the Event Sponsors and Your Audience as Barometers to Determine If You're Sitting on the Right Shelf

Event sponsors' reactions to agent pitches will be the first consumer testing you and your speech topics will get. Hopefully your agent will relay that feedback to you. Perhaps saying something like, *I pitched you for a conference at a corporate event for the spring and the event sponsor was really interested.* Or, *I'm getting more responses from colleges than nonprofits.*

And just as with any other product, you and your speeches will eventually be subject to broader market testing—a real live audience. It should go without saying that starting with your very first speech, the audience is your best barometer as to whether you're on the right shelf and to what works and what doesn't. So keep an observant and critical eye before, during, and after each speech. Listen to the audience. Look at them. Do they seem engaged? What specific parts of your speech seemed to move them the most? Were there lulls? When did they laugh? How was the applause? Did they swarm you with questions after your speech?

There are two things about audiences that are worth noting. Each and every one is different, and each person in attendance will internalize your message in his or her own way—despite the fact that they listened to the same speech. Someone speaking about coaching an NFL football team can affect everyone in the audience differently. One person may take away a message about inner strength and another might take away a message about teamwork. But the important thing is that the speaker resonates in one way or another with everyone in the audience—or else you're likely on the wrong shelf.

Never forget that as much as this is business and is about money and PR and brand-building, speeches also change and even save lives. For example, I booked a nonprofit leader to speak at a number of corporations—including Gatorade—and each time he absolutely nailed it. He delivered a message about the importance of cancer screening for men. He did so with a personal story, and by tapping into emotions that ran far deeper than the more obvious spoken message. He delivered a message that was carried by an emotion that was universally relatable, and by getting that message out in front of target audiences beyond the obvious of cancer groups, he undoubtedly saved lives. He was on the right shelf.

Case Study: Great Speaker, Wrong Audience—and How to Fix It

Why Defining the Best Target Audience Is More Art than Science

I once represented the founder of ESPN—the largest sports television network in the world. Bill was a great guy and easy to work with. Initially, we thought that his bookings would be almost exclusively for corporate audiences. After all, he built a great company and was a visionary—we were convinced that employees at corporations would love to learn from him. As it turned out, we were wrong. We discovered that companies weren't all that interested, and when we went back to try to figure out why, we decided that it was because the way his topics were framed there wasn't a distinct lesson corporate audiences could extrapolate and utilize from his particular experiences. He'd failed to deliver the first mandate of the USP; he didn't deliver a clear benefit to the audience.

And yet, the founding of ESPN in the 1970s—and its growth—is an incredible story. The problem, we learned, was that companies viewed him as more of a celebrity than anything else. He couldn't speak to innovation, largely because his message was dated. And he couldn't speak to brand management because most of the companies we were working with wanted a newer story—something they saw as more topical and more relevant. He could speak about sports, but that's not traditionally a topic that corporations are interested in. So, based on the market feedback we were receiving, we decided to try a different approach.

Since we couldn't avoid the celebrity angle and it was chasing away corporations, we changed his target audience to colleges and universities. Then we reframed Bill's topics and bio to reflect a new message—*following your dreams and finding success even when others don't believe in you.* We immediately began pitching him to colleges and universities with our new materials and started getting bookings in the $25,000 range right away.

For students, Bill's new message was spot on. Event sponsors wanted their students to learn about the value of pursuing your passion and fighting for what you believe in—and they also loved the celebrity aspect that had not worked with corporate clients. After all, college students watch a lot of ESPN. So, colleges also liked the fact that they could say that the founder of ESPN was appearing on campus. Bill drew hundreds, and sometimes thousands, of students to his events and received rave reviews from sponsors. He was thrilled, the event sponsors were ecstatic, and the agents at my agency were pitching him around the clock.

Case Study: The Converse

Michael was signed to my agency in 2012. He had founded a series of successful companies and wanted to speak about serial entrepreneurship, which was a very hot topic at the time. When we signed Michael, I assumed that he would be great for the university market—addressing students in MBA programs about how to become an entrepreneur.

Michael, as it turned out, only wanted to speak at corporations and had no interest in speaking at universities. I explained to him that it was unlikely that corporations would book him, since his topic was irrelevant to their business needs and also there could be fear of losing employees who might be inspired to quit and start their own companies following his speech. Nonetheless, he was adamant about speaking to the corporate market, so we decided to give it a shot. To my surprise, we secured a booking for him within the first few months at a major cereal company for $15,000.

And then we never booked him again. Three years went by and we parted ways. As far as I know, he went on to appear gratis at conferences and consortiums, but never signed with another agency and never gave another paid speech. Why did this happen? For one, we were pushing him to the wrong audience and, second, his topic was too narrow. There were dozens of other topics he could have spoken about—team-building, innovation, fund-raising, and management, to name a few. But all Michael wanted to speak about was how to be a serial entrepreneur—and only at corporations. And we all found out that there is barely a market for that. I learned several lessons from this failure, but Michael continued to be stubborn and believe that the fault lay with his agency, not with him.

When formulating and pitching your topics, remember that if you aren't finding success it might be because your message is too narrow, it might be being pitched to the wrong audiences, and it might be that your speech topic is not delivering a relatable takeaway—or it may be a bit of all of these things. But if you can be objective and look at yourself through the lens of event sponsors and audiences, chances are you'll find the right audience for you and improve your prospects of being booked.

TAKEAWAYS

Your best target audience will flow directly from your speech
topics

Your best audience may not be what you think it is, and the most
obvious audience is likely not going to be your bread and
butter—in fact, your message and your audience are often a
counterintuitive fit

Reposition yourself to appeal to different audiences if possible—it
can increase the number of bookings and increase income—
but keep your overall branding and brand consistency in mind
when doing so

Utilize market feedback to better position bookings in the future.
In fact, help confirm or redefine your audience by gathering relevant feedback, both from the feedback your agent gets from
event sponsors and the feedback—observed and spoken—you
receive for your speech

Speak frankly with the agents at your agency. They are constantly
receiving feedback in real time as they speak with potential event
sponsors. I've often received feedback along the lines of "He
seems great, but it sounds like this is more of a corporate talk."
Both agents and speakers should listen and learn from the market

12.

How to Set Your Rate

WHAT ARE YOU WORTH?

One of the most pressing questions every speaker wants answered is *What fee should I set?* They wonder, *How much can I charge? Am I a $5,000 speaker? $10,000? $15,000?* And what delineates these price points? *Who gets $25,000? What about $50,000 or $100,000? Who gets more than that—and why?*

For a whole lot of reasons, the answers to these questions aren't always easy.

For starters, speaker fees don't operate under clear and logical—or even consistent—pricing dynamics. Two speakers with very similar profiles may charge—and often get—very different rates. To add to the confusion, different agents may have different opinions as to where a particular speaker should be priced. So, it's fair to ask *What are the rules for setting a fee?*

In defense of what often appears to be almost random and nonsensical pricing, what we are selling—ideas delivered in a single performance before a live audience often for tens of thousands of dollars, if not more—is hard to put a price on. It's hard for agents and it's hard for event sponsors—so of course it's hard for speakers. Consider the college professor who makes $75,000 a year being offered $50,000 to give a keynote address at a corporate conference—*for an hour.* That's hard to wrap your head around. Then consider that the founder of a billion-dollar tech company, a hobbyist rock climber, a constitutional law scholar, or a fourth-grade teacher turned cupcake baker all may be pitched for the same event—and at the same fee. No matter who ends up getting booked for that particular event, the whole thing is hard to process, and those dollar values can be hard to assign and hard to keep in perspective.

Here's what we do know:

The more unique your branding and speech topics are, the greater your potential value. As soon as you aren't another product added to a speaking agency's website next to a long list of other similar looking and sounding speakers, you become worth more. Which of course is why we focused so intently on crafting a USP with great, singularly compelling speech topics and significant takeaways that an audience *can't get from anyone else.* We built your brand for optimum pricing—but now finding that exact price point can be tricky—and the process is loaded with potential pitfalls.

Here's what I can add to this:

Price too high and you won't get booked. Too low, and now you're labeled as having a certain value—and it's not premium. *You've been "bargain-binned,"* and you have to consider what that says about the value of what you have to say because—here's the real complication—*price is a big part of branding.*

Price can be brand-defining, and just like everything else we did, it makes a statement about the quality of your product. So, you need to ask, *When I finally put a price tag on myself, am I entering the market as the low-priced, affordable value brand, or the high-end, pricey, luxury brand? And what does that communicate and facilitate—or impede?* Remember, we're talking about the same exact product. All we're doing is slapping a price tag on the product we designed and packaged, and are now hoping to sell.

What complicates speaker pricing even more is that an individual speaker may be "worth" one amount one day and many times that just a few months later—or even on the same day to a different event sponsor. That speaker may also be worth one price in the corporate market and another in the college market. And, as we witnessed in the previous chapter, value may change greatly just by some shrewd rebranding. So you're left to wonder, *Is it better to start out with a (relatively) high fee and stick to it, or to start out with a low fee and attempt to increase it over time?* You've got to think about this because some speakers keep their fees static for years—decades even—and yet other speakers seem to see their fees rise meteorically. Why is that?

Even further adding to the confusion over pricing decisions is your *perceived value.* Not only your value as it's perceived by speaking agents and event sponsors—and even audiences—but your value as it's perceived by *you.* Often speakers complicate pricing decisions by viewing their fee as a dollar determination of self-worth. One that operates under real-world pricing metrics they understand—telling themselves some version of *I should be getting as much as so-and-so—or at least more than this guy. Look at him—he's a juggler and I have a PhD in mechanical engineering and four patents!* Or they flip the other way, and don't believe they are worthy of any amount of money to speak, confiding to their agent, when fee comes up, *Incredible, talented, pedigreed, accomplished people speak for free all the time—look at TED and TEDx—how can I charge anything at all?*

And then there's this: Some individuals only want to speak if they can get a certain amount of money, so the price they set—or want to set—has absolutely nothing to do with any type of actual industry market dynamics. I've had speakers turn down offers for $10,000 and $25,000—and $50,000. I've even had speakers turn down $250,000—not because they're actually worth more than that, but because the money doesn't mean anything to them.

Of course, logic says, *Just let the marketplace set the price*, but it's not that simple. Speakers are priced more *subjectively* than *objectively*; more like works of art than lumber or shampoo or bread. So, even if we look at speaker pricing from the accepted economic benchmark of supply and demand, it's hard to adhere to hard-and-fast rules.

As for supply, even though there may be dozens of paid speakers who have reasonably similar backgrounds and reasonably similar speaking topics, in the end, there's only one of you. You're an original—and that alone makes you difficult to price.

As for demand, that's not clear-cut either. Unlike many other products, demand for speakers isn't completely predicated by some kind of organic demand that originates in the marketplace. Granted, demand for speakers is in part dictated by a set number of event sponsors needing to book a set number of speakers for a set number of events, but that only dictates the overall market cap for the demand, not the demand metrics for any individual speaker. How much *in demand* a particular speaker is can be largely influenced by the sum total of their marketing and packaging—the value of their speech topics, the compelling story as penned in their bio, the strength of their collateral marketing materials, and even their fee.

But of equal—or perhaps arguably even greater—import, the demand for any particular speaker in the marketplace is, to a large degree, controlled by *who represents that speaker and how well the agents do it.* How often and how professionally the speaker is pitched. And for which events, and with what spin. In other words, good agents don't just stick speakers on store shelves—they market and sell them. Which means that agents— skilled agents—*create the demand for individual speakers.* That means that agents control the supply by whom they sign and how they are packaged, and then they manipulate the demand by whom they pitch and sell the hardest. And that confirms these two things:

▸ There isn't actually a free market.

▸ Initial pricing is very tricky—and brand-defining.

But on the upside, there's some good news here: All of this also means that there's a way to be smart, because baked into all of this mess there's pricing flexibility and the potential for explosive growth.

So, for a new speaker starting out, here's rule number one: *It's more important that you have a pricing strategy in place that is predicated on shrewd branding and optimum growth than it is to start out with a high fee.*

OK, got it. But there have to be some basic pricing parameters that underpin the paid speaking market, right?

Yes—of course there are.

Agents are always lumping speakers together in a ballpark kind of way, thinking or saying things like, *He's a $10,000 speaker any day of the week.* Or, *She's a $40,000–$50,000 speaker.* Or, *I can* *book her all day long for $5,000, but higher than that and we hit a wall.* And these generalizations exist for a reason—agents have experience. They know better than anyone whom and what they can sell, and for how much. The wild card here is that there are dynamics that can throw even experienced agents off too.

Here are a few more ballpark overviews to guide you:

Generally, new, inexperienced speakers who are represented by agencies receive between $5,000 and $7,500 per event—sometimes $10,000.* Which isn't too shabby, considering. If you have a book out with a major publisher that is selling decently, or if you are a more experienced speaker, $10,000–$15,000 tends to be the going rate. If the book is a first-time bestseller—meaning the author has no previous bestsellers—we can usually start at $15,000–$20,000 per event while the book is hot. While these examples refer to authors, we can apply a similar accomplishment hierarchy to speakers who don't have books. For example, if you're the founder of a company, your speaking rate will largely depend on the size of the company and how well known it is. Think of the inherent value and knowledge base of the founder of a national food franchise versus the owner of a small restaurant. The same applies to nonprofit leaders, professors, and other non-authors in general. But notice that all of the pricing generalizations above are independent of *what you are speaking about.* There are pricing dynamics that originate solely in the organic value of *who you are and what you've accomplished.* The biggest pricing dynamic will be defined by *what you have to say*—and this is where it gets complicated. It indicates the paramount importance of not forgetting that agents come to all

---

*   There are also a large number of highly established and successful speakers who operate in this price range long term.

these pricing conclusions based on the sum total of your specific branding—what you have to offer and how it's packaged and presented—which means that there is a lot you can do to impact those *This speaker is worth X* statements. Everything you should do should be driven by the fact that event sponsors are always moved more by *message* than *bio*—content over celebrity, story over pedigree—which is why that schoolteacher turned cupcake baker can sometimes be pitched for the same event as the constitutional law scholar, and get the gig.

There is also a lot you can do to ground and safeguard yourself against some of these confusing pricing metrics and pitfalls and to establish some constructive dynamics that will set the stage for a successful, progressive, sustainable pricing strategy. And simply understanding how pricing works will help tremendously.

For example, the lowest "going rate" in the paid speakers industry of $5,000–$7,500 per speech is driven by the underlying structure of the marketplace. Because agents work on commission, it's not financially sound to dip below that. This means that suggesting you can speak for $500 or $1,000 can backfire—your agent can't make any money.[†] And don't balk at this. There are tremendous $5,000 speakers and lots of events that have small budgets—and therefore money to be made. In fact, there are speakers who intentionally position themselves at $5,000 in order to be booked frequently.

Having said this, as argued in chapter 9, setting your fee at $5,000 can also work against you. So, pricing has to be considered

---

† There are some exceptions to this. If a speaker has incoming offers in the very low range and a lot of them, that sometimes can work, especially if tied to a strategy to eventually get that rate up, and there also may be a new or fledgling agency that will work with you for very low fee events.

on a case-by-case basis. What makes for a sound pricing strategy for one speaker doesn't necessarily work for another.

In addition to sponsors being more wowed by message than bio, they are also often swayed by *perceived value*—and a *higher price tag conveys greater value*. This means that sometimes a $5,000 speaker can thrive equally well when his fee is moved to $10,000, and yet to add to this confusing mess, other speakers are highly price sensitive and can't make that jump. The reasons for this aren't always apparent or easy to discern. Once you get up and running, I suggest using a strategy to determine how price-sensitive you are. Get your phone ringing with offers at $5,000, then work with your agent to move your fee up to $10,000. (This concept works for any price point or price jump.) If the number of offers declines by more than 50 percent—bump your rate back down. If you maintain your offers above that 50 percent benchmark, worst case scenario, you and your agent are making the same amount of money for half the work—assuming of course you doubled your rate.

Through all of these pricing decisions, just let your agents understand that you know that you are in a financial partnership. And let him or her know that you won't undermine that—that you won't insist that he or she employ a pricing strategy that may serve you and your needs, but will interfere with his or her ability to earn income.

Case Study: The Short Game or the Long Game?
Overpriced Speaker A or Underpriced Speaker B?

Speaker A signs with an agency. He's never given a paid speech before, but he's enormously accomplished. He's an acclaimed constitutional law scholar and tenured professor at Harvard

University who has written several highly respected books and regularly appears on cable news shows. He's not quite a household name, but he's an industry name, and has even been featured in several highbrow documentaries on PBS. Speaker A puts together compelling, timely speech topics with a hook; he has an intriguing and Unique Selling Proposition. He writes a great bio and when he meets with his agents, he tells them that he'd like to set his fee at $50,000 a night—after all, he argues, he has the academic chops to back up that price point.

The agents are excited about his pedigree and speech topics—they already have events and programs in mind that they think he'll be perfect for—but they think the fee he wants is too high. They gently explain that for someone who hasn't yet been paid to speak, setting his fee that high is probably a faulty pricing strategy that will likely make him difficult to book. The agents explain to Speaker A that one of the key selling points an agent has when speaking with an event sponsor—especially when trying to pitch a higher-priced speaker—is to be able to reference his recent gigs. They explain that at that price point event sponsors want to know that you've been booked at prestigious events and can deliver, and that you're an oft-requested speaker in high demand.

Speaker A scoffs at this and the agency reluctantly agrees to market him as a $50,000 speaker anyway—after all, they don't want to lose him and figure that despite the premium pricing maybe they'll be surprised and get lucky. They comfort themselves by thinking that the commissions on $50,000 bookings, although a long shot, are pretty nice.

Speaker B also signs with the same agency around the same time. He too is an acclaimed scholar of similar stature to Speaker A—not in constitutional law, but in the field of biotech. Speaker B has appeared on *60 Minutes*, has written several books, and advises some of the biggest companies in the world about new developments and growth opportunities in the biotech space. He too has compelling speech topics and a great overall one sheet with significant and broadly applicable audience takeaways—great stuff about what his experience in biotech can teach others about innovation and creative breakthroughs. And just like Speaker A, he has never yet been paid to give a speech other than a couple of honorariums at scientific conferences for a few hundred dollars. He too is perceived as a highly marketable speaker by the agents.

When Speaker B has his first conference call with his agents after signing, it's the first time they've discussed pricing and he is both excited and nervous. He has no idea what he is worth. The agents explain that an acclaimed scientist of his stature can generally expect to command $20,000 or more for each event. But they go on to say, since he hasn't done any paid speaking yet, they'd recommend pricing him below that—at $10,000. Speaker B asks the agents why, and they explain that they want to intentionally underprice him so he can get some gigs under his belt to build his speaking résumé, which will increase his perceived value. They further explain that once he's given a few speeches they'll likely be able to drive his fee up and, depending on how things go, perhaps even to a higher price point than the $20,000 a night they referenced as typical for someone with his pedigree. The agents explain to Speaker B that they are using a pricing strategy known as *pricing for penetration* in which you price something—or in this case someone—below market value to gain initial traction by increasing perceived value relative to the higher priced competition. In other words, the agents explain, compared to his peers, at $10,000, Speaker B will look like a bargain.

"Hold on," Speaker B asks. "Can't pricing for penetration

backfire? Once I'm put out there for one fee, how will I justify fee jumps? Especially if I want to move quickly? Nobody wants to pay double today for something they could have gotten for half the price yesterday."

The agents know that Speaker B is correct. Initially pricing a product under the market value can prove to be a problematic pricing strategy—consumers don't like big price hikes after they get used to seeing a lower price or paying less for something. But the agents also know that's only true for products that wear their prices on their sleeve, and that in the case of a paid speaker the problem can be completely averted by *never publishing fees*.*

The agents tell Speaker B that if the goal is to get a few gigs for his résumé, as long as his fee isn't ever published, pricing for penetration is a particularly valuable strategy. The agents further clarify that if the agency doesn't put a fee under Speaker B's name on their website any new event sponsors in the future will never know what he was paid for those early speeches.

Speaker B is intrigued. The agents go on to tell him that not publishing speaker fees is a protective, beneficial move that offers the speaker not only an opportunity to jump-start his career now, but also latitude in pricing across the board. They elaborate by saying:

▸ We can underprice you now to get early traction.

▸ Later on, you can safely accept below-fee deals when you want to—for whatever reason—without being tied to that lower rate in the future.

---

* Many speaking agencies list the price of each speaker on their websites.

▶ We can then raise your fee at any point, without event sponsors feeling that they've been ripped off. And if we get pullback from that higher price, we can safely slip back into the lower price under the radar.

Speaker B listens carefully to everything the agents tell him and, comforted by the fact that they have given this so much thought and the fact that they obviously have upward price mobility in mind, he agrees with their pricing strategy. The agents are thrilled and start pitching Speaker B immediately for $10,000 per night.

Meanwhile, Speaker A is being pitched for $50,000 as he spends the next two years teaching, appearing on television, and writing a new book that lands on the *New York Times* bestseller list. But he doesn't get a single booking. There is tremendous interest from event sponsors, but almost all immediately push back when they hear Speaker A's fee. When the agents can't justify the high fee by referencing where he's spoken before and can't provide rave event sponsor blurbs, it completely extinguishes any lingering interest. The consensus is that $50,000 is a lot to pay for someone who's never given a speech, regardless of credentials.

Speaker A, of course, doesn't want to hear this. He simply decides that his agents aren't doing a good job. And in the end, Speaker A is correct. They aren't.

After a while, the agents basically stop pitching Speaker A because he's so overpriced—and they need to get bookings. Frankly, the self-preservation decision they came to was that they couldn't afford to pitch Speaker A because he wasn't going to sell and if they pitched him, it was at the expense of speakers who they could actually book and from whom they could earn a commission. Speaker A, of course, doesn't know this. The agents can't tell him, so he just thinks that they aren't good at their jobs.

Speaker B, on the other hand, is rolling in offers and bookings. And not insignificantly, he has established a great working relationship with his agency. He spends the next two years advising companies, writing articles, and appearing on TV. Working together with his agents, toward the end of the first year, they decide to increase Speaker B's fee to $15,000—a small but welcome and well-deserved bump. Event sponsors don't bat an eyelash—he's proven that he's worth every penny—and he has the rave reviews from a long list of prestigious venues to back up that price point. And of course any new event sponsors he is being pitched to at his new rate don't know that he was paid less to speak before. During this two-year span, he is booked to speak thirteen times. He's gaining notoriety as a great, affordable speaker, worked out early kinks, improved his delivery, and even refined his topics a bit. Plus, he's pulled in over $100,000 after commissions. Not bad for someone who had no up-front costs, had never been paid to speak before, and started out with a below-market pricing strategy.

Collectively the agents then decide to bump Speaker B up again when the opportunity arises, and in year three he is booked nineteen times. Toward the end of his third year, one of his books becomes a *Wall Street Journal* bestseller—which makes sense. Through speaking, he's built his brand. He's gotten his face and his message out before a huge number of target book buyers and grown his network and email list. He speaks with the agents at his agency and they decide to increase his fee to $25,000—which is still, shrewdly, unpublished.

Speaker A was playing the short game—he wanted to earn a lot of money quickly and thought that he could cut to the front of the line and do that based on his credentials alone. And he earned exactly nothing. *Zero speaking dollars.*

Speaker B was playing the long game. He understood that the more speeches he gave, regardless of what he was paid for his early events, the greater his perceived—and real—value would be. He listened to his agents, showed respect for their professionalism and their financial partnership with him, and benefited enormously from it.

A Little Bit More about the Value of POA—Price on Application—and the Downside to Publishing Your Fee

As noted earlier, many agencies list speaker fees directly on their websites, and as the previous story illustrates, this is ill-advised for several reasons—and not only because of the price mobility point made above. To start, published price tags on speakers can chase prospective event sponsors away before they even contact your agency.

With your published price right there under your name, an event sponsor with a budget of $10,000 might visit your agency's website and see that your asking price is $15,000 and move on to a different speaker without bothering to enquire over the phone—a decision they made because of price alone. This means that a potential opportunity that you and your agents will never know existed was completely missed. And here's why it matters so much: *Inquiries and offers tell you and your agency a lot.* They indicate interest, where it's coming from, which of your speech topics attracted the buyer, and at what price point. Agents and event sponsors talk about speakers. Who else do the event sponsors see as comparable to you? What other speakers are they considering and why? What are those speakers' price points? Is one of your speaking topics particularly relevant now? Agents can use this information to help build your brand and help refine your speaking fee by framing their forward-moving decisions against how buyers are actually thinking—but only if they hear from them.

Remember, the most important thing in the speaking industry is getting offers, and it's better to have the chance to consider any and all offers—even if you turn some (or all) of them down— than it is to preemptively cut short opportunities before they are offered. Why? For starters, getting offers is *proof of concept*. Offers mean that your one sheet is appealing enough to attract buyers. Agents of course want to convert those offers to bookings to earn a commission but, as a speaker, you can always decline an invitation for any reason—including because it's below fee.

On top of that, if I have a buyer considering a speaker for a specific event and another buyer calls about the same date— and this happens sometimes—simply being able to share with the buyer that we *have an offer* for you that day already is more important than the dollar value of that offer because I never have to divulge what that dollar value actually is. This competing interest creates the impression that you are in demand—essentially flying off the shelf—and is validation of the buyer's interest in you in the first place.

In fact, there are numerous positive ways incoming below-fee inquiries can play out. For example, there may be additional context regarding a speaking event that may sway you when it comes to price. Perhaps the event sponsor with the lower-than-desired honorarium is with a nonprofit that is hosting an event you would have happily spoken at because of the cause. Or perhaps you have nothing else to do the day of the event and, if offered, would be thrilled to collect a $10,000 paycheck even though your stated fee is $15,000. Or maybe the event is nearby, meaning there is little travel and you can get in and out in one day. Perhaps it's a conference you are interested in with networking opportunities and good contacts for you to make—or it has a particularly large audience where you can capture data and get exposure. Perhaps it is an opportunity to attract readers to your blog, get additional speaking invitations, sell books, or generate donations—it's not only about the fee.

There is a strong argument that rather than sticking to a take-it-or-leave-it rate and publishing it, it's better to position yourself to see *all opportunities* and calculate the *other value* that is baked into a specific speaking opportunity than it is to never hear about the offers in the first place. So, think about flexible pricing models, nonmonetary currency, bulk book buys, charity, and goodwill. The idea is to do everything—even fee setting and fee transparency—with a long-term vision toward growing your brand, both in terms of price point and visibility. As good as it might feel to have your picture on an agency website with a lofty fee listed beneath it, it's far more constructive to position yourself to welcome any and all incoming inquiries, because the primary goal should be to encourage offers, regardless of the amount of money involved.

I've used the strategy of not publishing speaker fees for years, and it's an incredibly useful tactic that unleashes incredibly valuable information. Essentially, what you're doing is allowing the market to determine your price and it gives you, the speaker, a reference point in terms of which offers to accept and which to decline. But there is another significant value add to not publishing your fee. When you don't have a published or quoted fee, it encourages event sponsors to make their best offers based on their budgets. *By not quoting a price, it puts the onus on the event sponsor to decide your value.* And I've observed that their inclination is to offer *more* rather than to offer *less*. So that means that once a fee is listed, you are preemptively precluding above-fee offers, as well. Which means that you are, to a large degree, preventing fee growth—something you clearly don't want to do.

Remember the story earlier in the book about Charles, the speaker who got an incoming offer for $150,000 when his usual fee was $30,000? That only happened because he didn't have a published or quoted rate. As much as that was an opportunity we exploited, it wouldn't have happened at all if his price had been published. No one intentionally offers that much over ask. This only happened because the event sponsor independently arrived at such a high perceived value for Charles. Then, since he was who they wanted and they understood that the money would go to a good cause—and that was what they were offering for the event—we were able to execute the deal. And that story isn't a one-off—it happens all the time—not with that much swing of course, but with big enough dollar amounts and enough frequency to matter. *You want that edge.*

When an agent pitches you for an event or an event sponsor calls in with an inquiry, your agent knows your price point and can pitch you for that event by manipulating your rate either up or down depending on the broad parameters—and that's much harder to do when there is a published or outwardly quoted fee. A good agency will use the policy of not publishing fees to create *fee elasticity* to strategically increase your fee as you prove yourself in the marketplace and decrease it for opportunities that make sense. And not publishing fees isn't a "favor the speaker only" strategy either. It often helps event sponsors too. Flexible pricing allows that agent to get great speakers to favored event sponsors below fee without fear of uncomfortable feelings on either side. The agent will sell the speaker on the "other value" that event offers, and that isn't strictly self-serving on the agent's part. It's legitimate. I can't tell you how many new opportunities and how much growth have come from speakers accepting events that they thought they were doing solely for the below-fee honorarium.

And there's more. A speaker with an unpublished rate who accepts a below-fee offer doesn't have to feel embarrassed to be working for less since the event sponsor didn't negotiate off of a published number.

Once I set a fee, how long can I expect to stay at that price point?

There are some speakers who stay at the same price point for years and others who rapidly escalate. So how is it that one speaker's fee can be scaled from $5,000 per speech to $60,000, and another's from $7,000 per speech to $125,000, while other speaker's fees stay exactly the same? How and when should that rate increase, and why? Who decides? The marketplace? The agents? The speaker?

The answers to these questions are dependent on several factors. To start, agency policy. There are agencies that do not work with speakers to do much in the way of branding, career development, or to escalate fees. They book speakers—list and pitch—relying more on volume than strategizing and building careers. So, if you are signed with an agency that is not hands-on and proactive, you will likely find they have no interest in fee escalation strategies. Frankly, it's just more work than they may be willing to do.

One reason speakers who are at agencies that *do* work at career development might have trouble escaping their base fee is because if the agents regularly book a certain speaker at $10,000 a night, they may be hesitant to raise the fee because their number of bookings will go down. If bookings are consistent and event sponsors are happy, the agent is likely thinking, *Why mess with a good thing?* The fix here is to convince your agent to employ the strategy I outlined earlier and to say that you would like to experiment—but make it clear that your goal is not to earn less, and if it doesn't work, you'll revert. Remember, if you are asking someone who is working on spec to pitch something that is essentially overpriced and won't sell, they may decide to pitch other speakers. You need your agent to be on board with your decisions.

My strategy as an agent was always to have career development and fee escalation in mind. And typically, if a speaker could be booked ten times per year at a certain rate, it's time to see if you can increase that rate. I once worked with a speaker and author whose asking price was $20,000 a night, but he often accepted invitations for $10,000, and occasionally was offered speaking engagements at $25,000. After more than ten bookings in one year, we raised his rate to $25,000. A big jump, but since his fee was unpublished, it carried little risk. We simply quoted $25,000 to those who asked and listened to what was offered by those who didn't. In the next year, he ended up getting two speeches at $20,000, four speeches at an average of $17,500 and three "big ones" at $30,000, which totaled $200,000. This is exactly the same money as he would have generated for ten speeches at $20,000. In this case, for him it was a bit of a wash—but that's not always the case.

Case Study: Finding the Sweet Spot
The $10,000 Speaker and the $5,000 Death Swing
I once worked with a speaker who was getting booked twenty to twenty-five times a year at $10,000 per event. And it was like

clockwork. He had a popular book about the environment, and people loved his topics and his delivery. One day, we decided to increase his fee to $15,000—and we couldn't get a single bite. So, the speaker went from generating roughly $250,000 a year to maybe $45,000 a year. Of course, there's no benefit to anyone in a situation like this. And in this case, we were able to deduce that the failed fee escalation had nothing to do with his perceived value and everything to do with event sponsors' fixed budgets. *For universities, $10,000 is a good comfort point.* But $15,000 is often beyond their capacity. And since they are usually bidding with a fixed budget, they can't just go get more money. The outcome of this price hike hurt all three parties—the speaker, the event sponsors (because they lost access to a great speaker), and the agent—so we quickly recalibrated, which was easier to accomplish because his fee was never published.

This illustrates that another reason for price stagnation can simply be the marketplace. Some speakers, because of their branding, are only bookable at lower-paying programs. It's that simple. Their fees have to be set at a price that the market can bear—which, as this speaker proves, doesn't mean they can't make substantial money. They just have to do it by speaking more.

There are all sorts of established programs that have fixed budgets—Hispanic Heritage Month programs at universities, the English department, the African Studies department, the MBA program, and so on. If the budget for Hispanic Heritage Month speakers tends to hover around $5,000–$7,500 at the majority of universities—which is generally the case—speakers who talk about Hispanic heritage will end up with very few bookings if they set their fees at $10,000. This has nothing to do with their message or the quality of their speeches, it simply has to do with

budgets. Very few event sponsors can increase their budgets—
they are what they are.

Another reason that some speakers can never escape their
base fee is because they aren't being booked that often. If you
aren't getting a ton of bookings, it's hard for your agents to justify an increased fee. In fact, they may want to reduce your fee
in order to generate more bookings. And this isn't a bad idea,
as more bookings at a lower price can build a speaker's profile and jump-start a stagnant career, which can then—at least
theoretically—result in an increased fee down the line. Also,
don't forget that opportunities breed other opportunities. Who
are you meeting when you give a speech? What contacts do you
now have? There is far more to gain from speaking than just the
honorarium.

Having said all of this, if you feel stuck at a certain fee and
would like to increase it, talk with your agent. Agents tend to be
honest and they shoot from the hip. It's possible that they never
thought of increasing your fee because everyone, including you,
appeared to be happy with how things were going. Clear communication, and an in-depth understanding of the pricing dynamics
discussed above will help you to position yourself at the right
price point and grow your fee over time.

*Here's where the math intersects with motivation and the agent-
speaker relationship, and may get really problematic:* While there
may be no way to establish a "fair fee" for a speaker, there is a
way to establish a "perfect fee." If we consider all of the variables, from the price the speaker has been getting consistently to
how much and why the speaker wants to speak, we can ascertain
how much of that speaker's motivation to speak is solely based on
money, and how much the speaker is motivated by other value.
Where other value is a significant factor in the desire to speak,

if we decide to try a fee hike—even if it appears to work—it can actually backfire. If your motivation is up-selling or donations or data capture or networking and exposure, and a fee hike cuts down the number of gigs you get, even if you end up earning the same amount of money doing fewer, higher-fee gigs, the decrease in exposure can make this a detrimental move.

An additional consideration is how fewer gigs may impact your agent. If a speaker is regularly receiving $10,000 a day for a speech and booking ten events a year, that's $100,000 gross with $75,000 going to the speaker and $25,000 going to the agency. If we increase that fee to $15,000, and the number of events dips to six events per year, suddenly the speaker is making $67,500 instead of $75,000 ($7,500 less), but the agency's commission is reduced to $22,500 or a drop of $2,500. While this difference may be fine with the speaker—he's making less but traveled a whole lot less too—it's not as small to the agency. And here's why: If an agency has ten speakers at the same price point who increase their fees but reduce their number of bookings, based on the numbers above, that agency just lost $25,000. An agency with higher-fee speakers would lose even more. In both cases, the agencies would also likely lose event sponsors. So be clear about how much other value matters in your motivation to speak and clear your financial decisions that impact your agents *with* your agents. What might be best for you is not necessarily best for them, and like it or not, you are financial partners and it is to your advantage to compromise when needed.

A Little Bit More about How Speaking Agents Think about Fees

Speaking agents are in the business of *making money* and favor making money over whom they book. Toward that end, speaking agents first want to book high-priced speakers if they can because they'll make more on the commission and have only a fraction of the work—one sale, one contract, one set of travel arrangements instead of two or three, or even five or ten—for the same commission.

On the flip side, agents like to book lower-fee speakers if they know the speakers can be booked often. Every four $5,000 bookings yield the same commission dollars as one $20,000 booking. So, what agents need to serve their event sponsors individually and collectively is a roster that covers the gamut of low-, mid-, and high-priced speakers so that they can collect commissions across the whole spectrum, because there is nothing an agent likes less than leaving money on the table. When I would hear that an event sponsor was looking for a certain speaker or had an event that he or she didn't feel one of the speakers I represented would work for, I'd go searching off-roster for a speaker I could book for that event. Whether that meant cold-calling an unsuspecting "expert" or co-brokering with another agency, one way or another, I was determined to collect that commission. What this means for lower-priced speakers is *don't assume your agency doesn't value you.* You are filling an important spot on their roster that helps them serve their event sponsors who often have a variety of programs at different price points.

But what about commission rates?

This part, at least, is simple and clear cut.

Generally, the more established the speaker, the higher the fee, and the lower the commission rate. If an author with a bestselling book approaches an agency and is regularly receiving $40,000 a speech—say on average ten bookings a year—on her own or with her current agency and generates incoming offers, that author has already established a foothold in the market. If she signs with a new agency, they will gladly take her at a 20 percent commission despite the industry norm of 25 percent. *That's $80,000 in commissions walking in the door.* Now, don't get me wrong. The agents will still work for that. They will negotiate, pitch, and handle event details, contracts, fee distribution, and taxes, etc., but those incoming requests are a lot easier to close than cold-call deals for brand-new speakers.

So, as noted earlier, if you're just starting out and have no—or little—booking history, you should expect to pay a commission rate of 25 percent and in some cases even 30 percent. After all, your agent is taking a risk by signing you and will be working gratis until you get booked—and there is no guarantee that you will actually be booked—which means that agent has far more to lose than you do. Remember, 100 percent of nothing is nothing and as a new speaker with no track record, I would gladly pay a 30 percent commission to an agent if it meant I had a chance to get paid speaking offers.

Why Everyone Else's Rate Is Irrelevant

When it comes to who earns what, this isn't an industry where it pays to make direct comparisons. If there's a speaker you compare yourself to because she speaks about a similar topic—let's say the importance of clean drinking water in the developing world—who receives $30,000 a night, it doesn't mean that you should be getting $30,000. Maybe you should be getting more—or maybe you should be getting less. There may be significant differentiating variables that you can't see or calibrate—but the market will. The difference may be clear—that $30,000 speaker might run a massive nonprofit organization, and you might be running a one-person shop out of your garage. Or perhaps the $30,000 speaker who talks about the importance of clean drinking water in developing nations was recently featured on the cover of *Inc.* magazine—or just keynoted a large prestigious conference alongside luminaries, or has a highly regarded TED talk, or large following—which helps to justify her fee. At the same time, perhaps you just published a bestselling book—so maybe your fee should be $40,000. On the flip side, the difference that justifies the price differential may not be so easy to define. It may have to do with topical relevance, age, blurbs, social media presence, luck, contacts, and networks. But in each case, comparing yourself with the other speakers can be pointless or, worse yet, destructive. Because each speaker is unique—a one and only— each speaker should have a pricing plan that is coordinated with his or her specific goals. The reason *why* everyone else's rate is irrelevant is because you are participating in the speaking industry for yourself, by yourself—for your own goals and with your own branding, mission, and USP.

What about speaking for free—should I do it?

Yes and no.

The key is to separate the free speeches that are a waste of everyone's time and brand-eroding "freebies" from those that can be a smart investment. The difference comes down to what the speech offers other than financial compensation. Consider: *Will you receive a high-def video that is widely distributed? Do you get résumé-building bragging rights? Is it a high-visibility networking opportunity? Are you up-selling—a book or product or service where exposure has value? Does the offer include appealing free travel? Could your free speech be a catalyst for donations? Could it spark paid speaking offers? Is there a valuable payout instead of cash?*

For example, there are certain conference events like TED, TEDx, and Chicago Ideas Week that don't compensate their speakers but that record your speech in high resolution. High-quality videos can be a massive marketing tool for future paid speeches—assuming you do a good job, of course. These well-known and widely broadcast platforms also are prestigious and résumé-building. They are also excellent networking opportunities. In other words—brand-building.

And there are other exceptions. If a college asks you to speak for free and go out of pocket for travel, it might not be the best gig to accept—unless you work at a retail bank hoping to attract new banking customers. Or, perhaps you have a product or service you are trying to sell, in which case it might be worth the investment in travel expenses because your return on investment has less to do with honorarium and more to do with up-selling. If you are running a nonprofit and offered the opportunity to give a free speech about your mission to a group of one thousand business leaders, it's possible that you could walk out with significant donations or that one or two of those audience members will book you for a paid speech in the future. Or perhaps influential audience members will tweet about your talk.

I once represented a speaker named Lauren who was asked to give a free talk in front of 3,500 people in Las Vegas. The audience consisted of businessmen and businesswomen who specialized in financial planning. When I called her to share the invitation, Lauren—who ran a nonprofit focused on dog rescue—saw an opportunity to market herself to those 3,500 people. The event organizer was able to pay for her economy-class flight and a hotel room for two nights, so Lauren wasn't going out of pocket other than the "cost" of her time. She figured she could make enough connections that the event would be worthwhile. She absolutely nailed her talk and told her story in a way that was both emotional and impactful. What happened next still amazes me to this day. Several audience members, empowered by her presentation, formed a coalition to raise money for her cause. In one day they raised $100,000 in donations from the audience members. Furthermore, since this was a group of financial planners, she got offered free accounting and financial services from several of the people in attendance. Lauren had the foresight to see an opportunity, took a small risk, and ended up with $100,000 in additional funding for her nonprofit and free accounting and financial management from two leading executives. The money raised was nearly three times what she was able to generate in a year by herself, and it enabled her to hire two additional employees and paid for some much-needed marketing to help expand her nonprofit's visibility.

How to Convince Your Agent to Handle Unpaid Inquiries

Very rarely will an agent call you with an offer for a free talk— the agent makes no money but still has to do all of the work associated with a speaking event. However, if you want to try to leverage free speeches, talk with your agent about the possibility. For one, explain to your agent that certain free events might help to raise your speaking profile in the future—this means that the agent could be potentially making more money down the line by investing a little bit of sweat equity up front.

Second, depending on your agent's response, offer to handle all of the logistics yourself. This is a very common solution to free or low-fee invitations. If your agent knows that you'll handle travel arrangements, pre-event calls, and other logistics yourself, then the agent doesn't have to worry about all of the extra uncompensated work that comes along with a free event. And here's the thing—the free event might actually help your agent as well. Event sponsors often work on several events over the course of the year, and while one request might be a free-bie, the next request from the same institution might come with a substantial budget. While this doesn't help you unless you're booked again by the event sponsor—which is unlikely—it can help your agent massively. When it comes time to book a paid speaker, the event sponsor will remember the great agent who secured a free speaker for them and will likely come back to book the paid speaker.

If you explain this to your agent, there is a good chance she'll be on board with your plan. And this isn't to say that your agent should be pushing for free events. It's simply a question of acting on the opportunity when it arises by knowing that you are poten-tially available for a free speech when an event sponsor calls look-ing for one.

Warning: One of the biggest problems I find occurs when speakers accept a free engagement that is a few months away. As the event date becomes closer, the speech starts to feel less and less like a great idea—you have better things you could be doing that day, you overcommitted yourself to the sponsor, and there's a lot on the schedule, or you just gave three paid speeches and the idea of flying to Wisconsin in the middle of winter for a freebie now seems unappealing. So think long and hard before making these commitments.

Case Study: How I Leveraged Free Speeches to Get Paid Vacations All over the Word, Build My Business, and Enjoy Life

I absolutely love to travel. When my first book was released, I received many inquiries about giving free presentations to university and nonprofit audiences. At first I was hesitant to accept some of these events, but certain offers were very appealing. So I set a rule for myself that if I got a speaking offer in a city that I wanted to visit, I would accept the offer so long as my travel expenses were covered and I liked the group to whom I would be speaking.

This strategy became a way for me to visit places I had never been before—places I might not have ever visited were it not for the speaking invitations. Over the course of a few years, I sat on beaches in Mexico, ate steak tartare in Belgium, explored Taiwan on a moped, and visited incredible bars and music venues in Germany. My travel was paid by the sponsors, so I viewed each of these events as an excuse to take a small vacation. I worked for a few hours giving my speech, and then typically had three or four days to myself, allowing me to explore new cities, try new food, experience the nightlife, visit museums, and meet interesting people. I also got to lecture at prestigious institutions and companies including MIT, Microsoft, and Viacom.

For others, traveling to interesting locales may not be their cup of tea. Perhaps your interest lies in speaking at nonprofit events that cover a topic that you are passionate about. Or maybe you would be willing to speak for free if the event is nearby—it's good practice, and you might sell some books or meet some fascinating people while you network.

In my case, I was also able to leverage free speeches to help build my business. Since the event sponsors organizing these speeches were often also clients of my agency, these trips allowed me to meet with event sponsors face to face—a very rare thing in the speaking world. So while I was speaking for free, I was creating goodwill with sponsors who I knew would be coming back to me to book paid speakers down the line.

TAKEAWAYS

Speaking agents think about fees based on how often you can be booked. Listen to your agent's pricing thoughts—and participate in the conversation. Then ask about their growth strategy—and make sure they have one

Set a reasonable rate for yourself, and use successful speeches to grow it over time

Discuss the upside of not posting your fee with your agency. If your agency puts fees on their website, suggest the possibility of being listed as POA (price on application)

Just because you don't post a fee on your agency's website, it doesn't mean you and your agents shouldn't have a target fee in mind

When you do set that fee—or ideally, fee range—internally with your agency, don't view it as either a statement of personal worth or etched in stone. Your rate does not define your value, it is a means to an end

Understand that if you approach fee structure with a strategic pricing strategy in mind, you will get more offers, be booked more, and your fee will have a better chance of increasing over time

Use frequency of bookings to determine if your asking price is too low—or too high

Lack of bookings may be a result of an inflated asking price—or it may be something else entirely. Be analytical

If you are just starting out and have no speaking gigs under your belt yet, it's usually smart to start with a comparatively low fee—price position yourself to receive offers

The relationship between fees and commission rates are directly entwined—be smart before you try to negotiate a lower commission

Fly solo and identify the currency that you live by. When setting your rate, everyone else's rate is irrelevant

Consider speaking for free if there is valuable, leverageable, nonfinancial compensation

13.

How to Prepare for
Your First Paid Speech

...AND YOUR SECOND AND THIRD

Now that you've gotten a booking, let's examine everything you should do to prepare—not only for your first paid speech, but also for every paid speech to follow.

Get the Lay of the Land

First things first. Make sure you understand who the audience is and how the specific speech the event sponsor contracted you for relates to them. This is information that your agent should give to you even before you accept a paid speaking offer, and your agent should be hyper-specific. If you're speaking at a university, is it only for a specific group—say, the freshman class or the English department or a student organization—or will the event be open to the entire school, or even the larger community? If you're speaking at a nonprofit focused on aiding women in the workforce, is the audience going to be exclusively women?

If you're speaking at a corporation, it doesn't necessarily mean that you'll be talking to a broad corporate audience. Your audience could be a smaller group within that corporation, and you need to know if that is the case. Also, find out if there will be other speakers at the event, and if there is an overarching theme that you should be aware of. These are all important points to clarify with your agent that will impact your presentation in subtle ways.

Understand That Different Audiences Require Different Types of Preparation.

Even if you are giving the same core speech to colleges, corporations, and nonprofits, it's important to understand that the preparation required for each market—and each individual event—will be slightly different. Let's say, for example, that you have a speech titled "Crowd Funding and the Future of Entrepreneurship." There is a difference between presenting this talk to college students versus a corporate or nonprofit audience. The content of the speech doesn't necessarily need to change significantly, but the *tone* and *focus*—in addition to any side comments—likely need to be framed differently for each market and each specific audience. University students will probably be better served with somewhat more basic information about how to start a business via crowdfunding platforms than a nonprofit or corporate audience will be. Perhaps the students should walk away with a clear idea as to the process behind raising money to launch a start-up. But a corporate audience will likely be more sophisticated in their knowledge and might be more interested in understanding how your experience specifically applies to situations relevant to a more established business—or to their specific industry. These changes may manifest as subtle differences in content, spin, tone, and takeaways even though your core presentation remains the same—but can have a big impact on the success of a talk.

So, ask your agent questions. Lots of them. *How large will the audience be? What are the demographics? Do you need to customize your speech for the audience, or do they want one of the topics verbatim from your one sheet? Who was the last speaker they hosted? What is the room like? What is the overall company or school culture or vibe? Is the event formal or informal? What about the atmosphere? Are they expecting a PowerPoint presentation? What about handouts? Is there a dress code? Is anything expected of you beyond the speech?* For example, *Do they want a fifteen-minute question-and-answer session following your speech? Does the sponsor want a classroom visit or small-group breakout sessions in addition to your talk? Does the university want to host a private dinner with you and the dean? If working with a corporate client, are you expected to visit with employees in a specific department before or after your talk? Does the sponsor expect your speech to be longer than forty-five minutes? Or perhaps shorter?**

While these questions may seem obvious, it's important to understand that the more prepared you are, the better you'll do. This will manifest as a better event and garner better feedback, which will make it more likely that your agent will be able to secure bookings for you in the future. I've represented many speakers who don't ask these questions, but I always make it a point to provide the above information regardless of whether or not the speaker asks for it—so make sure you get it since it's imperative to have a clear idea as to what the event sponsor wants.

---

*   Some, but not all, of these specifics will be in your contract/deal memo.

Understand that there are situations in which the speech you sold from your topic description needs modification, and situations where none is necessary at all. I once represented a happiness expert (yes, there is such a thing) who received an invitation to speak to a group of wedding planners. The first thing she said after accepting the booking was "I'm going to go do a bunch of research about wedding planners." While a good instinct, in this case, that was a mistake—and I told her so. The wedding planners wanted her go-to speech about how to be happier, and I made that clear.* They already knew all about weddings and wedding planning and didn't need her insight on that topic. The idea was that the wedding planners would be able to extract elements from her happiness talk—the takeaways—and apply them to their daily work, thereby creating more happiness for themselves and for the clients they served. A good lesson was learned here by both the speaker, and me—the agent. There are times to customize your speech to a specific audience and there are times not to. She was trying to give the audience something they already had, information about wedding planning, and forgot for a moment to focus on what we had sold them, which was her Unique Selling Proposition—a route to happiness.

An important step in this process is to talk with the event sponsor to confirm exactly what that sponsor is looking for.

This is true for all three markets and every event. About a month prior to each event, there should be a conference call between you (the speaker), the agent, and the sponsor—and it should be arranged by your agent. The event sponsor will be thrilled to participate because she will be both nervous and

---

* In some cases, event sponsors want speakers to customize their talks to specifically fit the sponsors' particular businesses or event topics, while others don't.

excited about the event and will want to feel like she is part of the process. Rather than you simply showing up and giving a speech, by arranging for a call like this the sponsor feels important. You can communicate how seriously you are taking their event, and it allows the sponsor to feel that they know you. After the call, they'll be familiar with your voice and your personality, will have raised any of their own concerns about topic presentation and technicalities and—this is not insignificant—will also be excited that they got to speak with you, the talent. This call gives event sponsors confidence in the decision they made to hire you, it increases the chances that you will deliver what they are expecting, and it reduces the possibility of missteps on the day of the event. Your agent should welcome setting this up for you—after all, you already have a signed contract—and a call like this usually ensures a better experience for everyone.

Following the pre-event conference call, follow up separately with a call to your agent to get his or her take on the conversation. The agent often knows the sponsor and may have booked events with him or her before. A debrief with your agent will ensure that you didn't miss—or misread—anything mentioned on the call, and will help guarantee the best event possible.

Case Study: The Prepared Speaker versus the Unprepared Speaker

Speaker A or Speaker B?

Speaker A primarily speaks at corporations about leadership and company culture. He is a former executive of a midsize regional sales company and often receives invitations to speak to large audiences at well-known organizations. Whenever his agent calls with a speaking invitation, the first question Speaker A asks—after accepting the offer and signing the contract—is when the agent can arrange a conference call with the event sponsor. Although his agent has already provided the key details about the event, as well as the topic the sponsor wants him to speak about and the audience demographic, Speaker A always likes to get on the phone to learn more about what is expected of him directly from the event sponsor.

Speaker B primarily speaks at nonprofit organizations about management and employee training. She is a former non-profit leader who ran a well-known children's charity for over a decade. She receives roughly ten speaking invitations each year, and generally accepts all of them. Whenever her agent calls with a speaking invitation, Speaker B doesn't ask many questions at all, outside of the basics—what fee is being offered, the audience demographic, and how much travel is involved. She never asks to arrange a phone call with the event sponsor and balks when the agent suggests that it might be a good idea—so the agent lets it go.

Each time Speaker A hops on a conference call with his agent and the event sponsor, the speaker learns key pieces of information that help him customize his content—which in turn creates a better, more relevant speech. The sponsors are excited to talk with Speaker A, excited to form a relationship ahead of the event, and impressed that Speaker A cares so much about his speech and the audience to whom he will be speaking. "Last year, our keynote speaker refused to get on a conference call," one event sponsor tells him, and Speaker A is surprised, thinking, *Why wouldn't a speaker take twenty minutes to make sure his speech is on point?* After all, he is being paid a lot of money for his efforts and it's to his benefit to do so.

Speaker B, who hasn't requested a conference call, gets a

phone call from her agent asking if she would be willing to do a pre-event phone call that the sponsor specifically requested for their upcoming event. As expected, Speaker B pushes back— she has a busy schedule and is planning on giving her standard speech. In her mind there is nothing to talk about with the event sponsor that her agent hasn't already told her—so she says no.

Speaker B's agent now has to call the event sponsor and explain that the speaker isn't able to get on the phone—which is a really tough call to make. This is categorically disrespectful and puts the agent in a difficult position. After all, the agent has to tell the event sponsor that the speaker doesn't have twenty free minutes in the next thirty days to speak with him. Either that, or the speaker simply doesn't care about the event. The agent makes the call and it leaves a bad taste in the sponsor's mouth. The sponsor explains that he is paying a fair amount of money to Speaker B and feels that fifteen or twenty minutes to review the event isn't too much to ask for.

Speaker A delivers a great speech and gets wonderful reviews after the event. The sponsor's blurb raves about his commitment, and even references the fact that he got on the phone with the sponsor prior to the event to ensure that they were on the same page. This praise immediately goes on Speaker A's one sheet, which helps him to secure gigs in the future.

Speaker B delivers a solid speech but missed the mark when it came to the core problem the event sponsor was trying to address. The speech wasn't bad—Speaker B never gives a bad speech—but it wasn't a home run either. Further, the sponsor is annoyed that the event could have been vastly improved if the speaker had been willing to get on the phone. The event sponsor writes Speaker B a lukewarm review, and references the phone call the speaker refused. This blurb serves no value to the agency or to the speaker, and leaves the agent upset. It's going to be a while before the agent pitches Speaker B again because she has proven to be difficult to work with, and the agent has likely lost the event sponsor's business for future events, which directly affects his income.

In Addition to Being Well Informed, Remember to Manage Expectations

Don't promise the world to either your agents or event sponsors. Overhyped speakers can run into massive problems when the outcome of a speech doesn't meet inflated expectations. And this isn't to say that the speech delivered won't be great, but if the sponsor and audience are expecting lobster and get steak, they're likely going to be frustrated that they didn't get the lobster that was promised. This promise to overdeliver may start with your agent—the agent needs to convey the facts about you and your wonderful speaking abilities without overselling. Which means that you need to manage your agents' expectations—don't promise your agents more than you can deliver. If it's one of your first speeches, talk to the agent who booked it for you. You're still becoming familiar with the industry and getting used to stepping behind the podium—they understand that and can help. I don't care who you are, but there is no way your first or second speech is going to be as good as your tenth or twentieth. In not promising the world to your agent, and in your agent—and you—not promising the world to an event sponsor, you are setting yourself up for success. You will probably deliver a better speech than expected—essentially serving lobster to an audience expecting steak—and that's the desired outcome.

Remember that a good outcome for the speaker can be fundamentally different than a good outcome for the event sponsor—and that's important to take to heart as you prepare.

Obviously, everyone—speaker, agent, and sponsor—is focused on a great overall event. However, that can look radically different from the viewpoint of speaker and sponsor. For starters, the speaker is guaranteed a five- or six-figure fee just for showing up. This means that the speaker gets paid even if the speech is bad and that the event sponsor is bearing the majority of the risk. On top of that, the speaker is possibly even benefiting beyond the honorarium—whether that's general brand-building, book or product sales, generating donations, building email lists, networking, spreading an idea or message, or getting a positive review from the event sponsor.

The event sponsor, however—while hopeful that the speaker will deliver a great speech—has to be concerned with technicalities. Things like attendance, the event space, and room setup, electronic needs like sound systems, smart podiums, and PowerPoint connections, in addition to the pre-event marketing and promotion, day-of issues like transportation, speaker greeting, seating, and impressing their bosses with the quality of the event.

This means that the agent, speaker, and event sponsor have to be able to separate perceptions of the quality of the event carefully. The event may have a disappointing outcome for reasons that have nothing to do with the speaker—things like poor turnout or a failed sound system can lead to an unsatisfactory outcome—one the event sponsor may erroneously attribute to the speaker. Understanding these dynamics going into an event will help you on the day of.

Should I write a speech or wing it? Or should I do something in between?

This is tricky, and usually each speaker has to find his or her own way—and each event will have different requirements. For example, a panel discussion is one thing, but very few people can speak extemporaneously for something like a keynote speech successfully. Not only do you likely need to draft a speech for a formal presentation, but you need to practice it. Ideally, by giving it out loud before an audience—even an audience of friends and family*—and timing it. How many words and pages of material you need for a forty-five-minute keynote can vary based on the average number of words you speak per minute—and you don't want to run out of material, look at the clock, and see that twenty minutes are still left. Jokes that sound good on paper may land flat with an audience. Your speech may suffer from lack of clarity, your opening may be weak, or you may struggle with pacing. All of this can be prevented with practice. With practice you might also find that you don't know where to stand, or what to do with your hands, or where to look. You might decide that you want interactive material like PowerPoint slides to help anchor you while other speakers might find that they hate the technical encumbrance and find slides to be distracting. Some speakers are great on the fly, while other speakers find a drafted speech that they can memorize to be imperative. Some draft a speech word for word and then reduce it down to bullet points. Further, some of the best speeches appear to be one thing—off the top of the head—and they are in fact highly rehearsed and tested over and again before practice audiences. All of this needs to be worked through by each speaker and for each event—at least the first few

---

* There are a lot of creative ways you can do this. I once had a deal with an acting school in which I could have speakers give sample talks to an audience of acting students to get feedback on performance.

times each talk is given—and practice gives speakers confidence, so it's often best to over-prepare.

When Preparing—and Giving—Your Speech, Be Careful Not to Be Too "Salesy"

In my experience, it's *never* wise to sell from the stage—whether it's books, private coaching sessions, or the upcoming retreat you're hosting that still has tickets available. Frankly, it upsets the sponsors. They are paying for your speaking content, and don't want you to use their stage as a platform to sell something to the audience—unless that was specifically prearranged. This means that you should focus on delivering a great speech, not push something on the audience, mentioning perhaps that you have a new book out multiple times and that there is a bookseller on site if anyone wants to purchase a copy. Stick to delivering a great speech—which is the sale that's *already* been made and (with few exceptions) has the most monetary value, meaning if you are receiving $10,000 to deliver a speech you aren't going to make $10,000 selling books in the back of the room. The best way to handle sales is by simply mentioning once that you'd love to meet anyone who wants to talk with you and that you'll be signing books in the back of the room. This message is clear, to the point, and takes five seconds to deliver at the tail end of your presentation. Or you can weave the book—or whatever you are selling—into your talk *once* in a non-salesy way, perhaps saying something like, *When I wrote about this topic in my book* One Great Speech, *a well-known publication suggested...here's why I think they are wrong.* Or, *At my last seminar a participant told me...* That makes the back-end sale a part of your message, and gets the point across without being overbearing.

And Finally, a Few Tips for the Day of the Event

What do I wear?

I've represented speakers who arrive at their events in three-piece suits, and I've represented speakers who go on stage barefoot sporting a T-shirt and jeans. And guess what? Not one event sponsor has ever complained about the speaker's attire. Here's why: *In all cases the attire was on brand.*

The most important aspect of any given speech is authenticity; authenticity of message and authenticity of the speaker. Obviously, you should look professional and be dressed accordingly. If you're speaking at a sales conference in the finance industry, it might be wise to throw on a blazer or dress a bit nicer than you might for a family get-together, but—assuming your attire is aligned with your message and your overall brand—failing to do so probably isn't going to work against you. In other words, if you were hired to give a speech at that finance conference about finding inner peace through big wave surfing, the flip-flops might be on point even though the bankers are wearing suits. This is also a good question to ask your agent about when you accept the gig, or during your pre-event call.

What about day-of details and travel?

Your contract will likely stipulate specific provisions for things like food and beverage and a green room so you can rest and prepare prior to going on stage. There will also be stipulations for what is required of you in addition to the talk—so make sure you are familiar with what you are contracted to deliver beyond your actual speech.

Your travel will either be arranged for you by the event sponsor as part of your deal, or your agent will negotiate a buyout in which you will be paid a stipend above the honorarium to cover travel that you will then arrange for yourself or that your agency will arrange for you. Ideally, whoever arranges your travel will see to it that you have a safe travel window. For example, you don't want to cut it close and potentially miss your speech by flying in on the day of the event. Remember, if your flight is delayed or there is bad traffic, you might miss the event and therefore not get paid. In fact, not showing up is virtually the only way a speaker won't get paid for an event, so arriving early is both necessary and smart.

Case Study: What If Things Go Really Badly?

Speaker A and Speaker B

I was once invited to give a speech at MIT. I was really, really nervous but also really excited to be speaking at such a prestigious institution. The speaking topic was one of my favorites—social enterprise—and I looked forward to sharing my ideas with the audience. Upon arriving, the event sponsor who booked the speech warmly greeted me and made me feel right at home. Then things suddenly took a turn for the worse. A professor got on stage to introduce me. During his introduction, he said multiple times that my ideas were wrong, and that the information in my presentation was going to be incorrect. Imagine my horror as I stepped on stage to lecture to a group of students who had just been told that everything I was about to say was wrong.

Now this leads to an important question: If the professor thought my ideas were wrong, why was I invited to speak in the first place?

The answer is simple. The person who booked me for the speech was not the person who introduced me on stage. In other words, the professor didn't get the speaker he wanted, so he decided to embarrass me and the person who booked me. I had no choice other than to do my very best. Several students approached me after the speech to say what a great job I had done, and I walked away feeling bruised but content.

I've never heard of a situation like this in my career as a speaking agent, but it goes to show that you have to be ready for anything. And no story encapsulates that fact better than what happened to Speaker B, Teddy Roosevelt.

In 1912, Teddy Roosevelt—already a two-time president and seeking a third term in office—pulled off one of the most legendary speeches of all time. His opponents were Woodrow Wilson and William Taft, and many Americans were displeased that Roosevelt was seeking a third term on a third party—the progressive Bull Moose—ticket.

Ever the showman, Roosevelt took advantage of his popularity and toured the country to empower supporters. He regularly spoke on city streets, the front steps of hotels and at lodges—wherever there might be a supporter, Roosevelt was there preaching his message.

On October 14, 1912, in Milwaukee, Wisconsin, something amazing happened. Roosevelt left his hotel for his speech at a local auditorium carrying a folded, fifty-page version of his speech notes in his breast pocket. In front of Roosevelt's hotel, a local business owner named John Shrank fired a .38-caliber pistol, hitting Roosevelt in the chest. Amazingly, despite the bullet entering Roosevelt's body, the fifty pages in his pocket were enough to slow the bullet down so that it didn't kill him.

Roosevelt, bullet wound and all, proceeded to take the stage and deliver an impassioned eighty-four-minute speech: "Friends, I shall ask you to be as quiet as possible. I don't know whether you fully understand that I have just been shot; but it takes more than that to kill a Bull Moose. But fortunately I had my manuscript,

[He holds the folded manuscript up for the audience to see] so you see I was going to make a long speech, and there is a bullet—there is where the bullet went through—and it probably saved me from it going into my heart. The bullet is in me now, so that I cannot make a very long speech, but I will try my best."

TAKEAWAYS

Prepare for every speech by asking questions; be clear you understand who the audience is, understand exactly what is expected of you, and prepare accordingly. Have a conference call with your agent and event sponsor to become as informed as possible

Follow up with a call to your agent to make sure you understand everything completely

Remember that different audiences may require different types of preparation

Manage expectations by not overpromising

Go into a speech knowing that sometimes expectations don't align with the outcome, but that you can mitigate this in part by not overpromising

If a speech lands badly, ask your agent why, and what you can do to improve, but don't take the blame for things that are not your fault

Don't be too salesy on stage

Dress comfortably, authentically, and on brand

Create a safe travel window so you don't miss the event

If things go horribly wrong, know that you are not alone

14.

After the Speech

HOW CAN YOU LEVERAGE THE TALK YOU JUST GAVE GOING FORWARD?

Once you step off the stage you have a new job—leveraging the speech you just gave. Exactly how you do this will depend on what you are trying to accomplish by speaking. There are two component pieces to this post-speech assignment while you are still at the event.

The first is brand-building and marketing. If you are trying to network and build contacts, you will likely want to have a plan for data capture; for example, collecting email addresses. If you are selling something or promoting something—say an upcoming event, a nonprofit organization, or a new book—this is the time to work that angle. That may mean a book signing or bringing flyers or other promotional material to distribute.

The second component piece revolves around tying together the loose ends of the event itself. You will want to meet with the event sponsor and any other important people associated with the event and "work the room." To tie up an event, you want to be gracious and thankful and make yourself available to the sponsor and audience.

What is the best way to leverage the positive energy of a good speech while still on site and engage with audience members after the speech?

Post-speech interaction in one fashion or another is a normal part of what's expected at speaking events. It's also wise for your career—you never know who you are going to meet from that audience. Typically, event sponsors will have some sort of meet and greet, book signing, or reception set up following your speech. If not, see if you can get your agent to make this happen. The additional interaction will make the event sponsor feel good, as they feel they are getting more value—and it will be beneficial for you to meet people who likely enjoyed your speech and who want to interact with you.

I once worked with a speaker named Philip who had an incredible story about sailing his boat through a storm and almost dying at sea. He spoke about how to apply the lessons he learned and the tactics he used to survive to help others navigate the rough waters of everyday life. Philip had written a book about his experience, and he always made sure that his agents included a meet and greet at every event. This was part book signing, and part post-event conversation. Although the idea was Philip's, the agents at my company loved the fact that he was willing and eager to go the extra mile for the sponsor—even though it was mostly for his own benefit.

By engaging with audience members, Philip sold additional books and met college students and corporate employees with whom he otherwise never would have interacted. One day Philip called me after he gave a speech at a fairly large financial institution and told me that two of the audience members spoke with him after the event and were interested in helping him build a nonprofit organization that focused on teaching inner-city youth how to sail. Philip had mentioned his interest in doing so in his speech and had explained that research showed that when kids in the inner city get exposure to the outdoors it benefits them in the classroom. So simply by participating in a post-event meet and greet, Philip secured funding for the nonprofit he wanted to create. And this type of thing happens more often than you might think.

Case Study: Leveraging Up

The $500 Speech and the Six-Figure Donation

I once represented a speaker named Ally who worked at a non-profit that helped other nonprofits raise and deploy capital. She was a fairly popular speaker who was booked about six times a year, usually at other nonprofit organizations, and typically in the $7,500 range—a fee that went directly to the organization she worked for. Although she wasn't the founder, and didn't run the nonprofit herself, her boss was enthusiastic that Ally was representing his organization while he could stay in the office to focus on day-to-day management.

One day, we got an unusual request—an event sponsor asked if Ally would be interested in speaking on a panel to an audience of corporate leaders. The problem was that they could only offer her $500, plus travel expenses. The upside, as the sponsor explained, was that even though the speaking fee was low, the event could lead to donations to her nonprofit. The sponsor went on to explain that the year prior, a speaker raised $250,000 for his organization at this annual event.

I called Ally with the offer and explained what had happened the year prior. I also told her to take this information with a grain of salt. Event sponsors often make inflated—if not grandiose— comments in order to secure speakers at low prices. Ally spoke with her boss, did some research online, and decided that the event was worth the effort.

On the day of the event, Ally was part of a four-person panel and dominated the conversation in the best of ways. Following the event, she was mobbed by members of the audience who wanted to be involved, donate, and help in any way they could. Ally's nonprofit had set up a unique link for donations generated specifically by this event, information that Ally provided once onstage and on the business cards she handed out following her speech. Ten days later, Ally and her organization had raised in the vicinity of $225,000 directly from this event, simply as a result of her $500 panel appearance. This was more money than her organization had raised in the previous four years combined.

When considering events, it's wise to take into account the potential upside beyond the speaking fee. Ally's boss, and Ally herself, had the foresight to consider the potential benefits of exposure and networking. The potential downside in this case was that Ally would miss a day of work, but she did receive a $500 fee. The actual upside exceeded their wildest dreams—a cumulative six-figure donation and building massive awareness about their cause.

How should I approach data capture?

With a few exceptions, data capture via networking tends to occur more during corporate events, where meet and greets are more popular, than at universities. Having said that, I once had a client speaking at the University of North Carolina who provided a phone number that the audience could text message during the speech, and he received over one thousand text messages within two hours. Since the speaker was the CEO of a consumer packaged goods company, this type of data collection had significant value. Suddenly he had the email addresses and phone numbers for one thousand college tastemakers. Companies seek—and pay for—information like this. And if you're speaking to a rapt and targeted audience in a packed house, it can be very easy to collect useful information for free without coming off as a salesperson—if you approach it correctly. And data from corporate or nonprofit audiences can have more value than that from colleges since most college email addresses expire after graduation. But regardless of who you are trying to capture data from, it should be approached without being too aggressive.

You should offer a clear value to the audience as to why you are gathering contact information. It could be for your monthly newsletter or it could be to share updates about an upcoming book release, or any number of other things, but that value to the audience should be made evident. If speaking at a corporation, try to connect with as many people in the audience as you can, and focus on collecting business cards or email addresses after the speech—*but only if they are volunteered*. It can be shrewd to have a mailing list sign-up sheet on a clipboard. This way it won't come off as salesy or self-promoting—you're not actually asking for anything. Then, during the natural flow of conversation with audience members, *offer them your business card or a small flyer*. In my experience, most audience members are thrilled to connect with a speaker one-on-one, and this is an easy way to network.

As Philip's story just demonstrated, you never know when someone from the audience might reach out to you with a question, a proposition, or something else that's meaningful to your career—either as a speaker or related to other opportunities—and this can happen both on site and after you leave the event.

Case Study: Can I Have Your Contact Information?

Speaker A or Speaker B?

Speaker A is giving a speech at a conference about solar energy. He runs a small company based in New England and decides to incorporate an email address into his PowerPoint presentation. He figures that if people in the audience want to connect with him, they'll get the idea—after all, his email address is unassumingly placed in the lower right-hand corner of every slide, even though he doesn't mention it or invite anyone to contact him.

Speaker B is giving a presentation at a consortium of entrepreneurs who are focused on retail sales. Speaker B is the perfect speaker for an event like this because he has been in the retail industry for over thirty years. Prior to the event, he places a flyer on every seat in the auditorium with his contact information, asking each audience member for his or her name, phone number (for text message marketing), and email address.

Speaker A delivers a wonderful speech and gets a standing ovation. He speaks individually with audience members following the engagement, where he answers questions about his business, his unique offering, and even about how he got into the solar panel business to begin with. This is a great way to further engage the audience, and he does so without ever asking anyone for contact information.

Speaker B also delivers a great speech, and several members of the audience wait for him after the presentation to ask questions about sales challenges, how to expand in the incredibly competitive retail industry, and how he got to where he is. Speaker B asks each and every person he speaks with for their contact information, even though he already placed questionnaires on every seat in the auditorium.

Speaker A returns to his office the following day to find over two hundred emails from audience members in his inbox. Some have follow-up questions, and some are even looking to place orders through his company.

Speaker B collects the questionnaires from the auditorium, only to find that about twenty of them have been filled out. Since he gave such a great presentation, he doesn't understand why he didn't capture more data.

Why did Speaker B fail to collect contact information while Speaker A succeeded? The answer is simple. People are more likely to provide sensitive contact information when they feel that it's *their own choice*. By placing questionnaires on every seat in the venue, Speaker B made the audience feel pressured. He was asking for something that *he* could leverage—*their* contact info. While Speaker A quietly offered *his* contact information, asking nothing of the audience, he succeeded in allowing the people in attendance to feel safe, in control, and like they had a choice. He gave them something *they* could leverage if they chose to—*his* contact info.

In the technology sector, these techniques refer to active data and passive data collection (or explicit data and implicit data collection). Active data is data that needs to be requested from someone. Passive data is data that is collected without asking people for it. Speaker A succeeded in collecting useful information by taking the passive data approach—once someone from the audience emailed him, he now had their contact info. Plus, it was the contact information of a high-value prospect. Speaker B failed because he took the active data approach. And even if Speaker B had collected contact information on the questionnaires filled out prior to his speech, its value would be questionable. After all, he may have collected the contact information from people who hated his speech and had no interest in hearing from him.

So, remember that when thinking about collecting emails, phone numbers, or social media information, it is always important to consider the smartest way to do this, whether that means taking an active or passive approach.

Case Study: The Charter School Teacher and the Clipboard

I once worked with a charter school teacher named Liz. She was an expert on a variety of topics ranging from early childhood education to fund-raising, from building communities to how to train teachers to be their best when working in difficult—and sometimes dangerous—environments.

After her first several presentations, Liz was getting swarmed by teachers from the audience who had additional questions and ideas. Liz spoke with as many people as she could but lamented to me that she didn't feel like she was doing enough to capture contact information from members of the audience. She saw an opportunity to turn some of these audience members into paying clients for consulting down the road. At first, she was scribbling names and email addresses on scraps of paper, but by the time she got home she couldn't remember who was who. The solution to this problem was easy and effective. We set up a spreadsheet that simply asked for names, email addresses, and topics of interest. As Liz walked around the post-event conference rooms, she was able to direct everyone who had expressed interest in getting more help to the spreadsheet. And, as it turns out, many of those audience members ended up contacting Liz for private coaching, help with job placement, and even information about future seminars.

While creating a spreadsheet might sound painfully simple

and obvious, you'd be surprised how many speakers fail to do this. It's an easy solution to a common problem. Liz wasn't actively walking around with a clipboard signing people up for potential future services. She simply set up a way to capture the key information that she needed in order to stay in touch with interested parties. In addition to the spreadsheet, she also created a four-by-six-inch flyer with her name, contact information, and a list of the services she offered outside of speaking. She left the flyers right next to the spreadsheet, and on average went through about one hundred flyers per night.

Note the simple but significant difference in approach between Liz and Speaker B in the earlier example who left questionnaires on seats prior to the event and got nowhere. A sign-up sheet after the event self-selects high-value prospects. They've already been sold by your presentation. Requesting this information up front feels like an "ask" before the audience members know if they want to buy. And by laying the groundwork to create value in the future, Liz ensured that she was maximizing the outcomes of her speeches without being pushy or overly aggressive.

What if I'm selling something on the back end?

Lots of speakers have books that they are hoping to sell at each event. It's best to have a local bookseller who reports to BookScan* on site handling the sales rather than attempting to do it yourself. Invite a local vendor to come in, set up a table, and manage all of the book sales so that you can focus on your speech. This also makes you look more professional and your agent can set it up for you.

---

* NPD BookScan is a tracking service that provides authors and industry personnel with sales numbers for books sold, covering a large percentage of the retail market including POS data from major booksellers, independent bookstores, and mass merchandisers.

I once had a speaker mention his book being for sale over a dozen times during the course of his speech. The event sponsor was miffed and told me so when I followed up, saying, "We paid $25,000 for this speaker to visit and all he tried to do was push $20 book sales to our audience of three hundred college students." The speaker ended up selling about ten books, grossing $200, the entirety of which went to his publisher since he hadn't yet covered his advance. So, this speaker didn't provide the best speech possible and got a negative review all because he foolishly focused on the short money—pitching his book a dozen times from the stage.

So, don't sell from the stage. At most, make one mention of the book that will be for sale at the back of the venue toward the end of your speech. Perhaps saying at the close of your talk, "Thank you so much for inviting me. There are books available in the back of the auditorium for those who are interested."

Case Study: Leveraging Down
The $50,000 Speech and the Pushy Speaker

In April 2015, I booked a high-profile speaker who ran a T-shirt company for an annual retreat for bankers and people in the financial industry for $50,000. The speaker was excited about the invitation and prepared his standard speech—with one exception. Given the size of the crowd and the potential money in the audience, he decided to push his new book from the stage—and push it hard. About six months earlier he had self-published a book—meaning all of the proceeds would go to him as opposed to a publisher. This book was about following your passions, even if they seemed as silly as starting a T-shirt company.

During the speech, he made over fifteen references to his book being available both in the back of the speaking venue and online. Not only was the sponsor annoyed—this isn't what she was paying for—but the audience was annoyed as well. They felt like they were "watching a live infomercial" as the sponsor later explained to me on the phone. To make things worse, because this was a conference, there were a number of audience members who were in charge of booking speakers at *their* events, many of whom had already expressed interest to me in booking this speaker down the line.

Not a single event sponsor in the audience was still interested after seeing him speak. I figured that if even six or seven of the sponsors in the audience had followed through on their initial interest, we would have generated at least $300,000 in additional speaking fees—this was a household-name company, the speaker got $50,000 per event, and he had a big story. But instead, the speaker walked out of the event with a few book sales, which probably totaled a few hundred dollars, and lost out on hundreds of thousands of dollars or more in future bookings. In the following months, we were forced to reduce his speaking fee out of fear that he would do this again, and we were less confident in booking him. So, aside from annoying the audience and hurting the relationship the agency had with the sponsor, he also lost money on future bookings. By being pushy and forcing a sale from the stage, you can drive away potential business, positive reviews, and even your agents.

What if I am selling something on the back end bigger than a book? Say, up-selling? Beyond waiting until after the event, how do I do so tastefully?

At certain conferences and consortiums, some speakers are up-selling expensive offerings like seminars—but in these cases the event sponsor is aware that this will be happening, and the audience is prepared to be pitched on a product or service. As long as this is expected within the structure of the event, it's fine to do. But even in these situations, it's important to consider how you present your offering. Whether you're pushing a consumer packaged good, a retreat, or a service, consider that the best way to advertise anything is by first *demonstrating value*. And leading with content—as opposed to a sales pitch—is the best way to accomplish this. For example, it's better to get a good chunk of the speech out of the way before announcing your upcoming leadership retreat. And doing so will lead to more sales.

Early in my career I worked with a bestselling author who wrote and spoke about the "art" of picking up women. His primary audience was shy young men who had trouble approaching the opposite sex, and he regularly ran seminars outside of the paid speaking events he received. The sponsors accepted that the up-sell would be part of the presentation but only because it had been cleared ahead of time. And it worked to everyone's benefit. The audience members really wanted help and didn't mind being pitched, and his paid speeches were always well received. As a result the speaker was generally able to find a few audience members who were willing to spend the $10,000 he charged to attend his annual seminar in Las Vegas. Employing a clever advertising model, he had a reference to the up-sell annual retreat at the bottom of every slide in his PowerPoint presentation, but he only mentioned the retreat once, at the very end of his speech. It was a subtle yet effective way to passively advertise his up-sell without standing on stage and soliciting ticket sales or appearing salesy.

How should I best interact with the event sponsor after the event?

If the event sponsor wants to speak with you—or better yet spend time with you—after the speech, you should absolutely do so. This said, you should leave questions regarding audience feedback, audience engagement, and future bookings for your agent to handle. The post-event phone call is an important aspect of the agenting process for two reasons.

1. The event sponsor is always going to be more honest with your agent than she will be with you. In other words, a sponsor may tell you that you were great because it's difficult to be entirely honest with someone when speaking face to face.

2. Your agent likely works with this event sponsor regularly—or hopes to—and needs an excuse to follow up to see how things went. It works to your advantage to allow your agent the opportunity to do so.

I once worked with a speaker who always spoke with the event sponsor after his speeches, and he always got great feedback—according to him, anyway. But because the sponsor spoke with the speaker directly, when I called the speaker with constructive criticism I got from the sponsor he would push back, saying, "I spoke with the sponsor and she said I was the best speaker they've had in years." Suddenly my advice, which was a direct result of speaking candidly with the event sponsor, didn't hold water. The speaker thought he was the best thing since sliced bread and refused to listen to real feedback from me.

If I wallpaper my living room and invite my best friend over to my house to see it, she's going to tell me how great it looks. But if I show my living room to a wallpaper professional, he might give me feedback as to the small lumps underneath the paper, how certain pieces don't line up perfectly, or that I used too much water while papering. This is the importance of third-party feedback. By speaking with an objective individual with whom you can be honest, you can not only get the most accurate feedback, but also learn how to improve your performance in the future. As a speaker, you always want to be getting better, so allow your agent to do her job and provide you with objective feedback that can be used to further your career—whether it's more event bookings, increased fees, or both.

Why a "Bad" Speech Might Have Nothing to Do with Your Actual Speech

When an agent calls an event sponsor after your speech the agent usually receives feedback about your performance and then relays this information to you. As mentioned earlier, event sponsors, particularly the day-of contact, have a *lot* going on. They are counting tickets, worried about the sound system, worried about negative faculty or employee—or upper management—feedback, worried about keeping the speaker happy, and so on. In other words, the sponsor isn't only thinking about the speaker—or the actual speech—on the day of any given event.

Imagine the following scenario: you go out to dinner at a fancy new restaurant. The food is amazing, prepared by a three-star Michelin chef, and you have great conversation with your dinner party. Then, when it's time for dessert, the waiter trips and spills red wine all over your brand-new white shirt. You might be inclined to go on Yelp and post a negative review about the service. The thing is, short of the wine-spilling, the experience was great. So a *single miscue* can outweigh the positives and garner a negative review.

It is not unusual for similar things to happen in the speaking world. For example, you give a great speech but the auditorium is only half full. Or perhaps you give a great speech but the sound system cuts in and out, making it difficult to hear and you come off as unprofessional. These kinds of things can directly affect speaker reviews. If a school pays $10,000 for you to speak and there is a snowstorm that prevents people from attending, the event sponsor is likely upset that they "wasted" money on the event. But, of course, we can't control the weather or the attendance or the sound system.

So, in the follow-up call, it's important that your agent is asking the right questions. *Did you deliver the expected content? Were you engaged and approachable? Did you honor your contract?* If your agent isn't asking these questions, he should be. And if he is, you need to understand the distinct line between the *speech* and the *event*. Remember, event sponsors are under a lot of pressure too. In fact, they may feel like their job is on the line.

Now, if the feedback about your speech itself is negative, it's important to find out the specifics as to what was missed in the presentation. Maybe the talk leaned a little too much to the corporate side and you, the speaker, were presenting to a university audience. Maybe it's that you failed to engage with the audience at the level the speaker expected. Maybe the Q&A was weak. These are factors that you should consider when preparing for the next speech, with the goal of improving and growing in the process.

Case Study: How Not to Interact with an Event Sponsor

I once represented a speaker—Katherine—who always refused to participate in Q&A sessions. A few months into representing her, an event sponsor insisted on Q&A being part of the event—without the Q&A we wouldn't have a deal. I called Katherine and told her that we had a $10,000 offer but it was contingent upon a thirty-minute Q&A session. At first she balked but, deciding that the money was too significant to turn down, she accepted the gig. Our pre-event conference call went swimmingly, and I was confident that Katherine would deliver. On the day of the event, however, following her speech, she simply walked off the stage without participating in the Q&A session. The event sponsor wanted her to go back on stage to fulfill her contractual obligation—particularly because dozens of students were eagerly awaiting the opportunity to ask questions. Still Katherine refused, and the sponsor was faced with being in the awkward position of explaining to a room of five hundred people that the speaker wouldn't be participating in the Q&A session. And the sponsor didn't pull any punches—he specifically told the audience that despite signing a contract that stipulated Q&A, Katherine refused to participate. This kind of behavior is death in the speaking industry.

I got a call on my cell phone at ten o'clock that night from the sponsor, who was screaming. And I couldn't blame her. Rather than throwing the speaker under the bus, even though I was furious, I took the blame myself. After all, I provided a speaker who didn't deliver on what we promised. I told the sponsor that I should have known better, that I had known Katherine for a long time, and it was my fault for putting her in an uncomfortable situation. I should have made it clear with the event sponsor up front and suggested a different speaker, knowing that a Q&A session would be a problem for Katherine.

When I spoke with Katherine the following day, she explained to me that there were only five hundred people in a 1,500-capacity theater, and she felt misled by both me and the event sponsor as to the scope of the event. Of course, this is an unacceptable excuse, but it helped me to understand Katherine's frame of mind. She felt that because the turnout was poor she didn't need to fulfill her obligation to the five hundred people in the audience. Clearly, Katherine was wrong—it is not a contractual obligation of the sponsor to fill the room. I decided to offer the sponsor a $2,500 discount, which smoothed things over a bit, and I explained to Katherine that we were reducing her fee by 25 percent since she didn't honor her contract.

Managing expectations, and responding appropriately when those expectations are not met—for both the sponsor and the speaker—can be difficult waters to navigate. In this case, the speaker expected that there would be a packed house (which was unreasonable), and the sponsor expected Q&A with the audience (which was reasonable and contracted for). I explained to Katherine that she had to make a choice—either participate in events that have a Q&A component or turn down offers if they don't meet with her criteria. I also told her that the other agents in my office were aware of what happened, and they were concerned about pitching her to our valuable event sponsors in the future in fear of losing their business long term.

Katherine quickly apologized for her behavior, and when we dug deeper, we discovered that she was afraid to take questions from the audience because they weren't scripted and she felt uncomfortable, fearing that she might not come off as well as she did during her controlled speeches. So we found a solution— all questions in the future would be prescreened in advance so that Katherine would have the opportunity to prepare for them. When we shared this information with event sponsors, they were perfectly happy to have their questions prescreened and Katherine ended up including Q&A sessions in many of her future speeches. We learned a valuable lesson about managing expectations on both sides of the fence—Katherine needed the audience's questions ahead of time, and the event sponsors understood that this is what would help Katherine give her best performance. Sometimes it only takes some simple communication with all parties in order to avoid disasters and make an event successful for all involved.

How to Shake It Off If You Have a Bad Speech

So, you had a bad speech. This will eventually happen to everyone and you shouldn't let it destroy you—but you shouldn't dismiss it either. I almost always find that great speeches aren't as great as you think they are and bad speeches are never as bad as you think they are either. If you do give a bad speech, talk to your agent. Did you know it was bad during the event, or is this impression from sponsor feedback? Discuss what you could have done better, and be sure to take the critical feedback with a grain of salt. As discussed earlier, the sponsor may not be right; sometimes negative reviews have more to do with the audience, attendance, the weather, sound production, and dozens of other variables that have nothing to do with the speaker. There is also the possibility that you and your topic simply weren't a good fit for the program. In other cases, the speech itself actually wasn't that good, and the feedback from the sponsor can be incredibly helpful. Take the feedback as a challenge to do better the next time around. And keep working on improving. I once had a speaker vomit on stage—she was pregnant—and the reviews weren't great. But not because of the vomiting. The sponsor said she was impressed that the speaker made such an effort, even with morning sickness. But the speech wasn't well received because the speaker didn't deliver the content the event sponsor was looking for. This said, the speaker shook it off. She didn't quit. She learned from it, recovered, and went on to give many successful speeches.

TAKEAWAYS

Engage with audience members after the speech

Leverage the positive energy of a good speech while still on site through positive interaction

Don't be too "salesy," but don't be afraid to capture audience information

When selling something on the back end, be mindful not to offend the sponsor or audience

Interact with the buyer after the event without stepping on your agent's toes

Shake it off if you have a bad speech but learn from it—there will be more opportunities to come

15.

But What If I Tried and Failed?

BE RESILIENT AND PERSEVERE

Let's say you've met with a speaking agent or agency owner and are lucky enough to get signed to an exclusive contract. You're excited—and they're excited about working with you. They go to work on spec to get your materials—your speech topics, bio, and collateral marketing—formatted, in shape, and posted on their website. The agents familiarize themselves with your background and the topics you're hoping to lecture about and can now discuss you intelligently with potential event sponsors. They've likely had an agency-wide meeting to discuss all of the possible places and programs where you'd be a good fit.

Then the agents hit the phones and start pitching you. They spend hours talking with event sponsors at universities, corporations, and nonprofits, introducing you as a possible speaker when appropriate. They soft-pitch you to judge interest for panel discussions, conferences, consortiums, retreats, symposiums, and the like—anything for which you're a good candidate. They may even suggest creative ways to wrangle a first gig or two—saying perhaps, *I know we've already booked Paul and Alyssa for your innovation panel, but for a few more dollars I might be able to get you Francesca—she's a great speaker and has an interesting position on the future of health care.*

Hopefully offers start coming in. Hopefully you accept them, and you get your first few bookings and events under your belt.

Based on your experience, you learn a few things. You then refine your presentations, take the feedback your agent got from each event sponsor, and refine your topics even further. These early bookings are added to your résumé and the agents, invigorated by your success, continue to pitch you for the never-ending stream of speaking opportunities around the world, saying, *Francesca just got rave reviews for her last Fortune 100 keynote and I think she'd be perfect for your upcoming event.*

But let's say that doesn't happen. Instead, you sign with a speaking agency, upload your material, get pitched, and *you never get a single offer.* Crickets.

What then?

You're hugely disappointed. Some speakers even get angry when they aren't being booked, when they aren't getting booked enough, or when they aren't getting what they perceive as high enough fees or prestigious enough events. Getting booked at a pancake breakfast still pays, but it usually doesn't come with a high fee or carry the résumé-building gravitas that a university distinguished lecture series or a keynote speech at a major corporation does.

What you have to understand is that when you're signed exclusively to an agency and aren't getting booked, the agents are hugely disappointed too—perhaps even more so than you are. Remember, *the agency thought they could book you or they wouldn't have signed you.*

They've worked for many hours pitching you on the phone—on spec—to try to get you paid speaking engagements. And they, in most cases, have to make dollar and booking quotas to meet their draw, or they don't eat. And if they don't book speakers consistently, they will lose their jobs. So, despite what you might think, they are trying very hard to book you.

You, on the other hand, by signing with an agency, *face nothing but upside.* There's no up-front fee—so you haven't gone out of pocket for the opportunity—and if your agency is pitching you as they should be, your name, your face, and the name of your brand or your cause are all getting exposure, regardless of whether or not you are actually booked to speak anywhere. Which means that in the paid speaking industry, as counterintuitive as it sounds, if you're signed with an agency you almost can't fail—even if you are never booked. I like to think about speaking agency representation as secondary PR for which the speaker pays absolutely nothing. And it's PR that you may monetize in ways that don't mandate you getting speaking engagements.

Visitors to your speaking agency's website see your name and picture—and possibly your fee—and some will read your background material. Agents are actively pitching you on the phone to event buyers, more often than not at prestigious institutions with high visibility and enormous reach. *This is advertising you didn't pay for that's increasing your profile.*

Regardless of what field you work in, if you're applying for a job and a potential employer happens to Google you and sees your speaking profile and speech topics professionally presented on a reputable speaking agency website, it enhances your perceived value. You've been validated as an in-demand expert, even if you've never actually given a paid speech—something that potential employer probably isn't aware of.

If you go out to agents or publishers with a book proposal, your presence on a speaking agency website is validation of your expertise—and your commitment to marketing—as well. If you run a nonprofit, your organization's name and mission are also being discussed with event buyers, which can raise brand awareness and possibly lead to increased donations even without a single booking. The more you're out there and the higher your visibility, the greater the number of opportunities you'll receive—whether those opportunities manifest as paid speaking gigs or not.

Case Study: The Niche Beauty Brand and the Swag Bags

My agency had been pitching the founder of a relatively new beauty brand as a speaker and while we were getting him some gigs, we weren't getting him as many as he—or we—had hoped for. At one point, we pitched him for a keynote speech at a media company where the event sponsor had never heard of his brand—which is not that uncommon. Agents spend a lot of time explaining the qualifications of hugely successful potential speakers to event sponsors. If you happen to be an English professor who books events for a university's alumni association dinner, you don't necessarily know the name and reputation of the amazing expert on coral reefs or recognize the name of the Nobel Prize winner in physics, let alone know the founder of a niche beauty brand—even if his company's products are sold at major retail outlets.

In this case, we were presenting the founder of this beauty brand as innovative, creative, and funny. He was the caretaker of a young, growing company with a great line of products that were ethically sourced and had an intriguing tie to philanthropy in education, nutrition, and the health of young children.

The event sponsor at the media company liked everything she heard, but eventually decided to book someone else for the keynote address—which also isn't uncommon. *Everyone* we pitch is an interesting candidate with a unique background, and even the biggest speakers don't get booked for every event they're pitched for.

What we didn't know was that this particular media organization was also producing a music awards show that would be distributing gift bags to attendees. The event buyer had been so impressed with our spin on this niche beauty brand that she called back and offered to purchase $50,000 worth of product for the show's gift bags. This wouldn't have happened were it not for my agency's failed attempt at pitching the founder for a speaking opportunity. *Because he was signed to a speaking agency and was actively being pitched, he received $50,000 in sales without lifting a finger.*

Now, obviously, no bookings—or few bookings—is not the desired outcome. Not for you as a speaker, and not for your agency. But the lesson in this story is twofold:

▶ Remember that the speaking agency is taking on most of the risk in the speaker-agency relationship. *Understanding this will change both your behavior and your expectations.*

▶ A potential speaker can do a lot to prevent the sometimes inevitable—but hopefully avoidable—outcome of no bookings, few bookings, or stagnated growth. In other words, if you've already tried and failed to be a speaker, you may be able to fix it. And, if you're just starting out, you can make sure to present yourself in a manner that gives you the best possible shot at success.

TAKEAWAYS

In the paid speaking industry, as counterintuitive as it sounds, there is no failure

Being repped by an agency adds prestige to your personal brand

Sometimes a "non-booking" can turn into something extremely positive

Even the biggest speakers don't get booked for all the events they are pitched for

If you've tried and failed to be a paid speaker, there is a lot you can do to increase your chances of success

One Great Speech

THE MILLION-DOLLAR BALLOON

There is an old joke about a guy standing on a street corner selling balloons, and a man walks up to him and asks how much a balloon costs. The balloon salesman smiles and says, "One million dollars." The man, dumbfounded and baffled, scoffs and asks, "Why would you charge a million dollars for a balloon?" And the balloon salesman replies, "Because I only have to sell one."

One great speech can be your million-dollar balloon. Granted, we'll have to sell—and you'll have to give—that speech more than once. But if we can find—and perfectly brand and market—your speech, it can become your million-dollar balloon, the gift that keeps on giving.

The payoff for you can be in the form of speaker fees, or it can manifest in other ways. It can be the million-dollar brand you build for yourself or an increase in donations to your nonprofit—or it can be something far less quantifiable than either of those things. Your *one great speech* can be the million-dollar gift you give over and over again to audiences around the world by spreading a message that you feel passionate about. It can be the dissemination of your unique experience and knowledge told in your voice, with your own spin and perspective. You can have a million-dollar impact, become part of the human conversation.

The hallmarks of a singularly great speech? First, a universal, timeless message with significant audience takeaways.

Some topics are universally salable and have long legs. Some because they are *general*—for example, a speech about leadership during difficult times has long legs even though it faces a lot of competition. Some topics are universally salable because they are so *specific*—say, a particularly well-crafted concept that arose from a speaker's experience with a disability, a start-up, or a hobby. There are some topics that have expiration dates or limited markets or seasonal restrictions—or have no place in the commercial market at all. I once represented an undercover CIA agent who was in Osama bin Laden's inner circle—as a spy. He was featured in a segment of *60 Minutes* and had a bestselling book about 9/11. I remember the first time we met—there were armed guards in his office in New York City. I was certain that we could book him based on his credentials. And yet, it was an uphill battle. I learned that despite the enormous global magnitude of 9/11 and the massive loss of life, in the paid speaking market—at least with the event sponsors I worked with—9/11 is a seasonal request and the market is limited. Very few universities and no corporations were looking for speeches related to 9/11, and if they were, it was only around the anniversary of the terror attacks, which limits the market. Memorial events are limited in scope and generally don't require paid speakers—people *want* to speak at them for free. Speakers can get paid to talk about death and dying and cancer, but some messages and some topics should never come with a fee.

Second, one great speech also requires adaptability.

Hopefully, by launching with three solid, well-branded topics, one will stand out as the most viable for repeat bookings—and when it does, you'll know that you've found your *one great speech*. But you can't stop there. Successful professional speakers, particularly those who have found their *one great speech*, are great at modifying their presentations as needed or, as in the case of our happiness expert and the wedding planners, not modifying them at all. So, take your cues from the marketplace and welcome constructive criticism from event sponsors, audiences, agents—and your own gut.

Third, one great speech is properly priced and the speaker is easy to work with.

You can be the leading expert in the world on a particular topic, with the best speech in the world, but if your fee is unaffordable to most institutions, the world will never know that. So, price yourself appropriately.

Another common reality about booking speakers comes down to comfort. Your agent might get a phone call about booking a speaker who has more expertise than you do, but that speaker might be difficult to book due to his schedule or be difficult to work with in other ways. If you are positioned to buyers as a fairly priced expert who is easy to work with and gets great audience responses, you are halfway there.

Fourth, one great speech has to be proven in the marketplace.

Twelve bookings in a year is my benchmark for identifying *one great speech*. This means you're getting, on average, one booking a month. If your agent is able to book you that much, it means he or she is likely receiving three to four times as many inquiries about you. That means roughly an inquiry a week. Generally, do that consistently for two years—twenty-four bookings in twenty-four months—and you've proven your speech has legs. That is, as long as the topic you're being booked to speak about isn't time-sensitive. For example, you may get booked that frequently but your topic is about the upcoming presidential election, or is about your recent hot book, or is about an issue that is resolved, and therefore carries an expiration date.

But be careful here too—some books do have legs. I once worked with a speaker who wrote a Pulitzer Prize–winning book. The book has had long legs, was turned into a PBS documentary, and helped the author to cement himself as an incredibly successful, oft-requested speaker. Based on the success of the book, he didn't have to change his *one great speech* very much in the years after the book's publication.

Finally, one great speech demands a great relationship with your agency.

Don't ignore the importance of building a great relationship with your speaking agency. Accept gigs. Be a grateful speaker. Respect event sponsors and audiences. Overdeliver. Adapt and be flexible. It's all about relationships and mutual respect. Often the difference between *one great speech* that pays dividends for extended periods of time and *one great speech* that simply isn't being booked, is that one isn't being pitched all that often. Your agency wants you to find your *one great speech* just as much as you want to find it. It serves you both. So, work hard to establish that positive relationship.

Case Study: Who Is More Likely to Have One Great Speech?

Speaker A or Speaker B?

Speaker A is a holistic health speaker who teaches yoga and mindfulness. She gives presentations at universities and corporations about stress management, healthy living, and the impact they can have on performance at school, work, and in everyday life. She hasn't written a book but has a small blog with a few thousand followers. Every once in a while, she'll be asked to write an article for a newspaper, and she even appeared on the *Today Show* once to talk about these subjects.

Speaker B is a computer programmer who has worked on several popular video games. He speaks to university audiences about the joy he gets from designing games and working on a team. He has fantastic Q&A sessions at each event since the college students who come to his events are fervent gamers. When he speaks at corporations, he modifies his talk slightly to include more about team-building and the creative process. He has recently decided to leave his career as a video game designer to found a start-up focused on clean energy. He has never written a book, but he has been featured in several publications as one of the rising superstars in the gaming field.

Speaker A has been booked forty times in the last two years at events ranging from corporate retreats to college students during exam time. She keeps her price affordable—$10,000—and is willing to accept $7,500 if the circumstances are right. She has great reviews, a long list of places she's spoken, and an ever-growing mailing list as a result of all of her speaking events. So many contacts and followers, in fact, that she is considering writing a book for her expanding audience.

Speaker B has been booked twenty-two times in the last two years at events ranging from university arts programs to corporate conferences focused on technology. He keeps his price affordable too—$15,000—but is inflexible with his pricing due to the fact that it's costly for him to miss a day of work. Like Speaker A, he too has great reviews and a long list of places he's spoken but doesn't have a mailing list or a personal website. He has no interest in writing a book about gaming because he is focused on his new start-up venture.

Both Speaker A and Speaker B have generated roughly the same amount of money—$300,000—over the last two years. They've both given the number of required talks to have found their *one great speech*—roughly one booking a month for two years. But there is a distinct difference in these two speakers. One has found his or her *one great speech* and one hasn't.

Speaker A has *one great speech* and Speaker B doesn't. This is for a few reasons. Mainly, Speaker A's topic is never going to go out of style. Health and wellness is a big category, and interest in that space is not likely to wane. She will have steady demand and will probably have to change very little in her presentations for years to come. Students are always going to be stressed, corporations are always going to want to host wellness speakers, and happily she is flexible with her fee, which makes her easy to work with.

Speaker B, while booked the prerequisite number of times to qualify as having *one great speech*, is leaving his industry to found a new company that is unrelated to gaming. Further, video games are released, become hot, and then fade away when new games come out. It's highly likely that anyone booking a video game speaker or a coder won't be interested in Speaker B once he's left the industry and has no new games being released. After all, in some industries, you're only as popular as your last hit. And it's highly unlikely that Speaker B will find success—at least not immediately—in giving speeches about clean energy. He's new to the market, and there's massive competition in the speaking industry for these types of talks. But here is what truly separates Speaker A and Speaker B and propels the career of Speaker A and limits the career of Speaker B. *Speaker A built a brand and Speaker B did not.*

Case Study: How I Booked the Same Speech over One Hundred Times

I once represented a speaker who spoke about global warming and the environment. Alice had a popular book that was a common read at a number of universities. Because she had booked herself for several engagements prior to signing with my agency and she was confident that she knew what worked, she only had one speech topic—not two or three. She agreed to price herself affordably—$7,500–$10,000 a night—and after she signed with my agency, we started booking her almost immediately. The keys to Alice's success were that she had a universal topic (just like health and wellness, global warming is a popular subject that isn't going away anytime soon), she was affordable, her topic overlapped different academic departments that were often able to combine their budgets to meet her fee (for example, the English department, the science department, and the environmental studies department). Event sponsors loved that she came with great content and was affordable and, because her topic overlapped three areas of study—English (the writing aspect), science (the data that was driving her topic), and environment (what she was really speaking about)—they could not only draw from three budgets, but also they could draw from three distinct audience pools. This made her even more affordable and a greater value to the universities—she packed the rooms.

Within the first month, we booked Alice ten times. By month six, we had booked her thirty times. And by the end of the first year we were approaching forty-five total bookings. This number of bookings is highly unusual, but it demonstrates a critical point: a universal topic has a good shot at becoming that *one great speech* all speakers hope to find if it's priced to sell and delivered by an accomplished, polished, empowering speaker who is available, flexible, and willing to work. There was no point in Alice changing or modifying her topic other than to update information as new data became available, so she simply fell into a rhythm, as did the agents at my company. We booked, and she gave, the same speech over and over again.

Alice had found her *one great speech* and she ran with it. The agents at my agency never had to change their pitches, and she consistently got great reviews. She did this by meeting the mandate of any great brand; *she found a Unique Selling Proposition* and she built a brand around it:

▶ She identified and gave the audience a passionate takeaway about the health of our planet;

▶ With her book and credentials, she was uniquely qualified to give the talk;

▶ Her content moved the masses—it appealed to a lot of students;

▶ She was a great storyteller who wrapped her message about the environment in a compelling, engaging, and authentic story.

As a result, over the course of three years, Alice was booked over one hundred times.

That's close to a million dollars in revenue.

During my career as a speaking agent I have had a number of clients who have met with similar success. Only a few made this much through high volume, but many were able to accomplish it with higher fees. Fees that usually started out low but grew with a conscious branding and fee escalation strategy in place. Speeches can be sold repeatedly for years, for five- and sometimes six-figure fees. There are speakers who haven't changed or diverted from their one, go-to, bread-and-butter speech in over a decade, and it continues to sell. The question is, *Can you find yours?* Hopefully this book points you in the right direction. Hopefully it provides insight and guidance, forewarns you about the pitfalls, and paves a clear path to success. In the end, any product that has legs delivers something to the consumer that they need and want. With a speech, that thing the audience needs and wants is information that empowers them.

Hopefully, I've convinced you that even before you attempt to sign with an agency, you should work hard to craft compelling speech topics and construct a brand that is authentic and reflects your singularly Unique Selling Proposition. As you sign with an agency and after you get bookings, hopefully you now know enough to refine, market test, and tweak your topics and presentation using agent, event sponsor, and audience feedback. Hopefully you understand the value of professionalism from point of sale through delivery and follow-up.

In identifying your *one great speech*, remember that much of your success will have to do with persistence and grit, adaptability, market savvy, and building a great agency relationship— along with a lot of hard work and passion. And as much as success requires smarts and strategy, there's also an element of luck involved—both good luck and bad. But if you're the type of speaker who can light up a room and modify your topic based on the needs of each specific audience, are affable and easy to work with, are priced at an affordable rate for the market you target, and have strong agency backing, you will be well positioned to find success delivering the same speech for years.

So, work hard to find your *one great speech*. Perfect it. Develop a great relationship with a speaking agency. Build a personal brand.

Then go out and shake the world.

Acknowledgments

Writing a book is always a tremendous undertaking. I would like to extend my deepest gratitude to my agent, Leticia Gomez at Savvy Literary. Thank you for your vision and for making sure this book found the right home. I would also like to express my thanks to Anna Michels, my editor at Sourcebooks, and everyone on the Sourcebooks team for their dedication and passion for this project. I would be remiss if I didn't acknowledge the hundreds of speakers whom I've had the honor and privilege of representing over the last decade and counting. I've learned so much from so many of you—and without you this book wouldn't be possible. I made it a point to change many of the names mentioned throughout the text in order to protect the privacy of the speakers referenced, but all of you will know who you are through the stories I've shared. I would also like to extend my thanks to KJ White for her incredible wisdom. Finally, I would like to thank my family for their unwavering support—and for putting up with me while I tackled this project. Writing this book has been a passion project for me, and I owe the deepest of debts to all of you.

About the Author

Photo © Robert X. Fogarty

James Marshall Reilly is a speaking and literary consultant who has spent more than a decade in the paid speaking industry. During this time, he has represented in excess of one hundred exclusive speakers and has been responsible for more than one thousand events. As a speaker himself, he has given keynote presentations at Microsoft, Viacom, Chicago Ideas Week, and MIT, among others. He is also the author of *Shake the World: It's Not About Finding a Job, It's About Creating a Life*. His passion lies in connecting people and ideas and making events come to life. He currently serves as the Communications Manager at the Innocence Project. He resides in New York City.

For additional information, please visit
jamesmarshallreilly.com.

NOTES

EVELYN WAUGH

BRIDESHEAD REVISITED

WITH AN INTRODUCTION
BY FRANK KERMODE

EVERYMAN'S LIBRARY
Alfred A. Knopf   New York   London   Toronto

172

THIS IS A BORZOI BOOK
PUBLISHED BY ALFRED A. KNOPF

First included in Everyman's Library, 1993

Copyright information (UK):
First published by Chapman & Hall, 1945
Copyright 1945 by Evelyn Waugh
Revised edition published by Chapman & Hall, 1960
Published by arrangement with PFD on behalf of the Evelyn Waugh Trust

Copyright information (US):
Copyright © 1944, 1945 by Evelyn Waugh
Copyright renewed © 1972, 1973 by Mrs Laura Waugh
Published by arrangement with Little, Brown and Company, Inc.

Introduction, Bibliography and Chronology Copyright © 1993
by Everyman's Library
Typography by Peter B. Willberg
Tenth printing (US)

All rights reserved under International and Pan-American Copyright
Conventions. Published in the United States by Alfred A. Knopf,
a division of Random House, Inc., New York, and simultaneously in
Canada by Random House of Canada Limited, Toronto. Distributed
by Random House, Inc., New York. Published in the United Kingdom
by Everyman's Library, Northburgh House, 10 Northburgh Street,
London EC1V0AT, and distributed by Random House (UK) Ltd.

US website: www.randomhouse.com/everymans

ISBN: 978-0-679-42300-3 (US)
978-1-85715-172-5 (UK)
978-0-307-26996-6 (US Movie Tie-in)

A CIP catalogue reference for this book is available from the
British Library

Library of Congress Cataloging-in-Publication Data
Waugh, Evelyn, 1903–1966.
Brideshead revisited / Evelyn Waugh.
p.   cm.—(Everyman's library)
ISBN 0-679-42300-1
1. Upper classes—England—Fiction.
2. Catholics—England—Fiction.   3. Family—England—Fiction.
PR6045.A97B7   1993   93-1854
823'.912—dc20   CIP

Book design by Barbara de Wilde and Carol Devine Carson

Printed and bound in the United States of America

BRIDESHEAD
REVISITED

———

INTRODUCTION

The pre-publication history of *Brideshead Revisited*, probably Evelyn Waugh's most successful novel, is complicated and unusual. Its last pages were written in London in June 1944, while the Allied forces were landing in Normandy. Waugh, by this time as disillusioned with the army as the army was with him, had served for years in various branches of the service – he had been a Marine and a Commando, seen action in Crete, and damaged himself in a parachute jump. Having sought and got leave to write a novel – in itself surely an unusual achievement for an officer in any service in 1944 – he must have supposed that as the end of the war approached he was, at forty-one, finished with active service. He was not; the proofs of *Brideshead* were revised in Yugoslavia, where he had been sent on a mission with Randolph Churchill. Much later that mission provided the basis for the last section of his last novel, *Unconditional Surrender*.

He had written nothing of much substance since *Put Out More Flags*, published in 1942; it celebrated the 'phoney war' and what he described as 'the Churchillian renaissance' at its end. The unfinished *Work Suspended* also belongs to that year. Meanwhile he had repeatedly demonstrated both his desire for military action, however desperate, and his constitutional reluctance to accept the role of a junior officer. Already in his late thirties, and unaccustomed to strenuous exercise, he struggled to comply with the requirement of physical fitness and the relatively hard life of wartime soldiering, but he was prone to insult senior officers in various ways, not least when drunk.

In these circumstances the 'marriage' between Waugh and the army headed for breakdown. He long retained an earnest if, as it sometimes appeared from the conduct of associates, idiosyncratic interest in the idea of combat, but other military qualities were lacking; one commanding officer rated him highest for 'Zeal' and lowest for 'Judgment'. Having taken part in a useless expedition against the Free French at Dakar (to be remembered in *Men at Arms*) and an abortive raid on Bardia in Libya, he arrived in Crete just in time to take part in the British evacuation, so bitterly recounted in *Officers and Gentlemen*, the second volume of the war trilogy that was to be his last work of fiction.

Waugh greatly resented what he took to be the shameful character of that retreat. He genuinely could not understand why people were not as brave as he was – or, if they were afraid, why they did not conceal their fear. He began to withdraw his interest from the war, saying he had come to think of it as a matter for others: there were really, he remarked, two wars in progress – Russia *v.* Germany, and USA *v.* Japan – and 'England', he now thought, 'had no part in either of them'. Disillusioned as to the value and purpose of the conflict, he decided he had no part to play in its continuance, and sought to resume his life as an artist, to labour in his true vocation. Feeling the onset of a very ambitious novel, he wrote to Brendan Bracken, an acquaintance who was then Minister of Information, and to the War Office, requesting leave for three months. He explained that he was over forty, that he lacked physical agility and also such qualities as might make up for that lack – a knowledge of useful foreign languages, and so on. However, he remained able to write novels, and he asked for time to write one now, promising that three months would suffice for the purpose.

He eventually got his leave (though it was to be interrupted somewhat by the interference of military bureaucrats). Bracken earned little gratitude for his part in making this possible, for he was made to contribute to the character of Rex Mottram in the book that resulted. Waugh was contemplating, he said, a *magnum opus*, and for such a purpose the period of leave he requested might, though lengthy in view of the military situation, have looked barely adequate; but he was confident that he could bring it off, and indeed the book got written in a little over four months.

The story of its writing is as follows. From his diary we know he began it on 1 February 1944 in a hotel in Chagford, Devon: 'Up at 8.30, two and a half hours earlier than in London, and at work before 10. I found my mind stiff and my diction stilted but by dinner-time I had finished 1,300 words all of which were written twice and many three times before I got the time sequence and the transitions satisfactorily, but I think it is now all right.' On the following day we have 'Score at close of play 3,000 words odd.' Constantly rewriting, and under repeated threats of military recall, he was within a week managing 1,500–2,000 words a day, and on 14 February he wrote 3,000 words in three hours. By the 26th he had done 33,000 words, but was then forced back to 'military frivolities'. However, he managed to get another six weeks' leave and resumed work on 16 March (2,700 words). He then proceeded with extraordinary despatch, and by the end of March had half finished. On 4 May he complained about the difficulty of writing about 'love-making on a liner'. On 21 May he records that he has 'written about 15,000 words in the last week and am in alternate despondency and exultation about the book'. Lord Marchmain died on D-Day, 6 June: 'There only remains now the epilogue which is easy meat.' 'On Corpus Christi Day 1944 [10 June] ... I finished the last version of *Brideshead Revisited* and sent it to be typed.' It was, he wrote in a letter to his wife, the dedicatee, his first important book, and he was somewhat impatient for it to be recognized as such.

Waugh usually wrote fast when sure what he wanted to do, and if there is an unexpected touch of Trollope in this proud word-counting (and in the appended '*Chagford, February–June, 1944*') it is not to be thought that the work was as easily achieved as its completion in so short a time might suggest. The researches of Robert Murray Davis in the archives at Austin, Texas, and elsewhere have demonstrated the intensity of the labour devoted to the manuscript while the writing was in progress.

Waugh long wished to revise the book as it stood in 1944, and minor corrections were made in subsequent editions. In 1959 the publisher invited him to make any changes he wanted for a new edition, to be wholly reset, and the result was the version here reprinted. It differs in various respects from the first edition, even in physical characteristics – the trade edition of 1944 is printed on wartime 'economy' paper, the pages grey and fragile. More important were the alterations made, after mature consideration, to the structure and style of the work. These are referred to in the author's Preface. Observing that this book had won him celebrity but lost him esteem, he goes on to endorse its theme but criticizes its form and some aspects of its style. He deplores but excuses its celebration of gluttony; this, he says, he has now qualified, though not everything proper to the mood of 1944 could be removed simply because it seemed excessive in 1959. 'It would be impossible to bring it up to date without totally destroying it.'

The changes can be summarized thus. Waugh reverted to the three-book structure he had planned in the manuscript but reduced to two books in the 1944 version. He cut out or altered some of what he calls 'the grosser passages', trimming nostalgic accounts of luxurious eating and drinking (forgiveable as the self-indulgent reveries of the age of austerity in which the novel was written) and also instances of what Conor Cruise O'Brien, in an essay that mildly upset Waugh, referred to as 'elegiac afflatus'. But even after these changes the prose of *Brideshead* remains heavier, more elaborate, than that of any novel he had written before, and this is understandable considering that the subject is one of the gravest importance to the author – no less than 'the operation of divine grace on a group of diverse but closely connected characters'. Since the house itself has stood for the survival in apostate England of a remnant of Catholic aristocracy, though on the point of succumbing to atheistic modernity and the reign of the Hoopers, it seemed right to 'pile it on rather', and the same might be said for the reminiscences of the Oxford of Waugh's youth, which, as he says in his autobiography, was to him 'a Kingdom of Cockayne'.

To give a few instances of the reduction of the pile: Oxford, which in 1944 'exhaled the soft vapours of a thousand years of learning', in 1960 'exhaled the soft airs of centuries of youth' – a less extravagant and perhaps more accurate claim. In the account of the dinner at which Charles Ryder sees through the pretensions of Rex Mottram there was a long elegiac speech about Burgundy, now curtailed though not eliminated. Similarly there are beneficial cuts in the account of Sebastian

Flyte's Oxford luncheon party, which began 'a new epoch' in
Charles Ryder's life. The beginning of Book Three is quite
heavily cut. Anthony Blanche is introduced far less extrava-
gantly in the final than in the original version, no longer quite
as 'foreign as a Martian'.

On the other hand the blue pencil spared some rather
weighty editorializing, as at the opening of Book One,
Chapter 4: 'The languor of Youth – how unique and quintessential it is!', and so on to a comparison between that languor
and the experience of the Beatific Vision. In Book One,
Chapter 5, there is a passage, beginning 'The Charity matinée
was over', which explains how grievously Anthony Blanche
was missed when he failed to return to Oxford. It develops an
extremely elaborate theatrical figure and its success depends
on the ingenuity of that figure, and on the gravity of tone that
conveys it. It now seems strained or overdone, and as it was
surely dispensable one is surprised that it was spared.

There are more such passages: one in particular at the
outset of Book Three describes the behaviour of the pigeons in
the piazza of San Marco, and indicates their fugitive resemblance to human memories. The comparison near the beginning, between Ryder's disillusion with the army and the decay
of a marriage, extends over some three hundred words and
feels laboured. There is the very elaborate figure that occurs
after Charles' conversation with his boring and proper cousin,
to suggest that the wickedness of Oxford undergraduates can
be compared with the slow fermentation of port. (Waugh liked
this simile well enough to quote it in his autobiography.)

Such elaborately extended metaphors add a new gravity to
the tone of the novel. Waugh's prose, like his handling of
displaced autobiography, has induced some critics to compare
Brideshead with Proust's *A la Recherche du temps perdu*, but its
scale, though quite grand, is modest compared with that of
Proust, and the author's avowed purpose, to demonstrate the
workings of divine grace, wholly different.

One change in the final version has probably given rise to
more comment than any of the others. As I have already
noted, Waugh was not happy about the scene of love-making
on the liner, complaining that it was difficult to render sex

without being able to describe the sexual act in detail.

'I feel very much the futility of describing sexual emotions without describing the sexual act; I should like to give as much detail as I have of the meals, to the two coitions – with his wife and Julia. It would be no more or less obscene than to leave them to the reader's imagination, which in this case cannot be as acute as mine. There is a gap in which the reader will insert his own sexual habits instead of those of my characters.'

(*Diaries*, 9 May 1944)

In 1944 the love-making with Julia on the liner avoids any imputation of sexual excitement but goes in for rhetorical excess instead: 'I took formal possession of her as a lover ... Now on the rough water I was made free of her narrow loins and, it seemed now, assuaging that fierce appetite, cast a burden which I had borne all my life, toiled under, not knowing its nature – now, while the waves still broke and thundered on the prow, the act of possession was a symbol, a rite of ancient origin and solemn meaning.' Understandably discontented with this uneasily inflated prose, Waugh shortened the passage in 1960: 'Now on the rough water there was a formality to be observed, no more. It was as though a deed of conveyance of her narrow loins had been drawn and sealed. I was making my first entry as the freeholder of a property I would enjoy and develop at leisure.'

Not everybody will think this much of an improvement. From a rite observed in bad weather – accompanied by what Martin Stannard calls 'the lamentable phallic imagery of the ship' (Stannard, p. 106) – the lovemaking becomes an act of formal possession, as of a house. The figure of 'possession' and being made free of something has swollen into an elaborate trope about property, complete with a deed of conveyance; no fierce appetite is assuaged. Not surprisingly, some have complained that Ryder might almost be thinking about the inheritance of Brideshead made possible by this union, treating the coition as merely part of the negotiations for that supremely desirable residence.

Since these remarks about elaborate tropes and mannered gravity may have sounded a little disparaging, it should here be said that Waugh's dialogue is as edged and witty as ever; that he is extraordinarily skilful in making each of his characters speak in his or her own way, from Ryder's very original father to the bright child Cordelia. Waugh once argued for the value to writers of aristocratic English: 'only a continuous tradition of gentle speech, with all its implications – the avoidance of boredom and vulgarity, the exchange of complicated ideas, the observance of subtle nuances of word and phrase – can preserve the written tongue from death, and lifelong habitude to such speech alone schools a man to write his own tongue'. This rule may be of less general application than is here suggested, but it was one that the author himself obeyed, and with notable results. Nor is it merely a matter of upper-class dialect; one feels he heard his characters, distinguished their usages, reported idiolects.

On the whole most readers, I think, would agree that the purgation of the first version – not over-rigorous, for reasons Waugh suggests in his Preface – makes for improvement: the final version of the novel is preferable. Enough of the grand grave elaboration persists to convey the impression that this is the manner best suited to the mood in which the author attempted the work, the manner that best conveys the sense in which the novel is a personal record. To call the book displaced autobiography is of course not to suggest that Ryder is a self-portrait, but Waugh would certainly have seen conversion to Catholicism, with the attendant benefits and sacrifices, as evidence of the operation of grace in both his own life and his character's.

There are certainly reminiscences, however fictionalized, of episodes in the author's life. Important elements of the plot concern the Catholic prohibition of remarriage while a spouse remains alive, a difficulty Waugh had himself experienced, and one not to be dismissed as easily as Rex Mottram believed. Even more instrumental in the conception of the book was Waugh's anxiety about friends who remained, as he saw the matter, in schism (Anglicans, for instance, like John Betjeman) or others who had apostasized. He worried about the faith of Graham Greene, and at one remarkable moment succeeded in inducing a dying friend, Hubert Duggan, to see a priest. Duggan had lived out of wedlock with a woman now dead, and apparently felt it would be an insult to her memory if he were now to declare himself repentant on account of that relationship. A priest was brought in all the same, and succeeded in giving the dying man absolution; he was held to have assented and crossed himself (*Diaries*, 13 October 1943). This moment, a palpable intervention, as it was taken to be, of divine grace in a human life, was Waugh's inspiration for the account of the death of Lord Marchmain, who had also lived in sin.

*

The novel begins in a tedious and sleazy wartime present, in a military setting of that lowering variety, well known to survivors of Word War II, in which the absence or remoteness of action makes routine duties, moves, drills, orders and reprimands seem banal or irrelevant, causing all manner of petty irritation and bringing out the worst in everybody. This helps to account for Ryder's discontent, and has the additional thematic value of introducing the contemptibly irritating Hooper, the lowborn lowminded subaltern regarded by Ryder as representative of a new generation – a fellow innately incapable of understanding fine points of honour or discipline or indeed language, an enemy of the faith, and a threat, however negligible in himself, to the best people. Aimless troop movements undertaken in this company and this mood bring Ryder unexpectedly to Brideshead; whereupon the narrative retreats to the early twenties, when Ryder as an undergraduate fell under the spell of Sebastian Flyte, inhabitant of the paradisial Brideshead, Brideshead before the fall.

The Oxford memories in *Brideshead* may be thought of less as displaced than as transfigured autobiography. Waugh later wrote lovingly of his undergraduate life in *A Little Learning*, and others have contributed, in memoirs and admiring historical studies, to our idea of the place as Waugh experienced it in the early twenties. The beauty of the city itself, in the days before it was quite ruined by the motor car, was enhanced, at any rate for its transient occupants, by its being an almost exclusively male community. Waugh remarks that few of his contemporaries had 'any serious interest in women' though 'very few have developed into homosexuals'. They were in some respects, he says, sophisticated, in others barely adolescent. It was a time for warm male friendships, and that suited Waugh very well. At Oxford he was 'reborn'. He drank a lot, formed one homosexual relationship, and made friends with grander people from grander colleges than Hertford, where he was a scholar. He read too little and did not get on very well with dons, against one of whom he later conducted one of his relentless campaigns of teasing. He was fortunate in having as his Oxford contemporaries men of the calibre of Graham Greene, Henry Green, Anthony Powell, John Betjeman and Cyril Connolly, and he made several close friendships, but seems to have reserved his highest admiration for the affluent Alastair Graham and for Harold Acton and Brian Howard – 'a rich source of anecdote' who contributed much to the character of Anthony Blanche in *Brideshead*.

Oxford had also provided the opening scene of Waugh's first novel, *Decline and Fall*, which describes, with a degree of *schadenfreude* and teasing, the discomfiture of Paul Pennyfeather at the hands of drunken aristocratic rowdies of the 'Bollinger' Club, really the Bullingdon at Christ Church. (Tom Driberg remarked that the opening chapter of *Decline and Fall* gave 'a mild account of the night of any Bullingdon Club dinner'.) In *Brideshead* such people are not absent, nor is the slightly cruel fun – Blanche is an obvious quarry – but all is bathed in an elegiac glow, partly attributable to the 'mood of sentimental delusion' in which the novel was written.

Book One of the novel has an epigraph, 'Et in Arcadia Ego', a tag often used to suggest memories of a past idyllic time, though in fact the words, as Waugh understood very well, are supposed to be spoken by Death ('All fates,' said Waugh much later, 'are "worse than death"' (*Diaries*, p. 787). That time, like any time, could hold in perfection but a little moment, and the shadow of decay or death must be on Ryder's first outing with Sebastian, his first visit to Brideshead. Sebastian the beautiful, in any secular sense the doomed, the winsome lover of a teddy-bear, had vomited through the window into Ryder's room, so binding together two lives which, each in its way but also in concert, will illustrate the operation of grace in human existence, so that the mess left for the scout to clean up is, in a way, evidence of that operation.

After their meeting we are at once introduced to Ryder's father, eccentric, drily teasing, mildly malevolent, and his pompous cousin Jasper; they are from a world elsewhere, not the Flyte world, so 'madly charming'. What Ryder had already learnt, and what neither pompous cousin nor self-absorbed, ironic father ever would, was 'that to know and love one other human being is the root of all wisdom'. Like Blanche in his way, he had, in loving Sebastian, discovered a kind of holiness. He had also discovered, from Blanche, the delights of ostentatious and luxurious self-indulgence as well as a malevolence altogether preferable to his father's, as when Blanche at the George, having ordered 'four Alexandra cock-tails' at once, gossips wickedly about Sebastian's family. (In fact the cocktail was called an Alexander, not an Alexandra; but we cannot suppose the mistake to have been Blanche's.)

Eventually Sebastian allows Ryder to meet them, first Julia, who at once faintly arouses him; sex is also an agent, though a devious one, of grace. To be at Brideshead was for various reasons, and not only for its luxuries, to be 'very near heaven'. The spirit of that first stay is not particularly numinous or even very religious; Brideshead is 'not an old-established centre of Catholicism', and Ryder is aware of no supernatural solicitations. Yet the family is, as it were, vexed by its difference, its openness to calls unheard by those from whom they are different, including the young Ryder – its awareness of the enormous gulf existing between Catholics and others. Lord Marchmain, on his marriage, had entered into that difference; he tried to go back, but the end of the story is that when death approached he found himself, for all his worldli-ness and all his rage against the wife who had made him Catholic, compelled by the 'twitch upon the thread' to return to the condition of difference from which he had defected.

The twitch upon the thread is a central theme. The history of Lady Marchmain's relations with her husband and with Sebastian causes the latter to call her 'a femme fatale ... She killed at a touch.' Halfway through the book she announces that 'we must make a Catholic of Charles'. He will succumb to grace as it operates through the Flytes, and, eventually, concur even in her arguments in favour of wealth: '... it is possible for the rich to sin by coveting the privileges of the poor. The poor have always been the favourites of God.' Ryder is not at that point persuaded; he is preoccupied by Sebastian's apparent plight, described in another over-wrought figure as that of a Polynesian threatened by a colonist. But he is affected, and we are already wondering how the 'twitch on the thread' will be applied. That phrase, used as the title of Book Three, derives from one of Chesterton's Father Brown stories, earlier read as one of Lady Marchmain's after-dinner performances; in the words of Mark Amory, it is 'a fishing metaphor ... meaning that once someone has seen the Grace of God, however much time and space remove him, he can be retrieved' (*Letters*, p. 207).

There are different manifestations, many of which may seem improbable to sceptics, of the angling operations of grace. Sebastian's drunken decline, the interventions of Mr Samgrass, even Sebastian's running away like his father before him; or Lady Marchmain's introducing Ryder into her 'feminine' world, and telling him she had prayed for him: all these are part of the divine sport. All manner of apparently random events can constitute a divine plot.

Ryder cannot escape: professing to be with Sebastian *contra mundum*, seeing through what he takes to be the tricks of Lady Marchmain, he is nevertheless confounded in a conversation with Lord Brideshead, the pious, dull elder brother, regarded by Rex Mottram as just a 'half-baked monk'. Ryder cannot understand why Brideshead brings 'God into everything' and says, 'It seems to me that without your religion Sebastian would have a chance to be a happy and healthy man.' 'It's arguable,' replies Brideshead. Here the 'difference' is clearly expressed; Ryder cannot yet see either why God has to be in everything, nor why that chance of health and happiness is relatively unimportant; it will take time and much plotting to bring him to such an understanding.

Brideshead is fortunate in his unquestioned acceptance; he may be absurd in some ways (as he is, on the face of it, in his choice of wife) but in the one thing truly necessary he is both wise and lucky. His sister Julia, on the other hand, resents what seems to her the misfortune of being Catholic, but cannot break away: 'if she apostasized now, having been brought up in the Church, she would go to hell, while the Protestant girls of her acquaintance, schooled in happy ignorance, could marry eldest sons, live at peace with their world, and get to heaven before her'. The suggestion seems to be that to have the certain knowledge that comes with Catholicism can, for some, amount to a sort of curse; ignorant Protestants can avoid the troubles of conscience and deprivation entailed by adherence to the true religion and at the same time avoid the risk of hell. But out of love for Mottram, who has no understanding at all of the 'difference' – as the Jesuit who instructs him puts it, he has 'no sense of reality', is almost a 'semi-imbecile' – she does apostasize, or try to: 'I can't get all that sort of thing out of my mind, quite – Death, Judgment, Heaven, Hell, Nanny Hawkins and the catechism.' Mottram indeed turns out not to be 'a complete human being', but 'something absolutely modern that only this ghastly age could produce. A tiny bit of a man', rather like a Hooper become rich and powerful.

Wholeness in humanity is normally to be sought in the Catholic and well born; but the cost of being whole can be great. It is great for Sebastian, if only on a secular view; he comes to no earthly good. It is great for the family, who lose the chapel and Marchmain House. As Cordelia understands, it is a question of doing what the great plot irresistibly requires of you. 'If you haven't a vocation it's no good ... and if you have a vocation you can't get away from it, however much you hate it.'

Ryder's understanding of these matters is deferred. When the third and final book begins, after a lapse of ten years, he has become quite famous as an artist; he has travelled much and married badly; but, he says, 'I remained unchanged, still a small part of myself pretending to be a whole', and in that resembling Mottram more than a Catholic.

The understanding that there is a genuine impediment to his marriage with Julia, and that there is such a condition as 'living in sin', is the beginning of the twitch on Ryder's thread. Julia, it appears, is, like Sebastian, not an end but a 'fore-runner'. That understanding is also occasion for Julia's extra-ordinary outburst, partly excused, along with the moribund monologue of Lord Marchmain, by Waugh in his Preface. She thinks there is no turning back; wrongly, of course. The important thing is to be turned back before dying.

The death foreseen by Cordelia for Sebastian is that he will be picked up dying after a drinking bout and 'show by a mere flicker of the eyelid that he is conscious when they give him the last sacraments'. Ryder is by such speculations brought up close to the fence he had not known he must take before his own death. Dying is the most important moment in a life. It is fitting that the book should end with the peaceful death of Lord Marchmain ('They mean something so different by "peace"'). Julia, naturally understanding the importance of the moment, goes for a priest; Ryder deplores this act, but kneels in prayer as the absolution is given, and his prayer is answered. His reward is to be parted from Julia. By the time he returns in uniform to Brideshead it has been defiled by billeted troops, by the incursion of the age of Hooper; but the lamp burns again in the sanctuary of the chapel.

The reasons why, in the 1960 Preface, Waugh can say that this novel 'lost me such esteem as I once enjoyed among my contemporaries' are probably two. First, some readers, accus-tomed to the stringency and economy of his earlier prose, found his manner self-indulgent. Secondly, he was now angrily accused of snobbery, a snobbery that seemed to be closely associated with his championship of the religion to which he had been converted. Henry Reed's review in the *New Statesman* (23 June 1945), on the whole admiring, began with a condem-nation of this snobbery: 'A burden of respect for the peerage and for Eton, which those who belong to the former, or have been to the latter, seem able lightly to discard, weighs heavily upon him.' Reed singles out the scene with Mottram in the Paris restaurant as an instance of the narrator scoring off the lower-caste characters; in Waugh's 'testiness at other people's bad taste' he detects 'a special vulgarity'.

Waugh claimed not to be worried by such charges. 'Class

consciousness, particularly in England, has been so much inflamed these days that to mention a nobleman is like mentioning a prostitute sixty years ago. The new prudes say, "No doubt such people do exist but we would sooner not hear about them". I reserve the right to deal with the kind of people I know best.' He would not have wished to apologize for the famous passage in which Ryder reflects that Lady March-main's brothers, representative sons of 'the Catholic squires of England', were sacrificed in World War I 'to make a world for Hooper; they were the aborigines, vermin by right of law, to be shot off at leisure so that things might be safe for the travelling salesman, with his polygonal pince-nez, his fat wet hand-shake, his grinning dentures'.

What did upset him was any imputation that he believed the Catholic aristocracy to warrant special attentions from grace, attentions withheld from Mottrams and Hoopers and *hoi polloi*. Lady Marchmain's remarks about the spiritual privileges of the poor were perhaps inserted to forestall such interpretations; but they were forthcoming nevertheless. Conor Cruise O'Brien, an authority on the Catholic novel, pointed out, in the largely polite and admiring essay to which I referred earlier, that in Catholic countries (Ireland was perhaps in his mind) 'Catholicism is not romantic, not invaria-bly associated with big houses, or the fate of an aristocracy', adding that Waugh's Catholicism is 'dark and defeatist'. In a response to this article Waugh again admitted snobbery, but pointed out that at least two aristocrats in *Brideshead Revisited* – Mottram and Celia – are represented as 'worldly', and not 'sanctified' by his 'reverence for money and rank'. Given that Mottram is, in matters of religion, an ignoramus like Box-Bender in the later war trilogy, and Celia one of Waugh's pagan, rather dissolute upper-class women, like Guy Crouch-back's wife in the later work, this may seem a less than wholly satisfactory defence. But his main purpose in replying to O'Brien was 'the fear that a hasty reader [of O'Brien's notice] might conceive the doubt, which your reviewer scrupulously refrains from expressing, of the good faith of my conversion to Catholicism'.

Waugh expressed his shocked repudiation of such interpretations in a reply to an article by the present writer on the occasion of the publication of the 1960 edition of *Brideshead Revisited*. 'He imputes to me the absurd and blasphemous opinion that divine grace is "confined" to the highest and lowest class,' he wrote, citing a passage from *Helena* as proof that he did not hold that opinion.

My article had in fact emphasized, with evidence from *Helena*, Waugh's passionate concern for the *facts* of Catholic Christianity, and his confidence that 'the Faith is absolutely satisfactory to the mind ... that it is completely compelling to any who give it "indifferent and quiet audience"'' – a quotation from Waugh's book about the martyr Campion. I did not, when I wrote the piece, know Mr O'Brien's essay, and said at more length many of the same things, with a similar degree of admiration and respect, and with some quite modestly expressed reservations. The offensive words were these: 'But the operation of divine grace seems to be confined to those who say "chimney-piece" and the enviable poor. Hooper and his brothers may be hard to bear, but it seems outrageous to damn them for their manners.' This is too strongly expressed, though to take it in isolation from the lengthy (and, I find on re-reading it, accurate) characterization of the faith expressed in this and other novels was unfair. Unfairness of course is essential to Waugh's controversial manner, as it is to the fun and to the power of these works.

Returning to *Brideshead Revisited* after so many years, one is again impressed less by its preoccupation with luxury than by its preoccupation with death. Ryder speaks of the 'tragedy' in which he had participated, a tragedy which resulted from the acceptance of the truth, a truth of separation and death. There is, to use the word in a sense only indirectly related to the quality of aristocracy, a certain nobility in this attitude. Ryder, in the final pages, can, rather surprisingly, allow himself to tell Hooper that he is 'homeless, childless, middle-aged, loveless'. Waugh never pretended that religious belief should make one happy. In his ruined world, symbolized at the end by the great house now defaced, there is no abiding city, but there is the hope of heaven signified by the lamp 'of deplorable design'. All fates are worse than death, though many of them are amusing or even beautiful. Waugh, tired of the army, chose to be an artist in this book, and he never dissociated art from skill. This skill, devoted as it is to the narrative expression of a clear and unwavering faith, makes *Brideshead Revisited*, after all the necessary reservations are stated, a memorable work of art.

Frank Kermode

SELECT BIBLIOGRAPHY

THE NOVELS OF EVELYN WAUGH
(all published by Chapman & Hall)

Decline and Fall, 1928.
Vile Bodies, 1930.
Black Mischief, 1932.
A Handful of Dust, 1934.
Scoop, 1938.
Put Out More Flags, 1942.
Brideshead Revisited, 1945.
The Loved One, 1948.
Helena, 1950.
Men at Arms, 1952.
Officers and Gentlemen, 1955.
The Ordeal of Gilbert Pinfold, 1957.
Unconditional Surrender, 1961.
(*Men at Arms*, *Officers and Gentlemen*, and *Unconditional Surrender* form a trilogy later published in a revised version as *Sword of Honour*, 1965.)

BIOGRAPHY
The best biography of Evelyn Waugh is by Martin Stannard: vol. 1, *Evelyn Waugh: The Early Years*, Dent, 1986; vol. 2, *Evelyn Waugh: No Abiding City*, Dent, 1992. There is an earlier biography by the author's friend Christopher Sykes (*Evelyn Waugh: A Biography*, Collins, 1975). There are details in many memoirs and in the biographies of Waugh's contemporaries, e.g., the autobiographies of his brother Alec (*My Brother Evelyn and Other Profiles*, Cassell, 1967), of Anthony Powell, *To Keep the Ball Rolling*, vol. 2, Heinemann, 1978), and in Bevis Hillier's *Young Betjeman* (Murray, 1988). Waugh's *Letters* were edited by Mark Amory (Weidenfeld & Nicolson, 1980) and there are more letters in Artemis Cooper, ed., *Mr Wu and Mrs Stitch: The Letters of Evelyn Waugh and Diana Cooper* (Hodder & Stoughton, 1991). Michael Davie edited *The Diaries of Evelyn Waugh* (Methuen, 1983). Humphrey Carpenter's *The Brideshead Generation* (Weidenfeld & Nicolson, 1989) is a biography, written with special attention to the lives of Waugh's Oxford contemporaries.

CRITICISM
Criticism of Waugh's novels is well selected in Martin Stannard's

Evelyn Waugh: The Critical Heritage (Routledge & Kegan Paul, 1984).
Waugh himself approved of Frederick J. Stopp's *Evelyn Waugh: The
Portrait of an Artist* (Chapman & Hall, 1958). Other valuable works
are 'Donat O'Donnel' [Conor Cruise O'Brien], *Maria Cross: Imagin-
ative Patterns in a Group of Modern Catholic Writers* (Oxford, 1952) and
Robert Murray Davis, *Evelyn Waugh, Writer* (Oklahoma, Pilgrim
Books, 1981).

CHRONOLOGY

DATE	AUTHOR'S LIFE	LITERARY CONTEXT
1897	Birth of Alec Waugh, Evelyn's brother.	
1903	Birth of Evelyn Waugh to Arthur and Catherine Waugh in Hampstead.	James: *The Ambassadors.* Shaw: *Man and Superman.*
1904		James: *The Golden Bowl.* Conrad: *Nostromo.*
1907		Conrad: *The Secret Agent.*
1908		Forster: *A Room with a View.* Bennett: *The Old Wives' Tale.*
1910	Attends Heath Mount preparatory school. *The Curse of the Horse Race* (unpublished).	Forster: *Howards End.*
1911		Lawrence: *The White Peacock.*
1913		Lawrence: *Sons and Lovers.* Proust: *A la Recherche du temps perdu.*
1914		Conrad: *Chance.* Joyce: *Dubliners.*
1915		Madox Ford: *The Good Soldier.* Conrad: *Victory.* Buchan: *The Thirty-Nine Steps.* Woolf: *The Voyage Out.*
1916	Attends Lancing College. Starts to write diaries which continue throughout his life.	Joyce: *A Portrait of the Artist as a Young Man.* Shaw: *Pygmalion.*
1917		Yeats: *The Wild Swans at Coole.* Eliot: *Prufrock and Other Observations.*
1918		Brooke: *Collected Poems.* Pirandello: *Six Characters in Search of an Author.*
1919		Shaw: *Heartbreak House.*
1920		Pound: *Hugh Selwyn Mauberley.*
1921	Attends Hertford College, Oxford; also studies at the Ruskin School of Art.	Huxley: *Crome Yellow.*

Emmeline Pankhurst founds the Women's Social and Political Union.

Russo-Japanese War.

Asquith becomes Prime Minister.

Death of Edward VII. Liberals back in power.

Coronation of George V. Agadir crisis. Suffragette riots.

Outbreak of World War I.

Asquith forms coalition government with Balfour.

First battle of the Somme. Lloyd George becomes Prime Minister.

Russian revolution. US joins war. Third Battle of Ypres.

Armistice. Women over thirty gain vote.

Versailles peace conference.

League of Nations formed. Prohibition in the US.

DATE	AUTHOR'S LIFE	LITERARY CONTEXT
1922		Joyce: *Ulysses*.
		Eliot: *The Waste Land*.
		Housman: *Last Poems*.
		Fitzgerald: *The Beautiful and the Damned*.
1923	*Anthony, Who Sought Things That Were Lost*.	e e cummings: *The Enormous Room*.
		Huxley: *Antic Hay*.
1924	Leaves Oxford with a third class honours degree. Waugh then becomes a master at a preparatory school. *The Temple at Thatch* (unpublished).	Forster: *A Passage to India*.
		Shaw: *Saint Joan*.
1925		Fitzgerald: *The Great Gatsby*.
		Kafka: *The Trial*.
1926	Trains as a carpenter. *P.R.B. An Essay on the Pre-Raphaelite Brotherhood* (printed privately). *The Balance* (Georgian Papers).	Faulkner: *Soldiers' Pay*.
		Nabokov: *Mary*.
		Henry Green: *Blindness*.
1927	Meets and marries Evelyn Gardner. Publishes his first book, a biography of Dante Gabriel Rossetti.	Woolf: *To the Lighthouse*.
		Hemingway: *Men Without Women*.
		Dunne: *An Experiment with Time*.
1928	*Decline and Fall*.	Lawrence: *Lady Chatterley's Lover*.
		Woolf: *Orlando*.
		Yeats: *The Tower*.
		Lewis: *The Childermass*.
		Nabokov: *King, Queen, Knave*.
1929	Divorces his wife Evelyn.	Faulkner: *The Sound and the Fury*.
		Cocteau: *Les Enfants terribles*.
		Hemingway: *A Farewell to Arms*.
		Priestley: *The Good Companions*.
		Remarque: *All Quiet on the Western Front*.
1930	Converts to Roman Catholicism. *Vile Bodies, Labels*.	Eliot: *Ash Wednesday*.
		Faulkner: *As I Lay Dying*.
		Nabokov: *The Defence*.
1931	Travels around Africa and South America. *Remote People*.	Faulkner: *Sanctuary*.

CHRONOLOGY

Stalin becomes General Secretary of the Communist party Central Committee. Mussolini marches on Rome. Coalition falls and Bonar Law forms Conservative ministry.

Baldwin becomes Prime Minister. Hitler's coup in Munich fails. Women gain legal equality in divorce suits.

First Labour government formed by Ramsay MacDonald. Hitler in prison. Death of Lenin. Baldwin becomes Prime Minister again after a Conservative election victory.

Locarno conference.

British general strike. First television demonstrated. Stalin begins to oust Trotsky. French financial crisis.

German economy collapses.

Hoover becomes US president.

Wall Street crash.

Gandhi begins civil disobedience campaign in India. Nazis win seats from the moderates in German election.

DATE	AUTHOR'S LIFE	LITERARY CONTEXT
1932	*Black Mischief, Cruise, Bella Fleace Gave a Party, Incident in Anzania.*	Huxley: *Brave New World.* Faulkner: *Light in August.* Nabokov: *Glory.*
1933	*Out of Depth.*	Malraux: *La Condition humaine.* Stein: *The Autobiography of Alice B. Toklas.*
1934	*A Handful of Dust, Mr. Loveday's Little Outing, On Guard, Ninety-Two Days.*	
1935	*Winner Takes All,* also a biography of Edmund Campion.	Isherwood: *Mr. Norris Changes Trains.* Eliot: *Murder in the Cathedral.* Odets: *Waiting for Lefty.* Graham Greene: *England Made Me.*
1936	*Period Piece, Excursion in Reality, Waugh in Abyssinia, Love in the Slumps.*	Faulkner: *Absalom, Absalom!* Nabokov: *Despair.*
1937	Marries Laura Herbert.	Hemingway: *To Have and Have Not.* Orwell: *The Road to Wigan Pier.* Sartre: *La Nausée.* Steinbeck: *Of Mice and Men.*
1938	Birth of his daughter Teresa. *Scoop.*	Graham Greene: *Brighton Rock.* Beckett: *Murphy.* Orwell: *Homage to Catalonia.*
1939	Birth of his son Auberon. Joins the Royal Marines and then the Commandos, serving throughout the war. *An Englishman's Home, Robbery Under Law.*	Joyce: *Finnegans Wake.* Eliot: *The Family Reunion.* Steinbeck: *The Grapes of Wrath.* Henry Green: *Party Going.* Auden: *Journey to a War.* Isherwood: *Goodbye to Berlin.*
1940		Hemingway: *For Whom the Bell Tolls.* Graham Greene: *The Power and the Glory.* Dylan Thomas: *Portrait of the Artist as a Young Dog.* Faulkner: *The Hamlet.* Henry Green: *Pack my Bag: A Self-Portrait.*
1941		Acton: *Peonies and Ponies.* Fitzgerald: *The Last Tycoon.*

CHRONOLOGY

DATE	AUTHOR'S LIFE	LITERARY CONTEXT
1942	Birth of his daughter Margaret (died 1986). *Put Out More Flags* (a sequel to *Black Mischief*), *Work Suspended*.	Anouilh: *Eurydice*. Sartre: *Les Mouches*. Camus: *L'Etranger*. Camus: *Le Mythe de Sisyphe*.
1943		Davies: *Collected Poems*. Henry Green: *Caught*.
1944	Birth of his daughter Harriet.	Eliot: *Four Quartets*. Anouilh: *Antigone*. Camus: *Caligula*. Sartre: *Huis Clos*.
1945	*Brideshead Revisited, Charles Ryder's School Days*.	Broch: *The Death of Virgil*. Betjeman: *New Bats in Old Belfries*. Orwell: *Animal Farm*. Henry Green: *Loving*.
1946	Birth of his son James. *Scott-King's Modern Europe*, *When the Going Was Good*.	Rattigan: *The Winslow Boy*. Cocteau: *L'Aigle à deux têtes*. Henry Green: *Back*. Dylan Thomas: *Deaths and Entrances*.
1947	*Wine in Peace and War*.	Mann: *Doctor Faustus*. Camus: *La Peste*. Diary of Anne Frank is published. Henry Green: *Concluding*.
1948	*The Loved One*.	Eliot: *Notes Towards the Definition of Culture*. Graham Greene: *The Heart of the Matter*. Faulkner: *Intruder in the Dust*. Henry Green: *Nothing*.
1949		Acton: *Memoirs of an Aesthete*. Orwell: *Nineteen Eighty-Four*. De Beauvoir: *The Second Sex*. Graham Greene: *The Third Man*.
1950	Birth of his son Septimus. *Helena*.	Miller: *Death of a Salesman*. Lawrence Durrell: *Sappho*. Hemingway: *Across the River and into the Trees*. Eliot: *The Cocktail Party*. Henry Green: *Doting*.
1951		Salinger: *The Catcher in the Rye*. Powell: *A Question of Upbringing* (the first of the 12 novels comprising *A Dance to the Music of Time*: 1952–75).

CHRONOLOGY

HISTORICAL EVENTS

Germans retreat in Russia, Africa and Italy.

Germany is besieged.

Hitler commits suicide. World War II ends after atom bombs are dropped on Hiroshima and Nagasaki.

Iron curtain speech by Churchill.

Gruppe 47 founded by Young German Writers. Dead Sea scrolls are discovered.

Erhard launches the Deutschemark.

Germany is divided: Adenauer is Chancellor of West Germany, Ulbricht rules East.

Korea declares itself an independent state. Macarthy witch hunts – persecution of Communists throughout US.

DATE	AUTHOR'S LIFE	LITERARY CONTEXT
1952	*Men at Arms*, the first part of the *Sword of Honour* trilogy. *The Holy Places*.	Beckett: *Waiting for Godot*. Miller: *The Crucible*.
1953	*Love Among the Ruins*.	Hartley: *The Go-Between*.
1955	Moves to a large country house in Somerset with his family. *Officers and Gentlemen*, the second part of the *Sword of Honour* trilogy.	Nabokov: *Lolita*. Miller: *A View from the Bridge*. Graham Greene: *Loser Takes All*; *The Quiet American*. Murdoch: *Under The Net*.
1956		Beckett: *Molloy*. Camus: *The Fall*. Faulkner: *Requiem for a Nun*.
1957	*The Ordeal of Gilbert Pinfold*.	Camus: *L'Exil et le Royaume*. Pasternak: *Doctor Zhivago*. Pinter: *The Birthday Party*. Nabokov: *Pnin*. Spark: *The Comforters*.
1959	Publishes a biography of Ronald Knox.	Spark: *Memento Mori*. Eliot: *The Elder Statesman*. Graham Greene: *The Complaisant Lover*. Beckett: *Endgame*.
1960	*A Tourist in Africa*.	Spark: *The Ballad of Peckham Rye*. Updike: *Rabbit, Run*. Pinter: *The Caretaker*. Betjeman: *Summoned by Bells*.
1961	*Unconditional Surrender*, the final part of the *Sword of Honour* trilogy.	Graham Greene: *A Burnt-Out Case*. Albee: *The American Dream*. Huxley: *Religion without Revelation*. Spark: *The Prime of Miss Jean Brodie*.
1962	*Tactical Exercise*.	Albee: *Who's Afraid of Virginia Woolf?* Isherwood: *Down There on a Visit*.
1963	*Basil Seal Rides Again*.	Stoppard: *A Walk on Water*. Pinter: *The Lover*. Spark: *The Girls of Slender Means*.
1964	*A Little Learning*, an autobiography.	Sartre: *Les Mots*. Ayme: *The Minotaur*. Isherwood: *A Single Man*.
1965		Pinter: *The Homecoming*. Albee: *Tiny Alice*.
1966	Waugh dies at his home after Mass on Easter Sunday.	Albee: *A Delicate Balance*.

CHRONOLOGY

Burgess and Maclean defect to USSR.

Josef Stalin dies. USSR anti-Semite campaign.
USSR denounces its alliances with France and Britain. West Germany joins NATO.

Suez crisis and invasion of Hungary by USSR.

Macmillan becomes Prime Minister. Adenauer obtains an absolute majority in German elections. Gromyko becomes Minister for foreign affairs in the USSR. Suez canal re-opened.

De Gaulle becomes President of the French Republic. Castro becomes the leader of Cuba.

J. F. Kennedy becomes US President.

Khrushchev in UNO leads to a public scandal. Cuban missile crisis. Berlin wall is constructed. Britain applies to join the Common Market.

Spiegel affair in East Germany. Anglo-French agreement on the construction of Concorde.

Assassination of President Kennedy. Profumo affair. Douglas-Home becomes Prime Minister. Britain joins the Common Market.

Wilson becomes Prime Minister. Martin Luther King is awarded the Nobel Peace prize.

BRIDESHEAD REVISITED

The sacred and profane Memories
of Captain Charles Ryder

CONTENTS

To
LAURA

PREFACE

THIS novel, which is here re-issued with many small additions and some substantial cuts, lost me such esteem as I once enjoyed among my contemporaries and led me into an unfamiliar world of fan-mail and press photographers. Its theme – the operation of divine grace on a group of diverse but closely connected characters – was perhaps presumptuously large, but I make no apology for it. I am less happy about its form, whose more glaring defects may be blamed on the circumstances in which it was written.

In December 1943 I had the good fortune when parachuting to incur a minor injury which afforded me a rest from military service. This was extended by a sympathetic commanding officer, who let me remain unemployed until June 1944 when the book was finished. I wrote with a zest that was quite strange to me and also with impatience to get back to the war. It was a bleak period of present privation and threatening disaster – the period of soya beans and Basic English – and in consequence the book is infused with a kind of gluttony, for food and wine, for the splendours of the recent past, and for rhetorical and ornamental language, which now with a full stomach I find distasteful. I have modified the grosser passages but have not obliterated them because they are an essential part of the book.

I have been in two minds as to the treatment of Julia's outburst about mortal sin and Lord Marchmain's dying soliloquy. These passages were never, of course, intended to report words actually spoken. They belong to a different way of writing from, say, the early scenes between Charles and his father. I would not now introduce them into a novel which elsewhere aims at verisimilitude. But I have retained them here in something near their original form because, like the

I

Burgundy (misprinted in many editions) and the moonlight they were essentially of the mood of writing; also because many readers liked them, though that is not a consideration of first importance.

It was impossible to foresee, in the spring of 1944, the present cult of the English country house. It seemed then that the ancestral seats which were our chief national artistic achievement were doomed to decay and spoliation like the monasteries in the sixteenth century. So I piled it on rather, with passionate sincerity. Brideshead today would be open to trippers, its treasures rearranged by expert hands and the fabric better maintained than it was by Lord Marchmain. And the English aristocracy has maintained its identity to a degree that then seemed impossible. The advance of Hooper has been held up at several points. Much of this book therefore is a panegyric preached over an empty coffin. But it would be impossible to bring it up to date without totally destroying it. It is offered to a younger generation of readers as a souvenir of the Second War rather than of the twenties or of the thirties, with which it ostensibly deals.

                                                                E. W.

Combe Florey 1959

PROLOGUE
Brideshead Revisited

WHEN I reached 'C' Company lines, which were at the top of the hill, I paused and looked back at the camp, just coming into full view below me through the grey mist of early morning. We were leaving that day. When we marched in, three months before, the place was under snow; now the first leaves of spring were unfolding. I had reflected then that, whatever scenes of desolation lay ahead of us, I never feared one more brutal than this, and I reflected now that it had no single happy memory for me.

Here love had died between me and the army.

Here the tram-lines ended, so that men returning fuddled from Glasgow could doze in their seats until roused by their journey's end. There was some way to go from the tram-stop to the camp gates; quarter of a mile in which they could button their blouses and straighten their caps before passing the guard-room, quarter of a mile in which concrete gave place to grass at the road's edge. This was the extreme limit of the city. Here the close, homogeneous territory of housing estates and cinemas ended and the hinterland began.

The camp stood where, until quite lately, had been pasture and ploughland; the farmhouse still stood in a fold of the hill and had served us for battalion offices; ivy still supported part of what had once been the walls of a fruit garden; half an acre of mutilated old trees behind the wash-houses survived of an orchard. The place had been marked for destruction before the army came to it. Had there been another year of peace, there would have been no farmhouse, no wall, no apple trees. Already half a mile of concrete road lay between bare clay banks, and on either side a chequer of open ditches showed where the municipal contractors had designed a system of drainage. Another

year of peace would have made the place part of the neighbouring suburb. Now the huts where we had wintered waited their
turn for destruction.

Over the way, the subject of much ironical comment, half
hidden even in winter by its embosoming trees, lay the municipal lunatic asylum, whose cast-iron railings and noble gates put
our rough wire to shame. We could watch the madmen, on
clement days, sauntering and skipping among the trim gravel
walks and pleasantly planted lawns; happy collaborationists
who had given up the unequal struggle, all doubts resolved, all
duty done, the undisputed heirs-at-law of a century of progress,
enjoying the heritage at their ease. As we marched past, the
men used to shout greetings to them through the railings –
'Keep a bed warm for me, chum. I shan't be long' – but
Hooper, my newest-joined platoon-commander, grudged them
their life of privilege; 'Hitler would put them in a gas chamber,'
he said; 'I reckon we can learn a thing or two from him.'

Here, when we marched in at mid-winter, I brought a
company of strong and hopeful men; word had gone round
among them, as we moved from the moors to this dockland
area, that we were at last in transit for the Middle East. As the
days passed and we began clearing the snow and levelling a
parade ground, I saw their disappointment change to resignation. They snuffed the smell of the fried-fish shops and cocked
their ears to familiar, peace-time sounds of the works' siren and
the dance-hall band. On off-days they slouched now at street
corners and sidled away at the approach of an officer for fear
that, by saluting, they would lose face with their new mistresses.
In the company office there was a crop of minor charges and
requests for compassionate leave; while it was still half-light,
day began with the whine of the malingerer and the glum face
and fixed eye of the man with a grievance.

And I, who by every precept should have put heart into
them – how could I help them, who could so little help myself?
Here the colonel under whom we had formed, was promoted
out of our sight and succeeded by a younger and less lovable
man, cross-posted from another regiment. There were few left in

the mess now of the batch of volunteers who trained together at the outbreak of war; one way and another they were nearly all gone – some had been invalided out, some promoted to other battalions, some posted to staff jobs, some had volunteered for special service, one had got himself killed on the field firing range, one had been court-martialled – and their places were taken by conscripts; the wireless played incessantly in the ante-room nowadays, and much beer was drunk before dinner; it was not as it had been.

Here at the age of thirty-nine I began to be old. I felt stiff and weary in the evenings and reluctant to go out of camp; I developed proprietary claims to certain chairs and newspapers; I regularly drank three glasses of gin before dinner, never more or less, and went to bed immediately after the nine o'clock news. I was always awake and fretful an hour before reveille.

Here my last love died. There was nothing remarkable in the manner of its death. One day, not long before this last day in camp, as I lay awake before reveille, in the Nissen hut, gazing into the complete blackness, amid the deep breathing and muttering of the four other occupants, turning over in my mind what I had to do that day – had I put in the names of two corporals for the weapon-training course? Should I again have the largest number of men overstaying their leave in the batch due back that day? Could I trust Hooper to take the candidates class out map-reading? – as I lay in that dark hour, I was aghast to realize that something within me, long sickening, had quietly died, and felt as a husband might feel, who, in the fourth year of his marriage, suddenly knew that he had no longer any desire, or tenderness, or esteem, for a once-beloved wife; no pleasure in her company, no wish to please, no curiosity about anything she might ever do or say or think; no hope of setting things right, no self-reproach for the disaster. I knew it all, the whole drab compass of marital disillusion; we had been through it together, the Army and I, from the first importunate courtship until now, when nothing remained to us except the chill bonds of law and duty and custom. I had played every scene in the domestic tragedy, had found the early tiffs become more frequent, the tears less affecting, the reconciliations less sweet, till they engendered a mood of aloofness and cool criticism, and the growing conviction that it was not myself but the loved one who was at fault. I caught the false notes in her voice and learned to listen for them apprehensively; I recognized the blank, resentful stare of incomprehension in her eyes, and the selfish, hard set of the corners of her mouth. I learned her, as one must learn a woman one has kept house with, day in, day out, for three and a half years; I learned her slatternly ways, the routine and mechanism of her charm, her jealousy and self-seeking, and her nervous trick with the fingers when she was lying. She was stripped of all enchantment now and I knew her for an uncongenial stranger to whom I had bound myself indissolubly in a moment of folly.

So, on this morning of our move, I was entirely indifferent as to our destination. I would go on with my job, but I could bring to it nothing more than acquiescence. Our orders were to entrain at 0915 hours at a nearby siding, taking in the haversack the unexpired portion of the day's ration; that was all I needed to know. The company second-in-command had gone on with a small advance party. Company stores had been packed the day before. Hooper had been detailed to inspect the lines. The company was parading at 0730 hours with their kitbags piled before the huts. There had been many such moves since the wildly exhilarating morning in 1940 when we had erroneously believed ourselves destined for the defence of Calais. Three or four times a year since then we had changed our location; this time our new commanding officer was making an unusual display of 'security' and had even put us to the trouble of removing all distinguishing badges from our uniforms and transport. It was 'valuable training in active service conditions', he said. 'If I find any of these female camp followers waiting for us the other end, I'll know there's been a leakage.'

The smoke from the cook-houses drifted away in the mist and the camp lay revealed as a planless maze of short-cuts, superimposed on the unfinished housing-scheme, as though disinterred at a much later date by a party of archaeologists.

'*The Pollock diggings provide a valuable link between the citizen-slave communities of the twentieth century and the tribal anarchy which succeeded them. Here you see a people of advanced culture, capable of an elaborate draining system and the construction of permanent highways, over-run by a race of the lowest type.*'

Thus, I thought, the pundits of the future might write; and, turning away, I greeted the company sergeant-major: 'Has Mr Hooper been round?'

'Haven't seen him at all this morning, sir.'

We went to the dismantled company office, where I found a window newly broken since the barrack-damages book was completed. 'Wind-in-the-night, sir,' said the sergeant-major.

(All breakages were thus attributable or to 'Sappers'-demonstration, sir.')

Hooper appeared; he was a sallow youth with hair combed back, without parting, from his forehead, and a flat, Midland accent; he had been in the company two months.

The troops did not like Hooper because he knew too little about his work and would sometimes address them individually as 'George' at stand-easies, but I had a feeling which almost amounted to affection for him, largely by reason of an incident on his first evening in mess.

The new colonel had been with us less than a week at the time and we had not yet taken his measure. He had been standing rounds of gin in the ante-room and was slightly boisterous when he first took notice of Hooper.

'That young officer is one of yours, isn't he, Ryder?' he said to me. 'His hair wants cutting.'

'It does, sir,' I said. It did. 'I'll see that it's done.'

The colonel drank more gin and began to stare at Hooper, saying audibly, 'My God, the officers they send us now!'

Hooper seemed to obsess the colonel that evening. After dinner he suddenly said very loudly: 'In my late regiment if a young officer turned up like that, the other subalterns would bloody well have cut his hair for him.'

No one showed any enthusiasm for this sport, and our lack of response seemed to inflame the colonel. 'You,' he said, turning to a decent boy in 'A' Company, 'go and get a pair of scissors and cut that young officer's hair for him.'

'Is that an order, sir?'

'It's your commanding officer's wish and that's the best kind of order I know.'

'Very good, sir.'

And so, in an atmosphere of chilly embarrassment, Hooper sat in a chair while a few snips were made at the back of his head. At the beginning of the operation I left the ante-room, and later apologized to Hooper for his reception. 'It's not the sort of thing that usually happens in this regiment,' I said.

'Oh, no hard feelings,' said Hooper. 'I can take a bit of sport.'

Hooper had no illusions about the Army – or rather no special illusions distinguishable from the general, enveloping fog from which he observed the universe. He had come to it reluctantly, under compulsion, after he had made every feeble effort in his power to obtain deferment. He accepted it, he said, 'like the measles'. Hooper was no romantic. He had not as a child ridden with Rupert's horse or sat among the camp fires at Xanthus-side; at the age when my eyes were dry to all save poetry – that stoic, redskin interlude which our schools introduce between the fast-flowing tears of the child and the man – Hooper had wept often, but never for Henry's speech on St Crispin's day, nor for the epitaph at Thermopylae. The history they taught him had had few battles in it but, instead, a profusion of detail about humane legislation and recent industrial change. Gallipoli, Balaclava, Quebec, Lepanto, Bannockburn, Roncevales, and Marathon – these, and the Battle in the West where Arthur fell, and a hundred such names whose trumpet-notes, even now in my sere and lawless state, called to me irresistibly across the intervening years with all the clarity and strength of boyhood, sounded in vain to Hooper.

He seldom complained. Though himself a man to whom one could not confidently entrust the simplest duty, he had an over-mastering regard for efficiency and, drawing on his modest commercial experience, he would sometimes say of the ways of the Army in pay and supply and the use of 'man-hours': 'They couldn't get away with that in business.'

He slept sound while I lay awake fretting.

In the weeks that we were together Hooper became a symbol to me of Young England, so that whenever I read some public utterance proclaiming what Youth demanded in the Future and what the world owed to Youth, I would test these general statements by substituting 'Hooper' and seeing if they still seemed as plausible. Thus in the dark hour before reveille I sometimes pondered: 'Hooper Rallies', 'Hooper Hostels', 'International Hooper Cooperation', and 'the Religion of Hooper'. He was the acid test of all these alloys.

So far as he had changed at all, he was less soldierly now than when he arrived from his OCTU. This morning, laden with full equipment, he looked scarcely human. He came to attention with a kind of shuffling dance-step and spread a wool-gloved palm across his forehead.

'I want to speak to Mr Hooper, sergeant-major ... well, where the devil have you been? I told you to inspect the lines.'

''M I late? Sorry. Had a rush getting my gear together.'

'That's what you have a servant for.'

'Well, I suppose it is, strictly speaking. But you know how it is. He had his own stuff to do. If you get on the wrong side of these fellows they take it out of you other ways.'

'Well, go and inspect the lines now.'

'Rightyoh.'

'And for Christ's sake don't say "rightyoh".'

'Sorry. I do try to remember. It just slips out.'

When Hooper left the sergeant-major returned.

'C.O. just coming up the path, sir,' he said.

I went out to meet him.

There were beads of moisture on the hog-bristles of his little red moustache.

'Well, everything squared up here?'

'Yes, I think so, sir.'

'*Think so?* You ought to know.'

His eyes fell on the broken window. 'Has that been entered in the barrack damages?'

'Not yet, sir.'

'*Not yet?* I wonder when it would have been, if I hadn't seen it.'

He was not at ease with me, and much of his bluster rose from timidity, but I thought none the better of it for that.

He led me behind the huts to a wire fence which divided my area from the carrier-platoon's, skipped briskly over, and made for an overgrown ditch and bank which had once been a field boundary on the farm. Here he began grubbing with his walking-stick like a truffling pig and presently gave a cry of triumph. He had disclosed one of those deposits of rubbish, which are dear to the private soldier's sense of order: the head of a broom, the lid of a stove, a bucket rusted through, a sock, a loaf of bread, lay under the dock and nettle among cigarette packets and empty tins.

'Look at that,' said the commanding officer. 'Fine impression that gives to the regiment taking over from us.'

'That's bad,' I said.

'It's a disgrace. See everything there is burned before you leave camp.'

'Very good, sir. Sergeant-major, send over to the carrier-platoon and tell Captain Brown that the C.O. wants this ditch cleared up.'

I wondered whether the colonel would take this rebuff; so did he. He stood a moment irresolutely prodding the muck in the ditch, then he turned on his heel and strode away.

'You shouldn't do it, sir,' said the sergeant-major, who had been my guide and prop since I joined the company. 'You shouldn't really.'

'That wasn't our rubbish.'

'Maybe not, sir, but you know how it is. If you get on the wrong side of senior officers they take it out of you other ways.'

As we marched past the madhouse, two or three elderly inmates gibbered and mouthed politely behind the railings.

'Cheeroh, chum, we'll be seeing you'; 'We shan't be long now'; 'Keep smiling till we meet again', the men called to them.

I was marching with Hooper at the head of the leading platoon.

'I say, any idea where we're off to?'

'None.'

'D'you think it's the real thing?'

'No.'

'Just a flap?'

'Yes.'

'Everyone's been saying we're for it. I don't know what to think really. Seems so silly somehow, all this drill and training if we never go into action.'

'I shouldn't worry. There'll be plenty for everyone in time.'

'Oh, I don't want *much* you know. Just enough to say I've been in it.'

A train of antiquated coaches was waiting for us at the siding; an R.T.O. was in charge; a fatigue party was loading the last of the kit-bags from the trucks to the luggage vans. In half an hour we were ready to start and in an hour we started.

My three platoon commanders and myself had a carriage to ourselves. They ate sandwiches and chocolate, smoked and slept. None of them had a book. For the first three or four hours they noted the names of the towns and leaned out of the windows when, as often happened, we stopped between stations. Later they lost interest. At midday and again at dark some tepid cocoa was ladled from a container into our mugs. The train moved slowly south through flat, drab main-line scenery.

The chief incident in the day was the C.O.'s 'order group'. We assembled in his carriage, at the summons of an orderly, and found him and the adjutant wearing their steel helmets and equipment. The first thing he said was: 'This is an Order Group. I expect you to attend properly dressed. The fact that we happen to be in a train is immaterial.' I thought he was going to send us back but, after glaring at us, he said, 'Sit down.'

'The camp was left in a disgraceful condition. Wherever I went I found evidence that officers are not doing their duty. The state in which a camp is left is the best possible test of the efficiency of regimental officers. It is on such matters that the reputation of a battalion and its commander rests. And' – did he in fact say this or am I finding words for the resentment in his voice and eye? I think he left it unsaid – 'I do not intend to have my professional reputation compromised by the slackness of a few temporary officers.'

We sat with our note-books and pencils waiting to take down the details of our next jobs. A more sensitive man would have seen that he had failed to be impressive; perhaps he saw, for he added in a petulant schoolmasterish way: 'All I ask is loyal cooperation.'

Then he referred to his notes and read:

'Orders.

'Information. The battalion is now in transit between location A and location B. This is a major L of C and is liable to bombing and gas attack from the enemy.

'Intention. I intend to arrive at location B.

'Method. Train will arrive at destination at approximately 2315 hours ...' and so on.

The sting came at the end under the heading, 'Administration'. 'C' Company, less one platoon, was to unload the train on arrival at the siding where three three-tonners would be available for moving all stores to a battalion dump in the new camp; work to continue until completed; the remaining platoon was to find a guard on the dump and perimeter sentries for the camp area.

'Any questions?'

'Can we have an issue of cocoa for the working party?'

'No. Any more questions?'

When I told the sergeant-major of these orders he said: 'Poor old "C" Company struck unlucky again'; and I knew this to be a reproach for my having antagonized the commanding officer.

I told the platoon commanders.

'I say,' said Hooper, 'it makes it awfully awkward with the

chaps. They'll be fairly browned off. He always seems to pick on us for the dirty work.'

'You'll do guard.'

'Okeydoke. But I say, how am I to find the perimeter in the dark?'

Shortly after blackout we were disturbed by an orderly making his way lugubriously down the length of the train with a rattle. One of the more sophisticated sergeants called out '*Deuxième service.*'

'We are being sprayed with liquid mustard-gas,' I said. 'See that the windows are shut.' I then wrote a neat little situation-report to say that there were no casualties and nothing had been contaminated; that men had been detailed to decontaminate the outside of the coach before detraining. This seemed to satisfy the commanding officer, for we heard no more from him. After dark we all slept.

At last, very late, we came to our siding. It was part of our training in security and active service conditions that we should eschew stations and platforms. The drop from the running board to the cinder track made for disorder and breakages in the darkness.

'Fall in on the road below the embankment. "C" Company seem to be taking their time as usual, Captain Ryder.'

'Yes, sir. We're having a little difficulty with the bleach.'

'Bleach?'

'For decontaminating the outside of the coaches, sir.'

'Oh, very conscientious, I'm sure. Skip it and get a move on.'

By now my half-awake and sulky men were clattering into shape on the road. Soon Hooper's platoon had marched off into the darkness; I found the lorries, organized lines of men to pass the stores from hand to hand down the steep bank, and, presently, as they found themselves doing something with an apparent purpose in it, they got more cheerful. I handled stores with them for the first half hour; then broke off to meet the company second-in-command who came down with the first returning truck.

'It's not a bad camp,' he reported; 'big private house with

two or three lakes. Looks as if we might get some duck if we're lucky. Village with one pub and a post office. No town within miles. I've managed to get a hut between the two of us.'

By four in the morning the work was done. I drove in the last lorry, through tortuous lanes where the overhanging boughs whipped the windscreen; somewhere we left the lane and turned into a drive; somewhere we reached an open space where two drives converged and a ring of storm lanterns marked the heap of stores. Here we unloaded the truck and, at long last, followed the guides to our quarters, under a starless sky, with a fine drizzle of rain beginning now to fall.

I slept until my servant called me, rose wearily, dressed and shaved in silence. It was not till I reached the door that I asked the second-in-command, 'What's this place called?'

He told me and, on the instant, it was as though someone had switched off the wireless, and a voice that had been bawling in my ears, incessantly, fatuously, for days beyond number, had been suddenly cut short; an immense silence followed, empty at first, but gradually, as my outraged sense regained authority, full of a multitude of sweet and natural and long forgotten sounds: for he had spoken a name that was so familiar to me, a conjuror's name of such ancient power, that, at its mere sound, the phantoms of those haunted late years began to take flight.

Outside the hut I stood bemused. The rain had ceased but the clouds hung low and heavy overhead. It was a still morning and the smoke from the cook-house rose straight to the leaden sky. A cart-track, once metalled, then overgrown, now rutted and churned to mud, followed the contour of the hillside and dipped out of sight below a knoll, and on either side of it lay the haphazard litter of corrugated iron, from which rose the rattle and chatter and whistling and catcalls, all the zoo-noises of the battalion beginning a new day. Beyond and about us, more familiar still, lay an exquisite man-made landscape. It was a sequestered place, enclosed and embraced in a single, winding valley. Our camp lay along one gentle slope; opposite us the ground led, still unravished, to the neighbourly horizon, and between us flowed a stream – it was named the Bride and rose not two miles away at a farm called Bridesprings, where we used sometimes to walk to tea; it became a considerable river lower down before it joined the Avon – which had been dammed here to form three lakes, one no more than a wet slate among the reeds, but the others more spacious, reflecting the clouds and the mighty beeches at their margin. The woods were all of oak and beech, the oak grey and bare, the beech faintly dusted with green by the breaking buds; they made a simple, carefully designed pattern with the green glades and the wide green spaces – Did the fallow deer graze here still? – and, lest the eye wander aimlessly, a Doric temple stood by the water's edge, and an ivy-grown arch spanned the lowest of the connecting weirs. All this had been planned and planted a century and a half ago so that, at about this date, it might be seen in its maturity. From where I stood the house was hidden by a green spur, but I knew well how and where it lay, couched among the lime trees like a hind in the bracken.

Hooper came sidling up and greeted me with his much imitated but inimitable salute. His face was grey from his night's vigil and he had not yet shaved.

' "B" Company relieved us. I've sent the chaps off to get cleaned up.'

'Good.'

'The house is up there, round the corner.'

'Yes,' I said.

'Brigade Headquarters are coming there next week. Great barrack of a place. I've just had a snoop round. Very ornate, I'd call it. And a queer thing, there's a sort of R.C. Church attached. I looked in and there was a kind of service going on – just a padre and one old man. I felt very awkward. More in your line than mine.' Perhaps I seemed not to hear; in a final effort to excite my interest he said: 'There's a frightful great fountain, too, in front of the steps, all rocks and sort of carved animals. You never saw such a thing.'

'Yes, Hooper, I did. I've been here before.'

The words seemed to ring back to me enriched from the vaults of my dungeon.

'Oh well, you know all about it. I'll go and get cleaned up.'

I had been there before; I knew all about it.

BOOK ONE

ET IN ARCADIA EGO

CHAPTER I

'I HAVE been here before,' I said; I had been there before; first
with Sebastian more than twenty years ago on a cloudless day
in June, when the ditches were creamy with meadowsweet and
the air heavy with all the scents of summer; it was a day of
peculiar splendour, and though I had been there so often, in so
many moods, it was to that first visit that my heart returned on
this, my latest.

That day, too, I had come not knowing my destination. It
was Eights Week. Oxford – submerged now and obliterated,
irrecoverable as Lyonnesse, so quickly have the waters come
flooding in – Oxford, in those days, was still a city of aquatint.
In her spacious and quiet streets men walked and spoke as they
had done in Newman's day; her autumnal mists, her grey
springtime, and the rare glory of her summer days – such as that
day – when the chestnut was in flower and the bells rang out
high and clear over her gables and cupolas, exhaled the soft airs
of centuries of youth. It was this cloistral hush which gave our
laughter its resonance, and carried it still, joyously, over the
intervening clamour. Here, discordantly, in Eights Week, came
a rabble of womankind, some hundreds strong, twittering and
fluttering over the cobbles and up the steps, sight-seeing and
pleasure-seeking, drinking claret cup, eating cucumber sandwiches; pushed in punts about the river, herded in droves to the
college barges; greeted in the *Isis* and in the Union by a sudden
display of peculiar, facetious, wholly distressing Gilbert-and-
Sullivan badinage, and by peculiar choral effects in the College
chapels. Echoes of the intruders penetrated every corner, and in
my own College was no echo, but an original fount of the
grossest disturbance. We were giving a ball. The front quad,
where I lived, was floored and tented; palms and azaleas were

banked round the porter's lodge; worst of all, the don who lived above me, a mouse of a man connected with the Natural Sciences, had lent his rooms for a Ladies' Cloakroom, and a printed notice proclaiming this outrage hung not six inches from my oak.

No one felt more strongly about it than my scout.

'Gentlemen who haven't got ladies are asked as far as possible to take their meals out in the next few days,' he announced despondently. 'Will you be lunching in?'

'No, Lunt.'

'So as to give the servants a chance, they say. What a chance! I've got to buy a *pin-cushion* for the Ladies' Cloakroom. What do they want with dancing? I don't see the reason in it. There never was dancing before in Eights Week. Commem. now is another matter being in the vacation, but not in Eights Week, as if teas and the river wasn't enough. If you ask me, sir, it's all on account of the war. It couldn't have happened but for that.' For this was 1923 and for Lunt, as for thousands of others, things could never be the same as they had been in 1914. 'Now wine in the evening,' he continued, as was his habit half in and half out of the door, 'or one or two gentlemen to luncheon, there's reason in. But not dancing. It all came in with the men back from the war. They were too old and they didn't know and they wouldn't learn. That's the truth. And there's some even goes dancing with the town at the Masonic – but the proctors will get *them*, you see ... Well, here's Lord Sebastian. I mustn't stand here talking when there's pin-cushions to get.'

Sebastian entered – dove-grey flannel, white *crêpe de Chine*, a Charvet tie, my tie as it happened, a pattern of postage stamps – 'Charles – what in the world's happening at your college? Is there a circus? I've seen everything except elephants. I must say the whole of Oxford has become *most* peculiar suddenly. Last night it was pullulating with women. You're to come away at once, out of danger. I've got a motor-car and a basket of strawberries and a bottle of Château Peyraguey – which isn't a wine you've ever tasted, so don't pretend. It's heaven with strawberries.'

'Where are we going?'

'To see a friend.'

'Who?'

'Name of Hawkins. Bring some money in case we see anything we want to buy. The motor-car is the property of a man called Hardcastle. Return the bits to him if I kill myself; I'm not very good at driving.'

Beyond the gate, beyond the winter garden that was once the lodge, stood an open, two-seater Morris-Cowley. Sebastian's teddy-bear sat at the wheel. We put him between us – 'Take care he's not sick' – and drove off. The bells of St Mary's were chiming nine; we escaped collision with a clergyman, black-straw-hatted, white-bearded, pedalling quietly down the wrong side of the High Street, crossed Carfax, passed the station, and were soon in open country on the Botley Road; open country was easily reached in those days.

'Isn't it early?' said Sebastian. 'The women are still doing whatever women do to themselves before they come downstairs. Sloth has undone them. We're away. God bless Hardcastle.'

'Whoever he may be.'

'He thought he was coming with us. Sloth undid him too. Well, I did tell him *ten*. He's a very gloomy man in my college. He leads a double life. At least I assume he does. He couldn't go on being Hardcastle, day and night, always, could he? – or he'd die of it. He says he knows my father, which is impossible.'

'Why?'

'No one knows papa. He's a social leper. Hadn't you heard?'

'It's a pity neither of us can sing,' I said.

At Swindon we turned off the main road and, as the sun mounted high, we were among dry-stone walls and ashlar houses. It was about eleven when Sebastian, without warning, turned the car into a cart-track and stopped. It was hot enough now to make us seek the shade. On a sheep-cropped knoll under a clump of elms we ate the strawberries and drank the wine – as Sebastian promised, they were delicious together – and we lit fat, Turkish cigarettes and lay on our backs, Sebastian's eyes on the leaves above him, mine on his profile, while the blue-grey smoke rose, untroubled by any wind, to the blue-green shadows of foliage, and the sweet scent of the tobacco merged with the sweet summer scents around us and the fumes of the sweet, golden wine seemed to lift us a finger's breadth above the turf and hold us suspended.

'Just the place to bury a crock of gold,' said Sebastian. 'I should like to bury something precious in every place where I've been happy and then, when I was old and ugly and miserable, I could come back and dig it up and remember.'

This was my third term since matriculation, but I date my Oxford life from my first meeting with Sebastian, which had happened, by chance, in the middle of the term before. We were in different colleges and came from different schools; I might well have spent my three or four years in the University and never have met him, but for the chance of his getting drunk one evening in my college and of my having ground-floor rooms in the front quadrangle.

I had been warned against the dangers of these rooms by my cousin Jasper, who alone, when I first came up, thought me a suitable subject for detailed guidance. My father offered me none. Then, as always, he eschewed serious conversation with me. It was not until I was within a fortnight of going up that he mentioned the subject at all; then he said, shyly and rather slyly: 'I've been talking about you. I met your future Warden at the Athenaeum. I wanted to talk about Etruscan notions of immortality; he wanted to talk about extension lectures for the working class; so we compromised and talked about you. I asked him what your allowance should be. He said, 'Three hundred a year; on no account give him more; that's all most men have.' I thought that a deplorable answer. *I* had more than most men when *I* was up, and my recollection is that nowhere else in the world and at no other time, do a few hundred pounds, one way or the other, make so much difference to one's importance and popularity. I toyed with the idea of giving you six hundred,' said my father, snuffling a little, as he did when he was amused, 'but I reflected that, should the Warden come to hear of it, it might sound deliberately impolite. So I shall give you five hundred and fifty.'

I thanked him.

'Yes, it's indulgent of me, but it all comes out of capital, you know. ... I suppose this is the time I should give you advice. I never had any myself except once from your cousin Alfred. Do you know, in the summer before I was going up, your cousin Alfred rode over to Boughton especially to give me a piece of advice? And do you know what that advice was? 'Ned,' he said, 'there's one thing I must beg of you. *Always* wear a tall hat on Sundays during term. It is by that, more than anything, that a man is judged.' And do you know,' continued my father, snuffling deeply, 'I *always did*? Some men did, some didn't. I never saw any difference between them or heard it commented on, but I *always wore mine*. It only shows what effect judicious advice can have, properly delivered at the right moment. I wish I had some for you, but I haven't.'

My cousin Jasper made good the loss; he was the son of my father's elder brother, to whom he referred more than once, only half facetiously, as 'the Head of the Family'; he was in his fourth year and, the term before, had come within appreciable distance of getting his rowing blue; he was secretary of the Canning and president of the J.C.R.; a considerable person in college. He called on me formally during my first week and stayed to tea; he ate a very heavy meal of honey-buns, anchovy toast, and Fuller's walnut cake, then he lit his pipe and, lying back in the basket-chair, laid down the rules of conduct which I should follow; he covered most subjects; even today I could repeat much of what he said, word for word. '... You're reading History? A perfectly respectable school. The very worst is English literature and the next worst is Modern Greats. You want either a first or a fourth. There is no value in anything between. Time spent on a good second is time thrown away. You should go to the best lectures – Arkwright on Demosthenes for instance – irrespective of whether they are in your school or not. ... Clothes. Dress as you do in a country house. Never wear a tweed coat and flannel trousers – always a suit. And go to a

London tailor; you get better cut and longer credit. ... Clubs. Join the Carlton now and the Grid at the beginning of your second year. If you want to run for the Union – and it's not a bad thing to do – make your reputation *outside* first, at the Canning or the Chatham, and begin by speaking on the paper. ... Keep clear of Boar's Hill. ...' The sky over the opposing gables glowed and then darkened; I put more coal on the fire and turned on the light, revealing in their respectability his London-made plus-fours and his Leander tie. ... 'Don't treat dons like schoolmasters; treat them as you would the vicar at home. ... You'll find you spend half your second year shaking off the undesirable friends you made in your first. ... Beware of the Anglo-Catholics – they're all sodomites with unpleasant accents. In fact, steer clear of all the religious groups; they do nothing but harm. ...'

Finally, just as he was going, he said, 'One last point. Change your rooms.' – They were large, with deeply recessed windows and painted, eighteenth-century panelling; I was lucky as a freshman to get them. 'I've seen many a man ruined through having ground-floor rooms in the front quad,' said my cousin with deep gravity. 'People start dropping in. They leave their gowns here and come and collect them before hall; you start giving them sherry. Before you know where you are, you've opened a free bar for all the undesirables of the college.'

I do not know that I ever, consciously, followed any of this advice. I certainly never changed my rooms; there were gilly-flowers growing below the windows which on summer evenings filled them with fragrance.

It is easy, retrospectively, to endow one's youth with a false precocity or a false innocence; to tamper with the dates marking one's stature on the edge of the door. I should like to think – indeed I sometimes do think – that I decorated those rooms with Morris stuffs and Arundel prints and that my shelves were filled with seventeenth-century folios and French novels of the second empire in Russia-leather and watered silk. But this was not the truth. On my first afternoon I proudly hung a reproduction of Van Gogh's *Sunflowers* over the fire and set up a screen, painted by Roger Fry with a Provençal landscape, which I had bought inexpensively when the Omega workshops were sold up. I displayed also a poster by McKnight Kauffer and Rhyme Sheets from the Poetry Bookshop, and, most painful to recall, a porcelain figure of Polly Peachum which stood between black tapers on the chimney-piece. My books were meagre and commonplace – Roger Fry's *Vision and Design*, the Medici Press edition of *A Shropshire Lad*, *Eminent Victorians*, some volumes of *Georgian Poetry*, *Sinister Street* and *South Wind* – and my earliest friends fitted well into this background; they were Collins, a Wykehamist, an embryo don, a man of solid reading and childlike humour, and a small circle of college intellectuals, who maintained a middle course of culture between the flamboyant 'aesthetes' and the proletarian scholars who scrambled fiercely for facts in the lodging-houses of the Iffley Road and Wellington Square. It was by this circle that I found myself adopted during my first term; they provided the kind of company I had enjoyed in the sixth form at school, for which the sixth form had prepared me; but even in the earliest days, when the whole business of living at Oxford, with rooms of my own and my own cheque book, was a source of excitement, I felt at heart that this was not all which Oxford had to offer.

At Sebastian's approach these grey figures seemed quietly to fade into the landscape and vanish, like highland sheep in the misty heather. Collins had exposed the fallacy of modern aesthetics to me: '... the whole argument from Significant Form stands or falls by *volume*. If you allow Cézanne to represent a third dimension on his two-dimensional canvas, then you must allow Landseer his gleam of loyalty in the spaniel's eye' ... but it was not until Sebastian, idly turning the page of Clive Bell's *Art*, read: "Does anyone feel the same kind of emotion for a butterfly or a flower that he feels for a cathedral or a picture?" Yes. *I* do,' that my eyes were opened.

I knew Sebastian by sight long before I met him. That was unavoidable for, from his first week, he was the most conspicuous man of his year by reason of his beauty, which was arresting, and his eccentricities of behaviour, which seemed to know no bounds. My first sight of him was in the door of Germer's, and, on that occasion, I was struck less by his looks than by the fact that he was carrying a large teddy-bear.

'That,' said the barber, as I took his chair, 'was Lord Sebastian Flyte. A *most* amusing young gentleman.'

'Apparently,' I said coldly.

'The Marquis of Marchmain's second boy. His brother, the Earl of Brideshead, went down last term. Now he was *very* different, a very quiet gentleman, quite like an old man. What do you suppose Lord Sebastian wanted? A hair brush for his teddy-bear; it had to have very stiff bristles, *not*, Lord Sebastian said, to brush him with, but to threaten him with a spanking when he was sulky. He bought a very nice one with an ivory back and he's having "Aloysius" engraved on it – that's the bear's name.' The man, who, in his time, had had ample chance to tire of undergraduate fantasy, was plainly captivated. I, however, remained censorious, and subsequent glimpses of him, driving in a hansom cab and dining at the George in false whiskers, did not soften me, although Collins, who was reading Freud, had a number of technical terms to cover everything.

Nor, when at last we met, were the circumstances propitious. It was shortly before midnight in early March; I had been entertaining the college intellectuals to mulled claret; the fire was roaring, the air of my room heavy with smoke and spice, and my mind weary with metaphysics. I threw open my windows and from the quad outside came the not uncommon sounds of bibulous laughter and unsteady steps. A voice said: 'Hold up'; another, 'Come on'; another, 'Plenty of time ... House ... till Tom stops ringing'; and another, clearer than the rest, 'D'you know I feel most unaccountably unwell. I must leave you a minute,' and there appeared at my window the face I knew to be Sebastian's, but not, as I had formerly seen it, alive and alight with gaiety; he looked at me for a moment with unfocused eyes and then, leaning forward well into the room, he was sick.

It was not unusual for dinner parties to end in that way; there was in fact a recognized tariff for the scout on such occasions; we were all learning, by trial and error, to carry our wine. There was also a kind of insane and endearing orderliness about Sebastian's choice, in his extremity, of an open window. But, when all is said, it remained an unpropitious meeting.

His friends bore him to the gate and, in a few minutes, his host, an amiable Etonian of my year, returned to apologize. He, too, was tipsy and his explanations were repetitive and, towards the end, tearful. 'The wines were too various,' he said: 'it was neither the quality nor the quantity that was at fault. It was the mixture. Grasp that and you have the root of the matter. To understand all is to forgive all.'

'Yes,' I said, but it was with a sense of grievance that I faced Lunt's reproaches next morning.

'A couple of jugs of mulled claret between the five of you,' Lunt said, 'and *this* had to happen. Couldn't even get to the window. Those that can't keep it down are better without it.'

'It wasn't one of my party. It was someone from out of college.'

'Well, it's just as nasty clearing it up, whoever it was.'

'There's five shillings on the sideboard.'

'So I saw and thank you, but I'd rather not have the money and not have the mess, *any* morning.'

I took my gown and left him to his task. I still frequented the lecture-room in those days, and it was after eleven when I returned to college. I found my room full of flowers; what looked like, and, in fact, was, the entire day's stock of a market-stall stood in every conceivable vessel in every part of the room. Lunt was secreting the last of them in brown paper preparatory to taking them home.

'Lunt, *what* is all this?'

'The gentleman from last night, sir, he left a note for you.'

The note was written in *conté* crayon on a whole sheet of my choice Whatman H.P. drawing paper: *I am very contrite. Aloysius won't speak to me until he sees I am forgiven, so please come to luncheon today. Sebastian Flyte.* It was typical of him, I reflected, to assume I knew where he lived; but, then, I *did* know.

'A most amusing gentleman, I'm sure it's quite a pleasure to clean up after him. I take it you're lunching out, sir. I told Mr Collins and Mr Partridge so – they wanted to have their commons in here with you.'

'Yes, Lunt, lunching out.'

That luncheon party – for party it proved to be – was the beginning of a new epoch in my life.

I went there uncertainly, for it was foreign ground and there was a tiny, priggish, warning voice in my ear which in the tones of Collins told me it was seemly to hold back. But I was in search of love in those days, and I went full of curiosity and the faint, unrecognized apprehension that here, at last, I should find that low door in the wall, which others, I knew, had found before me, which opened on an enclosed and enchanted garden, which was somewhere, not overlooked by any window, in the heart of that grey city.

Sebastian lived at Christ Church, high in Meadow Buildings. He was alone when I came, peeling a plover's egg taken from the large nest of moss in the centre of his table.

'I've just counted them,' he said. 'There were five each and two over, so I'm having the two. I'm unaccountably hungry today. I put myself unreservedly in the hands of Dolbear and Goodall, and feel so drugged that I've begun to believe that the whole of yesterday evening was a dream. Please don't wake me up.'

He was entrancing, with that epicene beauty which in extreme youth sings aloud for love and withers at the first cold wind.

His room was filled with a strange jumble of objects – a harmonium in a gothic case, an elephant's-foot waste-paper basket, a dome of wax fruit, two disproportionately large Sèvres vases, framed drawings by Daumier – made all the more incongruous by the austere college furniture and the large luncheon table. His chimney-piece was covered in cards of invitation from London hostesses.

'That beast Hobson has put Aloysius next door,' he said. 'Perhaps it's as well, as there wouldn't have been any plovers' eggs for him. D'you know, Hobson hates Aloysius. I wish I had a scout like yours. He was sweet to me this morning where some people might have been quite strict.'

The party assembled. There were three Etonian freshmen, mild, elegant, detached young men who had all been to a dance in London the night before, and spoke of it as though it had been the funeral of a near but unloved kinsman. Each as he came into the room made first for the plovers' eggs, then noticed Sebastian and then myself with a polite lack of curiosity which seemed to say: 'We should not dream of being so offensive as to suggest that you never met us before.'

'The first this year,' they said. 'Where do you get them?'

'Mummy sends them from Brideshead. They always lay early for her.'

When the eggs were gone and we were eating the lobster Newburg, the last guest arrived.

'My dear,' he said, 'I couldn't get away before. I was lunching with my p-p-preposterous tutor. He thought it very odd my leaving when I did. I told him I had to change for *F-f-footer*.'

He was tall, slim, rather swarthy, with large saucy eyes. The rest of us wore rough tweeds and brogues. He had on a smooth chocolate-brown suit with loud white stripes, suède shoes, a large bow-tie and he drew off yellow, wash-leather gloves as he came into the room; part Gallic, part Yankee, part, perhaps, Jew; wholly exotic.

This, I did not need telling, was Anthony Blanche, the 'aesthete' *par excellence*, a byword of iniquity from Cherwell Edge to Somerville. He had been pointed out to me often in the streets, as he pranced along with his high peacock tread; I had heard his voice in the George challenging the conventions; and now meeting him, under the spell of Sebastian, I found myself enjoying him voraciously.

After luncheon he stood on the balcony with a megaphone which had appeared surprisingly among the bric-à-brac of Sebastian's room, and in languishing tones recited passages from *The Waste Land* to the sweatered and muffled throng that was on its way to the river.

'*I, Tiresias, have foresuffered all,*' he sobbed to them from the Venetian arches;

> '*Enacted on this same d-divan or b-bed,*
> *I who have sat by Thebes below the wall*
> *And walked among the l-l-lowest of the dead ...*'

And then, stepping lightly into the room, 'How I have surprised them! All b-boatmen are Grace Darlings to me.'

We sat on sipping Cointreau while the mildest and most detached of the Etonians sang: 'Home they brought her warrior dead' to his own accompaniment on the harmonium.

It was four o'clock before we broke up.

Anthony Blanche was the first to go. He took formal and complimentary leave of each of us in turn. To Sebastian he said: 'My dear, I should like to stick you full of barbed arrows like a p-p-pin-cushion,' and to me: 'I think it's perfectly brilliant of Sebastian to have discovered you. Where do you lurk? I shall come down your burrow and ch-chivvy you out like an old st-t-toat.'

The others left soon after him. I rose to go with them, but Sebastian said: 'Have some more Cointreau,' so I stayed and later he said, 'I must go to the Botanical Gardens.'

'Why?'

'To see the ivy.'

It seemed a good enough reason and I went with him. He took my arm as we walked under the walls of Merton.

'I've never been to the Botanical Gardens,' I said.

'Oh, Charles, what a lot you have to learn! There's a beautiful arch there and more different kinds of ivy than I knew existed. I don't know where I should be without the Botanical Gardens.'

When at length I returned to my rooms and found them exactly as I had left them that morning, I detected a jejune air that had not irked me before. What was wrong? Nothing except the golden daffodils seemed to be real. Was it the screen? I turned it face to the wall. That was better.

It was the end of the screen. Lunt never liked it, and after a few days he took it away, to an obscure refuge he had under the stairs, full of mops and buckets.

That day was the beginning of my friendship with Sebastian, and thus it came about, that morning in June, that I was lying beside him in the shade of the high elms watching the smoke from his lips drift up into the branches.

Presently we drove on and in another hour were hungry. We stopped at an inn, which was half farm also, and ate eggs and bacon, pickled walnuts and cheese, and drank our beer in a sunless parlour where an old clock ticked in the shadows and a cat slept by the empty grate.

We drove on and in the early afternoon came to our destination: wrought-iron gates and twin, classical lodges on a village green, an avenue, more gates, open parkland, a turn in the drive; and suddenly a new and secret landscape opened before us. We were at the head of a valley and below us, half a mile distant, grey and gold amid a screen of boskage, shone the dome and columns of an old house.

'Well?' said Sebastian, stopping the car. Beyond the dome lay receding steps of water and round it, guarding and hiding it, stood the soft hills.

'Well?'

'What a place to live in!' I said.

'You must see the garden front and the fountain.' He leaned forward and put the car into gear. 'It's where my family live'; and even then, rapt in the vision, I felt, momentarily, an ominous chill at the words he used – not, 'that is my house', but 'it's where my family live'.

'Don't worry,' he continued, 'they're all away. You won't have to meet them.'

'But I should like to.'

'Well, you can't. They're in London.'

We drove round the front into a side court – 'Everything's shut up. We'd better go in this way' – and entered through the fortress-like, stone-flagged, stone-vaulted passages of the servants' quarters – 'I want you to meet Nanny Hawkins. That's what we've come for' – and climbed uncarpeted, scrubbed elm stairs, followed more passages of wide boards covered in the centre by a thin strip of drugget, through passages covered by linoleum, passing the wells of many minor staircases and many rows of crimson and gold fire buckets, up a final staircase, gated at the head. The dome was false, designed to be seen from below like the cupolas of Chambord. Its drum was merely an additional storey full of segmental rooms. Here were the nurseries.

Sebastian's nanny was seated at the open window; the fountain lay before her, the lakes, the temple, and, far away on the last spur, a glittering obelisk; her hands lay open in her lap and, loosely between them, a rosary; she was fast asleep. Long hours of work in her youth, authority in middle life, repose and security in her age, had set their stamp on her lined and serene face.

'Well,' she said, waking; 'this *is* a surprise.'

Sebastian kissed her.

'Who's this?' she said, looking at me. 'I don't think I know him.'

Sebastian introduced us.

'You've come just the right time. Julia's here for the day. Such a time they're all having. It's dull without them. Just Mrs Chandler and two of the girls and old Bert. And then they're all going on holidays and the boiler's being done out in August and you going to see his Lordship in Italy, and the rest on visits, it'll be October before we're settled down again. Still, I suppose Julia must have her enjoyment the same as other young ladies, though what they always want to go to London for in the best of the summer and the gardens all out, I never have understood. Father Phipps was here on Thursday and I said exactly the same to him,' she added as though she had thus acquired sacerdotal authority for her opinion.

'D'you say Julia's here?'

'Yes, dear, you must have just missed her. It's the Conservative Women. Her Ladyship was to have done them, but she's poorly. Julia won't be long; she's leaving immediately after her speech, before the tea.'

'I'm afraid we may miss her again.'

'Don't do that, dear, it'll be such a surprise to her seeing you, though she ought to wait for the tea, I told her, it's what the Conservative Women come for. Now what's the news? Are you studying hard at your books?'

'Not very, I'm afraid, nanny.'

'Ah, cricketing all day long I expect, like your brother. He found time to study, too, though. He's not been here since Christmas, but he'll be here for the Agricultural, I expect. Did you see this piece about Julia in the paper? She brought it down for me. Not that it's nearly good enough of her, but what it says is *very* nice. "The lovely daughter whom Lady Marchmain is bringing out this season ... witty as well as ornamental ... the most popular débutante", well that's no more than the truth, though it was a shame to cut her hair; such a lovely head of hair she had, just like her Ladyship's. I said to Father Phipps it's not natural. He said: "Nuns do it," and I said, "Well, surely, father, you aren't going to make a nun out of Lady Julia? The very idea!" '

Sebastian and the old woman talked on. It was a charming room, oddly shaped to conform with the curve of the dome. The walls were papered in a pattern of ribbon and roses. There was a rocking-horse in the corner and an oleograph of the Sacred Heart over the mantelpiece; the empty grate was hidden by a bunch of pampas grass and bulrushes; laid out on the top of the chest of drawers and carefully dusted, were the collection of small presents which had been brought home to her at various times by her children, carved shell and lava, stamped leather, painted wood, china, bog-oak, damascened silver, blue-john, alabaster, coral, the souvenirs of many holidays.

Presently nanny said: 'Ring the bell, dear, and we'll have some tea. I usually go down to Mrs Chandler, but we'll have it up here today. My usual girl has gone to London with the others. The new one is just up from the village. She didn't know anything at first, but she's coming along nicely. Ring the bell.'

But Sebastian said we had to go.

'And miss Julia? She *will* be upset when she hears. It would have been *such* a surprise for her.'

'Poor nanny,' said Sebastian when we left the nursery. 'She does have such a dull life. I've a good mind to bring her to Oxford to live with me, only she'd always be trying to send me to church. We must go quickly before my sister gets back.'

'Which are you ashamed of, her or me?'

'I'm ashamed of myself,' said Sebastian gravely. 'I'm not going to have you get mixed up with my family. They're so madly charming. All my life they've been taking things away from me. If they once got hold of you with their charm, they'd make you *their* friend not mine, and I won't let them.'

'All right,' I said. 'I'm perfectly content. But am I not going to be allowed to see any more of the house?'

'It's all shut up. We came to see nanny. On Queen Alexandra's day it's all open for a shilling. Well, come and look if you want to. ...'

He led me through a baize door into a dark corridor; I could dimly see a gilt cornice and vaulted plaster above; then, opening a heavy, smooth-swinging, mahogany door, he led me into a darkened hall. Light streamed through the cracks in the shutters. Sebastian unbarred one, and folded it back; the mellow afternoon sun flooded in, over the bare floor, the vast, twin fireplaces of sculptured marble, the coved ceiling frescoed with classic deities and heroes, the gilt mirrors and *scagliola* pilasters, the islands of sheeted furniture. It was a glimpse only, such as might be had from the top of an omnibus into a lighted ballroom; then Sebastian quickly shut out the sun. 'You see,' he said, 'it's like this.'

His mood had changed since we had drunk our wine under the elm trees, since we had turned the corner of the drive and he had said: 'Well?'

'You see, there's nothing to see. A few pretty things I'd like to show you one day – not now. But there's the chapel. You must see that. It's a monument of *art nouveau*.'

The last architect to work at Brideshead had added a colonnade and flanking pavilions. One of these was the chapel. We entered it by the public porch (another door led direct to the house); Sebastian dipped his fingers in the water stoup, crossed himself, and genuflected; I copied him. 'Why do you do that?' he asked crossly.

'Just good manners.'

'Well, you needn't on my account. You wanted to do sight-seeing; how about this?'

The whole interior had been gutted, elaborately refurnished and redecorated in the arts-and-crafts style of the last decade of the nineteenth century. Angels in printed cotton smocks, rambler-roses, flower-spangled meadows, frisking lambs, texts in Celtic script, saints in armour, covered the walls in an intricate pattern of clear, bright colours. There was a triptych of pale oak, carved so as to give it the peculiar property of seeming to have been moulded in Plasticine. The sanctuary lamp and all the metal furniture were of bronze, hand-beaten to the patina of a pock-marked skin; the altar steps had a carpet of grass-green, strewn with white and gold daisies.

'Golly,' I said.

'It was papa's wedding present to mama. Now, if you've seen enough, we'll go.'

On the drive we passed a closed Rolls-Royce driven by a chauffeur; in the back was a vague, girlish figure who looked round at us through the window.

'Julia,' said Sebastian. 'We only just got away in time.'

We stopped to speak to a man with a bicycle – 'That was old Bat,' said Sebastian – and then were away, past the wrought-iron gates, past the lodges, and out on the road heading back to Oxford.

'I'm sorry,' said Sebastian after a time. 'I'm afraid I wasn't very nice this afternoon. Brideshead often has that effect on me. But I had to take you to see nanny.'

Why? I wondered; but said nothing – Sebastian's life was governed by a code of such imperatives. 'I *must* have pillar-box red pyjamas,' 'I *have* to stay in bed until the sun works round to the windows,' 'I've absolutely *got* to drink champagne tonight!' – except, 'It had quite the reverse effect on me.'

After a long pause he said petulantly, 'I don't keep asking you questions about *your* family.'

'Neither do I about yours.'

'But you look inquisitive.'

'Well, you're so mysterious about them.'

'I hoped I was mysterious about everything.'

'Perhaps I am rather curious about people's families – you see, it's not a thing I know about. There is only my father and myself. An aunt kept an eye on me for a time but my father drove her abroad. My mother was killed in the war.'

'Oh ... how very unusual.'

'She went to Serbia with the Red Cross. My father has been rather odd in the head ever since. He just lives alone in London with no friends and footles about collecting things.'

Sebastian said, 'You don't know what you've been saved. There are lots of us. Look them up in Debrett.'

His mood was lightening now. The further we drove from Brideshead, the more he seemed to cast off his uneasiness – the almost furtive restlessness and irritability that had possessed him. The sun was behind us as we drove, so that we seemed to be in pursuit of our own shadows.

'It's half past five. We'll get to Godstow in time for dinner, drink at the Trout, leave Hardcastle's motor-car, and walk back by the river. Wouldn't that be best?'

That is the full account of my first brief visit to Brideshead; could I have known then that it would one day be remembered with tears by a middle-aged captain of infantry?

CHAPTER II

Towards the end of that summer term I received the last visit and Grand Remonstrance of my cousin Jasper. I was just free of the schools, having taken the last paper of History Previous on the afternoon before; Jasper's subfusc suit and white tie proclaimed him still in the thick of it; he had, too, the exhausted but resentful air of one who fears he has failed to do himself full justice on the subject of Pindar's Orphism. Duty alone had brought him to my rooms that afternoon at great inconvenience to himself and, as it happened, to me, who, when he caught me in the door, was on my way to make final arrangements about a dinner I was giving that evening. It was one of several parties designed to comfort Hardcastle – one of the tasks that had lately fallen to Sebastian and me since, by leaving his car out, we had got him into grave trouble with the proctors.

Jasper would not sit down; this was to be no cosy chat; he stood with his back to the fireplace and, in his own phrase, talked to me 'like an uncle'.

'... I've tried to get in touch with you several times in the last week or two. In fact, I have the impression you are avoiding me. If that is so, Charles, I can't say I'm surprised.

'You may think it none of my business, but I feel a sense of responsibility. You know as well as I do that since your – well, since the war, your father has not been really in touch with things – lives in his own world. I don't want to sit back and see you making mistakes which a word in season might save you from.

'I expected you to make mistakes your first year. We all do. I got in with some thoroughly objectionable O.S.C.U. men who ran a mission to hop-pickers during the long vac. But you, my dear Charles, whether you realize it or not, have gone straight, hook line and sinker, into the *very worst set in the University*. You may think that, living in digs, I don't know what goes on in college; but I hear things. In fact, I hear all too much. I find that I've become a figure of mockery on your account at the Dining Club. There's that chap Sebastian Flyte you seem inseparable from. He may be all right, I don't know. His brother Brideshead was a very sound fellow. But this friend of yours looks odd to me and he gets himself talked about. Of course, they're an odd family. The Marchmains have lived apart since the war, you know. An extraordinary thing; everyone thought they were a devoted couple. Then he went off to France with his Yeomanry and just never came back. It was as if he'd been killed. She's a Roman Catholic, so she can't get a divorce – or *won't*, I expect. You can do anything at Rome with money, and they're enormously rich. Flyte *may* be all right, but *Anthony Blanche* – now there's a man there's absolutely no excuse for.'

'I don't particularly like him myself,' I said.

'Well, he's always hanging round here, and the stiffer element in college don't like it. They can't stand him at the House. He was in Mercury again last night. None of these people you go about with pull any weight in their own colleges, and that's the real test. They think because they've got a lot of money to throw about, they can do anything.

'And that's another thing. I don't know what allowance my uncle makes you, but I don't mind betting you're spending double. All *this*,' he said, including in a wide sweep of his hand the evidence of profligacy about him. It was true; my room had cast its austere winter garments, and, by not very slow stages, assumed a richer wardrobe. 'Is *that* paid for?' (the box of a hundred cabinet Partagas on the sideboard) 'or *those*?' (a dozen frivolous, new books on the table) 'or those?' (a Lalique decanter and glasses) 'or *that* peculiarly noisome object?' (a human skull lately purchased from the School of Medicine, which, resting in a bowl of roses, formed, at the moment, the chief decoration of my table. It bore the motto '*Et in Arcadia ego*' inscribed on its forehead.)

'Yes,' I said, glad to be clear of one charge. 'I had to pay cash for the skull.'

'You can't be doing any work. Not that that matters, particularly if you're making something of your career elsewhere – but are you? Have you spoken at the Union or at any of the clubs? Are you connected with any of the magazines? Are you even making a position in the O.U.D.S.? And *your clothes*!' continued my cousin. 'When you came up I remember advising you to dress as you would in a country house. Your present get-up seems an unhappy compromise between the correct wear for a theatrical party at Maidenhead and a glee-singing competition in a garden suburb.

'And drink – no one minds a man getting tight once or twice a term. In fact, he ought to, on certain occasions. But I hear you're constantly seen drunk in the middle of the afternoon.'

He paused, his duty discharged. Already the perplexities of

the examination school were beginning to reassert themselves in his mind.

'I'm sorry, Jasper,' I said. 'I know it must be embarrassing for you, but I happen to *like* this bad set. I *like* getting drunk at luncheon, and though I haven't yet spent quite double my allowance, I undoubtedly shall before the end of term. I usually have a glass of champagne about this time. Will you join me?'

So my cousin Jasper despaired and, I learned later, wrote to his father on the subject of my excesses who, in his turn, wrote to *my* father, who took no action or particular thought in the matter, partly because he had disliked my uncle for nearly sixty years and partly because, as Jasper had said, he lived in his own world now, since my mother's death.

Thus, in broad outline, Jasper sketched the more prominent features of my first year; some detail may be added on the same scale.

I had committed myself earlier to spend the Easter vacation with Collins and, though I would have broken my word without compunction, and left my former friend friendless, had Sebastian made a sign, no sign was made; accordingly Collins and I spent several economical and instructive weeks together in Ravenna. A bleak wind blew from the Adriatic among those mighty tombs. In an hotel bedroom designed for a warmer season, I wrote long letters to Sebastian and called daily at the post office for his answers. There were two, each from a different address, neither giving any plain news of himself, for he wrote in a style of remote fantasy – ... '*Mummy and two attendant poets have three bad colds in the head, so I have come here. It is the feast of S. Nichodemus of Thyatira, who was martyred by having goatskin nailed to his pate, and is accordingly the patron of bald heads. Tell Collins, who I am sure will be bald before us. There are too many people here, but one, praise heaven! has an ear-trumpet, and that keeps me in good humour. And now I must try to catch a fish. It is too far to send it to you so I will keep the backbone ...*' – which left me fretful. Collins made notes for a little thesis pointing out the inferiority of the original mosaics to their photographs. Here was planted the seed of what became his life's harvest. When, many years later, there appeared the first massive volume of his still unfinished work on Byzantine Art, I was touched to find among two pages of polite, preliminary acknowledgements of debt, my own name: '... *to Charles Ryder, with the aid of whose all-seeing eyes I first saw the Mausoleum of Galla Placidia and San Vitale ...*'

I sometimes wonder whether, had it not been for Sebastian, I might have trodden the same path as Collins round the cultural water-wheel. My father in his youth sat for All Souls and, in a year of hot competition, failed; other successes and honours came his way later, but that early failure impressed itself on him, and through him on me, so that I came up with an ill-considered sense that there lay the proper and natural goal of the life of reason. I, too, should doubtless have failed, but, having failed, I might perhaps have slipped into a less august academic life elsewhere. It is conceivable, but not, I believe, likely, for the hot spring of anarchy rose from depths where was no solid earth, and burst into the sunlight – a rainbow in its cooling vapours – with a power the rocks could not repress.

In the event, that Easter vacation formed a short stretch of level road in the precipitous descent of which Jasper warned me. Descent or ascent? It seems to me that I grew younger daily with each adult habit that I acquired. I had lived a lonely childhood and a boyhood straitened by war and overshadowed by bereavement; to the hard bachelordom of English adolescence, the premature dignity and authority of the school system, I had added a sad and grim strain of my own. Now, that summer term with Sebastian, it seemed as though I was being given a brief spell of what I had never known, a happy childhood, and though its toys were silk shirts and liqueurs and cigars and its naughtiness high in the catalogue of grave sins, there was something of nursery freshness about us that fell little short of the joy of innocence. At the end of the term I took my first schools; it was necessary to pass, if I was to remain at Oxford, and pass I did, after a week in which I forbade Sebastian my rooms and sat up to a late hour, with iced black coffee and charcoal biscuits, cramming myself with the neglected texts. I remember no syllable of them now, but the other, more ancient lore which I acquired that term will be with me in one shape or another to my last hour.

'I like this bad set and I like getting drunk at luncheon'; that was enough then. Is more needed now?

Looking back, now, after twenty years, there is little I would have left undone or done otherwise. I could match my cousin Jasper's game-cock maturity with a sturdier fowl. I could tell him that all the wickedness of that time was like the spirit they mix with the pure grape of the Douro, heady stuff full of dark ingredients; it at once enriched and retarded the whole process of adolescence as the spirit checks the fermentation of the wine, renders it undrinkable, so that it must lie in the dark, year in, year out, until it is brought up at last fit for the table.

I could tell him, too, that to know and love one other human being is the root of all wisdom. But I felt no need for these sophistries as I sat before my cousin, saw him, freed from his inconclusive struggle with Pindar, in his dark grey suit, his white tie, his scholar's gown; heard his grave tones and, all the time, savoured the gillyflowers in full bloom under my windows. I had my secret and sure defence, like a talisman worn in the bosom, felt for in the moment of danger, found and firmly grasped. So I told him what was not in fact the truth, that I usually had a glass of champagne about that time, and asked him to join me.

On the day after Jasper's Grand Remonstrance I received another, in different terms and from an unexpected source.

All the term I had been seeing rather more of Anthony Blanche than my liking for him warranted. I lived now among his friends, but our frequent meetings were more of his choosing than mine, for I held him in considerable awe.

In years, he was barely my senior, but he seemed then to be burdened with the experience of the Wandering Jew. He was indeed a nomad of no nationality.

An attempt had been made in his childhood to make an Englishman of him; he was two years at Eton; then in the middle of the war he had defied the submarines, rejoined his mother in the Argentine, and a clever and audacious schoolboy was added to the valet, the maid, the two chauffeurs, the pekinese, and the second husband. Criss-cross about the world he travelled with them, waxing in wickedness like a Hogarthian page boy. When peace came they returned to Europe, to hotels and furnished villas, spas, casinos, and bathing beaches. At the age of fifteen, for a wager, he was disguised as a girl and taken to play at the big table in the Jockey Club at Buenos Aires; he dined with Proust and Gide and was on closer terms with Cocteau and Diaghilev; Firbank sent him his novels with fervent inscriptions; he had aroused three irreconcilable feuds in Capri; by his own account he had practised black art in Cefalù and had been cured of drug-taking in California and of an Oedipus complex in Vienna.

At times we all seemed children beside him – at most times, but not always, for there was a bluster and zest in Anthony which the rest of us had shed somewhere in our more leisured adolescence, on the playing field or in the school-room; his vices flourished less in the pursuit of pleasure than in the wish to shock, and in the midst of his polished exhibitions I was often reminded of an urchin I had once seen in Naples, capering derisively, with obscene, unambiguous gestures, before a party of English tourists; as he told the tale of his evening at the gaming table, one could see in the roll of his eye just how he had glanced, covertly, over the dwindling pile of chips at his step-father's party; while we had been rolling one another in the mud at football and gorging ourselves with crumpets, Anthony had helped oil fading beauties on sub-tropical sands and had sipped his apéritif in smart little bars, so that the savage we had tamed was still rampant in him. He was cruel, too, in the wanton, insect-maiming manner of the very young, and fearless like a little boy, charging, head down, small fists whirling, at the school prefects.

He asked me to dinner, and I was a little disconcerted to find that we were to dine alone. 'We are going to Thame,' he said. 'There is a delightful hotel there, which luckily doesn't appeal to the Bullingdon. We will drink Rhine wine and imagine ourselves ... where? Not on a j-j-jaunt with J-J-Jorrocks, anyway. But first we will have our apéritif.'

At the George bar he ordered 'Four Alexandra cocktails, please,' ranged them before him with a loud 'Yum-yum' which drew every eye, outraged, upon him. 'I expect you would prefer sherry, but, my dear Charles, you are not going to *have* sherry. Isn't this a delicious concoction? You don't like it? Then I will drink it for you. One, two, three, four, down the red lane they go. *How* the students stare!' And he led me out to the waiting motor-car.

'I hope we shall find no undergraduates there. I am a little out of sympathy with them for the moment. You heard about their treatment of me on Thursday? It was too naughty. Luckily I was wearing my *oldest* pyjamas and it was an evening of oppressive heat, or I might have been seriously cross.' Anthony had a habit of putting his face near one when he spoke; the sweet and creamy cocktail had tainted his breath. I leaned away from him in the corner of the hired car.

'Picture me, my dear, alone and studious. I had just bought a rather forbidding book called *Antic Hay*, which I knew I must read before going to Garsington on Sunday, because everyone was bound to talk about it, and it's so banal saying you have not read the book of the moment, if you haven't. The solution I suppose is not to go to Garsington, but that didn't occur to me until this moment. *So*, my dear, I had an omelet and a peach and a bottle of Vichy water and put on my pyjamas and settled down to read. I must say my thoughts wandered, but I kept turning the pages and watching the light fade, which in Peckwater, my dear, is quite an experience – as darkness falls the stone seems positively to decay under one's eyes. I was reminded of some of those leprous façades in the *vieux port* at Marseille, until suddenly I was disturbed by such a bawling and caterwauling as you never heard, and there, down in the little piazza, I saw a mob of about twenty terrible young men, and do you know what they were chanting? "*We want Blanche. We want Blanche*," in a kind of litany. Such a *public* declaration! Well, I saw it was all up with Mr Huxley for the evening, and I must say I had reached a point of tedium when any interruption was welcome. I was stirred by the bellows, but, do you know, the louder they shouted, the shyer they seemed? They kept saying "Where's Boy?" "He's Boy Mulcaster's friend," "Boy must bring him down." Of course you've met Boy? He's always popping in and out of dear Sebastian's rooms. He's everything we dagos expect of an English lord. A great *parti* I can assure you. All the young ladies in London are after him. He's very hoity-toity with them, I'm told. My dear, he's scared stiff. A great oaf – that's Mulcaster – and what's more, my dear, a *cad*. He came to le Touquet at Easter and, in some extraordinary way, I seemed to have asked him to stay. He lost some infinitesimal sum at cards, and as a result expected me to pay for all his treats – well, Mulcaster was in this party; I could see his ungainly form shuffling about below and hear him saying: "It's no good. He's out. Let's go back and have a drink?" So then I put my head out of the window and called to him; "Good evening, Mulcaster, old sponge and toady, are you lurking among the hobbledehoys? Have you come to repay me the three hundred francs I lent you for the poor drab you picked up in the Casino? It was a niggardly sum for her trouble, and *what* a trouble, Mulcaster. Come up and pay me, poor hooligan!"

'That, my dear, seemed to put a little life into them, and up the stairs they came, clattering. About six of them came into my room, the rest stood mouthing outside. My dear, they looked *too* extraordinary. They had been having one of their ridiculous club dinners, and they were all wearing coloured tail-coats – a sort of livery. "My dears," I said to them, "you look like a lot of most disorderly footmen." Then one of them, rather a juicy little piece, accused me of unnatural vices. "My dear," I said, "I may be inverted but I am not insatiable. Come back when you are *alone*." Then they began to blaspheme in a very shocking manner, and suddenly I, too, began to be annoyed. "Really," I thought, "when I think of all the hullabaloo there was when I was seventeen, and the Duc de Vincennes (old Armand, of course, not Philippe) challenged me to a duel for an affair of the heart, and very much *more* than the heart, I assure you, with the duchess (Stefanie, of course, not old Poppy) – now, to submit to impertinence from these pimply, tipsy virgins . . ." Well, I gave up the light, bantering tone and let myself be just a *little* offensive.

'Then they began saying, "Get hold of him. Put him in Mercury." Now as you know I have two sculptures by Brancusi and several pretty things and I did not want them to start getting rough, so I said, pacifically, "Dear sweet clodhoppers, if you knew anything of sexual psychology you would know that nothing could give me keener pleasure than to be manhandled by you meaty boys. It would be an ecstasy of the very naughtiest kind. So if any of you wishes to be my partner in joy come and seize me. If, on the other hand, you simply wish to satisfy some obscure and less easily classified libido and see me bathe, come with me quietly, dear louts, to the fountain."

'Do you know, they all looked a little foolish at that? I walked down with them and no one came within a yard of me. Then I got into the fountain and, you know, it was really most refreshing, so I sported there a little and struck some attitudes, until they turned about and walked sulkily home, and I heard Boy Mulcaster saying, "Anyway, we *did* put him in Mercury." You know, Charles, that is just what they'll be saying in thirty years' time. When they're all married to scraggy little women like hens and have cretinous porcine sons like themselves getting drunk at the same club dinner in the same coloured coats, they'll still say, when my name is mentioned, "We put him in Mercury one night," and their barnyard daughters will snigger and think their father was quite a dog in his day, and what a pity he's grown so dull. Oh, *la fatigue du Nord!*'

It was not, I knew, the first time Anthony had been ducked, but the incident seemed much on his mind, for he reverted to it again at dinner.

'Now you can't imagine an *unpleasantness* like that happening to Sebastian, can you?'

'No,' I said; I could not.

'No, Sebastian has charm'; he held up his glass of hock to the candle-light and repeated, '*such* charm. Do you know, I went round to call on Sebastian next day? I thought the tale of my evening's adventures might amuse him. And what do you think I found – besides, of course, his *amusing* toy bear? Mulcaster and two of his cronies of the night before. *They* looked *very* foolish and Sebastian, as composed as Mrs P-p-ponsonby-de-Tomkyns in *P-p-punch*, said, "You know Lord Mulcaster, of course," and the oafs said, "Oh, we just came to see how Aloysius was," for they find the toy bear just as amusing as we do – or, shall I hint, just a *teeny* bit more? So off they went. And I said, "S-s-sebastian, do you realize that those s-sycophantic s-slugs insulted me last night, and but for the warmth of the weather might have given me a s-s-severe cold," and he said, "Poor things. I expect they were drunk." He has a kind word for everyone, you see; he has such charm.

'I can see he has completely captivated you, my dear Charles. Well, I'm not surprised. Of course, you haven't known him as long as I have. I was at school with him. You wouldn't believe it, but in those days people used to say he was a little *bitch*; just a few unkind boys who knew him well. Everyone in pop liked him, of course, and all the masters. I expect it was really that they were jealous of him. He never seemed to get into trouble. The rest of us were constantly being beaten in the most savage way, on the most frivolous pretexts, but never Sebastian. He was the only boy in my house who was never beaten at all. I can see him now, at the age of fifteen. He never had spots you know; all the other boys were spotty. Boy Mulcaster was positively scrofulous. But not Sebastian. Or did he have one, rather a stubborn one at the back of his neck? I think, now, that he did. Narcissus, with one pustule. He and I were both Catholics, so we used to go to mass together. He used to spend *such* a time in the confessional, I used to wonder what he had to say, because he never did anything wrong; never *quite*; at least, he never got punished. Perhaps he was just being charming through the grille. I left under what is called a cloud, you know – I can't think why it is called that; it seemed to me a glare of unwelcome light; the process involved a series of harrowing interviews with m' tutor. It was disconcerting to find how

observant that mild old man proved to be. The *things* he knew
about me, which I thought no one – except possibly Sebastian –
knew. It was a lesson never to trust mild old men – or charming
schoolboys; which?

'Shall we have another bottle of this wine, or of something
different? Something different, some bloody, old Burgundy, eh?
You see, Charles, I understand *all* your tastes. You must come to
France with me and drink the wine. We will go at the vintage. I
will take you to stay at the Vincennes. It is all made up with
them now, and he has the finest wine in France; he and the
Prince de Portallon – I will take you there, too. I think they
would amuse you, and of course they would *love* you. I want to
introduce you to a lot of my friends. I have told Cocteau about
you. He is all agog. You see, my dear Charles, you are that very
rare thing, An Artist. Oh yes, you must not look bashful. Behind
that cold, English, phlegmatic exterior you are An Artist. I have
seen those little drawings you keep hidden away in your room.
They are *exquisite*. And you, dear Charles, if you will understand
me, are *not* exquisite; but not at all. Artists are not exquisite. I
am; Sebastian, in a kind of way, is exquisite, but the artist is an
eternal type, solid, purposeful, observant – and, beneath it all,
p-p-passionate, eh, Charles?

'But who recognizes you? The other day I was speaking
to Sebastian about you, and I said, "But you know Charles
is *an artist*. He draws like a young Ingres," and do you know
what Sebastian said? – "Yes, Aloysius draws very prettily, too,
but of course he's rather more modern." *So* charming; *so*
amusing.

'Of course those that have charm don't really need brains.
Stefanie de Vincennes really tickled me four years ago. My
dear, I even used the same coloured varnish for my toe-nails. I
used her words and lit my cigarette in the same way and spoke
with her tone on the telephone so that the duke used to carry on
long and intimate conversations with me, thinking that I was
her. It was largely that which put his mind on pistol and sabres
in such an old-fashioned manner. My step-father thought it an
excellent education for me. He thought it would make me grow

out of what he calls my "English habits". Poor man, he is very South American. ... I never heard anyone speak an ill word of Stefanie, except the Duke: and *she*, my dear, is positively cretinous.'

Anthony had lost his stammer in the deep waters of his old romance. It came floating back to him, momentarily, with the coffee and liqueurs. 'Real G-g-green Chartreuse, made before the expulsion of the monks. There are five distinct tastes as it trickles over the tongue. It is like swallowing a sp-spectrum. Do you wish Sebastian was with us? Of course you do. Do I? I wonder. How our thoughts do run on that little bundle of charm to be sure. I think you must be mesmerizing me, Charles. I bring you here, at very considerable expense, my dear, simply to talk about myself, and I find I talk of no one except Sebastian. It's odd because there's really no mystery about him except how he came to be born of such a *very sinister* family.

'I forget if you know his family. I don't suppose he'll ever let you meet them. He's far too clever. They're quite, quite *gruesome*. Do you ever feel there is something a *teeny* bit gruesome about Sebastian? No? Perhaps I imagine it; it's simply that he *looks* so like the rest of them, sometimes.

'There's Brideshead who's something archaic, out of a cave that's been sealed for centuries. He has the face as though an Aztec sculptor had attempted a portrait of Sebastian; he's a learned bigot, a ceremonious barbarian, a snow-bound lama. ... Well, anything you like. And Julia, you know what *she* looks like. Who could help it? Her photograph appears as regularly in the illustrated papers as the advertisements for Beecham's Pills. A face of flawless Florentine *quattrocento* beauty; almost anyone else with those looks would have been tempted to become artistic; not Lady Julia; she's as smart as – well, as smart as Stefanie. Nothing greenery-yallery about her. So gay, so correct, so unaffected. I wonder if she's incestuous. I doubt it; all she wants is power. There ought to be an Inquisition especially set up to burn her. There's another sister, too, I believe, in the schoolroom. Nothing is known of her *yet* except that her governess went mad and drowned herself not long ago. I'm sure

she's abominable. So you see there was really very little left for
poor Sebastian to do except be sweet and charming.

'It's when one gets to the parents that a bottomless pit opens.
My dear, *such* a pair. *How does Lady Marchmain manage it?* It is one
of the questions of the age. You have seen her? Very, very
beautiful; no artifice, her hair just turning grey in elegant
silvery streaks, no rouge, very pale, huge-eyed – it is extraordinary how large those eyes look and how the lids are veined blue
where anyone else would have touched them with a finger-tip of
paint; pearls and a few great starlike jewels, heirlooms, in
ancient settings, a voice as quiet as a prayer, and as powerful.
And Lord Marchmain, well, a little fleshy perhaps, but *very*
handsome, a magnifico, a voluptuary, Byronic, bored, infec-
tiously slothful, not at all the sort of man you would expect to
see easily put down. And that Reinhardt nun, my dear, has
destroyed him – but utterly. He daren't show his great purple
face anywhere. He is the last, historic, authentic case of someone
being hounded out of society. Brideshead won't see him, the
girls mayn't, Sebastian does, of course, because he's so charming. No one else goes near him. Why, last September Lady
Marchmain was in Venice staying at the Palazzo Fogliere. To
tell you the truth she was just a teeny bit ridiculous in Venice.
She never went near the Lido, of course, but she was always
drifting about the canals in a gondola with Sir Adrian Porson –
such attitudes, my dear, like Madame Récamier; once I passed
them and I caught the eye of the Fogliere gondolier, whom, of
course, I knew, and, my dear, he gave me *such* a wink. She came
to all the parties in a sort of cocoon of gossamer, my dear, as
though she were part of some Celtic play or a heroine from
Maeterlinck; and she *would* go to church. Well, as you know,
Venice is the *one* town in Italy where *no one* ever *has* gone to
church. Anyway, she was rather a figure of fun that year, and
then who should turn up, in the Maltons' yacht, but poor Lord
Marchmain. He'd taken a little palace there, but was he
allowed in? Lord Malton put him and his valet into a dinghy,
my dear, and transhipped him there and then into the steamer
for Trieste. He hadn't even his mistress with him. It was her

yearly holiday. No one ever knew how they heard Lady Marchmain was there. And, do you know, for a week Lord Malton slunk about as if *he* was in disgrace? And he *was* in disgrace. The Principessa Fogliere gave a ball and Lord Malton was not asked nor anyone from his yacht – even the de Pañoses. *How does Lady Marchmain do it?* She has convinced the world that Lord Marchmain is a monster. And what is the truth? They were married for fifteen years or so and then Lord Marchmain went to the war; he never came back but formed a connexion with a highly talented dancer. There are a thousand such cases. She refuses to divorce him because she is so pious. Well, there have been cases of that before. Usually, it arouses sympathy for the adulterer; not for Lord Marchmain though. You would think that the old reprobate had tortured her, stolen her patrimony, flung her out of doors, roasted, stuffed, and eaten his children, and gone frolicking about wreathed in all the flowers of Sodom and Gomorrah; instead of what? Begetting four splendid children by her, handing over to her Brideshead and Marchmain House in St James's and all the money she can possibly want to spend, while he sits with a snowy shirt front at Larue's with a personable, middle-aged lady of the theatre, in most conventional Edwardian style. And she meanwhile keeps a small gang of enslaved and emaciated prisoners for her exclusive enjoyment. *She sucks their blood.* You can see the tooth marks all over Adrian Porson's shoulders when he is bathing. And he, my dear, was the greatest, the *only*, poet of our time. He's bled dry; there's nothing left of him. There are five or six others of all ages and sexes, like wraiths following her around. They never escape once she's had her teeth into them. It is witchcraft. There's no other explanation.

'So you see we mustn't blame Sebastian if at times he seems a little insipid – but then you don't blame him, do you, Charles? With that very murky background, what could he do except set up as being simple and charming, particularly as he isn't very well endowed in the Top Storey. We couldn't claim *that* for him, could we, much as we love him?

'Tell me candidly, have you ever heard Sebastian say

anything you have remembered for five minutes? You know, when I hear him talk, I am reminded of that in some ways nauseating picture of *"Bubbles"*. Conversation should be like juggling; up go the balls and the plates, up and over, in and out, good solid objects that glitter in the footlights and fall with a bang if you miss them. But when dear Sebastian speaks it is like a little sphere of soapsud drifting off the end of an old clay pipe, anywhere, full of rainbow light for a second and then – phut! vanished, with nothing left at all, nothing.'

And then Anthony spoke of the proper experiences of an artist, of the appreciation and criticism and stimulus he should expect from his friends, of the hazards he should take in the pursuit of emotion, of one thing and another while I fell drowsy and let my mind wander a little. So we drove home, but his words, as we swung over Magdalen Bridge, recalled the central theme of our dinner. 'Well, my dear, I've no doubt that first thing tomorrow you'll trot round to Sebastian and tell him *everything* I've said about him. And I will tell you two things; one, that it will not make the slightest difference to Sebastian's feeling for me and secondly, my dear – and I beg you to re-member this though I have plainly bored you into a condition of coma – that he will immediately start talking about that amusing bear of his. Good night. Sleep innocently.'

But I slept ill. Within an hour of tumbling drowsily to bed I was awake again, thirsty, restless, hot and cold by turns, and unnaturally excited. I had drunk a lot, but neither the mixture, nor the Chartreuse, nor the Mavrodaphne Trifle, nor even the fact that I had sat immobile and almost silent throughout the evening instead of clearing the fumes, as we normally did, in puppyish romps and tumbles, explains the distress of that hag-ridden night. No dream distorted the images of the evening into horrific shapes. I lay awake and clear-headed. I repeated to myself Anthony's words, catching his accent, soundlessly, and the stress and cadence of his speech, while under my closed lids I saw his pale, candle-lit face as it had fronted me across the dinner table. Once during the hours of darkness I brought to light the drawings in my sitting-room and sat at the open window, turning them over. Everything was black and dead-still in the quadrangle; only at the quarter-hours the bells awoke and sang over the gables. I drank soda-water and smoked and fretted, until light began to break and the rustle of a rising breeze turned me back to my bed.

When I awoke Lunt was at the open door. 'I let you lie,' he said. 'I didn't think you'd be going to the Corporate Communion.'

'You were quite right.'

'Most of the freshmen went and quite a few second and third year men. It's all on account of the new chaplain. There was never Corporate Communion before – just Holy Communion for those that wanted it and Chapel and Evening Chapel.'

It was the last Sunday of term; the last of the year. As I went to my bath, the quad filled with gowned and surpliced under-graduates drifting from chapel to hall. As I came back they were standing in groups, smoking; Jasper had bicycled in from his digs to be among them.

I walked down the empty Broad to breakfast, as I often did on Sundays, at a tea-shop opposite Balliol. The air was full of bells from the surrounding spires and the sun, casting long shadows across the open spaces, dispelled the fears of night. The tea-shop was hushed as a library; a few solitary men in bedroom slippers from Balliol and Trinity looked up as I entered, then turned back to their Sunday newspapers. I ate my scrambled eggs and bitter marmalade with the zest which in youth follows a restless night. I lit a cigarette and sat on, while one by one the Balliol and Trinity men paid their bills and shuffled away, slip-slop, across the street to their colleges. It was nearly eleven when I left, and during my walk I heard the change-ringing cease and, all over the town, give place to the single chime which warned the city that service was about to start.

None but church-goers seemed abroad that morning; under-graduates and graduates and wives and trades-people, walking with that unmistakable English church-going pace which eschewed equally both haste and idle sauntering; holding, bound in black lamb-skin and white celluloid, the liturgies of half a dozen conflicting sects; on their way to St Barnabas, St Columba, St Aloysius, St Mary's, Pusey House, Blackfriars, and heaven knows where besides; to restored Norman and revived Gothic, to travesties of Venice and Athens; all in the summer sunshine going to the temples of their race. Four proud infidels alone proclaimed their dissent; four Indians from the gates of Balliol, in freshly-laundered white flannels and neatly pressed blazers, with snow-white turbans on their heads, and in their plump, brown hands bright cushions, a picnic basket and the *Plays Unpleasant* of Bernard Shaw, making for the river.

In the Cornmarket a party of tourists stood on the steps of the Clarendon Hotel discussing a road map with their chauffeur, while opposite, through the venerable arch of the Golden Cross, I greeted a group of undergraduates from my college who had breakfasted there and now lingered with their pipes in the creeper-hung courtyard. A troop of boy scouts, church-bound, too, bright with coloured ribbons and badges, loped past in unmilitary array, and at Carfax I met the Mayor and corporation, in scarlet gowns and gold chains, preceded by wand-bearers and followed by no curious glances, in procession to the preaching at the City Church. In St Aldates I passed a crocodile of choir-boys, in starched collars and peculiar caps, on their way to Tom Gate and the Cathedral. So through a world of piety I made my way to Sebastian.

He was out. I read the letters, none of them very revealing, that littered his writing table and scrutinized the invitation cards on his chimney-piece – there were no new additions. Then I read *Lady into Fox* until he returned.

'I've been to mass at the Old Palace,' he said. 'I haven't been all this term, and Monsignor Bell asked me to dinner twice last week, and I know what that means. Mummy's been writing to him. So I sat bang in front where he couldn't help seeing me and absolutely shouted the Hail Marys at the end; so that's over. How was dinner with Antoine? What did you talk about?'

'Well, he did most of the talking. Tell me, did you know him at Eton?'

'He was sacked my first half. I remember seeing him about. He always has been a noticeable figure.'

'Did he go to church with you?'

'I don't think so, why?'

'Has he met any of your family?'

'Charles, how very peculiar you're being today. No. I don't suppose so.'

'Not your mother at Venice?'

'I believe she did say something about it. I forget what. I think she was staying with some Italian cousins of ours, the Foglieres, and Anthony turned up with his family at the hotel, and there was some party the Foglieres gave that they weren't asked to. I know Mummy said something about it when I told her he was a friend of mine. I can't think why he should want to go to a party at the Foglieres – the princess is so proud of her English blood that she talks of nothing else. Anyway, no one objected to Antoine – *much*, I gather. It was his mother they thought difficult.'

'And who is the Duchesse of Vincennes?'

'Poppy?'

'Stefanie.'

'You must ask Antoine that. He claims to have had an affair with her.'

'Did he?'

'I dare say. I think it's more or less compulsory at Cannes. Why all this interest?'

'I just wanted to find out how much truth there was in what Anthony said last night.'

'I shouldn't think a word. That's his great charm.'

'You may think it charming. I think it's devilish. Do you know he spent the whole of yesterday evening trying to turn me against you, and almost succeeded?'

'Did he? How silly. Aloysius wouldn't approve of that at all, would you, you pompous old bear?'

And then Boy Mulcaster came into the room.

CHAPTER III

I RETURNED home for the Long Vacation without plans and without money. To cover end-of-term expenses I had sold my Omega screen to Collins for ten pounds, of which I now kept four; my last cheque overdrew my account by a few shillings, and I had been told that, without my father's authority, I must draw no more. My next allowance was not due until October. I was thus faced with a bleak prospect and, turning the matter over in my mind, I felt something not far off remorse for the prodigality of the preceding weeks.

I had started the term with my battels paid and over a hundred pounds in hand. All that had gone, and not a penny paid out where I could get credit. There had been no reason for it, no great pleasure unattainable else; it had gone in ducks and drakes. Sebastian used to tease me – 'You spend money like a bookie' – but all of it went on and with him. His own finances were perpetually, vaguely distressed. 'It's all done by lawyers,' he said helplessly, 'and I suppose they embezzle a lot. Anyway, I never seem to get much. Of course, mummy would give me anything I asked for.'

'Then why don't you ask her for a proper allowance?'

'Oh, mummy likes everything to be a present. She's so sweet,' he said, adding one more line to the picture I was forming of her.

Now Sebastian had disappeared into that other life of his where I was not asked to follow, and I was left, instead, forlorn and regretful.

How ungenerously in later life we disclaim the virtuous moods of our youth, living in retrospect long, summer days of unreflecting dissipation. There is no candour in a story of early manhood which leaves out of account the home-sickness for nursery morality, the regrets and resolutions of amendment, the black hours which, like zero on the roulette table, turn up with roughly calculable regularity.

Thus I spent the first afternoon at home, wandering from

53

room to room, looking from the plate-glass windows in turn on the garden and the street, in a mood of vehement self-reproach.

My father, I knew, was in the house, but his library was inviolable, and it was not until just before dinner that he appeared to greet me. He was then in his late fifties, but it was his idiosyncrasy to seem much older than his years; to see him one might have put him at seventy, to hear him speak at nearly eighty. He came to me now, with the shuffling, mandarin-tread which he affected, and a shy smile of welcome. When he dined at home – and he seldom dined elsewhere – he wore a frogged velvet smoking-suit of the kind which had been fashionable many years before and was to be so again, but, at that time, was a deliberate archaism.

'My dear boy, they never told me you were here. Did you have a very exhausting journey? They gave you tea? You are well? I have just made a somewhat audacious purchase from Sonerscheins – a terra-cotta bull of the fifth century. I was examining it and forgot your arrival. Was the carriage *very* full? You had a corner seat?' (He travelled so rarely himself that to hear of others doing so always excited his solicitude.) 'Hayter brought you the evening paper? There is no news, of course – such a lot of nonsense.'

Dinner was announced. My father from long habit took a book with him to the table and then, remembering my presence, furtively dropped it under his chair. 'What do you like to drink? Hayter, what have we for Mr Charles to drink?'

'There's some whisky.'

'There's whisky. Perhaps you like something else? What else have we?'

'There isn't anything else in the house, sir.'

'There's nothing else. You must tell Hayter what you would like and he will get it in. I never keep any wine now. I am forbidden it and no one comes to see me. But while you are here, you must have what you like. You are here for long?'

'I'm not quite sure, father.'

'It's a *very* long vacation,' he said wistfully. 'In my day we used to go on what were called reading parties, always in mountainous areas. Why? Why', he repeated petulantly, 'should alpine scenery be thought conducive to study?'

'I thought of putting in some time at an art school – in the life class.'

'My dear boy, you'll find them all shut. The students go to Barbizon or such places and paint in the open air. There was an institution in my day called a "sketching club" – mixed sexes' (snuffle), 'bicycles' (snuffle), 'pepper-and-salt knickerbockers, holland umbrellas, and, it was popularly thought, free love' (snuffle), '*such* a lot of nonsense. I expect they still go on. You might try that.'

'One of the problems of the vacation is money, father.'

'Oh, I shouldn't worry about a thing like that at your age.'

'You see, I've run rather short.'

'Yes?' said my father without any sound of interest.

'In fact I don't quite know how I'm going to get through the next two months.'

'Well, I'm the worst person to come to for advice. I've never been "short" as you so painfully call it. And yet what else could you say? Hard up? Penurious? Distressed? Embarrassed? Stony-broke?' (snuffle). 'On the rocks? In Queer Street? Let us say you are in Queer Street and leave it at that. Your grandfather once said to me, "Live within your means, but if you do get into difficulties, come to me. Don't go to the Jews." Such a lot of nonsense. You try. Go to those gentlemen in Jermyn Street who offer advances on note of hand only. My dear boy, they won't give you a sovereign.'

'Then what do you suggest my doing?'

'Your cousin Melchior was imprudent with his investments and got into a very queer street. *He* went to Australia.'

I had not seen my father so gleeful since he found two pages of second-century papyrus between the leaves of a Lombardic breviary.

'Hayter, I've dropped my book.'

It was recovered for him from under his feet and propped against the épergne. For the rest of dinner he was silent save for an occasional snuffle of merriment which could not, I thought, be provoked by the work he read.

Presently we left the table and sat in the garden-room; and there, plainly, he put me out of his mind; his thoughts, I knew, were far away, in those distant ages where he moved at ease, where time passed in centuries and all the figures were defaced and the names of his companions were corrupt readings of words of quite other meaning. He sat in an attitude which to anyone else would have been one of extreme discomfort, askew in his upright armchair, with his book held high and obliquely to the light. Now and then he took a gold pencil-case from his watch-chain and made an entry in the margin. The windows were open to the summer night; the ticking of the clocks, the distant murmur of traffic on the Bayswater Road, and my father's regular turning of the pages were the only sounds. I had thought it impolitic to smoke a cigar while pleading poverty; now in desperation I went to my room and fetched one. My father did not look up. I pierced it, lit it, and with renewed confidence said, 'Father, you surely don't want me to spend the whole vacation here with you?'

'Eh?'

'Won't you find it rather a bore having me at home for so long?'

'I trust I should not betray such an emotion even if I felt it,' said my father mildly and turned back to his book.

The evening passed. Eventually all over the room clocks of diverse pattern musically chimed eleven. My father closed his book and removed his spectacles. 'You are very welcome, my dear boy,' he said. 'Stay as long as you find it convenient.' At the door he paused and turned back. 'Your cousin Melchior worked his passage to Australia *before the mast*.' (Snuffle.) 'What, I wonder, is "before the mast"?'

During the sultry week that followed, my relations with my father deteriorated sharply. I saw little of him during the day; he spent hours on end in the library; now and then he emerged and I would hear him calling over the banisters: 'Hayter, get me a cab.' Then he would be away, sometimes for half an hour or less, sometimes for a whole day; his errands were never explained. Often I saw trays going up to him at odd hours, laden with meagre nursery snacks – rusks, glasses of milk, bananas, and so forth. If we met in a passage or on the stairs he would look at me vacantly and say 'Ah-ha,' or 'Very warm,' or 'Splendid, splendid,' but in the evening, when he came to the garden-room in his velvet smoking suit, he always greeted me formally.

The dinner table was our battlefield.

On the second evening I took my book with me to the dining-room. His mild and wandering eye fastened on it with sudden attention, and as we passed through the hall he surreptitiously left his own on a side table. When we sat down, he said plaintively: 'I do think, Charles, you might talk to me. I've had a very exhausting day. I was looking forward to a little conversation.'

'Of course, father. What shall we talk about?'

'Cheer me up. Take me out of myself,' petulantly, 'tell me all about the new plays.'

'But I haven't been to any.'

'You should, you know, you really should. It's not natural in a young man to spend all his evenings at home.'

'Well, father, as I told you, I haven't much money to spare for theatre-going.'

'My dear boy, you must not let money become your master in this way. Why, at your age, your cousin Melchior was part-owner of a musical piece. It was one of his few happy ventures. You should go to the play as part of your education. If you read the lives of eminent men you will find that quite half of them made their first acquaintance with drama from the gallery. I am told there is no pleasure like it. It is there that you find the real critics and devotees. It is called "sitting with the gods". The expense is nugatory, and even while you wait for admission in the street you are diverted by "buskers". We will sit with the gods together one night. How do you find Mrs Abel's cooking?'

'Unchanged.'

'It was inspired by your Aunt Philippa. She gave Mrs Abel ten menus, and they have never been varied. When I am alone I do not notice what I eat, but now that you are here, we must have a change. What would you like? What is in season? Are you fond of lobsters? Hayter, tell Mrs Abel to give us lobsters tomorrow night.'

Dinner that evening consisted of a white, tasteless soup, over-fried fillets of sole with a pink sauce, lamb cutlets propped against a cone of mashed potato, stewed pears in jelly standing on a kind of sponge cake.

'It is purely out of respect for your Aunt Philippa that I dine at this length. She laid it down that a three-course dinner was middle-class. "If you once let the servants get their way," she said, "you will find yourself dining nightly off a single chop." There is nothing I should like more. In fact, that is exactly what I do when I go to my club on Mrs Abel's evening out. But your aunt ordained that at home I must have soup and three courses; some nights it is fish, meat, and savoury, on others it is meat, sweet, savoury – there are a number of possible permutations.

'It is remarkable how some people are able to put their opinions in lapidary form; your aunt had that gift.

'It is odd to think that she and I once dined together nightly – just as you and I do, my boy. Now *she* made unremitting efforts to take me out of myself. She used to tell me about her reading. It was in *her* mind to make a home with me, you know. She thought I should get into funny ways if I was left on my own. Perhaps I *have* got into funny ways. Have I? But it didn't do. I got her out in the end.'

There was an unmistakable note of menace in his voice as he said this.

It was largely by reason of my Aunt Philippa that I now found myself so much a stranger in my father's house. After my mother's death she came to live with my father and me, no doubt, as he said, with the idea of making her home with us. I knew nothing, then, of the nightly agonies at the dinner table. My aunt made herself my companion, and I accepted her without question. That was for a year. The first change was that she reopened her house in Surrey which she had meant to sell, and lived there during my school terms, coming to London only for a few days' shopping and entertainment. In the summer we went to lodgings together at the seaside. Then in my last year at school she left England. '*I got her out in the end*,' he said with derision and triumph of that kindly lady, and he knew that I heard in the words a challenge to myself.

As we left the dining-room my father said, 'Hayter, have you yet said anything to Mrs Abel about the lobsters I ordered for tomorrow?'

'No, sir.'

'Do not do so.'

'Very good, sir.'

And when we reached our chairs in the garden-room he said:

'I wonder whether Hayter had any intention of mentioning lobsters. I rather think not. Do you know, I believe he thought I was *joking*?'

Next day, by chance, a weapon came to hand. I met an old acquaintance of school-days, a contemporary of mine named Jorkins. I never had much liking for Jorkins. Once, in my Aunt Philippa's day, he had come to tea, and she had condemned him as being probably charming at heart, but unattractive at first sight. Now I greeted him with enthusiasm and asked him to dinner. He came and showed little alteration. My father must have been warned by Hayter that there was a guest, for instead of his velvet suit he wore a tail-coat; this, with a black waistcoat, very high collar, and very narrow white tie, was his evening dress; he wore it with an air of melancholy as though it were court mourning, which he had assumed in early youth and, finding the style sympathetic, had retained. He never possessed a dinner jacket.

'Good evening, good evening. So nice of you to come all this way.'

'Oh, it wasn't far,' said Jorkins, who lived in Sussex Square.

'Science annihilates distance,' said my father disconcertingly. 'You are over here on business?'

'Well, I'm *in* business, if that's what you mean.'

'I had a cousin who was in business – you wouldn't know him; it was before your time. I was telling Charles about him only the other night. He has been much in my mind. He came', my father paused to give full weight to the bizarre word – 'a *cropper*.'

Jorkins giggled nervously. My father fixed him with a look of reproach.

'You find his misfortune the subject of mirth? Or perhaps the word I used was unfamiliar; *you* no doubt would say that he "folded up".'

My father was master of the situation. He had made a little fantasy for himself, that Jorkins should be an American, and throughout the evening he played a delicate, one-sided parlour-game with him, explaining any peculiarly English terms that occurred in the conversation, translating pounds into dollars, and courteously deferring to him with such phrases as 'Of course, by *your* standards . . .'; 'All this must seem very parochial to Mr Jorkins'; 'In the vast spaces to which *you* are accustomed . . .' so that my guest was left with the vague sense that there was a misconception somewhere as to his identity, which he never got the chance of explaining. Again and again during dinner he sought my father's eye, thinking to read there the simple statement that this form of address was an elaborate joke, but met instead a look of such mild benignity that he was left baffled.

Once I thought my father had gone too far, when he said: 'I am afraid that, living in London, you must sadly miss your national game.'

'My national game?' asked Jorkins, slow in the uptake, but scenting that here, at last, was the opportunity for clearing the matter up.

My father glanced from him to me and his expression changed from kindness to malice; then back to kindness again as he turned once more to Jorkins. It was the look of a gambler who lays down fours against a full house. 'Your national game,' he said gently, '*cricket*,' and he snuffled uncontrollably, shaking all over and wiping his eyes with his napkin. 'Surely, working in the City, you find your time on the cricket-field greatly curtailed?'

At the door of the dining-room he left us. 'Good night, Mr Jorkins,' he said. 'I hope you will pay us another visit when you next "cross the herring pond".'

'I say, what did your governor mean by that? He seemed almost to think I was American.'

'He's rather odd at times.'

'I mean all that about advising me to visit Westminster Abbey. It seemed rum.'

'Yes. I can't quite explain.'

'I almost thought he was pulling my leg,' said Jorkins in puzzled tones.

My father's counter-attack was delivered a few days later. He sought me out and said, 'Mr Jorkins is still here?'

'No, father, of course not. He only came to dinner.'

'Oh, I hoped he was staying with us. Such a *versatile* young man. But you will be dining in?'

'Yes.'

'I am giving a little dinner party to diversify the rather monotonous series of your evenings at home. You think Mrs Abel is up to it? No. But our guests are not exacting. Sir Cuthbert and Lady Orme-Herrick are what might be called the nucleus. I hope for a little music afterwards. I have included in the invitations some young people for you.'

My presentiments of my father's plan were surpassed by the actuality. As the guests assembled in the room which my father, without self-consciousness, called 'the Gallery', it was plain to me that they had been carefully chosen for my discomfort. The 'young people' were Miss Gloria Orme-Herrick, a student of the cello; her fiancé, a bald young man from the British Museum; and a monoglot Munich publisher. I saw my father snuffling at me from behind a case of ceramics as he stood with them. That evening he wore, like a chivalric badge of battle, a small red rose in his button-hole.

Dinner was long and chosen, like the guests, in a spirit of

careful mockery. It was not of Aunt Philippa's choosing, but had been reconstructed from a much earlier period, long before he was of an age to dine downstairs. The dishes were ornamental in appearance and regularly alternated in colour between red and white. They and the wine were equally tasteless. After dinner my father led the German publisher to the piano and then, while he played, left the drawing-room to show Sir Cuthbert Orme-Herrick the Etruscan bull in the gallery.

It was a gruesome evening, and I was astonished to find, when at last the party broke up, that it was only a few minutes after eleven. My father helped himself to a glass of barley-water and said: 'What very dull friends I have! You know, without the spur of your presence I should never have roused myself to invite them. I have been very negligent about entertaining lately. Now that you are paying me such a long visit, I will have many such evenings. You liked Miss Gloria Orme-Herrick?'

'No.'

'No? Was it her little moustache you objected to or her very large feet? Do you think she enjoyed herself?'

'No.'

'That was my impression also. I doubt if any of our guests will count this as one of their happiest evenings. That young foreigner played atrociously, I thought. Where can I have met him? And Miss Constantia Smethwick – where can I have met *her*? But the obligations of hospitality must be observed. As long as you are here, you shall not be dull.'

Strife was internecine during the next fortnight, but I suffered the more, for my father had greater reserves to draw on and a wider territory for manoeuvre, while I was pinned to my bridgehead between the uplands and the sea. He never declared his war aims, and I do not to this day know whether they were purely punitive – whether he had really at the back of his mind some geopolitical idea of getting me out of the country, as my Aunt Philippa had been driven to Bordighera and cousin Melchior to Darwin, or whether, as seems most likely, he fought for the sheer love of a battle in which indeed he shone.

I received one letter from Sebastian, a conspicuous object

which was brought to me in my father's presence one day when he was lunching at home; I saw him look curiously at it and bore it away to read in solitude. It was written on, and enveloped in, heavy late-Victorian mourning paper, black-coroneted and black-bordered. I read it eagerly:

> Brideshead Castle,
> Wiltshire.
> *I wonder what the date is*

Dearest Charles,

I found a box of this paper at the back of a bureau so I must write to you as I am mourning for my lost innocence. It never looked like living. The doctors despaired of it from the start.

Soon I am off to Venice to stay with my papa in his palace of sin. I wish you were coming. I wish you were here.

I am never quite alone. Members of my family keep turning up and collecting luggage and going away again but the white raspberries are ripe.

I have a good mind not to take Aloysius to Venice. I don't want him to meet a lot of horrid Italian bears and pick up bad habits.

Love or what you will.

> *S.*

I knew his letters of old; I had had them at Ravenna; I should not have been disappointed; but that day, as I tore the stiff sheet across and let it fall into the basket, and gazed resentfully across the grimy gardens and irregular backs of Bayswater, at the jumble of soil-pipes and fire-escapes and protuberant little conservatories, I saw, in my mind's eye, the pale face of Anthony Blanche, peering through the straggling leaves as it had peered through the candle flames at Thame, and heard, above the murmur of traffic, his clear tones . . . 'You mustn't blame Sebastian if at times he seems a little insipid. . . . When I hear him talk I am reminded of that in some ways nauseating picture of "*Bubbles*".'

For days after that I thought I hated Sebastian; then one Sunday afternoon a telegram came from him, which dispelled that shadow, adding a new and darker one of its own.

My father was out and returned to find me in a condition of feverish anxiety. He stood in the hall with his panama hat still on his head and beamed at me.

'You'll never guess how I have spent the day; I have been to the Zoo. It was most agreeable; the animals seem to enjoy the sunshine so much.'

'Father, I've got to leave at once.'

'Yes?'

'A great friend of mine – he's had a terrible accident. I must go to him at once. Hayter's packing for me, now. There's a train in half an hour.'

I showed him the telegram, which read simply: *'Gravely injured come at once Sebastian.'*

'Well,' said my father. 'I'm sorry you are upset. Reading this message I should not say that the accident was as serious as you seem to think – otherwise it would hardly be signed by the victim himself. Still, of course, he may well be fully conscious but blind or paralysed with a broken back. Why exactly is your presence so necessary? You have no medical knowledge. You are not in holy orders. Do you hope for a legacy?'

'I told you, he is a great friend.'

'Well, Orme-Herrick is a great friend of mine, but I should not go tearing off to his death-bed on a warm Sunday afternoon. I should doubt whether Lady Orme-Herrick would welcome me. However, I see you have no such doubts. I shall miss you, my dear boy, but do not hurry back on my account.'

Paddington Station on that August Sunday evening, with the sun streaming through the obscure panes of its roof, the bookstalls shut, and the few passengers strolling unhurried beside their porters, would have soothed a mind less agitated than mine. The train was nearly empty. I had my suitcase put in the corner of a third-class carriage and took a seat in the dining-car. 'First dinner after Reading, sir; about seven o'clock. Can I get you anything now?' I ordered gin and vermouth; it was brought to me as we pulled out of the station. The knives and forks set up their regular jingle; the bright landscape rolled past the windows. But I had no mind for these smooth things;

instead, fear worked like yeast in my thoughts, and the fermentation brought to the surface, in great gobs of scum, the images
of disaster; a loaded gun held carelessly at a stile, a horse rearing
and rolling over, a shaded pool with a submerged stake, an elm
bough falling suddenly on a still morning, a car at a blind
corner; all the catalogue of threats to civilized life rose and
haunted me; I even pictured a homicidal maniac mouthing in
the shadows, swinging a length of lead pipe. The cornfields and
heavy woodland sped past, deep in the golden evening, and the
throb of the wheels repeated monotonously in my ears, 'You've
come too late. You've come too late. He's dead. He's dead. He's
dead.'

I dined and changed trains to the local line, and in twilight
came to Melstead Carbury, which was my destination.

'Brideshead, sir? Yes, Lady Julia's in the yard.'

She was sitting at the wheel of an open car. I recognized her
at once; I could not have failed to do so.

'You're Mr Ryder? Jump in.' Her voice was Sebastian's and
his her way of speaking.

'How is he?'

'Sebastian? Oh, he's fine. Have you had dinner? Well, I
expect it was beastly. There's some more at home. Sebastian
and I are alone, so we thought we'd wait for you.'

'What's happened to him?'

'Didn't he say? I expect he thought you wouldn't come if you
knew. He's cracked a bone in his ankle so small that it hasn't a
name. But they X-rayed it yesterday, and told him to keep it up
for a month. It's a great bore to him, putting out all his plans;
he's been making the most enormous fuss. . . . Everyone else has
gone. He tried to make me stay back with him. Well, I expect
you know how maddeningly pathetic he can be. I almost gave
in, and then I said: "Surely there must be *someone* you can get
hold of," and he said everybody was away or busy and, anyway,
no one else would do. But at last he agreed to try you, and I
promised I'd stay if you failed him, so you can imagine how
popular you are with me. I must say it's noble of you to come all
this way at a moment's notice.' But as she said it, I heard, or

thought I heard, a tiny note of contempt in her voice that I should be so readily available.

'How did he do it?'

'Believe it or not, playing croquet. He lost his temper and tripped over a hoop. *Not* a very honourable scar.'

She so much resembled Sebastian that, sitting beside her in the gathering dusk, I was confused by the double illusion of familiarity and strangeness. Thus, looking through strong lenses, one may watch a man approaching from afar, study every detail of his face and clothes, believe one has only to put out a hand to touch him, marvel that he does not hear one and look up as one moves, and then, seeing him with the naked eye, suddenly remember that one is to him a distant speck, doubtfully human. I knew her and she did not know me. Her dark hair was scarcely longer than Sebastian's, and it blew back from her forehead as his did; her eyes on the darkling road were his, but larger; her painted mouth was less friendly to the world. She wore a bangle of charms on her wrist and in her ears little gold rings. Her light coat revealed an inch or two of flowered silk; skirts were short in those days, and her legs, stretched forward to the controls of the car, were spindly, as was also the fashion. Because her sex was the palpable difference between the familiar and the strange, it seemed to fill the space between us, so that I felt her to be especially female, as I had felt of no woman before.

'I'm terrified of driving at this time of the evening,' she said. 'There doesn't seem anyone left at home who can drive a car. Sebastian and I are practically camping out here. I hope you haven't come expecting a pompous party.' She leaned forward to the locker for a box of cigarettes.

'No thanks.'

'Light one for me, will you?'

It was the first time in my life that anyone had asked this of me, and as I took the cigarette from my lips and put it in hers, I caught a thin bat's squeak of sexuality, inaudible to any but me.

'Thanks. You've been here before. Nanny reported it. We both thought it very odd of you not to stay to tea with me.'

'That was Sebastian.'

'You seem to let him boss you about a good deal. You shouldn't. It's very bad for him.'

We had turned the corner of the drive now; the colour had died in the woods and sky, and the house seemed painted in *grisaille*, save for the central golden square at the open doors. A man was waiting to take my luggage.

'Here we are.'

She led me up the steps and into the hall, flung her coat on a marble table, and stooped to fondle a dog which came to greet her. 'I wouldn't put it past Sebastian to have started dinner.'

At that moment he appeared between the pillars at the further end, propelling himself in a wheel-chair. He was in pyjamas and dressing gown, with one foot heavily bandaged.

'Well, darling, I've collected your chum,' she said, again with a barely perceptible note of contempt.

'I thought you were dying,' I said, conscious then, as I had been ever since I arrived, of the predominating emotion of vexation, rather than of relief, that I had been bilked of my expectations of a grand tragedy.

'I thought I was, too. The pain was excruciating. Julia, do you think, if *you* asked him, Wilcox would give us champagne tonight?'

'I hate champagne and Mr Ryder has had dinner.'

'*Mister* Ryder? *Mister* Ryder? Charles drinks champagne at all hours. Do you know, seeing this great swaddled foot of mine, I can't get it out of my mind that I have gout, and that gives me a craving for champagne.'

We dined in a room they called 'the Painted Parlour'. It was a spacious octagon, later in design than the rest of the house; its walls were adorned with wreathed medallions, and across its dome prim Pompeian figures stood in pastoral groups. They and the satin-wood and ormolu furniture, the carpet, the hanging bronze candelabrum, the mirrors and sconces, were all a single composition, the design of one illustrious hand. 'We usually eat here when we're alone,' said Sebastian, 'it's so cosy.'

While they dined I ate a peach and told them of the war with my father.

'He sounds a perfect poppet,' said Julia. 'And now I'm going to leave you boys.'

'Where are you off to?'

'The nursery. I promised nanny a last game of halma.' She kissed the top of Sebastian's head. I opened the door for her. 'Good night, Mr Ryder, and good-bye. I don't suppose we'll meet tomorrow. I'm leaving early. I can't tell you how grateful I am to you for relieving me at the sick-bed.'

'My sister's very pompous tonight,' said Sebastian, when she was gone.

'I don't think she cares for me,' I said.

'I don't think she cares for anyone much. I love her. She's so like me.'

'*Do you? Is she?*'

'In looks I mean and the way she talks. I wouldn't love anyone with a character like mine.'

When we had drunk our port, I walked beside Sebastian's chair through the pillared hall to the library, where we sat that night and nearly every night of the ensuing month. It lay on the side of the house that overlooked the lakes; the windows were open to the stars and the scented air, to the indigo and silver, moonlit landscape of the valley and the sound of water falling in the fountain.

'We'll have a heavenly time alone,' said Sebastian, and when next morning, while I was shaving, I saw from my bathroom window Julia, with luggage at her back, drive from the fore-court and disappear at the hill's crest, without a backward glance, I felt a sense of liberation and peace such as I was to know years later when, after a night of unrest, the sirens sounded the 'All Clear'.

CHAPTER IV

THE languor of Youth – how unique and quintessential it is! How quickly, how irrecoverably, lost! The zest, the generous affections, the illusions, the despair, all the traditional attributes of Youth – all save this – come and go with us through life. These things are a part of life itself; but languor – the relaxation of yet unwearied sinews, the mind sequestered and self-regarding – that belongs to Youth alone and dies with it. Perhaps in the mansions of Limbo the heroes enjoy some such compensation for their loss of the Beatific Vision; perhaps the Beatific Vision itself has some remote kinship with this lowly experience; I, at any rate, believed myself very near heaven, during those languid days at Brideshead.

'Why is this house called a "Castle"?'
'It used to be one until they moved it.'
'What can you mean?'
'Just that. We had a castle a mile away, down by the village. Then we took a fancy to the valley and pulled the castle down, carted the stones up here, and built a new house. I'm glad they did, aren't you?'
'If it was mine I'd never live anywhere else.'
'But you see, Charles, it isn't mine. Just at the moment it is, but usually it's full of ravening beasts. If it could only be like this always – always summer, always alone, the fruit always ripe, and Aloysius in a good temper. ...'

It is thus I like to remember Sebastian, as he was that summer, when we wandered alone together through that enchanted palace; Sebastian in his wheel-chair spinning down the box-edged walks of the kitchen gardens in search of alpine strawberries and warm figs, propelling himself through the succession of hot-houses, from scent to scent and climate to climate, to cut the muscat grapes and choose orchids for our button-holes; Sebastian hobbling with a pantomime of difficulty to the old nurseries, sitting beside me on the threadbare,

flowered carpet with the toy-cupboard empty about us and
Nanny Hawkins stitching complacently in the corner, saying,
'You're one as bad as the other; a pair of children the two of
you. Is that what they teach you at College?' Sebastian supine
on the sunny seat in the colonnade, as he was now, and I in a
hard chair beside him, trying to draw the fountain.

'Is the dome by Inigo Jones, too? It looks later.'

'Oh, Charles, don't be such a tourist. What does it matter
when it was built, if it's pretty?'

'It's the sort of thing I like to know.'

'Oh dear, I thought I'd cured you of all that – the terrible
Mr Collins.'

It was an aesthetic education to live within those walls, to
wander from room to room, from the Soanesque library to the
Chinese drawing-room, adazzle with gilt pagodas and nodding
mandarins, painted paper and Chippendale fretwork, from the
Pompeian parlour to the great tapestry-hung hall which stood
unchanged, as it had been designed two hundred and fifty years
before; to sit, hour after hour, in the shade looking out on the
terrace.

This terrace was the final consummation of the house's plan;
it stood on massive stone ramparts above the lakes, so that from
the hall steps it seemed to overhang them, as though, standing
by the balustrade, one could have dropped a pebble into the
first of them immediately below one's feet. It was embraced by
the two arms of the colonnade; beyond the pavilions groves of
lime led to the wooded hillsides. Part of the terrace was paved,
part planted with flower-beds and arabesques of dwarf box;
taller box grew in a dense hedge, making a wide oval, cut into
niches and interspersed with statuary, and, in the centre,
dominating the whole splendid space rose the fountain; such a
fountain as one might expect to find in a piazza of southern
Italy; such a fountain as was, indeed, found there a century ago
by one of Sebastian's ancestors; found, purchased, imported,
and re-erected in an alien but welcoming climate.

Sebastian set me to draw it. It was an ambitious subject for
an amateur – an oval basin with an island of sculptured rocks at

its centre; on the rocks grew, in stone, formal tropical vegetation and wild English fern in its natural fronds; through them ran a dozen streams that counterfeited springs, and round them sported fantastic tropical animals, camels and camelopards and an ebullient lion, all vomiting water; on the rocks, to the height of the pediment, stood an Egyptian obelisk of red sandstone – but, by some odd chance, for the thing was far beyond me, I brought it off and, by judicious omissions and some stylish tricks, produced a very passable echo of Piranesi. 'Shall I give it to your mother?' I asked.

'Why? You don't know her.'

'It seems polite. I'm staying in her house.'

'Give it to nanny,' said Sebastian.

I did so, and she put it among the collection on the top of her chest of drawers, remarking that it had quite a look of the thing, which she had often heard admired but could never see the beauty of, herself.

For me the beauty was new-found.

Since the days when, as a schoolboy, I used to bicycle round the neighbouring parishes, rubbing brasses and photographing fonts, I had nursed a love of architecture, but, though in opinion I had made that easy leap, characteristic of my generation, from the puritanism of Ruskin to the puritanism of Roger Fry, my sentiments at heart were insular and medieval.

This was my conversion to the Baroque. Here under that high and insolent dome, under those coffered ceilings; here, as I passed through those arches and broken pediments to the pillared shade beyond and sat, hour by hour, before the fountain, probing its shadows, tracing its lingering echoes, rejoicing in all its clustered feats of daring and invention, I felt a whole new system of nerves alive within me, as though the water that spurted and bubbled among its stones, was indeed a life-giving spring.

One day in a cupboard we found a large japanned-tin box of oil-paints still in workable condition.

'Mummy bought them a year or two ago. Someone told her

that you could only appreciate the beauty of the world by trying to paint it. We laughed at her a great deal about it. She couldn't draw at all, and however bright the colours were in the tubes, by the time mummy had mixed them up, they came out a kind of khaki.' Various dry, muddy smears on the palette confirmed this statement. 'Cordelia was always made to wash the brushes. In the end we all protested and made mummy stop.'

The paints gave us the idea of decorating the office; this was a small room opening on the colonnade; it had once been used for estate business, but was now derelict, holding only some garden games and a tub of dead aloes; it had plainly been designed for a softer use, perhaps as a tea-room or study, for the plaster walls were decorated with delicate Rococo panels and the roof was prettily groined. Here, in one of the smaller oval frames, I sketched a romantic landscape, and in the days that followed filled it out in colour, and, by luck and the happy mood of the moment, made a success of it. The brush seemed somehow to do what was wanted of it. It was a landscape without figures, a summer scene of white cloud and blue distances, with an ivy-clad ruin in the foreground, rocks and a waterfall affording a rugged introduction to the receding park-land behind. I knew little of oil-painting and learned its ways as I worked. When, in a week, it was finished, Sebastian was eager for me to start on one of the larger panels. I made some sketches. He called for a *fête champêtre* with a ribboned swing and a Negro page and a shepherd playing the pipes, but the thing languished. I knew it was good chance that had made my landscape, and that this elaborate pastiche was too much for me.

One day we went down to the cellars with Wilcox and saw the empty bays which had once held a vast store of wine; one transept only was used now; there the bins were well stocked, some of them with vintages fifty years old.

'There's been nothing added since his Lordship went abroad,' said Wilcox. 'A lot of the old wine wants drinking up. We ought to have laid down the eighteens and twenties. I've had several letters about it from the wine merchants, but her Ladyship says to ask Lord Brideshead, and he says to ask his Lordship, and his Lordship says to ask the lawyers. That's how we get low. There's enough here for ten years at the rate it's going, but how shall we be then?'

Wilcox welcomed our interest; we had bottles brought up from every bin, and it was during those tranquil evenings with Sebastian that I first made a serious acquaintance with wine and sowed the seed of that rich harvest which was to be my stay in many barren years. We would sit, he and I, in the Painted Parlour with three bottles open on the table and three glasses before each of us; Sebastian had found a book on wine-tasting, and we followed its instructions in detail. We warmed the glass slightly at a candle, filled it a third high, swirled the wine round, nursed it in our hands, held it to the light, breathed it, sipped it, filled our mouths with it, and rolled it over the tongue, ringing it on the palate like a coin on a counter, tilted our heads back and let it trickle down the throat. Then we talked of it and nibbled Bath Oliver biscuits, and passed on to another wine; then back to the first, then on to another, until all three were in circulation and the order of glasses got confused, and we fell out over which was which, and we passed the glasses to and fro between us until there were six glasses, some of them with mixed wines in them which we had filled from the wrong bottle, till we were obliged to start again with three clean glasses each, and the bottles were empty and our praise of them wilder and more exotic.

'. . . It is a little, shy wine like a gazelle.'
'Like a leprechaun.'
'Dappled, in a tapestry meadow.'
'Like a flute by still water.'
'. . . And this is a wise old wine.'
'A prophet in a cave.'
'. . . And this is a necklace of pearls on a white neck.'
'Like a swan.'
'Like the last unicorn.'
And we would leave the golden candle-light of the dining-

room for the starlight outside and sit on the edge of the fountain, cooling our hands in the water and listening drunkenly to its splash and gurgle over the rocks.

'Ought we to be drunk *every* night?' Sebastian asked one morning.

'Yes, I think so.'

'I think so too.'

We saw few strangers. There was the agent, a lean and pouchy colonel, who crossed our path occasionally and once came to tea. Usually we managed to hide from him. On Sundays a monk was fetched from a neighbouring monastery to say mass and breakfast with us. He was the first priest I ever met; I noticed how unlike he was to a parson, but Brideshead was a place of such enchantment to me that I expected everything and everyone to be unique; Father Phipps was in fact a bland, bun-faced man with an interest in county cricket which he obstinately believed us to share.

'You know, father, Charles and I simply don't *know* about cricket.'

'I wish I'd seen Tennyson make that fifty-eight last Thursday. That must have been an innings. The account in *The Times* was excellent. Did you see him against the South Africans?'

'I've never seen him.'

'Neither have I. I haven't seen a first-class match for years – not since Father Graves took me when we were passing through Leeds, after we'd been to the induction of the Abbot at Ampleforth. Father Graves managed to look up a train which gave us three hours to wait on the afternoon of the match against Lancashire. That *was* an afternoon. I remember every ball of it. Since then I've had to go by the papers. You seldom go to see cricket?'

'Never,' I said, and he looked at me with the expression I have seen since in the religious, of innocent wonder that those who expose themselves to the dangers of the world should avail themselves so little of its varied solace.

Sebastian always heard his mass, which was ill-attended.

Brideshead was not an old-established centre of Catholicism. Lady Marchmain had introduced a few Catholic servants, but the majority of them, and all the cottagers, prayed, if anywhere, among the Flyte tombs in the little grey church at the gates.

Sebastian's faith was an enigma to me at that time, but not one which I felt particularly concerned to solve. I had no religion. I was taken to church weekly as a child, and at school attended chapel daily, but, as though in compensation, from the time I went to my public school I was excused church in the holidays. The masters who taught me Divinity told me that biblical texts were highly untrustworthy. They never suggested I should try to pray. My father did not go to church except on family occasions and then with derision. My mother, I think, was devout. It once seemed odd to me that she should have thought it her duty to leave my father and me and go off with an ambulance, to Serbia, to die of exhaustion in the snow in Bosnia. But later I recognized some such spirit in myself. Later, too, I have come to accept claims which then, in 1923, I never troubled to examine, and to accept the supernatural as the real. I was aware of no such needs that summer at Brideshead.

Often, almost daily, since I had known Sebastian, some chance word in his conversation had reminded me that he was a Catholic, but I took it as a foible, like his teddy-bear. We never discussed the matter until on the second Sunday at Brideshead, when Father Phipps had left us and we sat in the colonnade with the papers, he surprised me by saying: 'Oh dear, it's very difficult being a Catholic.'

'Does it make much difference to you?'

'Of course. All the time.'

'Well, I can't say I've noticed it. Are you struggling against temptation? You don't seem much more virtuous than me.'

'I'm very, very much wickeder,' said Sebastian indignantly.

'Well then?'

'Who was it used to pray, "O God, make me good, but not yet"?'

'I don't know. You, I should think.'

'Why, yes, *I* do, every day. But it isn't that.' He turned back to the pages of the *News of the World* and said, 'Another naughty scout-master.'

'I suppose they try and make you believe an awful lot of nonsense?'

'Is it nonsense? I wish it were. It sometimes sounds terribly sensible to me.'

'But my dear Sebastian, you can't seriously *believe* it all.'

'Can't I?'

'I mean about Christmas and the star and the three kings and the ox and the ass.'

'Oh yes, I believe that. It's a lovely idea.'

'But you can't *believe* things because they're a lovely idea.'

'But I *do*. That's how I believe.'

'And in prayers? Do you think you can kneel down in front of a statue and say a few words, not even out loud, just in your mind, and change the weather; or that some saints are more influential than others, and you must get hold of the right one to help you on the right problem?'

'Oh yes. Don't you remember last term when I took Aloysius and left him behind I didn't know where. I prayed like mad to St Anthony of Padua that morning, and immediately after lunch there was Mr Nichols at Canterbury Gate with Aloysius in his arms, saying I'd left him in his cab.'

'Well,' I said, 'If you can believe all that and you don't want to be good, where's the difficulty about your religion?'

'If you can't see, you can't.'

'Well, where?'

'Oh, don't be a *bore*, Charles. I want to read about a woman in Hull who's been using an instrument.'

'You started the subject. I was just getting interested.'

'I'll never mention it again ... thirty-eight other cases were taken into consideration in sentencing her to six months – golly!'

But he did mention it again, some ten days later, as we were lying on the roof of the house, sunbathing and watching through a telescope the Agricultural Show which was in progress in the park below us. It was a modest two-day show

serving the neighbouring parishes, and surviving more as a fair
and social gathering than as a centre of serious competition. A
ring was marked out in flags, and round it had been pitched half
a dozen tents of varying size; there was a judges' box and some
pens for livestock; the largest marquee was for refreshments, and
there the farmers congregated in numbers. Preparations had
been going on for a week. 'We shall have to hide,' said Sebastian
as the day approached. 'My brother will be here. He's a big
part of the Agricultural Show.' So we lay on the roof under the
balustrade.

Brideshead came down by train in the morning and lunched
with Colonel Fender, the agent. I met him for five minutes on
his arrival. Anthony Blanche's description was peculiarly apt;
he had the Flyte face, carved by an Aztec. We could see him
now, through the telescope, moving awkwardly among the
tenants, stopping to greet the judges in their box, leaning over a
pen gazing seriously at the cattle.

'Queer fellow, my brother,' said Sebastian.

'He looks normal enough.'

'Oh, but he's not. If you only knew, he's much the craziest of
us, only it doesn't come out at all. He's all twisted inside. He
wanted to be a priest, you know.'

'I didn't.'

'I think he still does. He nearly became a Jesuit, straight
from Stonyhurst. It was awful for mummy. She couldn't exactly
try and stop him, but of course it was the last thing she wanted.
Think what people would have said – the eldest son; it's not as if
it had been me. And poor papa. The Church has been enough
trouble to him without that happening. There was a frightful
to-do – monks and monsignori running round the house like
mice, and Brideshead just sitting glum and talking about the
will of God. He was the most upset, you see, when papa went
abroad – much more than mummy really. Finally they persuaded him to go to Oxford and think it over for three years.
Now he's trying to make up his mind. He talks of going into the
Guards and into the House of Commons and of marrying. He
doesn't know what he wants. I wonder if I should have been like

that, if I'd gone to Stonyhurst. I should have gone, only papa went abroad before I was old enough, and the first thing he insisted on was my going to Eton.'

'Has your father given up religion?'

'Well, he's had to in a way; he only took to it when he married mummy. When he went off, he left that behind with the rest of us. You must meet him. He's a very nice man.'

Sebastian had never spoken seriously of his father before.

I said: 'It must have upset you all when your father went away.'

'All but Cordelia. She was too young. It upset *me* at the time. Mummy tried to explain it to the three eldest of us so that we wouldn't hate papa. I was the only one who didn't. I believe she wishes I did. I was always his favourite. I should be staying with him now, if it wasn't for this foot. I'm the only one who goes. Why don't you come too? You'd like him.'

A man with a megaphone was shouting the results of the last event in the field below; his voice came faintly to us.

'So you see we're a mixed family religiously. Brideshead and Cordelia are both fervent Catholics; he's miserable, she's bird-happy; Julia and I are half-heathen; I am happy, I rather think Julia isn't; mummy is popularly believed to be a saint and papa is excommunicated – and I wouldn't know which of them was happy. Anyway, however you look at it, happiness doesn't seem to have much to do with it, and that's all I want. ... I wish I liked Catholics more.'

'They seem just like other people.'

'My dear Charles, that's exactly what they're not – particularly in this country, where they're so few. It's not just that they're a clique – as a matter of fact, they're at least four cliques all blackguarding each other half the time – but they've got an entirely different outlook on life; everything they think important is different from other people. They try and hide it as much as they can, but it comes out all the time. It's quite natural, really, that they should. But you see it's difficult for semi-heathens like Julia and me.'

We were interrupted in this unusually grave conversation by

loud, childish cries from beyond the chimney-stacks, 'Sebastian, Sebastian.'

'Good heavens!' said Sebastian, reaching for a blanket. 'That sounds like my sister Cordelia. Cover yourself up.'

'Where are you?'

There came into view a robust child of ten or eleven; she had the unmistakable family characteristics, but had them ill-arranged in a frank and chubby plainness; two thick old-fashioned pigtails hung down her back.

'Go away, Cordelia. We've got no clothes on.'

'Why? You're quite decent. I guessed you were here. You didn't know I was about, did you? I came down with Bridey and stopped to see Francis Xavier.' (To me) 'He's my pig. Then we had lunch with Colonel Fender and then the show. Francis Xavier got a special mention. That beast Randal got first with a mangy animal. *Darling* Sebastian, I am pleased to see you again. How's your poor foot?'

'Say how-d'you-do to Mr Ryder.'

'Oh, sorry. How d'you do?' All the family charm was in her smile. 'They're all getting pretty boozy down there, so I came away. I say, who's been painting the office? I went in to look for a shooting-stick and saw it.'

'Be careful what you say. It's Mr Ryder.'

'But it's *lovely*. I say, did you really? You *are* clever. Why don't you both dress and come down? There's no one about.'

'Bridey's sure to bring the judges in.'

'But he won't. I heard him making plans not to. He's very sour today. He didn't want me to have dinner with you, but I fixed that. Come on. I'll be in the nursery when you're fit to be seen.'

We were a sombre little party that evening. Only Cordelia was perfectly at ease, rejoicing in the food, the lateness of the hour, and her brothers' company. Brideshead was three years older than Sebastian and I, but he seemed of another generation. He had the physical tricks of his family, and his smile, when it rarely came, was as lovely as theirs; he spoke, in their voice, with a gravity and restraint which in my cousin Jasper would have sounded pompous and false, but in him was plainly unassumed and unconscious.

'I am so sorry to miss so much of your visit,' he said to me. 'You are being looked after properly? I hope Sebastian is seeing to the wine. Wilcox is apt to be rather grudging when he is on his own.'

'He's treated us very liberally.'

'I am delighted to hear it. You are fond of wine?'

'Very.'

'I wish I were. It is such a bond with other men. At Magdalen I tried to get drunk more than once, but I did not enjoy it. Beer and whisky I find even less appetizing. Events like this afternoon's are a torment to me in consequence.'

'I like wine,' said Cordelia.

'My sister Cordelia's last report said that she was not only the worst girl in the school, but the worst there had ever been in the memory of the oldest nun.'

'That's because I refused to be an Enfant de Marie. Reverend Mother said that if I didn't keep my room tidier I couldn't be one, so I said, well, I won't be one, and I don't believe our Blessed Lady cares two hoots whether I put my gym shoes on the left or the right of my dancing shoes. Reverend Mother was livid.'

'Our Lady cares about obedience.'

'Bridey, you mustn't be pious,' said Sebastian. 'We've got an atheist with us.'

'Agnostic,' I said.

'Really? Is there much of that at your college? There was a certain amount at Magdalen.'

'I really don't know. I was one long before I went to Oxford.'

'It's everywhere,' said Brideshead.

Religion seemed an inevitable topic that day. For some time we talked about the Agricultural Show. Then Brideshead said, 'I saw the Bishop in London last week. You know, he wants to close our chapel.'

'Oh, he couldn't,' said Cordelia.

'I don't think mummy will let him,' said Sebastian.

'It's too far away,' said Brideshead. 'There are a dozen families round Melstead who can't get here. He wants to open a mass centre there.'

'But what about us?' said Sebastian. 'Do we have to drive out on winter mornings?'

'We must have the Blessed Sacrament here,' said Cordelia. 'I like popping in at odd times; so does mummy.'

'So do I,' said Brideshead, 'but there are so few of us. It's not as though we were old Catholics with everyone on the estate coming to mass. It'll have to go sooner or later, perhaps after mummy's time. The point is whether it wouldn't be better to let it go now. You are an artist, Ryder, what do you think of it aesthetically?'

'I think it's *beautiful*,' said Cordelia with tears in her eyes.

'Is it Good Art?'

'Well, I don't quite know what you mean,' I said warily. 'I think it's a remarkable example of its period. Probably in eighty years it will be greatly admired.'

'But surely it can't be good twenty years ago and good in eighty years, and not good now?'

'Well, it may be *good* now. All I mean is that I don't happen to like it much.'

'But is there a difference between liking a thing and thinking it good?'

'Bridey, don't be so Jesuitical,' said Sebastian, but I knew that this disagreement was not a matter of words only, but expressed a deep and impassable division between us; neither had any understanding of the other, nor ever could.

'Isn't that just the distinction you made about wine?'

'No. I like and think good the end to which wine is sometimes the means – the promotion of sympathy between man and man. But in my own case it does not achieve that end, so I neither like it nor think it good for me.'

'Bridey, do stop.'

'I'm sorry,' he said, 'I thought it rather an interesting point.'

'Thank God I went to Eton,' said Sebastian.

After dinner Brideshead said: 'I'm afraid I must take Sebastian away for half an hour. I shall be busy all day tomorrow, and I'm off immediately after the show. I've a lot of papers for father to sign. Sebastian must take them out and explain them to him. It's time you were in bed, Cordelia.'

'Must digest first,' she said. 'I'm not used to gorging like this at night. I'll talk to Charles.'

' "*Charles*"?' said Sebastian. ' "*Charles*"? "Mr Ryder" to you, child.'

'Come on, Charles.'

When we were alone she said: 'Are you really an agnostic?'

'Does your family always talk about religion all the time?'

'Not all the time. It's a subject that just comes up naturally, doesn't it?'

'Does it? It never has with me before.'

'Then perhaps you *are* an agnostic. I'll pray for you.'

'That's very kind of you.'

'I can't spare you a whole rosary you know. Just a decade. I've got such a long list of people. I take them in order and they get a decade about once a week.'

'I'm sure it's more than I deserve.'

'Oh, I've got some harder cases than you. Lloyd George and the Kaiser and Olive Banks.'

'Who is she?'

'She was bunked from the convent last term. I don't quite know what for. Reverend Mother found something she'd been writing. D'you know, if you weren't an agnostic, I should ask you for five shillings to buy a black god-daughter.'

'Nothing will surprise me about your religion.'

'It's a new thing a missionary priest started last term. You send five bob to some nuns in Africa and they christen a baby and name her after you. I've got six black Cordelias already. Isn't it lovely?'

When Brideshead and Sebastian returned, Cordelia was sent to bed. Brideshead began again on our discussion.

'Of course, you are right really,' he said. 'You take art as a means not as an end. That is strict theology, but it's unusual to find an agnostic believing it.'

'Cordelia has promised to pray for me,' I said.

'She made a novena for her pig,' said Sebastian.

'You know all this is very puzzling to me,' I said.

'I think we're causing scandal,' said Brideshead.

That night I began to realize how little I really knew of Sebastian, and to understand why he had always sought to keep me apart from the rest of his life. He was like a friend made on board ship, on the high seas; now we had come to his home port.

Brideshead and Cordelia went away; the tents were struck on the show ground, the flags uprooted; the trampled grass began to regain its colour; the month that had started in leisurely fashion came swiftly to its end. Sebastian walked without a stick now and had forgotten his injury.

'I think you'd better come with me to Venice,' he said.

'No money.'

'I thought of that. We live on papa when we get there. The lawyers pay my fare – first class and sleeper. We can both travel third for that.'

And so we went; first by the long, cheap sea-crossing to Dunkirk, sitting all night on deck under a clear sky, watching the grey dawn break over the sand dunes; then to Paris, on wooden seats, where we drove to the Lotti, had baths and shaved, lunched at Foyot's, which was hot and half-empty, loitered sleepily among the shops, and sat long in a café waiting till the time of our train; then in the warm, dusty evening to the Gare de Lyon, to the slow train south, again the wooden seats, a carriage full of the poor, visiting their families – travelling, as the poor do in Northern countries, with a multitude of small bundles and an air of patient submission to authority – and sailors returning from leave. We slept fitfully, jolting and stopping, changed once in the night, slept again and awoke in an empty carriage, with pine woods passing the windows and the distant view of mountain peaks. New uniforms at the frontier, coffee and bread at the station buffet, people round us of Southern grace and gaiety; on again into the plains, conifers

changing to vine and olive, a change of trains at Milan; garlic
sausage, bread, and a flask of Orvieto bought from a trolley (we
had spent all our money save for a few francs, in Paris); the sun
mounted high and the country glowed with heat; the carriage
filled with peasants, ebbing and flowing at each station, the
smell of garlic was overwhelming in the hot carriage. At last in
the evening we arrived at Venice.

A sombre figure was there to meet us. 'Papa's valet, Plender.'

'I met the express,' said Plender. 'His Lordship thought you
must have looked up the train wrong. This seemed only to come
from Milan.'

'We travelled third.'

Plender tittered politely. 'I have the gondola here. I shall
follow with the luggage in the *vaporetto*. His Lordship had gone
to the Lido. He was not sure he would be home before you –
that was when we expected you on the Express. He should be
there by now.'

He led us to the waiting boat. The gondoliers wore green
and white livery and silver plaques on their chests; they smiled
and bowed.

'*Palazzo. Pronto.*'

'*Sì, signore Plender.*'

And we floated away.

'You've been here before?'

'No.'

'I came once before – from the sea. This is the way to
arrive.'

'*Ecco ci siamo, signori.*'

The palace was a little less than it sounded, a narrow
Palladian façade, mossy steps, a dark archway of rusticated
stone. One boatman leapt ashore, made fast to the post, rang
the bell; the other stood on the prow keeping the craft in to the
steps. The doors opened; a man in rather raffish summer livery
of striped linen led us up the stairs from shadow into light; the
piano nobile was in full sunshine, ablaze with frescoes of the school
of Tintoretto.

Our rooms were on the floor above, reached by a precipitous

marble staircase; they were shuttered against the afternoon sun; the butler threw them open and we looked out on the Grand Canal; the beds had mosquito nets.

'*Mostica* not now.'

There was a little bulbous press in each room, a misty, gilt-framed mirror, and no other furniture. The floor was of bare marble slabs.

'A bit bleak?' asked Sebastian.

'Bleak? Look at that.' I led him again to the window and the incomparable pageant below and about us.

'No, you couldn't call it bleak.'

A tremendous explosion drew us next door. We found a bathroom which seemed to have been built in a chimney. There was no ceiling; instead the walls ran straight through the floor above to the open sky. The butler was almost invisible in the steam of an antiquated geyser. There was an overpowering smell of gas and a tiny trickle of cold water.

'No good.'

'*Sì, Sì, subito, signori.*'

The butler ran to the top of the staircase and began to shout down it; a female voice, more strident than his, answered. Sebastian and I returned to the spectacle below our windows. Presently the argument came to an end and a woman and child appeared, who smiled at us, scowled at the butler, and put on Sebastian's press a silver basin and ewer of boiling water. The butler meanwhile unpacked and folded our clothes and, lapsing into Italian, told us of the unrecognized merits of the geyser, until suddenly cocking his head sideways he became alert, said '*Il marchese*,' and darted downstairs.

'We'd better look respectable before meeting papa,' said Sebastian. 'We needn't dress. I gather he's alone at the moment.'

I was full of curiosity to meet Lord Marchmain. When I did so I was first struck by his normality, which, as I saw more of him, I found to be studied. It was as though he were conscious of a Byronic aura, which he considered to be in bad taste and was at pains to suppress. He was standing on the balcony of the saloon and, as he turned to greet us, his face was in deep shadow. I was aware only of a tall and upright figure.

'Darling papa,' said Sebastian, 'how young you are looking!'

He kissed Lord Marchmain on the cheek and I, who had not kissed my father since I left the nursery, stood shyly behind him.

'This is Charles. Don't you think my father very handsome, Charles?'

Lord Marchmain shook my hand.

'Whoever looked up your train,' he said – and his voice also was Sebastian's – 'made a *bêtise*. There's no such one.'

'We came on it.'

'You can't have. There was only a slow train from Milan at that time. I was at the Lido. I have taken to playing tennis there with the professional in the early evening. It is the only time of day when it is not too hot. I hope you boys will be fairly comfortable upstairs. This house seems to have been designed for the comfort of only one person, and I am that one. I have a room the size of this and a very decent dressing-room. Cara has taken possession of the other sizeable room.'

I was fascinated to hear him speak of his mistress so simply and casually; later I suspected that it was done for effect, for me.

'How is she?'

'Cara? Well, I hope. She will be back with us tomorrow. She is visiting some American friends at a villa on the Brenta canal. Where shall we dine? We might go to the Luna, but it is filling up with English now. Would you be too dull at home? Cara is sure to want to go out tomorrow, and the cook here is really quite excellent.'

He had moved away from the window and now stood in the full evening sunlight, with the red damask of the walls behind him. It was a noble face, a controlled one, just, it seemed, as he planned it to be; slightly weary, slightly sardonic, slightly voluptuous. He seemed in the prime of life; it was odd to think that he was only a few years younger than my father.

We dined at a marble table in the windows; everything was either of marble, or velvet, or dull, gilt *gesso*, in this house. Lord

Marchmain said, 'And how do you plan your time here? Bathing or sight-seeing?'

'*Some* sight-seeing, anyway,' I said.

'Cara will like that – she, as Sebastian will have told you, is your hostess here. You can't do both, you know. Once you go to the Lido there is no escaping – you play backgammon, you get caught at the bar, you get stupefied by the sun. Stick to the churches.'

'Charles is very keen on painting,' said Sebastian.

'Yes?' I noticed the hint of deep boredom which I knew so well in my own father. 'Yes? Any particular Venetian painter?'

'Bellini,' I answered rather wildly.

'Yes? Which?'

'I'm afraid I didn't know there were two of them.'

'Three to be precise. You will find that in the great ages painting was very much a family business. How did you leave England?'

'It has been lovely,' said Sebastian.

'Was it? *Was* it? It has been my tragedy that I abominate the English countryside. I suppose it is a disgraceful thing to inherit great responsibilities and to be entirely indifferent to them. I am all the Socialists would have me be, and a great stumbling-block to my own party. Well, my elder son will change all that, I've no doubt, if they leave him anything to inherit. . . . Why, I wonder, are Italian sweets always thought to be so good? There was always an Italian pastry-cook at Brideshead until my father's day. He had an Austrian, so much better. And now I suppose there is some British matron with beefy forearms.'

After dinner we left the palace by the street door and walked through a maze of bridges and squares and alleys, to Florian's for coffee, and watched the grave crowds crossing and recrossing under the campanile. 'There is nothing quite like a Venetian crowd,' said Lord Marchmain. 'The city is crawling with Anarchists, but an American woman tried to sit here the other night with bare shoulders and they drove her away by coming to stare at her, quite silently; they were like circling gulls coming back and back to her, until she left. Our countrymen are much less dignified when they attempt to express moral disapproval.'

An English party had just then come from the waterfront, made for a table near us, and then suddenly moved to the other side, where they looked askance at us and talked with their heads close together. 'That is a man and his wife I used to know when I was in politics. A prominent member of your church, Sebastian.'

As we went up to bed that night Sebastian said: 'He's rather a poppet, isn't he?'

Lord Marchmain's mistress arrived next day. I was nineteen years old and completely ignorant of women. I could not with any certainty recognize a prostitute in the streets. I was therefore not indifferent to the fact of living under the roof of an adulterous couple, but I was old enough to hide my interest. Lord Marchmain's mistress, therefore, found me with a multitude of conflicting expectations about her, all of which were, for the moment, disappointed by her appearance. She was not a voluptuous Toulouse-Lautrec odalisque; she was not a 'little bit of fluff'; she was a middle-aged, well-preserved, well-dressed, well-mannered woman such as I had seen in countless public places and occasionally met. Nor did she seem marked by any social stigma. On the day of her arrival we lunched at the Lido, where she was greeted at almost every table.

'Vittoria Corombona has asked us all to her ball on Saturday.'

'It is very kind of her. You know I do not dance,' said Lord Marchmain.

'But for the boys? It is a thing to be seen – the Corombona palace lit up for the ball. One does not know how many such balls there will be in the future.'

'The boys can do as they like. We must refuse.'

'And I have asked Mrs Hacking Brunner to luncheon. She has a charming daughter. Sebastian and his friend will like her.'

'Sebastian and his friend are more interested in Bellini than heiresses.'

'But that is what I have always wished,' said Cara, changing her point of attack adroitly. 'I have been here more times than I can count and Alex has not once let me inside San Marco even. We will become *tourists*, yes?'

We became tourists; Cara enlisted as guide a midget Venetian nobleman to whom all doors were open, and with him at her side and a guide book in her hand, she came with us, flagging sometimes but never giving up, a neat, prosaic figure amid the immense splendours of the place.

The fortnight at Venice passed quickly and sweetly – perhaps too sweetly; I was drowning in honey, stingless. On some days life kept pace with the gondola, as we nosed through the side-canals and the boatman uttered his plaintive musical bird-cry of warning; on other days with the speed-boat bouncing over the lagoon in a stream of sun-lit foam; it left a confused memory of fierce sunlight on the sands and cool, marble interiors; of water everywhere, lapping on smooth stone, reflected in a dapple of light on painted ceilings; of a night at the Corombona palace such as Byron might have known, and another Byronic night fishing for scampi in the shallows of Chioggia, the phosphorescent wake of the little ship, the lantern swinging in the prow, and the net coming up full of weed and sand and floundering fishes; of melon and *prosciutto* on the balcony in the cool of the morning; of hot cheese sandwiches and champagne cocktails at Harry's bar.

I remember Sebastian looking up at the Colleoni statue and saying, 'It's rather sad to think that whatever happens you and I can never possibly get involved in a war.'

I remember most particularly one conversation towards the end of my visit.

Sebastian had gone to play tennis with his father and Cara at last admitted to fatigue. We sat in the late afternoon at the windows overlooking the Grand Canal, she on the sofa with a piece of needlework, I in an armchair, idle. It was the first time we had been alone together.

'I think you are very fond of Sebastian,' she said.

'Why, certainly.'

'I know of these romantic friendships of the English and the

Germans. They are not Latin. I think they are very good if they do not go on too long.'

She was so composed and matter-of-fact that I could not take her amiss, but I failed to find an answer. She seemed not to expect one but continued stitching, pausing sometimes to match the silk from a work-bag at her side.

'It is a kind of love that comes to children before they know its meaning. In England it comes when you are almost men; I think I like that. It is better to have that kind of love for another boy than for a girl. Alex you see had it for a girl, for his wife. Do you think he loves *me*?'

'Really, Cara, you ask the most embarrassing questions. How should I know? I assume ...'

'He does not. But not the littlest piece. Then why does he stay with me? I will tell you; because I protect him from Lady Marchmain. He hates her; but you can have no conception how he hates her. You would think him so calm and English – the milord, rather blasé, all passion dead, wishing to be comfortable and not to be worried, following the sun, with me to look after that one thing that no man can do for himself. My friend, he is a volcano of hate. He cannot breathe the same air as she. He will not set foot in England because it is her home; he can scarcely be happy with Sebastian because he is her son. But Sebastian hates her too.'

'I'm sure you're wrong there.'

'He may not admit it to you. He may not admit it to himself; they are full of hate – hate of themselves. Alex and his family. . . . Why do you think he will never go into Society?'

'I always thought people had turned against him.'

'My dear boy, you are very young. People turn against a handsome, clever, wealthy man like Alex? Never in your life. It is he who has driven them away. Even now they come back again and again to be snubbed and laughed at. And all for Lady Marchmain. He will not touch a hand which may have touched hers. When we have guests I see him thinking, "Have they perhaps just come from Brideshead? Are they on their way to Marchmain House? Will they speak of me to my wife? Are they a link between me and her whom I hate?" But, seriously, with my heart, that is how he thinks. He is mad. And how has she deserved all this hate? She has done nothing except to be loved by someone who was not grown up. I have never met Lady Marchmain; I have seen her once only; but if you live with a man you come to know the other woman he has loved. I know Lady Marchmain very well. She is a good and simple woman who has been loved in the wrong way.

'When people hate with all that energy, it is something in themselves they are hating. Alex is hating all the illusions of boyhood – innocence, God, hope. Poor Lady Marchmain has to bear all that. A woman has not all these ways of loving.

'Now Alex is very fond of me and I protect him from his own innocence. We are comfortable.

'Sebastian is in love with his own childhood. That will make him very unhappy. His teddy-bear, his nanny ... and he is nineteen years old. ...'

She stirred on her sofa, shifting her weight so that she could look down at the passing boats, and said in fond, mocking tones: 'How good it is to sit in the shade and talk of love,' and then added with a sudden swoop to earth, 'Sebastian drinks too much.'

'I suppose we both do.'

'With you it does not matter. I have watched you together. With Sebastian it is different. He will be a drunkard if someone does not come to stop him. I have known so many. Alex was nearly a drunkard when he met me; it is in the blood. I see it in the *way* Sebastian drinks. It is not your way.'

We arrived in London on the day before term began. On the way from Charing Cross I dropped Sebastian in the forecourt of his mother's house; 'Here is "Marchers",' he said with a sigh which meant the end of a holiday. 'I won't ask you in, the place is probably full of my family. We'll meet at Oxford'; I drove across the park to my home.

My father greeted me with his usual air of mild regret.

'Here today,' he said; 'gone tomorrow. I seem to see very

little of you. Perhaps it is dull for you here. How could it be otherwise? You have enjoyed yourself?'

'Very much. I went to Venice.'

'Yes. Yes. I suppose so. The weather was fine?'

When he went to bed after an evening of silent study, he paused to ask: 'The friend you were so much concerned about, did he die?'

'No.'

'I am very thankful. You should have written to tell me. I worried about him so much.'

CHAPTER V

'It is typical of Oxford,' I said, 'to start the new year in autumn.'

Everywhere, on cobble and gravel and lawn, the leaves were falling and in the college gardens the smoke of the bonfires joined the wet river mist, drifting across the grey walls; the flags were oily underfoot and as, one by one, the lamps were lit in the windows round the quad, the golden lights were diffuse and remote, new figures in new gowns wandered through the twilight under the arches and the familiar bells now spoke of a year's memories.

The autumnal mood possessed us both – as though the riotous exuberance of June had died with the gillyflowers, whose scent at my windows now yielded to the damp leaves, smouldering in a corner of the quad.

It was the first Sunday evening of term.

'I feel precisely one hundred years old,' said Sebastian.

He had come up the night before, a day earlier than I, and this was our first meeting since we parted in the taxi.

'I've had a talking-to from Mgr Bell this afternoon. That makes the fourth since I came up – my tutor, the junior dean, Mr Samgrass of All Souls, and now Mgr Bell.'

'Who is Mr Samgrass of All Souls?'

'Just someone of mummy's. They all say that I made a very bad start last year, that I have been *noticed*, and that if I don't mend my ways I shall get sent down. How does one mend one's ways? I suppose one joins the League of Nations Union, and reads the *Isis* every week, and drinks coffee in the morning at the Cadena café, and smokes a great pipe and plays hockey and goes out to tea on Boar's Hill and to lectures at Keble, and rides a bicycle with a little tray full of note-books and drinks cocoa in the evening and discusses sex seriously. Oh, Charles, what has happened since last term? I feel so old.'

'I feel middle-aged. That is infinitely worse. I believe we have had all the fun we can expect here.'

We sat silent in the firelight as darkness fell.

'Anthony Blanche has gone down.'

'Why?'

'He wrote to me. Apparently he's taken a flat in Munich – he has formed an attachment to a policeman there.'

'I shall miss him.'

'I suppose I shall, too, in a way.'

We fell silent again and sat so still in the firelight that a man who came in to see me, stood for a moment in the door and then went away thinking the room empty.

'This is no way to start a new year,' said Sebastian; but this sombre October evening seemed to breathe its chill, moist air over the succeeding weeks. All that term and all that year Sebastian and I lived more and more in the shadows and, like a fetish, hidden first from the missionary and at length forgotten, the toy bear, Aloysius, sat unregarded on the chest-of-drawers in Sebastian's bedroom.

There was a change in both of us. We had lost the sense of discovery which had infused the anarchy of our first year. I began to settle down.

Unexpectedly, I missed my cousin Jasper, who had got his first in Greats and was now cumbrously setting about a life of public mischief in London; I needed him to shock; without that massive presence the college seemed to lack solidity; it no longer provoked and gave point to outrage as it had done in the summer. Moreover, I had come back glutted and a little chastened; with the resolve to go slow. Never again would I expose myself to my father's humour; his whimsical persecution had convinced me, as no rebuke could have done, of the folly of living beyond my means. I had had no talking-to this term; my success in History Previous and a beta minus in one of my Collections papers had put me on easy terms with my tutor which I managed to maintain without undue effort.

I kept a tenuous connexion with the History School, wrote my two essays a week, and attended an occasional lecture. Besides this I started my second year by joining the Ruskin School of Art; two or three mornings a week we met, about a dozen of us – half, at least, the daughters of north Oxford – among the casts from the antique at the Ashmolean Museum; twice a week we drew from the nude in a small room over a teashop; some pains were taken by the authorities to exclude any hint of lubricity on these evenings, and the young woman who sat to us was brought from London for the day and not allowed to reside in the University city; one flank, that nearer the oil stove, I remember, was always rosy and the other mottled and puckered as though it had been plucked. There, in the smell of the oil lamp, we sat astride the donkey stools and evoked a barely visible wraith of Trilby. My drawings were worthless; in my own rooms I designed elaborate little pastiches, some of which, preserved by friends of the period, come to light occasionally to embarrass me.

We were instructed by a man of about my age, who treated us with defensive hostility; he wore very dark blue shirts, a lemon-yellow tie, and horn-rimmed glasses, and it was largely by reason of this warning that I modified my own style of dress until it approximated to what my cousin Jasper would have thought suitable for country-house visiting. Thus soberly dressed and happily employed I became a fairly respectable member of my college.

With Sebastian it was different. His year of anarchy had filled a deep, interior need of his, the escape from reality, and as he found himself increasingly hemmed in, where he once felt himself free, he became at times listless and morose, even with me.

We kept very much to our own company that term, each so much bound up in the other that we did not look elsewhere for friends. My cousin Jasper had told me that it was normal to spend one's second year shaking off the friends of one's first, and it happened as he said. Most of my friends were those I had made through Sebastian; together we shed them and made no others. There was no renunciation. At first we seemed to see them as often as ever; we went to parties but gave few of our own. I was not concerned to impress the new freshmen who, like their London sisters, were here being launched in Society; there were strange faces now at every party and I, who a few months back had been voracious of new acquaintances, now felt surfeited; even our small circle of intimates, so lively in the summer sunshine, seemed dimmed and muted now in the pervading fog, the river-borne twilight that softened and ob-scured all that year for me. Anthony Blanche had taken some-thing away with him when he went; he had locked a door and hung the key on his chain; and all his friends, among whom he had always been a stranger, needed him now.

The Charity matinée was over, I felt; the impresario had buttoned his astrakhan coat and taken his fee and the disconso-late ladies of the company were without a leader. Without him they forgot their cues and garbled their lines; they needed him to ring the curtain up at the right moment; they needed him to direct the lime-lights; they needed his whisper in the wings, and his imperious eye on the leader of the band; without him there were no photographers from the weekly press, no prearranged goodwill and expectation of pleasure. No stronger bond held them together than common service; now the gold lace and velvet were packed away and returned to the costumier and the drab uniform of the day put on in its stead. For a few happy hours of rehearsal, for a few ecstatic minutes of performance, they had played splendid parts, their own great ancestors, the famous paintings they were thought to resemble; now it was over and in the bleak light of day they must go back to their homes; to the husband who came to London too often, to the lover who lost at cards, and to the child who grew too fast.

Anthony Blanche's set broke up and became a bare dozen lethargic, adolescent Englishmen. Sometimes in later life they would say: 'Do you remember that extraordinary fellow we used all to know at Oxford – Anthony Blanche? I wonder what became of him.' They lumbered back into the herd from which they had been so capriciously chosen and grew less and less individually recognizable. The change was not so apparent to them as to us, and they still congregated on occasions in our rooms; but we gave up seeking them. Instead we formed the taste for lower company and spent our evenings, as often as not, in Hogarthian little inns in St Ebb's and St Clement's and the streets between the old market and the canal, where we managed to be gay and were, I believe, well liked by the company. The Gardener's Arms and the Nag's Head, the Druid's Head near the theatre, and the Turf in Hell Passage knew us well; but in the last of these we were liable to meet other undergraduates – pub-crawling hearties from BNC – and Sebastian became possessed by a kind of phobia, like that which sometimes comes over men in uniform against their own service, so that many an evening was spoilt by their intrusion, and he would leave his glass half empty and turn sulkily back to college.

It was thus that Lady Marchmain found us when, early in that Michaelmas term, she came for a week to Oxford. She found Sebastian subdued, with all his host of friends reduced to one, myself. She accepted me as Sebastian's friend and sought to make me hers also, and in doing so, unwittingly struck at the roots of our friendship. That is the single reproach I have to set against her abundant kindness to me.

Her business in Oxford was with Mr Samgrass of All Souls, who now began to play an increasingly large part in our lives. Lady Marchmain was engaged in making a memorial book for circulation among her friends, about her brother, Ned, the eldest of three legendary heroes all killed between Mons and Passchendaele; he had left a quantity of papers – poems, letters, speeches, articles; to edit them, even for a restricted circle, needed tact and countless decisions in which the judgement of an adoring sister was liable to err. Acknowledging this, she had sought outside advice, and Mr Samgrass had been found to help her.

He was a young history don, a short, plump man, dapper in dress, with sparse hair brushed flat on an over-large head, neat hands, small feet, and the general appearance of being too often bathed. His manner was genial and his speech idiosyncratic. We came to know him well.

It was Mr Samgrass's particular aptitude to help others with their work, but he was himself the author of several stylish little books. He was a great delver in muniment-rooms and had a sharp nose for the picturesque. Sebastian spoke less than the truth when he described him as 'someone of mummy's'; he was someone of almost everyone's who possessed anything to attract him.

Mr Samgrass was a genealogist and a legitimist; he loved dispossessed royalty and knew the exact validity of the rival claims of the pretenders to many thrones; he was not a man of religious habit, but he knew more than most Catholics about their Church; he had friends in the Vatican and could talk at length of policy and appointments, saying which contemporary ecclesiastics were in good favour, which in bad, what recent theological hypothesis was suspect, and how this or that Jesuit or Dominican had skated on thin ice or sailed near the wind in his Lenten discourses; he had everything except the Faith, and later liked to attend benediction in the chapel of Brideshead and see the ladies of the family with their necks arched in devotion under their black lace mantillas; he loved forgotten scandals in high life and was an expert in putative parentage; he claimed to love the past, but I always felt that he thought all the splendid company, living or dead, with whom he associated slightly absurd; it was Mr Samgrass who was real, the rest were an insubstantial pageant. He was the Victorian tourist, solid and patronizing, for whose amusement these foreign things were paraded. And there was something a little too brisk about his literary manners; I suspected the existence of a dictaphone somewhere in his panelled rooms.

He was with Lady Marchmain when I first met them, and I thought then that she could not have found a greater contrast to herself than this intellectual-on-the-make, nor a better foil to her own charm. It was not her way to make a conspicuous entry into anyone's life, but towards the end of that week Sebastian said rather sourly: 'You and mummy seem very thick,' and I realized that in fact I was being drawn into intimacy by swift, imperceptible stages, for she was impatient of any human relationship that fell short of it. By the time that she left I had promised to spend all next vacation, except Christmas itself, at Brideshead.

One Monday morning a week or two later I was in Sebastian's room waiting for him to return from a tutorial, when Julia walked in, followed by a large man whom she introduced as 'Mr Mottram' and addressed as 'Rex'. They were motoring up from a house where they had spent the week-end, they explained. Rex Mottram was warm and confident in a check ulster; Julia cold and rather shy in furs; she made straight for the fire and crouched over it shivering.

'We hoped Sebastian might give us luncheon,' she said. 'Failing him we can always try Boy Mulcaster, but I somehow thought we should eat better with Sebastian, and we're very hungry. We've been literally starved all the week-end at the Chasms.'

'He and Sebastian are both lunching with me. Come too.'

So, without demur, they joined the party in my rooms, one of the last of the old kind that I gave. Rex Mottram exerted himself to make an impression. He was a handsome fellow with dark hair growing low on his forehead and heavy black eyebrows. He spoke with an engaging Canadian accent. One quickly learned all that he wished one to know about him, that he was a lucky man with money, a member of parliament, a gambler, a good fellow; that he played golf regularly with the Prince of Wales and was on easy terms with 'Max' and 'F.E.' and 'Gertie' Lawrence and Augustus John and Carpentier – with anyone, it seemed, who happened to be mentioned. Of the University he said: 'No, I was never here. It just means you start life three years behind the other fellow.'

His life, so far as he made it known, began in the war, where he had got a good M.C. serving with the Canadians and had ended as A.D.C. to a popular general.

He cannot have been more than thirty at the time we met him, but he seemed very old to us in Oxford. Julia treated him, as she seemed to treat all the world, with mild disdain, but with an air of possession. During luncheon she sent him to the car for her cigarettes, and once or twice when he was talking very big, she apologized for him, saying: 'Remember he's a colonial,' to which he replied with boisterous laughter.

When he had gone I asked who he was.

'Oh, just someone of Julia's,' said Sebastian.

We were slightly surprised a week later to get a telegram from him asking us and Boy Mulcaster to dinner in London on the following night for 'a party of Julia's'.

'I don't think he knows anyone young,' said Sebastian; 'all his friends are leathery old sharks in the City and the House of Commons. Shall we go?'

We discussed it, and because our life at Oxford was now so much in the shadows, we decided that we would.

'Why does he want Boy?'

'Julia and I have known him all our lives. I suppose, finding him at lunch with you, he thought he was a chum.'

We had no great liking for Mulcaster, but the three of us were in high spirits when, having got leave for the night from our colleges, we drove off on the London road in Hardcastle's car.

We were to spend the night at Marchmain House. We went there to dress and, while we dressed, drank a bottle of champagne, going in and out of one another's rooms which were together three floors up and rather shabby compared with the splendours below. As we came downstairs Julia passed us going up to her room still in her day clothes.

'I'm going to be late,' she said; 'you boys had better go on to Rex's. It's heavenly of you to come.'

'What is this party?'

'A ghastly charity ball I'm involved with. Rex insisted on giving a dinner party for it. See you there.'

Rex Mottram lived within walking distance of Marchmain House.

'Julia's going to be late,' we said, 'she's only just gone up to dress.'

'That means an hour. We'd better have some wine.'

A woman who was introduced as 'Mrs Champion' said: 'I'm sure she'd sooner we started, Rex.'

'Well, let's have some wine first anyway.'

'Why a Jeroboam, Rex?' she said peevishly. 'You always want to have everything too big.'

'Won't be too big for us,' he said, taking the bottle in his own hands and easing the cork.

There were two girls there, contemporaries of Julia's; they all seemed involved in the management of the ball. Mulcaster knew them of old and they, without much relish I thought, knew him. Mrs Champion talked to Rex. Sebastian and I found ourselves drinking alone together as we always did.

At length Julia arrived, unhurried, exquisite, unrepentant. 'You shouldn't have let him wait,' she said. 'It's his Canadian courtesy.'

Rex Mottram was a liberal host, and by the end of dinner the three of us who had come from Oxford were rather drunk. While we were standing in the hall waiting for the girls to come down and Rex and Mrs Champion had drawn away from us, talking, acrimoniously, in low voices, Mulcaster said, 'I say, let's slip away from this ghastly dance and go to Ma Mayfield's.'

'Who is Ma Mayfield?'

'You know Ma Mayfield. Everyone knows Ma Mayfield of the Old Hundredth. I've got a regular there – a sweet little thing called Effie. There'd be the devil to pay if Effie heard I'd been to London and hadn't been in to see her. Come and meet Effie at Ma Mayfield's.'

'All right,' said Sebastian, 'let's meet Effie at Ma Mayfield's.'

'We'll take another bottle of pop off the good Mottram and then leave the bloody dance and go to the Old Hundredth. How about that?'

It was not a difficult matter to leave the ball; the girls whom

Rex Mottram had collected had many friends there and, after we had danced together once or twice, our table began to fill up; Rex Mottram ordered more and more wine; presently the three of us were together on the pavement.

'D'you know where this place is?'

'Of course I do. A hundred Sink Street.'

'Where's that?'

'Just off Leicester Square. Better take the car.'

'Why?'

'Always better to have one's own car on an occasion like this.'

We did not question this reasoning, and there lay our mistake. The car was in the forecourt of Marchmain House within a hundred yards of the hotel where we had been dancing. Mulcaster drove and, after some wandering, brought us safely to Sink Street. A commissionaire at one side of a dark doorway and a middle-aged man in evening dress on the other side of it, standing with his face to the wall cooling his forehead on the bricks, indicated our destination.

'Keep out, you'll be poisoned,' said the middle-aged man.

'Members?' said the commissionaire.

'The name is Mulcaster,' said Mulcaster. 'Viscount Mulcaster.'

'Well, try inside,' said the commissionaire.

'You'll be robbed, poisoned and infected and robbed,' said the middle-aged man.

Inside the dark doorway was a bright hatch.

'Members?' asked a stout woman, in evening dress.

'I like that,' said Mulcaster. 'You ought to know me by now.'

'Yes, dearie,' said the woman without interest. 'Ten bob each.'

'Oh, look here, I've never paid before.'

'Daresay not, dearie. We're full up tonight so it's ten bob. Anyone who comes after you will have to pay a quid. You're lucky.'

'Let me speak to Mrs Mayfield.'

'I'm Mrs Mayfield. Ten bob each.'

'Why, Ma, I didn't recognize you in your finery. You know me, don't you? Boy Mulcaster.'

'Yes, duckie. Ten bob each.'

We paid, and the man who had been standing between us and the inner door now made way for us. Inside it was hot and crowded, for the Old Hundredth was then at the height of its success. We found a table and ordered a bottle; the waiter took payment before he opened it.

'Where's Effie tonight?' asked Mulcaster.

'Effie 'oo?'

'Effie, one of the girls who's always here. The pretty dark one.'

'There's lots of girls works here. Some of them's dark and some of them's fair. You might call some of them pretty. I haven't the time to know them by name.'

'I'll go and look for her,' said Mulcaster.

While he was away two girls stopped near our table and looked at us curiously. 'Come on,' said one to the other, 'we're wasting our time. They're only fairies.'

Presently Mulcaster returned in triumph with Effie to whom, without its being ordered, the waiter immediately brought a plate of eggs and bacon.

'First bite I've had all the evening,' she said. 'Only thing that's any good here is the breakfast; makes you fair peckish hanging about.'

'That's another six bob,' said the waiter.

When her hunger was appeased, Effie dabbed her mouth and looked at us.

'I've seen you here before, often, haven't I?' she said to me.

'I'm afraid not.'

'But I've seen *you*?' to Mulcaster.

'Well, I should rather hope so. You haven't forgotten our little evening in September?'

'No, darling, of course not. You were the boy in the Guards who cut your toe, weren't you?'

'Now, Effie, don't be a tease.'

'No, that was another night, wasn't it? I know – you were

with Bunty the time the police were in and we all hid in the place they keep the dust-bins.'

'Effie loves pulling my leg, don't you, Effie? She's annoyed with me for staying away so long, aren't you?'

'Whatever you say, I know I *have* seen you before somewhere.'

'Stop teasing.'

'I wasn't meaning to tease. Honest. Want to dance?'

'Not at the minute.'

'Thank the Lord. My shoes pinch something terrible tonight.'

Soon she and Mulcaster were deep in conversation. Sebastian leaned back and said to me: 'I'm going to ask that pair to join us.'

The two unattached women who had considered us earlier, were again circling towards us. Sebastian smiled and rose to greet them: soon they, too, were eating heartily. One had the face of a skull, the other of a sickly child. The Death's Head seemed destined for me. 'How about a little party,' she said, 'just the six of us over at my place?'

'Certainly,' said Sebastian.

'We thought you were fairies when you came in.'

'That was our extreme youth.'

Death's Head giggled. 'You're a good sport,' she said.

'You're very sweet really,' said the Sickly Child. 'I must just tell Mrs Mayfield we're going out.'

It was still early, not long after midnight, when we regained the street. The commissionaire tried to persuade us to take a taxi. 'I'll look after your car, sir, I wouldn't drive yourself, sir, really I wouldn't.'

But Sebastian took the wheel and the two women sat one on the other beside him, to show him the way. Effie and Mulcaster and I sat in the back. I think we cheered a little as we drove off.

We did not drive far. We turned into Shaftesbury Avenue and were making for Piccadilly when we narrowly escaped a head-on collision with a taxi-cab.

'For Christ's sake,' said Effie, 'look where you're going. D'you want to murder us all?'

'Careless fellow that,' said Sebastian.

'It isn't safe the way you're driving,' said Death's Head. 'Besides, we ought to be on the other side of the road.'

'So we should,' said Sebastian, swinging abruptly across.

'Here, stop. I'd sooner walk.'

'Stop? Certainly.'

He put on the brakes and we came abruptly to a halt broadside across the road. Two policemen quickened their stride and approached us.

'Let me out of this,' said Effie, and made her escape with a leap and a scamper.

The rest of us were caught.

'I'm sorry if I am impeding the traffic, officer,' said Sebastian with care, 'but the lady insisted on my stopping for her to get out. She would take no denial. As you will have observed, she was pressed for time. A matter of nerves you know.'

'Let me talk to him,' said Death's Head. 'Be a sport, handsome; no one's seen anything but you. The boys don't mean any harm. I'll get them into a taxi and see them home quiet.'

The policemen looked us over, deliberately, forming their own judgement. Even then everything might have been well had not Mulcaster joined in. 'Look here, my good man,' he said. 'There's no need for you to notice anything. We've just come from Ma Mayfield's. I reckon she pays you a nice retainer to keep your eyes shut. Well, you can keep 'em shut on us too, and you won't be the losers by it.'

That resolved any doubts which the policemen may have felt. In a short time we were in the cells.

I remember little of the journey there or the process of admission. Mulcaster, I think, protested vigorously and, when we were made to empty our pockets, accused his gaolers of theft. Then we were locked in, and my first clear memory is of tiled walls with a lamp set high up under thick glass, a bunk, and a door which had no handle on my side. Somewhere to the left of me Sebastian and Mulcaster were raising Cain. Sebastian had been steady on his legs and fairly composed on the way to the station; now, shut in, he seemed in a frenzy and was pounding the door, and shouting: 'Damn you, I'm not drunk. Open this door. I insist on seeing the doctor. I tell you I'm not drunk,' while Mulcaster, beyond, cried: 'My God, you'll pay for this! You're making a great mistake, I can tell you. Telephone the Home Secretary. Send for my solicitors. I will have *habeas corpus.*'

Groans of protest rose from the other cells where various tramps and pickpockets were trying to get some sleep: 'Aw, pipe down!' 'Give a man some peace, can't yer?' ... 'Is this a blinking lock-up or a looney-house?' – and the sergeant, going his rounds, admonished them through the grille. 'You'll be here all night if you don't sober up.'

I sat on the bunk in low spirits and dozed a little. Presently the racket subsided and Sebastian called: 'I say, Charles, are you there?'

'Here I am.'

'This is the hell of a business.'

'Can't we get bail or something?'

Mulcaster seemed to have fallen asleep.

'I tell you the man – Rex Mottram. He'd be in his element here.'

We had some difficulty in getting in touch with him; it was half an hour before the policeman in charge answered my bell. At last he consented, rather sceptically, to send a telephone message to the hotel where the ball was being held. There was another long delay and then our prison doors were opened.

Seeping through the squalid air of the police station, the sour smell of dirt and disinfectant, came the sweet, rich smoke of a Havana cigar – of two Havana cigars, for the sergeant in charge was smoking also.

Rex stood in the charge-room looking the embodiment – indeed, the burlesque – of power and prosperity; he wore a fur-lined overcoat with broad astrakhan lapels and a silk hat. The police were deferential and eager to help.

'We had to do our duty,' they said. 'Took the young gentlemen into custody for their own protection.'

Mulcaster looked crapulous and began a confused complaint that he had been denied legal representation and civil rights. Rex said: 'Better leave all the talking to me.'

I was clear-headed now and watched and listened with fascination while Rex settled our business. He examined the charge sheets, spoke affably to the men who had made the arrest; with the slightest perceptible nuance he opened the way for bribery and quickly covered it when he saw that things had now lasted too long and the knowledge had been too widely shared; he undertook to deliver us at the magistrate's court at ten next morning, and then led us away. His car was outside.

'It's no use discussing things tonight. Where are you sleeping?'

'Marchers,' said Sebastian.

'You'd better come to me. I can fix you up for tonight. Leave everything to me.'

It was plain that he rejoiced in his efficiency.

Next morning the display was even more impressive. I awoke with the startled and puzzled sense of being in a strange room, and in the first seconds of consciousness the memory of the evening before returned, first as though of a nightmare, then of reality. Rex's valet was unpacking a suitcase. On seeing me move he went to the wash-hand stand and poured something from a bottle. 'I think I have everything from Marchmain House,' he said. 'Mr Mottram sent round to Heppell's for this.'

I took the draught and felt better.

A man was there from Trumper's to shave us.

Rex joined us at breakfast. 'It's important to make a good appearance at the court,' he said. 'Luckily none of you look much the worse for wear.'

After breakfast the barrister arrived and Rex delivered a summary of the case.

'Sebastian's in a jam,' he said. 'He's liable to anything up to six months' imprisonment for being drunk in charge of a car. You'll come up before Grigg unfortunately. He takes rather a grim view of cases of this sort. All that will happen this morning is that we shall ask to have Sebastian held over for a week to prepare the defence. You two will plead guilty, say you're sorry, and pay your five bob fine. I'll see what can be done about squaring the evening papers. The *Star* may be difficult.

'Remember, the important thing is to keep out all mention of the Old Hundredth. Luckily the tarts were sober and aren't being charged, but their names have been taken as witnesses. If we try and break down the police evidence, they'll be called. We've got to avoid that at all costs, so we shall have to swallow the police story whole and appeal to the magistrate's good nature not to wreck a young man's career for a single boyish indiscretion. It'll work all right. We shall need a don to give evidence of good character. Julia tells me you have a tame one called Samgrass. He'll do. Meanwhile *your* story is simply that you came up from Oxford for a perfectly respectable dance, weren't used to wine, had too much, and lost the way driving home.

'After that we shall have to see about fixing things with your authorities at Oxford.'

'I told them to call my solicitors,' said Mulcaster, 'and they refused. They've put themselves hopelessly in the wrong, and I don't see why they should get away with it.'

'For heaven's sake don't start any kind of argument. Just plead guilty and pay up. Understand?'

Mulcaster grumbled but submitted.

Everything happened at court as Rex had predicted. At half past ten we stood in Bow Street, Mulcaster and I free men, Sebastian bound over to appear in a week's time. Mulcaster had kept silent about his grievance; he and I were admonished and fined five shillings each and fifteen shillings costs. Mulcaster was becoming rather irksome to us, and it was with relief that we heard his plea of other business in London. The barrister bustled off and Sebastian and I were left alone and disconsolate.

'I suppose mummy's got to hear about it,' he said. 'Damn, damn, damn! It's cold. I won't go home. I've nowhere to go. Let's just slip back to Oxford and wait for *them* to bother *us*.'

The raffish habitués of the police court came and went, up and down the steps; still we stood on the windy corner, undecided.

'Why not get hold of Julia?'

'I might go abroad.'

'My dear Sebastian, you'll only be given a talking-to and fined a few pounds.'

'Yes, but it's all the *bother* – mummy and Bridey and all the family and the dons. I'd sooner go to prison. If I just slip away abroad they can't get me back, can they? That's what people do when the police are after them. I know mummy will make it seem she has to bear the whole brunt of the business.'

'Let's telephone Julia and get her to meet us somewhere and talk it over.'

We met at Gunter's in Berkeley Square. Julia, like most women then, wore a green hat pulled down to her eyes with a diamond arrow in it; she had a small dog under her arm, three-quarters buried in the fur of her coat. She greeted us with an unusual show of interest.

'Well, you are a pair of pickles; I must say you look remarkably well on it. The only time I got tight I was paralysed all the next day. I do think you might have taken me with you. The ball was positively lethal, and I've always longed to go to the Old Hundredth. No one will ever take me. Is it heaven?'

'So you know all about that, too?'

'Rex telephoned me this morning and told me everything. What were your girl friends like?'

'Don't be prurient,' said Sebastian.

'Mine was like a skull.'

'Mine was like a consumptive.'

'*Goodness.*' It had clearly raised us in Julia's estimation that we had been out with women; to her they were the point of interest.

'Does mummy know?'

'Not about your skulls and consumptives. She knows you were in the clink. I told her. She was divine about it, of course. You know anything Uncle Ned did was always perfect, and he got locked up once for taking a bear into one of Lloyd George's meetings, so she really feels quite human about the whole thing. She wants you both to lunch with her.'

'Oh God!'

'The only trouble is the papers and the family. Have you got an awful family, Charles?'

'Only a father. He'll never hear about it.'

'Ours are awful. Poor mummy is in for a ghastly time with them. They'll be writing letters and paying visits of sympathy, and all the time at the back of their minds one half will be saying, "That's what comes of bringing the boy up a Catholic," and the other half will say, "That's what comes of sending him to Eton instead of Stonyhurst." Poor mummy can't get it right.'

We lunched with Lady Marchmain. She accepted the whole thing with humorous resignation. Her only reproach was: 'I can't think why you went off and stayed with Mr Mottram. You might have come and told me about it first.'

'How am I going to explain it to all the family?' she asked. 'They will be so shocked to find that they're more upset about it than I am. Do you know my sister-in-law, Fanny Rosscommon? She has always thought I brought the children up badly. Now I am beginning to think she must be right.'

When we left I said: 'She couldn't have been more charming. What were you so worried about?'

'I can't explain,' said Sebastian miserably.

A week later when Sebastian came up for trial he was fined ten pounds. The newspapers reported it with painful prominence, one of them under the ironic headline: '*Marquis's son unused to wine*'. The magistrate said that it was only through the prompt action of the police that he was not up on a grave charge ... 'It is purely by good fortune that you do not bear the responsibility of a serious accident. ...' Mr Samgrass gave evidence that Sebastian bore an irreproachable character and that a brilliant future at the University was in jeopardy. The papers took hold of this too – '*Model Student's Career at Stake*'. But for Mr Samgrass's evidence, said the magistrate, he would have been disposed to give an exemplary sentence; the law was the same for an Oxford undergraduate as for any young hooligan; indeed the better the home the more shameful the offence. . . .

It was not only at Bow Street that Mr Samgrass was of value. At Oxford he showed all the zeal and acumen which were Rex Mottram's in London. He interviewed the college authorities, the proctors, the Vice-Chancellor; he induced Mgr Bell to call on the Dean of Christ Church; he arranged for Lady March-main to talk to the Chancellor himself; and, as a result of all this, the three of us were gated for the rest of the term. Hardcastle, for no very clear reason, was again deprived of the use of his car, and the affair blew over. The most lasting penalty we suffered was our intimacy with Rex Mottram and Mr Samgrass, but since Rex's life was in London in a world of politics and high finance and Mr Samgrass's nearer to our own at Oxford, it was from him we suffered the more.

For the rest of that term he haunted us. Now that we were 'gated' we could not spend our evenings together, and from nine o'clock onwards were alone and at Mr Samgrass's mercy. Hardly an evening seemed to pass but he called on one or the other of us. He spoke of 'our little escapade' as though he, too, had been in the cells, and had that bond with us. . . . Once I climbed out of college and Mr Samgrass found me in Sebas-tian's rooms after the gate was shut and that, too, he made into a bond. It did not surprise me, therefore, when I arrived at Brideshead, after Christmas, to find Mr Samgrass, as though in wait for me, sitting alone before the fire in the room they called the 'Tapestry Hall'.

'You find me in solitary possession,' he said, and indeed he seemed to possess the hall and the sombre scenes of venery that hung round it, to possess the caryatids on either side of the fireplace, to possess me, as he rose to take my hand and greet me like a host: 'This morning,' he continued, 'we had a lawn meet of the Marchmain Hounds – a deliciously archaic spectacle – and all our young friends are foxhunting, even Sebastian who, you will not be surprised to hear, looked remarkably elegant in his pink coat. Brideshead was impressive rather than elegant; he is Joint-master with a local figure of fun named Sir Walter Strickland-Venables. I wish the two of them could be included in these rather humdrum tapestries – they would give a note of fantasy.

'Our hostess remained at home; also a convalescent Dominican who has read too much Maritain and too little Hegel; Sir Adrian Porson, of course, and two rather forbidding Magyar cousins – I have tried them in German and in French, but in neither tongue are they diverting. All these have now driven off to visit a neighbour. I have been spending a cosy afternoon before the fire with the incomparable Charlus. Your arrival emboldens me to ring for some tea. How can I prepare you for the party? Alas, it breaks up tomorrow. Lady Julia departs to celebrate the New Year elsewhere, and takes the *beau-monde* with her. I shall miss the pretty creatures about the house – particularly one Celia; she is the sister of our old companion in adversity, Boy Mulcaster, and wonderfully unlike him. She has a birdlike style of conversation, pecking away at the subject in a way I find most engaging, and a school-monitor style of dress which I can only call "saucy". I shall miss her, for I do not go tomorrow. Tomorrow I start work in earnest on our hostess's book – which, believe me, is a treasure-house of period gems; pure authentic 1914.'

Tea was brought and, soon after it, Sebastian returned; he had lost the hunt early, he said, and hacked home; the others were not long after him, having been fetched by car at the end of the day; Brideshead was absent; he had business at the kennels and Cordelia had gone with him. The rest filled the hall and were soon eating scrambled eggs and crumpets; and Mr Samgrass, who had lunched at home and dozed all the afternoon before the fire, ate eggs and crumpets with them. Presently Lady Marchmain's party returned, and when, before we went upstairs to dress for dinner, she said 'Who's coming to chapel for the Rosary?' and Sebastian and Julia said they must have their baths at once, Mr Samgrass went with her and the friar.

'I wish Mr Samgrass would go,' said Sebastian, in his bath; 'I'm sick of being grateful to him.'

In the course of the next fortnight distaste for Mr Samgrass came to be a little unspoken secret throughout the house; in his presence Sir Adrian Porson's fine old eyes seemed to search a distant horizon and his lips set in classic pessimism. Only the Hungarian cousins who, mistaking the status of tutor, took him for an unusually privileged upper servant, were unaffected by his presence.

Mr Samgrass, Sir Adrian Porson, the Hungarians, the friar, Brideshead, Sebastian, Cordelia were all who remained of the Christmas party.

Religion predominated in the house; not only in its practices – the daily mass and Rosary, morning and evening in the chapel – but in all its intercourse. 'We must make a Catholic of Charles,' Lady Marchmain said, and we had many little talks together during my visits when she delicately steered the subject into a holy quarter. After the first of these Sebastian said: 'Has mummy been having one of her "little talks" with you? She's always doing it. I wish to hell she wouldn't.'

One was never summoned for a little talk, or consciously led to it; it merely happened, when she wished to speak intimately, that one found oneself alone with her, if it was summer, in a secluded walk by the lakes or in a corner of the walled rose-gardens; if it was winter, in her sitting-room on the first floor.

This room was all her own; she had taken it for herself and changed it so that, entering, one seemed to be in another house. She had lowered the ceiling and the elaborate cornice which, in one form or another, graced every room was lost to view; the walls, one panelled in brocade, were stripped and washed blue and spotted with innumerable little water-colours of fond association; the air was sweet with the fresh scent of flowers and musty potpourri; her library in soft leather covers, well-read works of poetry and piety, filled a small rosewood bookcase; the chimney-piece was covered with small personal treasures – an ivory Madonna, a plaster St Joseph, posthumous miniatures of her three soldier brothers. When Sebastian and I lived alone at

Brideshead during that brilliant August we had kept out of his mother's room.

Scraps of conversation come back to me with the memory of her room. I remember her saying: 'When I was a girl we were comparatively poor, but still much richer than most of the world, and when I married I became very rich. It used to worry me, and I thought it wrong to have so many beautiful things when others had nothing. Now I realize that it is possible for the rich to sin by coveting the privileges of the poor. The poor have always been the favourites of God and his saints, but I believe that it is one of the special achievements of Grace to sanctify the whole of life, riches included. Wealth in pagan Rome was necessarily something cruel; it's not any more.'

I said something about a camel and the eye of a needle and she rose happily to the point.

'But of *course*,' she said, 'it's very unexpected for a camel to go through the eye of a needle, but the gospel is simply a catalogue of unexpected things. It's not to be *expected* that an ox and an ass should worship at the crib. Animals are always doing the oddest things in the lives of the saints. It's all part of the poetry, the Alice-in-Wonderland side, of religion.'

But I was as untouched by her faith as I was by her charm: or, rather, I was touched by both alike. I had no mind then for anything except Sebastian, and I saw him already as being threatened, though I did not yet know how black was the threat. His constant, despairing prayer was to be let alone. By the blue waters and rustling palms of his own mind he was happy and harmless as a Polynesian; only when the big ship dropped anchor beyond the coral reef, and the cutter beached in the lagoon, and, up the slope that had never known the print of a boot, there trod the grim invasion of trader, administrator, missionary, and tourist – only then was it time to disinter the archaic weapons of the tribe and sound the drums in the hills; or, more easily, to turn from the sunlit door and lie alone in the darkness, where the impotent, painted deities paraded the walls in vain, and cough his heart out among the rum bottles.

And since Sebastian counted among the intruders his own

conscience and all claims of human affection, his days in Arcadia were numbered. For in this, to me, tranquil time Sebastian took fright. I knew him well in that mood of alertness and suspicion, like a deer suddenly lifting his head at the far notes of the hunt; I had seen him grow wary at the thought of his family or his religion, now I found I, too, was suspect. He did not fail in love, but he lost his joy of it, for I was no longer part of his solitude. As my intimacy with his family grew, I became part of the world which he sought to escape; I became one of the bonds which held him. That was the part for which his mother, in all our little talks, was seeking to fit me. Everything was left unsaid. It was only dimly and at rare moments that I suspected what was afoot.

Outwardly Mr Samgrass was the only enemy. For a fortnight Sebastian and I remained at Brideshead, leading our own life. His brother was engaged in sport and estate management; Mr Samgrass was at work in the library on Lady Marchmain's book; Sir Adrian Porson demanded most of Lady Marchmain's time. We saw little of them except in the evenings; there was room under that domed roof for a wide variety of independent lives.

After a fortnight Sebastian said: 'I can't stand Mr Samgrass any more. Let's go to London,' so he came to stay with me and now began to use my home in preference to 'Marchers'. My father liked him. 'I think your friend very amusing,' he said. 'Ask him *often*.'

Then, back at Oxford, we took up again the life that seemed to be shrinking in the cold air. The sadness that had been strong in Sebastian the term before gave place to a kind of sullenness even towards me. He was sick at heart somewhere, I did not know how, and I grieved for him, unable to help.

When he was gay now it was usually because he was drunk, and when drunk he developed an obsession of 'mocking Mr Samgrass'. He composed a ditty of which the refrain was, 'Green arse, Samgrass – Samgrass green arse', sung to the tune of St Mary's chime, and he would thus serenade him, perhaps once a week, under his windows. Mr Samgrass was distinguished as being the first don to have a private telephone installed in his rooms. Sebastian in his cups used to ring him up and sing him this simple song. And all this Mr Samgrass took in good part, as it is called, smiling obsequiously when we met, but with growing confidence, as though each outrage in some way strengthened his hold on Sebastian.

It was during this term that I began to realize that Sebastian was a drunkard in quite a different sense to myself. I got drunk often, but through an excess of high spirits, in the love of the moment, and the wish to prolong and enhance it; Sebastian drank to escape. As we together grew older and more serious I drank less, he more. I found that sometimes after I had gone back to my college, he sat up late and alone, soaking. A succession of disasters came on him so swiftly and with such unexpected violence that it is hard to say when exactly I recognized that my friend was in deep trouble. I knew it well enough in the Easter vacation.

Julia used to say, 'Poor Sebastian. It's something chemical in him.'

That was the cant phrase of the time, derived from heaven knows what misconception of popular science. 'There's something chemical between them' was used to explain the overmastering hate or love of any two people. It was the old concept of determinism in a new form. I do not believe there was anything chemical in my friend.

The Easter party at Brideshead was a bitter time, culminating in a small but unforgettably painful incident. Sebastian got very drunk before dinner in his mother's house, and thus marked the beginning of a new epoch in his melancholy record, another stride in the flight from his family which brought him to ruin.

It was at the end of the day when the large Easter party left Brideshead. It was called the Easter party, though in fact it began on the Tuesday of Easter Week, for the Flytes all went into retreat at the guest-house of a monastery from Maundy Thursday until Easter. This year Sebastian had said he would not go, but at the last moment had yielded, and came home in a state of acute depression from which I totally failed to raise him.

He had been drinking very hard for a week – only I knew how hard – and drinking in a nervous, surreptitious way, totally unlike his old habit. During the party there was always a grog tray in the library, and Sebastian took to slipping in there at odd moments during the day without saying anything even to me. The house was largely deserted during the day. I was at work painting another panel in the little garden-room in the colonnade. Sebastian complained of a cold, stayed in, and during all that time was never quite sober; he escaped attention by being silent. Now and then I noticed him attract curious glances, but most of the party knew him too slightly to see the change in him, while his own family were occupied, each with their particular guests.

When I remonstrated he said, 'I can't stand all these people about,' but it was when they finally left and he had to face his family at close quarters that he broke down.

The normal practice was for a cocktail tray to be brought into the drawing-room at six; we mixed our own drinks and the bottles were removed when we went to dress; later, just before dinner, cocktails appeared again, this time handed round by the footmen.

Sebastian disappeared after tea; the light had gone and I spent the next hour playing mah-jong with Cordelia. At six I was alone in the drawing-room, when he returned; he was frowning in a way I knew all too well, and when he spoke I recognized the drunken thickening in his voice.

'Haven't they brought the cocktails yet?' He pulled clumsily on the bell-rope.

I said, 'Where have you been?'

'Up with nanny.'

'I don't believe it. You've been drinking somewhere.'

'I've been reading in my room. My cold's worse today.'

When the tray arrived he slopped gin and vermouth into a tumbler and carried it out of the room with him. I followed him upstairs, where he shut his bedroom door in my face and turned the key.

I returned to the drawing-room full of dismay and foreboding.

The family assembled. Lady Marchmain said: 'What's become of Sebastian?'

'He's gone to lie down. His cold is worse.'

'Oh dear, I hope he isn't getting flu. I thought he had a feverish look once or twice lately. Is there anything he wants?'

'No, he particularly asked not to be disturbed.'

I wondered whether I ought to speak to Brideshead, but that grim, rock-crystal mask forbade all confidence. Instead, on the way upstairs to dress, I told Julia.

'Sebastian's drunk.'

'He can't be. He didn't even come for a cocktail.'

'He's been drinking in his room all the afternoon.'

'How very peculiar! What a bore he is! Will he be all right for dinner?'

'No.'

'Well, *you* must deal with him. It's no business of mine. Does he often do this?'

'He has lately.'

'How very boring.'

I tried Sebastian's door, found it locked, and hoped he was sleeping, but, when I came back from my bath, I found him sitting in the chair before my fire; he was dressed for dinner, all but his shoes, but his tie was awry and his hair on end; he was very red in the face and squinting slightly. He spoke indistinctly.

'Charles, what you said was quite true. Not with nanny. Been drinking whisky up here. None in the library now party's gone. Now party's gone and only mummy. Feeling rather drunk. Think I'd better have something-on-a-tray up here. Not dinner with mummy.'

'Go to bed,' I told him. 'I'll say your cold's worse.'

'Much worse.'

I took him to his room which was next to mine and tried to

get him to bed, but he sat in front of his dressing table squinnying at himself in the glass, trying to remake his bow-tie. On the writing table by the fire was a half-empty decanter of whisky. I took it up, thinking he would not see, but he spun round from the mirror and said: 'You put that down.'

'Don't be an ass, Sebastian. You've had enough.'

'What the devil's it got to do with you? You're only a guest here – *my* guest. I drink what I want to in my own house.'

He would have fought me for it at that moment.

'Very well,' I said, putting the decanter back, 'only for God's sake keep out of sight.'

'Oh, mind your own business. You came here as my friend; now you're spying on me for my mother, I know. Well, you can get out, and tell her from me that I'll choose my friends and she her spies in future.'

So I left him and went down to dinner.

'I've been in to Sebastian,' I said. 'His cold has come on rather badly. He's gone to bed and says he doesn't want anything.'

'Poor Sebastian,' said Lady Marchmain. 'He'd better have a glass of hot whisky. I'll go and have a look at him.'

'Don't, mummy, I'll go,' said Julia rising.

'*I'll* go,' said Cordelia, who was dining down that night, for a treat to celebrate the departure of the guests. She was at the door and through it before anyone could stop her.

Julia caught my eye and gave a tiny, sad shrug.

In a few minutes Cordelia was back, looking grave. 'No, he doesn't seem to want anything,' she said.

'How was he?'

'Well, I don't *know*, but I *think* he's very drunk,' she said.

'*Cordelia*.'

Suddenly the child began to giggle. ' "Marquis's Son Unused to Wine",' she quoted. ' "Model Student's Career Threatened".'

'Charles, is this true?' asked Lady Marchmain.

'Yes.'

Then dinner was announced, and we went to the dining-room where the subject was not mentioned.

When Brideshead and I were left alone he said: 'Did you say Sebastian was drunk?'

'Yes.'

'Extraordinary time to choose. Couldn't you stop him?'

'No.'

'No,' said Brideshead, 'I don't suppose you could. I once saw my father drunk, in this room. I wasn't more than about ten at the time. You can't stop people if they want to get drunk. My mother couldn't stop my father, you know.'

He spoke in his odd, impersonal way. The more I saw of this family, I reflected, the more singular I found them. 'I shall ask my mother to read to us tonight.'

It was the custom, I learned later, always to ask Lady Marchmain to read aloud on evenings of family tension. She had a beautiful voice and great humour of expression. That night she read part of *The Wisdom of Father Brown*. Julia sat with a stool covered with manicure things and carefully revarnished her nails; Cordelia nursed Julia's Pekinese; Brideshead played patience; I sat unoccupied studying the pretty group they made, and mourning my friend upstairs.

But the horrors of that evening were not yet over.

It was sometimes Lady Marchmain's practice, when the family were alone, to visit the chapel before going to bed. She had just closed her book and proposed going there when the door opened and Sebastian appeared. He was dressed as I had last seen him, but now instead of being flushed he was deathly pale.

'Come to apologize,' he said.

'Sebastian, dear, do go back to your room,' said Lady Marchmain. 'We can talk about it in the morning.'

'Not to you. Come to apologize to Charles. I was bloody to him and he's my guest. He's my guest and my only friend and I was bloody to him.'

A chill spread over us. I led him back to his room; his family went to their prayers. I noticed when we got upstairs that the decanter was now empty. 'It's time you were in bed,' I said.

Sebastian began to weep. 'Why do you take their side

against me? I knew you would if I let you meet them. Why do you spy on me?'

He said more than I can bear to remember, even at twenty years' distance. At last I got him to sleep and very sadly went to bed myself.

Next morning, he came to my room very early, while the house still slept; he drew the curtains and the sound of it woke me, to find him there fully dressed, smoking, with his back to me, looking out of the windows to where the long dawn-shadows lay across the dew and the first birds were chattering in the budding tree-tops. When I spoke he turned a face which showed no ravages of the evening before, but was fresh and sullen as a disappointed child's.

'Well,' I said. 'How do you feel?'

'Rather odd. I think perhaps I'm still a little drunk. I've just been down to the stables trying to get a car but everything was locked. We're off.'

He drank from the water-bottle by my pillow, threw his cigarette from the window, and lit another with hands which trembled like an old man's.

'Where are you going?'

'I don't know. London, I suppose. Can I come and stay with you?'

'Of course.'

'Well, get dressed. They can send our luggage on by train.'

'We can't just go like this.'

'We can't stay.'

He sat on the window seat looking away from me, out of the window. Presently he said: 'There's smoke coming from some of the chimneys. They must have opened the stables now. Come on.'

'I can't go,' I said. 'I must say good-bye to your mother.'

'Sweet bulldog.'

'Well, I don't happen to like running away.'

'And I couldn't care less. And I shall go on running away, as far and as fast as I can. You can hatch up any plot you like with my mother; I shan't come back.'

'That's how you talked last night.'

'I know. I'm sorry, Charles. I told you I was still drunk. If it's any comfort to you, I absolutely detest myself.'

'It's no comfort at all.'

'It must be a little, I should have thought. Well, if you won't come, give my love to nanny.'

'You're really going?'

'Of course.'

'Shall I see you in London?'

'Yes, I'm coming to stay with you.'

He left me but I did not sleep again; nearly two hours later a footman came with tea and bread and butter and set my clothes out for a new day.

Later that morning I sought Lady Marchmain; the wind had freshened and we stayed indoors; I sat near her before the fire in her room, while she bent over her needlework and the budding creeper rattled on the window-panes.

'I wish I had not *seen* him,' she said. 'That was cruel. I do not mind the *idea* of his being drunk. It is a thing all men do when they are young. I am used to the *idea* of it. My brothers were wild at his age. What hurt last night was that there was nothing *happy* about him.'

'I know,' I said. 'I've never seen him like that before.'

'And last night of all nights . . . when everyone had gone and there were only ourselves here – you see, Charles, I look on you very much as one of ourselves. Sebastian loves you – when there was no need for him to make an effort to be gay. And he wasn't gay. I slept very little last night, and all the time I kept coming back to that one thing; he was so unhappy.'

It was impossible for me to explain to her what I only half understood myself; even then I felt, 'She will learn it soon enough. Perhaps she knows it now.'

'It was horrible,' I said. 'But please don't think that's his usual way.'

'Mr Samgrass told me he was drinking too much all last term.'

'Yes, but not like that – never before.'

'Then why now? here? with us? All night I have been thinking and praying and wondering what I was to say to him, and now, this morning, he isn't here at all. That was cruel of him, leaving without a word. I don't want him to be ashamed – it's being ashamed that makes it all so wrong of him.'

'He's ashamed of being unhappy,' I said.

'Mr Samgrass says he is noisy and high-spirited. I believe,' she said, with a faint light of humour streaking the clouds, 'I believe you and he tease Mr Samgrass rather. It's naughty of you. I'm very fond of Mr Samgrass, and you should be too, after all he's done for you. But I think perhaps if I were your age and a man, I might be just a little inclined to tease Mr Samgrass myself. No, I don't mind that, but last night and this morning are something quite different. You see, *it's all happened before.*'

'I can only say I've seen him drunk often and I've been drunk with him often, but last night was quite new to me.'

'Oh, I don't mean with Sebastian. I mean years ago. I've been through it all before with someone else whom I loved. Well, you must know what I mean – with his father. He used to be drunk in just that way. Someone told me he is not like that now. I pray God it's true and thank God for it with all my heart, if it is. But the *running away* – *he* ran away, too, you know. It was as you said just now, he was ashamed of being unhappy. Both of them unhappy, ashamed, and running away. It's too pitiful. The men I grew up with' – and her great eyes moved from the embroidery to the three miniatures in the folding leather case on the chimney-piece – 'were not like that. I simply don't understand it. Do you, Charles?'

'Only very little.'

'And yet Sebastian is fonder of you than of any of us, you know. You've got to help him. I can't.'

I have here compressed into a few sentences what, there, required many. Lady Marchmain was not diffuse, but she took hold of her subject in a feminine, flirtatious way, circling, approaching, retreating, feinting; she hovered over it like a butterfly; she played 'grandmother's steps' with it, getting nearer the real point imperceptibly while one's back was turned, standing rooted when she was observed. The unhappiness, the running away – these made up her sorrow, and in her own way she exposed the whole of it, before she was done. It was an hour before she had said all she meant to say. Then, as I rose to leave her, she added as though in an afterthought: 'I wonder have you seen my brothers' book? It has just come out.'

I told her I had looked through it in Sebastian's rooms.

'I should like you to have a copy. May I give you one? They were three splendid men; Ned was the best of them. He was the last to be killed, and when the telegram came, as I knew it would come, I thought: 'Now it's my son's turn to do what Ned can never do now.' I was alone then. He was just going to Eton. If you read Ned's book you'll understand.'

She had a copy lying ready on her bureau. I thought at the time, 'She planned this parting before ever I came in. Had she rehearsed all the interview? If things had gone differently would she have put the book back in the drawer?'

She wrote her name and mine on the fly leaf, the date and place.

'I prayed for you, too, in the night,' she said.

I closed the door behind me, shutting out the *bondieuserie*, the low ceiling, the chintz, the lambskin bindings, the views of Florence, the bowls of hyacinth and potpourri, the *petit-point*, the intimate feminine, modern world, and was back under the coved and coffered roof, the columns and entablature of the central hall, in the august, masculine atmosphere of a better age.

I was no fool; I was old enough to know that an attempt had been made to suborn me and young enough to have found the experience agreeable.

I did not see Julia that morning, but just as I was leaving Cordelia ran to the door of the car and said: 'Will you be seeing Sebastian? Please give him my special love. Will you remember – my *special* love?'

In the train to London I read the book Lady Marchmain

had given me. The frontispiece reproduced the photograph of a young man in Grenadier uniform, and I saw plainly revealed there the origin of that grim mask which, in Brideshead, overlaid the gracious features of his father's family; this was a man of the woods and caves, a hunter, a judge of the tribal council, the repository of the harsh traditions of a people at war with their environment. There were other illustrations in the book, snapshots of the three brothers on holiday, and in each I traced the same archaic lines; and remembering Lady March-main, starry and delicate, I could find no likeness to her in these sombre men.

She appeared seldom in the book; she was older than the eldest of them by nine years and had married and left home while they were schoolboys; between her and them stood two other sisters; after the birth of the third daughter there had been pilgrimages and pious benefactions in request for a son, for theirs was a wide property and an ancient name; male heirs had come late and, when they came, in a profusion which at the time seemed to promise continuity to the line which, in the tragic event, ended abruptly with them.

The family history was typical of the Catholic squires of England; from Elizabeth's reign till Victoria's they lived seques-tered lives, among their tenantry and kinsmen, sending their sons to school abroad, often marrying there, inter-marrying, if not, with a score of families like themselves, debarred from all preferment, and learning, in those lost generations, lessons which could still be read in the lives of the last three men of the house.

Mr Samgrass's deft editorship had assembled and arranged a curiously homogeneous little body of writing – poetry, letters, scraps of a journal, an unpublished essay or two, which all exhaled the same high-spirited, serious, chivalrous, other-worldly air; and the letters from their contemporaries, written after their deaths, all in varying degrees of articulateness, told the same tale of men who were, in all the full flood of academic and athletic success, of popularity and the promise of great rewards ahead, seen somehow as set apart from their fellows, garlanded victims, devoted to the sacrifice. These men must die to make a world for Hooper; they were the aborigines, vermin by right of law, to be shot off at leisure so that things might be safe for the travelling salesman, with his polygonal pince-nez, his fat wet hand-shake, his grinning dentures. I wondered, as the train carried me farther and farther from Lady Marchmain, whether perhaps there was not on her, too, the same blaze, marking her and hers for destruction by other ways than war. Did she see a sign in the red centre of her cosy grate and hear it in the rattle of creeper on the window-pane, this whisper of doom?

Then I reached Paddington and, returning home, found Sebastian there, and the sense of tragedy vanished, for he was gay and free as when I first met him.

'Cordelia sent you her special love.'

'Did you have a "little talk" with mummy?'

'Yes.'

'Have you gone over to her side?'

The day before I would have said: 'There aren't two sides'; that day I said, 'No, I'm with you, "Sebastian *contra mundum*".'

And that was all the conversation we had on the subject, then or ever.

But the shadows were closing round Sebastian. We returned to Oxford and once again the gillyflowers bloomed under my windows and the chestnut lit the streets and the warm stones strewed their flakes upon the cobble; but it was not as it had been; there was mid-winter in Sebastian's heart.

The weeks went by; we looked for lodgings for the coming term and found them in Merton Street, a secluded, expensive little house near the tennis court.

Meeting Mr Samgrass, whom we had seen less often of late, I told him of our choice. He was standing at the table in Blackwell's where recent German books were displayed, setting aside a little heap of purchases.

'You're sharing digs with Sebastian?' he said. 'So he *is* coming up next term?'

'I suppose so. Why shouldn't he be?'

'I don't know why; I somehow thought perhaps he wasn't. I'm always wrong about things like that. I like Merton Street.'

He showed me the books he was buying, which, since I knew no German, were not of interest to me. As I left him he said: 'Don't think me interfering, you know, but I shouldn't make any *definite* arrangement in Merton Street until you're sure.'

I told Sebastian of this conversation and he said: 'Yes, there's a plot on. Mummy wants me to go and live with Mgr Bell.'

'Why didn't you tell me about it?'

'Because I'm *not* going to live with Mgr Bell.'

'I still think you might have told me. When did it start?'

'Oh, it's been going on. Mummy's very clever, you know. She saw she'd failed with you. I expect it was the letter you wrote after reading Uncle Ned's book.'

'I hardly said anything.'

'That was it. If you were going to be any help to her, you would have said a lot. Uncle Ned is the test, you know.'

But it seemed she had not quite despaired, for a few days later I got a note from her which said: '*I shall be passing through Oxford on Tuesday and hope to see you and Sebastian. I would like to see you alone for five minutes before I see him. Is that too much to ask? I will come to your rooms at about twelve.*'

She came; she admired my rooms. . . . 'My brothers Simon and Ned were here, you know. Ned had rooms on the garden front. I wanted Sebastian to come here, too, but my husband was at Christ Church and, as you know, he took charge of Sebastian's education'; she admired my drawings . . . '*everyone* loves your paintings in the garden-room. We shall never forgive you if you don't finish them.' Finally, she came to her point.

'I expect you've guessed already what I have come to ask. Quite simply, is Sebastian drinking too much this term?'

I had guessed; I answered: 'If he were, I shouldn't answer. As it is, I can say, "No".'

She said: 'I believe you. Thank God!' and we went together to luncheon at Christ Church.

That night Sebastian had his third disaster and was found by the junior dean at one o'clock, wandering round Tom Quad hopelessly drunk.

I had left him morose but completely sober at a few minutes before twelve. In the succeeding hour he had drunk half a bottle of whisky alone. He did not remember much about it when he came to tell me next morning.

'Have you been doing that a lot,' I asked, 'drinking by yourself after I've gone?'

'About twice; perhaps four times. It's only when they start bothering me. I'd be all right if they'd only leave me alone.'

'They won't now,' I said.

'I know.'

We both knew that this was a crisis. I had no love for Sebastian that morning; he needed it, but I had none to give.

'Really,' I said, 'if you are going to embark on a solitary bout of drinking every time you see a member of your family, it's perfectly hopeless.'

'Oh, yes,' said Sebastian with great sadness. 'I *know*. It's hopeless.'

But my pride was stung because I had been made to look a liar and I could not respond to his need.

'Well, what do you propose to do?'

'I shan't do anything. They'll do it all.'

And I let him go without comfort.

Then the machinery began to move again, and I saw it all repeated as it had happened in December; Mr Samgrass and Mgr Bell saw the Dean of Christ Church; Brideshead came up for a night; the heavy wheels stirred and the small wheels spun. Everyone was exceedingly sorry for Lady Marchmain, whose brothers' names stood in letters of gold on the war memorial, whose brothers' memory was fresh in many breasts.

She came to see me and, again, I must reduce to a few words a conversation which took us from Holywell to the Parks, through Mesopotamia, and over the ferry to north Oxford, where she was staying the night with a houseful of nuns who were in some way under her protection.

'You *must* believe', I said, 'that when I told you Sebastian was not drinking, I was telling you the truth, as I knew it.'

'I know you wish to be a good friend to him.'

'That is not what I mean. I believed what I told you. I still believe it to some extent. I believe he has been drunk two or three times before, not more.'

'It's no good, Charles,' she said. 'All you can mean is that you have not as much influence or knowledge of him as I thought. It is no good either of us trying to believe him. I've known drunkards before. One of the most terrible things about them is their deceit. Love of truth is the first thing that goes.

'After that happy luncheon together. When you left he was so sweet to me, just as he used to be as a little boy, and I agreed to all he wanted. You know I had been doubtful about his sharing rooms with you. I know you'll understand me when I say that. You know that we are all fond of you apart from your being Sebastian's friend. We should miss you so much if you ever stopped coming to stay with us. But I want Sebastian to have all sorts of friends, not just one. Mgr Bell tells me he never mixes with the other Catholics, never goes to the Newman, very rarely goes to mass even. Heaven forbid that he should only know Catholics, but he must know *some*. It needs a very strong faith to stand entirely alone and Sebastian's isn't strong.

'But I was so happy at luncheon on Tuesday that I gave up all my objections; I went round with him and saw the rooms you had chosen. They are charming. And we decided on some furniture you could have from London to make them nicer. And then, on the very night after I had seen him! – No, Charles, it is not in the Logic of the Thing.'

As she said it I thought, 'That's a phrase she's picked up from one of her intellectual hangers-on.'

'Well,' I said, 'have you a remedy?'

'The college are being extraordinarily kind. They say they will not send him down provided he goes to live with Mgr Bell. It's not a thing I could have suggested myself, but it was the Monsignor's own idea. He specially sent a message to you to say how welcome you would always be. There's not room for you actually in the Old Palace, but I daresay you wouldn't want that yourself.'

'Lady Marchmain, if you want to make him a drunkard that's the way to do it. Don't you see that any idea of his being *watched* would be fatal?'

'Oh, dear, it's no good trying to explain. Protestants always think Catholic priests are spies.'

'I don't mean that.' I tried to explain but made a poor business of it. 'He must feel free.'

'But he's been free, always, up till now, and look at the result.'

We had reached the ferry; we had reached a deadlock. With scarcely another word I saw her to the convent, then took the bus back to Carfax.

Sebastian was in my rooms waiting for me. 'I'm going to cable to papa,' he said. 'He won't let them force me into this priest's house.'

'But if they make it a condition of your coming up?'

'I shan't come up. Can you imagine me – serving mass twice a week, helping at tea parties for shy Catholic freshmen, dining with the visiting lecturer at the Newman, drinking a glass of port when we have guests, with Mgr Bell's eye on me to see I don't get too much, being explained, when I was out of the room, as the rather embarrassing local inebriate who's being taken in because his mother is so charming?'

'I told her it wouldn't do,' I said.

'Shall we get really drunk tonight?'

'It's the one time it could do no conceivable harm,' I said.

'*Contra mundum?*'

'*Contra mundum.*'

'Bless you, Charles. There aren't many evenings left to us.'

And that night, the first time for many weeks, we got deliriously drunk together; I saw him to the gate as all the bells were striking midnight, and reeled back to my rooms under a starry heaven which swam dizzily among the towers, and fell asleep in my clothes as I had not done for a year.

Next day Lady Marchmain left Oxford, taking Sebastian with her. Brideshead and I went to his rooms to sort out what he would have sent on and what leave behind.

Brideshead was as grave and impersonal as ever. 'It's a pity Sebastian doesn't know Mgr Bell better,' he said. 'He'd find him a charming man to live with. I was there my last year. My mother believes Sebastian is a confirmed drunkard. Is he?'

'He's in danger of becoming one.'

'I believe God prefers drunkards to a lot of respectable people.'

'For God's sake,' I said, for I was near to tears that morning, 'why bring God into everything?'

'I'm sorry. I forgot. But you know that's an extremely funny question.'

'Is it?'

'To me. Not to you.'

'No, not to me. It seems to me that without your religion Sebastian would have the chance to be a happy and healthy man.'

'It's arguable,' said Brideshead. 'Do you think he will need this elephant's foot again?'

That evening I went across the quad to visit Collins. He was alone with his texts, working by the failing light at his open window. 'Hullo,' he said. 'Come in. I haven't seen you all the term. I'm afraid I've nothing to offer you. Why have you deserted the smart set?'

'I'm the loneliest man in Oxford,' I said. 'Sebastian Flyte's been sent down.'

Presently I asked him what he was doing in the long vacation. He told me; it sounded excruciatingly dull. Then I asked him if he had got digs for next term. Yes, he told me, rather far out but very comfortable. He was sharing with Tyngate, the secretary of the college Essay Society.

'There's one room we haven't filled yet. Barker was coming, but he feels, now he's standing for president of the Union, he ought to be nearer in.'

It was in both our minds that perhaps I might take that room.

'Where are you going?'

'I *was* going to Merton Street with Sebastian Flyte. That's no use now.'

Still neither of us made the suggestion and the moment passed. When I left he said: 'I hope you find someone for Merton Street,' and I said, 'I hope you find someone for the Iffley Road,' and I never spoke to him again.

There was only ten days of term to go; I got through them somehow and returned to London as I had done in such different circumstances the year before, with no plans made.

'That very good-looking friend of yours,' asked my father. 'Is he not with you?'

'No.'

'I quite thought he had taken this over as his home. I'm sorry, I liked him.'

'Father, do you particularly want me to take my degree?'

'*I* want you to? Good gracious, why should *I* want such a thing? No use to me. Not much use to you either, as far as I've seen.'

'That's exactly what I've been thinking. I thought perhaps it was rather a waste of time going back to Oxford.'

Until then my father had taken only a limited interest in what I was saying: now he put down his book, took off his spectacles, and looked at me hard. 'You've been sent down,' he said. 'My brother warned me of this.'

'No, I've not.'

'Well, then, what's all the talk about?' he asked testily, resuming his spectacles, searching for his place on the page. 'Everyone stays up at least three years. I knew one man who took seven to get a pass degree in theology.'

'I only thought that if I was not going to take up one of the professions where a degree is necessary, it might be best to start now on what I intend doing. I intend to be a painter.'

But to this my father made no answer at the time.

The idea, however, seemed to take root in his mind; by the time we spoke of the matter again it was firmly established.

'When you're a painter,' he said at Sunday luncheon, 'you'll need a studio.'

'Yes.'

'Well, there isn't a studio here. There isn't even a room you could use decently as a studio. I'm not going to have you painting in the gallery.'

'No. I never meant to.'

'Nor will I have undraped models all over the house, nor critics with their horrible jargon. And I don't like the smell of turpentine. I presume you intend to do the thing thoroughly and use oil-paint?' My father belonged to a generation which divided painters into the serious and the amateur, according as they used oil or water.

'I don't suppose I should do much painting the first year. Anyway, I should be working at a school.'

'Abroad?' asked my father hopefully. 'There are some excellent schools abroad, I believe.'

It was all happening rather faster than I intended.

'Abroad or here. I should have to look round first.'

'Look round abroad,' he said.

'Then you agree to my leaving Oxford?'

'Agree? Agree? My dear boy, you're twenty-two.'

'Twenty,' I said, 'twenty-one in October.'

'Is that all? It seems *much* longer.'

A letter from Lady Marchmain completes this episode.

'*My dear Charles,*' she wrote, '*Sebastian left me this morning to join his father abroad. Before he went I asked him if he had written to you. He said no, so I must write, tho' I can hardly hope to say in a letter what I could not say on our last walk. But you must not be left in silence.*

'*The college has sent Sebastian down for a term only, and will take him back after Christmas on condition he goes to live with Mgr Bell. It is for him to decide. Meanwhile Mr Samgrass has very kindly consented to take charge of him. As soon as his visit to his father is over Mr Samgrass will pick him up and they will go together to the Levant, where Mr*

Samgrass has long been anxious to investigate a number of orthodox monasteries. He hopes this may be a new interest for Sebastian.

'*Sebastian's stay here has not been happy.*

'*When they come home at Christmas I know Sebastian will want to see you, and so shall we all. I hope your arrangements for next term have not been too much upset and that everything will go well with you.*

Yours sincerely,

Teresa Marchmain.

'*I went to the garden-room this morning and was so very sorry.*'

BOOK TWO

BRIDESHEAD DESERTED

CHAPTER I

'AND when we reached the top of the pass,' said Mr Samgrass, 'we heard the galloping horses behind, and two soldiers rode up to the head of the caravan and turned us back. The General had sent them, and they reached us only just in time. There was a Band, not a mile ahead.'

He paused, and his small audience sat silent, conscious that he had sought to impress them but in doubt as to how they could politely show their interest.

'*A Band?*' said Julia. '*Goodness!*'

Still he seemed to expect more. At last Lady Marchmain said, 'I suppose the sort of folk-music you get in those parts *is* very monotonous.'

'Dear Lady Marchmain, a Band of *Brigands*.' Cordelia, beside me on the sofa, began to giggle noiselessly. 'The mountains are full of them. Stragglers from Kemal's army; Greeks who got cut off in the retreat. Very desperate fellows, I assure you.'

'Do pinch me,' whispered Cordelia.

I pinched her and the agitation of the sofa-springs ceased. 'Thanks,' she said, wiping her eyes with the back of her hand.

'So you never got to wherever-it-was,' said Julia. 'Weren't you terribly disappointed, Sebastian?'

'Me?' said Sebastian from the shadows beyond the lamplight, beyond the warmth of the burning logs, beyond the family circle, and the photographs spread out on the card-table. 'Me? Oh, I don't think I was there that day, was I, Sammy?'

'That was the day you were ill.'

'I was ill,' he repeated like an echo, 'so I never should have got to wherever-it-was, should I, Sammy?'

'Now *this*, Lady Marchmain, is the caravan at Aleppo in the courtyard of the inn. That's our Armenian cook, Begedbian; that's me on the pony; that's the tent folded up; that's a rather tiresome Kurd who would follow us about at the time. . . . Here I am in Pontus, Ephesus, Trebizond, Krak-des-chevaliers, Samothrace, Batum – of course, I haven't got them in chronological order yet.'

'All guides and ruins and mules,' said Cordelia. 'Where's Sebastian?'

'He,' said Mr Samgrass, with a hint of triumph in his voice, as though he had expected the question and prepared the answer, 'he held the camera. He became quite an expert as soon as he learned not to put his hand over the lens, didn't you, Sebastian?'

There was no answer from the shadows. Mr Samgrass delved again into his pigskin satchel.

'Here,' he said, 'is a group taken by a street photographer on the terrace of the St George Hotel at Beirut. There's Sebastian.'

'Why,' I said, 'there's Anthony Blanche, surely?'

'Yes, we saw quite a lot of him; met him by chance at Constantinople. A delightful companion. I can't think how I missed knowing him. He came with us all the way to Beirut.'

Tea had been cleared away and the curtains drawn. It was two days after Christmas, the first evening of my visit; the first, too, of Sebastian's and Mr Samgrass's, whom to my surprise I had found on the platform when I arrived.

Lady Marchmain had written three weeks before: '*I have just heard from Mr Samgrass that he and Sebastian will be home for Christmas as we hoped. I had not heard from them for so long that I was afraid they were lost and did not want to make any arrangements until I knew. Sebastian will be longing to see you. Do come to us for Christmas if you can manage it, or as soon after as you can.*'

Christmas with my uncle was an engagement I could not break, so I travelled across country and joined the local train midway, expecting to find Sebastian already established; there he was, however, in the next carriage to mine, and when I asked him what he was doing, Mr Samgrass replied with such glibness and at such length, telling me of mislaid luggage and of Cook's being shut over the holidays, that I was at once aware of some other explanation which was being withheld.

Mr Samgrass was not at ease; he maintained all the physical habits of self-confidence, but guilt hung about him like stale cigar smoke, and in Lady Marchmain's greeting of him I caught a note of anticipation. He kept up a lively account of his tour during tea, and then Lady Marchmain drew him away with her, upstairs, for a 'little talk'. I watched him go with something near compassion; it was plain to anyone with a poker sense that Mr Samgrass held a very imperfect hand and, as I watched him at tea, I began to suspect that he was not only bluffing but cheating. There was something he must say, did not want to say, and did not quite know how to say to Lady Marchmain about his doings over Christmas, but, more than that, I guessed, there was a great deal he ought to say and had no intention at all of saying, about the whole Levantine tour.

'Come and see nanny,' said Sebastian.

'Please, can I come, too?' said Cordelia.

'Come on.'

We climbed to the nursery in the dome. On the way Cordelia said: 'Aren't you at all pleased to be home?'

'Of course I'm pleased,' said Sebastian.

'Well, you might show it a bit. I've been looking forward to it so much.'

Nanny did not particularly wish to be talked to; she liked visitors best when they paid no attention to her and let her knit away, and watch their faces and think of them as she had known them as small children; their present goings-on did not signify much beside those early illnesses and crimes.

'Well,' she said, 'you *are* looking peaky. I expect it's all that foreign food doesn't agree with you. You must fatten up now you're back. Looks as though you'd been having some late nights, too, by the look of your eyes – dancing, I suppose.' (It was ever Nanny Hawkins's belief that the upper classes spent most of their leisure evenings in the ballroom.) 'And that shirt wants darning. Bring it to me before it goes to the wash.'

Sebastian certainly did look ill; five months had wrought the change of years in him. He was paler, thinner, pouchy under the eyes, drooping in the corners of his mouth, and he showed the scars of a boil on the side of his chin; his voice seemed flatter and his movements alternately listless and jumpy; he looked down-at-heel, too, with clothes and hair, which formerly had been happily negligent, now unkempt; worst of all, there was a wariness in his eye which I had surprised there at Easter, and which now seemed habitual to him.

Restrained by this wariness I asked him nothing of himself, but told him instead about my autumn and winter. I told him about my rooms in the Île Saint-Louis and the art school, and how good the old teachers were and how bad the students.

'They never go near the Louvre,' I said, 'or, if they do, it's only because one of their absurd reviews has suddenly "discovered" a master who fits in with that month's aesthetic theory. Half of them are out to make a popular splash like Picabia; the other half quite simply want to earn their living doing advertisements for *Vogue* and decorating night clubs. And the teachers still go on trying to make them paint like Delacroix.'

'Charles,' said Cordelia, 'Modern Art is all bosh, isn't it?'

'Great bosh.'

'Oh, I'm so glad. I had an argument with one of our nuns and she said we shouldn't try and criticize what we didn't understand. Now I shall tell her I have had it straight from a real artist, and snubs to her.'

Presently it was time for Cordelia to go to her supper, and for Sebastian and me to go down to the drawing-room for our cocktails. Brideshead was there alone, but Wilcox followed on our heels to say to him: 'Her Ladyship would like to speak to you upstairs, my Lord.'

'That's unlike mummy, sending for anyone. She usually lures them up herself.'

There was no sign of the cocktail tray. After a few minutes Sebastian rang the bell. A footman answered. 'Mr Wilcox is upstairs with her Ladyship.'

'Well, never mind, bring in the cocktail things.'

'Mr Wilcox has the keys, my Lord.'

'Oh ... well, send him in with them when he comes down.'

We talked a little about Anthony Blanche – 'He had a beard in Istanbul, but I made him take it off' – and after ten minutes Sebastian said: 'Well, I don't want a cocktail, anyway; I'm off to my bath,' and left the room.

It was half past seven; I supposed the others had gone to dress, but, as I was going to follow them, I met Brideshead coming down.

'Just a moment, Charles, there's something I've got to explain. My mother has given orders that no drinks are to be left in any of the rooms. You'll understand why. If you want anything, ring and ask Wilcox – only better wait until you're alone. I'm sorry, but there it is.'

'Is that necessary?'

'I gather very necessary. You may or may not have heard, Sebastian had another outbreak as soon as he got back to England. He was lost over Christmas. Mr Samgrass only found him yesterday evening.'

'I guessed something of the kind had happened. Are you sure this is the best way of dealing with it?'

'It's my mother's way. Will you have a cocktail, now that he's gone upstairs?'

'It would choke me.'

I was always given the room I had on my first visit; it was next to Sebastian's, and we shared what had once been a dressing-room and had been changed to a bathroom twenty years back by the substitution for the bed of a deep, copper, mahogany-framed bath, that was filled by pulling a brass lever heavy as a piece of marine engineering; the rest of the room remained unchanged; a coal fire always burned there in winter. I often think of that bathroom – the water-colours dimmed by steam and the huge towel warming on the back of the chintz armchair – and contrast it with the uniform, clinical, little chambers, glittering with chromium-plate and looking-glass, which pass for luxury in the modern world.

I lay in the bath and then dried slowly by the fire, thinking all the time of my friend's black home-coming. Then I put on my dressing gown and went to Sebastian's room, entering, as I always did, without knocking. He was sitting by his fire half-dressed, and he started angrily when he heard me and put down a tooth glass.

'Oh, it's you. You gave me a fright.'

'So you got a drink,' I said.

'I don't know what you mean.'

'For Christ's sake,' I said, 'you don't have to pretend with me! You might offer me some.'

'It's just something I had in my flask. I've finished it now.'

'What's going on?'

'Nothing. A lot. I'll tell you some time.'

I dressed and called in for Sebastian, but found him still sitting as I had left him, half-dressed over his fire.

Julia was alone in the drawing-room.

'Well,' I asked, 'what's going on?'

'Oh, just another boring family *potin*. Sebastian got tight again, so we've all got to keep an eye on him. It's too tedious.'

'It's pretty boring for him, too.'

'Well, it's his fault. Why can't he behave like anyone else? Talking of keeping an eye on people, what about Mr Samgrass? Charles, do you notice anything at all fishy about that man?'

'Very fishy. Do you think your mother saw it?'

'Mummy only sees what suits her. She can't have the whole household under surveillance. *I'm* causing anxiety, too, you know.'

'I didn't know,' I said, adding humbly, 'I've only just come from Paris,' so as to avoid giving the impression that any trouble she might be in was not widely notorious.

It was an evening of peculiar gloom. We dined in the Painted Parlour. Sebastian was late, and so painfully excited were we that I think it was in all our minds that he would make some sort of low-comedy entrance, reeling and hiccuping. When he came it was, of course, with perfect propriety; he apologized, sat in the empty place, and allowed Mr Samgrass to resume his mono-logue, uninterrupted and, it seemed, unheard. Druses, patriarchs, icons, bed-bugs, Romanesque remains, curious dishes of goat and sheeps' eyes, French and Turkish officials – all the catalogue of Near Eastern travel was provided for our amusement.

I watched the champagne go round the table. When it came to Sebastian he said: 'I'll have whisky, please,' and I saw Wilcox glance over his head to Lady Marchmain and saw her give a tiny, hardly perceptible nod. At Brideshead they used small individual spirit decanters which held about a quarter of a bottle, and were always placed, full, before anyone who asked for it; the decanter which Wilcox put before Sebastian was half-empty. Sebastian raised it very deliberately, tilted it, looked at it, and then in silence poured the liquor into his glass, where it covered two fingers. We all began talking at once, all except Sebastian, so that for a moment Mr Samgrass found himself talking to no one, telling the candlesticks about the Maronites; but soon we fell silent again, and he had the table until Lady Marchmain and Julia left the room.

'Don't be long, Bridey,' she said, at the door, as she always said, and that evening we had no inclination to delay. Our glasses were filled with port and the decanter was at once taken from the room. We drank quickly and went to the drawing-room, where Brideshead asked his mother to read, and she read *The Diary of a Nobody* with great spirit until ten o'clock, when she closed the book and said she was unaccountably tired, so tired that she would not visit the chapel that night.

'Who's hunting tomorrow?' she asked.

'Cordelia,' said Brideshead. 'I'm taking that young horse of Julia's, just to show him the hounds; I shan't keep him out more than a couple of hours.'

'Rex is arriving some time,' said Julia. 'I'd better stay in to greet him.'

'Where's the meet?' said Sebastian suddenly.

'Just here at Flyte St Mary.'

'Then I'd like to hunt, please, if there's anything for me.'

'Of course. That's delightful. I'd have asked you, only you always used to complain so of being made to go out. You can have Tinkerbell. She's been going very nicely this season.'

Everyone was suddenly pleased that Sebastian wanted to hunt; it seemed to undo some of the mischief of the evening. Brideshead rang the bell for whisky.

'Anyone else want any?'

'Bring me some, too,' said Sebastian, and, though it was a footman this time and not Wilcox, I saw the same exchange of glance and nod between the servant and Lady Marchmain. Everyone had been warned. The two drinks were brought in, poured out already in the glasses, like 'doubles' at a bar, and all our eyes followed the tray, as though we were dogs in a dining-room smelling game.

The good humour engendered by Sebastian's wish to hunt persisted, however; Brideshead wrote out a note for the stables, and we all went to bed quite cheerfully.

Sebastian got straight to bed; I sat by his fire and smoked a pipe. I said: 'I rather wish I was coming out with you tomorrow.'

'Well,' he said, 'you wouldn't see much sport. I can tell you exactly what I'm going to do. I shall leave Bridey at the first covert, hack over to the nearest good pub, and spend the entire day quietly soaking in the bar parlour. If they treat me like a dipsomaniac, they can bloody well have a dipsomaniac. I hate hunting, anyway.'

'Well, I can't stop you.'

'You can, as a matter of fact – by not giving me any money. They stopped my banking account, you know, in the summer. It's been one of my chief difficulties. I pawned my watch and cigarette case to ensure a happy Christmas, so I shall have to come to you tomorrow for my day's expenses.'

'I won't. You know perfectly well I can't.'

'Won't you, Charles? Well, I daresay I shall manage on my own somehow. I've got rather clever at that lately – managing on my own. I've had to.'

'Sebastian, what *have* you and Mr Samgrass been up to?'

'He told you at dinner – ruins and guides and mules, that's what Sammy's been up to. We decided to go our own ways, that's all. Poor Sammy's really behaved rather well so far. I hoped he would keep it up, but he seems to have been very indiscreet about my happy Christmas. I suppose he thought if he gave too good an account of me, he might lose his job as keeper.

'He makes quite a good thing out of it, you know. I don't mean that he steals. I should think he's fairly honest about money. He certainly keeps an embarrassing little note-book in which he puts down all the travellers' cheques he cashes and what he spends it on, for mummy and the lawyer to see. But he wanted to go to all these places, and it's very convenient for him to have me to take him in comfort, instead of going as dons usually do. The only disadvantage was having to put up with my company, and we soon solved that for him.

'We began very much on a Grand Tour, you know, with letters to all the chief people everywhere, and stayed with the Military Governor at Rhodes and the Ambassador at Constantinople. That was what Sammy had signed on for in the first place. Of course, he had his work cut out keeping his eye on me, but he warned all our hosts beforehand that I was not responsible.'

'Sebastian.'

'Not *quite* responsible – and as I had no money to spend I couldn't get away very much. He even did the tipping for me, put the note into the man's hand and jotted the amount down then and there in his note-book. My lucky time was at Constantinople. I managed to make some money at cards one evening when Sammy wasn't looking. Next day I gave him the slip and was having a very happy hour in the bar at the Tokatlian when who should come in but Anthony Blanche with a beard and a Jew boy. Anthony lent me a tenner just before Sammy came panting in and recaptured me. After that I didn't get a minute out of sight; the Embassy staff put us in the boat to Piraeus and watched us sail away. But in Athens it was easy. I simply walked out of the Legation one day after lunch, changed my money at Cook's, and asked about sailings to Alexandria just to fox Sammy, then went down to the port in a bus, found a sailor who spoke American, lay up with him till his ship sailed, and popped back to Constantinople, and that was that.

'Anthony and the Jew boy shared a very nice, tumble-down house near the bazaars. I stayed there till it got too cold, then Anthony and I drifted south till we met Sammy by appointment in Syria three weeks ago.'

'Didn't Sammy mind?'

'Oh, I think he quite enjoyed himself in his own ghastly way – only of course there was no more high life for him. I think he was a bit anxious at first. I didn't want him to get the whole Mediterranean Fleet out, so I cabled him from Constantinople that I was quite well and would he send money to the Ottoman Bank. He came hopping over as soon as he got my cable. Of course he was in a difficult position, because I'm of age and not certified yet, so he couldn't have me arrested. He couldn't leave me to starve while he was living on my money, and he couldn't tell mummy without looking pretty silly. I had him all ways, poor Sammy. My original idea had been to leave him flat, but Anthony was very helpful about that, and said it was far better to arrange things amicably; and he *did* arrange things very amicably. So here I am.'

'After Christmas.'

'Yes, I was determined to have a happy Christmas.'

'Did you?'

'I think so. I don't remember it much, and that's always a good sign, isn't it?'

Next morning at breakfast Brideshead wore scarlet; Cordelia, very smart herself, with her chin held high over her white stock, wailed when Sebastian appeared in a tweed coat: '*Oh, Sebastian*, you can't come out like that. Do go and change. You look so lovely in hunting clothes.'

'Locked away somewhere. Gibbs couldn't find them.'

'That's a fib. I helped get them out myself before you were called.'

'Half the things are missing.'

'It just encourages the Strickland-Venableses. They're behaving rottenly. They've even taken their grooms out of top hats.'

It was a quarter to eleven before the horses were brought round, but no one else appeared downstairs; it was as though they were in hiding, listening for Sebastian's retreating hooves before showing themselves.

Just as he was about to start, when the others were already mounted, Sebastian beckoned me into the hall. On the table beside his hat, gloves, whip, and sandwiches, lay the flask he had put out to be filled. He picked it up and shook it; it was empty.

'You see,' he said, 'I can't even be trusted that far. It's they who are mad, not me. Now you can't refuse me money.'

I gave him a pound.

'More,' he said.

I gave him another and watched him mount and trot after his brother and sister.

Then, as though it were his cue on the stage, Mr Samgrass came to my elbow, put an arm in mine, and led me back to the fire. He warmed his neat little hands and then turned to warm his seat.

'So Sebastian is in pursuit of the fox,' he said, 'and our little problem is shelved for an hour or two?'

I was not going to stand this from Mr Samgrass.

'I heard all about your Grand Tour, last night,' I said.

'Ah, I rather supposed you might have.' Mr Samgrass was undismayed, relieved, it seemed, to have someone else in the know. 'I did not harrow our hostess with all that. After all, it turned out far better than one had any right to expect. I did feel, however, that some explanation was due to her of Sebastian's Christmas festivities. You may have observed last night that there were certain precautions.'

'I did.'

'You thought them excessive? I am with you, particularly as they tend to compromise the comfort of our own little visit. I have seen Lady Marchmain this morning. You must not suppose I am just out of bed. I have had a little talk upstairs with our hostess. I think we may hope for some relaxation tonight. Yesterday was *not* an evening that any of us would wish to have repeated. I earned less gratitude than I deserved, I think, for my efforts to distract you.'

It was repugnant to me to talk about Sebastian to Mr Samgrass, but I was compelled to say: 'I'm not sure that tonight would be the best time to start the relaxation.'

'But surely? Why not tonight, after a day in the field under Brideshead's inquisitorial eye? Could one choose better?'

'Oh, I suppose it's none of my business really.'

'Nor mine, strictly, now that he is safely home. Lady Marchmain did me the honour of consulting me. But it is less Sebastian's welfare than our own I have at heart at the moment. I need my third glass of port; I need that hospitable tray in the library. And yet you specifically advise against it *tonight*. I wonder why. Sebastian can come to no mischief today. For one thing, he has no money. I happen to know. I saw to it. I even have his watch and cigarette case upstairs. He will be quite harmless . . . as long as no one is so wicked as to give him any. . . . Ah, Lady Julia, good morning to you, good morning. And how is the peke this hunting morning?'

'Oh, the peke's all right. Listen. I've got Rex Mottram coming here today. We simply can't have another evening like last night. Someone must speak to mummy.'

'Someone *has*. I spoke. I think it will be all right.'

'Thank God for that. Are you painting today, Charles?'

It had been the custom that on every visit to Brideshead I painted a medallion on the walls of the garden-room. The custom suited me well, for it gave me a good reason to detach myself from the rest of the party; when the house was full, the garden-room became a rival to the nursery, where from time to time people took refuge to complain about the others; thus without effort I kept in touch with the gossip of the place. There were three finished medallions now, each rather pretty in its way, but unhappily each in a different way, for my tastes had changed and I had become more dexterous in the eighteen months since the series was begun. As a decorative scheme, they were a failure. That morning was typical of the many mornings when I had found the garden-room a sanctuary. There I went and was soon at work. Julia came with me to see me started and we talked, inevitably, of Sebastian.

'Don't you get bored with the subject?' she asked. 'Why must everyone make such a Thing about it?'

'Just because we're fond of him.'

'Well, I'm fond of him too, in a way, I suppose, only I wish he'd behave like anybody else. I've grown up with one family skeleton, you know – papa. Not to be talked of before the servants, not to be talked of before us when we were children. If mummy is going to start making a skeleton out of Sebastian, it's *too* much. If he wants to be always tight, why doesn't he go to Kenya or somewhere where it doesn't matter?'

'Why does it matter less being unhappy in Kenya than anywhere else?'

'Don't pretend to be stupid, Charles. You understand perfectly.'

'You mean there won't be so many embarrassing situations for you? Well, all I was trying to say was that I'm afraid there may be an embarrassing situation tonight if Sebastian gets the chance. He's in a bad mood.'

'Oh, a day's hunting will put that all right.'

It was touching to see the faith which everybody put in the value of a day's hunting. Lady Marchmain, who looked in on me during the morning, mocked herself for it with that delicate irony for which she was famous.

'I've always detested hunting,' she said, 'because it seems to produce a particularly gross kind of caddishness in the nicest people. I don't know what it is, but the moment they dress up and get on a horse they become like a lot of Prussians. And so boastful after it. The evenings I've sat at dinner appalled at seeing the men and women I know, transformed into half-awake, self-opinionated, monomaniac louts! ... and yet, you know, – it must be something derived from centuries ago – my heart is quite light today to think of Sebastian out with them. "There's nothing wrong with him really," I say, "he's gone hunting" – as though it were an answer to prayer.'

She asked me about my life in Paris. I told her of my rooms

with their view of the river and the towers of Notre Dame. 'I'm hoping Sebastian will come and stay with me when I go back.'

'It would have been lovely,' said Lady Marchmain, sighing as though for the unattainable.

'I hope he's coming to stay with me in London.'

'Charles, you know it isn't possible. London's the worst place. Even Mr Samgrass couldn't hold him there. We have no secrets in this house. He was *lost*, you know, all through Christmas. Mr Samgrass only found him because he couldn't pay his bill in the place where he was, so they telephoned our house. It's too horrible. No, London is impossible; if he can't behave himself here, with us ... We must keep him happy and healthy here for a bit, hunting, and then send him abroad again with Mr Samgrass. ... You see, I've been through all this before.'

The retort was there, unspoken, well-understood by both of us – 'You couldn't keep *him*; *he* ran away. So will Sebastian. Because they both hate you.'

A horn and the huntsman's cry sounded in the valley below us.

'There they go now, drawing the home woods. I hope he's having a good day.'

Thus with Julia and Lady Marchmain I reached deadlock, not because we failed to understand one another, but because we understood too well. With Brideshead, who came home to luncheon and talked to me on the subject – for the subject was everywhere in the house like a fire deep in the hold of a ship, below the water-line, black and red in the darkness, coming to light in acrid wisps of smoke that oozed under hatches and billowed suddenly from the scuttles and air pipes – with Brideshead, I was in a strange world, a dead world to me, in a moon-landscape of barren lava, a high place of toiling lungs.

He said: 'I hope it is dipsomania. That is simply a great misfortune that we must all help him bear. What I used to fear was that he just got drunk deliberately when he liked and because he liked.'

'That's exactly what he did – what we both did. It's what he does with me now. I can keep him to that, if only your mother would trust me. If you worry him with keepers and cures he'll be a physical wreck in a few years.'

'There's nothing *wrong* in being a physical wreck, you know. There's no moral obligation to be Postmaster-General or Master of Foxhounds or to live to walk ten miles at eighty.'

'*Wrong*,' I said. '*Moral obligation* – now you're back on religion again.'

'I never left it,' said Brideshead.

'D'you know, Bridey, if I ever felt for a moment like becoming a Catholic, I should only have to talk to you for five minutes to be cured. You manage to reduce what seem quite sensible propositions to stark nonsense.'

'It's odd you should say that. I've heard it before from other people. It's one of the many reasons why I don't think I should make a good priest. It's something in the way my mind works, I suppose.'

At luncheon Julia had no thoughts except for her guest who was coming that day. She drove to the station to meet him and brought him home to tea.

'Mummy, do look at Rex's Christmas present.'

It was a small tortoise with Julia's initials set in diamonds in the living shell, and this slightly obscene object, now slipping impotently on the polished boards, now striding across the card-table, now lumbering over a rug, now withdrawn at a touch, now stretching its neck and swaying its withered, antediluvian head, became a memorable part of the evening, one of those needle-hooks of experience which catch the attention when larger matters are at stake.

'Dear me,' said Lady Marchmain. 'I wonder if it eats the same sort of things as an ordinary tortoise.'

'What will you do when it's dead?' asked Mr Samgrass. 'Can you have another tortoise fitted into the shell?'

Rex had been told about the problem of Sebastian – he could scarcely have endured in that atmosphere without – and had a solution pat. He propounded it cheerfully and openly at tea, and after a day of whispering it was a relief to hear the thing discussed. 'Send him to Borethus at Zürich. Borethus is the man. He works miracles every day at that sanatorium of his. You know how Charlie Kilcartney used to drink.'

'No,' said Lady Marchmain, with that sweet irony of hers. 'No, I'm afraid I don't know how Charlie Kilcartney drank.'

Julia, hearing her lover mocked, frowned at the tortoise, but Rex Mottram was impervious to such delicate mischief.

'Two wives despaired of him,' he said. 'When he got engaged to Sylvia, she made it a condition that he should take the cure at Zürich. And it worked. He came back in three months a different man. And he hasn't touched a drop since, even though Sylvia walked out on him.'

'Why did she do that?'

'Well, poor Charlie got rather a bore when he stopped drinking. But that's not really the point of the story.'

'No, I suppose not. In fact, I suppose, really, it's meant to be an encouraging story.'

Julia scowled at her jewelled tortoise.

'He takes sex cases, too, you know.'

'Oh dear, what very peculiar friends poor Sebastian will make in Zürich.'

'He's booked up for months ahead, but I think he'd find room if I asked him. I could telephone him from here tonight.'

(In his kindest moments Rex displayed a kind of hectoring zeal as if he were thrusting a vacuum cleaner on an unwilling housewife.)

'We'll think about it.'

And we were thinking about it when Cordelia returned from hunting.

'Oh, Julia, *what's* that? How *beastly*.'

'It's Rex's Christmas present.'

'Oh, sorry. I'm always putting my foot in it. But how cruel! It must have hurt frightfully.'

'They can't feel.'

'How d'you know? Bet they can.'

She kissed her mother, whom she had not seen that day, shook hands with Rex, and rang for eggs.

'I had one tea at Mrs Barney's, where I telephoned for the car, but I'm still hungry. It was a spiffing day. Jean Strickland-Venables fell in the mud. We ran from Bengers to Upper Eastrey without a check. I reckon that's five miles, don't you, Bridey?'

'Three.'

'Not as he ran. ...' Between mouthfuls of scrambled egg she told us about the hunt. '... You should have seen Jean when she came out of the mud.'

'Where's Sebastian?'

'He's in disgrace.' The words, in that clear, child's voice had the ring of a bell tolling, but she went on: 'Coming out in that beastly rat-catcher coat and mean little tie like something from Captain Morvin's Riding Academy. I just didn't recognize him at the meet, and I hope nobody else did. Isn't he back? I expect he got lost.'

When Wilcox came to clear the tea, Lady Marchmain asked: 'No sign of Lord Sebastian?'

'No, my Lady.'

'He must have stopped for tea with someone. How very unlike him.'

Half an hour later, when Wilcox brought in the cocktail tray, he said: 'Lord Sebastian has just rung up to be fetched from South Twining.'

'South Twining? Who lives there?'

'He was speaking from the hotel, my Lady.'

'South Twining?' said Cordelia. 'Goodness, he *did* get lost!'

When he arrived he was flushed and his eyes were feverishly bright; I saw that he was two-thirds drunk.

'Dear boy,' said Lady Marchmain. 'How nice to see you looking so well again. Your day in the open has done you good. The drinks are on the table; do help yourself.'

There was nothing unusual in her speech but the fact of her saying it. Six months ago it would not have been said.

'Thanks,' said Sebastian. 'I will.'

A blow, expected, repeated, falling on a bruise, with no smart or shock of surprise, only a dull and sickening pain and the doubt whether another like it could be borne – that was how it felt, sitting opposite Sebastian at dinner that night, seeing his clouded eye and groping movements, hearing his thickened voice breaking in, ineptly, after long brutish silences. When at length Lady Marchmain and Julia and the servants left us, Brideshead said: 'You'd best go to bed, Sebastian.'

'Have some port first.'

'Yes, have some port if you want it. But don't come into the drawing-room.'

'Too bloody drunk,' said Sebastian nodding heavily. 'Like olden times. Gentlemen always too drunk join ladies in olden times.'

('And yet, you know, it *wasn't*,' said Mr Samgrass, trying to be chatty with me about it afterwards, 'it wasn't at all like olden times. I wonder where the difference lies. The lack of good humour? The lack of companionship? You know I think he must have been drinking by himself today. Where did he get the money?')

'Sebastian's gone up,' said Brideshead when we reached the drawing-room.

'Yes? Shall I read?'

Julia and Rex played bezique; the tortoise, teased by the pekinese, withdrew into his shell; Lady Marchmain read *The Diary of a Nobody* aloud until, quite early, she said it was time for bed.

'Can't I stay up and play a little longer, mummy? Just three games?'

'Very well, darling. Come in and see me before you go to bed. I shan't be asleep.'

It was plain to Mr Samgrass and me that Julia and Rex wanted to be left alone, so we went, too; it was not plain to Brideshead, who settled down to read *The Times*, which he had not yet seen that day. Then, going to our side of the house, Mr Samgrass said: 'It wasn't at all like olden times.'

Next morning I said to Sebastian: 'Tell me honestly, do you want me to stay on here?'

'No, Charles, I don't believe I do.'

'I'm no help?'

'No help.'

So I went to make my excuses to his mother.

'There's something I must ask you, Charles. Did you give Sebastian money yesterday?'

'Yes.'

'Knowing how he was likely to spend it?'

'Yes.'

'I don't understand it,' she said. 'I simply don't understand how anyone can be so callously wicked.'

She paused, but I do not think she expected any answer; there was nothing I could say unless I were to start all over again on that familiar, endless argument.

'I'm not going to reproach you,' she said. 'God knows it's not for me to reproach anyone. Any failure in my children is my failure. But I don't understand it. I don't understand how you can have been so nice in so many ways, and then do something so wantonly cruel. I don't understand how we all liked you so much. Did you hate us all the time? I don't understand how we deserved it.'

I was unmoved; there was no part of me remotely touched by her distress. It was as I had often imagined being expelled from school. I almost expected to hear her say: 'I have already written to inform your unhappy father.' But as I drove away and turned back in the car to take what promised to be my last view of the house, I felt that I was leaving part of myself behind, and that wherever I went afterwards I should feel the lack of it, and search for it hopelessly, as ghosts are said to do, frequenting the spots where they buried material treasures without which they cannot pay their way to the nether world.

'I shall never go back,' I said to myself.

A door had shut, the low door in the wall I had sought and found in Oxford; open it now and I should find no enchanted garden.

I had come to the surface, into the light of common day and the fresh sea-air, after long captivity in the sunless coral palaces and waving forests of the ocean bed.

I had left behind me – what? Youth? Adolescence? Romance? The conjuring stuff of these things, 'the Young Magician's Compendium', that neat cabinet where the ebony wand had its place beside the delusive billiard balls, the penny that folded double, and the feather flowers that could be drawn into a hollow candle.

'I have left behind illusion,' I said to myself. 'Henceforth I live in a world of three dimensions – with the aid of my five senses.'

I have since learned that there is no such world, but then, as the car turned out of sight of the house, I thought it took no finding, but lay all about me at the end of the avenue.

Thus I returned to Paris, and to the friends I had found there and the habits I had formed. I thought I should hear no more of Brideshead, but life has few separations as sharp as that. It was not three weeks before I received a letter in Cordelia's Frenchified convent hand:

'*Darling Charles*,' she said. '*I was so very miserable when you went. You might have come and said good-bye!*

'*I heard all about your disgrace, and I am writing to say that I am in disgrace, too. I sneaked Wilcox's keys and got whisky for Sebastian and got caught. He did seem to want it so. And there was (and is) an awful row.*

'*Mr Samgrass has gone (good!), and I think he is a bit in disgrace, too, but I don't know why.*

'*Mr Mottram is very popular with Julia (bad!) and is taking Sebastian away (bad! bad!) to a German doctor.*

'*Julia's tortoise disappeared. We think it buried itself, as they do, so there goes a packet (expression of Mr Mottram's).*

'*I am very well.*

'*With love from*
                    Cordelia.'

It must have been about a week after receiving this letter that I returned to my rooms one afternoon to find Rex waiting for me.

It was about four, for the light began to fail early in the studio at that time of year. I could see by the expression on the concierge's face, when she told me I had a visitor waiting, that there was something impressive upstairs; she had a vivid gift of expressing differences of age or attraction; this was the expression which meant someone of the first consequence, and Rex indeed seemed to justify it, as I found him in his big travelling coat, filling the window that looked over the river.

'Well,' I said. 'Well.'

'I came this morning. They told me where you usually lunched but I couldn't see you there. Have you got him?'

I did not need to ask whom. 'So he's given you the slip, too?'

'We got here last night and were going on to Zürich today. I left him at the Lotti after dinner, as he said he was tired, and went round to the Travellers' for a game.'

I noticed how, even with me, he was making excuses, as though rehearsing his story for retelling elsewhere. 'As he said he was tired' was good. I could not well imagine Rex letting a half-tipsy boy interfere with his cards.

'So you came back and found him gone?'

'Not at all. I wish I had. I found him sitting up for me. I had a run of luck at the Travellers' and cleaned up a packet. Sebastian pinched the lot while I was asleep. All he left me was two first-class tickets to Zürich stuck in the edge of the looking-glass. I had nearly three hundred quid, blast him!'

'And now he may be almost anywhere.'

'Anywhere. You're *not* hiding him by any chance?'

'No. My dealings with that family are over.'

'I think mine are just beginning,' said Rex. 'I say, I've got a lot to talk about, and I promised a chap at the Travellers' I'd give him his revenge this afternoon. Won't you dine with me?'

'Yes. Where?'

'I usually go to Ciro's.'

'Why not Paillard's?'

'Never heard of it. I'm paying you know.'

'I know you are. Let me order dinner.'

'Well, all right. What's the place again?' I wrote it down for him. 'Is it the sort of place you see native life?'

'Yes, you might call it that.'

'Well, it'll be an experience. Order something good.'

'That's my intention.'

I was there twenty minutes before Rex. If I had to spend an evening with him, it should, at any rate, be in my own way. I remember the dinner well – soup of *oseille*, a sole quite simply cooked in a white-wine sauce, a *caneton à la presse*, a lemon soufflé. At the last minute, fearing that the whole thing was too simple for Rex, I added *caviar aux blinis*. And for wine I let him give me a bottle of 1906 Montrachet, then at its prime, and, with the duck, a Clos de Bèze of 1904.

Living was easy in France then; with the exchange as it was, my allowance went a long way and I did not live frugally. It was very seldom, however, that I had a dinner like this, and I felt well disposed to Rex, when at last he arrived and gave up his hat and coat with the air of not expecting to see them again. He looked round the sombre little place with suspicion as though hoping to see apaches or a drinking party of students. All he saw was four senators with napkins tucked under their beards eating in absolute silence. I could imagine him telling his commercial friends later: '... interesting fellow I know; an art student living in Paris. Took me to a funny little restaurant – sort of place you'd pass without looking at – where there was some of the best food I ever ate. There were half a dozen senators there, too, which shows you it was the right place. Wasn't at all cheap, either.'

'Any sign of Sebastian?' he asked.

'There won't be,' I said, 'until he needs money.'

'It's a bit thick, going off like that. I was rather hoping that if I made a good job of him, it might do me a bit of good in another direction.'

He plainly wished to talk of his own affairs; they could wait, I thought, for the hour of tolerance and repletion, for the cognac; they could wait until the attention was blunted and one could listen with half the mind only; now in the keen moment when the *maître d'hôtel* was turning the blinis over in the pan, and, in the background, two humbler men were preparing the press, we would talk of myself.

'Did you stay long at Brideshead? Was my name mentioned after I left?'

'Was it mentioned? I got sick of the sound of it, old boy. The Marchioness got what she called a 'bad conscience' about you. She piled it on pretty thick, I gather, at your last meeting.'

' "Callously wicked", "wantonly cruel".'

'Hard words.'

' "It doesn't matter what people call you unless they call you pigeon pie and eat you up." '

'Eh?'

'A saying.'

'Ah.' The cream and hot butter mingled and overflowed, separating each glaucous bead of caviar from its fellows, capping it in white and gold.

'I like a bit of chopped onion with mine,' said Rex. 'Chap-who-knew told me it brought out the flavour.'

'Try it without first,' I said. 'And tell me more news of myself.'

'Well, of course, Greenacre, or whatever he was called – the snooty don – he came a cropper. That was well received by all. He was the blue-eyed boy for a day or two after you left. Shouldn't wonder if he hadn't put the old girl up to pitching you out. He was always being pushed down our throats, so in the end Julia couldn't bear it any more and gave him away.'

'*Julia* did?'

'Well, he'd begun to stick his nose into *our* affairs, you see. Julia spotted he was a fake, and one afternoon when Sebastian was tight – he was tight most of the time – she got the whole story of the Grand Tour out of him. And that was the end of Mr Samgrass. After that the Marchioness began to think she might have been a bit rough with you.'

'And what about the row with Cordelia?'

'That eclipsed everything. That kid's a walking marvel – she'd been feeding Sebastian whisky right under our noses for a week. We couldn't think where he was getting it. That's when the Marchioness finally crumbled.'

The soup was delicious after the rich blinis – hot, thin, bitter, frothy.

'I'll tell you a thing, Charles, that Ma Marchmain hasn't let on to anyone. She's a very sick woman. Might peg out any minute. George Anstruther saw her in the autumn and put it at two years.'

'How on earth do you know?'

'It's the kind of thing I hear. With the way her family are going on at the moment, I wouldn't give her a year. I know just the man for her in Vienna. He put Sonia Bamfshire on her feet when everyone including Anstruther had despaired of her. But Ma Marchmain won't do anything about it. I suppose it's something to do with her crack-brain religion, not to take care of the body.'

The sole was so simple and unobtrusive that Rex failed to notice it. We ate to the music of the press – the crunch of the bones, the drip of blood and marrow, the tap of the spoon basting the thin slices of breast. There was a pause here of a quarter of an hour, while I drank the first glass of the Clos de Bèze and Rex smoked his first cigarette. He leaned back, blew a cloud of smoke across the table, and remarked, 'You know, the food here isn't half bad; someone ought to take this place up and make something of it.'

Presently he began again on the Marchmains:

'I'll tell you another thing, too – they'll get a jolt financially soon if they don't look out.'

'I thought they were enormously rich.'

'Well, they are rich in the way people are who just let their money sit quiet. Everyone of that sort is poorer than they were in 1914, and the Flytes don't seem to realize it. I reckon those lawyers who manage their affairs find it convenient to give them all the cash they want and no questions asked. Look at the way they live – Brideshead and Marchmain House both going full blast, pack of foxhounds, no rents raised, nobody sacked, dozens of old servants doing damn all, being waited on by other servants, and then besides all that there's the old boy setting up a separate establishment – and setting it up on no humble scale either. D'you know how much they're overdrawn?'

'Of course I don't.'

'Jolly near a hundred thousand in London. I don't know what they owe elsewhere. Well, that's quite a packet, you know, for people who aren't *using* their money. Ninety-eight thousand last November. It's the kind of thing I hear.'

Those were the kind of things he heard, mortal illness and debt, I thought.

I rejoiced in the Burgundy. It seemed a reminder that the world was an older and better place than Rex knew, that mankind in its long passion had learned another wisdom than his. By chance I met this same wine again, lunching with my wine merchant in St James's Street, in the first autumn of the war; it had softened and faded in the intervening years, but it still spoke in the pure, authentic accent of its prime, the same words of hope.

'I don't mean that they'll be paupers; the old boy will always be good for an odd thirty thousand a year, but there'll be a shake-up coming soon, and when the upper classes get the wind up, their first idea is usually to cut down on the girls. I'd like to get the little matter of a marriage settlement through, before it comes.'

We had by no means reached the cognac, but here we were on the subject of himself. In twenty minutes I should have been ready for all he had to tell. I closed my mind to him as best I could and gave myself to the food before me, but sentences came breaking in on my happiness, recalling me to the harsh, acquisitive world which Rex inhabited. He wanted a woman; he wanted the best on the market, and he wanted her at his own price; that was what it amounted to.

'... Ma Marchmain doesn't like me. Well, I'm not asking her to. It's not her I want to marry. She hasn't the guts to say openly: "You're not a gentleman. You're an adventurer from the Colonies." She says we live in different atmospheres. That's all right, but Julia happens to fancy my atmosphere. ... Then she brings up religion. I've nothing against her Church; we don't take much account of Catholics in Canada, but that's different; in Europe you've got some very posh Catholics. All right, Julia can go to church whenever she wants to. I shan't try and stop her. It doesn't mean two pins to her, as a matter of fact, but I like a girl to have religion. What's more, she can bring the children up Catholic. I'll make all the "promises" they want. ... Then there's my past. "We know so little about you." She knows a sight too much. You may know I've been tied up with someone else for a year or two.'

I knew; everyone who had ever met Rex knew of his affair with Brenda Champion; knew also that it was from this affair that he derived everything which distinguished him from every other stock-jobber; his golf with the Prince of Wales, his membership of Bratt's, even his smoking-room comradeship at the House of Commons, for, when he first appeared there, his party chiefs did not say of him, 'Look, there is the promising young member for north Gridley who spoke so well on Rent Restrictions.' They said: 'There's Brenda Champion's latest'; it had done him a great deal of good with men; women he could usually charm.

'Well, that's all washed up. Ma Marchmain was too delicate to mention the subject; all she said was that I had "notoriety". Well, what does she expect as a son-in-law – a sort of half-baked monk like Brideshead? Julia knows all about the other thing; if she doesn't care, I don't see it's anyone else's business.'

After the duck came a salad of watercress and chicory in a faint mist of chives. I tried to think only of the salad. I succeeded for a time in thinking only of the soufflé. Then came the cognac and the proper hour for these confidences. '... Julia's just rising twenty. I don't want to wait till she's of age. Anyway, I don't want to marry without doing the thing properly ... nothing hole-in-corner. ... I have to see she isn't jockeyed out of her proper settlement. So as the Marchioness won't play ball I'm off to see the old man and square him. I gather he's likely to agree to anything he knows will upset her. He's at Monte Carlo at the moment. I'd planned to go there after dropping Sebastian off at Zürich. That's why it's such a bloody bore having lost him.'

The cognac was not to Rex's taste. It was clear and pale and it came to us in a bottle free from grime and Napoleonic cyphers. It was only a year or two older than Rex and lately bottled. They gave it to us in very thin tulip-shaped glasses of modest size.

'Brandy's one of the things I do know a bit about,' said Rex. 'This is a bad colour. What's more, I can't taste it in this thimble.'

They brought him a balloon the size of his head. He made them warm it over the spirit lamp. Then he rolled the splendid spirit round, buried his face in the fumes, and pronounced it the sort of stuff he put soda in at home.

So, shamefacedly, they wheeled out of its hiding place the vast and mouldy bottle they kept for people of Rex's sort.

'That's the stuff,' he said, tilting the treacly concoction till it left dark rings round the sides of his glass. 'They've always got some tucked away, but they won't bring it out unless you make a fuss. Have some.'

'I'm quite happy with this.'

'Well, it's a crime to drink it, if you don't really appreciate it.'

He lit his cigar and sat back at peace with the world; I, too, was at peace in another world than his. We both were happy. He talked of Julia and I heard his voice, unintelligible at a great distance, like a dog's barking miles away on a still night.

At the beginning of May the engagement was announced. I saw the notice in the *Continental Daily Mail* and assumed that Rex had 'squared the old man'. But things did not go as were expected. The next news I had of them was in the middle of June, when I read that they had been married very quietly at the Savoy Chapel. No royalty was present; nor was the Prime Minister; nor were any of Julia's family. It sounded like a 'hole-in-the-corner' affair, but it was not for several years that I heard the full story.

CHAPTER II

It is time to speak of Julia, who till now has played an intermittent and somewhat enigmatic part in Sebastian's drama. It was thus she appeared to me at the time, and I to her. We pursued separate aims which brought us near to one another, but we remained strangers. She told me later that she had made a kind of note of me in her mind, as, scanning the shelf for a particular book, one will sometimes have one's attention caught by another, take it down, glance at the title page and, saying 'I must read that, too, when I've the time,' replace it, and continue the search. On my side the interest was keener, for there was always the physical likeness between brother and sister, which, caught repeatedly in different poses, under different lights, each time pierced me anew; and, as Sebastian in his sharp decline seemed daily to fade and crumble, so much the more did Julia stand out clear and firm.

She was thin in those days, flat-chested, leggy; she seemed all limbs and neck, bodiless, spidery; thus far she conformed to the fashion, but the hair-cut and the hats of the period, and the blank stare and gape of the period, and the clownish dabs of rouge high on the cheekbones, could not reduce her to type.

When I first met her, when she met me in the station yard and drove me home through the twilight, that high summer of 1923, she was just eighteen and fresh from her first London season.

Some said it was the most brilliant season since the war, that things were getting into their stride again. Julia was at the centre of it. There were then remaining perhaps half a dozen London houses which could be called 'historic'; Marchmain House in St James's was one of them, and the ball given for Julia, in spite of the ignoble costume of the time, was by all accounts a splendid spectacle. Sebastian went down for it and half-heartedly suggested my coming with him; I refused and came to regret my refusal, for it was the last ball of its kind given there; the last of a splendid series.

How could I have known? There seemed time for everything in those days; the world was open to be explored at leisure. I was so full of Oxford that summer; London could wait, I thought.

The other great houses belonged to kinsmen or to childhood friends of Julia's, and besides them there were countless substantial houses in the squares of Mayfair and Belgravia, alight and thronged, one or other of them, night after night. Foreigners returning on post from their own waste lands wrote home that here they seemed to catch a glimpse of the world they had believed lost for ever among the mud and wire, and through those halcyon weeks Julia darted and shone, part of the sunshine between the trees, part of the candle-light in the mirror's spectrum, so that elderly men and women, sitting aside with their memories, saw her as herself the blue-bird. ' "Bridey" Marchmain's eldest girl,' they said. 'Pity he can't see her tonight.'

That night and the night after and the night after, wherever she went, always in her own little circle of intimates, she brought a moment of joy, such as strikes deep to the heart on the river's bank when the kingfisher suddenly flares across the water.

This was the creature, neither child nor woman, that drove me through the dusk that summer evening, untroubled by love, taken aback by the power of her own beauty, hesitating on the cool edge of life; one who had suddenly found herself armed, unawares; the heroine of a fairy story turning over in her hands the magic ring; she had only to stroke it with her fingertips and whisper the charmed word, for the earth to open at her feet and belch forth her titanic servant, the fawning monster who would bring her whatever she asked, but bring it, perhaps, in unwelcome shape.

She had no interest in me that evening; the jinn rumbled below us uncalled; she lived apart in a little world, within a little world, the innermost of a system of concentric spheres, like the ivory balls laboriously carved in China; a little problem troubling her mind – little, as she saw it, in abstract terms and symbols. She was wondering, dispassionately and leagues distant from reality, whom she should marry. Thus strategists hesitate over the map, the few pins and lines of coloured chalk, contemplating a change in the pins and lines, a matter of inches, which outside the room, out of sight of the studious officers, may engulf past, present, and future in ruin or life. She was a symbol to herself then, lacking the life of both child and woman; victory and defeat were changes of pin and line; she knew nothing of war.

'If only one lived abroad,' she thought, 'where these things are arranged between parents and lawyers.'

To be married, soon and splendidly, was the aim of all her friends. If she looked further than the wedding, it was to see marriage as the beginning of individual existence; the skirmish where one gained one's spurs, from which one set out on the true quests of life.

She outshone by far all the girls of her age, but she knew that, in that little world within a world which she inhabited, there were certain grave disabilities from which she suffered. On the sofas against the wall where the old people counted up the points, there were things against her. There was the scandal of her father; that slight, inherited stain upon her brightness that seemed deepened by something in her own way of life – waywardness and wilfulness, a less disciplined habit than most of her contemporaries'; but for that, who knows? ...

One subject eclipsed all others in importance for the ladies along the wall; who would the young princes marry? They could not hope for purer lineage or a more gracious presence than Julia's; but there was this faint shadow on her that unfitted her for the highest honours; there was also her religion.

Nothing could have been further from Julia's ambitions than a royal marriage. She knew, or thought she knew, what she wanted and it was not that. But wherever she turned, it seemed, her religion stood as a barrier between her and her natural goal.

As it seemed to her, the thing was a dead loss. If she apostatized now, having been brought up in the Church, she would go to hell, while the Protestant girls of her acquaintance, schooled in happy ignorance, could marry eldest sons, live at peace with their world, and get to heaven before her. There could be no eldest son for her, and younger sons were indelicate things, necessary, but not to be much spoken of. Younger sons had none of the privileges of obscurity; it was their plain duty to remain hidden until some disaster perchance promoted them to their brothers' places, and, since this was their function, it was desirable that they should keep themselves wholly suitable for succession. Perhaps in a family of three or four boys, a Catholic might get the youngest without opposition. There were of course the Catholics themselves, but these came seldom into the little world Julia had made for herself; those who did were her mother's kinsmen, who, to her, seemed grim and eccentric. Of the dozen or so rich and noble Catholic families, none at that time had an heir of the right age. Foreigners – there were many among her mother's family – were tricky about money, odd in their ways, and a sure mark of failure in the English girl who wed them. What was there left?

This was Julia's problem after her weeks of triumph in London. She knew it was not insurmountable. There must, she thought, be a number of people outside her own world who were well qualified to be drawn into it; the shame was that she must seek them. Not for her the cruel, delicate luxury of choice, the indolent, cat-and-mouse pastimes of the hearth-rug. No Penelope she; she must hunt in the forest.

She had made a preposterous little picture of the kind of man who would do: he was an English diplomat of great but not very virile beauty, now abroad, with a house smaller than Brides-head, nearer to London; he was old, thirty-two or -three, and had been recently and tragically widowed; Julia thought she would prefer a man a little subdued by earlier grief. He had a great career before him but had grown listless in his loneliness; she was not sure he was not in danger of falling into the hands of an unscrupulous foreign adventuress; he needed a new infusion of young life to carry him to the Embassy at Paris. While professing a mild agnosticism himself, he had a liking for the shows of religion and was perfectly agreeable to having his children brought up Catholic; he believed, however, in the prudent restriction of his family to two boys and a girl, comfortably spaced over twelve years, and did not demand, as a Catholic husband might, yearly pregnancies. He had twelve thousand a year above his pay, and no near relations. Someone like that would do, Julia thought, and she was in search of him when she met me at the railway station. I was not her man. She told me as much, without a word, when she took the cigarette from my lips.

All this I learned about Julia, bit by bit, as one does learn the former – as it seems at the time, the preparatory – life of a woman one loves, so that one thinks of oneself as having been part of it, directing it by devious ways, towards oneself.

Julia left Sebastian and me at Brideshead and went to stay with an aunt, Lady Rosscommon, in her villa at Cap Ferrat. All the way she pondered her problem. She had given a name to her widower-diplomat; she called him 'Eustace', and from that moment he became a figure of fun to her, a little interior, incommunicable joke, so that when at last such a man did cross her path – though he was not a diplomat but a wistful major in the Life Guards – and fall in love with her and offer her just those gifts she had chosen, she sent him away moodier and more wistful than ever; for by that time she had met Rex Mottram.

Rex's age was greatly in his favour, for among Julia's friends there was a kind of gerontophilic snobbery; young men were held to be gauche and pimply; it was thought very much more chic to be seen lunching alone at the Ritz – a thing, in any case, allowed to few girls of that day, to the tiny circle of Julia's intimates; a thing looked at askance by the elders who kept the score, chatting pleasantly against the walls of the ballrooms – at the table on the left as you came in, with a starched and wrinkled old roué whom your mother had been warned of as a girl, than in the centre of the room with a party of exuberant young bloods. Rex, indeed, was neither starched nor wrinkled; his seniors thought him a pushful young cad, but Julia recognized the unmistakable chic – the flavour of 'Max' and 'F.E.'

and the Prince of Wales, of the big table in the Sporting Club, the second magnum, and the fourth cigar, of the chauffeur kept waiting hour after hour without compunction – which her friends would envy. His social position was unique; it had an air of mystery, even of crime, about it; people said Rex went about armed. Julia and her friends had a fascinated abhorrence of what they called 'Pont Street'; they collected phrases that damned their user, and among themselves – and often, disconcertingly, in public – talked a language made up of them. It was 'Pont Street' to wear a signet ring and to give chocolates at the theatre; it was 'Pont Street' at a dance to say, 'Can I forage for you?' Whatever Rex might be, he was definitely not 'Pont Street'. He had stepped straight from the underworld into the world of Brenda Champion who was herself the innermost of a number of concentric ivory spheres. Perhaps Julia recognized in Brenda Champion an intimation of what she and her friends might be in twelve years' time; there was an antagonism between the girl and the woman that was hard to explain otherwise. Certainly the fact of his being Brenda Champion's property sharpened Julia's appetite for Rex.

Rex and Brenda Champion were staying at the next villa on Cap Ferrat, taken that year by a newspaper magnate and frequented by politicians. They would not normally have come within Lady Rosscommon's ambit, but, living so close, the parties mingled and at once Rex began warily to pay his court.

All that summer he had been feeling restless. Mrs Champion had proved a dead end; it had all been intensely exciting at first, but now the bonds had begun to chafe. Mrs Champion lived as, he found, the English seemed apt to do, in a little world within a little world; Rex demanded a wider horizon. He wanted to consolidate his gains; to strike the black ensign, go ashore, hang the cutlass up over the chimney, and think about the crops. It was time he married; he, too, was in search of a 'Eustace', but, living as he did, he met few girls. He knew of Julia; she was by all accounts top débutante, a suitable prize.

With Mrs Champion's cold eyes watching behind her sunglasses, there was little Rex could do at Cap Ferrat except establish a friendliness which could be widened later. He was never entirely alone with Julia, but he saw to it that she was included in most things they did; he taught her chemin-de-fer, he arranged that it was always in his car that they drove to Monte Carlo or Nice; he did enough to make Lady Rosscommon write to Lady Marchmain, and Mrs Champion move him, sooner than they had planned, to Antibes.

Julia went to Salzburg to join her mother.

'Aunt Fanny tells me you made great friends with Mr Mottram. I'm sure he can't be very nice.'

'I don't think he is,' said Julia. 'I don't know that I like nice people.'

There is proverbially a mystery among most men of new wealth, how they made their first ten thousand; it is the qualities they showed then, before they became bullies, when every man was someone to be placated, when only hope sustained them and they could count on nothing from the world but what could be charmed from it, that make them, if they survive their triumph, successful with women. Rex, in the comparative freedom of London, became abject to Julia; he planned his life about hers, going where he would meet her, ingratiating himself with those who could report well of him to her; he sat on a number of charitable committees in order to be near Lady Marchmain; he offered his services to Brideshead in getting him a seat in Parliament (but was there rebuffed); he expressed a keen interest in the Catholic Church until he found that this was no way to Julia's heart. He was always ready to drive her in his Hispano wherever she wanted to go; he took her and parties of her friends to ring-side seats at prize-fights and introduced them afterwards to the pugilists; and all the time he never once made love to her. From being agreeable, he became indispensable to her; from having been proud of him in public she became a little ashamed, but by that time, between Christmas and Easter, he had become indispensable. And then, without in the least expecting it, she suddenly found herself in love.

It came to her, this disturbing and unsought revelation, one evening in May, when Rex had told her he would be busy at the

House, and, driving by chance down Charles Street, she saw him leaving what she knew to be Brenda Champion's house. She was so hurt and angry that she could barely keep up appearances through dinner; as soon as she could, she went home and cried bitterly for ten minutes; then she felt hungry, wished she had eaten more at dinner, ordered some bread-and-milk, and went to bed saying: 'When Mr Mottram telephones in the morning, whatever time it is, say I am not to be disturbed.'

Next day she breakfasted in bed as usual, read the papers, telephoned to her friends. Finally she asked: 'Did Mr Mottram ring up by any chance?'

'Oh yes, my lady, four times. Shall I put him through when he rings again?'

'Yes. No. Say I've gone out.'

When she came downstairs there was a message for her on the hall table. *Mr Mottram expects Lady Julia at the Ritz at 1.30.* 'I shall lunch at home today,' she said.

That afternoon she went shopping with her mother; they had tea with an aunt and returned at six.

'Mr Mottram is waiting, my Lady. I've shown him into the library.'

'Oh, mummy, I can't be bothered with him. Do tell him to go home.'

'That's not at all kind, Julia. I've often said he's not my favourite among your friends, but I have grown quite used to him, almost to like him. You really mustn't take people up and drop them like this – particularly people like Mr Mottram.'

'Oh, mummy, *must* I see him? There'll be a scene if I do.'

'Nonsense, Julia, you twist that poor man round your finger.'

So Julia went into the library and came out an hour later engaged to be married.

'Oh, mummy, I warned you this would happen if I went in there.'

'You did nothing of the kind. You merely said there would be a scene. I never conceived of a scene of *this* kind.'

'Anyway, you do like him, mummy. You said so.'

'He has been very kind in a number of ways. I regard him as entirely unsuitable as your husband. So will everyone.'

'Damn everybody.'

'We know nothing about him. He may have black blood – in fact he is suspiciously dark. Darling, the whole thing's impossible. I can't see how you can have been so foolish.'

'Well, what right have I got otherwise to be angry with him if he goes with that horrible old woman? You make a great thing about rescuing fallen women. Well, I'm rescuing a fallen man for a change. I'm saving Rex from mortal sin.'

'Don't be irreverent, Julia.'

'Well, isn't it mortal sin to sleep with Brenda Champion?'

'Or indecent.'

'He's promised never to see her again. I couldn't ask him to do that unless I admitted I was in love with him could I?'

'Mrs Champion's morals, thank God, are not my business. Your happiness is. If you must know, I think Mr Mottram a kind and useful friend, but I wouldn't trust him an inch, and I'm sure he'll have very unpleasant children. They always revert. I've no doubt you'll regret the whole thing in a few days. Meanwhile *nothing is to be done.* No one must be told anything or allowed to suspect. You must stop lunching with him. You may see him here, of course, but nowhere in public. You had better send him to me and I will have a little talk to him about it.'

Thus began a year's secret engagement for Julia; a time of great stress, for Rex made love to her that afternoon for the first time; not, as had happened to her once or twice before with sentimental and uncertain boys, but with a passion that disclosed the corner of something like it in her. Their passion frightened her, and she came back from the confessional one day determined to put an end to it.

'Otherwise I must stop seeing you,' she said.

Rex was humble at once, just as he had been in the winter, day after day, when he used to wait for her in the cold in his big car.

'If only we could be married immediately,' she said.

For six weeks they remained at arm's length, kissing when they met and parted, sitting meantime at a distance, talking of what they would do and where they would live and of Rex's chances of an under-secretaryship. Julia was content, deep in love, living in the future. Then, just before the end of the session, she learned that Rex had been staying the week-end with a stockbroker at Sunningdale, when he said he was at his constituency, and that Mrs Champion had been there, too.

On the evening she heard of this, when Rex came as usual to Marchmain House, they re-enacted the scene of two months before.

'What do you expect?' he said. 'What right have you to ask so much, when you give so little?'

She took her problem to Farm Street and propounded it in general terms, not in the confessional, but in a dark little parlour kept for such interviews.

'Surely, Father, it can't be wrong to commit a small sin myself in order to keep him from a much worse one?'

But the gentle old Jesuit was unyielding. She barely listened to him; he was refusing her what she wanted, that was all she needed to know.

When he had finished he said, 'Now you had better make your confession.'

'No, thank you,' she said, as though refusing the offer of something in a shop. 'I don't think I want to today,' and walked angrily home.

From that moment she shut her mind against her religion.

And Lady Marchmain saw this and added it to her new grief for Sebastian and her old grief for her husband and to the deadly sickness in her body, and took all these sorrows with her daily to church; it seemed her heart was transfixed with the swords of her dolours, a living heart to match the plaster and paint; what comfort she took home with her, God knows.

So the year wore on and the secret of the engagement spread from Julia's confidantes to their confidantes, until, like ripples at last breaking on the mud-verge, there were hints of it in the

Press, and Lady Rosscommon as Lady-in-Waiting was closely questioned about it, and something had to be done. Then, after Julia had refused to make her Christmas communion and Lady Marchmain had found herself betrayed first by me, then by Mr Samgrass, then by Cordelia, in the first grey days of 1925, she decided to act. She forbade all talk of an engagement; she forbade Julia and Rex ever to meet; she made plans for shutting Marchmain House for six months and taking Julia on a tour of visits to their foreign kinsmen. It was characteristic of an old, atavistic callousness that went with her delicacy that, even at this crisis, she did not think it unreasonable to put Sebastian in Rex's charge on the journey to Dr Borethus, and Rex, having failed her in that matter, went on to Monte Carlo, where he completed her rout. Lord Marchmain did not concern himself with the finer points of Rex's character; those, he believed, were his daughter's business. Rex seemed a rough, healthy, prosperous fellow whose name was already familiar to him from reading the political reports; he gambled in an open-handed but sensible manner; he seemed to keep reasonably good company; he had a future; Lady Marchmain disliked him. Lord Marchmain was, on the whole, relieved that Julia should have chosen so well, and gave his consent to an immediate marriage.

Rex gave himself to the preparations with gusto. He bought her a ring, not, as she expected, from a tray at Cartier's, but in a back room in Hatton Garden from a man who brought stones out of a safe in little bags and displayed them for her on a writing-desk; then another man in another back room made designs for the setting with a stub of pencil on a sheet of note-paper, and the result excited the admiration of all her friends.

'How d'you know about these things, Rex?' she asked.

She was daily surprised by the things he knew and the things he did not know; both, at the time, added to his attraction.

His present house in Hertford Street was large enough for them both, and had lately been furnished and decorated by the most expensive firm. Julia said she did not want a house in the country yet; they could always take places furnished when they wanted to go away.

There was trouble about the marriage settlement with which Julia refused to interest herself. The lawyers were in despair. Rex absolutely refused to settle any capital. 'What do I want with trustee stock?' he asked.

'I don't know, darling.'

'I make money work for me,' he said. 'I expect fifteen, twenty per cent and I get it. It's pure waste tying up capital at three and a half.'

'I'm sure it is, darling.'

'These fellows talk as though I were trying to rob you. It's *they* who are doing the robbing. They want to rob you of two-thirds of the income I can make you.'

'Does it matter, Rex? We've got heaps, haven't we?'

Rex hoped to have the whole of Julia's dowry in his hands, to make it work for him. The lawyers insisted on tying it up, but they could not get, as they asked, a like sum from him. Finally, grudgingly, he agreed to insure his life, after explaining at length to the lawyers that this was merely a device for putting part of his legitimate profits into other people's pockets; but he had some connexion with an insurance office which made the arrangement slightly less painful to him, by which he took for himself the agent's commission which the lawyers were themselves expecting.

Last and least came the question of Rex's religion. He had once attended a royal wedding in Madrid, and he wanted something of the kind for himself.

'That's one thing your Church can do,' he said, 'put on a good show. You never saw anything to equal the cardinals. How many do you have in England?'

'Only one, darling.'

'Only *one*? Can we hire some others from abroad?'

It was then explained to him that a mixed marriage was a very unostentatious affair.

'How d'you mean "mixed"? I'm not a nigger or anything.'

'No, darling, between a Catholic and a Protestant.'

'Oh, *that*? Well, if that's all, it's soon unmixed. I'll become a Catholic. What does one have to do?'

Lady Marchmain was dismayed and perplexed by this new development; it was no good her telling herself that in charity she must assume his good faith; it brought back memories of another courtship and another conversion.

'Rex,' she said. 'I sometimes wonder if you realize how big a thing you are taking on in the Faith. It would be very wicked to take a step like this without believing sincerely.'

He was masterly in his treatment of her.

'I don't pretend to be a very devout man,' he said, 'nor much of a theologian, but I know it's a bad plan to have two religions in one house. A man needs a religion. If your Church is good enough for Julia, it's good enough for me.'

'Very well,' she said, 'I will see about having you instructed.'

'Look, Lady Marchmain, I haven't the time. Instruction will be wasted on me. Just you give me the form and I'll sign on the dotted line.'

'It usually takes some months – often a lifetime.'

'Well, I'm a quick learner. Try me.'

So Rex was sent to Farm Street to Father Mowbray, a priest renowned for his triumphs with obdurate catechumens. After the third interview he came to tea with Lady Marchmain.

'Well, how do you find my future son-in-law?'

'He's the most difficult convert I have ever met.'

'Oh dear, I thought he was going to make it so easy.'

'That's exactly it. I can't get anywhere near him. He doesn't seem to have the least intellectual curiosity or natural piety.

'The first day I wanted to find out what sort of religious life he had till now, so I asked him what he meant by prayer. He said: "*I* don't mean anything. *You tell me.*" I tried to, in a few words, and he said: "Right. So much for prayer. What's the next thing?" I gave him the catechism to take away. Yesterday I asked him whether Our Lord had more than one nature. He said: "Just as many as you say, Father."

'Then again I asked him: "Supposing the Pope looked up and saw a cloud and said 'It's going to rain', would that be bound to happen?" "Oh, yes, Father." "But supposing it didn't?" He thought a moment and said, "I suppose it would be sort of raining spiritually, only we were too sinful to see it."

'Lady Marchmain, he doesn't correspond to any degree of paganism known to the missionaries.'

'Julia,' said Lady Marchmain, when the priest had gone, 'are you sure that Rex isn't doing this thing purely with the idea of pleasing us?'

'I don't think it enters his head,' said Julia.

'He's really sincere in his conversion?'

'He's absolutely determined to become a Catholic, mummy,' and to herself she said: 'In her long history the Church must have had some pretty queer converts. I don't suppose all Clovis's army were exactly Catholic-minded. One more won't hurt.'

Next week the Jesuit came to tea again. It was the Easter holidays and Cordelia was there, too.

'Lady Marchmain,' he said. 'You should have chosen one of the younger fathers for this task. I shall be dead long before Rex is a Catholic.'

'Oh dear, I thought it was going so well.'

'It was, in a sense. He was exceptionally docile, said he accepted everything I told him, remembered bits of it, asked no questions. I wasn't happy about him. He seemed to have no sense of reality, but I knew he was coming under a steady Catholic influence, so I was willing to receive him. One has to take a chance sometimes – with semi-imbeciles, for instance. You never know quite how much they have understood. As long as you know there's someone to keep an eye on them, you *do* take the chance.'

'How I wish Rex could hear this!' said Cordelia.

'But yesterday I got a regular eye-opener. The trouble with modern education is you never know how ignorant people are. With anyone over fifty you can be fairly confident what's been taught and what's been left out. But these young people have such an intelligent, knowledgeable surface, and then the crust suddenly breaks and you look down into the depths of confusion you didn't know existed. Take yesterday. He seemed to be doing very well. He learned large bits of the catechism by heart, and the Lord's Prayer, and the Hail Mary. Then I asked him as usual if there was anything troubling him, and he looked at me in a crafty way and said, "Look, Father, I don't think you're being straight with me. I want to join your Church and I'm going to join your Church, but you're holding too much back." I asked what he meant, and he said: "I've had a long talk with a Catholic – a very pious, well-educated one, and I've learned a thing or two. For instance, that you have to sleep with your feet pointing East because that's the direction of heaven, and if you die in the night you can walk there. Now I'll sleep with my feet pointing any way that suits Julia, but d'you expect a grown man to believe about walking to heaven? And what about the Pope who made one of his horses a Cardinal? And what about the box you keep in the church porch, and if you put in a pound note with someone's name on it, they get sent to hell. I don't say there mayn't be a good reason for all this," he said, "but you ought to tell me about it and not let me find out for myself."'

'What *can* the poor man have meant?' said Lady Marchmain.

'You see he's a long way from the Church yet,' said Father Mowbray.

'But who can he have been talking to? Did he dream it all? Cordelia, what's the matter?'

'What a chump! Oh, mummy, what a glorious chump!'

'Cordelia, it was *you*.'

'Oh, mummy, who could have dreamed he'd swallow it? I told him such a lot besides. About the sacred monkeys in the Vatican – all kinds of things.'

'Well, you've very considerably increased *my* work,' said Father Mowbray.

'Poor Rex,' said Lady Marchmain. 'You know, I think it makes him rather lovable. You must treat him like an idiot child, Father Mowbray.'

So the instruction was continued, and Father Mowbray at length consented to receive Rex a week before his wedding.

'You'd think they'd be all over themselves to have me in,' Rex complained. 'I can be a lot of help to them one way and another; instead they're like the chaps who issue cards for a casino. What's more,' he added, 'Cordelia's got me so muddled I don't know what's in the catechism and what she's invented.'

Thus things stood three weeks before the wedding; the cards had gone out, presents were coming in fast, the bridesmaids were delighted with their dresses. Then came what Julia called 'Bridey's bombshell'.

With characteristic ruthlessness he tossed his load of explosive without warning into what, till then, had been a happy family party. The library at Marchmain House was being devoted to wedding presents; Lady Marchmain, Julia, Cordelia, and Rex were busy unpacking and listing them. Brideshead came in and watched them for a moment.

'Chinky vases from Aunt Betty,' said Cordelia. 'Old stuff. I remember them on the stairs at Buckborne.'

'What's all this?' asked Brideshead.

'Mr, Mrs, *and* Miss Pendle-Garthwaite, one early morning tea set. Goode's, thirty shillings, jolly mean.'

'You'd better pack all that stuff up again.'

'Bridey, what *do* you mean?'

'Only that the wedding's off.'

'*Bridey.*'

'I thought I'd better make some inquiries about my prospective brother-in-law, as no one else seemed interested,' said Brideshead. 'I got the final answer tonight. He was married in Montreal in 1915 to a Miss Sarah Evangeline Cutler, who is still living there.'

'Rex, is this true?'

Rex stood with a jade dragon in his hand looking at it critically; then he set it carefully on its ebony stand and smiled openly and innocently at them all.

'Sure it's true,' he said. 'What about it? What are you all looking so het up about? She isn't a thing to me. She never meant any good. I was only a kid, anyhow. The sort of mistake anyone might make. I got my divorce back in 1919. I didn't even know where she was living till Bridey here told me. What's all the rumpus?'

'You might have told me,' said Julia.

'You never asked. Honest, I've not given her a thought in years.'

His sincerity was so plain that they had to sit down and talk about it calmly.

'Don't you realize, you poor sweet oaf,' said Julia, 'that you can't get married as a Catholic when you've another wife alive?'

'But I *haven't*. Didn't I just tell you we were divorced six years ago.'

'But you *can't* be divorced as a Catholic.'

'I wasn't a Catholic and I was divorced. I've got the papers somewhere.'

'But didn't Father Mowbray explain to you about marriage?'

'He said I wasn't to be divorced from you. Well, I don't want to be. I can't remember all he told me – sacred monkeys, plenary indulgences, four last things – if I remembered all he told me I shouldn't have time for anything else. Anyhow, what about your Italian cousin, Francesca? – she married twice.'

'She had an annulment.'

'All right then, I'll get an annulment. What does it cost? Who do I get it from? Has Father Mowbray got one? I only want to do what's right. Nobody told me.'

It was a long time before Rex could be convinced of the existence of a serious impediment to his marriage. The discussion took them to dinner, lay dormant in the presence of the servants, started again as soon as they were alone, and lasted long after midnight. Up, down, and round the argument circled and swooped like a gull, now out to sea, out of sight, cloud-bound, among irrelevances and repetitions, now right on the patch where the offal floated.

'What d'you want me to do? Who should I see?' Rex kept asking. 'Don't tell me there isn't someone who can fix this.'

'There's nothing to do, Rex,' said Brideshead. 'It simply means your marriage can't take place. I'm sorry from every-one's point of view that it's come so suddenly. You ought to have told us yourself.'

'Look,' said Rex. 'Maybe what you say is right; maybe strictly by law I shouldn't get married in your cathedral. But the cathedral is booked; no one there is asking any questions; the Cardinal knows nothing about it; Father Mowbray knows nothing about it. Nobody except us knows a thing. So why make a lot of trouble? Just stay mum and let the thing go through, as if nothing had happened. Who loses anything by that? Maybe I risk going to hell. Well, I'll risk it. What's it got to do with anyone else?'

'Why not?' said Julia. 'I don't believe these priests know everything. I don't believe in hell for things like that. I don't know that I believe in it for anything. Anyway, that's our look out. We're not asking you to risk your souls. Just keep away.'

'Julia, I hate you,' said Cordelia, and left the room.

'We're all tired,' said Lady Marchmain. 'If there was anything to say, I'd suggest our discussing it in the morning.'

'But there's nothing to discuss,' said Brideshead, 'except what is the least offensive way we can close the whole incident. Mother and I will decide that. We must put a notice in *The Times* and the *Morning Post*; the presents will have to go back. I don't know what is usual about the bridesmaids' dresses.'

'Just a moment,' said Rex. 'Just a moment. Maybe you can stop us marrying in your Cathedral. All right, to hell, we'll be married in a Protestant church.'

'I can stop that, too,' said Lady Marchmain.

'But I don't think you will, mummy,' said Julia. 'You see, I've been Rex's mistress for some time now, and I shall go on being, married or not.'

'Rex, is this true?'

'No damn it, it's not,' said Rex. 'I wish it were.'

'I see we *shall* have to discuss it all again in the morning,' said Lady Marchmain faintly. 'I can't go on any more now.'

And she needed her son's help up the stairs.

'What on earth made you tell your mother that?' I asked, when, years later, Julia described the scene to me.

'That's exactly what Rex wanted to know. I suppose because

I thought it was true. Not literally – though you must remember I was only twenty, and no one really knows the "facts of life" by being told them – but, of course, I didn't mean it was true literally. I didn't know how else to express it. I meant I was much too deep with Rex just to be able to say "the marriage arranged will not now take place", and leave it at that. I wanted to be made an honest woman. I've been wanting it ever since – come to think of it.'

'And then?'

'And then the talks went on and on. Poor mummy. And priests came into it and aunts came into it. There were all kinds of suggestions – that Rex should go to Canada, that Father Mowbray should go to Rome and see if there were any possible grounds for an annulment; that I should go abroad for a year. In the middle of it Rex just telegraphed to papa: "Julia and I prefer wedding ceremony take place by Protestant rites. Have you any objection?" He answered, "Delighted", and that settled the matter as far as mummy stopping us legally went. There was a lot of personal appeal after that. I was sent to talk to priests and nuns and aunts. Rex just went on quietly – or fairly quietly – with the plans.

'Oh, Charles, what a squalid wedding! The Savoy Chapel was the place where divorced couples got married in those days – a poky little place not at all what Rex had intended. I wanted just to slip into a registry office one morning and get the thing over with a couple of charwomen as witnesses, but nothing else would do but Rex had to have bridesmaids and orange-blossom and the Wedding March. It was gruesome.

'Poor mummy behaved like a martyr and insisted on my having her lace in spite of everything. Well, she more or less had to – the dress had been planned round it. My own friends came, of course, and the curious accomplices Rex called *his* friends; the rest of the party were very oddly assorted. None of mummy's family came, of course; one or two of papa's. All the stuffy people stayed away – you know, the Anchorages and Chasms and Vanbrughs – and I thought, "Thank God for that, they always look down their noses at me, anyhow," but Rex was furious, because it was just them he wanted apparently.

'I hoped at one moment there'd be no party at all. Mummy said we couldn't use Marchers, and Rex wanted to telegraph papa and invade the place with an army of caterers headed by the family solicitor. In the end it was decided to have a party the evening before at home to see the presents – apparently that was all right according to Father Mowbray. Well, no one can ever resist going to see her own present, so that was quite a success, but the reception Rex gave next day at the Savoy for the wedding guests was very squalid.

'There was great awkwardness about the tenants. In the end Bridey went down and gave them a dinner and bonfire there which wasn't at all what they expected in return for their silver soup tureen.

'Poor Cordelia took it hardest. She had looked forward so much to being my bridesmaid – it was a thing we used to talk about long before I came out – and of course she was a very pious child, too. At first she wouldn't speak to me. Then on the morning of the wedding – I'd moved to Aunt Fanny Rosscommon's the evening before; it was thought more suitable – she came bursting in before I was up, straight from Farm Street, in floods of tears, begged me not to marry, then hugged me, gave me a dear little brooch she'd bought, and said she prayed I'd always be happy. *Always happy*, Charles!

'It was an awfully unpopular wedding, you know. Everyone took mummy's side, as everyone always did – not that she got any benefit from it. All through her life mummy had all the sympathy of everyone except those she loved. They all said I'd behaved abominably to her. In fact, poor Rex found he'd married an outcast, which was exactly the opposite of all he'd wanted.

'So you see things never looked like going right. There was a hoodoo on us from the start. But I was still nuts about Rex.

'Funny to think of, isn't it?

'You know Father Mowbray hit on the truth about Rex at once, that it took me a year of marriage to see. He simply wasn't all there. He wasn't a complete human being at all. He was a tiny bit of one, unnaturally developed; something in a bottle, an organ kept alive in a laboratory. I thought he was a sort of primitive savage, but he was something absolutely modern and up-to-date that only this ghastly age could produce. A tiny bit of a man pretending he was the whole.

'Well, it's all over now.'

It was ten years later that she said this to me in a storm in the Atlantic.

CHAPTER III

I RETURNED to London in the spring of 1926 for the General Strike.

It was the topic of Paris. The French, exultant as always at the discomfiture of their former friends, and transposing into their own precise terms our mistier notions from across the Channel, foretold revolution and civil war. Every evening the kiosks displayed texts of doom, and, in the cafés, acquaintances greeted one half-derisively with: 'Ha, my friend, you are better off here than at home, are you not?' until I and several friends in circumstances like my own came seriously to believe that our country was in danger and that our duty lay there. We were joined by a Belgian Futurist, who lived under the, I think, assumed name of Jean de Brissac la Motte, and claimed the right to bear arms in any battle anywhere against the lower classes.

We crossed together, in a high-spirited, male party, expecting to find unfolding before us at Dover the history so often repeated of late, with so few variations, from all parts of Europe, that I, at any rate, had formed in my mind a clear, composite picture of 'Revolution' – the red flag on the post office, the overturned tram, the drunken N.C.O.s, the gaol open and gangs of released criminals prowling the streets, the train from the capital that did not arrive. One had read it in the papers, seen it in the films, heard it at café tables again and again for six or seven years now, till it had become part of one's experience, at second hand, like the mud of Flanders and the flies of Mesopotamia.

Then we landed and met the old routine of the customs-sheds, the punctual boat-train, the porters lining the platform at Victoria and converging on the first-class carriages; the long line of waiting taxis.

'We'll separate,' we said, 'and see what's happening. We'll meet and compare notes at dinner,' but we knew already in our hearts that nothing was happening; nothing, at any rate, which needed our presence.

'Oh dear,' said my father, meeting me by chance on the stairs, 'how delightful to see you again so soon.' (I had been abroad fifteen months.) 'You've come at a very awkward time, you know. They're having another of those strikes in two days – such a lot of nonsense – and I don't know when you'll be able to get away.'

I thought of the evening I was forgoing, with the lights coming out along the banks of the Seine, and the company I should have had there – for I was at the time concerned with two emancipated American girls who shared a *garçonnière* in Auteuil – and wished I had not come.

We dined that night at the Café Royal. There things were a little more warlike, for the Café was full of undergraduates who had come down for 'National Service'. One group, from Cambridge, had that afternoon signed on to run messages for Transport House, and their table backed on another group's, who were enrolled as special constables. Now and then one or other party would shout provocatively over the shoulder, but it is hard to come into serious conflict back to back, and the affair ended with their giving each other tall glasses of lager beer.

'You should have been in Budapest when Horthy marched in,' said Jean. '*That* was politics.'

A party was being given that night in Regent's Park for the 'Black Birds' who had newly arrived in England. One of us had been asked and thither we all went.

To us, who frequented Bricktop's and the Bal Nègre in the Rue Blomet, there was nothing particularly remarkable in the spectacle; I was scarcely inside the door when I heard an unmistakable voice, an echo from what now seemed a distant past.

'*No*,' it said, 'they are not animals in a *zoo*, Mulcaster, to be *goggled at*. They are *artists*, my dear, very great artists, to be *revered*.'

Anthony Blanche and Boy Mulcaster were at the table where the wine stood.

'Thank God here's someone I know,' said Mulcaster, as I joined them. 'Girl brought me. Can't see her anywhere.'

'She's given you the *slip*, my dear, and do you know why? Because you look ridiculously *out of place*, Mulcaster. It isn't your kind of party at all; you ought not to be here; you ought to go away, you know, to the Old Hundredth or some lugubrious dance in Belgrave Square.'

'Just come from one,' said Mulcaster. 'Too early for the Old Hundredth. I'll stay on a bit. Things may cheer up.'

'I spit on you,' said Anthony. 'Let me talk to *you*, Charles.'

We took a bottle and our glasses and found a corner in another room. At our feet five members of the 'Black Birds' orchestra squatted on their heels and threw dice.

'*That* one,' said Anthony, 'the rather *pale* one, my dear, conked Mrs Arnold Frickheimer the other morning on the *nut*, my dear, with a bottle of milk.'

Almost immediately, inevitably, we began to talk of Sebastian.

'My dear, he's such a *sot*. He came to live with me in Marseille last year when you threw him over, and really it was as much as I could stand. Sip, sip, sip like a dowager all day long. And so *sly*. I was always missing little things, my dear, things I rather liked; once I lost two suits that had arrived from Lesley and Roberts that morning. Of course, I didn't *know* it was Sebastian – there were some rather queer fish, my dear, in and out of my little apartment. Who knows better than you my taste for queer fish? Well, eventually, my dear, we found the pawnshop where Sebastian was p-p-popping them and *then* he hadn't got the tickets; there was a market for them, too, at the bistro.

'I can see that puritanical, disapproving look in your eye, dear Charles, as though you thought I had led the boy on. It's one of Sebastian's less lovable qualities that he always gives the impression of being l-l-led on – like a little horse at a circus. But I assure you I did everything. I said to him again and again, "Why drink? If you want to be intoxicated there are so many much more delicious things." I took him to quite the best man; well, you know him as well as I do, Nada Alopov and Jean Luxmore and *everyone we know* has been to him for years – he's always in the Regina Bar – and then we had trouble over that because Sebastian gave him a bad cheque – a *s-s-stumer*, my dear – and a whole lot of very menacing men came round to the flat – *thugs*, my dear – and Sebastian was making no sense at the time and it was all most unpleasant.'

Boy Mulcaster wandered towards us and sat down, without encouragement, by my side.

'Drink running short in there,' he said, helping himself from our bottle and emptying it. 'Not a soul in the place I ever set eyes on before – all black fellows.'

Anthony ignored him and continued: 'So then we left Marseille and went to Tangier, and *there*, my dear, Sebastian took up with his *new* friend. How can I describe him? He is like the footman in *Warning Shadows* – a great clod of a German who'd been in the Foreign Legion. He got out by shooting off his great toe. It hadn't healed yet. Sebastian found him, starving as tout to one of the houses in the Kasbah, and brought him to stay with us. It was *too* macabre. So back I came, my dear, to good old England – *Good old England*,' he repeated, embracing with a flourish of his hand the Negroes gambling at our feet, Mulcaster staring blankly before him, and our hostess who, in pyjamas, now introduced herself to us.

'Never seen you before,' she said. 'Never asked you. Who are all this white trash, anyway? Seems to me I must be in the wrong house.'

'A time of national emergency,' said Mulcaster. 'Anything may happen.'

'Is the party going well?' she asked anxiously. 'D'you think Florence Mills would sing? We've met before,' she added to Anthony.

'Often, my dear, but you never asked me tonight.'

'Oh dear, perhaps I don't like you. I thought I liked everyone.'

'Do you think,' asked Mulcaster, when our hostess had left us, 'that it might be witty to give the fire alarm?'

'Yes, Boy, run away and ring it.'

'Might cheer things up, I mean.'

'Exactly.'

So Mulcaster left us in search of the telephone.

'I think Sebastian and his lame chum went to French Morocco,' continued Anthony. 'They were in trouble with the Tangier police when I left them. The Marchioness has been a positive pest ever since I came to London, trying to make me get into touch with them. What a time that poor woman's having! It only shows there's some justice in life.'

Presently Miss Mills began to sing and everyone, except the crap players, crowded to the next room.

'That's my girl,' said Mulcaster. 'Over there with that black fellow. That's the girl who brought me.'

'She seems to have forgotten you now.'

'Yes. I wish I hadn't come. Let's go somewhere.'

Two fire engines drove up as we left and a host of helmeted figures joined the throng upstairs.

'That chap, Blanche,' said Mulcaster, '*not* a good fellow. I put him in Mercury once.'

We went to a number of night clubs. In two years Mulcaster seemed to have attained his simple ambition of being known and liked in such places. At the last of them he and I were kindled by a great flame of patriotism.

'You and I,' he said, 'were too young to fight in the war. Other chaps fought, millions of them dead. Not us. We'll show them. We'll show the dead chaps we can fight, too.'

'That's why I'm here,' I said. 'Come from overseas, rallying to old country in hour of need.'

'Like Australians.'

'Like the poor dead Australians.'

'What you in?'

'Nothing yet. War not ready.'

'Only one thing to join – Bill Meadows' show – Defence Corps. All good chaps. Being fixed in Bratt's.'

'I'll join.'

'You remember Bratt's?'

'No. I'll join that, too.'

'That's right. All good chaps like the dead chaps.'

So I joined Bill Meadows' show, which was a flying squad, protecting food deliveries in the poorest parts of London. First I was enrolled in the Defence Corps, took an oath of loyalty, and was given a helmet and truncheon; then I was put up for Bratt's Club and, with a number of other recruits, elected at a committee meeting specially called for the occasion. For a week we sat under orders in Bratt's, and thrice a day we drove out in a lorry at the head of a convoy of milk vans. We were jeered at and sometimes pelted with muck, but only once did we go into action.

We were sitting round after luncheon that day when Bill Meadows came back from the telephone in high spirits.

'Come on,' he said. 'There's a perfectly good battle in the Commercial Road.'

We drove at great speed and arrived to find a steel hawser stretched between lamp posts, an overturned truck and a policeman, alone on the pavement, being kicked by half a dozen youths. On either side of this centre of disturbance, and at a little distance from it, two opposing parties had formed. Near us, as we disembarked, a second policeman was sitting on the pavement, dazed, with his head in his hands and blood running through his fingers; two or three sympathizers were standing over him; on the other side of the hawser was a hostile knot of young dockers. We charged in cheerfully, relieved the policeman, and were just falling upon the main body of the enemy when we came into collision with a party of local clergy and town councillors who arrived simultaneously by another route to try persuasion. They were our only victims, for just as they went down there was a cry of 'Look out. The coppers,' and a lorry-load of police drew up in our rear.

The crowd broke and disappeared. We picked up the peacemakers (only one of whom was seriously hurt), patrolled some of the side streets looking for trouble and finding none, and at length returned to Bratt's. Next day the General Strike was called off and the country everywhere, except in the coal fields, returned to normal. It was as though a beast long fabled for its ferocity had emerged for an hour, scented danger, and slunk back to its lair. It had not been worth leaving Paris.

Jean, who joined another company, had a pot of ferns dropped on his head by an elderly widow in Camden Town and was in hospital for a week.

It was through my membership of Bill Meadows' squad that Julia learned I was in England. She telephoned to say her mother was anxious to see me.

'You'll find her terribly ill,' she said.

I went to Marchmain House on the first morning of peace. Sir Adrian Porson passed me in the hall, leaving, as I arrived; he held a bandanna handkerchief to his face and felt blindly for his hat and stick; he was in tears.

I was shown into the library and in less than a minute Julia joined me. She shook hands with a gentleness and gravity that were unfamiliar; in the gloom of that room she seemed a ghost.

'It's sweet of you to come. Mummy has kept asking for you, but I don't know if she'll be able to see you now, after all. She's just said "good-bye" to Adrian Porson and it's tired her.'

'Good-bye?'

'Yes. She's dying. She may live a week or two or she may go at any minute. She's so weak. I'll go and ask nurse.'

The stillness of death seemed in the house already. No one ever sat in the library at Marchmain House. It was the one ugly room in either of their houses. The bookcases of Victorian oak held volumes of Hansard and obsolete encyclopedias that were never opened; the bare mahogany table seemed set for the meeting of a committee; the place had the air of being both public and unfrequented; outside lay the forecourt, the railings, the quiet cul-de-sac.

Presently Julia returned.

'No, I'm afraid you can't see her. She's asleep. She may lie like that for hours; I can tell you what she wanted. Let's go somewhere else. I hate this room.'

We went across the hall to the small drawing-room where luncheon parties used to assemble, and sat on either side of the fireplace. Julia seemed to reflect the crimson and gold of the walls and lose some of her warmness.

'First, I know, mummy wanted to say how sorry she is she was so beastly to you last time you met. She's spoken of it often. She knows now she was wrong about you. I'm quite sure you understood and put it out of your mind immediately, but it's the kind of thing mummy can never forgive *herself* – it's the kind of thing she so seldom did.'

'Do tell her I understood completely.'

'The other thing, of course, you have guessed – Sebastian. She wants him. I don't know if that's possible. Is it?'

'I hear he's in a very bad way.'

'We heard that, too. We cabled to the last address we had, but there was no answer. There still may be time for him to see her. I thought of you as the only hope, as soon as I heard you were in England. Will you try and get him? It's an awful lot to ask, but I think Sebastian would want it, too, if he realized.'

'I'll try.'

'There's no one else we can ask. Rex is so busy.'

'Yes. I heard reports of all he's been doing organizing the gas works.'

'Oh yes,' Julia said with a touch of her old dryness. 'He's made a lot of kudos out of the strike.'

Then we talked for a few minutes about the Bratt's squad. She told me Brideshead had refused to take any public service because he was not satisfied with the justice of the cause; Cordelia was in London, in bed now, as she had been watching by her mother all night. I told her I had taken up architectural painting and that I enjoyed it. All this talk was nothing; we had said all we had to say in the first two minutes; I stayed for tea and then left her.

Air France ran a service of a kind to Casablanca; there I took the bus to Fez, starting at dawn and arriving in the new town at evening. I telephoned from the hotel to the British Consul and dined with him that evening, in his charming house by the walls of the old town. He was a kind, serious man.

'I'm delighted someone has come to look after young Flyte at last,' he said. 'He's been something of a thorn in our sides here. This is no place for a remittance man. The French don't understand him at all. They think everyone who's not engaged in trade is a spy. It's not as though he lived like a Milord. Things aren't easy here. There's war going on not thirty miles from this house, though you might not think it. We had some young fools on bicycles only last week who'd come to volunteer for Abdul Krim's army.

'Then the Moors are a tricky lot; they don't hold with drink and our young friend, as you may know, spends most of his day drinking. What does he want to come here for? There's plenty of room for him at Rabat or Tangier, where they cater for tourists. He's taken a house in the native town, you know. I tried to stop him, but he got it from a Frenchman in the Department of Arts. I don't say there's any harm in him, but he's an anxiety. There's an awful fellow sponging on him – a German out of the Foreign Legion. A thoroughly bad hat by all accounts. There's bound to be trouble.

'Mind you, I *like* Flyte. I don't see much of him. He used to come here for baths until he got fixed up at his house. He was always perfectly charming, and my wife took a great fancy to him. What he needs is occupation.'

I explained my errand.

'You'll probably find him at home now. Goodness knows there's nowhere to go in the evenings in the old town. If you like I'll send the porter to show you the way.'

So I set out after dinner, with the consular porter going ahead lantern in hand. Morocco was a new and strange country to me. Driving that day, mile after mile, up the smooth, strategic road, past the vineyards and military posts and the new, white settlements and the early crops already standing high in the vast, open fields, and the hoardings advertising the staples of France – Dubonnet, Michelin, Magasin du Louvre – I had thought it all very suburban and up-to-date; now, under the stars, in the walled city, whose streets were gentle, dusty stairways, and whose walls rose windowless on either side, closed overhead, then opened again to the stars; where the dust lay thick among the smooth paving-stones and figures passed silently, robed in white, on soft slippers or hard, bare soles; where the air was scented with cloves and incense and wood smoke – now I knew what had drawn Sebastian here and held him so long.

The consular porter strode arrogantly ahead with his light swinging and his tall cane banging; sometimes an open doorway revealed a silent group seated in golden lamplight round a brazier.

'Very dirty peoples,' the porter said scornfully, over his shoulder. 'No education. French leave them dirty. Not like British peoples. My peoples,' he said, 'always very British peoples.'

For he was from the Sudan Police, and regarded this ancient centre of his culture as a New Zealander might regard Rome.

At length we came to the last of many studded doors, and the porter beat on it with his stick.

'British Lord's house,' he said.

Lamplight and a dark face appeared at the grating. The consular porter spoke peremptorily; bolts were withdrawn and we entered a small courtyard with a well in its centre and a vine trained overhead.

'I wait here,' said the porter. 'You go with this native fellow.'

I entered the house; down a step and into the living-room I found a gramophone, an oil-stove and, between them, a young man. Later, when I looked about me, I noticed other, more agreeable things – the rugs on the floor, the embroidered silk on the walls, the carved and painted beams of the ceiling, the heavy, pierced lamp that hung from a chain and cast soft shadows of its own tracery about the room. But on first entering these three things, the gramophone for its noise – it was playing a French record of a jazz band – the stove for its smell, and the young man for his wolfish look, struck my senses. He was lolling in a basket chair, with a bandaged foot stuck forward on a box; he was dressed in a kind of thin, mid-European imitation tweed with a tennis shirt open at the neck; the unwounded foot wore a brown canvas shoe. There was a brass tray by his side on wooden legs, and on it were two beer bottles, a dirty plate, and a saucer full of cigarette ends; he held a glass of beer in his hand and a cigarette lay on his lower lip and stuck there when he spoke. He had long fair hair combed back without a parting and a face that was unnaturally lined for a man of his obvious youth; one of his front teeth was missing, so that his sibilants came sometimes with a lisp, sometimes with a disconcerting whistle, which he covered with a giggle; the teeth he had were stained with tobacco and set far apart.

This was plainly the 'thoroughly bad hat' of the consul's description, the film footman of Anthony's.

'I'm looking for Sebastian Flyte. This is his house, is it not?' I spoke loudly to make myself heard above the dance music, but he answered softly in English fluent enough to suggest that it was now habitual to him.

'Yeth. But he isn't here. There's no one but me.'

'I've come from England to see him on important business. Can you tell me where I can find him?'

The record came to its end. The German turned it over, wound up the machine, and started it playing again before answering.

'Sebastian's sick. The brothers took him away to the Infirmary. Maybe they'll let you thee him, maybe not. I got to go there myself one day thoon to have my foot dressed. I'll ask them then. When he's better they'll let you thee him, maybe.'

There was another chair and I sat down on it. Seeing that I meant to stay, the German offered me some beer.

'You're not Thebastian's brother?' he said. 'Cousin maybe? Maybe you married hith thister?'

'I'm only a friend. We were at the university together.'

'I had a friend at the university. We studied History. My

friend was cleverer than me; a little weak fellow – I used to pick him up and shake him when I was angry – but *tho* clever. Then one day we said: "What the hell? There is no work in Germany. Germany is down the drain," so we said good-bye to our professors, and they said: "Yes, Germany is down the drain. There is nothing for a student to do here now," and we went away and walked and walked and at last we came here. Then we said, "There is no army in Germany now, but we must be tholdiers," so we joined the Legion. My friend died of dysentery last year, campaigning in the Atlas. When he was dead, I said, "What the hell?" so I shot my foot. It is now full of pus, though I have done it one year.'

'Yes,' I said. 'That's very interesting. But my immediate concern is with Sebastian. Perhaps you would tell me about him.'

'He is a very good fellow, Sebastian. He is all right for me. Tangier was a stinking place. He brought me here – nice house, nice food, nice servant – everything is all right for me here, I reckon. I like it all right.'

'His mother is very ill,' I said. 'I have come to tell him.'

'She rich?'

'Yes.'

'Why don't she give him more money? Then we could live at Casablanca, maybe, in a nice flat. You know her well? You could make her give him more money?'

'What's the matter with him?'

'I don't know. I reckon maybe he drink too much. The brothers will look after him. It's all right for him there. The brothers are good fellows. Very cheap there.'

He clapped his hands and ordered more beer.

'You thee? A nice thervant to look after me. It is all right.'

When I had got the name of the hospital I left.

'Tell Thebastian I am still here and all right. I reckon he's worrying about me, maybe.'

The hospital, where I went next morning, was a collection of bungalows between the old and the new towns. It was kept by

Franciscans. I made my way through a crowd of diseased Moors to the doctor's room. He was a layman, clean shaven, dressed in white, starched overalls. We spoke in French, and he told me Sebastian was in no danger, but quite unfit to travel. He had had the grippe, with one lung slightly affected; he was very weak; he lacked resistance; what could one expect? He was an alcoholic. The doctor spoke dispassionately, almost brutally, with the relish men of science sometimes have for limiting themselves to inessentials, for pruning back their work to the point of sterility; but the bearded, barefooted brother in whose charge he put me, the man of no scientific pretensions who did the dirty jobs of the ward, had a different story.

'He's so patient. Not like a young man at all. He lies there and never complains – and there is much to complain of. We have no facilities. The Government give us what they can spare from the soldiers. And he is so kind. There is a poor German boy with a foot that will not heal and secondary syphilis, who comes here for treatment. Lord Flyte found him starving in Tangier and took him in and gave him a home. A real Samaritan.'

'Poor simple monk,' I thought, 'poor booby.' God forgive me!

Sebastian was in the wing kept for Europeans, where the beds were divided by low partitions into cubicles with some air of privacy. He was lying with his hands on the quilt staring at the wall, where the only ornament was a religious oleograph.

'Your friend,' said the brother.

He looked round slowly.

'Oh, I thought he meant Kurt. What are *you* doing here, Charles?'

He was more than ever emaciated; drink, which made others fat and red, seemed to wither Sebastian. The brother left us, and I sat by his bed and talked about his illness.

'I was out of my mind for a day or two,' he said. 'I kept thinking I was back in Oxford. You went to my house? Did you like it? Is Kurt still there? I won't ask you if you liked Kurt; no one does. It's funny – I couldn't get on without him, you know.'

Then I told him about his mother. He said nothing for some

time, but lay gazing at the oleograph of the Seven Dolours.
Then:

'Poor mummy. She really was a *femme fatale*, wasn't she? She
killed at a touch.'

I telegraphed to Julia that Sebastian was unable to travel,
and stayed a week at Fez, visiting the hospital daily until he was
well enough to move. His first sign of returning strength, on the
second day of my visit, was to ask for brandy. By next day he
had got some, somehow, and kept it under the bedclothes.

The doctor said: 'Your friend is drinking again. It is forbidden here. What can I do? This is not a reformatory school. I
cannot police the wards. I am here to cure people, not to protect
them from vicious habits, or teach them self-control. Cognac
will not hurt him now. It will make him weaker for the next
time he is ill, and then one day some little trouble will carry him
off, pouff. This is not a home for inebriates. He must go at the
end of the week.'

The lay brother said: 'Your friend is so much happier today,
it is like one transfigured.'

'Poor simple monk,' I thought, 'poor booby'; but he added,
'You know why? He has a bottle of cognac in bed with him. It is
the second I have found. No sooner do I take one away than he
gets another. He is so naughty. It is the Arab boys who fetch it
for him. But it is good to see him happy again when he has been
so sad.'

On my last afternoon I said, 'Sebastian, now your mother's
dead' – for the news had reached us that morning – 'do you
think of going back to England?'

'It *would* be lovely, in some ways,' he said, 'but do you think
Kurt would like it?'

'For God's sake,' I said, 'you don't mean to spend your life
with Kurt, do you?'

'I don't know. He seems to mean to spend it with me. "It'th
all right for him, I reckon, maybe,"' he said, mimicking Kurt's
accent, and then he added what, if I had paid more attention,
should have given me the key I lacked; at the time I heard and
remembered it, without taking notice. 'You know, Charles,' he

said, 'it's rather a pleasant change when all your life you've had people looking after you, to have someone to look after yourself. Only of course it has to be someone pretty hopeless to need looking after by *me*.'

I was able to straighten his money affairs before I left. He had lived till then by getting into difficulties and then telegraphing for odd sums to his lawyers. I saw the branch manager of the bank and arranged for him, if funds were forthcoming from London, to receive Sebastian's quarterly allowance and pay him a weekly sum of pocket money with a reserve to be drawn in emergencies. This sum was only to be given to Sebastian personally, and only when the manager was satisfied that he had a proper use for it. Sebastian agreed readily to all this.

'Otherwise,' he said, 'Kurt will get me to sign a cheque for the whole lot when I'm tight and then he'll go off and get into all kinds of trouble.'

I saw Sebastian home from the hospital. He seemed weaker in his basket chair than he had been in bed. The two sick men, he and Kurt, sat opposite one another with the gramophone between them.

'It was time you came back,' said Kurt. 'I need you.'

'Do you, Kurt?'

'I reckon so. It's not so good being alone when you're sick. That boy's a lazy fellow – always slipping off when I want him. Once he stayed out all night and there was no one to make my coffee when I woke up. It's no good having a foot full of pus. Times I can't sleep good. Maybe another time I shall slip off, too, and go where I can be looked after.' He clapped his hands but no servant came. 'You see?' he said.

'What d'you want?'

'Cigarettes. I got some in the bag under my bed.'

Sebastian began painfully to rise from his chair.

'I'll get them,' I said. 'Where's his bed?'

'No, that's my job,' said Sebastian.

'Yeth,' said Kurt, 'I reckon that's Sebastian's job.'

So I left him with his friend in the little enclosed house at the end of the alley. There was nothing more I could do for Sebastian.

I had meant to return direct to Paris, but this business of Sebastian's allowance meant that I must go to London and see Brideshead. I travelled by sea, taking the P. & O. from Tangier, and was home in early June.

'Do you consider,' asked Brideshead, 'that there is anything vicious in my brother's connexion with this German?'

'No. I'm sure not. It's simply a case of two waifs coming together.'

'You say he is a criminal?'

'I said "a criminal type". He's been in the military prison and was dishonourably discharged.'

'And the doctor says Sebastian is killing himself with drink?'

'Weakening himself. He hasn't D.T.s or cirrhosis.'

'He's not insane?'

'Certainly not. He's found a companion he happens to like and a place where he happens to like living.'

'Then he must have his allowance as you suggest. The thing is quite clear.'

In some ways Brideshead was an easy man to deal with. He had a kind of mad certainty about everything which made his decisions swift and easy.

'Would you like to paint this house?' he asked suddenly. 'A picture of the front, another of the back on the park, another of the staircase, another of the big drawing-room? Four small oils; that is what my father wants done for a record, to keep at Brideshead. I don't know any painters. Julia said you specialized in architecture.'

'Yes,' I said. 'I should like to very much.'

'You know it's being pulled down? My father's selling it. They are going to put up a block of flats here. They're keeping the name – we can't stop them apparently.'

'What a sad thing.'

'Well, I'm sorry of course. But you think it good architecturally?'

'One of the most beautiful houses I know.'

'Can't see it. I've always thought it rather ugly. Perhaps your pictures will make me see it differently.'

This was my first commission; I had to work against time, for the contractors were only waiting for the final signature to start their work of destruction. In spite, or perhaps, because, of that – for it is my vice to spend too long on a canvas, never content to leave well alone – those four paintings are particular favourites of mine, and it was their success, both with myself and others, that confirmed me in what has since been my career.

I began in the long drawing-room, for they were anxious to shift the furniture, which had stood there since it was built. It was a long, elaborate, symmetrical Adam room, with two bays of windows opening into Green Park. The light, streaming in from the west on the afternoon when I began to paint there, was fresh green from the young trees outside.

I had the perspective set out in pencil and the detail carefully placed. I held back from painting, like a diver on the water's edge; once in I found myself buoyed and exhilarated. I was normally a slow and deliberate painter; that afternoon and all next day, and the day after, I worked fast. I could do nothing wrong. At the end of each passage I paused, tense, afraid to start the next, fearing, like a gambler, that luck must turn and the pile be lost. Bit by bit, minute by minute, the thing came into being. There were no difficulties; the intricate multiplicity of light and colour became a whole; the right colour was where I wanted it on the palette; each brush stroke, as soon as it was complete, seemed to have been there always.

Presently on the last afternoon I heard a voice behind me say: 'May I stay here and watch?'

I turned and found Cordelia.

'Yes,' I said, 'if you don't talk,' and I worked on, oblivious of her, until the failing sun made me put up my brushes.

'It must be lovely to be able to do that.'

I had forgotten she was there.

'It is.'

I could not even now leave my picture, although the sun was

down and the room fading to monochrome. I took it from the easel and held it up to the windows, put it back and lightened a shadow. Then, suddenly weary in head and eyes and back and arm, I gave it up for the evening and turned to Cordelia.

She was now fifteen and had grown tall, nearly to her full height, in the last eighteen months. She had not the promise of Julia's full *quattrocento* loveliness; there was a touch of Brideshead already in her length of nose and high cheekbone; she was in black, mourning for her mother.

'I'm tired,' I said.

'I bet you are. Is it finished?'

'Practically. I must go over it again tomorrow.'

'D'you know it's long past dinner time? There's no one here to cook anything now. I only came up today, and didn't realize how far the decay had gone. You wouldn't like to take me out to dinner, would you?'

We left by the garden door, into the park, and walked in the twilight to the Ritz Grill.

'You've seen Sebastian? He won't come home, even now?'

I did not realize till then that she had understood so much. I said so.

'Well, I love him more than anyone,' she said. 'It's sad about Marchers, isn't it? Do you know they're going to build a block of flats, and that Rex wanted to take what he called a "penthouse" at the top. Isn't it like him? Poor Julia. That was too much for her. He couldn't understand at all; he thought she would like to keep up with her old home. Things have all come to an end very quickly, haven't they? Apparently papa has been terribly in debt for a long time. Selling Marchers has put him straight again and saved I don't know how much a year in rates. But it seems a shame to pull it down. Julia says she'd sooner that than to have someone else live there.'

'What's going to happen to you?'

'What, indeed? There are all kinds of suggestions. Aunt Fanny Rosscommon wants me to live with her. Then Rex and Julia talk of taking over half Brideshead and living there. Papa won't come back. We thought he might, but no.

'They've closed the chapel at Brideshead, Bridey and the Bishop; mummy's Requiem was the last mass said there. After she was buried the priest came in – I was there alone. I don't think he saw me – and took out the altar stone and put it in his bag; then he burned the wads of wool with the holy oil on them and threw the ash outside; he emptied the holy-water stoop and blew out the lamp in the sanctuary, and left the tabernacle open and empty, as though from now on it was always to be Good Friday. I suppose none of this makes any sense to you, Charles, poor agnostic. I stayed there till he was gone, and then, suddenly, there wasn't any chapel there any more, just an oddly decorated room. I can't tell you what it felt like. You've never been to Tenebrae, I suppose?'

'Never.'

'Well, if you had you'd know what the Jews felt about their temple. *Quomodo sedet sola civitas* ... it's a beautiful chant. You ought to go once, just to hear it.'

'Still trying to convert me, Cordelia?'

'Oh, no. That's all over, too. D'you know what papa said when he became a Catholic? Mummy told me once. He said to her: "You have brought back my family to the faith of their ancestors." Pompous, you know. It takes people different ways. Anyhow, the family haven't been very constant, have they? There's him gone and Sebastian gone and Julia gone. But God won't let them go for long, you know. I wonder if you remember the story mummy read us the evening Sebastian first got drunk – I mean the *bad* evening. "Father Brown" said something like "I caught him" (the thief) "with an unseen hook and an invisible line which is long enough to let him wander to the ends of the world and still to bring him back with a twitch upon the thread."'

We scarcely mentioned her mother. All the time we talked, she ate voraciously. Once she said:

'Did you see Sir Adrian Porson's poem in *The Times*? It's funny: he knew her best of anyone – he loved her all his life, you know – and yet it doesn't seem to have anything to do with her at all.

'I got on best with her of any of us, but I don't believe I ever really loved her. Not as she wanted or deserved. It's odd I didn't, because I'm full of natural affections.'

'I never really knew your Mother,' I said.

'You didn't like her. I sometimes think when people wanted to hate God they hated mummy.'

'What do you mean by that, Cordelia?'

'Well, you see, she was saintly but she wasn't a saint. No one could really hate a saint, could they? They can't really hate God either. When they want to hate him and his saints they have to find something like themselves and pretend it's God and hate that. I suppose you think that's all bosh.'

'I heard almost the same thing once before – from someone very different.'

'Oh, I'm quite serious. I've thought about it a lot. It seems to explain poor mummy.'

Then this odd child tucked into her dinner with renewed relish. 'First time I've ever been taken out to dinner alone at a restaurant,' she said.

Later: 'When Julia heard they were selling Marchers she said: "Poor Cordelia. She won't have her coming-out ball there after all." It's a thing we used to talk about – like my being her bridesmaid. That didn't come off either. When Julia had her ball I was allowed down for an hour, to sit in the corner with Aunt Fanny, and she said, "In six years' time you'll have all this." ... I hope I've got a vocation.'

'I don't know what that means.'

'It means you can be a nun. If you haven't a vocation it's no good however much you want to be; and if you have a vocation, you can't get away from it, however much you hate it. Bridey thinks he has a vocation and hasn't. I used to think Sebastian had and hated it – but I don't know now. Everything has changed so much suddenly.'

But I had no patience with this convent chatter. I had felt the brush take life in my hand that afternoon; I had had my finger in the great, succulent pie of creation. I was a man of the Renaissance that evening – of Browning's renaissance. I, who had walked the streets of Rome in Genoa velvet and had seen the stars through Galileo's tube, spurned the friars, with their dusty tomes and their sunken, jealous eyes and their crabbed hair-splitting speech.

'You'll fall in love,' I said.

'Oh, pray not. I say, do you think I could have another of those scrumptious meringues?'

BOOK THREE

A TWITCH UPON
THE THREAD

CHAPTER I

My theme is memory, that winged host that soared about me one grey morning of war-time.

These memories, which are my life – for we possess nothing certainly except the past – were always with me. Like the pigeons of St Mark's, they were everywhere, under my feet, singly, in pairs, in little honey-voiced congregations, nodding, strutting, winking, rolling the tender feathers of their necks, perching sometimes, if I stood still, on my shoulder; until, suddenly, the noon gun boomed and in a moment, with a flutter and sweep of wings, the pavement was bare and the whole sky above dark with a tumult of fowl. Thus it was that morning of war-time.

For nearly ten dead years after that evening with Cordelia I was borne along a road outwardly full of change and incident, but never during that time, except sometimes in my painting – and that at longer and longer intervals – did I come alive as I had been during the time of my friendship with Sebastian. I took it to be youth, not life, that I was losing. My work upheld me, for I had chosen to do what I could do well, did better daily, and liked doing; incidentally it was something which no one else at that time was attempting to do. I became an architectural painter.

More even than the work of the great architects, I loved buildings that grew silently with the centuries, catching and keeping the best of each generation, while time curbed the artist's pride and the Philistine's vulgarity, and repaired the clumsiness of the dull workman. In such buildings England abounded, and, in the last decade of their grandeur, English-men seemed for the first time to become conscious of what before was taken for granted, and to salute their achievement at the moment of extinction. Hence my prosperity, far beyond my merits; my work had nothing to recommend it except my growing technical skill, enthusiasm for my subject, and independence of popular notions.

The financial slump of the period, which left many painters without employment, served to enhance my success, which was, indeed, itself a symptom of the decline. When the water-holes were dry people sought to drink at the mirage. After my first exhibition I was called to all parts of the country to make portraits of houses that were soon to be deserted or debased; indeed, my arrival seemed often to be only a few paces ahead of the auctioneer's, a presage of doom.

I published three splendid folios – *Ryder's Country Seats, Ryder's English Homes,* and *Ryder's Village and Provincial Architecture,* which each sold its thousand copies at five guineas apiece. I seldom failed to please, for there was no conflict between myself and my patrons; we both wanted the same thing. But, as the years passed, I began to mourn the loss of something I had known in the drawing-room of Marchmain House and once or twice since, the intensity and singleness and the belief that it was not all done by hand – in a word, the inspiration.

In quest of this fading light I went abroad, in the augustan manner, laden with the apparatus of my trade, for two years' refreshment among alien styles. I did not go to Europe; her treasures were safe, too safe, swaddled in expert care, obscured by reverence. Europe could wait. There would be a time for Europe, I thought; all too soon the days would come when I should need a man at my side to put up my easel and carry my paints; when I could not venture more than an hour's journey from a good hotel; when I should need soft breezes and mellow sunshine all day long; then I would take my old eyes to Germany and Italy. Now while I had the strength I would go to the wild lands where man had deserted his post and the jungle was creeping back to its old strongholds.

Accordingly, by slow but not easy stages, I travelled through Mexico and Central America in a world which had all I needed, and the change from parkland and hall should have quickened me and set me right with myself. I sought inspiration among gutted palaces and cloisters embowered in weed, derelict churches where the vampire-bats hung in the dome like dry seed-pods and only the ants were ceaselessly astir tunnelling in the rich stalls; cities where no road led, and mausoleums where a single, agued family of Indians sheltered from the rains. There in great labour, sickness, and occasionally in some danger, I made the first drawings for *Ryder's Latin America*. Every few weeks I came to rest, finding myself once more in the zone of trade or tourism, recuperated, set up my studio, transcribed my sketches, anxiously packed the complete canvases, dispatched them to my New York agent, and then set out again, with my small retinue, into the wastes.

I was in no great pains to keep in touch with England. I followed local advice for my itinerary and had no settled route, so that much of my mail never reached me, and the rest accumulated until there was more than could be read at a sitting. I used to stuff a bundle of letters into my bag and read them when I felt inclined, which was in circumstances so incongruous – swinging in my hammock, under the net, by the light of a storm-lantern; drifting down river, amidships in the canoe, with the boys astern of me lazily keeping our nose out of the bank, with the dark water keeping pace with us, in the green shade, with the great trees towering above us and the monkeys screeching in the sunlight, high overhead among the flowers on the roof of the forest; on the veranda of a hospitable ranch, where the ice and the dice clicked, and a tiger cat played with its chain on the mown grass – that they seemed voices so distant as to be meaningless; their matter passed clean through the mind, and out, leaving no mark, like the facts about themselves which fellow travellers distribute so freely in American railway trains.

But despite this isolation and this long sojourn in a strange world, I remained unchanged, still a small part of myself pretending to be whole. I discarded the experiences of those two years with my tropical kit and returned to New York as I had set out. I had a fine haul – eleven paintings and fifty odd drawings – and when eventually I exhibited them in London, the art critics, many of whom hitherto had been patronizing in tone, as my success invited, acclaimed a new and richer note in my work. *Mr Ryder*, the most respected of them wrote, *rises like a fresh young trout to the hypodermic injection of a new culture and discloses a powerful facet in the vista of his potentialities ... By focusing the frankly traditional battery of his elegance and erudition on the maelstrom of barbarism, Mr Ryder has at last found himself.*

Grateful words, but, alas, not true by a long chalk. My wife, who crossed to New York to meet me and saw the fruits of our separation displayed in my agent's office, summed the thing up better by saying: 'Of course, I can see they're perfectly brilliant and really rather beautiful in a sinister way, but somehow I don't feel they are quite *you*.'

In Europe my wife was sometimes taken for an American because of her dapper and jaunty way of dressing, and the curiously hygienic quality of her prettiness; in America she assumed an English softness and reticence. She arrived a day or two before me, and was on the pier when my ship docked.

'It has been a long time,' she said fondly when we met.

She had not joined the expedition; she explained to our friends that the country was unsuitable and she had her son at home. There was also a daughter now, she remarked, and it came back to me that there had been talk of this before I started, as an additional reason for her staying behind. There had been some mention of it, too, in her letters.

'I don't believe you read my letters,' she said that night, when at last, late, after a dinner party and some hours at a cabaret, we found ourselves alone in our hotel bedroom.

'Some went astray. I remember distinctly your telling me that the daffodils in the orchard were a dream, that the nursery-maid was a jewel, that the Regency four-poster was a find, but frankly I do not remember hearing that your new baby was called Caroline. Why did you call it that?'

'After Charles, of course.'

'Ah!'

'I made Bertha Van Halt godmother. I thought she was safe for a good present. What do you think she gave?'

'Bertha Van Halt is a well-known trap. What?'

'A fifteen shilling book-token. Now that Johnjohn has a companion –'

'Who?'

'Your son, darling. You haven't forgotten him, too?'

'For Christ's sake,' I said, 'why do you call him that?'

'It's the name he invented for himself. Don't you think it sweet? Now that Johnjohn has a companion I think we'd better not have any more for some time, don't you?'

'Just as you please.'

'Johnjohn talks of you such a lot. He prays every night for your safe return.'

She talked in this way while she undressed, with an effort to appear at ease; then she sat at the dressing table, ran a comb through her hair, and with her bare back towards me, looking at herself in the glass, said: 'Shall I put my face to bed?'

It was a familiar phrase, one that I did not like; she meant, should she remove her make-up, cover herself with grease and put her hair in a net.

'No,' I said, 'not at once.'

Then she knew what was wanted. She had neat, hygienic ways for that too, but there were both relief and triumph in her smile of welcome; later we parted and lay in our twin beds a yard or two distant, smoking. I looked at my watch; it was four o'clock, but neither of us was ready to sleep, for in that city there is neurosis in the air which the inhabitants mistake for energy.

'I don't believe you've changed at all, Charles.'

'No, I'm afraid not.'

'D'you want to change?'

'It's the only evidence of life.'

'But you might change so that you didn't love me any more.'

'There is that risk.'

'Charles, you haven't stopped loving me?'

'You said yourself I hadn't changed.'

'Well, I'm beginning to think you have. I haven't.'

'No,' I said, 'no; I can see that.'

'Were you at all frightened at meeting me today?'

'Not the least.'

'You didn't wonder if I should have fallen in love with someone else in the meantime?'

'No. Have you?'

'You know I haven't. Have you?'

'No. I'm not in love.'

My wife seemed content with this answer. She had married me six years ago at the time of my first exhibition, and had done much since then to push our interests. People said she had 'made' me, but she herself took credit only for supplying me with a congenial background; she had firm faith in my genius and in the 'artistic temperament', and in the principle that things done on the sly are not really done at all.

Presently she said: 'Looking forward to getting home?' (My father gave me as a wedding present the price of a house, and I bought an old rectory in my wife's part of the country.) 'I've got a surprise for you.'

'Yes?'

'I've turned the old barn into a studio for you, so that you needn't be disturbed by the children or when we have people to stay. I got Emden to do it. Everyone thinks it a great success. There was an article on it in *Country Life*; I brought it for you to see.'

She showed me the article: '... *happy example of architectural good manners.* ... *Sir Joseph Emden's tactful adaptation of traditional material to modern needs ...*'; there were some photographs; wide oak boards now covered the earthen floor; a high, stone-mullioned bay-window had been built in the north wall, and the great timbered roof, which before had been lost in shadow, now stood out stark, well lit, with clean white plaster between the beams; it looked like a village hall. I remembered the smell of the place, which would now be lost.

'I rather liked that barn,' I said.

'But you'll be able to work there, won't you?'

'After squatting in a cloud of sting-fly,' I said, 'under a sun which scorched the paper off the block as I drew, I could work on the top of an omnibus. I expect the vicar would like to borrow the place for whist drives.'

'There's a lot of work waiting for you. I promised Lady Anchorage you would do Anchorage House as soon as you got back. That's coming down, too, you know – shops underneath and two-roomed flats above. You don't think, do you, Charles, that all this exotic work you've been doing, is going to spoil you for that sort of thing?'

'Why should it?'

'Well, it's so different. Don't be cross.'

'It's just another jungle closing in.'

'I know just how you feel, darling. The Georgian Society made such a fuss, but we couldn't do anything. .... Did you ever get my letter about Boy?'

'Did I? What did it say?'

('Boy' Mulcaster was her brother.)

'About his engagement. It doesn't matter now because it's all off, but father and mother were terribly upset. She was an awful girl. They had to give her money in the end.'

'No, I heard nothing of Boy.'

'He and Johnjohn are tremendous friends, now. It's so sweet to see them together. Whenever he comes the first thing he does is to drive straight to the Old Rectory. He just walks into the house, pays no attention to anyone else, and hollers out: "Where's my chum Johnjohn?" and Johnjohn comes tumbling downstairs and off they go into the spinney together and play for hours. You'd think, to hear them talk to each other, they were the same age. It was really Johnjohn who made him see reason about that girl; seriously, you know, he's frightfully sharp. He must have heard mother and me talking because next time Boy came he said: "Uncle Boy shan't marry horrid girl and leave Johnjohn," and that was the very day he settled for two thousand pounds out of court. Johnjohn admires Boy so tremendously and imitates him in everything. It's so good for them both.'

I crossed the room and tried once more, ineffectively, to moderate the heat of the radiators; I drank some iced water and opened the window, but, besides the sharp night air, music was borne in from the next room where they were playing the wireless. I shut it and turned back towards my wife.

At length she began talking again, more drowsily. ...

'The garden's come on a lot. ... The box hedges you planted grew five inches last year. ... I had some men down from London to put the tennis court right ... first-class cook at the moment ...'

As the city below us began to wake, we both fell asleep, but not for long; the telephone rang and a voice of hermaphroditic gaiety said: 'Savoy-Carlton-Hotel-goodmorning. It is now a quarter to eight.'

'I didn't ask to be called, you know.'

'Pardon me?'

'Oh, it doesn't matter.'

'You're welcome.'

As I was shaving, my wife from the bath said: 'Just like old times. I'm not worrying any more, Charles.'

'Good.'

'I was so terribly afraid that two years might have made a difference. Now I know we can start again exactly where we left off.'

'When?' I asked. 'What? When we left off what?'

'When you went away, of course.'

'You are not thinking of something else, a little time before?'

'Oh, Charles, that's old history. That was nothing. It was never anything. It's all over and forgotten.'

'I just wanted to know,' I said. 'We're back as we were the day I went abroad, is that it?'

So we started that day exactly where we left off two years before, with my wife in tears.

My wife's softness and English reticence, her very white, small regular teeth, her neat rosy finger-nails, her schoolgirl air of innocent mischief and her schoolgirl dress, her modern jewellery, which was made at great expense to give the impression, at a distance, of having been mass produced, her ready, rewarding smile, her deference to me and her zeal in my interests, her motherly heart which made her cable daily to the nanny at home – in short, her peculiar charm – made her popular among the Americans, and our cabin on the day of departure was full of cellophane packages – flowers, fruit, sweets, books, toys for the children – from friends she had known for a week. Stewards, like sisters in a nursing home, used to judge their passengers' importance by the number and value of these trophies; we therefore started the voyage in high esteem.

My wife's first thought on coming aboard was of the passenger list.

'Such a lot of friends,' she said. 'It's going to be a lovely trip. Let's have a cocktail party this evening.'

The companion-ways were no sooner cast off than she was busy with the telephone.

'Julia. This is Celia – Celia Ryder. It's lovely to find you on board. What have you been up to? Come and have a cocktail this evening and tell me all about it.'

'Julia who?'

'Mottram. I haven't seen her for years.'

Nor had I; not, in fact, since my wedding day, not to speak to for any time, since the private view of my exhibition where the four canvases of Marchmain House, lent by Brideshead, had hung together attracting much attention. Those pictures were my last contact with the Flytes; our lives, so close for a year or two, had drawn apart. Sebastian, I knew, was still abroad; Rex and Julia, I sometimes heard said, were unhappy together. Rex was not prospering quite as well as had been predicted; he remained on the fringe of the Government, prominent but vaguely suspect. He lived among the very rich, and in his speeches seemed to incline to revolutionary policies, flirting, with Communists and Fascists. I heard the Mottrams' names in conversation; I saw their faces now and again peeping from the *Tatler*, as I turned the pages impatiently waiting for someone to come, but they and I had fallen apart, as one could in England

and only there, into separate worlds, little spinning planets of personal relationship; there is probably a perfect metaphor for the process to be found in physics, from the way in which, I dimly apprehend, particles of energy group and regroup themselves in separate magnetic systems; a metaphor ready to hand for the man who can speak of these things with assurance; not for me, who can only say that England abounded in these small companies of intimate friends, so that, as in this case of Julia and myself, we could live in the same street in London, see at times, a few miles distant, the same rural horizon, could have a liking one for the other, a mild curiosity about the other's fortunes, a regret, even, that we should be separated, and the knowledge that either of us had only to pick up the telephone and speak by the other's pillow, enjoy the intimacies of the levee, coming in, as it were, with the morning orange juice and the sun, yet be restrained from doing so by the centripetal force of our own worlds, and the cold, interstellar space between them.

My wife, perched on the back of the sofa in a litter of cellophane and silk ribbons, continued telephoning, working brightly through the passenger list ... 'Yes, do of course bring him, I'm told he's sweet. .... Yes, I've got Charles back from the wilds at last; isn't it lovely. .... What a treat seeing your name in the list! It's made my trip ... darling, we were at the Savoy-Carlton, too; how can we have missed you?' ... Sometimes she turned to me and said: 'I have to make sure you're still really there. I haven't got used to it yet.'

I went up and out as we steamed slowly down the river to one of the great glass cases where the passengers stood to watch the land slip by. 'Such a lot of friends,' my wife had said. They looked a strange crowd to me; the emotions of leave-taking were just beginning to subside; some of them, who had been drinking till the last moment with those who were seeing them off, were still boisterous; others were planning where they would have their deck chairs; the band played unnoticed – all were as restless as ants.

I turned into some of the halls of the ship, which were huge without any splendour, as though they had been designed for a railway coach and preposterously magnified. I passed through vast bronze gates on which paper-thin Assyrian animals cavorted; I trod carpets the colour of blotting paper; the painted panels of the walls were like blotting paper, too – kindergarten work in flat, drab colours – and between the walls were yards and yards of biscuit-coloured wood which no carpenter's tool had ever touched, wood that had been bent round corners, invisibly joined strip to strip, steamed and squeezed and polished; all over the blotting-paper carpet were strewn tables designed perhaps by a sanitary engineer, square blocks of stuffing, with square holes for sitting in, and uphol-stered, it seemed, in blotting paper also; the light of the hall was suffused from scores of hollows, giving an even glow, casting no shadows – the whole place hummed from its hundred ventila-tors and vibrated with the turn of the great engines below.

'Here I am,' I thought, 'back from the jungle, back from the ruins. Here, where wealth is no longer gorgeous and power has no dignity. *Quomodo sedet sola civitas*' (for I had heard that great lament, which Cordelia once quoted to me in the drawing-room of Marchmain House, sung by a half-caste choir in Guatemala, nearly a year ago).

A steward came up to me.

'Can I get you anything, sir?'

'A whisky and soda, not iced.'

'I'm sorry, sir, *all* the soda is iced.'

'Is the water iced, too?'

'Oh yes, sir.'

'Well, it doesn't matter.'

He trotted off, puzzled, soundless in the pervading hum.

'Charles.'

I looked behind me. Julia was sitting in a cube of blotting paper, her hands folded in her lap, so still that I had passed by without noticing her.

'I heard you were here. Celia telephoned to me. It's delightful.'

'What are you doing?'

She opened the empty hands in her lap with a little eloquent gesture. 'Waiting. My maid's unpacking; she's been so disagreeable ever since we left England. She's complaining now about my cabin. I can't think why. It seems a lap to me.'

The steward returned with whisky and two jugs, one of iced water, the other of boiling water; I mixed them to the right temperature. He watched and said: 'I'll remember that's how you take it, sir.'

Most passengers had fads; he was paid to fortify their self-esteem. Julia asked for a cup of hot chocolate. I sat by her in the next cube.

'I never see you now,' she said. 'I never seem to see anyone I like. I don't know why.'

But she spoke as though it were a matter of weeks rather than of years; as though, too, before our parting we had been firm friends. It was dead contrary to the common experience of such encounters, when time is found to have built its own defensive lines, camouflaged vulnerable points, and laid a field of mines across all but a few well-trodden paths, so that, more often than not, we can only signal to one another from either side of the tangle of wire. Here she and I, who were never friends before, met on terms of long and unbroken intimacy.

'What have you been doing in America?'

She looked up slowly from her chocolate and, her splendid, serious eyes in mine, said: 'Don't you know? I'll tell you about it sometime. I've been a mug. I thought I was in love with someone, but it didn't turn out that way.' And my mind went back ten years to the evening at Brideshead, when that lovely, spidery child of nineteen, as though brought in for an hour from the nursery and nettled by lack of attention from the grown-ups, had said: '*I'm* causing anxiety, too, you know,' and I had thought at the time, though scarcely, it now seemed to me, in long trousers myself, 'How important these girls make themselves with their love affairs.'

Now it was different; there was nothing but humility and friendly candour in the way she spoke.

I wished I could respond to her confidence, give some token

of acceptance, but there was nothing in my last, flat, eventful years that I could share with her. I began instead to talk of my time in the jungle, of the comic characters I had met and the lost places I had visited, but in this mood of old friendship the tale faltered and came to an end abruptly.

'I long to see the paintings,' she said.

'Celia wanted me to unpack some and stick them round the cabin for her cocktail party. I couldn't do that.'

'No ... is Celia as pretty as ever? I always thought she had the most delicious looks of any girl of my year.'

'She hasn't changed.'

'You have, Charles. So lean and grim; not at all the pretty boy Sebastian brought home with him. Harder, too.'

'And you're softer.'

'Yes, I think so ... and very patient now.'

She was not yet thirty, but was approaching the zenith of her loveliness, all her rich promise abundantly fulfilled. She had lost that fashionable, spidery look; the head that I used to think *quattrocento*, which had sat a little oddly on her, was now part of herself and not at all Florentine; not connected in any way with painting or the arts or with anything except herself, so that it would be idle to itemize and dissect her beauty, which was her own essence, and could only be known in her and by her authority and in the love I was soon to have for her.

Time had wrought another change, too; not for her the sly, complacent smile of la Gioconda; the years had been more than 'the sound of lyres and flutes', and had saddened her. She seemed to say: 'Look at me. I have done my share. I am beautiful. It is something quite out of the ordinary, this beauty of mine. I am made for delight. But what do *I* get out of it? Where is *my* reward?'

That was the change in her from ten years ago; that, indeed, was her reward, this haunting, magical sadness which spoke straight to the heart and struck silence; it was the completion of her beauty.

'Sadder, too,' I said.

'Oh yes, much sadder.'

My wife was in exuberant spirits when, two hours later, I returned to the cabin.

'I've had to do everything. How does it look?'

We had been given, without paying more for it, a large suite of rooms, one so large, in fact, that it was seldom booked except by directors of the line, and on most voyages, the chief purser admitted, was given to those he wished to honour. (My wife was adept in achieving such small advantages, first impressing the impressionable with her chic and my celebrity and, superiority once firmly established, changing quickly to a pose of almost flirtatious affability.) In token of her appreciation the chief purser had been asked to our party and he, in token of his appreciation, had sent before him the life-size effigy of a swan, moulded in ice and filled with caviar. This chilly piece of magnificence now dominated the room, standing on a table in the centre, thawing gently, dripping at the beak into its silver dish. The flowers of the morning delivery hid as much as possible of the panelling (for this room was a miniature of the monstrous hall above).

'You must get dressed at once. Where have you been all this time?'

'Talking to Julia Mottram.'

'D'you know her? Oh, of course, you were a friend of the dipso brother. Goodness, her glamour!'

'She greatly admires your looks, too.'

'She used to be a girl friend of Boy's.'

'Surely not?'

'He always said so.'

'Have you considered,' I asked, 'how your guests are going to eat this caviar?'

'I have. It's insoluble. But there's all this' – she revealed some trays of glassy titbits – 'and anyway, people always find ways of eating things at parties. D'you remember we once ate potted shrimps with a paper knife?'

'Did we?'

'Darling, it was the night you popped the question.'

'As I remember, you popped.'

'Well, the night we got engaged. But you haven't said how you like the arrangements.'

The arrangements, apart from the swan and the flowers, consisted of a steward already inextricably trapped in the corner behind an improvised bar, and another steward, tray in hand, in comparative freedom.

'A cinema actor's dream,' I said.

'Cinema actors,' said my wife; 'that's what I want to talk about.'

She came with me to my dressing-room and talked while I changed. It had occurred to her that, with my interest in architecture, my true *métier* was designing scenery for the films, and she had asked two Hollywood magnates to the party with whom she wished to ingratiate me.

We returned to the sitting-room.

'Darling, I believe you've taken against my bird. Don't be beastly about it in front of the purser. It was sweet of him to think of it. Besides, you know, if you had read about it in the description of a sixteenth-century banquet in Venice, you would have said those were the days to live.'

'In sixteenth-century Venice it would have been a somewhat different shape.'

'Here is Father Christmas. We were just in raptures over your swan.'

The chief purser came into the room and shook hands, powerfully.

'Dear Lady Celia,' he said, 'if you'll put on your warmest clothes and come on an expedition into the cold storage with me tomorrow, I can show you a whole Noah's Ark of such objects. The toast will be along in a minute. They're keeping it hot.'

'Toast!' said my wife, as though this was something beyond the dreams of gluttony. 'Do you hear that, Charles? *Toast.*'

Soon the guests began to arrive; there was nothing to delay them. 'Celia,' they said, 'what a grand cabin and what a beautiful swan!' and, for all that it was one of the largest in the ship, our room was soon painfully crowded; they began to put out their cigarettes in the little pool of ice-water which now surrounded the swan.

The purser made a sensation, as sailors like to do, by predicting a storm. 'How can you be so beastly?' asked my wife, conveying the flattering suggestion that not only the cabin and the caviar, but the waves, too, were at his command. 'Anyway, storms don't affect a ship like this, do they?'

'Might hold us back a bit.'

'But it wouldn't make us sick?'

'Depends if you're a good sailor. I'm always sick in storms, ever since I was a boy.'

'I don't believe it. He's just being sadistic. Come over here, there's something I want to show you.'

It was the latest photograph of her children. 'Charles hasn't even seen Caroline yet. Isn't it thrilling for him?'

There were no friends of mine there, but I knew about a third of the party, and talked away civilly enough. An elderly woman said to me, 'So you're Charles. I feel I know you, through and through, Celia's talked so much about you.'

'Through and through,' I thought. 'Through and through is a long way, madam. Can you indeed see into those dark places where my own eyes seek in vain to guide me? Can you tell me, dear Mrs Stuyvesant Oglander – if I am correct in thinking that is how I heard my wife speak of you – why it is that at this moment, while I talk to you, here, about my forthcoming exhibition, I am thinking all the time only of when Julia will come? Why can I talk like this to you, but not to her? Why have I already set her apart from humankind, and myself with her? What is going on in those secret places of my spirit with which you make so free? What is cooking, Mrs Stuyvesant Oglander?'

Still Julia did not come, and the noise of twenty people in that tiny room, which was so large that no one hired it, was the noise of a multitude.

Then I saw a curious thing. There was a little red-headed man whom no one seemed to know, a dowdy fellow quite unlike the general run of my wife's guests; he had been standing by the caviar for twenty minutes eating as fast as a rabbit. Now he wiped his mouth with his handkerchief and, on the impulse apparently, leaned forward and dabbed the beak of the swan, removing the drop of water that had been swelling there and would soon have fallen. Then he looked round furtively to see if he had been observed, caught my eye, and giggled nervously.

'Been wanting to do that for a long time,' he said. 'Bet you don't know how many drops to the minute. I do, I counted.'

'I've no idea.'

'Guess. Tanner if you're wrong; half a dollar if you're right. That's fair.'

'Three,' I said.

'Coo, you're a sharp one. Been counting 'em yourself.' But he showed no inclination to pay this debt. Instead he said: 'How d'you figure this out. I'm an Englishman born and bred, but this is my first time on the Atlantic.'

'You flew out perhaps?'

'No, nor over it.'

'Then I presume you went round the world and came across the Pacific.'

'You *are* a sharp one and no mistake. I've made quite a bit getting into arguments over that one.'

'What was your route?' I asked, wishing to be agreeable.

'Ah, that'd be telling. Well, I must skedaddle. So long.'

'Charles,' said my wife, 'this is Mr Kramm, of Interastral Films.'

'So you are Mr Charles Ryder,' said Mr Kramm.

'Yes.'

'Well, well, well,' he paused. I waited. 'The purser here says we're heading for dirty weather. What d'you know about that?'

'Far less than the purser.'

'Pardon me, Mr Ryder, I don't quite get you.'

'I mean I know less than the purser.'

'Is that so? Well, well, well. I've enjoyed our talk very much. I hope that it will be the first of many.'

An Englishwoman said: 'Oh, that swan! Six weeks in America has given me an absolute phobia of ice. Do tell me, how did it feel meeting Celia again after two years? I know I should feel indecently bridal. But Celia's never quite got the orange blossom out of her hair, has she?'

Another woman said: 'Isn't it heaven saying good-bye and knowing we shall meet again in half an hour and go on meeting every half-hour for days?'

Our guests began to go, and each on leaving informed me of something my wife had promised to bring me to in the near future; it was the theme of the evening that we should all be seeing a lot of each other, that we had formed one of those molecular systems that physicists can illustrate. At last the swan was wheeled out, too, and I said to my wife, 'Julia never came.'

'No, she telephoned. I couldn't hear what she said, there was such a noise going on – something about a dress. Quite lucky really, there wasn't room for a cat. It was a lovely party, wasn't it? Did you hate it very much? You behaved beautifully and looked so distinguished. Who was your red-haired chum?'

'No chum of mine.'

'How *very* peculiar! Did you say anything to Mr Kramm about working in Hollywood?'

'Of course not.'

'Oh, Charles, you are a worry to me. It's not enough just to stand about looking distinguished and a martyr for Art. Let's go to dinner. We're at the Captain's table. I don't suppose he'll dine down tonight, but it's polite to be fairly punctual.'

By the time that we reached the table the rest of the party had arranged themselves. On either side of the Captain's empty chair sat Julia and Mrs Stuyvesant Oglander; besides them there was an English diplomat and his wife, Senator Stuyvesant Oglander, and an American clergyman at present totally isolated between two pairs of empty chairs. This clergyman later described himself – redundantly it seemed – as an Episcopalian Bishop. Husbands and wives sat together here. My wife was confronted with a quick decision, and although the steward attempted to direct us otherwise, sat so that she had the senator and I the Bishop. Julia gave us both a little dismal signal of sympathy.

'I'm miserable about the party,' she said, 'my beastly maid

totally disappeared with every dress I have. She only turned up half an hour ago. She'd been playing ping-pong.'

'I've been telling the Senator what he missed,' said Mrs Stuyvesant Oglander. 'Wherever Celia is, you'll find she knows all the significant people.'

'On my right,' said the Bishop, 'a significant couple are expected. They take all their meals in their cabin except when they have been informed in advance that the Captain will be present.'

We were a gruesome circle; even my wife's high social spirit faltered. At moments I heard bits of her conversation.

'... an extraordinary little red-haired man. Captain Foulenough in person.'

'But I understood you to say, Lady Celia, that you were unacquainted with him.'

'I meant he was *like* Captain Foulenough.'

'I begin to comprehend. He impersonated this friend of yours in order to come to your party.'

'No, no. Captain Foulenough is simply a comic character.'

'There seems to have been nothing very amusing about this other man. Your friend is a comedian?'

'No, no. Captain Foulenough is an imaginary character in an English paper. You know, like your "Popeye".'

The senator laid down knife and fork. 'To recapitulate: an imposter came to your party and you admitted him because of a fancied resemblance to a fictitious character in a cartoon.'

'Yes, I suppose that was it really.'

The senator looked at his wife as much as to say: 'Significant people, huh!'

I heard Julia across the table trying to trace, for the benefit of the diplomat, the marriage-connexions of her Hungarian and Italian cousins. The diamonds flashed in her hair and on her fingers, but her hands were nervously rolling little balls of crumb, and her starry head drooped in despair.

The Bishop told me of the goodwill mission on which he was travelling to Barcelona ... 'a very, very valuable work of clearance has been performed, Mr Ryder. The time has now come to rebuild on broader foundations. I have made it my aim to reconcile the so-called Anarchists and the so-called Communists, and with that in view I and my committee have digested all the available documentation of the subject. Our conclusion, Mr Ryder, is unanimous. There is *no* fundamental diversity between the two ideologies. It is a matter of personalities, Mr Ryder, and what personalities have put asunder personalities can unite. . . .'

On the other side I heard: 'And may I make so bold as to ask what institutions sponsored your husband's expedition?'

The diplomat's wife bravely engaged the Bishop across the gulf that separated them.

'And what language will you speak when you get to Barcelona?'

'The language of Reason and Brotherhood, madam,' and, turning back to me, 'The speech of the coming century is in thoughts not in words. Do you not agree, Mr Ryder?'

'Yes,' I said. 'Yes.'

'What are words?' said the Bishop.

'What indeed?'

'Mere conventional symbols, Mr Ryder, and this is an age rightly sceptical of conventional symbols.'

My mind reeled; after the parrot-house fever of my wife's party, and unplumbed emotions of the afternoon, after all the exertions of my wife's pleasures in New York, after the months of solitude in the steaming, green shadows of the jungle, this was too much. I felt like Lear on the heath, like the Duchess of Malfi bayed by madmen. I summoned cataracts and hurricanoes, and as if by conjury the call was immediately answered.

For some time now, though whether it was a mere trick of the nerves I did not then know, I had felt a recurrent and persistently growing motion – a heave and shudder of the large dining-room as of the breast of a man in deep sleep. Now my wife turned to me and said: 'Either I am a little drunk or it's getting rough,' and, even as she spoke we found ourselves leaning sideways in our chairs; there was a crash and tinkle of falling cutlery by the wall, and on our table the wine glasses all together toppled and rolled over, while each of us steadied the plate and forks and looked at the other with expressions that varied between frank horror in the diplomat's wife and relief in Julia.

The gale which, unheard, unseen, unfelt, in our enclosed and insulated world had, for an hour, been mounting over us, had now veered and fallen full on our bows.

Silence followed the crash, then a high, nervous babble of laughter. Stewards laid napkins on the pools of spilt wine. We tried to resume the conversation, but all were waiting, as the little ginger man had watched the drop swell and fall from the swan's beak, for the next great blow; it came, heavier than the last.

'This is where I say good night to you all,' said the diplomat's wife, rising.

Her husband led her to their cabin. The dining-room was emptying fast. Soon only Julia, my wife, and I were left at the table, and, telepathically, Julia said, 'Like King Lear.'

'Only each of us is all three of them.'

'What can you mean?' asked my wife.

'Lear, Kent, Fool.'

'Oh, dear, it's like that agonizing Foulenough conversation over again. Don't try and explain.'

'I doubt if I could,' I said.

Another climb, another vast drop. The stewards were at work making things fast, shutting things up, hustling away unstable ornaments.

'Well, we've finished dinner and set a fine example of British phlegm,' said my wife. 'Let's go and see what's on.'

Once, on our way to the lounge, we had all three to cling to a pillar; when we got there we found it almost deserted; the band played but no one danced; the tables were set for tombola but no one bought a card, and the ship's officer, who made a speciality of calling the numbers with all the patter of the lower deck – 'sweet sixteen and never been kissed – key of the door, twenty-one – clickety-click, sixty-six' – was idly talking to his colleagues; there were a score of scattered novel readers, a few games of bridge, some brandy drinking in the smoking-room, but all our guests of two hours before had disappeared.

The three of us sat for a little by the empty dance floor; my wife was full of schemes by which, without impoliteness, we could move to another table in the dining-room. 'It's crazy to go to the restaurant,' she said, 'and pay extra for exactly the same dinner. Only film people go there, anyway. I don't see why we should be made to.'

Presently she said: 'It's making my head ache and I'm tired, anyway. I'm going to bed.'

Julia went with her. I walked round the ship, on one of the covered decks where the wind howled and the spray leaped up from the darkness and smashed white and brown against the glass screen; men were posted to keep the passengers off the open decks. Then I, too, went below.

In my dressing-room everything breakable had been stowed away, the door to the cabin was hooked open, and my wife called plaintively from within.

'I feel terrible. I didn't know a ship of this size could pitch like this,' she said, and her eyes were full of consternation and resentment, like those of a woman who, at the end of her time, at length realizes that however luxurious the nursing home, and however well paid the doctor, her labour is inevitable; and the lift and fall of the ship came regularly as the pains of childbirth.

I slept next door; or, rather, I lay there between dreaming and waking. In a narrow bunk, on a hard mattress, there might have been rest, but here the beds were broad and buoyant; I collected what cushions I could find and tried to wedge myself firm, but through the night I turned with each swing and twist of the ship – she was rolling now as well as pitching – and my head rang with the creak and thud.

Once, an hour before dawn, my wife appeared like a ghost in the doorway, supporting herself with either hand on the jambs, saying: 'Are you awake? Can't you do something? Can't you get something from the doctor?'

I rang for the night steward, who had a draught ready prepared, which comforted her a little.

And all night between dreaming and waking I thought of Julia; in my brief dreams she took a hundred fantastic and terrible and obscene forms, but in my waking thoughts she returned with her sad, starry head just as I had seen her at dinner.

After first light I slept for an hour or two, then awoke clear-headed, with a joyous sense of anticipation.

The wind had dropped a little, the steward told me, but was still blowing hard and there was a very heavy swell; 'which there's nothing worse than a heavy swell', he said, 'for the enjoyment of the passengers. There's not many breakfasts wanted this morning.'

I looked in at my wife, found her sleeping, and closed the door between us; then I ate salmon kedgeree and cold Braden-ham ham and telephoned for a barber to come and shave me.

'There's a lot of stuff in the sitting-room for the lady,' said the steward; 'shall I leave it for the time?'

I went to see. There was a second delivery of cellophane parcels from the shops on board, some ordered by radio from friends in New York whose secretaries had failed to remind them of our departure in time, some by our guests as they left the cocktail party. It was no day for flower vases; I told him to leave them on the floor and then, struck by the thought, removed the card from Mr Kramm's roses and sent them with my love to Julia.

She telephoned while I was being shaved.

'What a deplorable thing to do, Charles! How unlike you!'

'Don't you like them?'

'What can I do with roses on a day like this?'

'Smell them.'

There was a pause and a rustle of unpacking. 'They've absolutely no smell at all.'

'What have you had for breakfast?'

'Muscat grapes and cantaloup.'

'When shall I see you?'

'Before lunch. I'm busy till then with a masseuse.'

'A masseuse?'

'Yes, isn't it peculiar? I've never had one before, except once when I hurt my shoulder hunting. What is it about being on a boat that makes everyone behave like a film star?'

'I don't.'

'How about these very embarrassing roses?'

The barber did his work with extraordinary dexterity – indeed, with agility, for he stood like a swordsman in a ballet sometimes on the point of one foot, sometimes on the other, lightly flicking the lather off his blade, and swooping back to my chin as the ship righted herself; I should not have dared use a safety razor on myself.

The telephone rang again.

It was my wife.

'How are you, Charles?'

'Tired.'

'Aren't you coming to see me?'

'I came once. I'll be in again.'

I brought her the flowers from the sitting-room; they completed the atmosphere of a maternity ward which she had managed to create in the cabin; the stewardess had the air of a midwife, standing by the bed, a pillar of starched linen and composure. My wife turned her head on the pillow and smiled wanly; she stretched out a bare arm and caressed with the tips of her fingers the cellophane and silk ribbons of the largest bouquet. 'How sweet people are,' she said faintly, as though the gale were a private misfortune of her own for which the world in its love was condoling with her.

'I take it you're not getting up.'

'Oh no, Mrs Clark is being so sweet'; she was always quick to get servants' names. 'Don't bother. Come in sometimes and tell me what's going on.'

'Now, now, dear,' said the stewardess, 'the less we are disturbed today the better.'

My wife seemed to make a sacred, female rite even of seasickness.

Julia's cabin, I knew, was somewhere below ours. I waited

for her by the lift on the main deck; when she came we walked
once round the promenade; I held the rail; she took my other
arm. It was hard going; through the streaming glass we saw a
distorted world of grey sky and black water. When the ship
rolled heavily I swung her round so that she could hold the rail
with her other hand; the howl of the wind was subdued, but the
whole ship creaked with strain. We made the circuit once, then
Julia said: 'It's no good. That woman beat hell out of me, and I
feel limp, anyway. Let's sit down.'

The great bronze doors of the lounge had torn away from
their hooks and were swinging free with the roll of the ship;
regularly and, it seemed, irresistibly, first one, then the other,
opened and shut; they paused at the completion of each half
circle, began to move slowly and finished fast with a resounding
clash. There was no real risk in passing them, except of slipping
and being caught by that swift, final blow; there was ample time
to walk through unhurried but there was something forbidding
in the sight of that great weight of uncontrolled metal, flapping
to and fro, which might have made a timid man flinch or skip
through too quickly; I rejoiced to feel Julia's hand perfectly
steady on my arm and know, as I walked beside her, that she
was wholly undismayed.

'Bravo,' said a man sitting nearby. 'I confess I went round
the other way. I didn't like the look of those doors somehow.
They've been trying to fix them all the morning.'

There were few people about that day, and that few seemed
bound together by a camaraderie of reciprocal esteem; they did
nothing except sit rather glumly in their armchairs, drink
occasionally, and exchange congratulations on not being
seasick.

'You're the first lady I've seen,' said the man.

'I'm very lucky.'

'*We* are very lucky,' he said, with a movement which began
as a bow and ended as a lurch forward to his knees, as the
blotting-paper floor dipped steeply between us. The roll carried
us away from him, clinging together but still on our feet, and we
quickly sat where our dance led us, on the further side, in

isolation; a web of life-lines had been stretched across the lounge, and we seemed like boxers, roped into the ring.

The steward approached. 'Your usual, sir? Whisky and tepid water, I think. And for the lady? Might I suggest a nip of champagne?'

'D'you know, the awful thing is I *would* like champagne very much,' said Julia. 'What a life of pleasure – roses, half an hour with a female pugilist, and now champagne!'

'I wish you wouldn't go on about the roses. It wasn't my idea in the first place. Someone sent them to Celia.'

'Oh, that's quite different. It lets you out completely. But it makes my massage worse.'

'I was shaved in bed.'

'I'm glad about the roses,' said Julia. 'Frankly, they were a shock. They made me think we were starting the day on the wrong foot.'

I knew what she meant, and in that moment felt as though I had shaken off some of the dust and grit of ten dry years; then and always, however she spoke to me, in half sentences, single words, stock phrases of contemporary jargon, in scarcely perceptible movements of eyes or lips or hands, however inexpressible her thought, however quick and far it had glanced from the matter in hand, however deep it had plunged, as it often did, straight from the surface to the depths, I knew; even that day when I still stood on the extreme verge of love, I knew what she meant.

We drank our wine and soon our new friend came lurching towards us down the life-line.

'Mind if I join you? Nothing like a bit of rough weather for bringing people together. This is my tenth crossing, and I've never seen anything like it. I can see you are an experienced sailor, young lady.'

'No. As a matter of fact, I've never been at sea before except coming to New York and, of course, crossing the Channel. I don't feel sick, thank God, but I feel tired. I thought at first it was only the massage, but I'm coming to the conclusion it's the ship.'

'My wife's in a terrible way. She's an experienced sailor. Only shows, doesn't it?'

He joined us at luncheon, and I did not mind his being there; he had clearly taken a fancy to Julia, and he thought we were man and wife; this misconception and his gallantry seemed in some way to bring her and me closer together. 'Saw you two last night at the Captain's table,' he said, 'with all the nobs.'

'Very dull nobs.'

'If you ask me, nobs always are. When you get a storm like this you find out what people are really made of.'

'You have a predilection for good sailors?'

'Well, put like that I don't know that I do – what I mean is, it makes for getting together.'

'Yes.'

'Take us for example. But for this we might never have met. I've had some very romantic encounters at sea in my time. If the lady will excuse me, I'd like to tell you about a little adventure I had in the Gulf of Lions when I was younger than I am now.'

We were both weary; lack of sleep, the incessant din, and the strain every movement required, wore us down. We spent that afternoon apart in our cabins. I slept and when I awoke the sea was as high as ever, inky clouds swept over us, and the glass streamed still with water, but I had grown used to the storm in my sleep, had made its rhythm mine, had become part of it, so that I arose strongly and confidently and found Julia already up and in the same temper.

'What d'you think?' she said. 'That man's giving a little "get-together party" tonight in the smoking-room for all the good sailors. He asked me to bring my husband.'

'Are we going?'

'Of course. ... I wonder if I ought to feel like the lady our friend met on the way to Barcelona. I don't, Charles, not a bit.'

There were eighteen people at the 'get-together party'; we had nothing in common except immunity from seasickness. We drank champagne, and presently our host said: 'Tell you what, I've got a roulette wheel. Trouble is we can't go to my cabin on account of the wife, and we aren't allowed to play in public.'

So the party adjourned to my sitting-room and we played for low stakes until late into the night, when Julia left and our host had drunk too much wine to be surprised that she and I were not in the same quarters. When all but he had gone, he fell asleep in his chair, and I left him there. It was the last I saw of him, for later – so the steward told me when he came from returning the roulette things to the man's cabin – he broke his thigh, falling in the corridor, and was taken to the ship's hospital.

All next day Julia and I spent together without interruption; talking, scarcely moving, held in our chairs by the swell of the sea. After luncheon the last hardy passengers went to rest and we were alone as though the place had been cleared for us, as though tact on a titanic scale had sent everyone tip-toeing out to leave us to one another.

The bronze doors of the lounge had been fixed, but not before two seamen had been badly injured. They had tried various devices, lashing with ropes and, later, when these failed, with steel hawsers, but there was nothing to which they could be made fast; finally, they drove wooden wedges under them, catching them in the brief moment of repose when they were full open, and these held firm.

When, before dinner, she went to her cabin to get ready (no one dressed that night) and I came with her, uninvited, unopposed, expected, and behind closed doors took her in my arms and first kissed her, there was no alteration from the mood of the afternoon. Later, turning it over in my mind, as I turned in my bed with the rise and fall of the ship, through the long, lonely, drowsy night, I recalled the courtships of the past, dead, ten years; how, knotting my tie before setting out, putting the gardenia in my button-hole, I would plan my evening and think at such and such a time, at such and such an opportunity, I shall cross the start-line and open my attack for better or worse; 'this phase of the battle has gone on long enough', I would think; 'a decision must be reached.' With Julia there were no phases, no start-line, no tactics at all.

But later that night when she went to bed and I followed her to her door, she stopped me.

'No, Charles, not yet. Perhaps never. I don't know. I don't know if I want love.'

Then something, some surviving ghost from those dead ten years – for one cannot die, even for a little, without some loss – made me say, 'Love? I'm not asking for love.'

'Oh yes, Charles, you are,' she said, and putting up her hand gently stroked my cheek; then shut her door.

And I reeled back, first on one wall, then on the other, of the long, softly lighted, empty corridor; for the storm, it appeared, had the form of a ring; all day we had been sailing through its still centre; now we were once more in the full fury of the wind – and that night was to be rougher than the one before.

Ten hours of talking: what had we to say? Plain fact mostly, the record of our two lives, so long widely separate, now being knit to one. Through all that storm-tossed night I rehearsed what she had told me; she was no longer the alternate succubus and starry vision of the night before; she had given all that was transferable of her past into my keeping. She told me, as I have already retold, of her courtship and marriage; she told me, as though fondly turning the pages of an old nursery-book, of her childhood, and I lived long, sunny days with her in the meadows, with Nanny Hawkins on her camp stool and Cordelia asleep in the pram, slept quiet nights under the dome with the religious pictures fading round the cot as the nightlight burned low and the embers settled in the grate. She told me of her life with Rex and of the secret, vicious, disastrous escapade that had taken her to New York. She, too, had had her dead years. She told me of her long struggle with Rex as to whether she should have a child; at first she wanted one, but learned after a year that an operation was needed to make it possible; by that time Rex and she were out of love, but he still wanted his child, and when at last she consented, it was born dead.

'Rex has never been unkind to me intentionally,' she said. 'It's just that he isn't a real person at all; he's just a few faculties of a man highly developed; the rest simply isn't there. He couldn't imagine why it hurt me to find two months after we came back to London from our honeymoon, that he was still keeping up with Brenda Champion.'

'I was glad when I found Celia was unfaithful,' I said. 'I felt it was all right for me to dislike her.'

'Is she? Do you? I'm glad. I don't like her either. Why did you marry her?'

'Physical attraction. Ambition. Everyone agrees she's the ideal wife for a painter. Loneliness, missing Sebastian.'

'You loved him, didn't you?'

'Oh yes. He was the forerunner.'

Julia understood.

The ship creaked and shuddered, rose and fell. My wife called to me from the next room: 'Charles, are you there?'

'Yes.'

'I've been asleep such a long while. What time is it?'

'Half past three.'

'It's no better, is it?'

'Worse.'

'I feel a little better, though. D'you think they'd bring me some tea or something if I rang the bell?'

I got her some tea and biscuits from the night steward.

'Did you have an amusing evening?'

'Everyone's seasick.'

'Poor Charles. It was going to have been such a lovely trip, too. It may be better tomorrow.'

I turned out the light and shut the door between us.

Waking and dreaming, through the strain and creak and heave of the long night, firm on my back with my arms and legs spread wide to check the roll, and my eyes open to the darkness, I lay thinking of Julia.

'... We thought papa might come back to England after mummy died, or that he might marry again, but he lives just as he did. Rex and I often go to see him now. I've grown fond of him. ... Sebastian's disappeared completely ... Cordelia's in Spain with an ambulance ... Bridey leads his own extraordinary life. He wanted to shut Brideshead after mummy died, but papa wouldn't have it for some reason, so Rex and I live there now, and Bridey has two rooms up in the dome, next to Nanny Hawkins, part of the old nurseries. He's like a character from Chekhov. One meets him sometimes coming out of the library or on the stairs – I never know when he's at home – and now and then he suddenly comes in to dinner like a ghost quite unexpectedly.

'... Oh, Rex's parties! Politics and money. They can't do anything except for money; if they walk round the lake they have to make bets about how many swans they see ... sitting up till two, amusing Rex's girls, hearing them gossip, rattling away endlessly on the backgammon board while the men play cards and smoke cigars. The cigar smoke. I can smell it in my hair when I wake up in the morning; it's in my clothes when I dress at night. Do I smell of it now? D'you think that woman who rubbed me, felt it in my skin?

'... At first I used to stay away with Rex in his friends' houses. He doesn't make me any more. He was ashamed of me when he found I didn't cut the kind of figure he wanted, ashamed of himself for having been taken in. I wasn't at all the article he'd bargained for. He can't see the point of me, but whenever he's made up his mind there isn't a point and he's begun to feel comfortable, he gets a surprise – some man, or even woman, he respects, takes a fancy to me and he suddenly sees that there is a whole world of things we understand and he doesn't ... he was upset when I went away. He'll be delighted to have me back. I was faithful to him until this last thing came along. There's nothing like a good upbringing. Do you know last year, when I thought I was going to have a child, I'd decided to have it brought up a Catholic? I hadn't thought about religion before; I haven't since; but just at that time, when I was waiting for the birth, I thought, "That's one thing I can give her. It doesn't seem to have done me much good, but my child shall have it." It was odd, wanting to give something one had lost oneself. Then, in the end, I couldn't even give that: I couldn't even give her life. I never saw her; I was too ill to know what was going on, and afterwards, for a long time, until now, I didn't want to speak about her – she was a daughter, so Rex didn't so much mind her being dead.

'I've been punished a little for marrying Rex. You see, I can't get all that sort of thing out of my mind, quite – Death, Judgement, Heaven, Hell, Nanny Hawkins, and the catechism. It becomes part of oneself, if they give it one early enough. And yet I wanted my child to have it ... now I suppose I shall be punished for what I've just done. Perhaps that is why you and I are here together like this ... part of a plan.'

That was almost the last thing she said to me – 'part of a plan' – before we went below and I left her at the cabin door.

Next day the wind had again dropped, and again we were wallowing in the swell. The talk was less of seasickness now than of broken bones; people had been thrown about in the night, and there had been many nasty accidents on bathroom floors.

That day, because we had talked so much the day before and because what we had to say needed few words, we spoke little. We had books; Julia found a game she liked. When after long silences we spoke, our thoughts, we found, had kept pace together side by side.

Once I said, 'You are standing guard over your sadness.'

'It's all I have earned. You said yesterday. My wages.'

'An I.O.U. from life. A promise to pay on demand.'

Rain ceased at midday; at evening the clouds dispersed and the sun, astern of us, suddenly broke into the lounge where we sat, putting all the lights to shame.

'Sunset,' said Julia, 'the end of our day.'

She rose and, though the roll and pitch of the ship seemed unabated, led me up to the boat-deck. She put her arm through mine and her hand into mine, in my great-coat pocket. The deck was dry and empty, swept only by the wind of the ship's speed. As we made our halting, laborious way forward, away from the flying smuts of the smoke stack, we were alternately jostled together, then strained, nearly sundered, arms and fingers interlocked as I held the rail and Julia clung to me, thrust together again, drawn apart; then, in a plunge deeper than the rest, I found myself flung across her, pressing her against the rail, warding myself off her with the arms that held her prisoner on either side, and as the ship paused at the end of its drop as though gathering strength for the ascent, we stood thus embraced, in the open, cheek against cheek, her hair blowing across my eyes; the dark horizon of tumbling water, flashing now with gold, stood still above us, then came sweeping down till I was staring through Julia's dark hair into a wide and golden sky, and she was thrown forward on my heart, held up by my hands on the rail, her face still pressed to mine.

In that minute, with her lips to my ear and her breath warm in the salt wind, Julia said, though I had not spoken, 'Yes, now,' and as the ship righted herself and for the moment ran into calmer waters, Julia led me below.

It was no time for the sweets of luxury; they would come, in their season, with the swallow and the lime flowers. Now on the rough water there was a formality to be observed, no more. It was as though a deed of conveyance of her narrow loins had been drawn and sealed. I was making my first entry as the freeholder of a property I would enjoy and develop at leisure.

We dined that night high up in the ship, in the restaurant, and saw through the bow windows the stars come out and sweep across the sky as once, I remembered, I had seen them sweep above the towers and gables of Oxford. The stewards promised that tomorrow night the band would play again and the place be full. We had better book now, they said, if we wanted a good table.

'Oh dear,' said Julia, 'where can we hide in fair weather, we orphans of the storm?'

I could not leave her that night, but early next morning, as once again I made my way back along the corridor, I found I could walk without difficulty; the ship rode easily on a smooth sea, and I knew that our solitude was broken.

My wife called joyously from her cabin: 'Charles, Charles, I feel so well. What do you think I am having for breakfast?'

I went to see. She was eating a beefsteak.

'I've fixed up for a visit to the hairdresser – do you know they couldn't take me till four o'clock this afternoon, they're so busy suddenly? So I shan't appear till the evening, but lots of people are coming in to see us this morning, and I've asked Miles and Janet to lunch with us in our sitting-room. I'm afraid I've been a worthless wife to you the last two days. What have you been up to?'

'One gay evening', I said, 'we played roulette till two o'clock, next door in the sitting-room, and our host passed out.'

'Goodness. It sounds very disreputable. Have you been behaving, Charles? You haven't been picking up sirens?'

'There was scarcely a woman about. I spent most of the time with Julia.'

'Oh, good. I always wanted to bring you together. She's one of my friends I knew you'd like. I expect you were a godsend to her. She's had rather a gloomy time lately. I don't expect she mentioned it, but ...' my wife proceeded to relate a current version of Julia's journey to New York. 'I'll ask her to cocktails this morning,' she concluded.

Julia came among the others, and it was happiness enough, now merely to be near her.

'I hear you've been looking after my husband for me,' my wife said.

'Yes, we've become very matey. He and I and a man whose name we don't know.'

'Mr Kramm, what have you done to your arm?'

'It was the bathroom floor,' said Mr Kramm, and explained at length how he had fallen.

That night the captain dined at his table and the circle was complete, for claimants came to the chairs on the Bishop's right, two Japanese who expressed deep interest in his projects for world-brotherhood. The captain was full of chaff at Julia's endurance in the storm, offering to engage her as a seaman; years of sea-going had given him jokes for every occasion. My wife, fresh from the beauty parlour, was unmarked by her three days of distress, and in the eyes of many seemed to outshine

Julia, whose sadness had gone and been replaced by an incommunicable content and tranquillity; incommunicable save to me; she and I, separated by the crowd, sat alone together close enwrapped, as we had lain in each other's arms the night before.

There was a gala spirit in the ship that night. Though it meant rising at dawn to pack, everyone was determined that for this one night he would enjoy the luxury the storm had denied him. There was no solitude. Every corner of the ship was thronged; dance music and high, excited chatter, stewards darting everywhere with trays of glasses, the voice of the officer in charge of tombola – 'Kelly's eye – number one; legs, eleven; and we'll Shake the Bag' – Mrs Stuyvesant Oglander in a paper cap, Mr Kramm and his bandages, the two Japanese decorously throwing paper streamers and hissing like geese.

I did not speak to Julia, alone, all that evening.

We met for a minute next day on the starboard side of the ship while everyone else crowded to port to see the officials come aboard and to gaze at the green coastline of Devon.

'What are your plans?'

'London for a bit,' she said.

'Celia's going straight home. She wants to see the children.'

'You, too?'

'No.'

'In London then.'

'Charles, the little red-haired man – Foulenough. Did you see? Two plain clothes police have taken him off.'

'I missed it. There was such a crowd on that side of the ship.'

'I found out the trains and sent a telegram. We shall be home by dinner. The children will be asleep. Perhaps we might wake Johnjohn up, just for once.'

'You go down,' I said. 'I shall have to stay in London.'

'Oh, but Charles, you *must* come. You haven't seen Caroline.'

'Will she change much in a week or two?'

'Darling, she changes every day.'

'Then what's the point of seeing her now? I'm sorry, my dear, but I must get the pictures unpacked and see how they've travelled. I must fix up for the exhibition right away.'

'Must you?' she said, but I knew that her resistance ended when I appealed to the mysteries of my trade. 'It's very disappointing. Besides, I don't know if Andrew and Cynthia will be out of the flat. They took it till the end of the month.'

'I can go to an hotel.'

'But that's so grim. I can't bear you to be alone your first night home. I'll stay and go down tomorrow.'

'You mustn't disappoint the children.'

'No.' Her children, my art, the two mysteries of our trades.

'Will you come for the week-end?'

'If I can.'

'All British passports to the smoking-room, please,' said a steward.

'I've arranged with that sweet Foreign Office man at our table to get us off early with him,' said my wife.

CHAPTER II

IT was my wife's idea to hold the private view on Friday.

'We are out to catch the critics this time,' she said. 'It's high time they began to take you seriously, and they know it. This is their chance. If you open on Monday, they'll most of them have just come up from the country, and they'll dash off a few paragraphs before dinner – I'm only worrying about the weeklies of course. If we give them the week-end to think about it, we shall have them in an urbane Sunday-in-the-country mood. They'll settle down after a good luncheon, tuck up their cuffs, and turn out a nice, leisurely full-length essay, which they'll reprint later in a nice little book. Nothing less will do this time.'

She was up and down from the Old Rectory several times during the month of preparation, revising the list of invitations and helping with the hanging.

On the morning of the private view I telephoned to Julia

and said: 'I'm sick of the pictures already and never want to see them again, but I suppose I shall have to put in an appearance.'

'D'you want me to come?'

'I'd much rather you didn't.'

'Celia sent a card with "Bring everyone" written across it in green ink. When do we meet?'

'In the train. You might pick up my luggage.'

'If you'll have it packed soon I'll pick you up, too, and drop you at the gallery. I've got a fitting next door at twelve.'

When I reached the gallery my wife was standing looking through the window to the street. Behind her half a dozen unknown picture-lovers were moving from canvas to canvas, catalogue in hand; they were people who had once bought a wood-cut and were consequently on the gallery's list of patrons.

'No one has come yet,' said my wife. 'I've been here since ten and it's been very dull. Whose car was that you came in?'

'Julia's.'

'Julia's? Why didn't you bring her in? Oddly enough, I've just been talking about Brideshead to a funny little man who seemed to know us very well. He said he was called Mr Samgrass. Apparently he's one of Lord Copper's middle-aged young men on the *Daily Beast*. I tried to feed him some paragraphs, but he seemed to know more about you than I do. He said he'd met me years ago at Brideshead. I wish Julia had come in; then we could have asked her about him.'

'I remember him well. He's a crook.'

'Yes, that stuck out a mile. He's been talking all about what he calls the "Brideshead set". Apparently Rex Mottram has made the place a nest of party mutiny. Did you know? What would Teresa Marchmain have thought?'

'I'm going there tonight.'

'Not tonight, Charles; you can't go there *tonight*. You're expected at home. You promised, as soon as the exhibition was ready, you'd come home. Johnjohn and Nanny have made a banner with "Welcome" on it. And you haven't seen Caroline yet.'

'I'm sorry, it's all settled.'

'Besides, Daddy will think it so odd. And Boy is home for Sunday. And you haven't seen the new studio. You can't go tonight. Did they ask me?'

'Of course; but I knew you wouldn't be able to come.'

'I can't now. I could have, if you'd let me know earlier. I should adore to see the "Brideshead set" at home. I do think you're perfectly beastly, but this is no time for a family rumpus. The Clarences promised to come in before luncheon; they may be here any minute.'

We were interrupted, however, not by royalty, but by a woman reporter from one of the dailies, whom the manager of the gallery now led up to us. She had not come to see the pictures but to get a 'human story' of the dangers of my journey. I left her to my wife, and next day read in her paper: *Charles "Stately Homes" Ryder steps off the map. That the snakes and vampires of the jungle have nothing on Mayfair is the opinion of socialite artist Ryder, who has abandoned the houses of the great for the ruins of equatorial Africa. ...*'

The rooms began to fill and I was soon busy being civil. My wife was everywhere, greeting people, introducing people, deftly transforming the crowd into a party. I saw her lead friends forward one after another to the subscription list that had been opened for the book of *Ryder's Latin America*; I heard her say: 'No, darling, I'm not at all surprised, but you wouldn't expect *me* to be, would you? You see Charles lives for one thing – Beauty. I think he got bored with finding it ready-made in England; he had to go and create it for himself. He wanted new worlds to conquer. After all, he has said the last word about country houses, hasn't he? Not, I mean, that he's given that up altogether. I'm sure he'll always do one or two more for *friends*.'

A photographer brought us together, flashed a lamp in our faces, and let us part.

Presently there was the slight hush and edging away which follows the entry of a royal party. I saw my wife curtsey and heard her say: 'Oh, sir, you are sweet'; then I was led into the clearing and the Duke of Clarence said: 'Pretty hot out there I should think.'

'It was, sir.'

'Awfully clever the way you've hit off the impression of heat. Makes me feel quite uncomfortable in my great-coat.'

'Ha, ha.'

When they had gone my wife said: 'Goodness, we're late for lunch. Margot's giving a party in your honour,' and in the taxi she said: 'I've just thought of something. Why don't you write and ask the Duchess of Clarence's permission to dedicate *Latin America* to her?'

'Why should I?'

'She'd love it so.'

'I wasn't thinking of dedicating it to anyone.'

'There you are; that's typical of you, Charles. Why miss an opportunity to give pleasure?'

There were a dozen at luncheon, and though it pleased my hostess and my wife to say that they were there in my honour, it was plain to me that half of them did not know of my exhibition and had come because they had been invited and had no other engagement. Throughout luncheon they talked, without stopping, of Mrs Simpson, but they all, or nearly all, came back with us to the gallery.

The hour after luncheon was the busiest time. There were representatives of the Tate Gallery and the National Art Collections Fund, who all promised to return shortly with colleagues and, in the meantime, reserved certain pictures for further consideration. The most influential critic, who in the past had dismissed me with a few wounding commendations, peered out at me from between his slouch hat and woollen muffler, gripped my arm, and said: 'I knew you had it. I saw it there. I've been waiting for it.'

From fashionable and unfashionable lips alike I heard fragments of praise. 'If you'd asked me to guess,' I overheard, 'Ryder's is the last name would have occurred to me. They're so virile, so passionate.'

They all thought they had found something new. It had not been thus at my last exhibition in these same rooms, shortly before my going abroad. Then there had been an unmistakable note of weariness. Then the talk had been less of me than of the houses, anecdotes of their owners. That same woman, it came back to me, who now applauded my virility and passion, had stood quite near me, before a painfully laboured canvas, and said, 'So facile'.

I remembered the exhibition, too, for another reason; it was the week I detected my wife in adultery. Then, as now, she was a tireless hostess, and I heard her say: 'Whenever I see anything lovely nowadays – a building or a piece of scenery – I think to myself, "that's by Charles". I see everything through his eyes. He *is* England to me.'

I heard her say that; it was the sort of thing she had the habit of saying. Throughout our married life, again and again, I had felt my bowels shrivel within me at the things she said. But that day, in this gallery, I heard her unmoved, and suddenly realized that she was powerless to hurt me any more; I was a free man; she had given me my manumission in that brief, sly lapse of hers; my cuckold's horns made me lord of the forest.

At the end of the day my wife said: 'Darling, I must go. It's been a terrific success, hasn't it? I'll think of something to tell them at home, but I wish it hadn't got to happen quite this way.'

'So she knows,' I thought. 'She's a sharp one. She's had her nose down since luncheon and picked up the scent.'

I let her get clear of the place and was about to follow – the rooms were nearly empty – when I heard a voice at the turnstile I had not heard for many years, an unforgettable self-taught stammer, a sharp cadence of remonstration.

'No. I have *not* brought a card of invitation. I do not even know whether I received one. I have not come to a social function; I do not seek to scrape acquaintance with Lady Celia; I do not want my photograph in the *Tatler*; I have not come to exhibit myself. I have come to see the *pictures*. Perhaps you are unaware that there are any pictures here. I happen to have a personal interest in the *artist* – if that word has any meaning for you.'

'Antoine,' I said, 'come in.'

'My dear, there is a g-g-gorgon here who thinks I am g-g-gate-crashing. I only arrived in London yesterday, and heard quite by chance at luncheon that you were having an exhibition, so of course I dashed impetuously to the shrine to pay homage. Have I changed? Would you recognize me? Where are the pictures? Let me explain them to you.'

Anthony Blanche had not changed from when I last saw him; not, indeed, from when I first saw him. He swept lightly across the room to the most prominent canvas – a jungle landscape – paused a moment, his head cocked like a knowing terrier, and asked: 'Where, my dear Charles, did you find this sumptuous greenery? The corner of a hothouse at T-t-trent or T-t-tring? What gorgeous usurer nurtured these fronds for your pleasure?'

Then he made a tour of the two rooms; once or twice he sighed deeply, otherwise he kept silence. When he came to the end he sighed once more, more deeply than ever, and said: 'But they tell me, my dear, you are happy in love. That is everything, is it not, or nearly everything?'

'Are they as bad as that?'

Anthony dropped his voice to a piercing whisper: 'My dear, let us not expose your little imposture before these good, plain people' – he gave a conspiratorial glance to the last remnants of the crowd – 'let us not spoil their innocent pleasure. We know, you and I, that this is all t-t-terrible t-t-tripe. Let us go, before we offend the connoisseurs. I know of a *louche* little bar quite near here. Let us go there and talk of your other c-c-conquests.'

It needed this voice from the past to recall me; the indiscriminate chatter of praise all that crowded day had worked on me like a succession of advertisement hoardings on a long road, kilometre after kilometre between the poplars, commanding one to stay at some new hotel, so that when at the end of the drive, stiff and dusty, one arrives at the destination, it seems inevitable to turn into the yard under the name that had first bored, then angered one, and finally become an inseparable part of one's fatigue.

Anthony led me from the gallery and down a side street to a door between a disreputable newsagent and a disreputable chemist, painted with the words 'Blue Grotto Club. Members only.'

'Not quite your milieu, my dear, but mine, I assure you. After all, you have been in your milieu all day.'

He led me downstairs, from a smell of cats to a smell of gin and cigarette-ends and the sound of a wireless.

'I was given the address by a dirty old man in the Boeuf sur le Toit. I am most grateful to him. I have been out of England so long, and really sympathetic little joints like this change so fast. I presented myself here for the first time yesterday evening, and already I feel *quite* at home. Good evening, Cyril.'

' 'Lo, Toni, back again?' said the youth behind the bar.

'We will take our drinks and sit in a corner. You must remember, my dear, that *here* you are just as conspicuous and, may I say, abnormal, my dear, as I should be in B-b-bratt's.'

The place was painted cobalt; there was cobalt linoleum on the floor. Fishes of silver and gold paper had been pasted haphazard on ceiling and walls. Half a dozen youths were drinking and playing with the slot-machines; an older, natty, crapulous-looking man seemed to be in control; there was some sniggering round the fruit-gum machine; then one of the youths came up to us and said, 'Would your friend care to rhumba?'

'No, Tom, he would *not*, and I'm not going to give you a drink; not yet, anyway. That's a very impudent boy, a regular little gold-digger, my dear.'

'Well,' I said, affecting an ease I was far from feeling in that den, 'what have you been up to all these years?'

'My dear, it is what *you* have been up to that we are here to talk about. I've been watching you, my dear. I'm a faithful old body and I've kept my eye on you.' As he spoke the bar and the bar-tender, the blue wicker furniture, the gambling-machines, the gramophone, the couple of youths dancing on the oilcloth, the youths sniggering round the slots, the purple-veined, stiffly-dressed elderly man drinking in the corner opposite us, the whole drab and furtive joint seemed to fade, and I was back in

Oxford looking out over Christ Church meadow through a window of Ruskin-Gothic. 'I went to your first exhibition,' said Anthony; 'I found it – charming. There was an interior of Marchmain House, very English, very correct, but quite delicious. "Charles has done something," I said; "not all he will do, not all he can do, but something."

'Even then, my dear, I wondered a little. It seemed to me that there was something a little *gentlemanly* about your painting. You must remember I am not English; I cannot understand this keen zest to be well-bred. English snobbery is more macabre to me even than English morals. However, I said, "Charles has done something delicious. What will he do next?"

'The next thing I saw was your very handsome volume – *Village and Provincial Architecture*, was it called? Quite a tome, my dear, and what did I find? Charm again. "Not quite my cup of tea," I thought; "this is too English." I have the fancy for rather spicy things, you know, not for the shade of the cedar tree, the cucumber sandwich, the silver cream-jug, the English girl dressed in whatever English girls do wear for tennis – not that, not Jane Austen, *not* M-m-miss M-m-mitford. Then, to be frank, dear Charles, I despaired of you. "I am a degenerate old d-d-dago," I said "and Charles – I speak of your art, my dear – is a dean's daughter in flowered muslin."

'Imagine then my excitement at luncheon today. Everyone was talking about you. My hostess was a friend of my mother's, a Mrs Stuyvesant Oglander; a friend of yours, too, my dear. Such a frump! Not at all the society I imagined you to keep. However, they had all been to your exhibition, but it was *you* they talked of, how you had broken away, my dear, gone to the tropics, become a Gauguin, a Rimbaud. You can imagine how my old heart leaped.

' "Poor Celia," they said, "after all she's done for him." "He owes everything to her. It's too bad." "And with Julia," they said, "after the way she behaved in America." "Just as she was going back to Rex."

' "But the pictures," I said; "Tell me about *them*."

' "Oh, the pictures," they said; "they're most peculiar."

"Not at all what he usually does." "Very forceful." "Quite barbaric." "I call them downright unhealthy," said Mrs Stuyvesant Oglander.

'My dear, I could hardly keep still in my chair. I wanted to dash out of the house and leap in a taxi and say, "Take me to Charles's unhealthy pictures." Well, I went, but the gallery after luncheon was so full of absurd women in the sort of hats they should be made to *eat*, that I rested a little – I rested here with Cyril and Tom and these saucy boys. Then I came back at the unfashionable time of five o'clock, all agog, my dear; and what did I find? I found, my dear, a very naughty and very successful practical joke. It reminded me of dear Sebastian when he liked so much to dress up in false whiskers. It was charm again, my dear, simple, creamy English charm, playing tigers.'

'You're quite right,' I said.

'My dear, of course I'm right. I was right years ago – more years, I am happy to say, than either of us shows – when I *warned* you. I took you out to dinner to warn you of charm. I warned you expressly and in great detail of the Flyte family. Charm is the great English blight. It does not exist outside these damp islands. It spots and kills anything it touches. It kills love; it kills art; I greatly fear, my dear Charles, it has killed *you*.'

The youth called Tom approached us again. 'Don't be a tease, Toni; buy me a drink.' I remembered my train and left Anthony with him.

As I stood on the platform by the restaurant-car I saw my luggage and Julia's go past with Julia's sour-faced maid strutting beside the porter. They had begun shutting the carriage doors when Julia arrived, unhurried, and took her place in front of me. I had a table for two. This was a very convenient train; there was half an hour before dinner and half an hour after it; then, instead of changing to the branch line, as had been the rule in Lady Marchmain's day, we were met at the junction. It was night as we drew out of Paddington, and the glow of the town gave place first to the scattered lights of the suburbs, then to the darkness of the fields.

'It seems days since I saw you,' I said.

'Six hours; and we were together all yesterday. You look worn out.'

'It's been a day of nightmare – crowds, critics, the Clarences, a luncheon party at Margot's, ending up with half an hour's well-reasoned abuse of my pictures in a pansy bar. ... I think Celia knows about us.'

'Well, she had to know some time.'

'Everyone seems to know. My pansy friend had not been in London twenty-four hours before he'd heard.'

'Damn everybody.'

'What about Rex?'

'Rex isn't anybody at all,' said Julia; 'he just doesn't exist.'

The knives and forks jingled on the tables as we sped through the darkness; the little circle of gin and vermouth in the glasses lengthened to oval, contracted again, with the sway of the carriage, touched the lip, lapped back again, never spilt; I was leaving the day behind me. Julia pulled off her hat and tossed it into the rack above her, and shook her night-dark hair with a little sigh of ease – a sigh fit for the pillow, the sinking firelight, and a bedroom window open to the stars and the whisper of bare trees.

'It's great to have you back, Charles; like the old days.'

'Like the old days?' I thought.

Rex, in his early forties, had grown heavy and ruddy; he had lost his Canadian accent and acquired instead the hoarse, loud tone that was common to all his friends, as though their voices were perpetually strained to make themselves heard above a crowd, as though, with youth forsaking them, there was no time to wait the opportunity to speak, no time to listen, no time to reply; time for a laugh – a throaty mirthless laugh, the base currency of goodwill.

There were half a dozen of these friends in the Tapestry Hall: politicians; 'young Conservatives' in the early forties, with sparse hair and high blood-pressure; a Socialist from the coal-mines who had already caught their clear accents, whose cigars came to pieces on his lips, whose hand shook when he poured himself out a drink; a financier older than the rest, and, one might guess from the way they treated him, richer; a love-sick columnist, who alone was silent, gloating sombrely on the only woman of the party; a woman they called 'Grizel', a knowing rake whom, in their hearts, they all feared a little.

They all feared Julia, too, Grizel included. She greeted them and apologized for not being there to welcome them, with a formality which hushed them for a minute; then she came and sat with me near the fire, and the storm of talk arose once more and whirled about our ears.

'Of course, he can marry her and make her queen tomorrow.'

'We had our chance in October. Why didn't we send the Italian fleet to the bottom of Mare Nostrum? Why didn't we blow Spezia to blazes? Why didn't we land on Pantelleria?'

'Franco's simply a German agent. They tried to put him in to prepare air bases to bomb France. That bluff has been called, anyway.'

'It would make the monarchy stronger than it's been since Tudor times. The people are with him.'

'The Press are with him.'

'I'm with him.'

'Who cares about divorce now except a few old maids who aren't married, anyway?'

'If he has a show-down with the old gang, they'll just disappear like, like ...'

'Why didn't we close the canal? Why didn't we bomb Rome?'

'It wouldn't have been necessary. One firm note ...'

'One firm speech.'

'One show-down.'

'Anyway, Franco will soon be skipping back to Morocco. Chap I saw today just come from Barcelona. ...'

'... Chap just come from Fort Belvedere. ...'

'... Chap just come from the Palazzo Venezia. ...'

'All we want is a show-down.'

'A show-down with Baldwin.'

'A show-down with Hitler.'

'A show-down with the Old Gang.'

'... That I should live to see my country, the land of Clive and Nelson. ...'

'... *My* country of Hawkins and Drake.'

'... *My* country of Palmerston. ...'

'Would you very much mind not doing that?' said Grizel to the columnist, who had been attempting in a maudlin manner to twist her wrist; 'I don't happen to enjoy it.'

'I wonder which is the more horrible,' I said, 'Celia's Art and Fashion or Rex's Politics and Money.'

'Why worry about them?'

'Oh, my darling, why is it that love makes me hate the world? It's supposed to have quite the opposite effect. I feel as though all mankind, and God, too, were in a conspiracy against us.'

'They are, they are.'

'But we've got our happiness in spite of them; here and now, we've taken possession of it. They can't hurt us, can they?'

'Not tonight; not now.'

'Not for how many nights?'

CHAPTER III

'Do you remember,' said Julia, in the tranquil, lime-scented evening, 'do you remember the storm?'

'The bronze doors banging.'

'The roses in cellophane.'

'The man who gave the "get-together" party and was never seen again.'

'Do you remember how the sun came out on our last evening just as it has done today?'

It had been an afternoon of low cloud and summer squalls, so overcast that at times I had stopped work and roused Julia from the light trance in which she sat – she had sat so often;

I never tired of painting her, forever finding in her new wealth and delicacy – until at length we had gone early to our baths and, on coming down, dressed for dinner, in the last half-hour of the day, we found the world transformed; the sun had emerged; the wind had fallen to a soft breeze which gently stirred the blossom in the limes and carried its fragrance, fresh from the late rains, to merge with the sweet breath of box and the drying stone. The shadow of the obelisk spanned the terrace.

I had carried two garden cushions from the shelter of the colonnade and put them on the rim of the fountain. There Julia sat, in a tight little gold tunic and a white gown, one hand in the water idly turning an emerald ring to catch the fire of the sunset; the carved animals mounted over her dark head in a cumulus of green moss and glowing stone and dense shadow, and the waters round them flashed and bubbled and broke into scattered flames.

'. . . So much to remember,' she said. 'How many days have there been since then, when we haven't seen each other; a hundred, do you think?'

'Not so many.'

'Two Christmases' – those bleak, annual excursions into propriety. Boughton, home of my family, home of my cousin Jasper, with what glum memories of childhood I revisited its pitch-pine corridors and dripping walls! How querulously my father and I, seated side by side in my uncle's Humber, approached the avenue of Wellingtonias knowing that at the end of the drive we should find my uncle, my aunt, my Aunt Philippa, my cousin Jasper, and, of recent years, Jasper's wife and children; and besides them, perhaps already arrived, perhaps every moment expected, my wife and my children. This annual sacrifice united us; here among the holly and mistletoe and the cut spruce, the parlour games ritually performed, the brandy-butter and the Carlsbad plums, the village choir in the pitch-pine minstrels' gallery, gold twine and sprigged wrapping-paper, she and I were accepted, whatever ugly rumours had been afloat in the past year, as man and wife. 'We must keep it up, whatever it costs us, for the sake of the children,' my wife said.

'Yes, two Christmases. ... And the three days of good taste before I followed you to Capri.'

'Our first summer.'

'Do you remember how I hung about Naples, then followed, how we met by arrangement on the hill path and how flat it fell?'

'I went back to the villa and said, "Papa, who do you think has arrived at the hotel?" and he said, "Charles Ryder, I suppose." I said, "Why did you think of him?" and papa replied, "Cara came back from Paris with the news that you and he were inseparable. He seems to have a penchant for my children. However, bring him here; I think we have the room."'

'There was the time you had jaundice and wouldn't let me see you.'

'And when I had flu and you were afraid to come.'

'Countless visits to Rex's constituency.'

'And Coronation Week, when you ran away from London. Your goodwill mission to your father-in-law. The time you went to Oxford to paint the picture they didn't like. Oh, yes, quite a hundred days.'

'A hundred days wasted out of two years and a bit ... not a day's coldness or mistrust or disappointment.'

'Never that.'

We fell silent; only the birds spoke in a multitude of small, clear voices in the lime trees; only the waters spoke among their carved stones.

Julia took the handkerchief from my breast pocket and dried her hand; then lit a cigarette. I feared to break the spell of memories, but for once our thoughts had not kept pace together, for when at length Julia spoke, she said sadly: 'How many more? Another hundred?'

'A lifetime.'

'I want to marry you, Charles.'

'One day; why now?'

'War,' she said, 'this year, next year, sometime soon. I want a day or two with you of real peace.'

'Isn't this peace?'

The sun had sunk now to the line of woodland beyond the valley; all the opposing slope was already in twilight, but the lakes below us were aflame; the light grew in strength and splendour as it neared death, drawing long shadows across the pasture, falling full on the rich stone spaces of the house, firing the panes in the windows, glowing on cornices and colonnade and dome, spreading out all the stacked merchandise of colour and scent from earth and stone and leaf, glorifying the head and golden shoulders of the woman beside me.

'What do you mean by "peace", if not this?'

'So much more'; and then in a chill, matter-of-fact tone she continued: 'Marriage isn't a thing we can take when the impulse moves us. There must be a divorce – two divorces. We must make plans.'

'Plans, divorce, war – on an evening like this.'

'Sometimes,' said Julia, 'I feel the past and the future pressing so hard on either side that there's no room for the present at all.'

Then Wilcox came down the steps into the sunset to tell us that dinner was ready.

Shutters were up, curtains drawn, candles lit, in the Painted Parlour.

'Hullo, it's laid for three.'

'Lord Brideshead arrived half an hour ago, my lady. He sent a message would you please not wait dinner for him as he may be a little late.'

'It seems months since he was here last,' said Julia. 'What *does* he do in London?'

It was often a matter for speculation between us – giving birth to many fantasies, for Bridey was a mystery; a creature from underground; a hard-snouted, burrowing, hibernating animal who shunned the light. He had been completely without action in all his years of adult life; the talk of his going into the army and into parliament and into a monastery, had all come to nothing. All that he was known with certainty to have done –

and this because in a season of scant news it had formed the subject of a newspaper article entitled '*Peer's Unusual Hobby*' – was to form a collection of match-boxes; he kept them mounted on boards, card-indexed, yearly occupying a larger and larger space in his small house in Westminster. At first he was bashful about the notoriety which the newspaper caused, but later greatly pleased, for he found it the means of his getting into touch with other collectors in all parts of the world with whom he now corresponded and swapped duplicates. Other than this he was not known to have any interests. He remained Joint-Master of the Marchmain and hunted with them dutifully on their two days a week when he was at home; he never hunted with the neighbouring pack, who had the better country. He had no real zest for sport, and had not been out a dozen times that season; he had few friends; he visited his aunts; he went to public dinners held in the Catholic interest. At Brideshead he performed all unavoidable local duties, bringing with him to platform and fête and committee room his own thin mist of clumsiness and aloofness.

'There was a girl found strangled with a piece of barbed wire at Wandsworth last week,' I said, reviving an old fantasy.

'That must be Bridey. He is naughty.'

When we had been a quarter of an hour at the table, he joined us, coming ponderously into the room in the bottle-green velvet smoking suit which he kept at Brideshead and always wore when he was there. At thirty-eight he had grown heavy and bald, and might have been taken for forty-five.

'Well,' he said, 'well, only you two; I hoped to find Rex here.'

I often wondered what he made of me and of my continual presence; he seemed to accept me, without curiosity, as one of the household. Twice in the past two years he had surprised me by what seemed to be acts of friendship; that Christmas he had sent me a photograph of himself in the robes of a Knight of Malta, and shortly afterwards asked me to go with him to a dining club. Both acts had an explanation: he had had more copies of his portrait printed than he knew what to do with; he was proud of his club. It was a surprising association of men quite eminent in their professions who met once a month for an evening of ceremonious buffoonery; each had his sobriquet – Bridey was called 'Brother Grandee' – and a specially designed jewel worn like an order of chivalry, symbolizing it; they had club buttons for their waistcoats and an elaborate ritual for the introduction of guests; after dinner a paper was read and facetious speeches were made. There was plainly some competition to bring guests of distinction, and since Bridey had few friends, and since I was tolerably well known, I was invited. Even on that convivial evening I could feel my host emanating little magnetic waves of social uneasiness, creating, rather, a pool of general embarrassment about himself in which he floated with log-like calm.

He sat down opposite me and bowed his sparse, pink head over his plate.

'Well, Bridey. What's the news?'

'As a matter of fact,' he said, 'I have some news. But it can wait.'

'Tell us now.'

He made a grimace which I took to mean 'not in front of the servants', and said, 'How is the painting, Charles?'

'Which painting?'

'Whatever you have on the stocks.'

'I began a sketch of Julia, but the light was tricky all today.'

'Julia? I thought you'd done her before. I suppose it's a change from architecture, and much more difficult.'

His conversation abounded in long pauses during which his mind seemed to remain motionless; he always brought one back with a start to the exact point where he had stopped. Now after more than a minute he said: 'The world is full of different subjects.'

'Very true, Bridey.'

'If I were a painter,' he said, 'I should choose an entirely different subject every time; subjects with plenty of action in them like ...' Another pause. What, I wondered was coming? The Flying Scotsman? The Charge of the Light Brigade?

Henley Regatta? Then surprisingly he said: '. . . like Macbeth.' There was something supremely preposterous in the idea of Bridey as a painter of action pictures; he was usually preposterous yet somehow achieved a certain dignity by his remoteness and agelessness; he was still half-child, already half-veteran; there seemed no spark of contemporary life in him; he had a kind of massive rectitude and impermeability, an indifference to the world, which compelled respect. Though we often laughed at him, he was never wholly ridiculous; at times he was even formidable.

We talked of the news from central Europe until, suddenly cutting across this barren topic, Bridey asked: 'Where are mummy's jewels?'

'This was hers,' said Julia, 'and this. Cordelia and I had all her own things. The family jewels went to the bank.'

'It's so long since I've seen them – I don't know that I ever saw them all. What is there? Aren't there some rather famous rubies, someone was telling me?'

'Yes, a necklace. Mummy used often to wear it, don't you remember? And there are the pearls – she always had those out. But most of it stayed in the bank year after year. There are some hideous diamond fenders, I remember, and a Victorian diamond collar no one could wear now. There's a mass of good stones. Why?'

'I'd like to have a look at them some day.'

'I say, papa isn't going to pop them, is he? He hasn't got into debt again?'

'No, no, nothing like that.'

Bridey was a slow and copious eater. Julia and I watched him between the candles. Presently he said: 'If I was Rex' – his mind seemed full of such suppositions: 'If I was Archbishop of Westminster', 'If I was head of the Great Western Railway', 'If I was an actress', as though it were a mere trick of fate that he was none of these things, and he might awake any morning to find the matter adjusted – 'if I was Rex I should want to live in my constituency.'

'Rex says it saves four days' work a week not to.'

'I'm sorry he's not here. I have a little announcement to make.'

'Bridey, don't be so mysterious. Out with it.'

He made the grimace which seemed to mean 'not before the servants'.

Later when port was on the table and we three were alone Julia said: 'I'm not going till I hear the announcement.'

'Well,' said Bridey, sitting back in his chair and gazing fixedly at his glass. 'You have only to wait until Monday to see it in black and white in the newspapers. I am engaged to be married. I hope you are pleased.'

'Bridey. How ... how very exciting! Who to?'

'Oh, no one you know.'

'Is she pretty?'

'I don't think you would exactly call her pretty; 'comely' is the word I think of in her connexion. She is a big woman.'

'Fat?'

'No, big. She is called Mrs Muspratt; her Christian name is Beryl. I have known her for a long time, but until last year she had a husband; now she is a widow. Why do you laugh?'

'I'm sorry. It isn't the least funny. It's just so unexpected. Is she ... is she about your own age?'

'Just about, I believe. She has three children, the eldest boy has just gone to Ampleforth. She is not at all well off.'

'But, Bridey, where did you find her?'

'Her late husband, Admiral Muspratt, collected match-boxes,' he said with complete gravity.

Julia trembled on the verge of laughter, recovered her self-possession, and asked: 'You're not marrying her for her match-boxes?'

'No, no; the whole collection was left to the Falmouth Town Library. I have a great affection for her. In spite of all her difficulties she is a very cheerful woman, very fond of acting. She is connected with the Catholic Players' Guild.'

'Does papa know?'

'I had a letter from him this morning giving me his approval. He has been urging me to marry for some time.'

It occurred both to Julia and myself simultaneously that we were allowing curiosity and surprise to predominate; now we congratulated him in gentler tones from which mockery was almost excluded.

'Thank you,' he said, 'thank you. I think I am very fortunate.'

'But when are we going to meet her? I do think you might have brought her down with you.'

He said nothing, sipped and gazed.

'Bridey,' said Julia. 'You sly, smug old brute, why haven't you brought her here?'

'Oh, I couldn't do that, you know.'

'Why couldn't you? I'm dying to meet her. Let's ring her up now and invite her. She'll think us most peculiar leaving her alone at a time like this.'

'She has the children,' said Brideshead. 'Besides, you *are* peculiar, aren't you?'

'What can you mean?'

Brideshead raised his head and looked solemnly at his sister, and continued in the same simple way, as though he were saying nothing particularly different from what had gone before, 'I couldn't ask her here, as things are. It wouldn't be suitable. After all, I am a lodger here. This is Rex's house at the moment, so far as it's anybody's. What goes on here is his business. But I couldn't bring Beryl here.'

'I simply don't understand,' said Julia rather sharply. I looked at her. All the gentle mockery had gone; she was alert, almost scared, it seemed. 'Of course, Rex and I want her to come.'

'Oh, yes, I don't doubt that. The difficulty is quite otherwise.' He finished his port, refilled his glass, and pushed the decanter towards me. 'You must understand that Beryl is a woman of strict Catholic principle fortified by the prejudices of the middle class. I couldn't possibly bring her here. It is a matter of indifference whether you choose to live in sin with Rex or Charles or both – I have always avoided inquiry into the details of your *ménage* – but in no case would Beryl consent to be your guest.'

Julia rose. 'Why, you pompous ass . . .' she said, stopped, and turned towards the door.

At first I thought she was overcome by laughter; then, as I opened the door to her, I saw with consternation that she was in tears. I hesitated. She slipped past me without a glance.

'I may have given the impression that this was a marriage of convenience,' Brideshead continued placidly. 'I cannot speak for Beryl; no doubt the security of my position has some influence on her. Indeed, she has said as much. But for myself, let me emphasize, I am ardently attracted.'

'Bridey, what a bloody offensive thing to say to Julia!'

'There was nothing she should object to. I was merely stating a fact well known to her.'

She was not in the library; I mounted to her room, but she was not there. I paused by her laden dressing table wondering if she would come. Then through the open window, as the light streamed out across the terrace into the dusk, to the fountain which in that house seemed always to draw us to itself for comfort and refreshment, I caught the glimpse of a white skirt against the stones. It was nearly night. I found her in the darkest refuge, on a wooden seat, in a bay of the clipped box which encircled the basin. I took her in my arms and she pressed her face to my heart.

'Aren't you cold out here?'

She did not answer, only clung closer to me, and shook with sobs.

'My darling, what is it? Why do you mind? What does it matter what that old booby says?'

'I don't; it doesn't. It's just the shock. Don't laugh at me.'

In the two years of our love, which seemed a lifetime, I had not seen her so moved or felt so powerless to help.

'How dare he speak to you like that?' I said. 'The cold-blooded old humbug . . .' But I was failing her in sympathy.

'No,' she said, 'it's not that. He's quite right. They know all about it, Bridey and his widow; they've got it in black and white; they bought it for a penny at the church door. You can get anything there for a penny, in black and white, and nobody to see that you pay; only an old woman with a broom at the other end, rattling round the confessionals, and a young woman lighting a candle at the Seven Dolours. Put a penny in the box, or not, just as you like; take your tract. There you've got it, in black and white.

'All in one word, too, one little, flat, deadly word that covers a lifetime.

' "Living in Sin"; not just doing wrong, as I did when I went to America; doing wrong, knowing it is wrong, stopping doing it, forgetting. That's not what they mean. That's not Bridey's pennyworth. He means just what it says in black and white.

'*Living in sin*, with sin, always the same, like an idiot child carefully nursed, guarded from the world. "Poor Julia," they say, "she can't go out. She's got to take care of her sin. A pity it ever lived," they say, "but it's so strong. Children like that always are. Julia's so good to her little, mad sin." '

'An hour ago,' I thought, 'under the sunset, she sat turning her ring in the water and counting the days of happiness; now under the first stars and the last grey whisper of day, all this mysterious tumult of sorrow! What had happened to us in the Painted Parlour? What shadow had fallen in the candlelight? Two rough sentences and a trite phrase.' She was beside herself; her voice, now muffled in my breast, now clear and anguished, came to me in single words and broken sentences.

'Past and future; the years when I was trying to be a good wife, in the cigar smoke, while the counters clicked on the backgammon board, and the man who was "dummy" at the men's table filled the glasses; when I was trying to bear his child, torn in pieces by something already dead; putting him away, forgetting him, finding you, the past two years with you, all the future with you, all the future with or without you, war coming, world ending – sin.

'A word from so long ago, from Nanny Hawkins stitching by the hearth and the nightlight burning before the Sacred Heart. Cordelia and me with the catechism, in mummy's room, before luncheon on Sundays. Mummy carrying my sin with her to church, bowed under it and the black lace veil, in the chapel; slipping out with it in London before the fires were lit; taking it with her through the empty streets, where the milkman's ponies stood with their forefeet on the pavement; mummy dying with my sin eating at her, more cruelly than her own deadly illness.

'Mummy dying with it; Christ dying with it, nailed hand and foot; hanging over the bed in the night-nursery; hanging year after year in the dark little study at Farm Street with the shining oilcloth; hanging in the dark church where only the old charwoman raises the dust and one candle burns; hanging at noon, high among the crowds and the soldiers; no comfort except a sponge of vinegar and the kind words of a thief; hanging for ever; never the cool sepulchre and the grave clothes spread on the stone slab, never the oil and spices in the dark cave; always the midday sun and the dice clicking for the seamless coat.

'No way back; the gates barred; all the saints and angels posted along the walls. Thrown away, scrapped, rotting down; the old man with lupus and the forked stick who limps out at nightfall to turn the rubbish, hoping for something to put in his sack, something marketable, turns away with disgust.

'Nameless and dead, like the baby they wrapped up and took away before I had seen her.'

Between her tears she talked herself into silence. I could do nothing; I was adrift in a strange sea; my hands on the metal-spun threads of her tunic were cold and stiff, my eyes dry; I was as far from her in spirit, as she clung to me in the darkness, as when years ago I had lit her cigarette on the way from the station; as far as when she was out of mind, in the dry, empty years at the Old Rectory, and in the jungle.

Tears spring from speech; presently in her silence her weeping stopped. She sat up, away from me, took my handkerchief, shivered, rose to her feet.

'Well,' she said, in a voice much like normal. 'Bridey is one for bombshells, isn't he?'

I followed her into the house and to her room; she sat at her looking-glass. 'Considering that I've just recovered from a fit of hysteria,' she said, 'I don't call that at all bad.' Her eyes seemed unnaturally large and bright, her cheeks pale with two spots of high colour, where, as a girl, she used to put a dab of rouge. 'Most hysterical women look as if they had a bad cold. You'd better change your shirt before going down; it's all tears and lipstick.'

'Are we going down?'

'Of course, we mustn't leave poor Bridey on his engagement night.'

'When I went back to her she said: 'I'm sorry for that appalling scene, Charles. I can't explain.'

Brideshead was in the library, smoking his pipe, placidly reading a detective story.

'Was it nice out? If I'd known you were going I'd have come, too.'

'Rather cold.'

'I hope it's not going to be inconvenient for Rex moving out of here. You see, Barton Street is much too small for us and the three children. Besides, Beryl likes the country. In his letter papa proposed making over the whole estate right away.'

I remembered how Rex had greeted me on my first arrival at Brideshead as Julia's guest. 'A very happy arrangement,' he had said. 'Suits me down to the ground. The old boy keeps the place up; Bridey does all the feudal stuff with the tenants; I have the run of the house rent free. All it costs me is the food and the wages of the indoor servants. Couldn't ask fairer than that, could you?'

'I should think he'll be sorry to go,' I said.

'Oh, he'll find another bargain somewhere,' said Julia; 'trust him.'

'Beryl's got some furniture of her own she's very attached to. I don't know if it would go very well here. You know, oak dressers and coffin stools and things. I thought she could put it in mummy's old room.'

'Yes, that would be the place.'

So brother and sister sat and talked about the arrangement of the house until bedtime. 'An hour ago,' I thought, 'in the black refuge in the box hedge, she wept her heart out for the death of her God; now she is discussing whether Beryl's children shall take the old smoking-room or the school-room for their own.' I was all at sea.

'Julia,' I said later, when Brideshead had gone upstairs, 'have you ever seen a picture of Holman Hunt's called "The Awakened Conscience"?'

'No.'

I had seen a copy of *Pre-Raphaelitism* in the library some days before; I found it again and read her Ruskin's description. She laughed quite happily.

'You're perfectly right. That's exactly what I did feel.'

'But, darling, I won't believe that great spout of tears came just from a few words of Bridey's. You must have been thinking about it before.'

'Hardly at all; now and then; more, lately, with the Last Trump so near.'

'Of course it's a thing psychologists could explain; a precon-ditioning from childhood; feelings of guilt from the nonsense you were taught in the nursery. You do know at heart that it's all bosh, don't you?'

'How I wish it was!'

'Sebastian once said almost the same thing to me.'

'He's gone back to the Church, you know. Of course, he never left it as definitely as I did. I've gone too far; there's no turning back now; I know that, if that's what you mean by thinking it all bosh. All I can hope to do is to put my life in some sort of order in a human way, before all human order comes to an end. That's why I want to marry you. I should like to have a child. That's one thing I can do. ... Let's go out again. The moon should be up by now.'

The moon was full and high. We walked round the house; under the limes Julia paused and idly snapped off one of the long shoots, last year's growth, that fringed their boles, and stripped it as she walked, making a switch, as children do, but with petulant movements that were not a child's, snatching nervously at the leaves and crumbling them between her fingers; she began peeling the bark, scratching it with her nails.

Once more we stood by the fountain.

'It's like the setting of a comedy,' I said. 'Scene: a Baroque fountain in a nobleman's grounds. Act one, sunset; act two, dusk; act three, moonlight. The characters keep assembling at the fountain for no very clear reason.'

'Comedy?'

'Drama. Tragedy. Farce. What you will. This is the reconciliation scene.'

'Was there a quarrel?'

'Estrangement and misunderstanding in act two.'

'Oh, don't talk in that damned bounderish way. Why must you see everything second-hand? Why must this be a play? Why must my conscience be a pre-Raphaelite picture?'

'It's a way I have.'

'I hate it.'

Her anger was as unexpected as every change on this evening of swift veering moods. Suddenly she cut me across the face with her switch, a vicious, stinging little blow as hard as she could strike.

'Now do you see how I hate it?'

She hit me again.

'All right,' I said, 'go on.'

Then, though her hand was raised, she stopped and threw the half-peeled wand into the water, where it floated white and black in the moonlight.

'Did that hurt?'

'Yes.'

'Did it? ... Did I?'

In the instant her rage was gone; her tears, newly flowing, were on my cheek. I held her at arm's length and she put down her head, stroking my hand on her shoulder with her face, cat-like, but, unlike a cat, leaving a tear there.

'Cat on the roof-top,' I said.

'Beast!'

She bit at my hand, but when I did not move it and her

teeth touched me, she changed the bite to a kiss, the kiss to a lick of her tongue.

'Cat in the moonlight.'

This was the mood I knew. We turned towards the house. When we came to the lighted hall she said: 'Your poor face,' touching the weals with her fingers. 'Will there be a mark tomorrow?'

'I expect so.'

'Charles, am I going crazy? What's happened tonight? I'm so tired.'

She yawned; a fit of yawning took her. She sat at her dressing table, head bowed, hair over her face, yawning helplessly; when she looked up I saw over her shoulder in the glass a face that was dazed with weariness like a retreating soldier's, and beside it my own, streaked with two crimson lines.

'So tired,' she repeated, taking off her gold tunic and letting it fall to the floor, 'tired and crazy and good for nothing.'

I saw her to bed; the blue lids fell over her eyes; her pale lips moved on the pillow, but whether to wish me good night or to murmur a prayer – a jingle of the nursery that came to her now in the twilight world between sorrow and sleep: some ancient pious rhyme that had come down to Nanny Hawkins from centuries of bedtime whispering, through all the changes of language, from the days of pack-horses on the Pilgrim's Way – I did not know.

Next night Rex and his political associates were with us.

'They won't fight.'

'They can't fight. They haven't the money; they haven't the oil.'

'They haven't the wolfram; they haven't the men.'

'They haven't the guts.'

'They're afraid.'

'Scared of the French; scared of the Czechs; scared of the Slovaks; scared of us.'

'It's a bluff.'

'Of course it's a bluff. Where's their tungsten? Where's their manganese?'

'Where's their chrome?'

'I'll tell you a thing ...'

'Listen to this; it'll be good; Rex will tell you a thing.'

'... Friend of mine motoring in the Black Forest, only the other day, just came back and told me about it while we played a round of golf. Well, this friend driving along, turned down a lane into the high road. What should he find but a military convoy? Couldn't stop, drove right into it, smack into a tank, broadside on. Gave himself up for dead. ... Hold on, this is the funny part.'

'This is the funny part.'

'Drove clean through it, didn't scratch his paint. What do you think? It was made of canvas – a bamboo frame and painted canvas.'

'They haven't the steel.'

'They haven't the tools. They haven't the labour. They're half starving. They haven't the fats. The children have rickets.'

'The women are barren.'

'The men are impotent.'

'They haven't the doctors.'

'The doctors were Jewish.'

'Now they've got consumption.'

'Now they've got syphilis.'

'Goering told a friend of mine ...'

'Goebbels told a friend of mine ...'

'Ribbentrop told me that the army just kept Hitler in power so long as he was able to get things for nothing. The moment anyone stands up to him, he's finished. The army will shoot him.'

'The Liberals will hang him.'

'The Communists will tear him limb from limb.'

'He'll scupper himself.'

'He'd do it now if it wasn't for Chamberlain.'

'If it wasn't for Halifax.'

'If it wasn't for Sir Samuel Hoare.'

'And the 1922 Committee.'

'Peace Pledge.'

'Foreign Office.'

'New York Banks.'

'All that's wanted is a good strong line.'

'A line from Rex.'

'And a line from me.'

'We'll give Europe a good strong line. Europe is waiting for a speech from Rex.'

'And a speech from me.'

'And a speech from me. Rally the freedom-loving peoples of the world. Germany will rise; Austria will rise. The Czechs and the Slovaks are bound to rise.'

'To a speech from Rex and a speech from me.'

'What about a rubber? How about a whisky? Which of you chaps will have a big cigar? Hullo, you two going out?'

'Yes, Rex,' said Julia. 'Charles and I are going into the moonlight.'

We shut the windows behind us and the voices ceased; the moonlight lay like hoar-frost on the terrace and the music of the fountain crept in our ears; the stone balustrade of the terrace might have been the Trojan walls, and in the silent park might have stood the Grecian tents where Cressid lay that night.

'A few days, a few months.'

'No time to be lost.'

'A lifetime between the rising of the moon and its setting. Then the dark.'

CHAPTER IV

'And of course Celia will have custody of the children.'

'Of course.'

'Then what about the Old Rectory? I don't imagine you'll want to settle down with Julia bang at our gates. The children look on it as their home, you know. Robin's got no place of his own till his uncle dies. After all, you never used the studio, did you? Robin was saying only the other day what a good play-room it would make – big enough for Badminton.'

'Robin can have the Old Rectory.'

'Now with regard to money, Celia and Robin naturally don't want to accept anything for themselves, but there's the question of the children's education.'

'That will be all right. I'll see the lawyers about it.'

'Well, I think that's everything,' said Mulcaster. 'You know, I've seen a few divorces in my time, and I've never known one work out so happily for all concerned. Almost always, however matey people are at the start, bad blood crops up when they get down to detail. Mind you, I don't mind saying there have been times in the last two years when I thought you were treating Celia a bit rough. It's hard to tell with one's own sister, but I've always thought her a jolly attractive girl, the sort of girl any chap would be glad to have – artistic, too, just down your street. But I must admit you're a good picker. I've always had a soft spot for Julia. Anyway, as things have turned out everyone seems satisfied. Robin's been mad about Celia for a year or more. D'you know him?'

'Vaguely. A half-baked, pimply youth as I remember him.'

'Oh, I wouldn't quite say that. He's rather young, of course, but the great thing is that Johnjohn and Caroline adore him. You've got two grand kids there, Charles. Remember me to Julia; wish her all the best for old times' sake.'

'So you're being divorced,' said my father. 'Isn't that rather unnecessary, after you've been happy together all these years?'

'We weren't particularly happy, you know.'

'Weren't you? Were you not? I distinctly remember last Christmas seeing you together and thinking how happy you looked, and wondering why. You'll find it very disturbing, you know, starting off again. How old are you – thirty-four? That's no age to be starting. You ought to be settling down. Have you made any plans?'

'Yes. I'm marrying again as soon as the divorce is through.'

'Well, I do call that a lot of nonsense. I can understand a man wishing he hadn't married and trying to get out of it – though I never felt anything of the kind myself – but to get rid of one wife and take up with another immediately, is beyond all reason. Celia was always perfectly civil to me. I had quite a liking for her, in a way. If you couldn't be happy with her, why on earth should you expect to be happy with anyone else? Take my advice, my dear boy, and give up the whole idea.'

'Why bring Julia and me into this?' asked Rex. 'If Celia wants to marry again, well and good; let her. That's your business and hers. But I should have thought Julia and I were quite happy as we are. You can't say I've been difficult. Lots of chaps would have cut up nasty. I hope I'm a man of the world. I've had my own fish to fry, too. But a divorce is a different thing altogether; I've never known a divorce do anyone any good.'

'That's your affair and Julia's.'

'Oh, Julia's set on it. What I hoped was, you might be able to talk her round. I've tried to keep out of the way as much as I could; if I've been around too much, just tell me; I shan't mind. But there's too much going on altogether at the moment, what with Bridey wanting me to clear out of the house; it's disturbing, and I've got a lot on my mind.'

Rex's public life was approaching a climacteric. Things had not gone as smoothly with him as he had planned. I knew nothing of finance, but I heard it said that his dealings were badly looked on by orthodox Conservatives; even his good qualities of geniality and impetuosity counted against him, for his parties at Brideshead got talked about. There was always too much about him in the papers; he was one with the Press lords and their sad-eyed, smiling hangers-on; in his speeches he said the sort of thing which 'made a story' in Fleet Street, and that did him no good with his party chiefs; only war could put Rex's fortunes right and carry him into power. A divorce would do him no great harm; it was rather that with a big bank running he could not look up from the table.

'If Julia insists on a divorce, I suppose she must have it,' he said. 'But she couldn't have chosen a worse time. Tell her to hang on a bit, Charles, there's a good fellow.'

'Bridey's widow said: "So you're divorcing one divorced

man and marrying another. It sounds rather complicated, but my dear'' – she called me ''my dear'' about twenty times – ''I've usually found every Catholic family has one lapsed member, and it's often the nicest.'' '

Julia had just returned from a luncheon party given by Lady Rosscommon in honour of Brideshead's engagement.

'What's she like?'

'Majestic and voluptuous; common, of course; husky voice, big mouth, small eyes, dyed hair – I'll tell you one thing, she's lied to Bridey about her age. She's a good forty-five. I don't see her providing an heir. Bridey can't take his eyes off her. He was gloating on her in the most revolting way all through luncheon.'

'Friendly?'

'Goodness, yes, in a condescending way. You see, I imagine she's been used to bossing things rather in naval circles, with flag-lieutenants trotting round and young officers on-the-make sucking up to her. Well, she clearly couldn't do a great deal of bossing at Aunt Fanny's, so it put her rather at ease to have me there as the black sheep. She concentrated on me in fact, asked my advice about shops and things, said, rather pointedly, she hoped to see me often *in London*. I think Bridey's scruples only extend to her sleeping under the same roof with me. Apparently I can do her no serious harm in a hat-shop or hairdresser's or lunching at the Ritz. The scruples are all on Bridey's part, anyway; the widow is madly tough.'

'Does she boss him?'

'Not yet, much. He's in an amorous stupor, poor beast, and doesn't quite know where he is. She's just a good-hearted woman who wants a good home for her children and isn't going to let anything get in her way. She's playing up the religious stuff at the moment for all it's worth. I daresay she'll go easier when she's settled.'

The divorces were much talked of, among our friends; even in that summer of general alarm there were still corners where private affairs commanded first attention. My wife was able to make it understood that the business was at the same time a matter of congratulation for her and reproach for me; that she had behaved wonderfully, had stood it longer than anyone but she would have done. Robin was seven years younger and a little immature for his age, they whispered in their private corners, but he was absolutely devoted to poor Celia, and really she deserved it after all she had been through. As for Julia and me, that was an old story. 'To put it crudely,' said my cousin Jasper, as though he had ever in his life put anything otherwise: 'I don't see why you bother to marry.'

Summer passed; delirious crowds cheered Neville Chamberlain's return from Munich; Rex made a rabid speech in the House of Commons which sealed his fate one way or the other; sealed it, as is sometimes done with naval orders, to be opened later at sea. Julia's family lawyers, whose black, tin boxes, painted 'Marquis of Marchmain', seemed to fill a room, began the slow process of her divorce; my own, brisker firm, two doors down, were weeks ahead with my affairs. It was necessary for Rex and Julia to separate formally, and since, for the time being, Brideshead was still her home, she remained there and Rex removed his trunks and valet to their house in London. Evidence was taken against Julia and me in my flat. A date was fixed for Brideshead's wedding, early in the Christmas holidays, so that his future step-children might take part.

One afternoon in November Julia and I stood at a window in the drawing-room watching the wind at work stripping the lime trees, sweeping down the yellow leaves, sweeping them up and round and along the terrace and lawns, trailing them through puddles and over the wet grass, pasting them on walls and window-panes, leaving them at length in sodden piles against the stonework.

'We shan't see them in spring,' said Julia; 'perhaps never again.'

'Once before,' I said, 'I went away, thinking I should never return.'

'Perhaps years later, to what's left of it, with what's left of us . . .'

A door opened and shut in the darkling room behind us.

Wilcox approached through the firelight into the dusk about the long windows.

'A telephone message, my Lady, from Lady Cordelia.'

'Lady Cordelia! Where was she?'

'In London, my Lady.'

'Wilcox, how lovely! Is she coming home?'

'She was just starting for the station. She will be here after dinner.'

'I haven't seen her for twelve years,' I said – not since the evening when we dined together and she spoke of being a nun; the evening when I painted the drawing-room at Marchmain House. 'She was an enchanting child.'

'She's had an odd life. First, the convent; then, when that was no good, the war in Spain. I've not seen her since then. The other girls who went with the ambulance came back when the war was over; she stayed on, getting people back to their homes, helping in the prison-camps. An odd girl. She's grown up quite plain, you know.'

'Does she know about us?'

'Yes, she wrote me a sweet letter.'

It hurt to think of Cordelia growing up 'quite plain'; to think of all that burning love spending itself on serum-injections and de-lousing powder. When she arrived, tired from her journey, rather shabby, moving in the manner of one who has no interest in pleasing, I thought her an ugly woman. It was odd, I thought, how the same ingredients, differently dispensed, could produce Brideshead, Sebastian, Julia, and her. She was unmistakably their sister, without any of Julia's or Sebastian's grace, without Brideshead's gravity. She seemed brisk and matter-of-fact, steeped in the atmosphere of camp and dressing-station, so accustomed to gross suffering as to lose the finer shades of pleasure. She looked more than her twenty-six years; hard living had roughened her; constant intercourse in a foreign tongue had worn away the nuances of speech; she straddled a little as she sat by the fire, and when she said, 'It's wonderful to be home,' it sounded to my ears like the grunt of an animal returning to its basket.

Those were the impressions of the first half hour, sharpened by the contrast with Julia's white skin and silk and jewelled hair and with my memories of her as a child.

'My job's over in Spain,' she said; 'the authorities were very polite, thanked me for all I'd done, gave me a medal, and sent me packing. It looks as though there'll be plenty of the same sort of work over here soon.'

Then she said: 'Is it too late to see nanny?'

'No, she sits up to all hours with her wireless.'

We went up, all three together, to the old nursery. Julia and I always spent part of our day there. Nanny Hawkins and my father were two people who seemed impervious to change, neither an hour older than when I first knew them. A wireless set had now been added to Nanny Hawkins' small assembly of pleasures – the rosary, the Peerage with its neat brown-paper wrapping protecting the red and gold covers, the photographs, and holiday souvenirs – on her table. When we broke it to her that Julia and I were to be married, she said: 'Well, dear, I hope it's all for the best,' for it was not part of her religion to question the propriety of Julia's actions.

Brideshead had never been a favourite with her; she greeted the news of his engagement with: 'He's certainly taken long enough to make up his mind,' and, when the search through Debrett afforded no information about Mrs Muspratt's connexions: 'she's caught him, I daresay.'

We found her, as always in the evening, at the fireside with her teapot, and the wool rug she was making.

'I knew you'd be up,' she said. 'Mr Wilcox sent to tell me you were coming.'

'I brought you some lace.'

'Well, dear, that is nice. Just like her poor Ladyship used to wear at mass. Though why they made it black I never did understand, seeing lace is white naturally. That is very welcome, I'm sure.'

'May I turn off the wireless, nanny?'

'Why, of course; I didn't notice it was on, in the pleasure of seeing you. What have you done to your hair?'

'I know it's terrible. I must get all that put right now I'm back. Darling nanny.'

As we sat there talking, and I saw Cordelia's fond eyes on all of us, I began to realize that she, too, had a beauty of her own.

'I saw Sebastian last month.'

'What a time he's been gone! Was he quite well?'

'Not very. That's why I went. It's quite near you know from Spain to Tunis. He's with the monks there.'

'I hope they look after him properly. I expect they find him a regular handful. He always sends to me at Christmas, but it's not the same as having him home. Why you must all always be going abroad I never did understand. Just like his Lordship. When there was that talk about going to war with Munich, I said to myself, "There's Cordelia and Sebastian and his Lordship all abroad; that'll be very awkward for them."'

'I wanted him to come home with me, but he wouldn't. He's got a beard now, you know, and he's very religious.'

'That I won't believe, not even if I see it. He was always a little heathen. Brideshead was one for church, not Sebastian. And a beard, only fancy; such a nice fair skin as he had; always looked clean though he'd not been near water all day, while Brideshead there was no doing anything with, scrub as you might.'

'It's frightening,' Julia once said, 'to think how completely you have forgotten Sebastian.'

'He was the forerunner.'

'That's what you said in the storm. I've thought since, perhaps I am only a forerunner, too.'

'Perhaps,' I thought, while her words still hung in the air between us like a wisp of tobacco smoke – a thought to fade and vanish like smoke without a trace – 'perhaps all our loves are merely hints and symbols; vagabond-language scrawled on gate-posts and paving-stones along the weary road that others have tramped before us; perhaps you and I are types and this sadness which sometimes falls between us springs from disappointment in our search, each straining through and beyond the other, snatching a glimpse now and then of the shadow which turns the corner always a pace or two ahead of us.'

I had not forgotten Sebastian. He was with me daily in Julia; or rather it was Julia I had known in him, in those distant Arcadian days.

'That's cold comfort for a girl,' she said when I tried to explain. 'How do I know I shan't suddenly turn out to be somebody else? It's an easy way to chuck.'

I had not forgotten Sebastian; every stone of the house had a memory of him, and hearing him spoken of by Cordelia as someone she had seen a month ago, my lost friend filled my thoughts. When we left the nursery, I said, 'I want to hear all about Sebastian.'

'Tomorrow. It's a long story.'

And next day, walking through the wind-swept park, she told me:

'I heard he was dying,' she said. 'A journalist in Burgos told me, who'd just arrived from North Africa. A down-and-out called Flyte, who people said was an English lord, whom the fathers had found starving and taken in at a monastery near Carthage. That was how the story reached me. I knew it couldn't be quite true – however little we did for Sebastian, he at least got his money sent him – but I started off at once.

'It was all quite easy. I went to the consulate first and they knew all about him; he was in the infirmary of the head house of some missionary fathers. The consul's story was that Sebastian had turned up in Tunis one day in a motor bus from Algiers, and had applied to be taken on as a missionary lay brother. The Fathers took one look at him and turned him down. Then he started drinking. He lived in a little hotel on the edge of the Arab quarter. I went to see the place later; it was a bar with a few rooms over it, kept by a Greek, smelling of hot oil and garlic and stale wine and old clothes, a place where the small Greek traders came and played draughts and listened to the wireless. He stayed there a month drinking Greek absinthe, occasionally wandering out, they didn't know where, coming back and drinking again. They were afraid he would come to harm and followed him sometimes, but he only went to the church or took a car to the monastery outside the town. They loved him there. He's still loved, you see, wherever he goes, whatever condition he's in. It's a thing about him he'll never lose. You should have heard the proprietor and his family talk of him, tears running down their cheeks; they'd clearly robbed him right and left, but they'd looked after him and tried to make him eat his food. That was the thing that shocked them about him; that he wouldn't eat; there he was with all that money, so thin. Some of the clients of the place came in while we were talking in very peculiar French; they all had the same story; such a *good* man, they said, it made them unhappy to see him so low. They thought very ill of his family for leaving him like that; it couldn't happen with their people, they said, and I daresay they're right.

'Anyway, that was later; after the consulate I went straight to the monastery and saw the Superior. He was a grim old Dutchman who had spent fifty years in Central Africa. He told me his part of the story; how Sebastian had turned up, just as the consul said, with his beard and a suitcase, and asked to be admitted as a lay brother. "He was very earnest," the Superior said' – Cordelia imitated his guttural tones; she had an aptitude for mimicry, I remembered, in the school-room – "Please do not think there is any doubt of that – he is quite sane and quite in earnest." He wanted to go to the bush, as far away as he could get, among the simplest people, to the cannibals. The Superior said: "We have no cannibals in our missions." He said, well, pygmies would do, or just a primitive village somewhere on a river, or lepers, lepers would do best of anything. The Superior said: "We have plenty of lepers, but they live in our settlements with doctors and nuns. It is all very orderly." He thought again, and said perhaps lepers were not what he wanted, was there not some small church by a river – he always wanted a river you see – which he could look after when the priest was away. The Superior said: "Yes, there are such churches. Now tell me about yourself." "Oh, I'm nothing," he said. "We see some queer fish," ' Cordelia lapsed again into mimicry; "he was a queer fish but he was very earnest." The Superior told him about the novitiate and the training and said: "You are not a young man. You do not seem strong to me." He said: "No, I don't want to be trained. I don't want to do things that need training." The Superior said: "My friend, you need a missionary for yourself," and he said: "Yes, of course." Then he sent him away.

'Next day he came back again. He had been drinking. He said he had decided to become a novice and be trained. "Well," said the Superior, "there are certain things that are impossible for a man in the bush. One of them is drinking. It is not the worst thing, but it is nevertheless quite fatal. I sent him away." Then he kept coming two or three times a week, always drunk, until the Superior gave orders that the porter was to keep him out. I said, "Oh dear, I'm afraid he was a terrible nuisance to you," but of course that's a thing they don't understand in a place like that. The Superior simply said, "I did not think there was anything I could do to help him except pray." He was a very holy old man and recognized it in others.'

'Holiness?'

'Oh yes, Charles, that's what you've got to understand about Sebastian.

'Well, finally one day they found Sebastian lying outside the main gate unconscious, he had walked out – usually he took a car – and fallen down and lain there all night. At first they thought he was merely drunk again; then they realized he was very ill, so they put him in the infirmary, where he'd been ever since.

'I stayed a fortnight with him till he was over the worst of his illness. He looked terrible, any age, rather bald with a straggling beard, but he had his old sweet manner. They'd given him a room to himself; it was barely more than a monk's cell with a bed and a crucifix and white walls. At first he couldn't talk much and was not at all surprised to see me; then he was surprised and wouldn't talk much, until just before I was going, when he told me all that had been happening to him. It was mostly about Kurt, his German friend. Well, you met him, so you know all about that. He sounds gruesome, but as long as Sebastian had him to look after, he was happy. He told me he'd practically given up drinking at one time while he and Kurt lived together. Kurt was ill and had a wound that wouldn't heal. Sebastian saw him through that. Then they went to Greece when Kurt got well. You know how Germans sometimes seem to discover a sense of decency when they get to a classical country. It seems to have worked with Kurt. Sebastian says he became quite human in Athens. Then he got sent to prison; I couldn't quite make out why; apparently it wasn't particularly his fault – some brawl with an official. Once he was locked up the German authorities got at him. It was the time when they were rounding up all their nationals from all parts of the world to make them into Nazis. Kurt didn't want to leave Greece, but the Greeks didn't want him, and he was marched straight from prison with a lot of other toughs into a German boat and shipped home.

'Sebastian went after him, and for a year could find no trace. Then in the end he ran him to earth dressed as a storm-trooper in a provincial town. At first he wouldn't have anything to do with Sebastian; spouted all the official jargon about the rebirth of his country, and his belonging to his country, and finding self-realization in the life of the race. But it was only skin deep with him. Six years of Sebastian had taught him more than a year of Hitler; eventually he chucked it, admitted he hated Germany, and wanted to get out. I don't know how much it was simply the call of the easy life, sponging on Sebastian, bathing in the Mediterranean, sitting about in cafés, having his shoes polished. Sebastian says it wasn't entirely that; Kurt had just begun to grow up in Athens. It may be he's right. Anyway, he decided to try and get out. But it didn't work. He always got into trouble whatever he did, Sebastian said. They caught him and put him in a concentration camp. Sebastian couldn't get near him or hear a word of him; he couldn't even find what camp he was in; he hung about for nearly a year in Germany, drinking again, until one day in his cups he took up with a man who was just out of the camp where Kurt had been, and learned that he had hanged himself in his hut the first week.

'So that was the end of Europe for Sebastian. He went back

to Morocco, where he had been happy, and gradually drifted down the coast, from place to place, until one day when he had sobered up – his drinking goes in pretty regular bouts now – he conceived the idea of escaping to the savages. And there he was.

'I didn't suggest his coming home. I knew he wouldn't, and he was too weak still to argue it out. He seemed quite happy by the time I left. He'll never be able to go into the bush, of course, or join the order, but the Father Superior is going to take charge of him. They had the idea of making him a sort of under-porter; there are usually a few odd hangers-on in a religious house, you know; people who can't quite fit in either to the world or the monastic rule. I suppose I'm something of the sort myself. But as I don't happen to drink, I'm more employable.'

We had reached the turn in our walk, the stone bridge at the foot of the last and smallest lake, under which the swollen waters fell in a cataract to the stream below; beyond, the path doubled back towards the house. We paused at the parapet looking down into the dark water.

'I once had a governess who jumped off this bridge and drowned herself.'

'Yes, I know.'

'How could you know?'

'It was the first thing I ever heard about you – before I ever met you.'

'How very odd. . . .'

'Have you told Julia this about Sebastian?'

'The substance of it; not quite as I told you. She never loved him, you know, as we do.'

'*Do*'. The word reproached me; there was no past tense in Cordelia's verb 'to love'.

'Poor Sebastian!' I said. 'It's too pitiful. How will it end?'

'I think I can tell you exactly, Charles. I've seen others like him, and I believe they are very near and dear to God. He'll live on, half in, half out of, the community, a familiar figure pottering round with his broom and his bunch of keys. He'll be a great favourite with the old fathers, something of a joke to the novices. Everyone will know about his drinking; he'll disappear for two or three days every month or so, and they'll all nod and smile and say in their various accents, "Old Sebastian's on the spree again," and then he'll come back dishevelled and shame-faced and be more devout for a day or two in the chapel. He'll probably have little hiding places about the garden where he keeps a bottle and takes a swig now and then on the sly. They'll bring him forward to act as guide, whenever they have an English-speaking visitor, and he will be completely charming so that before they go, they'll ask about him and perhaps be given a hint that he has high connexions at home. If he lives long enough, generations of missionaries in all kinds of remote places will think of him as a queer old character who was somehow part of the Home of their student days, and remember him in their masses. He'll develop little eccentricities of devotion, intense personal cults of his own; he'll be found in the chapel at odd times and missed when he's expected. Then one morning, after one of his drinking bouts, he'll be picked up at the gate dying, and show by a mere flicker of the eyelid that he is conscious when they give him the last sacraments. It's not such a bad way of getting through one's life.'

I thought of the youth with the teddy-bear under the flowering chestnuts. 'It's not what one would have foretold,' I said. 'I suppose he doesn't suffer?'

'Oh, yes, I think he does. One can have no idea what the suffering may be, to be maimed as he is – no dignity, no power of will. No one is ever holy without suffering. It's taken that form with him. ... I've seen so much suffering in the last few years; there's so much coming for everybody soon. It's the spring of love ...' and then in condescension to my paganism, she added: 'He's in a very beautiful place, you know, by the sea – white cloisters, a bell tower, rows of green vegetables, and a monk watering them when the sun is low.'

I laughed. 'You knew I wouldn't understand?'

'You and Julia ...' she said. And then, as we moved on towards the house, 'When you met me last night did you think, "Poor Cordelia, such an engaging child, grown up a plain and pious spinster, full of good works"? Did you think "thwarted"?'

It was no time for prevarication. 'Yes,' I said, 'I did; I don't now, so much.'

'It's funny,' she said, 'that's exactly the word I thought of for you and Julia. When we were up in the nursery with nanny. "Thwarted passion," I thought.'

She spoke with that gentle, infinitesimal inflexion of mockery which descended to her from her mother, but later that evening the words came back to me poignantly.

Julia wore the embroidered Chinese robe which she often used when we were dining alone at Brideshead; it was a robe whose weight and stiff folds stressed her repose; her neck rose exquisitely from the plain gold circle at her throat; her hands lay still among the dragons in her lap. It was thus that I had rejoiced to see her nights without number, and that night, watching her as she sat between the firelight and the shaded lamp, unable to look away for love of her beauty, I suddenly thought, 'When else have I seen her like this? Why am I reminded of another moment of vision?' And it came back to me that this was how she had sat in the liner, before the storm; this was how she had looked, and I realized that she had regained what I thought she had lost for ever, the magical sadness which had drawn me to her, the thwarted look that had seemed to say, 'Surely I was made for some other purpose than this?'

That night I woke in the darkness and lay awake turning over in my mind the conversation with Cordelia. How I had said, 'You knew I would not understand.' How often, it seemed to me, I was brought up short, like a horse in full stride suddenly refusing an obstacle, backing against the spurs, too shy even to put his nose at it and look at the thing.

And another image came to me, of an arctic hut and a trapper alone with his furs and oil lamp and log fire; everything dry and ship-shape and warm inside, and outside the last blizzard of winter raging and the snow piling up against the door. Quite silently a great weight forming against the timber; the bolt straining in its socket; minute by minute in the darkness outside the white heap sealing the door, until quite soon when the wind dropped and the sun came out on the ice slopes and the thaw set in a block would move, slide, and tumble, high above, gather weight, till the whole hillside seemed to be falling, and the little lighted place would open and splinter and disappear, rolling with the avalanche into the ravine.

CHAPTER V

MY divorce case, or rather my wife's, was due to be heard at about the same time as Brideshead was to be married. Julia's would not come up till the following term; meanwhile the game of General Post – moving my property from the Old Rectory to my flat, my wife's from my flat to the Old Rectory, Julia's from Rex's house and from Brideshead to my flat, Rex's from Brideshead to his house, and Mrs Muspratt's from Falmouth to Brideshead – was in full swing and we were all, in varying degrees, homeless, when a halt was called and Lord March-main, with a taste for the dramatically inopportune which was plainly the prototype of his elder son's, declared his intention, in view of the international situation, of returning to England and passing his declining years in his old home.

The only member of the family to whom this change promised any benefit was Cordelia, who had been sadly abandoned in the turmoil. Brideshead, indeed, had made a formal request to her to consider his house her home for as long as it suited her, but when she learned that her sister-in-law proposed to install her children there for the holidays immediately after the wedding, in the charge of a sister of hers and the sister's friend, Cordelia had decided to move, too, and was talking of setting up alone in London. She now found herself, Cinderella-like, promoted *châtelaine*, while her brother and his wife who had till that moment expected to find themselves, within a matter of days, in absolute command, were without a roof; the deeds of conveyance, engrossed and ready for signing, were rolled up, tied, and put away in one of the black tin boxes in Lincoln's Inn. It was bitter for Mrs Muspratt; she was not an ambitious woman; something very much less grand than Brideshead would have contented her heartily, but she did aspire to find some shelter for her children over Christmas. The house at Falmouth was stripped and up for sale; moreover, Mrs Muspratt had taken leave of the place with some justifiably rather large talk of her new establishment; they could not return there. She was obliged in a hurry to move her furniture from Lady Marchmain's room to a disused coach-house and to take a furnished villa at Torquay. She was not, as I have said, a woman of high ambition, but, having had her expectations so much raised, it was disconcerting to be brought so low so suddenly. In the village the working party who had been preparing the decorations for the bridal entry, began unpicking the Bs on the bunting and substituting Ms, obliterating the Earl's points and stencilling balls and strawberry leaves on the painted coronets, in preparation for Lord Marchmain's return.

News of his intentions came first to the solicitors, then to Cordelia, then to Julia and me, in a rapid succession of contradictory cables. Lord Marchmain would arrive in time for the wedding; he would arrive after the wedding, having seen Lord and Lady Brideshead on their way through Paris; he would see them in Rome. He was not well enough to travel at all; he was just starting; he had unhappy memories of winter at Brideshead and would not come until spring was well advanced and the heating apparatus overhauled; he was coming alone; he was bringing his Italian household; he wished his return to be unannounced and to lead a life of complete seclusion; he would give a ball. At last a date in January was chosen which proved to be the correct one.

Plender preceded him by some days; there was a difficulty here. Plender was not an original member of the Brideshead household; he had been Lord Marchmain's servant in the yeomanry, and had only once met Wilcox on the painful occasion of the removal of his master's luggage when it was decided not to return from the war; then Plender had been valet, as, officially, he still was, but he had in the past years introduced a kind of suffragan, a Swiss body-servant, to attend to the wardrobe and also, when occasion arose, lend a hand with less dignified tasks about the house, and had in effect become major-domo of that fluctuating and mobile household; sometimes he even referred to himself on the telephone as 'the secretary'. There was an acre of thin ice between him and Wilcox.

Fortunately the two men took a liking to one another, and the thing was solved in a series of three-cornered discussions with Cordelia. Plender and Wilcox became joint grooms of the chambers, like 'Blues' and Life Guards with equal precedence, Plender having as his particular province his Lordship's own apartments and Wilcox a sphere of influence in the public rooms; the senior footman was given a black coat and promoted butler, the nondescript Swiss, on arrival, was to have plain clothes and full valet's status; there was a general increase in wages to meet the new dignities, and all were content.

Julia and I, who had left Brideshead a month before, thinking we should not return, moved back for the reception. When the day came, Cordelia went to the station and we remained to greet him at home. It was a bleak and gusty day. Cottages and lodges were decorated; plans for a bonfire that night and for the village silver band to play on the terrace, were put down, but the house flag, that had not flown for twenty-five years, was hoisted over the pediment, and flapped sharply against the leaden sky. Whatever harsh voices might be bawling into the microphones of central Europe, and whatever lathes spinning in the armament factories, the return of Lord March-main was a matter of first importance in his own neighbourhood.

He was due at three o'clock. Julia and I waited in the drawing-room until Wilcox, who had arranged with the stationmaster to be kept informed, announced 'the train is signalled', and a minute later, 'the train is in; his Lordship is on the way.' Then we went to the front portico and waited there with the upper servants. Soon the Rolls appeared at the turn in the drive, followed at some distance by the two vans. It drew up; first Cordelia got out, then Cara; there was a pause, a rug was handed to the chauffeur, a stick to the footman; then a leg was cautiously thrust forward. Plender was by now at the car door;

another servant – the Swiss valet – had emerged from a van; together they lifted Lord Marchmain out and set him on his feet; he felt for his stick, grasped it, and stood for a minute collecting his strength for the few low steps which led to the front door.

Julia gave a little sigh of surprise and touched my hand. We had seen him nine months ago at Monte Carlo, when he had been an upright and stately figure, little changed from when I first met him in Venice. Now he was an old man. Plender had told us his master had been unwell lately: he had not prepared us for this.

Lord Marchmain stood bowed and shrunken, weighed down by his great-coat, a white muffler fluttering untidily at his throat, a cloth cap pulled low on his forehead, his face white and lined, his nose coloured by the cold; the tears which gathered in his eyes came not from emotion but from the east wind; he breathed heavily. Cara tucked in the end of his muffler and whispered something to him. He raised a gloved hand – a schoolboy's glove of grey wool – and made a small, weary gesture of greeting to the group at the door; then, very slowly, with his eyes on the ground before him, he made his way into the house.

They took off his coat and cap and muffler and the kind of leather jerkin which he wore under them; thus stripped he seemed more than ever wasted but more elegant; he had cast the shabbiness of extreme fatigue. Cara straightened his tie; he wiped his eyes with a bandanna handkerchief and shuffled with his stick to the hall fire.

There was a little heraldic chair by the chimney-piece, one of a set which stood against the walls, a little, inhospitable, flat-seated thing, a mere excuse for the elaborate armorial painting on its back, on which, perhaps, no one, not even a weary footman, had ever sat since it was made; there Lord Marchmain sat and wiped his eyes.

'It's the cold,' he said. 'I'd forgotten how cold it is in England. Quite bowled me over.'

'Can I get you anything, my lord?'

'Nothing, thank you. Cara, where are those confounded pills?'

'Alex, the doctor said not more than three times a day.'

'Damn the doctor. I feel quite bowled over.'

Cara produced a blue bottle from her bag and Lord Marchmain took a pill. Whatever was in it, seemed to revive him. He remained seated, his long legs stuck out before him, his cane between them, his chin on its ivory handle, but he began to take notice of us all, to greet us and to give orders.

'I'm afraid I'm not at all the thing today; the journey's taken it out of me. Ought to have waited a night at Dover. Wilcox, what rooms have you prepared for me?'

'Your old ones, my Lord.'

'Won't do; not till I'm fit again. Too many stairs; must be on the ground floor. Plender, get a bed made up for me downstairs.'

Plender and Wilcox exchanged an anxious glance.

'Very good, my Lord. Which room shall we put it in?'

Lord Marchmain thought for a moment. 'The Chinese drawing-room; and, Wilcox, the "Queen's bed".'

'The Chinese drawing-room, my lord, the "Queen's bed"?'

'Yes, yes. I may be spending some time there in the next few weeks.'

The Chinese drawing-room was one I had never seen used; in fact one could not normally go further into it than a small roped area round the door, where sight-seers were corralled on the days the house was open to the public; it was a splendid, uninhabitable museum of Chippendale carving and porcelain and lacquer and painted hangings; the Queen's bed, too, was an exhibition piece, a vast velvet tent like the *baldacchino* at St Peter's. Had Lord Marchmain planned this lying-in-state for himself, I wondered, before he left the sunshine of Italy? Had he thought of it during the scudding rain of his long, fretful journey? Had it come to him at that moment, an awakened memory of childhood, a dream in the nursery – 'When I'm grown up I'll sleep in the Queen's bed in the Chinese drawing-room' – the apotheosis of adult grandeur?

Few things, certainly, could have caused more stir in the house. What had been foreseen as a day of formality became one of fierce exertion; housemaids began making a fire, removing covers, unfolding linen; men in aprons, never normally seen, shifted furniture; the estate carpenters were collected to dismantle the bed. It came down the main staircase in pieces, at intervals during the afternoon; huge sections of Rococo, velvet-covered cornice; the twisted, gilt and velvet columns which formed its posts; beams of unpolished wood, made not to be seen, which performed invisible, structural functions below the draperies; plumes of dyed feathers, which sprang from gold-mounted ostrich eggs and crowned the canopy; finally, the mattresses with four toiling men to each. Lord Marchmain seemed to derive comfort from the consequences of his whim; he sat by the fire watching the bustle, while we stood in a half circle – Cara, Cordelia, Julia, and I – and talked to him.

Colour came back to his cheeks and light to his eyes. 'Brideshead and his wife dined with me in Rome,' he said. 'Since we are all members of the family' – and his eye moved ironically from Cara to me – 'I can speak without reserve. I found her deplorable. Her former consort, I understand, was a seafaring man and, presumably, the less exacting, but how my son, at the ripe age of thirty-eight, with, unless things have changed very much, a very free choice among the women of England, can have settled on – I suppose I must call her so – *Beryl*. ...' He left the sentence eloquently unfinished.

Lord Marchmain showed no inclination to move, so presently we drew up chairs – the little, heraldic chairs, for everything else in the hall was ponderous – and sat round him.

'I daresay I shall not be really fit again until summer comes,' he said. 'I look to you four to amuse me.'

There seemed little we could do at the moment to lighten the rather sombre mood; he, indeed, was the most cheerful of us. 'Tell me', he said, 'the circumstances of Brideshead's courtship.'

We told him what we knew.

'Match-boxes,' he said. 'Match-boxes. I think she's past child-bearing.'

Tea was brought us at the hall fireplace.

'In Italy,' he said, 'no one believes there will be a war. They think it will all be "arranged". I suppose, Julia, you no longer have access to political information? Cara, here, is fortunately a British subject by marriage. It is not a thing she customarily mentions, but it may prove valuable. She is legally Mrs Hicks, are you not, my dear? We know little of Hicks, but we shall be grateful to him, none the less, if it comes to war. And you,' he said, turning the attack to me, 'you will no doubt become an official artist?'

'No. As a matter of fact I am negotiating now for a commission in the Special Reserve.'

'Oh, but you should be an artist. I had one with my squadron during the last war, for weeks – until we went up to the line.'

This waspishness was new. I had always been aware of a frame of malevolence under his urbanity; now it protruded like his own sharp bones through the sunken skin.

It was dark before the bed was finished; we went to see it, Lord Marchmain stepping quite briskly now through the intervening rooms.

'I congratulate you. It really looks remarkably well. Wilcox, I seem to remember a silver basin and ewer – they stood in a room we called "the Cardinal's dressing-room", I think – suppose we had them here on the console. Then if you will send Plender and Gaston to me, the luggage can wait till tomorrow – simply the dressing case and what I need for the night. Plender will know. If you will leave me with Plender and Gaston, I will go to bed. We will meet later; you will dine here and keep me amused.'

We turned to go; as I was at the door he called me back.

'It looks very well, does it not?'

'Very well.'

'You might paint it, eh – and call it the *Death Bed*?'

'Yes,' said Cara, 'he has come home to die.'

'But when he first arrived he was talking so confidently of recovery.'

'That was because he was so ill. When he is himself, he knows he is dying and accepts it. His sickness is up and down; one day, sometimes for several days on end, he is strong and lively and then he is ready for death, then he is down and afraid. I do not know how it will be when he is more and more down. That must come in good time. The doctors in Rome gave him less than a year. There is someone coming from London, I think tomorrow, who will tell us more.'

'What is it?'

'His heart; some long word at the heart. He is dying of a long word.'

That evening Lord Marchmain was in good spirits; the room had a Hogarthian aspect, with the dinner-table set for the four of us by the grotesque, *chinoiserie* chimney-piece, and the old man propped among his pillows, sipping champagne, tasting, praising, and failing to eat, the succession of dishes which had been prepared for his homecoming. Wilcox had brought out for the occasion the gold plate, which I had not before seen in use; that, the gilt mirrors, and the lacquer and the drapery of the great bed and Julia's mandarin coat gave the scene an air of pantomime, of Aladdin's cave.

Just at the end, when the time came for us to go, his spirits flagged.

'I shall not sleep,' he said. 'Who is going to sit with me? Cara, *carissima*, you are fatigued. Cordelia, will you watch for an hour in this Gethsemane?'

Next morning I asked her how the night had passed.

'He went to sleep almost at once. I came in to see him at two to make up the fire; the lights were on, but he was asleep again. He must have woken up and turned them on; he had to get out of bed to do that. I think perhaps he is afraid of the dark.'

It was natural, with her hospital experience, that Cordelia should take charge of her father. When the doctors came that day they gave their instructions to her, instinctively.

'Until he gets worse,' she said, 'I and the valet can look after him. We don't want nurses in the house before they are needed.'

At this stage the doctors had nothing to recommend except

to keep him comfortable and administer certain drugs when his attacks came on.

'How long will it be?'

'Lady Cordelia, there are men walking about in hearty old age whom their doctors gave a week to live. I have learned one thing in medicine; never prophesy.'

These two men had made a long journey to tell her this; the local doctor was there to accept the same advice in technical phrases.

That night Lord Marchmain reverted to the topic of his new daughter-in-law; it had never been long out of his mind, finding expression in various sly hints throughout the day; now he lay back in his pillows and talked of her at length.

'I have never been much moved by family piety until now,' he said, 'but I am frankly appalled at the prospect of – of Beryl taking what was once my mother's place in this house. Why should that uncouth pair sit here childless while the place crumbles about their ears? I will not disguise from you that I have taken a dislike to Beryl.

'Perhaps it was unfortunate that we met in Rome. Anywhere else might have been more sympathetic. And yet, if one comes to consider it, where could I have met her without repugnance? We dined at Ranieri's; it is a quiet little restaurant I have frequented for years – no doubt you know it. Beryl seemed to fill the place. I, of course, was host, though to hear Beryl press my son with food, you might have thought otherwise. Brideshead was always a greedy boy; a wife who has his best interests at heart should seek to restrain him. However, that is a matter of small importance.

'She had no doubt heard of me as a man of irregular life. I can only describe her manner to me as roguish. A naughty old man, that's what she thought I was. I suppose she had met naughty old admirals and knew how they should be humoured … I could not attempt to reproduce her conversation. I will give you one example.

'They had been to an audience at the Vatican that morning; a blessing for their marriage – I did not follow attentively –

something of the kind had happened before, I gathered, some previous husband, some previous Pope. She described, rather vivaciously, how on this earlier occasion she had gone with a whole body of newly married couples, mostly Italians of all ranks, some of the simpler girls in their wedding dresses, and how each had appraised the other, the bridegrooms looking the brides over, comparing their own with one another's, and so forth. Then she said, "This time, of course, we were in private, but do you know, Lord Marchmain, I felt as though it was I who was leading in the bride."

'It was said with great indelicacy. I have not yet quite fathomed her meaning. Was she making a play on my son's name, or was she, do you think, referring to his undoubted virginity? I fancy the latter. Anyway, it was with pleasantries of that kind that we passed the evening.

'I don't think she would be quite in her proper element here, do you? Who shall I leave it to? The entail ended with me, you know. Sebastian, alas, is out of the question. Who wants it? *Quis?* Would you like it, Cara? No, of course you would not. Cordelia? I think I shall leave it to Julia and Charles.'

'Of course not, papa, it's Bridey's.'

'And ... Beryl's? I will have Gregson down one day soon and go over the matter. It is time I brought my will up to date; it is full of anomalies and anachronisms ... I have rather a fancy for the idea of installing Julia here; so beautiful this evening, my dear; so beautiful always; much, much more suitable.'

Shortly after this he sent to London for his solicitor, but, on the day he came, Lord Marchmain was suffering from an attack and would not see him. 'Plenty of time,' he said, between painful gasps for breath, 'another day, when I am stronger,' but the choice of his heir was constantly in his mind, and he referred often to the time when Julia and I should be married and in possession.

'Do you think he really means to leave it to us?' I asked Julia.

'Yes, I think he does.'

'But it's monstrous for Bridey.'

'Is it? I don't think he cares much for the place. I do, you know. He and Beryl would be much more content in some little house somewhere.'

'You mean to accept it?'

'Certainly. It's papa's to leave as he likes. I think you and I could be very happy here.'

It opened a prospect; the prospect one gained at the turn of the avenue, as I had first seen it with Sebastian, of the secluded valley, the lakes falling away one below the other, the old house in the foreground, the rest of the world abandoned and forgotten; a world of its own of peace and love and beauty; a soldier's dream in a foreign bivouac; such a prospect perhaps as a high pinnacle of the temple afforded after the hungry days in the desert and the jackal-haunted nights. Need I reproach myself if sometimes I was taken by the vision?

The weeks of illness wore on and the life of the house kept pace with the faltering strength of the sick man. There were days when Lord Marchmain was dressed, when he stood at the window or moved on his valet's arm from fire to fire through the rooms of the ground floor, when visitors came and went – neighbours and people from the estate, men of business from London – parcels of new books were opened and discussed, a piano was moved into the Chinese drawing-room; once at the end of February, on a single, unexpected day of brilliant sunshine, he called for a car and got as far as the hall, had on his fur coat, and reached the front door. Then suddenly he lost interest in the drive, said 'Not now. Later. One day in the summer,' took his man's arm again and was led back to his chair. Once he had the humour of changing his room and gave detailed orders for a move to the Painted Parlour; the *chinoiserie*, he said, disturbed his rest – he kept the lights full on at night – but again lost heart, countermanded everything, and kept his room.

On other days the house was hushed as he sat high in bed, propped by his pillows, with labouring breath; even then he wanted to have us round him; night or day he could not bear to be alone; when he could not speak his eyes followed us, and if anyone left the room he would look distressed, and Cara, sitting often for hours at a time by his side against the pillows with an arm in his, would say, 'It's all right, Alex, she's coming back.'

Brideshead and his wife returned from their honeymoon and stayed a few nights; it was one of the bad times, and Lord Marchmain refused to have them near him. It was Beryl's first visit, and she would have been unnatural if she had shown no curiosity about what had nearly been, and now again promised soon to be, her home. Beryl was natural enough, and surveyed the place fairly thoroughly in the days she was there. In the strange disorder caused by Lord Marchmain's illness, it must have seemed capable of much improvement; she referred once or twice to the way in which establishments of similar size had been managed at various Government Houses she had visited. Brideshead took her visiting among the tenants by day, and in the evenings, she talked to me of painting, or to Cordelia of hospitals, or to Julia of clothes, with cheerful assurance. The shadow of betrayal, the knowledge of how precarious were their just expectations, was all one-sided. I was not easy with them; but that was no new thing to Brideshead; in the little circle of shyness in which he was used to move, my guilt passed unseen.

Eventually it became clear that Lord Marchmain did not intend to see more of them. Brideshead was admitted alone for a minute's leave-taking; then they left.

'There's nothing we can do here,' said Brideshead, 'and it's very distressing for Beryl. We'll come back if things get worse.'

The bad spells became longer and more frequent; a nurse was engaged. 'I never saw such a room,' she said, 'nothing like it anywhere; no conveniences of any sort.' She tried to have her patient moved upstairs, where there was running water, a dressing-room for herself, a 'sensible' narrow bed she could 'get round' – what she was used to – but Lord Marchmain would not budge. Soon, as days and nights became indistinguishable to him, a second nurse was installed; the specialists came again from London; they recommended a new and rather daring treatment, but his body seemed weary of all drugs and did not respond. Presently there were no good spells, merely brief fluctuations in the speed of his decline.

Brideshead was called. It was the Easter holidays and Beryl was busy with her children. He came alone, and having stood silently for some minutes beside his father, who sat silently looking at him, he left the room and, joining the rest of us, who were in the library, said, 'Papa must see a priest.'

It was not the first time the topic had come up. In the early days, when Lord Marchmain first arrived, the parish priest – since the chapel was shut there was a new church and presbytery in Melstead – had come to call as a matter of politeness. Cordelia had put him off with apologies and excuses, but when he was gone she said: 'Not yet. Papa doesn't want him yet.'

Julia, Cara, and I were there at the time; we each had something to say, began to speak, and thought better of it. It was never mentioned between the four of us, but Julia, alone with me, said, 'Charles, I see great Church trouble ahead.'

'Can't they even let him die in peace?'

'They mean something so different by "peace".'

'It would be an outrage. No one could have made it clearer, all his life, what he thought of religion. They'll come now, when his mind's wandering and he hasn't the strength to resist, and claim him as a death-bed penitent. I've had a certain respect for their Church up till now. If they do a thing like that I shall know that everything stupid people say about them is quite true – that it's all superstition and trickery.' Julia said nothing. 'Don't you agree?' Still Julia said nothing. 'Don't you agree?'

'I don't know, Charles. I simply don't know.'

And, though none of us spoke of it, I felt the question ever present, growing through all the weeks of Lord Marchmain's illness; I saw it when Cordelia drove off early in the mornings to mass; I saw it as Cara took to going with her; this little cloud, the size of a man's hand, that was going to swell into a storm among us.

Now Brideshead, in his heavy, ruthless way, planted the problem down before us.

'Oh, Bridey, do you think he would?' asked Cordelia.

'I shall see that he does,' said Brideshead. 'I shall take Father Mackay in to him tomorrow.'

Still the clouds gathered and did not break; none of us spoke. Cara and Cordelia went back to the sickroom; Brideshead looked for a book, found one, and left us.

'Julia,' I said, 'how can we stop this tomfoolery?'

She did not answer for some time; then: 'Why should we?'

'You know as well as I do. It's just – just an unseemly incident.'

'Who am I to object to unseemly incidents?' she asked sadly. 'Anyway, what harm can it do? Let's ask the doctor.'

We asked the doctor, who said: 'It's hard to say. It might alarm him of course; on the other hand, I have known cases where it has had a wonderfully soothing effect on a patient; I've even known it act as a positive stimulant. It certainly is usually a great comfort to the relations. Really I think it's a thing for Lord Brideshead to decide. Mind you, there is no need for immediate anxiety. Lord Marchmain is very weak today; tomorrow he may be quite strong again. Is it not usual to wait a little?'

'Well, he wasn't much help,' I said to Julia, when we left him.

'Help? I really can't quite see why you've taken it so much to heart that my father shall not have the last sacraments.'

'It's such a lot of witchcraft and hypocrisy.'

'Is it? Anyway, it's been going on for nearly two thousand years. I don't know why you should suddenly get in a rage now.' Her voice rose; she was swift to anger of late months. 'For Christ's sake, write to *The Times*; get up and make a speech in Hyde Park; start a "No Popery" riot, but don't bore me about it. What's it got to do with you or me whether my father sees his parish priest?'

I knew these fierce moods of Julia's, such as had overtaken her at the fountain in moonlight, and dimly surmised their origin; I knew they could not be assuaged by words. Nor could I have spoken, for the answer to her question was still unformed; the sense that the fate of more souls than one was at issue; that the snow was beginning to shift on the high slopes.

Brideshead and I breakfasted together next morning with the night-nurse, who had just come off duty.

'He's much brighter today,' she said. 'He slept very nicely for nearly three hours. When Gaston came to shave him he was quite chatty.'

'Good,' said Brideshead. 'Cordelia went to mass. She's driving Father Mackay back here to breakfast.'

I had met Father Mackay several times; he was a stocky, middle-aged, genial Glasgow-Irishman who, when we met, was apt to ask me such questions as, 'Would you say now, Mr Ryder, that the painter Titian was more truly artistic than the painter Raphael?' and, more disconcertingly still, to remember my answers: 'To revert, Mr Ryder, to what you said when last I had the pleasure to meet you, would it be right now to say that the painter Titian ...' usually ending with some such reflection as: 'Ah, it's a grand resource for a man to have the talent you have, Mr Ryder, and the time to indulge it.' Cordelia could imitate him.

This morning he made a hearty breakfast, glanced at the headlines of the paper, and then said with professional briskness: 'And now, Lord Brideshead, would the poor soul be ready to see me, do you think?'

Brideshead led him out; Cordelia followed, and I was left alone among the breakfast things. In less than a minute I heard the voices of all three outside the door.

'... can only apologize.'

'... poor soul. Mark you, it was seeing a strange face; depend upon it, it was that – an unexpected stranger. I well understand it.'

'... Father, I am sorry ... bringing you all this way ...'

'Don't think about it at all, Lady Cordelia. Why, I've had bottles thrown at me in the Gorbals. ... Give him time. I've known worse cases make beautiful deaths. Pray for him ... I'll come again ... and now if you'll excuse me I'll just pay a little visit to Mrs Hawkins. Yes, indeed, I know the way well.'

Then Cordelia and Brideshead came into the room.

'I gather the visit was not a success.'

'It was not. Cordelia, will you drive Father Mackay home when he comes down from nanny? I'm going to telephone to Beryl and see when she needs me home.'

'Bridey, it was horrible. What are we to do?'

'We've done everything we can at the moment.' He left the room.

Cordelia's face was grave; she took a piece of bacon from the dish, dipped it in mustard and ate it. 'Damn Bridey,' she said, 'I knew it wouldn't work.'

'What happened?'

'Would you like to know? We walked in there in a line; Cara was reading the paper aloud to papa. Bridey said, "I've brought Father Mackay to see you"; papa said, "Father Mackay, I am afraid you have been brought here under a misapprehension. I am not *in extremis*, and I have not been a practising member of your Church for twenty-five years. Brideshead, show Father Mackay the way out." Then we all turned about and walked away, and I heard Cara start reading the paper again, and that, Charles, was that.'

I carried the news to Julia, who lay with her bed-table amid a litter of newspapers and envelopes. 'Mumbo-jumbo is off,' I said. 'The witch-doctor has gone.'

'Poor papa.'

'It's great sucks to Bridey.'

I felt triumphant. I had been right, everyone else had been wrong, truth had prevailed; the threat that I had felt hanging over Julia and me ever since that evening at the fountain, had been averted, perhaps dispelled for ever; and there was also – I can now confess it – another unexpressed, inexpressible, indecent little victory that I was furtively celebrating. I guessed that that morning's business had put Brideshead some considerable way further from his rightful inheritance.

In that I was correct; a man was sent for from the solicitors in London; in a day or two he came and it was known throughout the house that Lord Marchmain had made a new will. But I was wrong in thinking that the religious controversy was quashed; it flamed up again after dinner on Brideshead's last evening.

'... What papa said was, "I am not *in extremis*, I have not been a practising member of the Church for twenty-five years."'

'Not "*the* Church", "your Church".'

'I don't see the difference.'

'There's every difference.'

'Bridey, it's quite plain what he meant.'

'I presume he meant what he said. He meant that he had not been accustomed regularly to receive the sacraments, and since he was not at the moment dying, he did not mean to change his ways – *yet*.'

'That's simply a quibble.'

'Why do people always think that one is quibbling when one tries to be precise? His plain meaning was that he did not want to see a priest that day, but that he would when he was "*in extremis*".'

'I wish someone would explain to me,' I said, 'quite what the significance of these sacraments is. Do you mean that if he dies alone he goes to hell, and that if a priest puts oil on him –'

'Oh, it's not the oil,' said Cordelia, 'that's to heal him.'

'Odder still – well, whatever it is the priest does – that he then goes to heaven. Is that what you believe?'

Cara then interposed: 'I think my nurse told me, someone did anyway, that if the priest got there before the body was cold it was all right. That's so, isn't it?'

The others turned on her.

'No, Cara, it's not.'

'Of course not.'

'You've got it all wrong, Cara.'

'Well, I remember when Alphonse de Grenet died, Madame de Grenet had a priest hidden outside the door – he couldn't bear the sight of a priest – and brought him in *before the body was cold*; she told me herself, and they had a full Requiem for him, and I went to it.'

'Having a Requiem doesn't mean you go to heaven necessarily.'

'Madame de Grenet thought it did.'

'Well, she was wrong.'

'Do any of you Catholics know what good you think this priest can do?' I asked. 'Do you simply want to arrange it so that your father can have Christian burial? Do you want to keep him out of hell? I only want to be told.'

Brideshead told me at some length, and when he had finished Cara slightly marred the unity of the Catholic front by saying in simple wonder, 'I never heard that before.'

'Let's get this clear,' I said; 'he has to make an act of will; he has to be contrite and wish to be reconciled; is that right? But only God knows whether he has really made an act of will; the priest can't tell; and if there isn't a priest there, and he makes the act of will alone, that's as good as if there were a priest. And it's quite possible that the will may still be working when a man is too weak to make any outward sign of it; is that right? He may be lying, as though for dead, and willing all the time, and being reconciled, and God understands that; is that right?'

'More or less,' said Brideshead.

'Well, for heaven's sake,' I said, 'what is the priest for?'

There was a pause in which Julia sighed and Brideshead drew breath as though to start further subdividing the propositions. In the silence Cara said, 'All I know is that *I* shall take very good care to have a priest.'

'Bless you,' said Cordelia, 'I believe that's the best answer.'

And we let the argument drop, each for different reasons, thinking it had been inconclusive.

Later Julia said: 'I wish you wouldn't start these religious arguments.'

'I didn't start it.'

'You don't convince anyone else and you don't really convince yourself.'

'I only want to know what these people believe. They say it's all based on logic.'

'If you'd let Bridey finish, he would have made it all quite logical.'

'There were four of you,' I said. 'Cara didn't know the first thing it was about, and may or may not have believed it; you knew a bit and didn't believe a word; Cordelia knew about as much and believed it madly; only poor Bridey knew and believed, and I thought he made a pretty poor show when it came to explaining. And people go round saying, "At least Catholics know what they believe." We had a fair cross-section tonight –'

'Oh, Charles, don't rant. I shall begin to think you're getting doubts yourself.'

The weeks passed and still Lord Marchmain lived on. In June my divorce was made absolute and my former wife married for the second time. Julia would be free in September. The nearer our marriage got, the more wistfully, I noticed, Julia spoke of it; war was growing nearer, too – we neither of us doubted that – but Julia's tender, remote, it sometimes seemed, desperate longing did not come from any uncertainty outside herself; it suddenly darkened, too, into brief accesses of hate when she seemed to throw herself against the restraints of her love for me like a caged animal against the bars.

I was summoned to the War Office, interviewed, and put on a list in case of emergency; Cordelia also, on another list; lists were becoming part of our lives once more, as they had been at school. Everything was being got ready for the coming 'Emergency'. No one in that dark office spoke the word 'war'; it was taboo; we should be called for if there was 'an emergency' – not in case of strife, an act of human will; nothing so clear and simple as wrath or retribution; an emergency; something coming out of the waters, a monster with sightless face and thrashing tail thrown up from the depths.

Lord Marchmain took little interest in events outside his own room; we took him the papers daily and made the attempt to read to him, but he turned his head on the pillows and with his eyes followed the intricate patterns about him. 'Shall I go on?' 'Please do if it's not boring you.' But he was not listening; occasionally at a familiar name he would whisper: 'Irwin ... I knew him – a mediocre fellow'; occasionally some remote comment: 'Czechs make good coachmen; nothing else'; but his mind was far from world affairs; it was there, on the spot, turned in on himself; he had no strength for any other war than his own solitary struggle to keep alive.

I said to the doctor, who was with us daily: 'He's got a wonderful will to live, hasn't he?'

'Would you put it like that? I should say a great fear of death.'

'Is there a difference?'

'Oh dear, yes. He doesn't derive any strength from his fear, you know. It's wearing him out.'

Next to death, perhaps because they are like death, he feared darkness and loneliness. He liked to have us in his room and the lights burnt all night among the gilt figures; he did not wish us to speak much, but he talked himself, so quietly that we often could not hear him; he talked, I think, because his was the only voice he could trust, when it assured him that he was still alive; what he said was not for us, nor for any ears but his own.

'Better today. Better today. I can see now, in the corner of the fireplace, where the mandarin is holding his gold bell and the crooked tree is in flower below his feet, where yesterday I was confused and took the little tower for another man. Soon I shall see the bridge and the three storks and know where the path leads over the hill.

'Better tomorrow. We live long in our family and marry late. Seventy-three is no great age. Aunt Julia, my father's aunt, lived to be eighty-eight, born and died here, never married, saw the fire on beacon hill for the battle of Trafalgar, always called it "the New House"; that was the name they had for it in the nursery and in the fields when unlettered men had long memories. You can see where the old house stood near the village church; they call the field "Castle Hill", Horlick's field where the ground's uneven and half of it is waste, nettle, and brier in hollows too deep for ploughing. They dug to the foundations to carry the stone for the new house; the house that was a century old when Aunt Julia was born. Those were our roots in the waste hollows of Castle Hill, in the brier and nettle; among the tombs in the old church and the chantry where no clerk sings.

'Aunt Julia knew the tombs, cross-legged knight and doubleted earl, marquis like a Roman senator, limestone, alabaster, and Italian marble; tapped the escutcheons with her ebony cane, made the casque ring over old Sir Roger. We were knights then, barons since Agincourt, the larger honours came with the Georges. They came the last and they'll go the first; the barony goes on. When all of you are dead Julia's son will be called by the name his fathers bore before the fat days; the days of wool shearing and the wide corn lands, the days of growth and building, when the marshes were drained and the waste land brought under the plough, when one built the house, his son added the dome, his son spread the wings and dammed the river. Aunt Julia watched them build the fountain; it was old before it came here, weathered two hundred years by the suns of Naples, brought by man-o'-war in the days of Nelson. Soon the fountain will be dry till the rain fills it, setting the fallen leaves afloat in the basin; and over the lakes the reeds will spread and close. Better today.

'Better today. I have lived carefully, sheltered myself from the cold winds, eaten moderately of what was in season, drunk fine claret, slept in my own sheets; I shall live long. I was fifty when they dismounted us and sent us into the line; old men stay at the base, the orders said, but Walter Venables, my commanding officer, my nearest neighbour, said: "You're as fit as the youngest of them, Alex." So I was; so I am now, if I could only breathe.

'No air; no wind stirring under the velvet canopy. When the summer comes,' said Lord Marchmain, oblivious of the deep corn and swelling fruit and the surfeited bees who slowly sought their hives in the heavy afternoon sunlight outside his windows, 'when the summer comes, I shall leave my bed and sit in the open air and breathe more easily.

'Who would have thought that all these little gold men, gentlemen in their own country, could live so long without breathing? Like toads in the coal, down a deep mine, untroubled. God take it, why have they dug a hole for me? Must a man stifle to death in his own cellars? Plender, Gaston, open the windows.'

'The windows are all wide open, my lord.'

A cylinder of oxygen was placed beside his bed, with a long tube, a face-piece, and a little stop-cock he could work himself. Often he said: 'It's empty; look nurse, there's nothing comes out.'

'No, Lord Marchmain, it's quite full; the bubble here in the glass bulb shows that; it's at full pressure; listen, don't you hear it hiss? Try and breathe slowly, Lord Marchmain; quite gently, then you get the benefit.'

'Free as air; that's what they say – "free as air". Now they bring me my air in an iron barrel.'

Once he said: 'Cordelia, what became of the chapel?'

'They locked it up, papa, when mummy died.'

'It was hers, I gave it to her. We've always been builders in our family. I built it for her; in the shade of the pavilion; rebuilt with the old stones behind the old walls; it was the last of the new house to come, the first to go. There used to be a chaplain until the war. Do you remember him?'

'I was too young.'

'Then I went away – left her in the chapel praying. It was hers. It was the place for her. I never came back to disturb her prayers. They said we were fighting for freedom; I had my own victory. Was it a crime?'

'I think it was, papa.'

'Crying to heaven for vengeance? Is that why they've locked me in this cave, do you think, with a black tube of air and the little yellow men along the walls, who live without breathing? Do you think that, child? But the wind will come soon, tomorrow perhaps, and we'll breathe again. The ill wind that will blow me good. Better tomorrow.'

Thus, till mid-July, Lord Marchmain lay dying, wearing himself down in the struggle to live. Then, since there was no reason to expect an immediate change, Cordelia went to London to see her women's organization about the coming 'emergency'. That day Lord Marchmain became suddenly worse. He lay silent and quite still, breathing laboriously; only his open eyes, which sometimes moved about the room, gave any sign of consciousness.

'Is this the end?' Julia asked.

'It is impossible to say,' the doctor answered; 'when he does die it will probably be like this. He may recover from the present attack. The only thing is not to disturb him. The least shock will be fatal.'

'I'm going for Father Mackay,' she said.

I was not surprised. I had seen it in her mind all the summer. When she had gone I said to the doctor, 'We must stop this nonsense.'

He said: 'My business is with the body. It's not my business to argue whether people are better alive or dead, or what happens to them after death. I only try to keep them alive.'

'And you said just now any shock would kill him. What could be worse for a man who fears death, as he does, than to have a priest brought to him – a priest he turned out when he had the strength?'

'I think it may kill him.'

'Then will you forbid it?'

'I've no authority to forbid anything. I can only give my opinion.'

'Cara, what do you think?'

'I don't want him made unhappy. That is all there is to hope for now; that he'll die without knowing it. But I should like the priest there, all the same.'

'Will you try and persuade Julia to keep him away – until the end? After that he can do no harm.'

'I will ask her to leave Alex happy, yes.'

In half an hour Julia was back with Father Mackay. We all met in the library.

'I've telegraphed for Bridey and Cordelia,' I said. 'I hope you agree that nothing must be done till they arrive.'

'I wish they were here,' said Julia.

'You can't take the responsibility alone,' I said; 'everyone else is against you. Doctor Grant, tell her what you said to me just now.'

'I said that the shock of seeing a priest might well kill him; without that he may survive this attack. As his medical man I must protest against anything being done to disturb him.'

'Cara?'

'Julia, dear, I know you are thinking for the best, but, you know, Alex was not a religious man. He scoffed always. We mustn't take advantage of him, now he's weak, to comfort our own consciences. If Father Mackay comes to him when he is unconscious, then he can be buried in the proper way, can he not, Father?'

'I'll go and see how he is,' said the doctor, leaving us.

'Father Mackay,' I said. 'You know how Lord Marchmain greeted you last time you came; do you think it possible he can have changed now?'

'Thank God, by his grace it is possible.'

'Perhaps,' said Cara, 'you could slip in while he is sleeping, say the words of absolution over him; he would never know.'

'I have seen so many men and women die,' said the priest; 'I never knew them sorry to have me there at the end.'

'But they were Catholics; Lord Marchmain has never been one except in name – at any rate, not for years. He was a scoffer, Cara said so.'

'Christ came to call, not the righteous, but sinners to repentance.'

The doctor returned. 'There's no change,' he said.

'Now doctor,' said the priest, 'how would I be a shock to anyone?' He turned his bland, innocent, matter-of-fact face first on the doctor, then upon the rest of us. 'Do you know what I want to do? It is something so small, no show about it. I don't wear special clothes, you know. I go just as I am. He knows the look of me now. There's nothing alarming. I just want to ask him if he is sorry for his sins. I want him to make some little sign of assent; I want him, anyway, not to refuse me; then I want to give him God's pardon. Then, though that's not essential, I want to anoint him. It is nothing, a touch of the fingers, just some oil from this little box, look it is nothing to hurt him.'

'Oh, Julia,' said Cara, 'what are we to say? Let me speak to him.'

She went to the Chinese drawing-room; we waited in silence; there was a wall of fire between Julia and me. Presently Cara returned.

'I don't think he heard,' she said. 'I thought I knew how to put it to him. I said: "Alex, you remember the priest from Melstead. You were very naughty when he came to see you. You hurt his feelings very much. Now he's here again. I want you to see him just for my sake, to make friends." But he didn't answer. If he's unconscious, it couldn't make him unhappy to see the priest, could it, doctor?'

Julia, who had been standing still and silent, suddenly moved.

'Thank you for your advice, doctor,' she said. 'I take full responsibility for whatever happens. Father Mackay, will you please come and see my father now,' and without looking at me, led him to the door.

We all followed. Lord Marchmain was lying as I had seen him that morning, but his eyes were now shut; his hands lay, palm upwards, above the bed-clothes; the nurse had her fingers on the pulse of one of them. 'Come in,' she said brightly, 'you won't disturb him now.'

'D'you mean . . . ?'

'No, no, but he's past noticing anything.'

She held the oxygen apparatus to his face and the hiss of escaping gas was the only sound at the bedside.

The priest bent over Lord Marchmain and blessed him. Julia and Cara knelt at the foot of the bed. The doctor, the nurse, and I stood behind them.

'Now,' said the priest, 'I know you are sorry for all the sins of your life, aren't you? Make a sign, if you can. You're sorry, aren't you?' But there was no sign. 'Try and remember your sins; tell God you are sorry. I am going to give you absolution. While I am giving it, tell God you are sorry you have offended him.' He began to speak in Latin. I recognized the words '*ego te absolvo in nomine Patris . . .*' and saw the priest make the sign of the cross. Then I knelt, too, and prayed: 'O God, if there is a God, forgive him his sins, if there is such a thing as sin,' and the man on the bed opened his eyes and gave a sigh, the sort of sigh I had imagined people made at the moment of death, but his eyes moved so that we knew there was still life in him.

I suddenly felt the longing for a sign, if only of courtesy, if only for the sake of the woman I loved, who knelt in front of me, praying, I knew, for a sign. It seemed so small a thing that was asked, the bare acknowledgement of a present, a nod in the crowd. I prayed more simply; 'God forgive him his sins' and 'Please God, make him accept your forgiveness.'

So small a thing to ask.

The priest took the little silver box from his pocket and spoke again in Latin, touching the dying man with an oily wad; he finished what he had to do, put away the box and gave the final blessing. Suddenly Lord Marchmain moved his hand to his forehead; I thought he had felt the touch of the chrism and was wiping it away. 'O God,' I prayed, 'don't let him do that.' But there was no need for fear; the hand moved slowly down his breast, then to his shoulder, and Lord Marchmain made the sign of the cross. Then I knew that the sign I had asked for was not a little thing, not a passing nod of recognition, and a phrase came back to me from my childhood of the veil of the temple being rent from top to bottom.

It was over; we stood up; the nurse went back to the oxygen cylinder; the doctor bent over his patient. Julia whispered to me: 'Will you see Father Mackay out? I'm staying here for a little.'

Outside the door Father Mackay became the simple, genial man I had known before. 'Well, now, and that was a beautiful thing to see. I've known it happen that way again and again. The devil resists to the last moment and then the Grace of God is too much for him. You're not a Catholic I think, Mr Ryder, but at least you'll be glad for the ladies to have the comfort of it.'

As we were waiting for the chauffeur, it occurred to me that Father Mackay should be paid for his services. I asked him awkwardly. 'Why, don't think about it, Mr Ryder. It was a pleasure,' he said, 'but anything you care to give is useful in a parish like mine.' I found I had three pounds in my note-case

and gave them to him. 'Why, indeed, that's more than generous. God bless you, Mr Ryder. I'll call again, but I don't think
the poor soul has long for this world.'

Julia remained in the Chinese drawing-room until, at five
o'clock that evening, her father died, proving both sides right in
the dispute, priest and doctor.

Thus I come to the broken sentences which were the last
words spoken between Julia and me, the last memories.

When her father died Julia remained some minutes with his
body; the nurse came to the next room to announce the news
and I had a glimpse of her through the open door, kneeling at
the foot of the bed, and of Cara sitting by her. Presently the two
women came out together, and Julia said to me: 'Not now; I'm
just taking Cara up to her room; later.'

While she was still upstairs Brideshead and Cordelia arrived
from London; when at last we met alone it was by stealth, like
young lovers.

Julia said: 'Here in the shadow, in the corner of the stair – a
minute to say good-bye.'

'So long to say so little.'

'You knew?'

'Since this morning; since before this morning; all this year.'

'I didn't know till today. Oh, my dear, if you could only
understand. Then I could bear to part, or bear it better. I
should say my heart was breaking, if I believed in broken
hearts. I can't marry you, Charles; I can't be with you ever
again.'

'I know.'

'How can you know?'

'What will you do?'

'Just go on – alone. How can I tell what I shall do? You
know the whole of me. You know I'm not one for a life of
mourning. I've always been bad. Probably I shall be bad again,
punished again. But the worse I am, the more I need God. I
can't shut myself out from his mercy. That is what it would
mean; starting a life with you, without him. One can only hope

to see one step ahead. But I saw today there was one thing unforgivable – like things in the school-room, so bad they were unpunishable, that only mummy could deal with – the bad thing I was on the point of doing, that I'm not quite bad enough to do; to set up a rival good to God's. Why should I be allowed to understand that, and not you, Charles? It may be because of mummy, nanny, Cordelia, Sebastian – perhaps Bridey and Mrs Muspratt – keeping my name in their prayers; or it may be a private bargain between me and God, that if I give up this one thing I want so much, however bad I am, he won't quite despair of me in the end.

'Now we shall both be alone, and I shall have no way of making you understand.'

'I don't want to make it easier for you,' I said; 'I hope your heart may break; but I do understand.'

The avalanche was down, the hillside swept bare behind it; the last echoes died on the white slopes; the new mound glittered and lay still in the silent valley.

EPILOGUE

Brideshead Revisited

'THE worst place we've struck yet,' said the commanding officer; 'no facilities, no amenities, and Brigade sitting right on top of us. There's one pub in Flyte St Mary with capacity for about twenty – that, of course, will be out of bounds for officers; there's a Naafi in the camp area. I hope to run transport once a week to Melstead Carbury. Marchmain is ten miles away and damn-all when you get there. It will therefore be the first concern of company officers to organize recreation for their men. M.O., I want you to take a look at the lakes to see if they're fit for bathing.'

'Very good, sir.'

'Brigade expects us to clean up the house for them. I should have thought some of those half-shaven scrim-shankers I see lounging round Headquarters might have saved us the trouble; however ... Ryder, you will find a fatigue party of fifty and report to the Quartering Commandant at the house at 1045 hours; he'll show you what we're taking over.'

'Very good, sir.'

'Our predecessors do not seem to have been very enterprising. The valley has great potentialities for an assault course and a mortar range. Weapon-training officer, make a recce this morning and get something laid on before Brigade arrives.'

'Very good, sir.'

'I'm going out myself with the adjutant to recce training areas. Anyone happen to know this district?'

I said nothing.

'That's all then, get cracking.'

'Wonderful old place in its way,' said the Quartering Commandant; 'pity to knock it about too much.'

He was an old, retired, re-appointed lieutenant-colonel from some miles away. We met in the space before the main doors, where I had my half-company fallen-in, waiting for orders. 'Come in. I'll soon show you over. It's a great warren of a place, but we've only requisitioned the ground floor and half a dozen bedrooms. Everything else upstairs is still private property, mostly cram-full of furniture; you never saw such stuff, priceless some of it.

'There's a caretaker and a couple of old servants live at the top – they won't be any trouble to you – and a blitzed R.C. padre whom Lady Julia gave a home to – jittery old bird, but no trouble. He's opened the chapel; that's in bounds for the troops; surprising lot use it, too.

'The place belongs to Lady Julia Flyte, as she calls herself now. She was married to Mottram, the Minister of whatever-it-is. She's abroad in some woman's service, and I try to keep an eye on things for her. Queer thing the old marquis leaving everything to her – rough on the boys.

'Now this is where the last lot put the clerks; plenty of room, anyway. I've had the walls and fireplaces boarded up you see – valuable old work underneath. Hullo, someone seems to have been making a beast of himself here; destructive beggars, soldiers are! Lucky we spotted it, or it would have been charged to you chaps.

'This is another good-sized room, used to be full of tapestry. I'd advise you to use this for conferences.'

'I'm only here to clean up, sir. Someone from Brigade will allot the rooms.'

'Oh, well, you've got an easy job. Very decent fellows the last lot. They shouldn't have done that to the fireplace though. How did they manage it? Looks solid enough. I wonder if it can be mended?

'I expect the brigadier will take this for his office; the last did. It's got a lot of painting that can't be moved, done on the walls. As you see, I've covered it up as best I can, but soldiers get through anything – as the brigadier's done in the corner. There was another painted room, outside under pillars – modern work but, if you ask me, the prettiest in the place; it was the signal office and they made absolute hay of it; rather a shame.

'This eyesore is what they used as the mess; that's why I didn't cover it up; not that it would matter much if it did get damaged; always reminds me of one of the costlier knocking-shops, you know – "*Maison Japonaise*" ... and this was the ante-room ...'

It did not take us long to make our tour of the echoing rooms. Then we went outside on the terrace.

'Those are the other ranks' latrines and wash-house; can't think why they built them just there; it was done before I took the job over. All this used to be cut off from the front. We laid the road through the trees joining it up with the main drive; unsightly but very practical; awful lot of transport comes in and out; cuts the place up, too. Look where one careless devil went smack through the box hedge and carried away all that balus-trade; did it with a three-ton lorry, too; you'd think he had a Churchill tank at least.

'That fountain is rather a tender spot with our landlady; the young officers used to lark about in it on guest nights and it was looking a bit the worse for wear, so I wired it in and turned the water off. Looks a bit untidy now; all the drivers throw their cigarette-ends and the remains of the sandwiches there, and you can't get to it to clean it up, since I put the wire round it. Florid great thing, isn't it? ...

'Well, if you've seen everything I'll push off. Good day to you.'

His driver threw a cigarette into the dry basin of the fountain; saluted and opened the door of the car. I saluted and the Quartering Commandant drove away through the new, metalled gap in the lime trees.

'Hooper,' I said, when I had seen my men started, 'do you think I can safely leave you in charge of the work-party for half an hour?'

'I was just wondering where we could scrounge some tea.'

'For Christ's sake,' I said, 'they've only just begun work.'

'They're awfully browned off.'

'Keep them at it.'

'Rightyoh.'

I did not spend long in the desolate ground-floor rooms, but went upstairs and wandered down the familiar corridors, trying doors that were locked, opening doors into rooms piled to the ceiling with furniture. At length I met an old housemaid carrying a cup of tea. 'Why,' she said, 'isn't it Mr Ryder?'

'It is. I was wondering when I should meet someone I know.'

'Mrs Hawkins is up in her old room. I was just taking her some tea.'

'I'll take it for you,' I said, and passed through the baize doors, up the uncarpeted stairs, to the nursery.

Nanny Hawkins did not recognize me until I spoke, and my arrival threw her into some confusion; it was not until I had been sitting some time by her fireside that she recovered her old calm. She, who had changed so little in all the years I knew her, had lately become greatly aged. The changes of the last years had come too late in her life to be accepted and understood; her sight was failing, she told me, and she could see only the coarsest needlework. Her speech, sharpened by years of gentle conversation, had reverted now to the soft, peasant tones of its origin.

'... only myself here and the two girls and poor Father Membling who was blown up, not a roof to his head nor a stick of furniture till Julia took him in with the kind heart she's got, and his nerves something shocking. ... Lady Brideshead, too, Marchmain it is now, who I ought by rights to call her Ladyship now, but it doesn't come natural, it was the same with her. First, when Julia and Cordelia left to the war, she came here with the two boys and then the military turned them out, so they went to London, nor they hadn't been in their house not a month, and Bridey away with the yeomanry the same as his poor Lordship, when they were blown up too, everything gone, all the furniture she brought here and kept in the coach-house. Then she had another house outside London, and the military took that, too, and there she is now, when I last heard, in a hotel at the seaside, which isn't the same as your own home, is it? It doesn't seem right.

'... Did you listen to Mr Mottram last night? Very nasty he

was about Hitler. I said to the girl Effie who does for me: "If Hitler was listening, and if he understands English, which I doubt, he must feel very small." Who would have thought of Mr Mottram doing so well? And so many of his friends, too, that used to stay here? I said to Mr Wilcox, who comes to see me regular on the bus from Melstead twice a month, which is very good of him and I appreciate it, I said: "We were entertaining angels unawares," because Mr Wilcox never liked Mr Mottram's friends, which I never saw, but used to hear about from all of you, nor Julia didn't like them, but they've done very well, haven't they?'

At last I asked her: 'Have you heard from Julia?'

'From Cordelia, only last week, and they're together still as they have been all the time, and Julia sent me love at the bottom of the page. They're both very well, though they couldn't say where, but Father Membling said, reading between the lines, it was Palestine, which is where Bridey's yeomanry is, so that's very nice for them all. Cordelia said they were looking forward to coming home after the war, which I am sure we all are, though whether I live to see it, is another story.'

I stayed with her for half an hour, and left promising to return often. When I reached the hall I found no sign of work and Hooper looking guilty.

'They had to go off to draw the bed-straw. I didn't know till Sergeant Block told me. I don't know whether they're coming back.'

'Don't know? What orders did you give?'

'Well, I told Sergeant Block to bring them back if he thought it was worthwhile; I mean if there was time before dinner.'

It was nearly twelve. 'You've been hotted again, Hooper. That straw was to be drawn any time before six tonight.'

'Oh Lor; sorry, Ryder. Sergeant Block –'

'It's my own fault for going away. ... Fall in the same party immediately after dinner, bring them back here and keep them here till the job's done.'

'Rightyoh. I say, did you say you knew this place before?'

'Yes, very well. It belongs to friends of mine,' and as I said

the words they sounded as odd in my ears as Sebastian's had
done, when, instead of saying, 'It is my home,' he said, 'It is
where my family live.'

'It doesn't seem to make any sense – one family in a place
this size. What's the use of it?'

'Well, I suppose Brigade are finding it useful.'

'But that's not what it was built for, is it?'

'No,' I said, 'not what it was built for. Perhaps that's one of
the pleasures of building, like having a son, wondering how he'll
grow up. I don't know; I never built anything, and I forfeited
the right to watch my son grow up. I'm homeless, childless,
middle-aged, loveless, Hooper.' He looked to see if I was being
funny, decided that I was, and laughed. 'Now go back to camp,
keep out of the C.O.'s way, if he's back from his recce, and don't
let on to anyone that we've made a nonsense of the morning.'

'Okey, Ryder.'

There was one part of the house I had not yet visited, and I
went there now. The chapel showed no ill-effects of its long
neglect; the *art-nouveau* paint was as fresh and bright as ever; the
art-nouveau lamp burned once more before the altar. I said a
prayer, an ancient, newly-learned form of words, and left,
turning towards the camp; and as I walked back, and the cook-
house bugle sounded ahead of me, I thought:

'The builders did not know the uses to which their work
would descend; they made a new house with the stones of the
old castle; year by year, generation after generation, they
enriched and extended it; year by year the great harvest of
timber in the park grew to ripeness; until, in sudden frost, came
the age of Hooper; the place was desolate and the work all
brought to nothing; *Quomodo sedet sola civitas*. Vanity of vanities,
all is vanity.

'And yet,' I thought, stepping out more briskly towards the
camp, where the bugles after a pause had taken up the second
call and were sounding 'Pick-em-up, pick-em-up, hot potatoes',
'and yet that is not the last word; it is not even an apt word; it is
a dead word from ten years back.

'Something quite remote from anything the builders

intended, has come out of their work, and out of the fierce little human tragedy in which I played; something none of us thought about at the time; a small red flame – a beaten-copper lamp of deplorable design relit before the beaten-copper doors of a tabernacle; the flame which the old knights saw from their tombs, which they saw put out; that flame burns again for other soldiers, far from home, farther, in heart, than Acre or Jerusalem. It could not have been lit but for the builders and the tragedians, and there I found it this morning, burning anew among the old stones.'

I quickened my pace and reached the hut which served us for our ante-room.

'You're looking unusually cheerful today,' said the second-in-command.

ABOUT THE INTRODUCER

SIR FRANK KERMODE has been Northcliffe Professor of Modern English Literature at University College, London, King Edward VII Professor of English Literature at Cambridge and Charles Eliot Norton Professor of Poetry at Harvard. His many books include *The Sense of an Ending, Romantic Image* and a memoir, *Not Entitled.*

This book is set in BASKERVILLE. John
Baskerville of Birmingham formed his
ideas of letter-design during his
early career as a writing-master
and engraver of inscriptions.
He retired in middle age,
set up a press of his
own and produced
his first book
in 1757.